Social Demography, edited by Thomas R. Ford and Gordon F. De Jong, is a book of readings that focuses on these key questions: How do demographic variables influence social systems? And how do social variables influence demographic systems? The editors develop an analytical framework to examine the relationships between a demographic system and a social system. It is the area of intersection between these two systems that defines the field of social demography and the point of view of this book.

THOMAS R. FORD, Ph.D. Vanderbilt University, is Professor and Chairman of the Department of Sociology at the University of Kentucky.

GORDON F. DE JONG, Ph.D. University of Kentucky, is Associate Professor in the Department of Sociology at Pennsylvania State University.

SOCIAL
DEMOGRAPHY

SOCIAL DEMOGRAPHY

Edited by
THOMAS R. FORD
University of Kentucky

GORDON F. DE JONG
Pennsylvania State University

Prentice-Hall, Inc.,
Englewood Cliffs, N.J.

PRENTICE-HALL SOCIOLOGY SERIES
NEIL J. SMELSER, Editor

Current Printing (Last Digit):
10 9 8 7 6 5 4 3 2 1

13-815555-0

Library of Congress Catalog Card Number: 69–14426

Printed in the United States of America

PRENTICE-HALL INTERNATIONAL, INC., London
PRENTICE-HALL OF AUSTRALIA, PTY. LTD., Sydney
PRENTICE-HALL OF CANADA, LTD., Toronto
PRENTICE-HALL OF INDIA PRIVATE LTD., New Delhi
PRENTICE-HALL OF JAPAN, INC., Tokyo

This book developed in response to two questions that the editors often asked themselves and their students: How do demographic variables influence social systems? And how do social variables influence demographic systems? Asking these questions is in itself symptomatic of the emergence of demography as a separate discipline in the United States after a long period of captivity by sociology. For as long as the study of population was considered a subfield of sociology,

PREFACE

few sociologists thought of demographic variables as other than attributes of a generally ill-defined social system. This was not the case with demographers working outside the field of sociology who developed concepts of a population and the processes that change it that were analytically separable from social and ecological systems. But little effort was made to link their "pure" or "formal" demography to sociology. Instead, sociologists traditionally acknowledged a distinction between *formal demography*, restricted to the analysis of the basic components of population change, and *population studies*, concerned with the relations between demographic components and nondemographic variables of various types.

Quite properly, most sociologists have been primarily interested in population studies, but they have rarely sought to define the field, if it is a field at all. As characterized by Hauser and Duncan, "the field of population studies is at least as broad as interest in the 'determinants and consequences of population trends.' "[1] In our view,

[1] Philip M. Hauser and Otis Dudley Duncan, eds., *The Study of Population—An Inventory and Appraisal* (Chicago: The University of Chicago Press, 1959), pp. 2–3.

this concept is both too broad and too nebulous to provide a base for the development of useful theory. We have, therefore, tried to develop an analytical framework to deal with those aspects of population studies of greatest interest to the sociologists: the relationships between demographic and sociological variables. In so doing, we have retained the distinction between a population or demographic system and a social system. The area of intersection between the two systems defines the field we have called social demography. For illustrations of social demographic studies, we have read literally hundreds of articles and have selected those that most closely corresponded to our concept of the field. That few of the selections explicitly link demographic and social systems is to be expected, for this was not their original purpose. Undoubtedly, however, many of the papers would have benefited had their authors worked within a more clearly defined social demographic framework.

It should be made clear that this book is not intended as a conventional beginning text in population. The subject matter treated assumes some knowledge of both demography and sociology, at least to the extent of introductory courses in both fields. Neither is it oriented to the study of population problems of the Malthusian order. For while we share the growing social concern with the problems of world population growth, we also hold that the solutions to these problems are dependent upon an understanding of their complexities. Such an understanding is most likely to be gained within a systematic analytic framework.

With Frank S. Lorimer, we also share the belief that "significant demography is necessarily interdisciplinary." For this reason we have sought to clarify at least one area of interdisciplinary relationship. The need for further clarification we cheerfully acknowledge, for our attempt is only a beginning. We pose no claim to the ultimate superiority of our approach to the development of social demography. We offer only the affirmation that we and our students have found it useful and stimulating and the hope that others will find it equally so.

Thomas R. Ford

Gordon F. De Jong

CONTENTS

Introduction to Social Demography

A general knowledge of world population growth is now commonplace not only to the academician and planner but also to the informed layman. The steep rise of the world's population growth curve has led to a multitude of speculations about possible relations between population trends and human society; however, only very recently has this relationship been the subject of scientific investigation.

Consider, for example, the contemporary prob-

1

AN
ANALYTICAL
APPROACH

lem of the relation of population trends to social and economic development. As increased numbers of nations have faced the problems of stimulating social and economic development, attention has focused on population growth as one of the basic factors in the developmental process. Demographers now generally recognize that population growth is not an inexorable biological process limited only by the availability of the basic necessities of life. Contrary to the dire predictions of early Malthusianism, population growth in the technologically advanced societies has not constantly pressed against the limits of productivity. Indeed, not too many decades ago many nations of Western Europe were seriously concerned about their slow rates of population growth. But if population growth is not regulated solely by biological factors, neither is its control simply a matter of technological advancement. Most societies already possess the technical knowledge required to control population, but the availability of knowledge does not necessarily mean that it will be effectively utilized. When we ask why knowledge of population control is not more fully applied, we encounter a complex set of cultural and social factors. An analysis of how these factors affect fertility and the other demographic processes leads us well beyond the boundaries of traditional demographic analysis.

Although questions about the whys and wherefores of fertility may be currently in the spotlight of public interest, they are not the only demographic phenomena of scientific importance. The demographic processes produce changes in population size, composition, and distribution; these changes also raise significant questions of cause and effect. What is the influence of population density on social relations? What accounts for the rapid urbanization of population that is taking place in most countries of the world, including many in which the development of industry and commerce is still greatly retarded? What are the social effects of increasing proportions of old people in a population? How does population composition affect political activity? Does the employment of women in occupations that take them outside the home affect the rate of reproduction? How does population size influence efforts for economic development and cultural change? Answers to these and many similar questions involve a complex set of cultural and social factors. *The major concern of social demography is the analysis of how general social and cultural factors are related to population structure and process.*

THE AREA OF SOCIAL DEMOGRAPHY

The use of the term *social demography* has increased in recent years, but, as is true of most disciplinary areas, neither the context nor the boundaries of social demography can be defined with great exactitude. Conceived in general terms, social demography is concerned with the relationships between social and demographic phenomena. This concept is broader than the implicit definition provided by Kingsley Davis in his statement that social demography is distinguished by its interest in investigating the motivational linkages between changing conditions and demographic behavior and population trends.[1] Certainly a great deal of social demographic research is concerned not so much with the social causes as with the social consequences of demographic changes. On the other hand, social demography would appear to be somewhat more circumscribed than the nebulous field labeled "population studies" by Hauser and Duncan.[2] They use this term to designate "a body of subject

---

[1] Kingsley Davis, "Social Demography," in *The Behavioral Sciences Today*, ed. Bernard Berelson (New York: Harper Torchbook edition, 1964), p. 204.

matter which is of common interest to a number of diverse theoretical disciplines and to which are applied the techniques of demographic analysis."[3] Undoubtedly such a field is broad enough to encompass most social demographic studies, but it also explicitly includes a variety of natural science areas such as biology, zoology, and physical anthropology which lie outside the arena of social science.

There are two basic approaches to analyzing relationships between social and cultural factors and population variables. Social and cultural factors may be viewed as independent variables that account for empirical regularities in population structure or process. The influence of social mobility on fertility illustrates this type of relationship. Much of the research in social demography has been of this type. But social demographers are not exclusively interested in the social and cultural determinants of population structure and process. Questions about the way changes in population affect various aspects of society and culture are also important. From this view, social and cultural factors are treated as dependent variables with the intent of explaining how they are influenced by demographic factors. An illustration of this approach is the influence of population size on racial discrimination.

Of course not all studies neatly conform to these two general patterns. It should be recognized that the relationship between demographic and sociocultural factors is usually one of reciprocal influence, and factors are considered *independent* or *dependent* primarily for analytical purposes. The common thread of concern in all social demography studies is the relationship between aggregate demographic phenomena and regularities in other social and individual units of human behavior.

At its current stage of development, social demography can probably be more accurately characterized as an area of interest rather than a separate discipline with its own organized body of theory using specialized methods and techniques of study. More specifically, the area of interest of social demography lies at the intersection of demographic and sociological analysis, and social demographers draw their concepts, theory, and methods from both disciplines.

COMPARATIVE FRAMES OF REFERENCE

There have been previous attempts to develop conceptual systems that incorporate both demographic and social variables within a single framework. Social morphology as conceived by Durkheim and Halbwachs offers one such example. As elaborated by Halbwachs, the dis-

[2] Philip M. Hauser and Otis Dudley Duncan, "The Nature of Demography," in *The Study of Population, An Inventory and Appraisal,* eds. Hauser and Duncan (Chicago: University of Chicago Press, 1959), pp. 36–37.
[3] *Ibid.*

cipline focuses on the relationships among (1) the size and spatial distribution of a population; (2) the age and sex composition; (3) the types and forms of social structures defined by a "collective conscience," such as clans, families, and extended kinship groups; and (4) the forms, or structural features, of social institutions. A major task of social morphology as set forth by Halbwachs was "to show that the morphological structure of groups, and this alone, sometimes allows us to explain their internal states and changes, their institutions and their way of life."[4]

The analytical schema of social morphology, while widely used in French population studies, has found little application in American research, partly because the phenomena with which it is concerned are also treated within the analytical framework of human ecology. As defined by Hawley, one of the leading scholars in the field, human ecology is the study of the form and development of the community in the human population. Its concern with the community, as seen by Hawley, is limited to the "overt and measurable features" of social organization which emerge as men relate themselves to one another in order to live in their habitats. "Population is conceived as one of the principal permissive or limiting causes of social phenomena. Hence problems such as the implications of size, of biological structure, or rates of population change for the organization of relationships occupy a position of major importance in ecological work."[5]

Duncan has provided a somewhat clearer delineation of the boundaries of ecological analysis with his concept of the human ecological complex as the interdependent relations among the components of (1) population, (2) environment, (3) social organization, and (4) technology. In the analysis of this relational system, demographic variables may be treated as *independent variables* operating to influence or limit the system; as *dependent variables* responding to the influences or limitations of other aspects of the system; or as *indicators* of one or another aspect of the system.[6]

There is by no means complete agreement among human ecologists as to what social phenomena should be studied within the ecological framework, but even the broadest conceptions of the field would seem to exclude certain social factors that are generally thought to have significant demographic determinants or consequences. For instance, Duncan's ecological complex includes a social organization component but omits reference to such social components as values, attitudes, and beliefs.

[4] Maurice Halbwachs, *Morphologie Sociale* (Paris: Librairie Armand Colin, 1946).

[5] Amos H. Hawley, *Human Ecology* (New York: The Ronald Press Co., 1950), pp. 66–79.

[6] Otis Dudley Duncan, "Human Ecology and Population Studies," in *The Study of Population*, eds. Hauser and Duncan, pp. 683–684.

This is no criticism of the discipline, for every discipline must be selective of the phenomena with which it is concerned, but it does mean that not all subject matter of interest to social demographers can be fitted within the ecological framework.

AN ANALYTICAL SYSTEMS APPROACH

Whether a single integrated analytical system of social demography is possible remains a moot question. In its absence, however, it would appear possible to conduct a great deal of fruitful research using some of the existing analytical systems of sociology and demography and formulating more specifically their logical relationships. In this introduction we have sought to identify some of the analytical systems involved in social demographic studies without developing the systemic relationships to the degree that is desirable.

By an *analytical system* we mean simply a set of elements related to each other in some specified manner. Each element may be described in terms of certain properties of analytical interest. For instance, an *aggregate system*, viewed as a total unit, may be described in terms of system properties. Two properties of basic interest are the structural traits and the processes—the composition and change features of the system. The definition of any analytical system, its elements, traits, and processes, is largely arbitrary, although for purposes of scientific analysis the various properties are expected to have empirical referents.

The conceptualization of a system may be clarified by Table 1.1

TABLE 1.1.   TRAITS AND PROCESSES OF A DEMOGRAPHIC SYSTEM

Element trait	*Element process*	*System trait*	*System process*
Membership	Birth, death, and migration (in and out migration)	Size	Growth: gains through natality and in-migration minus loss through mortality and out-migration.
Age	Aging	Age composition	Recomposition by age
Sex	—	Sex composition	Recomposition by sex
Residence	Internal migration	Residential distribution	Redistribution by residence

which outlines the traits and processes of a simple demographic system. Consider the hypothetical case of a small country; a first concern in demographic analysis is to determine what is to be included in the system. This can be done in our example simply by defining the system as all residents of the country. But since no analytical system is concerned with all aspects of the population, particular traits or characteristics of the residents must be specified. Traditionally, the element traits of primary demographic concern are the age, sex, and location of individuals in the area.[7] At a given time, then, our entire demographic system, which includes all residents, might be represented by an age-sex pyramid with proper shading to show geographic distribution. The total system can now be described by the joint relations of the several characteristics of size, age-sex composition, and residential distribution.

In time the demographic system of our hypothetical country is changed by a patterned occurrence of events or processes. The events themselves happen to individual elements, but the joint effect is seen in the alteration of the total system. For example, the size of the system is changed by the combined effect of three processes: Some members of the system die; others are born; some migrate. The migrants may move out of the country and thus leave the system, or they may move into the country and thus become part of the system. The operation of these three processes—mortality, natality, and migration—also changes the age-sex composition of the population, and probably the residential composition as well. Internal migration, or the movement of persons within the country from city to rural areas or vice versa, also changes the residential composition but does not affect the age-sex composition of the total system. Another process that modifies the composition of the system is aging, for it is apparent that the age composition of the population would continue to change even if all the other processes were halted. Formal demography is concerned almost exclusively with the relationships among demographic *system* traits and processes, while social demography is concerned with the relationships among demographic system components (element traits and processes as well as system traits and processes) and components of various social systems.

A second type of analytical system utilized by social demographers is the *social action system*. The direct study of social behavior, which is of basic interest to most sociologists, is carried on within a social action

---

[7] Some demographers add to this list other social characteristics such as race, marital status, education, occupation, religion, etc. Since the determination is purely arbitrary, we shall restrict our element traits to the very basic biosocial characteristics of age and sex. Race is probably the most sensitive exclusion from the demographic system. We feel, however, that its conceptual and empirical treatment is more closely akin to that of other social characteristics than to the demographic characteristics of age and sex.

The status of residence as a social or demographic trait is also subject to discussion. All populations must be located in space and thus residence is a basic demographic element. However, residential categories are often treated as causative social variables and not as location coordinates. For instance, rural, rural nonfarm, city, suburban, metropolitan area, etc., are sometimes conceptualized as much in sociological as in geo-demographic terms. For operational purposes, we will consider residence as a necessary demographic trait.

system analytical framework. The chief characteristic of social action systems is their inclusion of various forms of interpersonal interaction as basic analytic components. That there is no clear consensus among sociologists regarding the elements, traits, and processes of a social action system is an understatement. But there does seem to be general agreement that interactional behavior, especially role behavior, is a major focus of interest. It is possible to explore the relationships among many more or less clearly conceptualized social action systems and the demographic system.

The social action system that has probably been investigated most frequently by social demographers is the family,[8] yet even it presents a multitude of analytical complexities. Each member of the family usually holds several statuses within the system (such as father, husband, uncle, grandfather, brother, brother-in-law, and so forth) which are defined by relations with other members of the system. Each status carries with it certain behavioral expectations which constitute its social role. There are thus various element processes associated with role performance and, in addition, a number of system processes relating to the functioning of the family as a social group. Clearly, several of the traits and processes of the family are closely related to demographic composition and change.

A full description of the family or any other social action system is beyond the scope of this book. Indeed, there are several approaches to the family, and those used in the reading selections presented in a subsequent section only illustrate the types of models available to relate the family as a social action system to demography.

An example from one of the readings may illustrate how the structure and functioning of the family affects demographic change. In their Puerto Rican study of fertility planning, Hill, Back, and Stycos employed an interactional role analysis of the nuclear family of procreation. It was hypothesized that one of the keys to effective fertility planning was interspouse communication. Their analysis revealed that while such communication was quite low, due primarily to norms of wifely modesty and respect for the husband, families having the best communication were most likely to exercise fertility control. Further, accuracy of perception by one spouse of the other spouse's attitudes on family size and birth control were also related to interspouse communication and

---

[8] Outstanding examples of social demographic studies of the family are: Judith Blake, *Family Structure in Jamaica: The Social Context of Reproduction* (New York: The Free Press of Glencoe, Inc., 1961); J. M. Stycos, *Family and Fertility in Puerto Rico: A Study of the Lower Income Group* (New York: Columbia University Press, 1955); Reuben Hill, *et al., The Family and Population Control: A Puerto Rican Experiment in Social Change* (Chapel Hill: University of North Carolina Press, 1959).

family limitation practices. The important point here is that, although the theoretical approaches to the family may differ from one study to another, the structure and functioning of the family system is affected by demographic factors and vice versa.

Social action systems that have developed to meet basic human needs are often referred to as *institutional systems*. The selections relating to social action systems in this volume are mainly concerned with major institutional systems. There are other types of social action systems, however, that are not considered basic institutional systems, such as informal groups, special interest organizations, and numerous other restricted associational forms. Although they may have important demographic consequences, they have rarely been studied by social demographers.

A third type of analytical system utilized by social demographers is what may be termed a *social aggregate system*. The vast majority of social demographic studies have involved social aggregate rather than social action systems. Aggregate systems in their simplest form are defined by elements possessing one or more common social traits and do not include interpersonal interaction as a process. Both social action and social aggregate systems may involve behavior expectations; however, social action systems characteristically focus on the specific expectations of concrete actors (such as the familial role of the working wife), while social aggregate systems relate to more generalized expectations of people who possess common social traits (such as married women in the labor force). The importance of sociological and demographic generalizations derived from social aggregate data attests to the predictability of generalized social expectations.

To illustrate a social aggregate system, let us consider the labor force of the hypothetical country used in explaining the demographic system. The elements of the labor force may be arbitrarily defined as all persons 14 years old or over who are gainfully employed or are seeking employment. The element traits of interest in our system are age, sex, and occupation. The first two of these are also demographic traits and form points of intersection between the demographic system and the labor force social aggregate system. Here the social demographer might be interested in what effect female participation in the labor force has on fertility. In addition to the element traits, we are also interested in certain characteristics of the whole labor force, namely its size, age composition, sex composition, and occupational composition.

As in the case of the demographic system, the social aggregate system may be modified by the operation of various processes. In the case of the labor force, individuals may enter the system for the first time (analogous to birth in the demographic system) by seeking or securing employment after age 14. They may also drop out of the system permanently (analogous to death in the demographic system), or they may drop out temporarily and reenter at a later date. A person may also change occupations within the system, a process of social mobility analytically equivalent to internal migration in the demographic system. The various traits and processes of the labor force system are shown in Table 1.2.

TABLE 1.2. TRAITS AND PROCESSES OF A LABOR FORCE SYSTEM AS A SOCIAL AGGREGATE SYSTEM

Element trait	*Element process*	*System trait*	*System process*
System membership	Entry, withdrawal	Size	Growth (entries minus withdrawals)
Age	Aging	Age composition	Recomposition by age
Sex	—	Sex composition	Recomposition by sex
Occupation	Occupational mobility	Occupational composition	Recomposition by occupation

The demographic system and changes that occur in it will have both direct and indirect effects upon the labor force system. As already noted, some traits and processes of the two systems are shared. In other cases, demographic processes of mortality and migration that involve members of the labor force will directly affect labor force growth and composition. Indirectly, births will probably be related to entry into the labor force some 14 years later.

Not all social aggregate systems are as closely related to the demographic system as is the labor force, but the intersystem relationships may still be of importance. For example, we might consider the social class system of our hypothetical country as an aggregate system. Assuming for purposes of simplicity that all members can be classified into one of three class categories—high, middle, and low—we may be concerned with only one element trait: social class status. The element process associated with this system is class mobility, or movement from one class to another. Since, by definition, every member of the population is a member of the class system, demographic processes play an important role in the recomposition of the system. Therefore, the sociologist interested in the dynamics of social class structure should be concerned not only with vertical mobility but also with class differences in natality, mortality, and migration. On the other hand, the demographer who is interested in predicting birth rates may find that the social class composition of the population will help to refine his predictions if fertility differentials are clearly associated with social class. Both the sociologist and the demographer may engage in social demographic studies to further their own disciplinary interests.

Again an example from a subsequent section of the book may illustrate our point. How does migration from the home community affect intergenerational social mobility? This question, which overlaps social policy as well as sociological and demographic issues, was posed by Scudder and Anderson in a study of a small Kentucky town. Their expectations, supported by the data, were that sons who leave their home community become detached from stable status relationships of the small town and manifest unusual vertical occupational mobility. Clearly the dynamics of the demographic system are relevant to the analysis of social stratification.

The influence of social psychological factors on demographic processes has become of increasing concern to social demographers. Studies of fertility attitudes and values as well as inquiries into the attitudinal base for migration illustrate this type of investigation. Largely unsettled, however, are the theoretical issues of how these studies relate to results from interaction system research on the one hand and generalizations from social aggregate studies on the other. A fairly extensive review of the literature in this area reveals that most social demographic studies do not treat such factors as values, attitudes, and beliefs in the context of interaction systems but rather as part of some largely undefined analytical system. The overwhelming majority of these studies report findings based on a sample survey of sociologically unrelated individuals instead of participants of various kinds of interaction systems. This treatment of social psychological factors is not fundamentally different from that used in other aggregate studies. Consequently we have included such social psychological factors as attitudes, values, and beliefs as components of analytically defined social aggregate systems (Fig. 1.1).

The failure to conceptualize adequately the analytical system in which social psychological factors are presumed to operate can be seen in the frequently reported opinion data on what is considered the "ideal family size." Clearly the referent points for such a question can be as varied as the respondents care to make them. Some respondents may use "ideal" conditions for a generalized "average" man as a reference, while others may answer in terms of personal or family issues and preferences. Even the improved inquiry into the number of children respondents "expect" to have suffers from the same imprecision. In calculating how many children he expects to have, the respondent may have to juggle the relative importance of such issues as his desires, the desires of his spouse and of other reference groups, the long-term financial situation, fecundity problems, and the use of contraception.[9] The difficulty in inter-

---

[9] For a discussion of some theoretical and methodological issues in ideal and expected family size investigations see Judith Blake, "Ideal Family Among White Americans: A Quarter of a Century's Evidence," *Demography*, III (1966), 160–163.

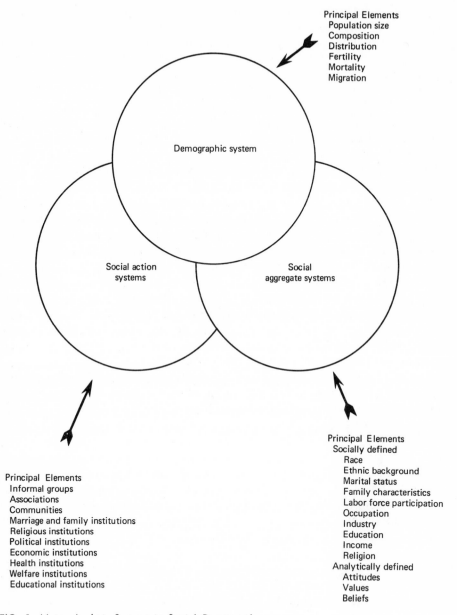

Principal Elements
Population size
Composition
Distribution
Fertility
Mortality
Migration

Demographic system

Social action
systems

Social
aggregate systems

Principal Elements
Informal groups
Associations
Communities
Marriage and family institutions
Religious institutions
Political institutions
Economic institutions
Health institutions
Welfare institutions
Educational institutions

Principal Elements
Socially defined
  Race
  Ethnic background
  Marital status
  Family characteristics
  Labor force participation
  Occupation
  Industry
  Education
  Income
  Religion
Analytically defined
  Attitudes
  Values
  Beliefs

FIG. 1. Major Analysis Systems in Social Demography

preting some of the observed relationships to demographic behavioral variables may be partially explained by the lack of precise conceptualization of the linkages between social psychological data and the variables of social aggregate and social action systems.

Similar interpretation difficulties can be noted for attitudinal responses to "why did you move" questions. Although it is usually assumed that the attitude questions are related to social behavior, the behavior itself is seldom studied in action system units. As a result, a direct relationship is seldom established between the demographic variables and social behavior but only between the demographic variables and assumed indicators of social behavior.

Aggregate analyses, then, are usually based on certain assumptions, sometimes explicit but often implicit, about the social behavior of the aggregate members. Indeed, for social aggregate analysis to have any significance this must be the case. A comparison of the mortality rates of farmers and coal miners, for example, is meaningful only because the occupational roles (which are studied as part of a social action system) carry with them different risks of death. By the same token, a comparison of the mortality rates of all people named Jones and Smith would be sociologically meaningless because there is no social behavior related to these surnames that would lead one to expect differences. A finding of differences might, of course, lead us in search of behavioral differences, and might even have utilitarian value for insurance companies in computing actuarial risks. But without further investigation, the knowledge of such differences would not contribute to our understanding of either social behavior or demographic processes. Unfortunately, not all demographic social aggregate studies make clear what the behavioral implications of observed differences are. In choosing readings for this volume the editors have tried to select those in which the behavioral assumptions underlying aggregate categories are either explicitly stated or reasonably common knowledge.

In résumé, the preceding discussion has emphasized the relationships between demography and general social and cultural factors in terms of element and system traits and processes. Element and system properties were delineated for several systems relevant to social demography. These include demographic, social aggregate, and social action systems. Figure 1.1 summarizes these major analysis systems in social demography.

PLAN OF THE VOLUME

The readings included in this book were selected to illustrate various aspects of the relationship between sociology and demography. The selections are presented in four major parts. Part Two presents readings that analyze some of the theoretical aspects of the relationships between social and demographic variables. Part Three considers the relationship between demography and various social action systems. Besides informal groups and communities, several major institutional areas are included: marriage and the family, economic, political, religious, and health, education, and welfare. Part Four focuses on the ties between social aggregate system characteristics and demography. Included are studies of racial and ethnic characteristics, social stratification and social mobility, and those attitudinal characteristics that researchers have considered as aggregate traits of a population. The final part considers the macrosocial demography issue of the reciprocal influences of demographic transition and social and economic change in total societies. In each of the first three parts of the book, articles are included that illustrate the relationship between social factors and the major demographic variables: fertility, mortality, migration, and population size and composition. Readings specifically focusing on social factors and population distribution are not included since distribution is often an explicit or certainly an implicit demographic factor in almost every selection. Just over half the readings illustrate general social and cultural determinants of population variables (which are treated as dependent variables), and an approximately equal number of readings analyze the consequences of population variables (which are treated as independent variables). The readings are also about equally divided between research within the United States and research in other countries.

Although the choice of selections was of necessity somewhat arbitrary, we did follow certain criteria. Our first criterion for a selection was its excellence in analyzing and specifying the relationships between demographic and sociological, sociocultural, and sociopsychological factors. In the first section of the book the primary concern is with theoretical statements, but in subsequent sections we tended to choose readings that emphasized carefully conducted empirical studies rather than speculative or programmatic discussions. The organization of the book dictated considerable attention to the choice of articles from the theoretically significant analytical systems that are related to social demography. But since social demographic research is not evenly represented in all categories, some unevenness in quality is an unavoidable result. A final major criterion was recency of publication. Most selections were from the literature of the past ten years. Recency of publication, of course, is no guarantee of excellence, but it does increase the probability of including studies that utilized new or improved theoretical perspectives and research designs.

It is hardly to be expected that studies conducted by individuals operating with a wide diversity of analytical frameworks should fit neatly into an organizational scheme for which they were not originally intended. Indeed, the variety of topics and analytical approaches represented in the readings exemplifies the general area of social demography at the present time. It is hoped, however, that, although they may reveal a lack of theoretical, conceptual, or methodological unity of a field, the studies will demonstrate the importance of understanding the ways in which demographic and social phenomena are related.

part
2

Explorations in Social Demographic Theory

Social demography, as noted in the introductory chapter, is concerned with relationships between social and demographic phenomena. It is thus distinguished from "pure demography" which deals with relationships among the demographic variables that constitute the demographic system, although it should be recognized that all demographic processes take place within an influencing social context. Most social demographic theory, therefore, is basically dependent upon

2

SOCIOLOGICAL ANALYSIS OF DEMOGRAPHIC PROCESSES

sociological theory or, perhaps more accurately, on sociological theories.

At present there does not exist within the field of sociology any single frame of reference with integrated sets of deductive and empirical propositions linking social and demographic variables that could properly be called social demographic theory. This is not to say that theoretical propositions are lacking, for they exist in abundance, as various studies in this volume indicate. Rather it is to say that they have not been brought together in any single organized schema or theoretical system.[1] Wilbert Moore has suggested that the

[1] A number of authors have recently developed sets of formal propositions relating to various aspects of social demography. Paul E. Mott's *The Organization of Society* (Englewood Cliffs, N.J.: Prentice-Hall, Inc., 1965) pre-

"structural-functional" approach in sociology offers one of the most promising frameworks for the development of social demographic theory in that it explicitly brings demographic variables into the scheme of sociological theory.[2] Kingsley Davis, who is one of the leading contemporary social demographers and a proponent of structural functional analysis, has warned, however, that "future advances [in demographic theory] will hardly be made by pretentious attempts to develop general theory or to 'integrate' the big 'ologies' with demography: it will more likely be made by individuals pursuing particular problems with all the conceptual and empirical tools they can find."[3]

The reading selections presented in this chapter provide some recent examples of the "pursuit of particular problems" that contribute to social demographic theory. Fittingly, the first paper is by Kingsley Davis and presents a theory of "multiphasic response" to demographic changes. Davis holds that demographic changes are both *reflexive* and *behavioral*. They are reflexive in that they affect other components of a social system, which in turn bring about changes in the component initiating the change. They are behavioral in that they involve human decisions. Societies faced with problems of prolonged population increase may choose any of a number of alternative methods of control. Characteristically, as Davis points out, they utilize more than one method. He discusses six methods employed in Japan and Western Europe: abortion, contraception, sterilization, migration, postponement of marriage, and permanent celibacy. There are, of course, other alternatives such as infanticide employed at various times by other societies. An issue of considerable sociological interest is what determines the choice of control methods. Contrary to other social demographers, Davis argues that demographic behavior is not to be explained as "a response either to absolute need or to some cultural idiosyncracy such as a particular 'value system' or 'custom.'" But as usual, it is easier to say what does not explain human behavior than what does.

In the second article, prepared as an introduction to an extensive

---

sents thirteen propositions relating population size to social organization. Donald O. Cowgill's "Transitional Theory as General Population Theory" (reproduced in Part V of this volume) offers twelve propositions that constitute a general theory of demographic transition. Everett S. Lee, "A Theory of Migration," *Demography*, III, No. 1 (1966), 47–57, provides propositional sets concerning the volume of migration stream and counter-stream, and characteristics of migrants.

A set of empirical generalizations in the field of social demography is presented in Bernard A. Berelson and Gary A. Steiner, *Human Behavior, An Inventory of Scientific Findings* (New York: Harcourt, Brace & World, Inc., 1964), pp. 588–604.

[2] Wilbert E. Moore, "Sociology and Demography," in *The Study of Population,* eds. Philip M. Hauser and Otis Dudley Duncan, pp. 832–849.

[3] Kingsley Davis, "The Sociology of Demographic Behavior," in *Sociology Today,* eds. Robert K. Merton, Leonard Broom, Leonard S. Cottrell, Jr. (New York: Basic Books, Inc., Publishers, 1959), p. 314.

1955,[1] although at the latter date the registration of abortions is estimated to have been only 50 to 75 per cent complete.[2] The resort to abortion has been the leading cause of probably the fastest drop in the birth rate ever exhibited by an entire nation, births per 1000 women aged 10–49 falling by 41 per cent between 1950 and 1957. Westerners profess to be astonished by this phenomenon, but they should not be. The behavior of the Japanese is essentially the same in kind as the behavior of West Europeans at a similar time in their social and demographic history. The main difference is that Japanese tolerance permits the abortion rate to be reasonably well known, whereas in the past of Europe the abortion rate has never been known and, for this reason, is usually ignored in population theory.

Yet there is indirect and approximate evidence that in the late nineteenth and early twentieth centuries in Western Europe abortion played a great role. David Glass, who in 1940 summarized the findings for eight northwest European countries, cited the records of women under a German sickness benefit fund which show a gradual climb in abortions from 38 per 100 births in 1908 to 113 per 100 in 1932.[3] In Belgium "there were many books explaining how to induce abortion and any woman could buy, for 60 centimes, a uterine syringe and use this to induce an abortion."[4] In both France and Germany advertisements by abortionists were freely published. In fact, one gets the impression that the attitude toward abortion in West European society was much less intolerant between 1900 and 1935 than it is today. A study of maternity cases in Israel in 1958 showed that, for women born in Europe, America, and Australia–New Zealand, 32 per cent of those having a third birth admitted having resorted to induced abortion.[5]

Finally, in five of the People's Republics in Eastern Europe, which have legalized abortion, the subsequent history of the rise of registered abortions, as summarized by Tietze,[6] is amazingly like that of Japan. In Hungary, for example, medical boards were established about 1953 for authorizing therapeutic abortions. "That these boards progressively liberalized their policies is reflected in the growing numbers of legal abortions from 1953 onward." After the decree of 1956 permitting "the interruption of pregnancy on request, the number of legal abortions increased rapidly until in 1959 it exceeded the number of live births."[7] Not only did the legal abortion rate

[1] Masabumi Kimura, "A Review of Induced Abortion Surveys in Japan." Paper No. 43 in mimeographed proceedings of the 1961 conference of the International Union for the Scientific Study of Population, p. 1.

[2] Minoru Muramatsu, "Effect of Induced Abortion on the Reduction of Births in Japan," *Milbank Memorial Fund Quarterly*, XXXVIII, No. 2 (April, 1960), 152–166.

[3] D. V. Glass, *Population Policies and Movements in Europe* (Oxford: Clarendon Press, 1940), pp. 278–280. Other health-fund data showed more abortions than births in the late 1920s.

[4] *Ibid.*, pp. 444–445.

[5] Roberto Bachi and Judah Matras, "Contraception and Induced Abortions among Jewish Maternity Cases in Israel," *Milbank Memorial Fund Quarterly*, XXXX, No. 2 (April, 1962), 227.

[6] Christopher Tietze, "Legal Abortion in Eastern Europe," *Journal of the American Medical Association*, CLXXV (April, 1961), 1149–1154; *idem*, "The Demographic Significance of Legal Abortion in Eastern Europe," paper presented at annual meeting, Population Association of America, April 25–27, 1963. Mimeographed.

[7] Tietze, "Legal Abortion in Eastern Europe," pp. 1149–1154.

bibliography of fertility studies, Ronald Freedman takes a comprehensive look at fertility from the standpoint of sociological analysis. Drawing on a tremendous variety of fertility research, Freedman derives a model of social factors that affect fertility and also poses some hypotheses relating specific social variables to fertility. The limitations of social demographic theory are evident both in the nature of some hypotheses and in the results of testing others. Weak hypotheses such as "the forms of holding property in interaction with the type of family organization have various effects on fertility" indicate that our knowledge is inadequate to state clearly the nature of a presumed relationship. In other cases where relatively strong hypotheses have been offered (e.g., "upward social mobility between social strata leads to relatively low fertility"), empirical tests have yielded inconsistent findings. The great value of Freedman's paper is that it provides a framework for classifying and accumulating the findings from social demographic studies of fertility, a task that remains to be done for studies of other demographic variables.

The third paper provides a much more limited treatment of another demographic process—mortality. Dr. Alfred Yankauer, a physician, discusses ways social and cultural values and practices contribute to infant mortality in India. He observes that "it is far easier to catalog aspects of culture that may influence infant mortality than it is to suggest ways of modifying them." Dr. Yankauer might have added that it is also easier to catalog such influences in cultures other than our own. Even fairly sophisticated members of American society often fail to appreciate the influence of cultural factors, other than those that are primarily technological, upon mortality levels. Consequently, American responses to high mortality rates tend to be technological responses —safer automobiles and highways, improved cigarette filters, or new surgical techniques. It is especially interesting that Dr. Yankauer sees applied social science as the most feasible approach to lowering infant mortality in India while recognizing that it is rarely used in Western society except in times of disaster.

In a fourth selection, S. N. Eisenstadt considers the absorption of immigrants by the society to which they migrate. Demographers are interested in migration as a process whereby individuals leave one population system and enter another. Their major concern is the extent to which the size and composition of the two systems is altered as a consequence. Eisenstadt's particular concern is with what factors determine the degree to which migrants adapt to, or are assimilated by, the society to which they migrate. The answer to this question is difficult because, as the author points out, no single index is adequate to measure the different modes of adjustment. Given an appropriate index or set of indexes, however, is it possible to predict in advance how well a given group will adjust, by whatever means, to life in a society to which it may migrate? If this is a useful question, we might further ask what are the most important predictors of a satisfactory adjustment.

Migration is also mainly responsible for the growth of metropolitan centers throughout the world. Partly as a result of increasing social and economic disorder in such centers, social planners and government officials have questioned the desirability of the continued concentration of population. A central issue is whether the mere fact of high population density has undesirable social effects. The supposition that it does is supported by studies that document the adverse effects of high population densities on animal behavior. Drawing on the implications of such studies, Halliman Winsborough examined the relationship between population density and various indicators of social well-being in the city of Chicago. His findings are given in the fourth reading selection and, admittedly, offer little basis for policy formulation. Winsborough suggests, however, that his results "are strong and curious enough to warrant further investigation." Granted the need for studies of the social and economic effects of population density, social demographers are faced with a variety of problems. What types of population units should be studied? What indicators of social and economic well-being might be used? And, similar to the issue of migrant adjustment raised by Eisenstadt, what are the criteria of a desirable standard of living?

In a final selection, Norman B. Ryder views social change from a new perspective that might be truly termed social demographic. Using the familiar demographic concept of a *cohort* (an aggregate of individuals within a population who have experienced the same event, such as birth or marriage, within the same time interval), Ryder proposes a new and intellectually exciting application of cohort analysis. His central proposition is that a cohort reflects "the circumstances of its unique organization and history" which tend to influence the behavior of its members throughout life. For example, the cohort born in the United States in the years immediately following World War II was subjected to fairly common experiences of crowding in schools, maturing during the Vietnamese War, and reaching voting age in a period of national social unrest reflected in urban riots, political assassinations, and student rebellions. Ryder holds such experiences, unique to a given cohort, are important to understanding both its present and later behavior.

A major research question is whether the effects of unique cohort experiences can actually be measured. Ryder assumes not only that they can but that they should be taken into account in seeking to explain behavioral variations between age cohorts or continuities in behavior

for a given cohort over time. Although they must still be speculative, Ryder's propositions are sufficiently plausible empirical testing.

The Theory of Change and Respo in Modern Demographic History

Kingsley Davis

The process of demographic change and response is not only continuous but also reflexive and behavioral—reflexive in the sense that a change in one component is eventually altered by the change it has induced in other components; behavioral in the sense that the process involves human decisions in the pursuit of goals with varying means and conditions. As a consequence, the subject has a frightening complexity—so much so that the temptation is great to escape from its intricacies. One method of escape is to eschew any comprehensive theory, simply describing computations or working on a single hypothesis at a time. Another is to adopt some convenient oversimplification, such as the assumption that population is simply a matter of two capacities—a "reproductive urge" on the one side and

"means of subsistence" —or, at an opposite ex demographic behavior is a a "traditional culture" or tem."

My purpose here is to t pass some of the com an overall analysis of change in the industrialize To do this, I prefer to Japan. Not only does Jap fully industrialized non-W try, furnish a perspecti other country can furnish phases of its population statistically better docume

ABC
DEMOGRAPHI

The phenomenon most and one commonly regarde iarly Japanese—is the ra the registered abortion 11.8 per 1000 women age 1949 to a peak of 50.2 p

* Kingsley Davis, "The Theory of Change and Response in Modern Demographic History," *Population Index*, XXIX, No. 4 (October, 1963), 345–366.

rise rapidly in all four countries but also, as in Japan again, there was a substantial nonlegal rate. The number of abortions per 100 births in 1961 was in Hungary, 145; Czechoslovakia, 55; Poland, 35; and Yugoslavia (1960), 34.

If, then, abortion was once a widespread practice in the most advanced countries of Western Europe, if it is now widespread in Eastern Europe, where it is legal and subject to record, and where economic development is behind that of Western Europe, there is no reason to regard the resort to abortion as peculiarly Japanese. It is not an outgrowth of ancient tradition

the people of northwest Europe were in their reproductive control. Now that it is reasonably safe when legalized,[8] it is an effective means of family limitation for Hungary and Poland as well as for Japan.

If Western prudery and Oriental realism have led to an exaggeration of the role of abortions in Japan, this tendency has been helped by a statistical illusion. Not only have abortions increased as births have fallen, but the sum of births and registered abortions for each year yields a combined rate per 1000 population that has changed little during the big fertility drop (Table 1).[9]

TABLE 1. Births and Abortions in Japan

	Annual totals (000's)			Sum per 1000 population
	Births	Abortions	Sum	
1949	2,697	102	2,798	34.4
1950	2,338	320	2,658	32.1
1951	2,138	459	2,596	30.8
1952	2,005	798	2,803	32.8
1953	1,868	1,067	2,935	33.9
1954	1,770	1,143	2,913	33.1
1955	1,727	1,170	2,897	32.6
1956	1,665	1,159	2,825	31.4
1957	1,563	1,122	2,686	29.6
1958	1,653	1,128	2,781	30.4
1959	1,626	1,099	2,725	29.5

Sources: Masabumi, Kimura "A Review of Induced Abortion Surveys in Japan," Paper No. 43 in mimeographed proceedings of the 1961 conference of the International Union for the Scientific Study of Population, *United Nations Demographic Yearbook 1960*, Part I.

in Tokugawa times; not an outgrowth of the absence of Christian ideology. It is a response to social and economic conditions arising in country after country at a particular time in the process of modernization. The fact that abortion was not safe earlier in the century shows how determined

---

[8] In Denmark and Sweden, 1953–57, there were only 6 or 7 deaths per 10,000 legal abortions. See: Christopher Tietze, "The Current Status of Fertility Control," *Law and Contemporary Problems*, XXV (Summer, 1960), 442.

[9] The combined rate would doubtless remain even more unchanging if the number of unregistered abortions were known.

This seems to say that an abortion was responsible for each birth saved. Actually, of course, abortions can and do occur much more frequently than births can.[10] Other factors must therefore have played a role in Japan's falling birth rate.

OTHER RESPONSES IN JAPAN

One such factor was contraception. Irene Taeuber points out that this practice increased rapidly after 1950 although abortions were available, relatively safe, and cheap.[11] Use prior to that time is shown by a 1950 national survey which found that a fifth of all couples were currently

before the great rise in reported abortions began, couples were increasingly controlling their births, especially at the older ages.[12]

Of late, further control has been achieved by sterilization. Reported operations, totaling 5,695 in 1949, averaged 42,843 per year during 1955–59, at which time they equalled 3.8 per cent of the reported abortions. There is even some indication of a small amount of infanticide.[13]

In addition, the Japanese migrated from their homeland in sizable members. The proportion of Japanese persons aged 15–59 outside to those inside the home islands was 2.8 per cent in 1920; 3.2 per cent in 1930; and 5.6 per cent in 1940.[14]

TABLE 2.   Japan :   Changing Proportion Ever Married, by Age

Age	Percentage ever married					
	Women			Men		
	1920	1940	1955	1920	1940	1955
15–19	17.7	4.3	1.8	2.8	0.4	0.1
20–24	68.6	46.5	33.9	29.1	10.0	9.8
25–29	90.8	86.5	79.8	74.3	58.0	59.3
30–34	95.9	94.7	92.0	91.8	89.7	90.8
35–39	97.3	97.1	96.0	95.9	95.6	97.0
40–44	97.9	98.0	97.6	97.2	97.3	98.3
45–49	98.1	98.4	98.3	97.7	98.0	98.8

Source of data: Irene B. Taeuber, *The Population of Japan* (Princeton: Princeton University Press, 1958), p. 211.

practicing contraception and that nearly a third had done so at some time. Furthermore, the age-pattern of change in marital fertility shows that,

---

[10] According to surveys in 1949–50 and 1953–54, the gestation preceding abortions in Japan lasted between 9 and 11 weeks, depending on the order of the abortion. Kimura, *op. cit.*, pp. 3, 9.
[11] Irene B. Taeuber, *The Population of Japan* (Princeton: Princeton University Press, 1958), p. 274.

[12] Legitimate births per 1000 married women :

Age of married women	1950 rate as % of 1925 rate
15–19	92.8
20–24	96.4
25–29	93.3
30–34	75.4
35–39	54.4
40–44	40.5
45–49	13.2

Derived from data in: Taeuber, *op. cit.*, p. 265.
[13] *Ibid.*, pp. 278–282.
[14] *Ibid.*, p. 203.

TABLE 3. Age at First Marriage, Selected Countries

Country and date	All marriages with age known	Percentage marrying at following ages					
		Under 20	20–24	25–29	30–34	35–39	40+
		Brides					
Japan, 1959	100	5.3	63.8	27.5	2.9	0.3	0.1
U. S. A., 1959	100	48.6	37.8	7.4	2.8	1.5	2.0
Sweden, 1950	100	13.5	45.0	24.6	8.3	4.1	4.6
Italy, 1951	100	14.1	46.0	27.0	6.9	3.2	2.8
		Grooms					
Japan	100	0.4	23.7	61.8	12.7	1.2	0.3
U. S. A.	100	16.1	53.5	18.5	6.1	2.6	3.2
Sweden	100	1.9	31.4	38.4	15.7	6.7	5.9
Italy	100	1.7	24.6	42.3	18.3	8.1	5.0

Sources of data: for Japan, *United Nations Demographic Yearbook 1961*, Table 28; for the United States (29 states only), *Vital Statistics of the United States 1959* (U. S. National Office of Vital Statistics), I, 61; for Sweden and Italy, *United Nations Demographic Yearbook 1958*, Table 22.

TABLE 4. Proportion Never Married Among Women Aged 40-44

Country and date	Per cent
Japan, 1955	2.4
U. S. A., 1950	8.1
New Zealand, 1951	11.3
England and Wales, 1951	14.2
Austria, 1951	14.3
Italy, 1951	15.7
Sweden, 1950	15.8
Finland, 1950	17.8
Portugal, 1950	18.5
Northern Ireland, 1951	23.0
Ireland, 1951	26.7

Finally, the Japanese have exhibited still another adjustment—postponement of marriage. The proportion ever married among girls aged 15–19 fell from 17.7 in 1920 to 1.8 per cent in 1955, and for women 20–24 it fell from 68.6 to 33.9 (Table 2). The shift for men was also drastic. Indeed, it may be that the age at marriage rose faster in Japan than in any other country in history. By 1959 the nation had a marital age higher than that of most Western countries (Table 3). In the United States in that year nearly half the brides in first marriages were under 20, but in Japan only one-nineteenth of them were that young. However, the Japanese concentrate their marriages more heavily in the modal ages

—20–24 for brides and 25–29 for grooms—than Western countries do, as Table 3 shows.

The one adjustment the Japanese have not adopted is celibacy. In 1955 the proportion of women aged 40–44 who had never married was only 2.4 per cent, whereas in the United States in 1950 it was 8.1, and in Italy in 1951 it was 15.7 per cent (see Table 4). It looks as though the age at marriage is flexible in Japan, but not the decision to marry or not to marry. However, even this may change. The women who in 1955 were aged 40–44 represent a generation whose marriages, occurring mainly in 1930–40, were still almost wholly arranged by parents. As the age at marriage gets later, and as mating becomes more a matter of individual selection, a rising contingent of women may never succeed in attracting a man they are willing to marry.

THE THEORY OF THE
MULTIPHASIC RESPONSE

What, then, is the picture that Japan presents? It is the picture of a people responding in almost every demographic manner then known to some powerful stimulus. Within a brief period they quickly postponed marriage, embraced contraception, began sterilization, utilized abortions, and migrated outward. It was a determined, *multiphasic response*, and it was extremely effective with respect to fertility. It brought down the gross reproduction rate, with only a brief wartime interruption, from 2.7 in 1920 to 0.99 in 1959.[15] A change

that took at least 60 years in the United States required only 40 years in Japan.

What was the stimulus that caused such a massive response? In my view, the demographic stimulus was the decline in mortality and the sustained natural increase to which it gave rise. The data prior to 1920, though not entirely trustworthy, do at least suggest a declining death rate.[16] This is consistent with the better established trend after 1920, when, in not quite 30 years, mortality dropped to an extent that had required, starting at the same level, 76 years in Sweden and 37 years in Germany. The resulting natural increase climbed above 10 per 1000 around the turn of the century and averaged 12.8 from 1900 to 1959. When, as in Fig. 1, these rates are plotted on the same chart as those for three Scandinavian countries averaged together (Denmark, Norway, and Sweden), with Japan lagged 50 years, the latter appears to be reenacting the history of natural increase in northwestern Europe, but more abruptly.[17]

But why the multiphasic reaction to sustained natural increase? Were the Japanese experiencing increased poverty? Were their "means of subsistence" disappearing under the impact of increased millions? No, such an explanation—of a type often called upon in demographic theory— has no relation to the facts. During the 45 years from 1913 to 1958 the average rate of growth of industrial

---

15 Annual gross reproduction rates, 1920–55 from: Taeuber, *op. cit.*, p. 232. Annual gross reproduction rates, 1956–59 from: *Population Index*, XXVIII, No. 2 (April, 1962), 205.

16 Taeuber, *op. cit.*, pp. 50–51.
17 Dudley Kirk pointed out in 1944 the similarity between the Japanese birth and death rates of 1921–41 and those of England and Wales in 1880–1900. ["Population Changes in the Postwar World," *American Sociological Review*, IX (Feb., 1944), 34.]

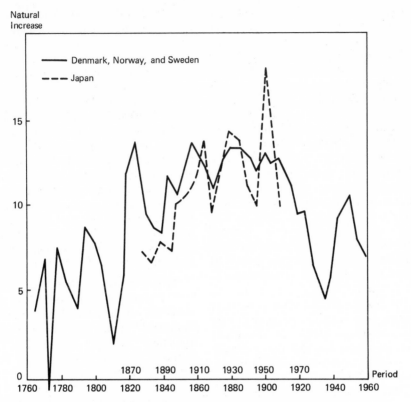

FIG. 1. Rates of Natural Increase in Denmark, Norway, Sweden (Averaged), and Japan, with Japan Lagged 50 Years.

output in Japan rose by 5.4 per cent per year, thus exceeding the 5-per-cent rate of Germany, Italy, and the U.S.A. from 1880 to 1913, and greatly exceeding the performance of the United Kingdom and France in any sustained period.[18] Obviously the demographic response of the Japanese is not to be explained in terms of spreading poverty or diminishing resources. Nor were the people influenced in their behavior by concern about national "overpopulation," for

they let their government proclaim a policy of population expansion during the "Co-prosperity" era. In short, an explanation of the vigorous Japanese response to sustained natural increase must account for the antagonism between such increase and prosperity, in terms of behavior prompted by personal rather than national goals.

WAS THE NORTHWEST EUROPEAN RESPONSE SIMILAR? Since the northwest European countries, years ahead of Japan, also had a sustained natural increase, did they manifest a similar multiphasic response? The answer is undeniably yes. Although generally

[18] Surendra J. Patel, "Rates of Industrial Growth in the Last Century, 1860–1958," *Economic Development and Cultural Change*, IX (April 1961), 317–318.

overlooked because of our preoccupation with the contraceptive issue, the fact is that every country in northwest Europe reacted to its persistent excess of births over deaths with virtually the entire range of possible responses. Regardless of nationality, language, and religion, each industrializing nation tended to postpone marriage, to increase celibacy, to resort to abortion, to practice contraception in some form, and to emigrate overseas. The timing and relative importance of the reactions were not identical in the various countries, and of course methods could not be used that were not then technically feasible for the public at large (e.g., harmless sterilization); but the remarkable thing is that all of the northwest European countries reacted, that they did so in each case with the reappearance of the whole range of responses, and that virtually the entire panorama was later repeated in Japan.

That the stimulus was also similar to that in Japan is clear. Our three Scandinavian countries in Fig. 1 reached a high plateau of natural increase around 1815 and *sustained it for more than a hundred years.* Since the plateau was reached long before a significant drop in the birth rate occurred, there were about six decades of what was then an unprecedented rate of human multiplication —sufficient to double the population every 61 years in the absence of emigration—before the birth rate began visibly to fall around 1870, and it took another 30 years or so before the drop in fertility could move fast enough to gain on the steadily falling mortality. Periods of substantial increase had of course been known before, but they were brief and virtually self-correcting, since each time

the death rate would soon rise again and wipe out the gain. What was unprecedented in northwest Europe was that self-correction was avoided so long over such a wide region. Local catastrophes did occur—as in the Irish potato famine of the 1840's —but it was characteristic of Europe at the time that these were accepted not as inescapable acts of God but as examples of what must be avoided at all costs by collective effort. Northwest Europe was winning the fight against death to a degree never before accomplished, and its success, with the resulting natural increase, explains the desperateness of the subsequent demographic response.

THE THEORY OF HOW THE STIMULUS PRODUCES RESPONSE. But how were the stimulus and the response connected? It was not true in Europe, any more than in Japan, that the connecting link was poverty. From 1860 to 1900, the gross domestic product grew on the average at almost 3 per cent per year in Denmark and Sweden, and almost 2 per cent in Norway.[19] When interpreting the effects of sustained population growth, most observers seem to assume that the question concerns the level of living. Was the population growth too fast, they ask, to maintain the general level? If the answer is "no," interest tends to vanish, because there is no "problem." If the answer is "yes," then all sorts of further consequences supposedly follow, because, with growing poverty,

---

[19] Based on average rates of growth over various specified periods, with constant prices, as given in: Simon Kuznets, "Quantitative Aspects of the Economic Growth of Nations: VI. Long-term Trends in Capital Formation Proportions," *Economic Development and Cultural Change*, IX (July, 1961), 76, 82, 88.

human beings must bestir themselves. But, as we have seen, the northwest Europeans and Japanese bestirred themselves in the face of prolonged natural increase without being goaded to do so by rising poverty. The answer to the central question about modern demographic history cannot be posed, then, in the framework of ordinary population theory, which assumes the sole "population factor" to be some relation between the population resources ratio and the collective level of living. It is doubtful that any question about demographic behavior can be satisfactorily posed in such terms, because human beings are not motivated by the population-resources ratio even when they know about it (which is seldom).

My own view is that no society has been geared to a sustained high rate of natural increase except by conquest. Under a prolonged drop in mortality with industrialization, people in northwest Europe and Japan found that their accustomed demographic behavior was handicapping them in their effort to take advantage of the opportunities being provided by the emerging economy. They accordingly began changing their behavior. Thus it was in a sense the rising prosperity itself, viewed from the standpoint of the individual's desire to get ahead and appear respectable, that forced a modification of his reproductive behavior.

Mortality decline impinged on the individual by enlarging his family. Unless something were done to offset this effect, it gave him, as a child, more siblings with whom to share whatever derived from his parents as well as more likelihood of reckoning with his parents for a longer period of life; and, as an adult, it gave him a more fragmented and more delayed

share of the patrimony with which to get married and found his own family, while at the same time it saddled him, in founding that family, with the task of providing for more children—for rearing them, educating them, endowing their marriages, etc., —in a manner assuring them a status no lower than his. The obligations of marriage and expanded parenthood were not easy, as Banks has shown so convincingly for nineteenth-century Britain,[20] in a changing society where one's position was threatened from every side and where one's children had to acquire new and costly forms of education. The parent needed to conserve some means for himself, because of longer life expectancy and because of the importance of capital for seizing opportunities or staving off disaster in the fluid situation of the times.

The inappropriateness of the old demographic behavior was not confined to one segment of society, such as the "middle class" or the towns and cities. Nor was it characteristic of some societies and not others. Whenever and wherever mortality declined on a sustained basis, there the continuation of old demographic patterns brought a train of disadvantages.

READJUSTMENTS IN THE AGRICULTURAL AREAS

Our view receives an acid test, for example, with respect to the peasantry, because a central tenet of population theory is that farmers lag behind other classes in altering their demographic behavior. We note, how-

---

[20] J. A. Banks, *Prosperity and Parenthood* (London: Routledge and Kegan Paul, Ltd., 1954).

ever, that the explanations given for this alleged fact are mutually contradictory. On the one hand, it is commonly taken for granted that no adjustment is made by farmers because none is needed: agrarian societies can assimilate natural increase indefinitely, because "children are an asset on the farm." This makes the farmer's unchanging reproductive behavior purely rational. However, it is hard to avoid seeing that a sustained natural increase in a delimited farming area will eventually mean "too many people for the land." This much granted, the theorist may explain rural demographic slowness by saying that farmers *feel* children to be an asset on the farm. Now, however, the farmer is no longer rational but irrational, and one must find an explanation for his stupidity. This is easy if one assumes that peasants are "traditional in their attitudes." By this route we are led to feel it is natural for modern attitudes and practices to begin in the cities and "diffuse" gradually to the countryside.

Such thinking appears to be a case of a nonexistent fact being "explained" by a plethora of unsubstantiated reasons. In Japan and northwest Europe, population increase was especially hard on the peasantry, with the consequence that their reaction was especially drastic. The structure of the rural societies was such that they could accommodate permanently growing populations only on one assumption—territorial expansion. Technological improvement provided no accommodation, because it called for fewer rather than more workers. As capital was increasingly applied to agriculture and the optimum size of farm unit rose, a young man found it more difficult, rather than less, to acquire what was necessary in agriculture to guarantee a satisfactory social status.

PROLONGED NATURAL INCREASE, INHERITANCE, AND AGRICULTURE. In the absence of long-run natural increase, there is no general problem of rural inheritance. The few parents with numerous surviving offspring are fortunate, for they have not only the child labor but also the eventual old-age security that children can furnish. Their children can receive enough land or substance to marry at a normal age, because each large family is matched by families that have died out entirely or have had only one child survive. Naturally, land and goods flow from the dead to the living in several ways—by purchase prior to death, by collateral relatives in the absence of true heirs, by remarriage of widows—and so large families acquire the means to endow their children for marriage. Without population growth, then, the demographic inequalities of one generation are ironed out in the next. There is no general problem of inheritance but only a problem for an occasional family that has lost out by ineptitude or has no heirs because of misfortune.

When, however, there is a sustained high rate of natural increase, inheritance becomes a chronic problem. Since the proportion of families with numerous surviving children is now much higher, these families are not matched by others that have land but few or no survivors. As a consequence, if their children are given land to marry with, the size of the farm will be reduced; if they are given cash or goods, its capital will be denuded. The parents are reluctant to do either, because they also have to live and, given their now greater life expectancy, they hang on to the land until much later in the life of the offspring. Young people are forced to postpone marriage, and some to forego it altogether. Thus the strictly agrarian system has very little capacity to absorb population increase.

This inability, be it noted, has nothing to do with "the inheritance system." The latter is concerned solely with the matter of discrimination among potential heirs, whereas our concern is with the growth of the total number of potential heirs (all with their social expectations) in relation to the resources available in agriculture. If there are more heirs than can be accommodated at the expected standard of living with the land available, no inheritance system can itself alter this fact. It can at best decide who gets hurt and who does not. In other words, if there is no sustained natural increase in a settled agrarian area, any system of inheritance will work. If the opposite is the case, then no inheritance system will work, unless, of course, there is some real solution available. Despite the vogue of inheritance systems in population theory, it is doubtful that they play any determinative role in demographic change. Rather, they simply reflect whatever demographic solutions are developed in the society. This view is strengthened when one realizes that fixed and rigid inheritance systems are figments of the social scientist's imagination. They are not something "laid on," which the people follow in the fashion of automatons; rather, they are fashioned and modified as changing conditions and interests demand.

"TRADITIONALISM" AND AGRARIAN DEMOGRAPHIC RESPONSE. If histor-ically the peasant communities of Japan and western Europe experienced a sustained natural increase, did they fail to respond successfully because "the peasant was wedded to his traditional value system"? To say so is to commit not only a factual error, as we shall see in a moment, but also a tautology. An explanation in terms of "tradition" has no value in social science, because "tradition" is merely a name for absence of change. A type of social behavior is like the momentum of a moving body: it will not change unless something forces it to change. If the absence of a contrary force is itself not explained, we have no real theory of the persistence but merely another name for it. As for the so-called values, they should be recognized as being a part, or aspect, of the behavior itself and, according-ly, as requiring to be explained rather than being used as the explanation. The fact that people migrate is not explained by their favorable evaluation of migration. By definition, nobody does anything voluntary without some purpose, however vague, in mind. The question of change or persistence is therefore a question of what did or did not act upon the total action (motive plus conduct). In other words, to say that fertility continues to be high in some group because of the group's "high-fertility values" is like saying that birds fly because they have wings.

In the case of the European peas-antry, however, the alleged fact to be explained—a lack of demographic response—is itself not true. The demographic behavior of the rural population did change, and it changed drastically, because it had to. The common assumption to the contrary seems to arise from our parochial tendency to ignore all changes except the reduction of marital fertility by contraception. If contraception was not at first adopted on a major scale in most of the agrarian sectors, it was because ready alternatives were available. One of these was migration. As the economic revolution advanced, the rural sections found in the rising cities an ever expanding outlet for their excess natural increase—an outlet that helped them to capitalize on the opportunities offered by continued industrialization.

Indeed, as we know, in all of the industrializing countries rural-urban migration removed not only the farmers' natural increase but also a substantial portion of the base population as well. In Japan, for example, Irene Taeuber estimates that, without migration, the rural population of 45.9 million in 1920 would have reached 62.6 million by 1940 instead of the actual 45.5 million.[21] The significance of rural-urban migration is that it involves a shift of occupation as well as residence. In fact, members of a farm family can leave agriculture, either part time or full time, without ever leaving home.[22] The best

indicator of rural migratory adjustment is therefore the diminution of the agricultural labor force. In Great Britain the greatest number of men employed in agriculture was 1.8 million in 1851. A hundred years later, when the total population was nearly 2½ times as great as in 1851, the agricultural male labor force was down to 1.1 million.[23] In Japan the population employed in agriculture, given as 15.7 million in 1876,[24] was 13.7 million in 1958[25] when the total population was more than 2½ times greater. Daughters often left the countryside in greater abundance than sons. Village girls in Japan went to work in cities as maids or in factories and shops, typically remaining away for six years, often saving enough to get married either upon returning home or while remaining in distant towns and cities.[26]

Thus it can hardly be said that

Foundation, 1953), mimeographed. Pp. 24–25.

[23] B. R. Mitchell and Phyllis Dean, *Abstract of British Historical Statistics* (Cambridge: Cambridge University Press, 1962), pp. 60–61. For data on agriculture's diminishing proportion of the labor force in the evolution of industrial countries, see: Simon Kuznets, "Industrial Distribution of National Product and Labor Force," *Economic Development and Cultural Change*, Supplement to V, No. 4 (July, 1957), Appendix Table 4.

[24] Ryoichi Ishii, *Population Pressure and Economic Life in Japan* (Chicago: University of Chicago Press, 1937), p. 78.

[25] Japan. Ministry of Foreign Affairs, *Statistical Survey of Economy of Japan 1959*, p. 9.

[26] In one village of 2,752 population in 1948, a total of 58 girls were working in the city. Out of 72 girls marrying in 1948, 16 married men in distant cities and towns (Ishino and Bennett, *op. cit.*, p. 91). The exodus of women out of agriculture in Japan is shown by the fact that the younger the age group, the smaller the proportion in farming (Taeuber, *op. cit.*, p. 94).

---

[21] *Op. cit.*, p. 145. Dr. Taeuber shows, p. 71, that the communes of less than 10,000 inhabitants—which in 1930 had 68.1 per cent of their occupied population in agriculture—lost 4.6 per cent of their population between 1920 and 1940, while the whole nation gained by 31.0 per cent. Since the farmland of Japan was densely settled already, "absorption of additional population would have jeopardized economic well-being, social organization, and political stability. The preservation of the status quo required the exodus of younger sons and daughters to urban areas and nonagricultural employment," p. 73.

[22] As a consequence, agricultural density may be highest in those areas where most farmers are only part-time in that occupation. See: Iwao Ishino and John W. Bennett, *Types of the Japanese Rural Economy* (Columbus: Ohio State University Research

rural population in industrializing countries made no demographic response. They responded to sustained natural increase by the drastic process of removing it. Their failure to feature contraception and abortion was not due to "traditional attitudes" (mass migration out of agriculture was not "traditional" either) but to the availability of an alternative which fitted the interests and structure of peasant families in the evolving economy.

The critical moment in the peasant family cycle, especially in northwest Europe, was the time when the surviving young people were to get married. Up until then their labor was useful on the farms and their consumption limited; but, if they were to marry, they had to have the means (i.e., adequate land) to support a family in a fully adult, independent, and respectable manner. The common process by which reproduction was brought into equilibrium with the agrarian economy was the postponement or hastening of marriage according to the socially defined scarcity or abundance of land. With a prolonged decline in mortality, there were more claimants to land for marriage and a greater reluctance on the part of elders to give it up; but the same progressive forces in the society which were bringing the mortality decline were also opening up opportunities for employment in nonagricultural sectors. The decision to stay in agriculture or to seize these new opportunities was made in the young person's life at about the same time as the marital decision. Indeed, the two decisions—whether to postpone marriage and whether to leave agriculture—were doubtless often made jointly. Leaving agriculture might be the only hope for getting married—

as in the case of Japanese girls who had to have a dowry. Migration out of agriculture was thus an adjustment that was congruent with the response pattern already built into the rural social structure.

This adjustment would not have been available, however, if it had not fitted into and aided the trend of the larger economy. Since industrialization by its very nature requires an exodus from agriculture,[27] the fact that economic development was occurring is proof enough that rural-urban migration was being rewarded. Many a farm got desperately needed capital, many a farm boy or farm girl achieved matrimony, because of receipts from the city. The adjustment of Japanese and European peasants was clearly not a descent into grim poverty and senseless subdivision; it was not a "resistance to the forces of modernization" in the name of a "traditional value system." It was, on the contrary, a utilization of the new opportunities of the economic revolution.

DELAYED MARRIAGE, A CONTINUED RURAL RESPONSE. The rural populations of industrializing nations did not respond to sustained natural increase by one means alone. In addition to out-migration, they adopted their old mechanism—postponement of marriage—to the new exigences, particularly in regions remote from urban centers. They did this, of course, not as a deliberate effort to reduce fertility or to solve the popu-

[27] K. Davis, "The Role of Class Mobility in Economic Development," *Population Review*, VI (July, 1962), pp. 67–73; and *idem*, "Internal Migration and Urbanization in Relation to Economic Development," *Proceedings of the World Population Conference 1954*, II (New York, 1955), pp. 783–801.

lation problem, but as a response to the complexity and insecurity of the new requirements for respectable adult status under changing circumstances. In Japan, as noted already, a dowry was required for a girl's marriage. Her farm family, short on land and long on surviving members, needed cash more than it needed girl power. Japanese factories and offices, on the other hand, needed cheap labor. It was therefore advantageous all around for rural girls to work under supervision, have their salaries returned home, and delay marriage for several years.[28] As a consequence, the age at marriage rose almost as fast in the rural areas of Japan as it did in the urban.[29] In neither sector was postponement a response to deepening poverty. Agriculture, as well as the total economy, was increasing in productivity.[30] In all sectors of the economy, then, families had to grasp the new opportunities of the evolving society or else face relative loss of social status and consumption. Their chances were not improved by demographic behavior that permitted the large family size made possible by declining mortality.

Rural marital postponement was particularly important in the eighteenth and early nineteenth centuries in northwest Europe, because outside opportunities were then too few to make out-migration work as the sole adjustment. Even in England and Wales, the country most conducive to rural-urban migration around 1800, less than 17 per cent of the population resided in places of more than 20,000 inhabitants. If within a decade the natural increase of the rest had migrated to cities, the urban population would have risen by approximately two-thirds instead of the actual one-fourth. In the United States, with plausible assumptions as to differential natural increase, one finds that, had all the natural increase of the farm population and one-half of that of the rural nonfarm population between 1840 and 1850 gone to the urban places, the latter would have increased by approximately 275 per cent during the decade, or three times as fast as they actually did. Apparently, the earlier in economic development the downward trend in mortality occurs, the more difficult it is, other things equal, to avoid solely by out-migration an increase of people on farms.[31]

---

[28] In 1930 some 435,800 girls, representing 4.2 per cent of the female labor force, lived in factory dormitories (Taeuber, *op. cit.*, pp. 87, 116).

[29] The proportion of women ever married by age was:

Age group	Shi (towns and cities)		
	1920	1935	Ratio
15–19	13.5	5.7	2.4
20–24	60.6	48.4	1.3
25–29	86.3	85.4	1.0
Gun group	(small towns and villages)		
	1920	1935	Ratio
15–19	18.9	8.7	2.2
20–24	70.9	59.8	1.2
25–29	92.0	91.1	1.0

From: Taeuber, *op. cit.*, p. 211.

[30] Between 1878–82 and 1913–17, land productivity in Japan rose by 80 per cent and labor productivity in agriculture by 136 per cent. See: Kazushi Ohkawa and Henry Rosovsky, "The Role of Agriculture in Modern Japanese Economic Development," *Economic Development and Cultural Change*, XI, Part II (Oct., 1960), p. 46.

[31] When the urban sector is small and the farm sector large, a rural-urban migratory stream that is big from the standpoint of cities will be insignificant from the standpoint of the countryside. See: K. Davis, "Internal Migration and Urbanization in Relation to Economic Development," *loc. cit.* However, it should be clear that there are other variables. One is the magnitude of the rural natural increase, which is greater

TABLE 5. Children Born and Surviving, and Age at Marriage, for Polish Mothers Born Between 1855 and 1880, by Size of Farm

		Size of farm (hectares)			
	Landless	0–1	1–4	4–7	7+
Number of mothers	9	36	110	31	15
Average year of birth for mothers	1872	1875	1875	1874	1874
Number of births per mother		3.9	5.4	6.4	7.7	9.1
Surviving children per mother[a]	2.9	4.1	5.0	5.9	8.0
Age at marriage of mother	31	25	24	22	20
Births per year from marriage to age 45	0.28	0.26	0.30	0.35	0.37
Births per year from marriage to birth of last child	0.43	0.35	0.36	0.39	0.41

[a] Evidently these were the children who survived to get married.
Source: W. Stys, "The Influence of Economic Conditions on the Fertility of Peasant Women," *Population Studies*, XI, No. 2 (1957), 136–148.

Even with both marital postponement and rural-urban migration, a decline in farm size often occurred in areas of northern Europe. A study of twenty villages in southern Poland finds, for example, that the average size fell from 7.24 hectares in 1787 to 3.17 in 1931, "although the whole area owned by peasants increased from 16,966 to 21,558 ha."[32] In Ireland there was evidently a similar shift, with the result that by 1841 more than half the holdings were of less than five acres.[33] Even in the United States, in the Southeastern region, the improved acreage per farm fell from 103.6 in 1860 to a low point of 37.9 in 1925.[34]

Forgetting the possibility of increased yields,[35] one tends to view such declines as the consequence of some "inheritance system" or as today in underdeveloped countries than it was in nineteenth-century Europe. This means that, given the same rural-urban distribution of the population, the out-migration from agriculture has a greater burden to carry in currently underdeveloped counties. See: K. Davis, "Urbanization in India: Past and Future," *India's Urban Future*, ed. Roy Turner (Berkeley: University of California Press, 1962).

[32] W. Stys, "The Influence of Economic Conditions on the Fertility of Peasant Women," *Population Studies*, XI, No. 2 (Nov., 1957), 136–148. The change is graphically shown, p. 148, by two maps of the farms in the area at the beginning and at the end of the period.

[33] My estimate based on: K. H. Connell, *The Population of Ireland, 1750–1845* (Oxford: Clarendon Press, 1950), pp. 163–164.

[34] Rupert B. Vance, *All These People* (Chapel Hill: University of North Carolina Press, 1945), p. 164.

[35] Per-acre productivity rose early in the economic transformation because of shifts in land use, better methods and instruments of tillage, and higher-yielding types of plants and animals. Thus "during the eighteenth century the traditional bias of Irish agriculture towards grazing had shifted to tillage," methods of tillage were steadily improved, and the potato, introduced in the sixteenth century and yielding more calories per acre than any other plant, became the main food crop. See: E. R. R. Green, "Agriculture," in *The Great Famine*, eds. R. Dudley Edwards and T. D. Williams (New York: New York University Press, 1957), p. 90. Also Connell, *op. cit.*, pp. 136, 158–159.

simply an indication of population pressure and deepening poverty; but they can more properly be viewed, in my opinion, partly as the maintenance of the same product per family with less land and partly as the consequence of a one- or two-generation lag of the adjustment mechanism behind the lowered mortality. That the adjustment mechanisms were there is evident in the twenty Polish villages. As can be seen in line 3 of Table 5, the number of children born per mother, during roughly the period 1872 to 1914, was almost twice on the largest farms what it was on the smallest. This positive association between completed fertility and size of farm has been reported often for peasants.[36] In the Polish case, differential mortality adds to the inequality in surviving children, but only slightly. The main factor in the differential fertility and in the number of surviving children alike is the age at marriage (line 5). That there is little limitation within marriage is shown by the sixth line—births per year between a woman's marriage and her 45th year. Comparison of the last two lines suggests, however, that the poorer peasant couples stopped their reproduction earlier (perhaps by abstinence and abortion), or suffered more impaired fecundity, for the births per year between marriage

and the last child (last line) show smaller class differences than those between marriage and the woman's 45th birthday (previous line).

The European peasants' response to sustained natural increase clearly reflected a social structure that held married couples responsible for their children. This feature—along with its corollary, postponement of marriage for those incapable of supporting children—was part of the independence and separateness accorded the nuclear family, as opposed to the joint household, in west European society. As such, it went back to medieval and post-medieval times;[37] and it tended to yield a later age at marriage than is found in most joint household systems. It did not necessarily produce a late marital age, however, because, with high mortality, individuals so unfortunate as to have to marry late were balanced by those lucky enough to marry early. When, in the late eighteenth and the nineteenth centuries, the rural areas were faced with a natural increase unprecedented in its size and duration, postponement of marriage appeared as one of the adjustments. This was by no means the only adjustment that enabled the peasants to avoid subdividing land to the point of severe poverty and resurgent mortality. In addition, the peasants maximized migration off the farm, increased permanent celibacy, and curtailed reproduction in the later years of marriage (probably by abortion, folk-contraception, and abstinence). Since, owing to the accelerating economic transformation, rural-urban

---

[36] E.g., Tsarist Russia, China between the two world wars, Japan in 1940, Bulgaria, and India. See in particular: G. Wm. Skinner, "A Study in Miniature of Chinese Population," *Population Studies*, V, No. 2 (Nov., 1951), 98–103. United Nations, *The Mysore Population Study* (New York, 1961), p. 86; A. Okazaki, *Investigation on Differential Fertility*, Japan, Welfare Ministry, Institute of Population Problems, Research Data, B, No. 2. Additional references, with tabular data for Germany and China, are in Stys, *op. cit.*, pp. 143–144.

[37] For evidence, references, and discussion, see: K. Davis and J. Blake, "Social Structure and Fertility: An Analytic Framework," *Economic Development and Cultural Change*, IV, No. 3 (April, 1956), 214–218.

migration became increasingly available, the forces tending to depress fertility, especially marital fertility, did not need to act so strongly as they did in towns and cities. In the latter places, migration out of agriculture was obviously not a possible alternative. The city-dweller's "migration" into a more lucrative occupation was mainly by acquiring education, skill, experience, and contacts—none of which was helped by an improvident marriage or a high marital fertility. His solution lay more in the direction of contraception and abortion, to which he had better access than the peasant.

IRELAND AS A TEST CASE

If correct, our analyis should hold not only for the different social classes but also for the various countries of northwest Europe, even in cases that are commonly regarded as demographically unique. Ireland, for example, is habitually cited as a country having in modern times a population history unlike that of any other nation. Not only did she experience a pronounced decline in population while her neighbors were all showing an unprecedented increase, but she exhibited a tendency toward late marriage and celibacy that strikes many observers as peculiar. On the assumption of uniqueness, particularistic explanations of her demographic history have been given—e.g., that it is a result of the Irish famine, the "land" situation, or extreme religious zeal.[38]

But how unique is Ireland? It is certainly not unique in having a marital age that was comparatively late to begin with and which grew later in the last half of the nineteenth century. In 1830–40 Irish women married reasonably early for Europeans: the proportion of brides who were under 21 was 28.1 per cent; under 26, it was 66.5 per cent—both proportions similar to those in England and Wales.[39] The Irish age at marriage evidently rose after that, reaching its highest point about 1911, at which time it started gradually down, as Table 6 shows. By 1957 the average age at marriage for Irish women was 27.6, only two years above the figure of 25.6 years for women in England and Wales.[40]

If the late age at marriage in Ireland is to be explained, it must therefore be explained in terms applicable to northwest Europe as a whole. In seventeen countries of that region around 1950, the proportion of brides at first marriage who were age 25 or older was 39.6 per cent, compared to 24.9 per cent in three East European nations and 21.5 per cent in five overseas industrial countries of European origin. The 1959 Irish figure of 53.1 per cent seems abnormally high until we realize that in 1950 the

---

[38] Honohan believes that the famine created "in the minds of the people a hard-headed and somewhat irrational scepticism in regard to the prospects and permanence of material betterment in Ireland," and that "a strong religious

faith" led to resistance to trends that developed elsewhere. (W. A. Honohan, "The Population of Ireland," *Journal of the Institute of Actuaries*, LXXXVI, Part 1, No. 372 (1960), 30–49. pp. 48–49.) He does not explain, however, why a famine should have an effect different in Ireland from the effect in India, why this attitude should last for a century, or why the Irish should happen to have such a strong religious faith. If the Irish were hard-headedly sceptical about future prospects in Ireland, why were they not also sceptical about the Roman clergy?

[39] Connell, *op. cit.*, p. 39.

[40] Honohan, *op. cit.*, p. 37.

TABLE 6. Percentage of Women in Young Age Groups Ever Married:
Ireland and Sweden

	Ireland				Sweden		
	Women					Women	
Date	15–19	20–24	25–29	Date	15–19	20–24	25–29
—	—	—	—	1750	4.4	27.3	56.6
—	—	—	—	1800	2.7	22.4	51.8
1851[a]	0.0	10.0	40.0	1850	0.8	16.5	49.4
1861	2.2	25.3	36.0	—	—	—	—
1871	1.9	21.9	51.0	1870	1.0	15.7	46.2
1891	0.8	14.0	40.9	—	—	—	—
1901	0.6	12.0	37.8[b]	1900	1.1	19.6	48.5
1911	0.5	11.6	34.4[b]	1910	1.1	19.8	48.6
1926	0.7	13.0	38.2	1920	1.1	20.3	49.3
1936	0.9	13.6	35.9	1930	1.0	19.6	48.3
1946	1.6	17.5	42.4	1945	3.3	36.1	69.7
1951	1.1	17.7	45.4[b]	1950	3.7	40.3	73.6

[a] These percentages relate to age groups " under 17," " 17–25," and " 25–35."

[b] For 1901, 1911, and 1951, data were available only for the age group 25–34. The figures here are our estimates derived by interpolation from earlier and later censuses giving the five age classifications.

Sources: Ireland: *Census of Population, 1946*, V, Part I, 34; *U. N. Demographic Yearbook, 1958*, p. 187; *British Sessional Papers, 1856*, XXXI, 1–99; *1863*, LX, 616; *1874*, Vol. LXXIV, Part II, Table 18; Sweden: *Historisk Statistik för Sverige, Vol. 1, 1720–1950* (Stockholm; 1955).

Spanish percentage was 50.4, the Norwegian 50.8, and the Swiss 46.7.

Granted that Ireland is part of the late-marrying wing of northwest Europe, one may explain this fact as due to her Roman Catholicism. But for five Catholic countries of the region,[41] the average percentage of first brides aged 25-plus was 40.4, as compared to 39.1 for ten non-Catholic countries. Even if Catholicism were involved in Irish marital postponement, how would it be? It would certainly not be because the church has an injunction against early marriage.

The usual interpretation is that the church defines marriage as second best, and hence gives no powerful encouragement to early marriage; but Belgium, an eminently Catholic country, has an earlier age at first marriage for females than does Norway, Sweden, or Scotland.

The way to understand Ireland's demographic career is hardly in such particularistic terms. Fascination with her late marriage should not blind us to the fact that she responded to long-continued natural increase by other means as well. She responded by permanent celibacy, for example, and here again Ireland was not an isolated case but rather an extreme exemplification of the northwest

---

[41] Austria, Belgium, Italy, Portugal, Spain. France is omitted because of some question about its being a "Catholic country."

TABLE 7. Regional Comparison of Average Percentage Single of Women Aged 45 or Over

	Number of countries	Average percentage single among women aged 45 or over
European[a]	30	12.6
Northwest European	22	15.7
Catholic	8	16.6
Non-Catholic	14	15.2
Eastern European	8	4.0
Overseas European industrial	5	9.8
Moslem (North Africa, Turkey, Pakistan)	7	2.0
Asian	12	2.2

[a] Ireland is excluded throughout. If added, the northwest Europe average rises to 16.1 and the "Catholic" group to 17.5. France is counted as a "non-Catholic" country. Scotland, Northern Ireland, and England and Wales are counted as separate countries.
Source of data: *United Nations Demographic Yearbook 1960*, Table 10.

European pattern, itself extreme. In 1951 some 24.7 per cent of the Irish women aged 45 or more had never been married. In 1950 the Icelandic figure was 21.5 per cent; the Norwegian and the Scottish, 20.9. The degree to which Europe stands out can be seen from [Table 7].

A third Irish response—again typically west-European and extreme in character—was the very high and prolonged rate of out-migration. The peak of Irish-born living abroad was reached about 1880, when, in four countries alone, they represented 60 per cent as many as lived in Ireland itself. From 1901 to 1956 the net emigration came to an estimated 1.34 million, an average of 24,300 per year. The loss during 1946 to 1956 amounted to about half the number of births.[42]

It is commonly claimed that the Irish postponed marriage or migrated as an alternative to practicing birth control within marriage. However, as

Glass has noted,[43] data from the 1946 census show class differences in marital fertility. Furthermore, a decline of 25 per cent occurred in overall marital fertility between 1911 and 1946. Couples in Ireland, as elsewhere in Europe, were apparently taking to birth control, though not to the same extent as in neighboring countries. One should note, of course, that a shift to a later age at marriage, other things equal, will independently bring a reduction in marital fertility by pushing a greater part of the marital exposure into the less fecund years of the reproductive span. It will cause an additional loss through the greater proportion of women who die before marrying. For these reasons the influence of a shift in the age at marriage is greater than the simple proportion of the

---

42 Honohan, *op. cit.*, p. 42.

43 David V. Glass, "Malthus and the Limitation of Population Growth," in *Introduction to Malthus*, ed. D. V. Glass (New York: John Wiley & Sons, Inc., 1953), p. 35–37.

reproductive years added or eliminated.

If, then, Ireland exhibited a multiphasic response similar to that shown by her neighbors, differing from theirs only in the relative emphasis placed on the various means and in its vigor—so drastic that it halved the absolute population within 80 years—the explanation must be in terms applicable to the rest of the region. A significant fact is that Ireland was, and has to a considerable degree remained, a *rural* part of northwest Europe. It was a rural backland when it belonged to Great Britain, and after its independence in 1922 it was cut off from its most industrial section, the northern six counties—much as if Mississippi, Arkansas, and Louisiana were given their independence but with New Orleans and the rest of the Gulf Coast removed. A late age at marriage, as we have seen, was particularly characteristic of rural northwest Europe; and in Ireland it prevailed more in the rural areas than in the towns. Ireland's continued rurality, together with the circumstance that Catholicism became a symbol and rallying point of Irish Nationalism as against the Protestant British, enabled the Catholic clergy to remain strong. Being in control to an unusual degree, the celibate clergy could implement its ascetic supervision over courtship and instill its negative attitude toward marriage, including state enforcement of the indissolubility of wedlock. It thus gave its blessing to marital postponement and lay celibacy, and at the same time kept down illegitimate fertility. Concomitantly, the exceptional power of the clergy tended, as in other Catholic countries, to discourage economic development and thus to keep the area rural.

As an agrarian region, Ireland partook of the exodus out of agriculture that accompanies modern economic development—except that, without economic development in its own territory, the migration out of agriculture was simultaneously a migration out of Ireland. In other words, international and overseas migration and rural-urban migration were one and the same thing for Ireland. The lack of economic opportunity at home powerfully discouraged marriage, while ecclesiastical determination of family, criminal, customs, and censorship laws made abortions, contraceptive materials, and birth control information and services difficult to obtain. Marriage tended to be postponed not only because the economic requirements for it were hard to secure, not only because it could not be dissolved if it proved personally obnoxious, but also because it was likely to lead to several children. In addition, clerical control, poor economic development, and rural community opinion worked together to discourage married women from entering the labor force, thus reducing still more the economic support for marriage. Recently the proportion of married women aged 15 to 65 in paid employment was less than 3 per cent, as compared to about 23 per cent in England and Wales.[44]

Ireland thus manifests a combination of the demographic responses of Europe, extreme in its totality and in its result but composed of familiar strands indeed, all understandable under the circumstances. It thus illustrates the principle that the explanation of as fundamental a feature of society as its demographic changes is not to be found in some

----

[44] Honohan, *op. cit.*, p. 39.

inflexible biological or economic law or in some particularistic cultural idiosyncrasy, but rather in the main features of the operating social organization on the one hand and, on the other, in the changing conditions which arise from past performance and the altering international politico-economic environment.

My thesis is that, faced with a persistent high rate of natural increase resulting from past success in controlling mortality, families tended to use every demographic means possible to maximize their new opportunities and to avoid relative loss of status. An understanding of this process in population theory has been hindered by a failure to see the multiphasic character of the response and by an interpretation of demographic behavior as a response either to absolute need or to some cultural idiosyncracy such as a particular "value system" or "custom." When the demographic history of industrialized nations is analyzed comparatively, an amazing similarity of the response syndrome seems to me to emerge. An explanation of a country's demographic behavior by reference to a peculiarity or accident of its culture fails to cope with this basic similarity of response. Curiously, we do not adopt such an easy way out with respect to mortality. We do not "explain" India's high death rate and

Sweden's low death rate by saying that the one "values" high mortality and the other low mortality. Yet we sometimes come perilously close to this in regard to other aspects of human demography, especially fertility.

As for the view that the motivational linkage between change and response depends on fear of absolute poverty, we have seen that it fails to account for the fact that the multiphasic effort to reduce population growth occurs simultaneously with a spectacular economic growth. Fear of hunger as a principal motive may fit some groups in an extreme stage of social disorganization or at a particular moment of crisis, but it fits none with which I am familiar and certainly none of the advanced peoples of western Europe and Japan. The fear of invidious deprivation apparently has greater force, and hence the absolute level of living acts more as an environmental condition than as a subjective stimulus. If each family is concerned with its prospective standing in comparison to other families within its reference group, we can understand why the peoples of the industrializing and hence prospering countries altered their demographic behavior in numerous ways that had the effect of reducing the population growth brought about by lowered mortality.

The Sociology of Human Fertility*

Ronald Freedman

POSTWAR INTEREST IN THE
SOCIOLOGY OF HUMAN
FERTILITY

Interest in the sociology of human
fertility has increased greatly in the
postwar period among social scientists, administrators, political leaders, and the informed public in many
countries. The background for this
increasing interest is an interrelated
complex of changes in society itself
and in knowledge about population
and society.

1. *There is an increasing realization that the problematic factor in
population growth today is the fertility rate.* Growth rates in most countries are little affected by international migration; they depend mainly
on mortality and fertility levels. In
the underdeveloped areas mortality
either already has fallen to low levels

---

* Abstracted by the editors of this
volume from Ronald Freedman, "The
Sociology of Human Fertility: A Trend
Report and Bibliography," *Current Sociology*, X/XI (1961–62), 35–42, 58–68.
The original monograph, from which this
material is abstracted, is the introduction to a long annotated bibliography
to which the summary of the literature
has reference. Both the original monograph and the abstract cover the period
from the end of World War II to 1961.
They do not cover either the population
trends or the literature since 1961—a
period during which there has been a
considerable development of organized
family-planning programs which have
begun to have an influence on fertility
trends in some countries. There has also
been a considerable body of new research
in the intervening period. However, the
author, Professor Freedman, believes
that the broad generalizations made in
the original monograph are still valid.

or can be predicted to do so soon with
the probable application of existing
knowledge. Since fertility rates are
expected to remain high for at least
a time, the increasingly rapid rate of
growth resulting from mortality decline is regarded by most development experts as a threat to programs
of economic and social development.
So, a variety of people concerned
with these programs are eager for
knowledge which can be used in
action programs to accelerate fertility
decline....

Before the war, most demographers simply expected fertility rates
to continue to decline or to stabilize
at very low levels as effective contraception spread in an increasingly
urbanized population. Since prewar
population projections erred mainly
in failing to allow adequately either
for the possibility of higher fertility
rates or for their volatility, demographers have begun to turn to more
broadly based social research on fertility for better predictions of this
element in population growth....

2. *A very recent stimulus to fertility research is the discovery that
the age structure of a population
depends much more on fertility than
mortality trends.* Even among social
scientists there are many who do not
know that the "aging" of Western
populations resulted mainly from the
decline in the birth rate rather than
from lower mortality. In the underdeveloped areas a decrease in mortality without a decrease in fertility
creates a younger rather than an
older population and greatly increases

the size of the dependent child population for which expensive overhead social services must be provided.

3. *Sociologists have been emphasizing once again the essential functions of the family even in an urban industrial society.* Prewar writing about the urban family emphasized its loss of functions to other specialized institutions and used the decline in family size as an important index of this trend.... Special social incentives to childbearing were widely discussed as a means to achieve the reproductive needs of the society in view of the presumed lack of individual motivation for having children. In the postwar period there has been a rediscovery by sociologists of the persistent strength of primary groups, and especially of the family....[1] The increasing use of sample surveys and other techniques for studying normal families has also provided evidence of the continuing importance of the nuclear and even the extended kinship relationship in the broader functioning of an urban society.[2] Once it is recognized that the family remains a viable institution of critical importance even in an urban society, it becomes meaningful and important to study how its size and the process of its growth is related to the other institutions and structural aspects of the society.

---

[1] E.g., E. Shils, "The Study of The Primary Group," in *The Policy Sciences*, eds. D. Lerner and H. Lasswell (Stanford: Stanford University Press, 1951).
[2] E.g., M. Young and P. Willmott, *Family and Kinship in East London* (London: Routledge & Kegan Paul, 1957); R. Firth, *Two Studies of Kinship in London* (London: The Athlone Press, 1956), London School of Economics Monographs on Social Anthropology, No. 15, 1956; and R. Freedman *et al.*, *Principles of Sociology* (New York: Henry Holt & Co., 1956), Chaps. 11 and 12.

4. *Methodological developments since the war also have increased the possibility of many kinds of fertility study.* Sample interview surveys have been used to study important variables closely related to fertility and formerly believed to be too personal and intimate for systematic study. Contraception, abortion, fecundity, and other presumably sensitive subjects have been studied in a variety of cultural settings with enough success to demonstrate that such investigations are feasible, although there are major problems of reliability and validity in measurement. The great increase since the war in the number of countries taking censuses and developing statistical reporting systems also has increased the resources for fertility studies....

A CLASSIFICATION OF THE VARIABLES THAT AFFECT FERTILITY

The variables that affect human fertility are numerous and complex in their interrelation. Most of the research studies understandably have concentrated on a very small part of the complex whole. A gross initial classification of the major types of variables that affect fertility may be useful in placing individual studies in a larger perspective specifying other major classes of variables that may condition or explain a particular relationship....

One model for the sociological analysis of fertility levels works backwards from measures of fertility to the following classes of variables affecting the fertility levels of a society or of strata or categories within the society.

1. *The means of fertility control which stand between the social organization and the social norms on the one hand and fertility on the other.* Davis and Blake have provided the following very useful classification of such means, which they call "intermediate variables":[3]

Factors Affecting Exposure to Intercourse ("Intercourse Variables")

(a) Those governing the formation and dissolution of unions in the reproductive period.

  (1) Age of entry into sexual unions.

  (2) Permanent celibacy: proportion of women never entering sexual unions.

  (3) Amount of reproductive period spent after or between unions.

    (a) When unions are broken by divorce, separation, or desertion.

    (b) When unions are broken by death of husband.

(b) Those governing the exposure to intercourse within unions.

  (4) Voluntary abstinence.

  (5) Involuntary abstinence (from impotence, illness, unavoidable but temporary separations).

  (6) Coital frequency (excluding periods of abstinence).

Factors Affecting Exposure to Conception ("Conception Variables")

  (7) Fecundity or infecundity,[4] as affected by involuntary causes.

  (8) Use or non-use of contraception.[5]

    (a) By mechanical and chemical means.

    (b) By other means.

  (9) Fecundity or infecundity, as affected by voluntary causes (sterilization, subincision, medical treatment, etc.)

Factors Affecting Gestation and Successful Parturition ("Gestation Variables")

  (10) Foetal mortality from involuntary causes.

  (11) Foetal mortality from voluntary causes....

2. *Social norms about what family size ought to be....*

3. *Social norms about each of the "intermediate variables."...*

4. *Any important aspects of the social organization which function explicitly or implicitly to support the norms for family size by providing important social rewards and punishments which depend on the numbers of children in the familial unit....*

5. *Other aspects of the social organization which affect fertility by their influence on the norms or actual values for the intermediate variables, either independently of or in relation to their effect on the norms about fertility....*

6. *The mortality level which determines how large a surplus of births is required to produce the normative number of children....*

7. *The net migration level, which determines the number and ages of persons available to the families and to the society as a whole and thus affects fertility....*

---

[3] Kingsley Davis and Judith Blake, "Social Structure and Fertility: An Analytic Framework," *Economic Development and Cultural Change*, IV, No. 2 (April, 1956), 221–235.

[4] Infecundity refers here to any physiological impairment to a normal rate of reproduction. It is not restricted to complete sterility.

[5] Contraception refers here to any means for avoiding conception, including prolonged or periodic abstinence, coitus interruptus, and any mechanical or chemical methods.

8. *Other factors in the environment which affect the intermediate variables in ways inconsistent with the fertility norms....*

In brief, this model specifies that the fertility of any social collectivity tends to correspond with a level prescribed by the social norms which are in turn an adjustment to the way in which varying numbers of children affect the achievement of socially valued objectives. In the long run, the net effect of the intermediate variables affecting fertility should approximately produce the normative reproductive level. However, in a complex and changing society the other organizational and environmental factors may affect the intermediate variables in ways that are inconsistent with the family size norms. It is not necessary to assume an equilibrium model to use this classification of the variables affecting fertility....

While we are considering fertility mainly as the dependent variable to be explained, it can interact with other social-economic variables both as a cause and effect. For example, there is a considerable literature on how family size affects intellectual development and educational attainment of the children. This problem can be turned around, so that the educational attainment of parents or their perception of the educational advantages of a small family are seen as the independent variables affecting their fertility. Similarly, economic status may affect or be affected by family size. These are not contradictory propositions. The observation over time by a large number of people that varying family sizes have differing consequences for socially valued goals affects the development of social norms about family size and motivates appropriate behavior. The study of the consequences of differing fertility levels probably is indispensable for understanding their causes....

FACTORS RELATED TO FERTILITY: ANALYTICAL HYPOTHESES

A. STRATIFICATION VARIABLES ... Unquestionably, the greatest volume of fertility research is concerned with stratification variables, partly because data are available in standard demographic sources, but also because stratification is important for both economic and social theory. Differences in life style associated with position in a status hierarchy presumably may influence any of the norms or intermediate variables affecting fertility. Among the important status indicators considered in various fertility studies are: occupation, income, education, wealth, power, prestige, caste, and general class indicators (e.g., divisions into "upper," "middle," "working class" or divisions into feudal strata). Probably there is a general agreement that no universally valid relation exists between status measures and fertility. Instead, research has been directed increasingly to the specific nature of the relationship in major types of society and for different measures of status.

1. Stys[6] and others have provided some evidence for the hypothesis that in a preindustrial society in which the family is the basic economic unit, status will tend to have a positive correlation with fertility, because higher status will carry with it resources for early marriage, multiple

---

[6] W. Stys, "The Influence of Economic Conditions on the Fertility of Peasant Women," *Population Studies*, XI, No. 2 (Nov., 1956), 136–148.

marriage, adequate diet, or other bases for increasing fertility.... But evidence is contradictory from a large number of recent Indian studies, which, presumably, are relevant to a preindustrial situation. Some studies indicate relatively low fertility in the lowest social stratum, some find no relationship to status, and others find a negative relationship....

2. A large number of studies document an inverse relation between status measures and fertility during the period of transition from high to low fertility....

There is significant evidence in a number of studies that the negative relationship of status with fertility can be explained, at least in part, by a positive relation between status and the age at marriage or the effective use of contraception or abortion. The other more sociological explanations are more speculative, being supported either by scattered partial evidence or by none at all.

3. Many scholars expect that in the mature urban society status differentials will change so that the correlation of status with fertility will become positive.[7] The basic argument here is that all strata are likely to learn effective family planning. Children, having lost their value as laborers in family enterprises or as social security resources, are valued as consumer goods. But since lower income groups must choose more often between children and other consumer goods, the higher income groups can afford more children. This hypothesis makes assumptions about the elasticity of demand for children which may be incorrect....

Many postwar studies in the West

[7] See, for example, A. Hawley, *Human Ecology* (New York: The Ronald Press Co., 1950), Chap. 7.

do show a tendency for status differentials to diminish, but there is little evidence of a significant positive relation yet. The relationships still are obscured by the fact that many families in all strata have had their first few children early in the postwar period. The ultimate status differentials may not emerge until data are available for the last part of the child-bearing period.

4. The hypothesis that upward social mobility between social strata leads to relatively low fertility has been investigated in a variety of settings. The primary rationale for the hypothesis is that: (1) those with relatively small families can utilize for their advancement the energy and resources that otherwise would be devoted to raising additional children (this may involve prior aspirations for mobility), (2) mobile persons become individuated and secular in outlook so that traditional group motivations for fertility are reduced....

5. Status variables are often treated as interchangeable indicators of an underlying status continuum, but some research suggests that fertility variations may result from discrepancies between statuses in different hierarchies....

6. Each of the status indicators may also have an effect that is independent of its role as a general class indicator but depending instead on its specific consequences. For example, education:

(1) may create interests and activities that will affect norms about family size (e.g., college-educated women are likely to acquire a wider range of non-familial interests and activities);

(2) may give greater access to information about family limita-

tion or help to develop attitudes, skills, or relationships increasing the probability that family limitation can be used successfully;

(3) is frequently a means for changing status or permitting identification with and participation in new status groups....

B. FAMILY STRUCTURE VARIABLES

1. We have already discussed ... the important general hypothesis that fertility is higher to the extent that socially valued goals are achieved in kinship-based organizations and that the specific forms of kinship organization affect the fertility level in various ways.

While the potential importance of hypotheses in this area is generally conceded, systematic research efforts are rare. There is need for analysis of how fertility is affected by the specific division of functions between familial and other institutions under various conditions.

2. There is systematic evidence that fertility declines as married women engage in nonfamilial activities, especially in work away from home. Presumably, her status then depends more on these other activities and less on her fertility. There is now evidence that the relationship runs in both directions with some women working because they can have only few children and some having few children because they want to work. In high-fertility societies, the role of the wife in supplying personnel for the all-important kinship unit is so important that her status is likely to depend on her ability to produce at least a minimum number....

3. Some hypotheses emphasize certain organizational requirements in the family for efficient fertility control and small families. For example, adequate communication between spouses and their organization for joint decisions have been cited as necessary means for efficient fertility control. An important study by Hill *et al.*[8] reports that the absence of efficient familial organization is an important cause of the high fertility in Puerto Rico despite expressed interest by the population in much lower fertility....

4. Dominance relations in the family may affect fertility because differing familial roles have distinctive interests in reproduction. A recurrent theme in discussion of this issue is that the wife has strong interests in family limitation but lacks the power to implement her interests.... There is some evidence that dominance is a conditioning variable in the U.S.A. affecting whether the husband's economic status or the wife's nonfamilial interests will determine family size.

5. Fertility may be affected by the requirement of a certain sex distribution among the children if the family is to function adequately in its society. There is considerable evidence of preference for sons for religious and economic reasons in many preindustrial societies, but in modern societies the evidence is not consistent as to preference for sons. There is some evidence of a desire for at least one child of each sex in industrial societies. Any sex preference of this kind may increase fertility to produce the desired minimal sex distribution.

6. Children may be valued because they strengthen the marital bond and

---

8 R. Hill, J. M. Stycos, and K. W. Back, *The Family and Population Control: A Puerto Rican Experiment in Social Change* (Chapel Hill: University of North Carolina Press, 1959).

thus ensure that the rewards of marriage will be available. Apart from direct statements of such a belief in some studies, there is indirect evidence in data showing lower divorce rates for couples with children (again the direction of the relationships is ambiguous).

7. Under current Western conditions, after one child is born, there is a fairly high probability the family will go on to have at least one more. Some interpretations are that this is because: (*a*) the marginal costs of a second child are small, (*b*) the socialization process is (or is believed to be) easier with several children.

C. Non-Familial Institutions or Groups with Explicit Programs for Influencing Fertility Norms or the Intermediate Variables

Apart from analyses of the origins of governmental pronatalist or antinatalist policies, most research in this area takes for granted a set of historical values about reproduction in a group or institution and deals with whether the group values actually affect the reproduction of its members. There is almost no investigation of the more difficult question of why the group or institution has developed or maintained distinctive values.

1. Sauvy[9] and others have pointed out that, at least in the short run, the interest of the state in reproduction at certain levels for economic or strategic reasons may be inconsistent with the cumulative results produced by the valuation of children by married

couples who act without reference to the needs of the larger society. An extensive literature about whether pronatalist governmental policies, such as family allowances, can increase fertility is inconclusive, although French demographers are convinced that this has been the effect in postwar France.

Official antinatalist policies in underdeveloped areas have not yet been successful.... The existence of large-scale antinatalist programs offers an important opportunity for studying this problem. The spectacular and unprecedented decline of Japanese fertility in the postwar period is associated in the literature with the legalization of abortions and with government support of birth control programs. It is not clear, however, to what extent government action precipitated the decline and to what extent it implemented demands created by preceding changes in Japanese society....

2. Religious organizations may foster specific norms about fertility or affect it diffusely by maintaining ideologies with specific if unintended effects on fertility. Most of the empirical research deals with the specific influence of the Roman Catholic church in limiting the use of many control measures and in supporting values for larger families. The results vary with the country studied, suggesting that the church's influence depends on other variables in the society as well as on variations in the character of the church itself....

3. Obviously the organized planned parenthood movement in many countries may have an effect in reducing fertility. However, there are few significant evaluation studies of the effect of specific programs. For most countries it is clear that the couples reach-

9 A. Sauvy, *De Malthus à Mao Tsé-Toung: le problème de la population dans le monde* (Paris: Denoel, 1958). English translation: *Fertility and Survival. Population Problems from Malthus to Mao Tse-Toung* (New York: Criterion Books, 1961).

ed directly by such programs are only a small part of the total group using contraception, but the indirect influence of the programs through their clients, through the mass media, or through other less formal communication channels is unknown. . . .

4. Organizations (e.g., medical) controlling access to the means for regulating fertility may have special interests which will affect the availability of these means. For example, in Japan, midwives charged with disseminating contraceptive information may feel that this activity reduces the number of deliveries to their disadvantage, and doctors specializing in legalized abortions may have a vested interest in this program. In the U.S.A. the relatively large number of Catholic hospitals and doctors exercise a considerable influence on medical practice that is related to fertility control. . . .

D. OTHER GENERAL CHARACTERISTICS OF SOCIAL AND ECONOMIC ORGANIZATION

1. The organization of society on the basis of rational, secular procedures rather than sacred, traditional practices has been related theoretically to efficient family planning and small families. Attempts to find such a relationship empirically within a single population in the Indianapolis Study were not very successful, but this is probably the kind of problem for which societies rather than individuals are the proper unit of analysis. . . .

2. The increasing organization of an urban society in bureaucratic structures which routinize social relations has been linked to higher fertility because such a structure minimizes future risks and defines the career patterns of the mobile. Insofar as bureaucratization also involves the routinization of work, it may reduce interest in work and lead to a greater interest in family and other nonwork associations. . . .

3. An increasing degree of institutional specialization at first decreases fertility by reducing the relative value of family and children. But in a mature, highly specialized urban society the family provides essential primary group functions unavailable in other ways because other groups are too impersonal or too transitory. In this connection, the family can be studied as linking the individual to the larger society, thus strengthening social bonds and providing for essential orientation and social control. . . .

4. Fertility is generally reported to decrease with increasing community size in industrialized countries, with the highest fertility in the farm sector. But this is not necessarily the case in preindustrial societies where the organization and functions of cities are quite different. . . . The question is whether community-size and farm-urban differentials reflect differentials in other variables which are changing (e.g., institutional specialization or the extent to which economic and other activity is based on a familial unit or education levels). This involves explaining why city size or rural-urban differences affect fertility in the first place.

5. In a society in which the production economy is not based on familial units, fertility may depend on the extent to which the production level is high enough to permit expenditures on "consumption" of additional children without sacrificing other consumer goods. This proposition leads to a rather complex series of questions about: the elasticity of demand for children in a society where they have

little productive economic value, whether "expensive children" are different from "inexpensive children," and whether noneconomic considerations affect the demand for children in a manner systematically related to income. . . .

6. Once contraception is widely available and family income depends on a highly organized but volatile economy, short-run fluctuations in economic conditions are associated with postponements and advancements of marriages and of births without necessary proportionate changes in reproductive norms or in completed fertility. However, there is also evidence that similar co-variations occurred earlier even in some predominantly agricultural societies.[10]

7. The forms of holding and inheriting property in interaction with the type of family organization have various effects on fertility.

8. Nonfamilial economic organizations encourage or discourage marriage and reproduction in indirect and diffuse ways depending on their interests. In many Western countries businesses encourage strong family ties in various ways as fringe benefits to improve employee morale and to increase the loyalty of employees with scarce skills (by scholarships for children, preference in employment to men with children, etc.). On the other hand, in Japan some companies subsidize contraceptive clinics and abortions (either directly or through health insurance). . . .

9. The extent to which the mass media and informal communication channels influence fertility norms and practices is still largely unexplored. This research area is particularly important because we know that in Western countries the long-run secular fertility decline is in no case attributable primarily to organized governmental or private programs. So, less formal and more diffuse influences need to be investigated. . . .

10. Extreme social disorganization or very rapid social change may lead to an increase in fertility by reducing conformity to traditional practices which keep fertility below the potential biological maximum. This hypothesis has been discussed in connection with the transition from preindustrial to industrial organization or the contrasts between industrial and preindustrial societies. . . .

E. TECHNOLOGICAL FACTORS Fertility changes may be indirectly produced by technological changes which affect almost all of the variables previously considered. For example, the development of a modern system of transportation and communication is a precondition for a highly specialized organization of society associated with a dispersion of familial functions to other institutions. . . . The following are only examples chosen from those involving somewhat more direct relationships:

1. The invention and economical production of efficient contraceptives obviously is relevant to fertility control, but whether the availability of mechanical or appliance contraceptives is necessary for low fertility is still a controversial question.

2. Early forms of urban industrial development with dense population concentrations in small housing units required by the technology sometimes are cited as discouraging to high fertility.

---

[10] For data on preindustrial Sweden, see D. S. Thomas, *Social and Economic Aspects of Swedish Population Movement, 1750–1933* (New York: The Macmillan Company, Publishers, 1941).

3. Technological developments leading to suburbanization in developed industrial societies may encourage higher fertility by providing a setting more suitable for children and family life.

4. The invention of appliances which increase the services and activities concentrated in the family home (e.g., television, washing machines, etc.) may increase fertility.

5. Housing conditions and facilities in underdeveloped areas are discussed as discouraging family limitation practices because of lack of privacy, water, storage facilities, etc.

F. SOCIAL-PSYCHOLOGICAL AND PSYCHOLOGICAL VARIABLES Psychological variables and hypotheses that have been considered relevant to fertility may be divided into two very broad classes: (1) those which are concerned with the process by which reproductive norms are learned, (2) those which are concerned with social attitudes, motivations, or personality traits which affect the norms or the actual level of fertility. We have very little systematic empirical evidence to establish the validity of most psychological hypotheses, but it is only fair to add that most of the scattered research has been done by sociologists rather than by psychologists. The major American efforts to relate psychological variables to fertility and family planning have been rather unsuccessful. . . .

An Approach to the Cultural Base of Infant Mortality in India*†

Alfred Yankauer

In 1909, at a time when the infant mortality rate in England and Wales was above 120 and some forty years after William Farr had demonstrated that tremendous variations in infant mortality were directly related to urban socio-economic differentials, Sir Arthur Newsholme wrote: "Infant mortality is the most sensitive index we possess of social welfare and sanitary administration, especially among

---

* The views expressed in this article are entirely personal and do not represent those of any organization with which the author is or has been associated.

† Alfred Yankauer, "An Approach to the Cultural Base of Infant Mortality in India," *Population Review*, III, No. 2 (July, 1959), 39–51.

urban conditions."[1] These are words which have been quoted often and thoughts which have been enshrined in textbooks. Not only medicine and public health but allied disciplines have been taught to think in these terms. Yet there are good reasons today to take a longer and harder look at them —first to be sure that their meaning is clear, and secondly to qualify their dogmatic assertions in the light of more recent observations on mortality rates and other indices of technological development.

The concept of "social welfare" is value laden. Therefore it takes on different shapes in the minds of men depending upon the values transmitted to them by their different cultures. Such shapes may not only differ, but may even diametrically oppose each other, as, for example, the shape of the central institution of human social life, the family, in India and in the U.S.A. Who is to say whether "social welfare" is better served by the human closeness and sense of duty engendered by growing up as a member of a large, joint, kinship-rooted family than by the individual freedom and the stress on initiative which are more characteristic of the small companionship family of the west? Or, in converse, that "social welfare" is worse served by the dependency and the intense but narrow social obligations that appear to be associated with the joint family than by the restlessness, tensions, and hurry that seem to characterize the western family?

This report will point up ways in which social institutions (such as the family), patterns of behavior, and

ways of thinking are etiologically related to infant mortality in India (as in all other countries). Therefore, it is important to recognize that the values of culture in their higher sense, the contributions made toward fulfillment purpose and contentment in life, are not the subject of discussion. Infant mortality is no measure of social welfare in this sense. What Newsholme meant by social welfare is more comparable to what is now called technological development, or material prosperity, or social welfare services. This is but one expression of the western industrialized, materialistic society of the twentieth century. There are many other expressions of this same society which can be judged inimical to social welfare, the most insistent and threatening of these being its propensity for self-destruction in a cloud of atomic dust. However, this same society has thus far succeeded in preventing premature death —particularly in infancy and early childhood, to an extent undreamed of by any previous order of civilization. The characteristics which have enabled it to do so are both physical, in the sense of a favorable balance of natural resources, scientific knowledge and population, and mental, in the sense of a culture or way of behavior and human interrelationships which could develop such resources and apply such knowledge efficiently and rapidly.

Whether the infant mortality rate is the most sensitive index of this type of technological development, however, is open to question. A number of observers in recent years have pointed out the key position of the 1–4 year age mortality rate in this connection.[2,3] Table 1 compares current mor-

---

[1] A. Newsholme, Report by the Medical Officer on Infant and Child Mortality, Supplement to the 30th Annual Report of the Local Government Board (London, 1910).

[2] Z. Verhoestraate, "International Aspects of Maternal and Child Health," *American Journal of Public Health,*

tality rates of different age groups from birth through 14 years of age in Madras City and in the U.S.A.[4] It will be observed that the greatest contrast in rates is in the 1–4 year age group, followed by the 1–11 month segment of infant mortality rather than its total. There are other vital statistics which are sensitive indices of technological development: weight at birth, the ratio of neonatal to postneonatal mortality, the average expectation of life at birth, even the age distribution of the population and the age distribution of its deaths. There is probably little point in arguing as to which of these indices is the most sensitive. All are useful reflections of differences and contribute to a description of a nation's health problems.

THE INFANT MORTALITY RATE

The really compelling characteristic of infant mortality is its size, for more deaths occur during this first year than at any other equivalent period of time of the human life span. Although this is characteristic of nations in all stages of technological development, the contrast is vastly greater in underdeveloped areas. Thus, in Madras City, infant deaths in 1956 formed 28 per cent of all deaths, while in New York State they formed only 5.3 per cent of all deaths. This

striking contrast is a reflection of the higher birth rate and the lower expectation of life, as well as the higher mortality in infancy in Madras.

It is conventional and convenient to separate the components of infant mortality into two parts: those whose origin lies in the natal, prenatal or preconception period, and those which act upon the infant only after its birth. In general, deleterious prenatal or natal factors cause death soon after birth so that even though medical certification of death may be incomplete or inaccurate, some insight into the relative importance of these components is obtained by examining the time of death in infancy. The most striking change which has occurred in these components in western countries is the sharp decline in mortality after one month of age, a change which has not been paralleled in India nor in other nations whose technological development has remained underprivileged. This is illustrated in Fig. 1 which compares the trend of infant mortality above and below one month of age in the U.S.A. for whites (a relatively privileged class) and nonwhites (a relatively underprivileged class) with that of Madras City for the past 40 years. It will be observed that the decline in neonatal mortality is comparable for all three groups; the decline in postneonatal mortality for American nonwhites parallels that for whites, indicating that they have shared equally in the benefits of material prosperity, although their relative status is unchanged. (A precisely similar effect has been noted in the U.K. in trends of neonatal and postneonatal mortality for social classes during the present century.[5] In

XLVI (1956), 19.

[3] C. D. Williams, "Social Medicine in Developing Countries," *Lancet*, I (1958), 863.

[4] In this report statistics and experiences from Madras City, New York State (excluding New York City) and the continental U.S.A. will be drawn upon because they are readily available to the writer. It is believed that they are fairly illustrative of India as a whole and its contrasts with the West.

[5] J. N. Morris and J. A. Heady, "Social and Biological Factors in Infant Mortality," *Lancet*, I (1955), 343.

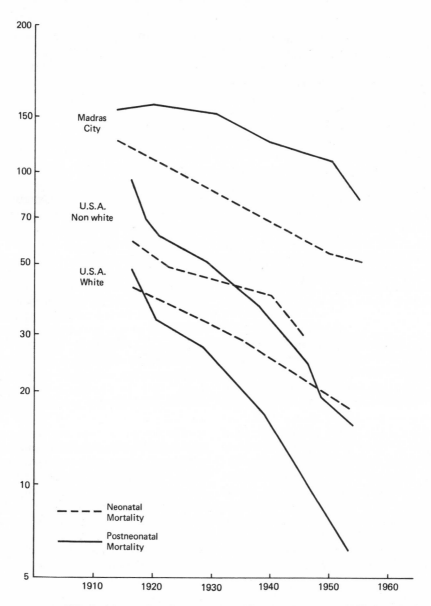

FIG. 1. Neonatal and Postneonatal Mortality Rates per 1000 Live Births in U.S.A. (White and Nonwhite) and Madras City, 1915–1955

contrast, the postneonatal mortality in Madras City has fallen no faster than its neonatal mortality and exceeds it to the same extent that it did 40 years ago, so that, in a comparative sense, ground has actually been lost. The total infant mortality rate in Madras was thrice that of U.S.A. in 1915. It

is almost six times that of the U.S.A. in 1954. The sharp fall in postneonatal mortality since 1950 in Madras is of interest, but too short a time period is involved to know whether this trend will continue. From the point of view of rates, the situation in Madras today is comparable to that in England and Wales at the beginning of the twentieth century. During the nineteenth century infant mortality and the ratio of neonatal to postneonatal deaths in Britain remained virtually stationary.[6] The drastic decline in postneonatal deaths did not begin until 50 years ago.

Causes of infant deaths, although inaccurately reported, reflect a similar picture. In Madras these causes are reported today in virtually the same relative proportion as they were 40 years ago[7] whereas in all technologically developed countries the relative proportion of deaths ascribed to infections (particularly gastrointestinal) has been drastically reduced.

In the West, the twentieth century has sometimes been called the century of the child. In the early 1900s social reform, economic development and the free milk and educational activities of the infant welfare movement supplemented each other to relieve poverty, hunger, and overcrowding and to substitute rational infant care for traditional practice. Together with advances in the science of medicine and public health and their application, this combination of circumstances accounts for the precipitous fall in post neonatal mortality in western countries. All these factors were interdependent and cross fertilized each

other to such an extent that it would be foolish to emphasize the exclusive importance of any one of them.

The potentials for reducing infant mortality in India today are quite different from those of Britain 50 year ago. Quite apart from differences in tradition, history, natural resources, and relationships with other nations' influences hard to compare, two obvious differences exist. In the first place there is more knowledge about the cause, cure, and prevention of disease to apply, and in the second place the government is in a stronger position to form policy and program and to translate it into action. This last difference has come about because of the increasing growth and acceptance of the idea of "the welfare state" which has accompanied technological development all over the world. In India this is manifest not only in the deliberate planning and controls of the Central Government, but in the stated objectives of the controlling Congress Party and its leaders. Although there may be some disadvantages to such a role for government, the potential for more rapid change which this role offers far outweighs them. In fact one may with some legitimacy ask why improvement in infant mortality has not been more striking and rapid up to the present time. The remainder of this discussion will focus primarily on the postneonatal segment of infant mortality, since it is this segment which has shown the least tendency to change in India.

Basically the causes of the excess infant postneonatal mortality in India are to be found in the nutritional status of its infants and in their overexposure to large doses of pathogenic microorganisms. This is obvious to the most casual observer and needs no special survey to substantiate it. These

---

6 J. Charles, in *Diseases of Children*, eds. A. Moncrieff and P. Evans (5th ed.; London: Edward Arnold Co., 1953), Vol. I, Part I, chap. i.

7 A. Yankauer, unpublished data.

two basic causes of death supplement and reinforce each other. Nutritional privation lowers resistance to infection and infection accentuates nutritional privation.

Purely medical methods and means, of course, have no bearing on the prevention, and little relevance to the permanent cure, of nutritional privation. With respect to infant deaths due to infections, the situation is more complicated. Immunizing agents against a number of specific diseases exist: pertussis, poliomyelitis, diphtheria, tetanus, tuberculosis, and smallpox. Mass immunization will effectively prevent deaths from these diseases and is economically sound. Malaria eradication is also economically sound. However, the number of infant deaths that would be prevented as a result of immunization and mosquito killing campaigns is relatively small (except in areas of high malarial endemicity). The vast excess of deaths due to the common diarrheal and respiratory infections would remain untouched by such campaigns.

Early, thorough and adequate treatment of these common infections could theoretically prevent most fatal outcomes. However, the expense of facilities, drugs, and other therapeutic agents, and the enormous numbers of trained personnel needed to carry out such a program would be beyond the dreams of the wildest planner. Furthermore, it is unsound to concentrate energy on repair work if there are ways of avoiding damage in the first place.

The application of modern methods of sanitary science to water supply, human waste disposal, and food production would surely prevent many of these excess deaths. However, such application is also hampered by the inordinate expense of facilities, the shortage of trained personnel, and by traditional modes of behavior which militate against the use of facilities even when provided. It would, however, be most useful to be able to establish priorities in the approach to disease control by sanitation. These could be set up if modern epidemiologic and bacteriologic methods were applied to the study of the cause, source and spread of infections in India. Such studies have not been carried out and one can only guess at the nature of the infecting agent and speculate about which of its several possible channels of spread are most important. The experiences of other countries cannot be drawn upon except as methodological models.

CULTURAL FACTORS

If medical and sanitary approaches to reducing infant mortality are of limited value, other approaches must be sought. When viewed broadly the basic causes of the excess infant deaths in India, undernutrition and overinfection, possess a material and a nonmaterial component. The material component exists because of Indian shortages in resources, capital and technological know-how. The nonmaterial component exists because of the human behavior, human relationships, motivations and values which compose India's culture. From the material point of view the problem of undernutrition exists because there is not enough food produced and distributed, not enough money to invest or enough technological know-how to apply modern methods of food production and distribution, not enough income per family to permit purchase of an adequate diet, etc. From the nonmaterial point of view, however, both the producer and the consumer of food have a choice even within the restricted economic range imposed upon them. The choice they make is not calculated to get the most nutritional value out of a product of comparable cost or availability. It is based purely and simply upon traditionally learned behavior and the symbolic significance of particular kinds of food in the Indian scale of values. Considerable thought and attention has been given to the material components of these bases of disease and death in infancy and to the development of programs which seek to eliminate them. In contrast, relatively little attention has been paid to the nonmaterial components and to the deliberate development of a program to modify them in such a way that they no longer contribute to disease and death. Although in this discussion attention is devoted mainly to cultural factors affecting postneonatal deaths, the same reasoning and approach could also be applied to neonatal deaths, but the specific examples and operational effects might differ.

It is significant that the cultural values and practices of India which (whatever their other significance) contribute to infant disease and death center around the three primal characteristics of all living matter: the ingestion of nutrients, the egestion of wastes, and the reproduction of the species. This is an indication of the deep-seated holds, their roots in early childhood experience, and their resistance to change. It is relatively easy to point out what they are, but relatively difficult to know how to change them. Yet change is occurring and will continue to occur in these cultural values and practices. Such change can be hastened by community action, and planning such action could well receive

as much attention as planning to raise the material level of living.

Any discussion of the relationship of culture to health in India is necessarily limited by the fact that cultural variations exist in different parts of the country and different segments of the population. Most of the features to be discussed have been observed in Madras. However, many, if not most of them are common to other parts of India, and to all segments of the population as evidenced by a number of written reports.[3,8] The discussion is also handicapped by the author's limited period of observation and limited ability to observe, understand and interpret. This is a more serious criticism. It can only be hoped that the discussion will stimulate further study and work in this important field. The details presented (whether accurate or inaccurate) are less important than the point of view they are used to illustrate.

FOOD

Cultural values and practices related to the ingestion of nutrients bear upon infant deaths by influencing the amount of a nutrient ingested and its absorption (thus affecting body needs directly) and by causing food to become a channel for the introduction of pathogens. The amount of nutrients ingested and absorbed is influenced by the following practices:

1. THE CUSTOM OF INTRODUCING SOLID FOODS AT A RELATIVELY LATE AGE. Breast milk contains relatively little Vitamin D, insufficient Vitamin C, and virtually no iron. Beyond the age of

---

[8] D. B. Jeliffe, "Cultural Variation and the Practical Pediatrician," *J. of Ped.*, XL (1956), 661.

6 months the quantity of breast milk is generally insufficient to meet the infant's caloric and protein needs. The scarcity and high cost of cow's milk (the most desirable major additional source of protein at this age) makes it all the more important that solid foods containing protein, iron, and vitamins be started, at the very latest, by 6 months of age. In Madras such a practice is quite uncommon. Prior to their first birthday only one out of two children will generally have received any food other than breast or cow's milk. Even at a year and a half a few children will have not yet been introduced to other foods.

2. PRACTICES WHICH DILUTE OR DE-STROY NUTRIENTS. Milk is commonly diluted when given to infants and children, and the degree of dilution is great and bears little relationship to age. This practice is harmful insofar as it deludes mothers into equating quantity with quality, a delusion most commonly encountered when the expensive, well advertised proprietary baby milk mixtures or food are being used. The practice of diluting milk may be economically rather than culturally determined, but this is by no means always true. Occasionally an artificially fed infant is being given a formula so dilute that he cannot possibly take it all and the full food value of the milk is lost to him. The prolonged cooking of food, often long before its consumption, tends to destroy its accessory food values, although without effect on other elements. Most children under two years of age receiving foods other than milk are fed out of the family pot, rather than given food especially prepared for them. Thus this is a relevant factor. The precise importance of

these particular practices is difficult if not impossible to measure.

3. PRACTICES WHICH INTERFERE WITH THE ABSORPTION OF NUTRIENTS IN FOOD. Practices which hasten bowel evacuation are the routine administration of castor oil and the use of irritating spices, chillies and peppers in food offered to children. The administration of castor oil daily or biweekly is quite common in Madras, and, as previously mentioned, feeding children from the family pot is customary. Like the previous factors of dilution and destruction, the importance of these practices is purely conjectural, although not illogically so.

4. CUSTOMS, BELIEFS AND PRACTICES INFLUENCING THE CHOICE OF FOODS. These constitute a wide and relatively unexplored spectrum of factors, whose details seem to vary (often to conflict with each other) according to geography, caste, and family. Sometimes even individuals of the same family will fail to agree upon them. Although details (such as the classification of a particular food) may vary, these factors do possess a number of common denominators:

(a) The system of classifying foods as "hot" or "cold," a practice prevalent in the folk belief of many parts of the world and incorporated in *Ayurveda,* influences choice not only because of the avoidance of certain "very hot" or "very cold" foods (particularly in babies) or the avoidance of too much of a series of hot or cold foods, but also because illnesses and their cures are also classified in terms of "hot" or "cold." Thus the presence of a mild diarrhea will tend to make for avoidance of "hot" and consumption of "cold" foods. Because of the enormous burden of illness in infancy, this latter practice has frequent scope for operation, even if other factors are considered less important. Children admitted to hospital for severe protein deprivation (kwashiorkor) have often been deliberately deprived of protein-containing foods because of some illness which by itself would not have been serious.

(b) Certain foods are apparently avoided because of what seems to be an imitative relationship to illness. In Madras, for example, it is commonly believed that ripe bananas cause diarrhea and that drinking water enhances diarrhea.

(c) Certain foods are deemed harmful only to particular classes of people, among whom lactating women and nursing infants are probably the most outstanding. Thus, meat or fish, although eaten by all other members of the family, will often not be given to the infant or young child.

(d) Although probably of relatively little significance, since it is practiced only by a small portion of the population, vegetarianism based on family tradition, religious custom, or moral conviction should also be listed as a factor influencing food choice. Of more significance is the religio-cultural status of cattle, a status which conflicts with their potential as a food source (beef) and a food producer (milk).[9]

(e) In almost every society certain foods are invested with a high degree of emotional and social significance whose meaning derives from early childhood experience and links closely with fundamental personality determinants. The strength and meaning

[9] *Report on India's Food Crisis and Steps to Meet It*, Agricultural Production Team (Ford Foundation), Govt. of India (New Delhi, 1959).

may be very great and influence food choice proportionately, particularly when economic factors operate as well. In South India rice and rice eating must exist not only because of custom and the nature of the agricultural economy, but also because rice itself is invested with emotional values, associations, and meanings. When the family budget permits, other foods will be consumed along with rice as part of a balanced diet. When the budget is limited, however (as is the case in the vast majority of families), foods other than rice will be sacrificed, regardless of their relative cost and nutritional value in order to procure enough rice to achieve some degree of satisfaction from eating.

Food may also serve as a carrier of pathogenic microorganisms. The manner in which food is prepared, stored, served, and eaten has obvious relationships to the presence or absence of such organisms. In general, existing practices of food preparation tend to eliminate microorganisms (viz., boiling of milk, customary purchase and storage of only small quantities of food, etc.). These practices also promote food preservation under tropical conditions. However, the use of fingers as eating utensils may facilitate the spread of microorganisms in infants and children. This practice is undoubtedly less significant for adults since what contaminates an individual's fingers is likely to enter his mouth regardless of how he eats. However, when combined with the fact that many adults and older siblings may feed the same child and that children are fed by others rather than allowed to feed themselves for a very much longer period of their life than in Western cultures, it seems possible that this custom may make some contribution to the excessive infections of infancy. Hands, banana leaves, and tumblers are often rinsed with water before food contacts them. However, the extent of rinsing is unlikely to eliminate many microorganisms. The practice of rinsing seems part of a larger trait, that of avoiding, eliminating, or hiding from view the obviously offensive. Since it is not based upon an understanding of the germ theory of disease, it may sometimes do more harm than good. Thus the mother who boils milk before giving it to her baby may (after boiling) contaminate the milk by straining it through an unsterile rag to remove scum particles.

A final cultural factor which may affect infant mortality by way of food and infection is the method of feeding fluids to small infants. The Western observer cannot help but be impressed by the contrast between the infant held closely in arms, head up and comfortable, to suck freely at the breast, and the infant laid flat on its back, helplessly restricted by its mother, while she pours milk or other fluids into its crying mouth. Apart from the psychological trauma of this common feeding practice, the possibility of its contributing to respiratory infections because of the aspiration of milk or other food cannot be ignored. Unfortunately no postmortem studies specifically searching out aspiration pneumonia are available to test this hypothetical point.

HUMAN WASTES

Urinary wastes rarely are carriers of microorganisms, whereas respiratory and gastrointestinal waste products frequently carry pathogens. The spread of disease through such channels depends partly upon how these wastes (sputum and feces) are disposed of and partly (since air is the only repository of expiration) upon how closely people live together. Closeness of living, to take the last factor first, is not determined solely by economic necessity. The joint family itself groups many under one roof and brings many adults in contact with one single infant, increasing the infant's exposure to germs. Some desire or need to live closely with others must account for the presence of densely packed village settlements in a rural economy which could as easily support isolated homes nearer the fields to be worked. In this sense culture contributes to overcrowding; the overexposure to infection in rural India is greater than in Western countries where families are small, infants are handled almost exclusively by their mothers, and individual dwelling units are occupied by fewer people in spite of the overwhelming urbanization of society.

Few could deny that promiscuous defecation and (to a lesser extent) expectoration, with the subsequent migration of pathogens to a new host via flies, water, dust, or food, constitute an important channel of disease spread in India. Although this chain can be broken at several places, the most obviously vulnerable point of attack is the behavior of the human being himself. More provision of sanitary latrines is no solution to this problem, as field experience has shown.[10] For latrines to be used, traditional behavior and attitudes must change as well.

The subject of defecation is not a topic of polite conversation. As an

---

[10] T. R. Baskharan, "Environmental Sanitation in NEFA," *Swasth Hind*, II (Sept., 1958), 226.

intimate body function, its discussion is apt to cause embarrassment. This is reflected by a general neglect of the human attitudes, motivations, and associations with this act in medical, public health, and social science literature. Even descriptive analyses of the act as it is followed by a community are singularly absent. Yet it would be useful to know something factual about place, time, efforts to cleanse or cover, if they are made, and other ascertainable details, and to relate actual practice to ancient ritual prescriptions or to expressed ideals. Casual observation in Madras City reveals that open places near water seem preferred; even when a segregated common spot that is cleansed out daily is used as a repository, feces are rarely deposited in a covered pot or covered with earth, although either precaution would be quite feasible and desirable.

Far less is known about bowel attitudes and personality formation in India, although Carstairs[11] has some interesting things to say on this score. Yet if change in behavior is sought it might be important to know more about these deeper associations also. One of the things which strikes a Western observer most forcibly is the "permissiveness" of toilet training in children, an attitude that can be characterized as psychologically healthy compared to the obsessional rigidity and emotional horror with which the Western parent generally approaches the subject. The relationship of this permissive attitude and the community personality which it expresses to the maintenance of community physical health and the spread of fecal-borne disease in India is worthy of further exploration.

[11] M. A. Carstairs, *The Twice Born* (London: Hogarth Press, 1957).

SEX

Sexual intercourse is also taboo to polite discussion although in recent years the urgent need to control population growth has caused medical and social science to focus attention on it. The act itself will not be considered here as it relates to spreading disease (venereal disease), but rather the organization and attitudes of society which have been built around the act in India.

High fertility and large family size must be considered an important contributory cause of infant mortality in the light of the underprivileged social and economic circumstances prevailing in India today. With a more favorable balance of material goods and habitable lands, these factors might be of negligible importance. As it is, in addition to other effects, they intensify (by dilution) the mass malnutrition and magnify (by concentration) the mass overinfection of infants and children. Cultural factors affecting fertility and family size in India have been discussed by others in more authoritative fashion than can be done here. Chandrasekhar[12] for example has pointed out that among other things, early and universal marriage, the banning of remarriage, the inferior position of women in society, and the difficulty of practicing contraception within joint family living conditions, all contribute to the problem.

One other factor which seems to have received relatively little attention in the literature is the relationship of the culturally defined purpose of the sexual act itself to fertility and family size. In Western society today sexual intercourse, by and large, is

[12] S. Chandrasekhar, *Population and Planned Parenthood in India* (London: Geo. Allen & Unwin, 1955).

apt to be consciously seen as the culmination of deeply felt love between two human beings and as an emotional experience whose achievement is an end in itself, even though some segments of society would consider such a purpose immoral. In India, its purpose, as formulated by the culture in which it exists, appears to be more directly related to the production of children, so that it is not as apt to be viewed as an experience valuable in itself. The expressed desire of many Indian families to limit the number of children they produce, a fact revealed by various surveys,[13] is in seeming conflict with such an observation. However, if this observation is correct, it would merely point up an ambiguity in motivation and add another cultural factor to the list of those interfering with a program of population control.

In India the joint family and caste system are the cultural institutions within which sexual intercourse is permissable and desirable. Although these institutions may be fast changing, they have certainly not disappeared so that their possible relationships to infant mortality (apart from their contribution to high fertility and large family size) are worth considering. One contribution, the assemblage of many relatives in one household unit and the resultant overcrowding and facilitation of disease spread, has already been mentioned. A second, the custom of intracaste and subcaste marriage, may also contribute by producing more defective fetuses than would be produced by more exogamous mating. No data are available on this point, however, and it must remain conjectural. A final and equally conjectural point is the set of values and the view of life and interpersonal relationships which are transmitted to the growing Indian child through family, clan, and (their extension) religion. In many small but obvious ways these values may affect infant mortality: by giving the purchase of a marriage gift for a relative a higher priority than purchasing needed medicine or food; by valuing the ritual purification of a dead body above the performance of a postmortem examination; by rendering performance of unplanned social obligations more important than the keeping of a planned medical appointment, etc. In a larger way, the disintegrating effect in today's world of the heritage of joint family, caste, and religious philosophy on interpersonal relationships and the functioning of the adult Hindu personality, and thus on infant mortality as on all else, is, perhaps, less obvious. Among others, Carstairs,[12] Panikkar,[13] and Narain[14] have commented on this point and it deserves notation at least in any discussion of the subject.

This brief catalog of culturally conditioned practices and attitudes which of themselves contribute to infant mortality has necessarily accentuated the negative. Cultural practices and attitudes which favor infant survival, such as the almost universal breast feeding, the inevitable boiling of animal milk, the affection lavished on most children, etc., have not been discussed. It is important to bear this point in mind lest the impression be gained that all cultural attitudes and practices in India contribute to infant mortality. It should also be pointed out that Western medical practice is as capable of creating and perpetuating its own unscientific rituals and

[13] K. M. Panikkar, *Hindu Society at Cross Roads* (2nd ed.; Bombay: Asia Pub. House, 1956).

[14] D. Narain, *Hindu Character*, University of Bombay Publications, Sociology Series, No. 8 (1957).

superstitions as any society. It is recognized today that beliefs once firmly preached, such as feeding by the clock and early toilet training, belong in the realm of prejudice rather than science. In the same way, some of the suggestions made earlier but unsupported by scientific observation, such as the harmfulness of castor oil and chillies or the practice of hand eating, may arise from unfounded prejudice.

CULTURAL CHANGE

The social institutions and the patterns of learned behavior, attitude, and feeling to which we give the name culture are as inseparable from the physical or material aspects of a society as the psyche and the soma of the individual man. Teleologically man's culture is a tool that enables him to extend his individual biological mastery of environment, but as his expenditure of energy for survival, food, and shelter becomes less, the environment itself is altered and this in turn affects the pattern of culture. This has occurred most strikingly in Western society since the advent of mechanization and industrialization with the result that the culture of the Western world has also become a tool that enables man to use and live with the machines he has created to master the physical aspects of his environment. Sometimes these machines themselves become a hazard to him, as with the automobile. Sometimes, when viewed from a universal frame, the culturally transmitted behavior of machine-centered man may seem ridiculous, as for example the compulsive need of a suburbanite to catch a train, to be at the office on time, to keep each appointment on schedule. Yet it is this same compulsive perfectionism that keeps

the wheels of a complex industrial society moving smoothly and that motivates a mother to prepare artificial foods for her baby which are as free from contamination as human breast milk. Sometimes the driving competitiveness of the Westerner seems excessive, yet it is this same source of energy which causes mothers to vie with each other to feed solids to their infants and have them immunized at the earliest possible age.

These interrelationships between the physical and cultural aspects of man's environment are worth bearing in mind. They point up the difficulty of isolating and modifying one small aspect of culture, such as an infant feeding practice considered harmful, without also changing the physical environment or, more significantly, without also changing the underlying personality traits which this one small practice reflects. But if these considerations point up difficulties, they also emphasize the necessity of viewing economic and social man together. If the physical and cultural aspects of his environment cannot be compartmentalized, neither can any approach to the prevention of disease and death to which these two aspects of his environment contribute.

It is far easier to catalog aspects of culture that may influence infant mortality than it is to suggest ways of modifying them. Indeed any serious approach to this subject necessarily verges into realms of religious thought and philosophies of governmental action. Rather than attempting to treat it in detail, some general principles will be discussed, out of which a program to reduce infant mortality by changing culturally conditioned practices and attitudes could grow.

There seem to be three ways of

hastening the change in human behavior and attitude that occurs naturally with growth and experience. Mass behavioral or cultural change can be effected in the same ways. The first way, by exhortation, persuasion, and reward or promise of reward, is most often associated with religion, but it is also used a great deal by medical practitioners. This is the method of "shoulds" and its effectiveness is directly related to the prestige and status of the preacher or doctor. To the Western observer this method seems to be used more often in Indian social, business, and political life than it is in the West. When applied to Indian child-rearing methods and attitudes its effectiveness may well be related to the status and prestige of grandmother or mother-in-law as compared to doctor, nurse, or political and religious leader. The more Westernized and urbanized the family, the greater the chance for its success.

The second way of change, by compulsion, regulation, punishment or threat of punishment, is most often associated with a martial existence and government by dictatorship. However, every society regulates its own welfare by a system of formal sanctions or laws as well as by the informal sanctions of its culture. It is only by the degree of regulated action and thought and in the thoroughness of regulatory enforcement that army and civilian life and governments differ. Laws can be a force for changing culture as well as for retaining its status quo. Unless the rationale of a law is understood and generally accepted by the people, however, its enforcement becomes either a mockery or a butchery.

If a given regulation will improve health and if it can be enforced without great difficulty there is no reason why any government as well as any army should not adopt it. Thus in the early part of the present century in the U.S.A. legal measures and public opinion united to virtually eliminate the fairly common practice of indiscriminate expectoration in public places; remnants of this campaign can still be seen in the signs on New York City subways notifying passengers that spitting is punishable by severe fine and imprisonment. This campaign was successful because public opinion supported it. It should be contrasted with the failure of legal measures to affect the indiscriminate elimination of human wastes in a city such as Madras. This failure cannot rightly be ascribed to a lack of sanitary facilities, because even the simplest sanitary precautions are ignored; it cannot be ascribed to a lack of law enforcement officers because the prohibited acts sometimes occur in their presence. It can only be ascribed to the observable fact that these illegal acts do not arouse in the people or police officers of Madras the same outraged sense of personal indignation that expectoration in the subways aroused in the people of New York City.

Other practices affecting infant mortality may yield more readily to the regulatory approach. The rationing of food, for example, was practiced during the last war in India with some degree of acceptance. Whether food rationing or subsidies as a means of favorably affecting food choice in India today is feasible or not would probably depend upon the educational efforts which accompanied it and its acceptance by the people as a drastic but necessary step for the welfare of all.

The third way of change, by insightful decision based on clarified understanding, is most often associated with psychoanalytic therapy. It is a way of change that can be used effectively with small groups as well as with individuals. Although this approach, if used on a mass scale, could also be labeled educational, it is education in a much deeper sense than imparting knowledge alone. It is not enough for man and wife to know how to practice contraception, the nature of their understanding of method must be fervent and large enough to guarantee that the method will be applied whatever the existing circumstances.

How can motivation of this nature be produced in an entire society as well as in individuals and small groups? This is a question which the advertising merchant, the political leader, and the public health official all ask themselves for their own reasons and purposes. If there were any single or easy answer in a society whose government is not totalitarian it would be well known.

Western experience does, however, offer a way to find out what these answers might be in a given society and to validate the answers in practice. This is the scientific method of research. Social science is young compared to physical science and the body of knowledge and research method it possesses might well be called immature. This is all the more reason to cultivate rather than ignore it. Its promise of holding a rational solution to man's human problems is the one constructive contribution of Western civilization to the problems it has created through its technology. Appreciation of the significance of social science research in public health is of relatively recent origin.[15] Almost unknown is the idea of taking official government cognizance of the relationship of cultural factors to health and assigning consultant missions to social scientists. A conspicuous example of this was the appointment and mission of the Committee on Food Habits of the National Research Council (U.S.A.) during the late war.[16] This committee of distinguished scientists initiated studies and made recommendations to government agencies concerning government policy which opened up entirely new vistas of thought and which were eminently practical. Unfortunately, the passing of the war emergency meant the termination of the Committee's work.

In many respects India's situation today has the character of an emergency. It would be salutary indeed if the problem of infant mortality were boldly faced as one reflecting primarily the economic and cultural development of the country, rather than as something to be shouldered by a public health program expected to work in isolation with nothing but medical or sanitary tools. If it were so faced, ways to reduce it by changing culturally conditioned behavior could be sought and applied in a thorough and scientific manner. The listing of cultural factors given earlier can be reevaluated in such a light. Some of them, as noted in the listing, are still conjectural, as, for example, the effect of finger feeding or force feeding in a supine position—for these, studies to establish or disprove their significance are needed. Others (both medical and anthropological) are not conjectural at all, as, for example, the late age at which solids are introduced and practices associated with the elimination of wastes. Studies (primarily social science based) could be designed on a broad scale to learn more about what

15 B. D. Paul, "Social Science in Public Health," *Am. J. Pub. Health*, XLVI (1956), 1390.

16 *The Problem of Changing Food Habits*, Bull. Nat. Research Council (U.S.A., No. 108, Oct., 1943).

these customs mean to people and what methods might be expected to change them. Later the actual results of the application of proposed methods could be evaluated as a scientific study. It is of vital importance, however, that these studies and the development of methods for cultural change should not be conducted within the narrow planes of medical and paramedical action, nor even within the conventional confines of what is called health education. They should embrace the whole potential range of man's economic and social life, including government policy, regulation, and service, and the action of other societal groups and individuals. The potential use of all methods of behavioral change—exhortation, compulsion, mass media or decision making by small groups—needs to be explored scientifically; indeed they might be applied in various combinations. The application must be thorough and many-pronged, not, as so often occurs in health education efforts, an isolated, undermanned sortie that merely forms one pressure among the many that impinge on a community and seek to modify its behavior.

Something like this research approach to the solution of a problem is now being carried out in the "research-cum-action" programs designed to promote the use of latrines in villages.[17] However, the amount and scope of these efforts are pitiably small when viewed against the background of need.

In summary, the excess infant (post neonatal) mortality in India, when compared to technologically more developed countries, has been

viewed as a product of the cultural as well as material factors of the Indian environment. Attention has been focused on the nature of the cultural factors and they may operate to help produce disease and death. The factors discussed centered around primal biological functions, ingestion of food, egestion of wastes, and reproduction of the species, an indication of their deep-seated holds. The concept of planning to reduce infant mortality by deliberately seeking to modify cultural practices and attitudes considered harmful and doing so within the framework of current economic development was presented. Exhortation, compulsion and the educational process of insightful change are potential methods of change, but the important factor is the application of studies to learn more about the relationship of culture and health, followed by the planned evaluation of considered action. This action must be part of a deliberate and total program rather than an isolated pitch.

TABLE 1.   Age-Specific Mortality Rates In U. S. A., 1954 and in Madras City, 1954–56

Age group	Madras City	U.S.A.	Ratio : Madras/ U.S.A.
Under 1 month[a]	55	19.1	3.5
1–11 months[a]	87	7.5	11.5
Total under 1 year	142	26.6	5.4
1–4 years[b]	47	1.2	42.0
5–14 years[b]	4.6	0.5	9.2

[a] Rate per 1,000 live births may be considered fairly accurate for both U.S.A. and Madras City.

[b] Rate per estimated 1,000 children. Population estimate for Madras City based on age distribution of 10 per cent sample of Madras State (1951 census) applied to estimated City total population, 1954–1956. Accuracy questionable.

---

17 P. Neurath, "Research-cum-Action as a Method in Public Health Work," *Swasth Hind*, II (Sept., 1958), 224.

This is an approach which has been pointed out by Western social science, but never utilized by Western society except in time of disaster. It can be adopted in India today with far more justice and urgency than in Western countries. To execute it, the problem of infant mortality must be viewed boldly and broadly as the product of both material and nonmaterial aspects of a total society and not merely as the product of a group of diseases which require only medical treatment and medically trained personnel for their prevention and cure. Remedial or preventive measures must be devised which are more far reaching and pervasive than health and welfare services in the usual sense of these terms—measures which will invest the day-to-day living and thinking of people with an ardour for progressive change.

Analysis of Patterns of Immigration and Absorption of Immigrants[*]

S. N. Eisenstadt

PART I

THE PROBLEM OF INDICES OF ADAPTATION OF IMMIGRANTS

Despite the voluminous literature on migration, absorption and assimilation of immigrants, and allied subjects, systematic and comparative analysis of the subject is still inadequate. Almost every work on this subject is confined to its own setting and specific problems, its own point of view, with only a minimal amount of more general orientation. This holds true largely, not only as between the different—although in reality interconnected—fields of scientific analysis, such as those of "pure demography"[1] and of sociology,[2] but

---

[*] S. N. Eisenstadt, "Analysis of Patterns of Immigration and Absorption of Immigrants," *Population Studies*, VII (November, 1953), 167–180.

[1] See, for instance, P. Fromont, *Démographie Economique* (Paris, 1947), pp. 174–201.

[2] The literature here is abundant. One of the "classics" is W. Thomas and F. Znaniecki, *The Polish Peasant in Europe and America*, 1927. For some attempts at systematization see, for instance, W. C. Smith, *Americans in the Making, The Natural History of the Assimilation of Immigrants* (New York, 1938); R. A. Schermerhorn, *These our People* (New York, 1949); Ll. Warner and L. Srole, *The Social Systems of American Ethnic Groups* (New Haven,

even of those within the same field. There is, in addition, a lack of explicitness in the assumptions underlying the different studies, and a consequent lack of interrelation between the various concrete indices used. At the same time, however, there are many implicit assumptions which underlie and direct the specific researches.

The first part of the present paper examines some of these implicit assumptions in order to estimate their importance for a framework of comparative analysis, and suggests such a tentative framework. The second part then attempts to apply this framework to the analysis of concrete cases of migration and assimilation of immigrants, and to draw conclusions for further research.[3]

Research on this subject tends to assume that there are three main interdependent indices of adaptation and assimilation of immigrants within their new country: (1) institutional integration, (2) "acculturation," (3) personal adjustment and integration of the immigrants.

_____

1942); R. A. Grauman, *Methods of Studying the Cultural Assimilation of Immigrants* (M.Sc. (Econ.) Thesis, University of London, 1951).

The most pertinent systematic analyses are to be found in the series of papers on "Cultural Assimilation of Immigrants," *Population Studies Supplement* (March, 1950), and in the book of E. Willems cited in n. 2, p. 174.

[3] The main outlines of this analysis derive from the various researches on the absorption of immigrants in Israel conducted by the author. See, for example, S. N. Eisenstadt, *The Absorption of Immigrants in Israel* (Jerusalem, 1951), and "Proposal for a Research Project on Adaptation of Immigrants," *International Social Science Bulletin* (Summer, 1951). The analysis presented here advances beyond the suppositions of these former papers, and has been greatly stimulated through discussions with Prof. D. V. Glass.

The first index refers mainly to the extent to which immigrants are "disseminated" within the main institutional spheres—family, economic, political, religious—of their new country; the second refers to the extent to which immigrants acquire the various norms, *mores*, and customs of the new country; and the third relates to the degree of personal integration which the immigrant succeeds in maintaining in the face of difficulties of transplantation and adjustment. While it is assumed that these three indices are the best indicators of adaptation and integration, nowhere do we find a full and explicit analysis of their *relative* importance and interrelations. In most of the literature, however, it is *implied* that the first criterion, that of institutional integration and dispersion, is the primary one. It is usually assumed that a group of immigrants is completely absorbed in so far as it no longer bears any particular symbols through which it can be distinguished from the rest of the population, or which may serve as a basis for its own particular identification.[4] The other two criteria appear to be subsumed under this one.

THE EMERGENCE OF A PLURALISTIC STRUCTURE AS A RESULT OF ABSORPTION OF IMMIGRANTS

While this criterion may hold true from a purely logical point of view, in reality it can serve only as a limiting—and very exceptional—case.[5] The

_____

[4] See, for instance, R. A. Schermerhorn, *op. cit.*

[5] As we shall try to show later, Jewish immigration to Palestine in some of its stages constituted such an exceptional case—but even then only partially.

absorption of any significant number of immigrants by a country may be provoked either by institutional needs and deficiencies of that country or by external exigencies (or, of course, a combination of both). In each instance this absorption gives rise to some change in the institutional structure of the country and in the relative distribution of different elements of the population between the various institutional spheres. The evolution of a new institutional structure is a long-term process, which cannot immediately obliterate the distinct identities of different (immigrant) groups but, at most, transforms and incorporates them within the new structure.

Consequently, from the absorption of large-scale immigration there usually develops a "pluralistic" structure or network of substructures—a society which is, to some extent, composed of different subsystems which are allocated to different immigrant ("ethnic") groups. While there are almost always some demands made on the immigrants to learn new roles characteristic of the absorbing population, this is not necessarily the case with regard to many secondary, alternative roles. So far as these latter are concerned, the immigrants may not only be allowed, but encouraged and expected, to remain distinct from the older inhabitants. Integration of these groups within the absorbing country cannot, then, be analyzed solely with reference to the exceptional case of complete obliteration of distinct identities, but also, and perhaps mainly, in terms of the extent to which evolution of a "pluralistic" structure does not put too heavy a strain on the society, and does not generate tensions which cannot be resolved in some way within the institutional structure.

Thus the study of absorption of immigrants is, from this point of view, mainly concerned with various types of "pluralistic" structures which develop within different societies, and the conditions in which they arise.

This analysis postulates from the beginning the possibility of tensions of the kind described above, and views the process of adaptation as a process of successful or unsuccessful solution of these tensions. They are postulated because they form a basic, systemic aspect of the process of migration and absorption of immigrants. They are not, therefore, random and contingent, but develop according to fundamental patterns and possibilities inherent in the process of migration. To be able to analyze them fully we must first consider certain basic characteristics of the process of migration and absorption.

SOME BASIC CHARACTERISTICS OF IMMIGRATION AND ADAPTATION

The process of immigration is a process of physical transition from one society to another, involving considerable frustrations and giving rise to many social problems among the immigrants. The initial immigration is usually motivated by some feelings of inadequacy and insecurity within the old social system, and by the hope of resolving this insecurity in the new one. In the first stages of transplantation the immigrant encounters, however, an additional element of insecurity, caused by two interdependent factors: first, the need to act in a new social field may increase the feeling of insecurity; and secondly, the process of transplantation involves a considerable shrinking of the immigrant's social life and participation. Immigration usually takes place in groups which do not encompass all the social spheres of the population, and for some time at least the immigrant is confined to such smaller groups for his main social participation and identification. Thus throughout this period the immigrant can perform adequately only some of his roles, as only in these smaller groups are his role-expectations more or less institutionalized. In other, wider spheres the immigrant lives in an unstable, unstructured field, with only minimal institutionalization of role-expectations. Thereafter, there may be an extension of the field of social participation through mutual adaptation of immigrants' role-expectations and the institutionalized norms of the absorbing society, and a consequent overcoming of the initial insecurity.

The institutionalization of roles and role-expectations is, however, not only a process of extension. It also involves a transformation of the existing basic group and of the behavior and roles sanctioned by it—i.e. transformation of the immigrants' entire range of behavior and social relations. This is necessarily a gradual process, which implies: (1) redefinition of old, established roles (especially those relating to the immigrants' basic group) so as to make them compatible with the alternative roles of the new society; (2) acquisition of new roles which have been, as it were, relinquished during the process of migration and which are necessary prerequisites for participation in the new society; and (3) transformation of the immigrants' basic identification— i.e. evolution of identification with the new society and its common, shared values and goals.

Such a transformation is possible because, first, the immigrants have some "idea" or "image" of the new country and some more or less definite role-expectations with regard to the wider social field. These role-expectations are among the most important determinants of the immigrants' perception of the new social structure, its institutional norms, and their own place within it. Secondly, from the outset some demands are made on them by the absorbing country to adapt themselves and to orient themselves toward their new setting. The nature of these attitudes and demands, and of the possibilities open to the immigrants in the new country, differs, however, from case to case, and it is their interplay which determines the extent of transformation of the immigrants' groups and behaviour, the type of pluralistic substructures evolved and tensions engendered.

THE MAIN TYPES OF SOCIAL TENSIONS INHERENT IN THE PROCESS OF ADAPTATION OF IMMIGRANTS

The tensions which may be engendered through the process of absorption emerge insofar as the institutionalization of roles is not achieved, and, consequently, as different fields of "unstructured" behavior develop. As these tensions are implied in the very process of transformation of the immigrants' groups and behavior, they may be analyzed in accordance with the main criteria of institutionalization of roles outlined above.

The following main types of tensions may thus be distinguished:

1. Lack of performance of stable roles by immigrants in various fields of social relations, which may be

classified by the institutional spheres (family, economic, political, etc.), and by the extent to which they relate to either the immigrants' basic group (family, etc.) or to the wider social structure. In extreme cases the lack of stability in role-performance and role-expectations may give rise to deviant behavior and to different types of personal disorganization, ranging from suicide to different types of personal regression and aggression.[6]

2. The inability to achieve positions which confer status established within the new country and which are recognized as valid by the immigrants. This type of tension does not necessarily refer to concrete situations different from the above, but is analytically distinct, as it emphasizes, not the extent of stability in the performance of roles, but the extent to which social status is not achieved through various degrees of performance of these roles.

3. Failure to achieve basic identification with the new society, and the maintenance or creation, instead, of identifications which are incompatible with it.

All these different aspects of tensions are associated with some ineffectiveness of communication between immigrants and their new social setting. Because of this, great importance must be attached to the various bearers and transmitters of communication, particularly the elites and leaders of the immigrants' groups, who may either block or foster the transformation of these values.[7]

This analysis does not assume that the mere existence of different substructures gives rise to tensions and constitutes a negative index of adaptation. The reverse is the case. It is not the plurality of groups which is of crucial importance, but the extent of instability of role-performance, of inability to achieve status, and of lack of identification with the new society.

These considerations are of help in understanding one of the main problems of adaptation, very often emphasized in the relevant literature—namely, that of the structure of the immigrant group and community.[8] There has usually been an implicit assumption that the mere existence of such a distinct community is a sign of lack of adaptation. But there is much evidence against such a conclusion. It is not the existence of an "ethnic" community that is an index of adaptation, but the extent to which its structure is balanced, both internally and in relation to the total social structure. And this balance may be evaluated with reference to the tension criteria discussed above.

If the analysis suggested here is valid—even if only in broad outline—then it makes possible a proper evaluation of the numerous criteria and indices of adaptation used and implied in the literature on immigration. The indices cannot be used as absolute measuring rods, or to compare the degree of absorption in various countries (e.g. the extent to which immigrants in the United States, Brazil, and Israel acquire the new language, attend schools, or achieve positions in industry). Such comparisons are not valid, for they assume that the impor-

---

6 These possibilities have been fully illustrated in Thomas and Znaniecki's work, cited above.

7 This problem has been analyzed in S. N. Eisenstadt, "The Place of Elites and Primary Groups in the Process of Absorption of Immigrants," *American Journal of Sociology*, 1951; and in "Com- munication Processes among Immigrants," *Public Opinion Quarterly*, 1952.

8 See, for instance, the analysis in Ll. Warner and L. Srole, *op. cit.*

tance of each index is equal in all these countries and at all periods of their evolution. In reality the importance of a criterion will vary in accordance with its function in the institutionalization of roles and in the evolution of a positive identification in each social type. The comparisons should, then, be made "through" the intervening variables outlined above, the concrete manifestations of which differ, of course, from one society to another. The working out of such comparisons is one of the main problems for further research.

PART II

ANALYSES OF CONCRETE TYPES OF MIGRATION AND ABSORPTION

The preceding analysis was stated in abstract terms, and in order to test it, it will be applied to concrete types of absorption of immigrants. There is no question of a complete inventory of types of immigrant communities, but only of a few illustrative examples. In each case we shall analyze very briefly both the main process of absorption and the main types of tension accruing from it. The pattern of migration in Asia will not be discussed.

AGRICULTURAL IMMIGRANTS IN EUROPE. This type of immigration is of great importance in some European countries, particularly in France and Belgium (and, earlier, also in Germany) ; but because of its special characteristics it has not been sufficiently analyzed.[9] The immigrants con-

sisted mostly of Polish and Italian peasants and farmworkers who came to settle in the eastern regions of France, where agricultural manpower was being diminished through depopulation and urbanization, and formed part of a much larger group of seasonal farm labourers.

The main motive for immigration on the part of these groups was improvement of their economic lot, either by earning money with which they could supplement their fortunes at home, or by more permanent settlement in the new country. In all cases their motives were firmly bound to the status of peasants, and they have maintained a strong orientation toward their homelands, and especially with the help of their leaders, priests, and in some cases (mostly among Italians) teachers, who either came with them or were "imported" from the homeland, and who tried to recreate in the new countries the original communities and peasant folkways of the countries of origin. The communal leadership of these groups was largely a continuation of the pattern of the countries of origin.

The cultural and social setting of rural areas in absorbing countries was usually quite adaptable to such a development, which occurred whenever a sufficiently large number of immigrants took root in a specific place. Only gradually did some discrepancies arise which either undermined the stability of these communities or showed the imperfect institutionalization of their roles within the absorbing social structure. Instability of relations was usually evidenced in the second generation, when (1) possibil-

---

[9] The most complete illustrative casebook on this type of migration is A. Demangeon and G. Mauco, *Documents pour servir à l'étude des l'étrangers dans l'agriculture française* (Paris, 1939). See also the more recent study by R. Poignant, "Etude sur l'assimilation de l'immigration polonaise dans le Pas de Calais," *Population*, IV (1949), 157–162.

ities of intermarriage with "local people" materialized, either due to a disproportionate sex-ratio or to the family's lessening orientation toward the homeland; and when (2) economic inducements drove them away from the rural communities to more urbanized sectors. Instability is also usually connected with encroachments on the formal universalistic roles inherent in a modern political and economic society—the demands of formal state education, of military service, and, to a much smaller extent, of political parties and economic and vocational organizations. It is in these spheres that the imperfect institutionalization of their roles could be seen. The semi-traditional particularistic pattern of peasant culture was well fitted to the rural framework of the absorbing countries, with its relative isolation from the modern industrial economy. Within this framework the very slow process of change of customs, acquisition of the new language, etc., did not deter the immigrants from achieving a more or less accepted place in the new setting. However, a strong cultural orientation toward their countries of origin, embedded in their communities, was potentially incompatible with the more basic, universalistic symbols and values of the country, which could bear a traditional substructure provided its symbols of identification were subsumed, as it were, under the more general ones. While the instability of the immigrants' groups was not of great structural importance because it usually involved a greater dispersion in the absorbing country, with a slow process of dilution of the original communities and their leadership and with only minimal personal disorganization,[10] the

incompatibility of orientation was of greater structural significance (as, for instance, in shirking military service and in cases of "double loyalty") —although, because of small numbers, such shirking never became a "problem".[11]

THE "PLANTATION PATTERN." A somewhat similar pattern can be seen in many other cases in which immigrants have been oriented toward a rural-agricultural setting, such as the Japanese in Kona[12] and the German settlers in Brazil.[13] The same initial "transplantation" of parts of autonomous and semi-self-sufficient communities took place in these cases, with a relatively strong orientation toward the country of origin. The process of adaptation and evolution of pluralistic societies differed, however, from that outlined above, because of (1) the different institutional setting of agriculture in the plantation-economy type of society, and (2) the development of different aspirational levels among the immigrants.

The rural setting in these cases was not of a purely traditional peasant type, but was part of a more formal economic structure based on market exchange and a high degree of spe-

---

10 See A. Demangeon and G. Mauco, *op. cit.*, chap. x.

11 An interesting analysis which clearly shows the relation between the immigrants' strong orientation toward the country of origin and slower dispersion, adaptation, and acquisition of loyalty to the new country is a comparison of Russian and Armenian immigrants in France. See R. Gessain and M. Doré, "Facteurs comparés d'assimilation chez des russes et des arméniens," *Population*, I (1946).

12 J. Embree, "Acculturation among the Japanese in Kona," *Memoir 59 of the American Anthropological Association*, 1941. For additional literature on similar types of Oriental immigration see, for example, E. Burrows, *Hawaiian Americans* (New Haven, 1947).

13 Emilio Willems, *Assimilacao e Populacoes Marginaes do Brasil*, 1940.

cialization. From the outset there were far fewer possibilities of maintaining a traditional setting, because of both the pressure of the absorbing country and the development of new types of economic aspiration-achievements oriented within urban settings. The formal, universalistic, political, and educational norms encroached to a very large extent on the autarchy of peasant communities, undermining the old type of identification and groups and giving rise to a faster tempo of acculturation, language acquisition, etc. This usually produced a crisis among the immigrants' traditional leaders and elites, especially insofar as they were strongly identified with the country of origin and its cultural patterns. At first attempts were made to resolve the conflict by adapting new means to serve the old goals—mainly by trying to use the more formal type of associations as bearers of traditional values.[14] The success of these attempts was usually temporary, particularly among the second and third generations, among whom the more formal activities tended to be geared increasingly to new goals and to the achievement of social status through economic advancement. (Emphasis on the achievement of recognized social status within the new society is much stronger among the Germans in Brazil than among the Oriental type of immigrant in Pacific countries.) The initial peasant—or plantation laborer—community was transformed into an ethnic group. Insofar, however, as the attachment to agriculture persisted, this transformation was a relatively slow one. In any case it provides many possibilities of incomplete institutionalization of roles. Whenever the strength of the initial orientation to-ward the original culture pattern is strongly upheld by the leaders and by the first generation, many personal tensions arise between the generations, resulting either in personal disorganization (e.g. suicide), delinquency, etc., or in the development of a quasi-leadership of a "marginal" type.[15] At the same time, the development of new status-aspirations may create, among the old inhabitants, fears of encroachment, especially since in most of these cases the immigrants' specific cultural identity and separateness has been maintained from the outset. Various practices of discrimination are evolved which may block the achievement of any *fully recognized* status. Consequently the transformation of identification may not be successful, and a negative attitude toward the absorbing social structure may arise—either of a regressive[16] or of a more aggressive type. In some cases this negative identification is encouraged by leaders with a strong cultural orientation toward their country of origin, who may try in this way to foster the old loyalties.

These possibilities remain in an embryonic stage when the immigrants are confined to the agricultural sector, in which, even in the "plantation pattern," the possibilities of maintaining particularistic and separate patterns are still large and, consequently, the process of transformation relatively slow. Nevertheless, compared with the traditional peasant type of migration, the tensions existing in this type of migration are of greater structural significance, because (1) there are more immigrants in relation to the host population, and (2) there is a more widespread diffusion of the

---

14 J. Embree, *op. cit.*

15 E. Willems, *op. cit.*, chaps. viii and x.

16 *Ibid.*

immigrants in the various institutional spheres of the absorbing society. Hence the maintenance or development of negative identification by the immigrants may be of great significance, and the tensions arising out of this situation may have many repercussions in the absorbing society.

IMMIGRATION AND "ETHNIC GROUPS" IN THE UNITED STATES. Among all countries of immigration studied, the United States holds the place of honour in relevant literature; its development sometimes serves as a prototype of modern immigration. But despite the comprehensiveness of the literature on this subject, there is as yet no full comparative and historical analysis of the problem.[17] Any attempt at a summary analysis is therefore made extremely difficult, if not impossible, and the present discussion will deal only with some crucial aspects, and in the most general way.

Migration to the United States may be described as largely motivated by an urge for economic improvement coupled with social advancement, and, in some cases, with political freedom. The great influx of immigrants was absorbed both through the development of the frontier[18] and of the industrial sector. At the same time the immigrants furthered these developments and provided one of their main driving forces. From the outset the immigrants were drawn into the universalistic framework of American society, with its strong emphasis on

formal criteria and achievement-orientated status which helped to dissolve their own traditional grouping and patterns of life.[19] At the same time neither the general, formal framework of the social structure nor the different (usually small) degrees of cultural identification between "old" inhabitants and new immigrants made possible the complete absorption and dispersion of the immigrants within the institutionalized spheres of the structure. Instead, there arose various types of "ethnic groups," one of the chief examples of "pluralistic" substructures. The most common characteristic of American ethnic groups is that they consist of immigrants from one country of origin, who maintain some sort of mutual identification (embodied in different institutional practices—mostly of a "cultural" character), and at the same time are, to some extent, oriented toward achievement of status within the absorbing society, within which, however, they are allocated roles (and status) according to criteria which differentiate them from other such groups and from "old" inhabitants.[20] The ethnic group arises, then, through the transformation of an original immigrant group within the new setting, at the same time maintaining some sort of particularistic identity. The most general agent of such transformation is usually the "formalized ethnic agency," i.e. a formal association patterned after the type prevalent in the absorbing society, whose membership is nevertheless largely confined

---

17 Useful surveys may be found in M. Davie, *World Immigration* (New York, 1936); D. Young, *American Minority Peoples* (New York, 1932); R. Schermerhorn, *op. cit.*; A. and C. Rose, *America Divided* (New York, 1949); M. L. Hansen, *The Immigrant in American History* (Cambridge, 1940).
18 This aspect of the problem has been succinctly analyzed by M. L. Hansen, *op. cit.*, pp. 53–77.

19 The conscious impact of American life on the immigrant has been described in the "Americanization" series, and recently in E. G. Hartman, *The Movement to Americanize the Immigrant* (Columbia, 1948).
20 For good instances see Ll. Warner and L. Srole, *op. cit.*; S. Koenig, *Immigrant Settlement in Connecticut*, 1938.

to the specific "ethnic group," and whose goals are, broadly speaking, the adaptation of some "ethnic" patterns and values to those of the absorbing society. It is through this formalized agency that transformation of the immigrants' self-association from a primary-communal to a secondary-associational one is usually effected.[21]

The extent and success of such transformation differ, however, from one group to another and from one historical period to another, and accordingly the emerging pluralistic patterns also differ. Three main types will be referred to, each of which demonstrates a different type of transformation problem. In the first type, the immigrants retain a high degree of exclusiveness, cling to their accustomed cultural patterns, and maintain (in the field of religion, housing, family ritual) a status structure of their own, while at the same time they form an accepted part of the general economic and political structure and achieve recognized status within it. They do this because (1) they concentrate either in a geographically isolated region or in the more "ascriptive" advanced sectors of the economic structure which are relatively high in the status hierarchy, and (2) because of relatively great cultural similarity to and identification with the upper strata of the absorbing society. Instances of this type may be found among some of the Norwegian and Danish groups.[22] Here the transformation of symbols of iden-

tification and of various group practices (especially in the direction of more formal associations, etc.) is most successful because it involves maintenance and achievement of a relatively highly status position and does not require too rapid a change of customs. A second type, parallel and yet somewhat opposite, may be found among those immigrant groups which succeed in maintaining some of their traditional patterns because they are confined, due to discriminatory practices and/or cultural incompatibility, to the lowest strata of the absorbing society, in what may be termed "negatively ascriptive" sectors. This holds true of Mexican immigrants, some Oriental immigrant groups,[23] etc. In this case the extent of cultural transformation and formalization is much smaller, but there may exist a cultural identification which would be purely neutral or even incompatible with that of the absorbing society (somewhat similar to the plantation pattern). Any large extent of cultural transformation due to the development of aspirations toward formalized associations usually undermines the traditional pattern (particularly the traditional family pattern), and involves personal stresses and disorganization.[24]

The third and most commonly described—and probably the most common—type of ethnic group is the one whose concrete variations are most manifold.[25] The main characteristics

---

21 See Ll. Warner and L. Srole, *op. cit.*; R. Schermerhorn, *op. cit.*
22 P. A. Munch, "Social Adjustment among Wisconsin Norwegians," *American Sociological Review*, XIV (1949), 780–787; H. Taba, *Adolescent Character and Personality*; C. J. Johansen, "Cultural Variables in the Ecology of an Ethnic Group," *American Sociological Review*, XIV, No. 1 (Feb., 1949).

23 R. Schermerhorn, *op. cit.*, chaps. ix and x; M. Gamio, *The Mexican Immigrant, His Life Story* (Chicago, 1931); R. H. Lee, "The Decline of Chinatowns in the United States," *American Journal of Sociology*, LIV (1949), 422–432.
24 E. Bogardus, "Second Generation Mexicans," *Sociology and Social Research*, Vol. XIII (1929).
25 The possibility of slow dispersion because of small numerical proportion, a "bad" sex ratio and gradual lessening of discrimination is seen among the

of this group are that its members are absorbed within the orbit of the new society's middle strata, in which formal achievement is greatly stressed; the degree of social and economic isolation is small, with varying levels of (though usually not complete) cultural compatibility and identification with the absorbing population, consequent upon the extent of discrimination and blocking of status-aspirations. It is within this type that the "formalized" agency is most prevalent, forming as it were the main avenue to status-conferring channels of behavior. It is also within this type that specific status structures and behavior evolve, which, though patterned after those of the absorbing society, tend to be confined to specific strata (usually "lower-middle"), and to exhibit in an exaggerated and vicarious way various status paraphernalia, symbols, and associations. The associations stress "ethnic" identification as part of the "American way of life," and stress also the basic compatibility between the two.[26]

The incomplete institutionalization of this pluralistic pattern usually arises through two parallel processes, already visible in an embryonic stage in the "plantation" pattern. First, the greater the incompatibility between the cultural pattern and orientation of the immigrants (especially among those coming from traditional peasant societies) and those of the absorbing country, and the stronger the immigrants' identification with their original patterns, the greater the tensions within the immigrants' own groups, particularly between different generations, and the consequent instability of roles and high degree of personal disorganization.[27] Secondly, in so far as the immigrants' status-aspirations are blocked by discriminatory practices or cultural and professional incompatibility, they may evolve negative ("regressive" or aggressive) symbols of identification, usually with the encouragement of those immigrant leaders who feel most acutely the different status dilemmas. The transformation of immigrant leadership from the traditional to the new accommodating and formal type is then neither smooth nor successful, and the new leaders, instead of promoting Americanization, become bearers of negative identification, and the various formal associations sponsored by them, foci of such resentment.[28]

In the U.S.A. the development of these various tensions is of great importance to the absorbing social structure—first, because many different immigrant groups interplay in this situation; secondly, because the immigrant groups are very large, both absolutely and relatively; and thirdly because, owing to the greater plasticity and "dissolving" power of the

Chinese. See R. H. Lee, *op. cit.* See also Ll. Warner and L. Srole, *op. cit.*; R. Schermerhorn, *op. cit.*, chaps. xi–xv; S. Koenig, *op. cit.*; J. M. Stylos, "The Spartan Greeks of Bridgetown: Community Cohesion," *Common Ground*, VIII (1948), 24–34; M. B. Treudley, "An Ethnic Group's View of the American Middle Class," *American Sociological Review*, XI (1946), 715–724.

26 Y. J. Myz and R. Lewis, "Agencies Organized by Nationality Groups in the United States," *Annals of the American Academy of Political and Social Science*, CCLXII (1949), 148–158; M. B. Treudley, "Formal Organization and the Americanization Process," *American Sociological Review*, XIV (Feb., 1949).

27 See, for instance, I. Child, *Italian or American* (New Haven, 1940), and the numerous illustrations in Thomas and Znaniecki, *op. cit.*

28 An interesting parallel instance may be found among the rural French Canadians migrating to towns. See E. Hughes, *French Canada in Transition* (London, 1946), particularly chaps. xiv and xix.

U.S.A. with regard to the immigrants and because of the historical importance of the immigrants in the development of the nation, they have become a more integrated part of the total structure. Consequently tensions arising out of incomplete institutionalization become as it were endemic to the social system, increasing on the one hand the number of sectors in which anomic behavior of the regressive and innovatory type is engendered, and on the other hand leading to different degrees of intergroup tensions, "prejudices," etc., which undermine the basic values of the absorbing society and which give rise to deviant personality-types.[29] This tendency is enhanced by the absorbing society's high degree of institutional plasticity, which, though it makes possible the "taking-in" of the immigrants, at the same time generates various possibilities of lack of social and psychological security which may result in a search for a scapegoat among the immigrants.[30]

JEWISH IMMIGRATION TO PALESTINE AND ISRAEL[31]

Among the various migrations, that of the Jews to Palestine up to 1947 may perhaps serve as a partial

---

[29] See A. and C. Rose, *op. cit.*; R. Schermerhorn, *op. cit.*, chap. xviii; and for an interesting case study, W. Whyte, *Street Corner Society* (Chicago, 1943).

[30] *Ibid.*, and B. Bettelheim and M. Janovitz, *Dynamics of Prejudice* (New York, 1950).

[31] Only a very summary account of the Jewish migration to Palestine will be given here. Fuller accounts may be found in the following publications by the author: "The Sociological Structure of the Jewish Community in Palestine," *Jewish Social Studies*, 1948; "The Oriental Jews in Israel," *Jewish Social Studies*, 1950; *The Absorption of Immigrants in Israel*, 1951.

example of total institutional dispersion of various waves of immigrants within the institutional spheres of the absorbing country. With the exception of the so-called "Oriental Jews," most Jewish immigrants were quickly disseminated within the economic, political, educational, and cultural sphere of life, giving up any separate identity based on their countries of origin and almost completely neutralizing the social heritage of those countries. This dissemination took place not only within the framework of formal settings and institutions, but also in the more informal spheres of the social structure, and was evidenced in the creation of common primary groups, a very high degree of intermarriage, etc. An important corollary of these processes is the fact that there was no "old" type of leadership among the immigrants, and that all the leading positions of society were built on the basis of new criteria common to most of the waves of immigrants.

Among the special reasons for this unique development, the following seem to be most important: (1) The initial motive for immigration was not economic, but mainly national, i.e. to rebuild the Jewish National Home in Palestine and to create a new society there. For this reason (2) the immigrants were not bound to their communities of origin, against which they had rebelled, but had a very high predisposition to change their behavior and identification in accordance with the demands of the new society. (3) Sometimes the change had already begun in the country of origin, where the prospective migrants formed special "preparatory-pioneering" groups. (4) Because of their strong national motivation, there was a very strong mutual identification among the immigrants, with a consequent minimal monopolization of the best economic positions by those who came earlier. (5) The economic and political development of the *Yishuv* (the Jewish community in Israel) was very much dependent on a constant—even if gradual—influx of immigrants and of immigrant capital.

The only exception was a section of the so-called "Oriental Jews," whose motivation for migration differed, being mainly of a "traditional Messianic" pattern with a minimal predisposition to change or identification with the new secular pattern of the *Yishuv*. Because of this the differences of educational and technical levels became of crucial importance for the allocation of roles within the new social structure, and the "Oriental Jews" evolved a specific "ethnic" pattern within the lower strata of the new society.

This general picture began to change with the establishment of the State of Israel in 1948 and the mass immigration which has almost doubled the population within three to four years. Although it is too early to evaluate fully the processes of integration of the new immigrants, it may easily be seen that they are not becoming rapidly disseminated within the institutional structure, and that they tend initially to cluster in specific groups and sectors of their own, with only a very gradual extension of their social relations. This seems to be due mainly to (1) the changing pattern of motivation for immigration—"revolutionary" pioneering motives giving way to motives of social and political security—and the consequent lower predisposition to change; (2) the maintenance of their own specific groups (in which immigration took place); (3) the growing proportion of immigrants to old inhabitants, which

minimizes the direct absorbing powers of the old society; (4) the economic difficulties connected with the absorption of new immigrants, due both to the lag in capital investment and to the low level of skill among the immigrants; and (5) the growing formalization and bureaucratization of the absorptive pattern of the old society.

CONCLUSIONS

The above analysis of some types of adaptation of immigrants has necessarily been cursory, and could not do justice to the fulness and variety of the materials at hand. It is hoped, however, that the discussion may serve both as a justification of the analytical scheme outlined in the first part of this paper, and as a starting point for more detailed examination of the existing data. At the same time, it is useful, even at this stage, to attempt to summarize some of the empirical conclusions arising from the present study, and to define both the conditions in which different types of pluralistic "immigrant" substructures arise, and the tensions they engender.

The types of pluralistic structures arising through the absorption of immigrants are determined by the immigrants' own motivations, by the demands made on them by the absorbing society, and by the possibilities open to them in that society. On the basis of the material presented here we may attempt to break down these factors into more specific variables, of which the following are the most important: (1) the immigrants' aspirations toward specific social and economic positions within the new society, the achievement of which constituted a basic motivation for immigration; (2) the type of cultural orientation and aspirations of the immigrants, which may be subdivided, first as to the basic cultural values which the immigrants hope to maintain or achieve in the new country, and, secondly, as to the extent to which their cultural orientation is tied up with the maintenance of a strong, basic identification with their country of origin; (3) the orientation of the immigrants as compared with that of the absorbing country and the strength of the pressure exerted on them to change their customs, patterns of communal life, etc.

The exact weight of each of these factors in various situations and societies has yet to be worked out in a series of concrete studies, and we shall here outline only some very general suggestions.

We may perhaps attempt here to state the conditions which determine the extent of institutional dissemination of immigrants. Such dissemination will be greater insofar as (1) the immigrants constitute new primary groups in their countries of origin which are culturally oriented toward the new country; (2) there is mutual identification and cultural and professional compatibility between immigrants and old inhabitants; (3) there is interdependence in economic and political spheres; and (4) economic development keeps pace with the influx of immigrants (and/or the immigrants do not constitute a significant numerical problem). Insofar as these conditions do not obtain, the extent of pluralistic substructures will be greater, though here also the exact weight of each of these factors has yet to be investigated and determined.

In almost no country of absorption will these favorable conditions be found fully operative and some type of pluralistic society will therefore arise.

Two main types of absorbing countries may be distinguished: those with a modern market economy and universalistic, formal political structure; and those of the "colonial" pattern. In each of these, different types of immigrant substructures and different processes of absorption arise.

The main characteristic of the first type is that in it there is a definite pressure for the acquisition of some of the basic common roles by the immigrants, and absorption involves integration into these roles. The strength of this pressure varies, however, and we may accordingly distinguish two main subtypes and substructures. In the first, immigrants continue to maintain a culturally closed and distinct community, based to a large extent on ascriptive (usually traditional) values, with little institutional change and intermingling with the formal economic and political structure. Such substructures may be maintained mainly in those sectors of the structure of the absorbing society which are relatively "isolated" from the main, formal, achievement-oriented pattern.

The second type of substructure is characterized by a more rapid dissolution of the immigrants' traditional community and patterns of life through participation in the formal organization and achievement-oriented status groups (mainly "middle-class" urban settings), in which, however, distinct roles are allocated to immigrants on the basis of their group identification, and in which they maintain some separate cultural identity, basically construed as one of the possible alternatives and variations of the formal pattern.

The main tensions possible in this pattern may arise from (1) cultural incompatibility between original immigrant group and formal structure, giving rise to different levels of instability and personal disorganization; and (2) the impossibility of realizing their levels of aspiration either because of or mainly because of (3) different degrees of discrimination on the part of the absorbing country —giving rise to aggressive feelings and negative attitudes toward the new country. These tensions are, as we have seen, of great structural significance to the absorbing country.

It may in general be suggested that whereas instability of behavior and deviancy are connected with cultural incompatibility (whenever status can be achieved), negative identifications are associated mainly with the inability to realize the levels of status-aspiration. The two are, however, interconnected to a very considerable, though varying, extent.

The pattern of immigrant substructures in the colonial type differs markedly from that in the first type. Here the initial pressure on the immigrants is not to participate in the (almost nonexistent) universal, common roles, but rather to establish separate sectors of their own. The principal tensions in this case arise when the development of modern political movements with universalistic-nationalistic aspirations undermines the former particularistic symbiosis. In this field, perhaps even more than in many others, additional detailed investigations are badly needed.

The analysis presented here does, we hope, show that no concrete index of acculturation—acquisition of language, customs, etc.—can serve as a universal criterion of adaptation. The importance of any index varies according to the basic social setting, and even the general importance of "acculturation" as such varies from place to place. The significance of the various indices can only be evaluated by examining the various types of immigrant-pluralistic societies.

The Social Consequences of High Population Density*†

Halliman H. Winsborough

The man who participates in decisions about urban affairs today seems a most unreasonably imposed-upon fellow. Not only is he called upon to be comfortable in both of C. P. Snow's two cultures (on the one hand considering engineering problems and on the other choosing among competing notions of urban esthetics), but he is frequently asked to show some familiarity with a third minor but lustily growing culture: that of the social sciences. To walk in the elegant and orderly garden of natural science and to trace subtle paths in search of taste no doubt offer some pleasure. To hack one's way through the tangled thicket of the social sciences, however, must frequently seem an imposition—especially so if one's major business lies elsewhere.

The motive of this paper is to offer some aid and comfort to the person who looks in the social sciences for assistance in making choices in urban planning.

Let us begin by arguing that most work in the social sciences can be divided into two kinds. The distinction between the two depends on

* Reprinted, by permission, from a symposium, *Immigration*, appearing in *Law and Contemporary Problems*, Vol. XXX, No. 1 (Winter, 1965); published by the Duke University School of Law, Durham, N.C. Copyright 1965, by Duke University.

† This paper is based on research supported by a grant from the Duke University Council on Research. Some of the computations involved were carried out in the Duke University Computing Laboratory which is supported, in part, by the National Science Foundation.

taste and judgment as to how things in the social world are to be explained. One group of social scientists, who may be designated behavioralists, explain things in terms of the actions which individuals take. From the point of view of the behavioralists, if we know enough about the causes, motives for, and constraints upon individual action we can account for the behavior of groups of people, or even of whole cities, by a process of aggregation.

The second group, whom we will call the structuralists, argue that the very collection of persons into groups provides possibilities and produces characteristics which are not to be derived from a summation of the characteristics of individuals. For example, the law of a country is not easily explained in terms of the motives and actions of the persons presently resident there.

Each of these points of view can be made persuasively by their adherents. Each has been productive of exciting research and discovery. When each is on its home ground all is well. However, when both points of view seem to apply at the same time, or when one tries to take both factors into account at once, the problem becomes complex and the dogmatic statements issuing from both camps become vociferous. It is at this juncture that one must keep one's head and, recognizing the limits as well as the extent of knowledge, try to assess the balance of effects in exercising decision.

Since all of the foregoing no doubt seems fairly abstracted from the everyday decision in urban affairs, let us consider an extended example. A not uncommon problem in urban planning concerns the proper level of population density for which to plan. Certainly various levels of density have various costs and various advantages. Supposing that an intrepid man began to search the literature in sociology in hopes of finding some guidance about the nature of these costs and advantages: What might he find?

He would discover that two somewhat separate traditions in sociology argue that the level of population density in a human society has important social consequences. Each tradition is based on the writings of one of the founding fathers of modern sociology and each has fairly vigorous present-day adherents. The consequences presumed by these two traditions are, however, rather different. On the one hand, the structuralists, following a Durkheimian point of view, see high population density, along with high population size, as a prerequisite for the development of division of labor.[1] On the other hand, behaviorally-oriented followers of Simmel stress the psychological—and even physiological—strain involved in the frequent stimulation and interaction concomitant with dense living.[2]

The Durkheimian position is succinctly summarized by Halbwachs as follows:[3]

In reality, the division of labor results from the expansion of human groups and from the increase in their density. These are necessary conditions, (1) for the appearance and development...of a great variety of aptitudes and also of needs; (2) for bringing aptitudes and needs together in reciprocal stimulation...and (3) for establishing increasingly precise adaptation between the techniques of the more and more specialized producers and the needs of the more and more diversified consumers.

This point of view has received theoretical and empirical elaboration in the development of central place theory. This theory argues that a certain number of consumers are necessary within a given radius of a center for the support of a specific good or service.[4] Whether a specific good or service becomes a central one, then, depends upon the population density of the area in question, that is, upon whether it will find a sufficient number of consumers within its range. Some recent developments in this theory suggest it may apply to the distribution of services in the city as well as the distribution of cities in space.[5]

---

[1] Emile Durkheim, *The Division of Labor in Society*, trans. George Simpson (New York: The Free Press of Glencoe, Inc., 1960), pp. 256–282.
[2] Simmel, "The Metropolis and Mental Life," in *Cities and Society*, eds. Paul K. Hatt and Albert J. Reiss (New York: The Free Press of Glencoe, Inc., 1957), 635–647.
[3] Maurice Halbwachs, *Population and Society 173*, trans. Otis Dudley Duncan

and Harold W. Pfauts (New York: The Free Press of Glencoe, Inc., 1960).
[4] A concise presentation of central place theory is given in Ullman, "A Theory of Location for Cities," in Hatt and Reiss, *op. cit. supra* note 2, pp. 227–236. For a more lengthy treatment, see August Losch, *The Economics of Location*, trans. William H. Woglam and Wolfgang F. Stolper (New Haven: Yale University Press, 1954). Additional citations can be found in Brian J. L. Berry and Allen Pred, *Central Place Studies: A Bibliography of Theory and Applications* (Philadelphia: Regional Science Research Institute, 1961).
[5] Carol, "The Hierarchy of Central Functions Within the City," *Annals of the Ass'n of Am. Geographers*, L (1960), 419. Some additional pertinent discussion is found in Ludlow, "Urban Densities and Their Costs: An Exploration

The Simmelian point of view has also received recent empirical support —a good deal of it from studies of animal behavior. In an attempt to investigate the relationship between animal behavior and population characteristics in a species living in the wild, Calhoun confined a group of wild rats to a quarter-acre enclosure.[6] He provided an abundance of food and relative freedom from predators. Population did not rise as expected because of an increase in infant mortality. This increase, Calhoun held, came about because stress from social interaction led to disruption of maternal behavior. Pursuing this hypothesis under laboratory conditions, Calhoun permitted caged populations of experimental rats to develop about twice the density which seemed to provide only moderate stress.[7] His results were dramatic. Many females became unable to carry pregnancy to full term. Many of those who did were unable to survive the delivery. Of those who survived, many subsequently fell so short in their maternal functions that infant mortality ran as high as ninety-six per cent in some experimental groups.

Males, too, exhibited strange behavior, ranging from sexual deviation to cannibalism, and from frenetic overactivity to pathological withdrawal.

Calhoun holds that these disturbances in behavior are the result of the stress from social interaction. Other investigators have found a direct relationship between density and adult animal mortality. Deevey cites some literature in support of this relationship and offers a physiological explanation of the relationship between the stimulation due to increased interaction and mortality.[8]

In summary, then, there is considerable evidence supporting both consequences of high levels of population density. Given the weight of the evidence it would seem unwise to simply disregard one or another of these effects. The problem becomes one of assessing the outcome of their joint influence. In a paper in which he speculates on the combination of these effects on human populations, Calhoun conceptualizes the problem as follows.[9] He associates the level of density which maximizes the division of labor with what he calls the economic climax state of the society. That level of density which minimizes psychological and physiological stress from interaction he associates with the social climax state. Of these he says:[10]

> It is logical to assume that the social climax can be achieved at a lower density than the economic climax. Thus the population characteristic of the economic climax community may serve as a yardstick of value judgment at what level the population should stabilize. Since this level is likely to be attained in the United States within the next 50 or 100 years, any individuals or groups who

into the Economics of Population Densities and Urban Patterns," in *Urban Redevelopment: Problems and Practices,* ed. Coleman Woodbury (1953), pp. 102–120.

[6] Calhoun, "A Method for Self-Control of Population Growth Among Mammals Living in the Wild," *Science,* CIX (1949), 92.

[7] Calhoun, "Population Density and Social Pathology," *Scientific American* (Feb., 1962), pp. 139–149.

[8] Deevy, "The Hare and the Haruspex: A Cautionary Tale," *Yale Rev.* XL (1959), 161.

[9] Calhoun, "Social Welfare As a Variable in Population Dynamics," *Cold Spring Harbor Symposia on Quantitative Biology,* XXII (1957), 339–356.

[10] *Idem,* 355.

encourage population growth at a rate likely to make this level to be exceeded, draw upon themselves the onus of contributing to the difficulties of achieving the climax social community.

Although Calhoun's statement may well be correct, it seems an over-simplification of a complex problem. First, it seems likely that, as with the problem of optimum city size, the optimum level of density, taking into account both stress and the division of labor, may vary with the characteristic to be optimized.[11] Further, there remains the question of the relative magnitude of the effects of stress and the division of labor upon a characteristic to be optimized. Given that the human animal is subject to the psychological and physiological stress due to interaction documented for other animals, it remains a question, for instance, whether easier access to medical facilities in a dense population may not significantly ameliorate effects of stress on adult human mortality.

By the time our urban decision-maker had reached this point in his search of the sociological literature, he would no doubt feel that his patience as well as the accumulated knowledge was exhausted. Not a great deal of specific information about the problem of the effects of various density levels within the urban community has been provided. In fact, about all that has been accomplished is to suggest that the decision about the level of population density is an important one.

Given all the foregoing information, how should a man try to influence the decision process with re-spect to population density levels? Certainly the behavioralists' findings are impressive. But in many circumstances the pressure of costs will argue for higher density. Since the latter argument has a kind of life of its own, perhaps one should use his influence to argue for lower density presuming that the net result will approximate Calhoun's social climax state.

Would such a decision be justified? Would further research on the problem make this decision strategy wrong? I was curious enough about these questions to try to carry the research process along another step in the hope of being able to make some pertinent assessment.

To begin this investigation, I returned to the original Simmelian topic of people living in the city. I investigated the relationships between population density and a series of variables similar to or suggested by Calhoun's work as they occurred in the seventy-five Community Areas in the city of Chicago. These Community Areas are a partitioning of the land area of the city which was accomplished some years ago and are convenient for this analysis because they demonstrate a considerable variability in population density.

Five variables suggested by Calhoun's writings were readily available.[12] They are the infant death rate, an over-all death rate which has been adjusted for differences between areas in age composition, a tuberculosis rate, an overall public assistance rate adjusted for differences in age composition, and a measure of the rate of public assistance to per-

---

11 Duncan, "Optimum Size of Cities," in Hatt and Reiss, *op. cit. supra* note 2, pp. 759–772.

12 Data are taken from Philip M. Hauser and Evelyn M. Kitagawa (eds.), *Local Community Fact Book for Chicago, 1950* (1953).

TABLE 1. Zero-Order and Partial Correlation of Gross Population Density and Stated Dependent Variable; Community Areas, City of Chicago, 1950

Dependent variable	Variable set held constant[a]	
	1	2
Infant deaths per 100 live births	0.32[b]	0.33[b]
Age standardized deaths per 1000 persons	0.14	—0.62[b]
Tuberculosis cases per 10,000 persons 15 years and older	0.20[c]	—0.67[b]
Age standardized public assistance per 1000 persons	0.37[b]	—0.39[b]
Quintile ranking of public assistance to persons under 18 per 1000 persons under 18	0.45[b]	0.14

[a]1. Zero-order correlations

2. Per cent of workers in professional, technical, and kindred occupations
   Median income of families
   Median years of school completed by persons 25 years and older
   Per cent of population foreign born white
   Per cent of population Negro
   Median age
   Per cent of dwelling units owner occupied
   Median rent of renter occupied dwelling units
   Per cent of dwelling units with no water, no bath, or dilapidated
   Per cent of dwellings built before 1920
   Per cent of dwellings with 1.5 or more persons per room
   Per cent of persons one year and older living in same household, 1949 and 1950

[b]   Significantly different from zero at the 0.01 level.

[c]   Significantly different from zero at the 0.05 level.

sons under 18 years old. Pearsonian correlation was used as a measure of the association between each of these variables and the level of population density over the community areas. These correlations are given in the first column of Table 1. All but one of the variables showed a positive correlation with population density. That is, the higher the density the higher the rates. The exception to this rule was the over-all death rate which showed no appreciable association with density.

These findings certainly suggest that increased density has a deleterious effect on the population. To assume that this effect is caused by increased stress is, however, a long logical leap. In fact, only a moderate acquaintance with cities would suggest an alternative explanation. People of lower socioeconomic status—people more likely, irrespective of density, to score higher on all of the rates investigated—tend to live closer to the center of the city than do persons of higher socioeconomic status. Further, population density declines in a regular way as one moves outward from the city center. These facts suggest that socioeconomic status may be confounding the relationships which we wish to investigate. Another variable which may confound the relationships is quality of housing, which also has association with density and with each of the rates. Finally, any effects of stress which may be present are confounded because the number of in-migrants to each area is likely to be different.

In order to avoid these confounding variables, then, one would like to investigate the associations between population density and each of the five rates "controlling" for socioeconomic status, quality of housing, and migration.[13] We have chosen to accomplish this by partial correlation, a fairly satisfactory technique which allows one to approach the "control" of the classical experiment. A list of the variables "partialed out" can be found in note a-2 of Table 1. The values of the partial correlations are given in column two of that table.

Removing the effects of socioeconomic status, quality of housing, and migration changes the pattern of the findings considerably. The over-all death rate, which had originally shown no relationship with density, changed to a strong negative association: the higher the density, the lower the rate. The infant mortality rate, however, which had originally been positively associated with density, continued virtually unchanged in its association with density. Thus, after control, one mortality rate is in the direction predicted by the behavioralists and another in the direction predicted by the structuralist argument. The tuberculosis rate, which originally had a positive association with density, becomes, under control,

strong and negative. This is a very odd finding, suggesting that, *ceteris paribus*, high density leads to low tuberculosis rates. Both public assistance measures were originally positively associated with density. After control, each has changed but in a somewhat different way. Over-all public assistance becomes negatively associated with density while assistance to persons under eighteen years of age demonstrates no appreciable association.

After control for the three confounding factors, then, we have a fairly mixed bag. One rate shows the positive association with density predicted by the behavioralists' argument.[14] Three show the negative association predicted by the structuralist argument. The final rate shows no association.

Perhaps the only order that we can bring to these heterogeneous findings is to suggest that the effects of density on the young seem to be different from the effects on the adult population. The findings certainly add

---

[13] It may be noted that one of the variables held constant, per cent of dwelling units having more than 1.51 persons per room, is related to the number of persons per room, a component of total density. This aspect of density was treated separately because of some thought that its effects might be different from those of total density. The finding was, however, that the pattern of partial correlations was similar to that for total density except that all correlations except for those for assistance to juveniles were smaller and that public assistance was signed positively and assistance to juveniles was signed negatively.

[14] An interesting methodological point arises in using the data in this fashion. At first blush, it appears that we are commiting the "fallacy of ecological correlation" in investigating a phenomenon which occurs at the individual level using aggregated data for census tracts. It seems to us, however, that our problem is rather different from that usually discussed in terms of the classical fallacy. Our problem is not to assess the existence of an individual effect of density on stress. Such an assessment can be performed with considerably greater elegance and precision in an experiment. In the main we find Calhoun's demonstration fairly compelling as to the existence of the effect. Rather, it is our aim to investigate the balance of effects, individual and aggregative, which derive from the variation in density. Thus we argue that, rather than being fallacious, an ecological correlation is a convenient device to investigate the balance of effects in the aggregate.

weight to the previously stated guess that the optimum level of density varies with the thing to be optimized.

Before proceeding further let me insert the scholar's usual note of caution. Clearly the foregoing findings are rather tentative. Inferences from high order partial correlation is a notoriously tricky game. I have investigated the effects of density as it varies within only one city. Clearly there might be different outcomes in other cities, and variation between cities might produce still other outcomes. Despite these demurs, the results of the analysis are strong and curious enough to warrant further investigation.

Where does all this leave the man who must arrive at some policy with respect to urban planning? Not very far along, I expect. The original strategy proposed before the statistical analysis seems to fare reasonably well. It might be modified only by suggesting that lower density should be accompanied with a diminution of the catchment area for medical facilities.

If all the foregoing is taken as a cautionary tale, I suppose its moral is to take with a grain of salt dogmatic claims by either behavioralists or structuralists when good sense or the pressure of realistic constraints suggests that variables from the opposite camp should be taken into consideration. No doubt some day the social sciences will offer a larger fund of demonstrated principles to aid the decision-maker. But it will certainly be a long time before solutions to problems in urban affairs can be spewed forth from a computer without the inclusion of a factor of good judgment.

The Cohort as a Concept in the Study of Social Change*

Norman B. Ryder

SOCIAL CHANGE AND DEMOGRAPHIC METABOLISM

This essay presents a demographic approach to the study of social change. The particular meaning here given to change is structural transformation rather than the network of actions and interactions predicated in the routine operation of the institu-

* Norman B. Ryder, "The Cohort as a Concept in the Study of Social Change," *American Sociological Review*, XXX (December, 1965), 843–861. (Pages 843–848 only are reproduced here.)

tional structure. Discussion is restricted to the variations in social organization that are reflected in measurements on individuals, summarized in aggregate distributions of performances and characteristics. Changes in an individual throughout his life are distinguishable from changes in the population of which he is a component. The biological ineluctability of the individual life cycle carries no necessary implication for transformation of the population. Every society has pretensions to an immortality beyond the reach of its members. The lives and deaths of individuals are, from the societal standpoint, a massive process of personnel replacement, which may be called "demographic metabolism." This essay is concerned with interdependencies between social change and population process, including in the latter both demographic metabolism and the life cycles of individuals considered in the aggregate.

Society is a functioning collectivity of organic components. It persists as if independent of its membership, continually receiving raw material by fertility and discharging depleted resources by mortality. To survive, it must meet the challenge to persistence implicit in this continual change of membership, and especially the incessant "invasion of barbarians." Every individual arrives on the social scene literally without sociopsychological configuration. As a requisite for effective performance, the society seeks and promotes a minimal degree of stability and predictability, and frequently succeeds. The agencies of socialization and social control are designed to give the new member a shape appropriate to the societal design.

Perhaps stability is a more likely institutional goal than innovation be-cause it is simpler and safer, at least in the short run, but any fixed set of solutions to problems posed by a threatening environment becomes a liability whenever such problems change. The capacity for societal transformation has an indispensable ally in the process of demographic metabolism. Mortality and fertility make flexibility possible just as they make stability problematic. The continual emergence of new participants in the social process and the continual withdrawal of their predecessor compensate the society for limited individual flexibility. For every species the inevitability of death impels the development of reproduction and thus variation and evolution; the same holds for societies. The society whose members were immortal would resemble a stagnant pond.[1] Of course death is no more an unmixed blessing to the society than it is an unmixed curse to the individual. Metabolism may make change likely, or at least possible, but it does not guarantee that the change will be beneficial. As a minimum, mortality permits perennial reappraisal of institutionalized formulae.

The aggregate by which the society counterbalances attrition is the birth cohort, those persons born in the same time interval and aging together. Each new cohort makes fresh contact with the contemporary social heritage and carries the impress of the encounter through life. This confrontation has been called the inter-

---

[1] Lemuel Gulliver reported that the Luggnaggians solved the problem with their Struldbruggs by desocializing them at 80. Comte hypothesized that progress is maximized by a length of life neither too ephemeral nor too protracted. Harriet Martineau, *The Positive Philosophy of Auguste Comte* (London: Trübner, n.d.), II, 152–153.

section of the innovative and the conservative forces in history.[2] The members of any cohort are entitled to participate in only one slice of life—their unique location in the stream of history. Because it embodies a temporally specific version of the heritage, each cohort is differentiated from all others, despite the minimization of variability by symbolically perpetuated institutions and by hierarchically graduated structures of authority.

To assert that the cause of social change is demographic replacement would be tantamount to explaining a variable by a constant, yet each fresh cohort is a possible intermediary in the transformation process, a vehicle for introducing new postures. The new cohorts provide the opportunity for social change to occur. They do not cause change; they permit it. If change does occur, it differentiates cohorts from one another, and the comparison of their careers becomes a way to study change. The minimal basis for expecting interdependency between intercohort differentiation and social change is that change has variant import for persons of unlike age, and that the consequences of change persist in the subsequent behavior of these individuals and thus of their cohorts.

For the most part, the literature on the cohort approach is divisible into two almost antipodal categories. On the one hand, the cohort concept, under the label "generation," has long been used by historians of the arts—in rebellion against the Procrustean frame of chronological sections favored by conventional historians—as well as by political journalists and

other humanistic interpreters of the passing scene.[3] The other field of application has been the work of demographers, particularly the recent redirection of the study of fertility time series away from the period-by-period format toward an appraisal of temporal variations from cohort to cohort.[4] Although written by a demographer, the present essay is concerned not with the many contributions to technical demography which utilize the cohort concept, but rather with the sociological arguments underlying it, and the conceptualization of social change it suggests.

THE COHORT FROM A MACROANALYTIC STANDPOINT

A cohort may be defined as the aggregate of individuals (within some population definition) who experienced the same event within the same time interval. In almost all cohort research to date the defining event has been birth, but this is only a special case of the more general approach. Cohort data are ordinarily assembled sequentially from observations of the time of occurrence of the behavior being studied, and the interval since occurrence of the cohort-defining event. For the birth cohort

---

2 Robert M. MacIver, *The Challenge of the Passing Years* (New York: Pocket Books, 1963), pp. 110–111.

3 Julius Petersen, *Die Literarischen Generationen* (Berlin: Junker and Dunnhaupt, 1930); Henri Peyre, *Les Générations Littéraires* (Paris: Bowin, 1948); Yves Renouard, "La notion de génération en histoire," *Revue Historique*, CCIX (1935), 1–23. The outstanding sociological contribution is: Karl Mannheim, "The Problem of Generations," in *Essays on the Sociology of Knowledge* (New York: Oxford University Press, 1952), pp. 276–322.

4 Norman B. Ryder, "La mesure des variations de la fécondité au cours du temps," *Population*, XI (1956), pp. 29–46.

this interval is age. If t is the time of occurrence and a is the age at that time, then observations for age a, time t, apply (approximately) to the cohort born in year t-a, as do observations for age a-1, time t-1, and so forth.

The cohort record is not merely a summation of a set of individual histories. Each cohort has a distinctive composition and character reflecting the circumstances of its unique origination and history. The lifetime data for one cohort may be analyzed and compared with those for other cohorts by all the procedures developed for a population in temporal cross-section. The movement of the cohort, within the politico-spatial boundaries defining the society, is a flow of person-years from time of birth to the death of the last survivor. This differs from a synthetic cross-section because time and age change *pari passu* for any cohort. A cohort has an age distribution of its person-years of exposure, provided by its successive sizes age by age. The age distribution varies from cohort to cohort because of mortality and migration. Thus a cohort experiences demographic transformation in ways that have no meaning at the individual level of analysis, because its composition is modified not only by status changes of the components, but also by selective changes of membership.

The most evident manifestation of intercohort differences is variation, and particularly abrupt fluctuation, in cohort size, attributable to changes in the numbers of births from year to year or, less commonly, from brief heavy migration or mortality the impact of which is limited to a narrow age span. A cohort's size relative to the sizes of its neighbors is a persistent and compelling feature of its life-

time environment. As the new cohort reaches each major juncture in the life cycle, the society has the problem of assimilating it. Any extraordinary size deviation is likely to leave an imprint on the cohort as well as on the society. In the United States today the cohorts entering adulthood are much larger than their predecessors. In consequence, they were raised in crowded housing, crammed together in schools, and are now threatening to be a glut on the labor market. Perhaps they will have to delay marriage, because of too few jobs or homes, and have fewer children. It is not entirely coincidental that the American cohorts whose fertility levels appear to be the highest in this century were those with the smallest numbers.

Size is only one characteristic by which the cohort aggregate is differentiated from its temporal neighbors. Many statistical facets of cohort composition, broadly influential as independent variables, differ at age zero from one cohort to the next, and remain approximately unchanged throughout the cohort's history. Consider the various inherited items like race, mother tongue, and birth-place. The cohort is not homogeneous in such characteristics, but the distribution of its heterogeneity tends to be fixed throughout its life in a shape which may differ from those of preceding and succeeding cohorts. Other birth and childhood characteristics are differentiating: for example, family structure by age, sex, and generation determines the relative frequency of only children, younger and older children of like or unlike sex, and younger or older parents. Intercohort variability in these characteristics may derive from fertility, mortality, or migration, to the extent that these are selective for the characteristic concerned and variable through time. Differential migration is the most striking influence in the short run, but differential natural replacement is generally more important in the long run.

Cohort differentiation is not confined to characteristics fixed at birth. Other status changes tend to be highly localized by age, relatively universal in occurrence, and influential in the rest of life.[5] Age is not only a general rubric for the consequences, rewards and penalties of experience; it is an important basis for role allocation in every society.[6] Age ascription is the cross-sectional counterpart of cohort differentiation. Similarities of experience within and differentiation of experience between age groups are observable in every culture. Similar functioning is imposed by society on those sharing an age at a particular time. Any legislation that is age-specific, either *de jure*, or, by virtue of its content, *de facto*, differentiates cohorts. Such norms give a distinctive age pattern to the life cycle of each cohort. If age-specific norms, or the context within which they are being applied, change through time, cohort experiences will be differentiated.

Thus marriage has a high probability of occurring within a narrow age span and is responsive to the exigencies of the moment. The members of a cohort are influenced in the age at which they marry, the persons they choose to marry and even their eventual likelihood of marriage by the

particular set of circumstances prevailing at the time they reach marriage age. The outcome is not so individualistic as the romantic love ethos might suggest. The state of the marriage market is an aggregate phenomenon: the probability of marriage depends not only on an individual's personal characteristics, but also on the comparative characteristics of all others of the same sex, and also on the availability of those of the opposite sex who meet the approximate criteria of nubility. Underlying this is the propitiousness of the period for marriage, the relevance of which for cohort delineation depends directly on the age variance of marriage for the cohort. The same is true of any major event in personal history which is concentrated by age.

The time of completing education is also highly age-specific in its location and influential both in personal futures and in societal change. The intimate relation of education to social change is properly emphasized in programs of social and economic development. It is "the modern world's cutting edge." Changes through time in the proportions completing various stages of education are familiar trends in modern life which provide an indelible differentiation of cohort character and behavior.[7] The differentiation encompasses not only mere duration but also the quality of teaching, the nature of instructional materials and the content of the curriculum.[8]

The consequences of distinctive educational preparation prevail in the

[5] Bernice L. Neugarten, J. W. Moore, and J. C. Lowe, "Age Norms, Age Constraints and Adult Socialization," *American Journal of Sociology*, LXX (1965), 710–717.

[6] Marion J. Levy, Jr., *The Structure of Society* (Princeton, N.J.: Princeton University Press, 1952), p. 307.

[7] Talcott Parsons, "The School Class as a Social System: Some of its Functions in American Society," *Harvard Educational Review*, XX (1959), 297–318.

[8] Nelson N. Foote, "Anachronism and Synchronism in Sociology," *Sociometry*, XXI (1958), 17–29.

cohort's occupational flow-chart. The experience of the cohort with employment and labor force status begins with the character of the employment market at its time of entry.[9] The cohort is distinctively marked by the career stage it occupies when prosperity or depression, and peace or war, impinge on it. The occupational structure of the cohort is not crystallized upon entry into the labor force, but the configuration imposed on individual economic histories has a high sequential dependence through time.[10] One explanation advanced for the baby boom is that the cohorts responsible had an unprecedented educational advantage when they sought their first jobs.[11] Projections of labor force participation rates for women have been successfully designed on a cohort basis, because of the observed continuity of differences between cohorts.[12]

The attractive simplicity of birth cohort membership as signified by age cannot conceal the ways in which this identification is cross-cut and attenuated by differentiation with respect to education, occupation, marital status, parity status, and so forth. Every birth cohort is heterogeneous.

To some extent all cohorts respond to any given period—specific stimulus. Rarely are changes so localized in either age or time that their burden falls exclusively on the shoulders of one cohort. Intercohort analysis is profitably supplemented with cross-classification by relevant compositional variables.[13] The meaning of sharing a common historical location is modified and adumbrated by these other identifying characteristics.[14] Different subsets of the cohort have different time patterns of development. Youth of manual and nonmanual origins differ in length of educational preparation and age at marriage. The various members of a cohort follow differently paced occupational lines. This may be especially true of intellectual histories. The differing tempi of careers in literature, music, and mathematics yield different productivity modes by age, and therefore responsiveness to different historical circumstances, despite membership in the same birth cohort.[15]

As a minimum, the cohort is a structural category with the same kind of analytic utility as a variable like social class.[16] Such structural categories have explanatory power be-

---

[9] Bracker noted that the graduates of American universities of the class of 1929 were united by the distinction of being educated for prosperity and then vaulted into depression. Milton Bracker, "There's No Class Like The Class of '29," *New York Times Magazine* (May 23, 1954), pp. 14 *et seq.*

[10] Abram J. Jaffe and Robert O. Carleton, *Occupational Mobility in the United States 1930–1960* (New York: Columbia University Press, 1954).

[11] Richard A. Easterlin, "The American Baby Boom in Historical Perspective," *American Economic Review*, LI (1961), 869–911.

[12] John D. Durand, *The Labor Force in the United States, 1890–1960* (New York: Social Science Research Council, 1948).

[13] William M. Evan, "Cohort Analysis of Survey Data: a Procedure for Studying Long-term Opinion Change," *Public Opinion Quarterly*, XXIII (1959), 63–72.

[14] Michel Ralea, "Le problème des générations et la jeunesse d'aujourd'hui," Rencontres Internationales de Genève, *La vie et le temps* (Neuchâtel: Baconnière, 1962), pp. 59–73.

[15] Bennett M. Berger, "How Long is a Generation?" *British Journal of Sociology*, XI (1960), 557–568.

[16] Seymour Martin Lipset, Paul G. Lazarsfeld, Allen H. Barton, and Juan Linz, "The Psychology of Voting: an Analysis of Political Behavior," in *Handbook of Social Psychology*, ed. Gardner Lindzey (Cambridge, Mass.: Addison-Wesley, 1954), II, 1124–1175.

cause they are surrogate indices for the common experiences of many persons in each category. Conceptually the cohort resembles most closely the ethnic group: membership is determined at birth, and often has considerable capacity to explain variance, but need not imply that the category is an organized group.

Two reseach suggestions may be advanced. In the first place, age should be so interpreted in every statistical table as to exploit its dual significance —as a point in the cohort life cycle and as a temporal location. Age is customarily used in statistical analyses merely in the former role, if not as a cross-sectional nuisance to be controlled by procedures like standardization. This implicitly static orientation ignores an important source of variation and inhibits the progress of temporal analysis. In the second place, age-cum-cohort should be used not only as a cross-classification to explain the internal variations of other groups, but as a group-defining variable in its own right, in terms of which distributions by other variables may be compared through time. In this way, research results may be compared in cumulated fashion, linking the outputs of the various studies using the same cohort identifications, just as has been done with other quasi-group categorizations. Each such study can enhance the significance of others for the same cohort. Comparison of such composite cohort biographies would yield the most direct and efficient measurement of the consequences of social change.

The proposed orientation to temporal differentiation of cohorts emphasizes the context prevailing at the time members of the cohort experience critical transitions. The approach can be generalized beyond the birth cohort to cohorts identified by common time of occurrence of any significant and enduring event in life history. Cohorts may be defined in terms of the year in which they completed their schooling, the year they married, the year in which they migrated to the city, or the year in which they entered the labor force full-time.[17] Each of these events is important in identifying the kinds of situation to which persons respond differently, and establishing a status to which future experiences are oriented. The research implication of this viewpoint is that more effort should be devoted to collecting items of dated information, to identify not only statuses but times of entry into them. Birth date serves as a surrogate for cohort identification by date of occurrence of other relevant events. It is a satisfactory approximation to the extent that variance in the age at which the event in question occurs is small. Thus the cohort approach may be generalized to consider any class of event in terms of the experience of successive cohorts defined by time of initial exposure to the risk of occurrence of that event.

The strategic focus for research on social change is the context under which each cohort is launched on its own path. The prototype is the cohort of persons entering the labor force each year. The annual meeting of prospective employers and employees produces an occupational distribution which manifests and foretells social change. The process requires macroanalysis because the possibility of

---

[17] As an exotic example, Hyman Enzer has recently completed a study of the cohort of all 118 American authors whose first novels came out in 1958. See David Dempsey, "First Novelists, Last Words," *Saturday Review*, LXVI (October 12, 1963), 34.

an individual finding a particular job, or of an employer securing a needed talent, is a function of the entire set of comparative characteristics of all participants in the market. The educational system has prepared the new labor force entrants for this confrontation. Although the stimulus for innovation is most likely to come from the employers, the feasibility of new directions depends in part on how well they have been anticipated by the educational system. Indeed the conditions determining labor supply go all the way back to the composition of the relevant cohorts at birth. The implicit link between reproduction in one year, and characteristics of the labor market some two decades later, is an important channel for transmission of disturbances through time.

Out of the confrontation of the cohort of any year and the societal structures into which it seeks entry, a shape is forged which influences the directions in which the structures will change. More generally, the proximate indication of direction of change is the movement of personnel from one status to another, as the result of quasi-market activity in one or another role sphere. The market metaphor extends into the consideration of differential rewards, and thus of changing role evaluations, cognate with the Davis-Moore theory of social differentiation.[18] The importance for social change of the kind of selectivity exercised in forming the cohort is largely obscured in this essay by exclusive attention to the birth cohort, which is more random in composition than any other cohort type. The study of the formation of cohorts defined in terms of specific role markets promises to provide a focused view of the processes that transform the different parts of the social system. . . .

---

[18] Kingsley Davis and Wilbert E. Moore, "Some Principles of Stratification," *American Sociological Review*, X (1945), 242–247.

Social Action Systems and Demographic Structure and Processes

The six chapters included in this part are concerned with the demographic determinants and consequences of various types of social action systems. As defined in Chap. 1, a social action system is chiefly characterized by the inclusion of social interaction of the system's members as an element process. A basic assumption of sociology is that personal interaction gives rise to social norms which govern social behavior. These norms have important influences on basic demographic processes of fertility, mortality, and migration and, through them, upon demographic structure. Reciprocally, the size, age structure, and sex composition of a population strongly affect the nature of personal interaction and hence, the functioning of social action systems.

Social action systems may be classified into institutional and non-institutional systems. Several of the latter, informal groups, associations, and communities, are treated in demographic perspective in Chap. 3. The succeeding chapters deal with marriage and the family, economic institutions, religious institutions, political institutions, and health, education and welfare institutions in listed order.

Social action systems can take many forms and characteristics. Perhaps the more prominent social action units are the family and other institutional forms of society, but interactive behavior is certainly not restricted to these. Informal groups, special purpose associations, and communities can be added to our consideration. These three are treated together in this section because of the paucity of social demographic research on any single category. No one theory in sociology sys-

3

INFORMAL GROUPS, ASSOCIATIONS, AND COMMUNITIES

tematically relates the structures and processes of all these social action systems, but there are some identifiable common features. In each system, interaction is a basic process; role relationships develop; and, based in part on primary group interactions, more general normative patterns are formed. The readings in this section indicate some of the ways in which informal groups, associations, and communities affect demographic behavior.

Informal groups are often studied under the more general topic of small-group research. Of traditional interest to researchers in this field have been the development of norms and sanctions, the decision-making process, cohesiveness, leadership, communication networks, and group size. Studies of these topics have rarely involved demographic factors, but some research in fertility shows points of intersection. Examples include efforts to assess (1) the role of informal group attachments in establishing fertility norms and behavior, and (2) the influence of communication networks and decision-making processes in fertility control programs. Many other relationships remain virtually unexplored, such as informal group influences on, decisions to migrate or the possible effects of specific group norms on mortality.

Special purpose associations encompass formal structure as well as informal relations within a single action system. Some of the major studies of associations have concerned businesses, corporations, and trade-unions—all of which can influence demographic behavior, especially migration. While sociologists generally have recognized the influence of population size on formal structure and informal relationships within associations, very few demographers have focused on possible reciprocal ties to population structure or processes.

The community is a more frequent unit of analysis for social demographers; however, most community research treats communities as aggregate systems rather than social action systems. In the study of communities, as of informal groups and associations, the action system approach emphasizes interactive behavior and role relationships. Hillery has suggested that the "community," in its most parsimonious conceptualization, is described by three components: (1) localization, or the ecological component, (2) the family, and (3) cooperation.[1] To these major components and their derivatives are related a variety of demographic variables, both in a causal and consequential context.

The selections presented in this section are indicative of theoretical and empirical contributions to social demography from informal group, association, and community research. A test of the influence of primary group relations on fertility is provided in the first selection by Robert Potter and John Kantner. By means of correlational analysis they examined the relationship between family sizes of couples and those of their siblings and close friends. Their objective was to test for "conformity," viewed as responsiveness to the fertility examples provided by relatives and friends. The results indicate that the number of children married couples have corresponds closely to the number their close friends have, but the extent to which this represents conformity to primary group norms is yet to be determined. Group interaction and group sanctions are two keys to an understanding of the process of developing family size norms. Theoretical and operational schemes, which include these concepts, are a next step.

The belief that social and psychic factors affect life expectancy is widely accepted but difficult to prove. In the second reading, Francis

---

[1] George A. Hillery, Jr., *Communal Organizations: A Study of Local Societies* (Chicago: University of Chicago Press, 1968).

Madigan considers how role satisfaction may affect length of life. How he measures role satisfaction obviously becomes an important issue. Father Madigan develops an ingenious design in studying an order of priests with severe life stresses but also high role satisfactions. The priests had a longer, instead of a shorter, life expectancy than comparable U.S. white males. Several hypotheses are discussed which could explain this finding, but Father Madigan believes the relation between role satisfaction and mortality experience is the most tenable.

Raymond Breton's research presented in the third reading treats the community as an arena for interpersonal relations of immigrants. Basic to this perspective is the sociological definition of migration which involves the breaking of interpersonal "fields" in one place and reconstructing them in another location. The thesis of the study is that the most critical factors bearing upon the absorption of immigrants are found in the social organization of the receiving communities. The immigrant usually establishes a network of social affiliations within one or a combination of three communities: the community of his ethnicity, the native or receiving community, or the other ethnic communities. While the direction of social integration is in part determined by the characteristics of the immigrant himself, the degree of institutional completeness of communities appears to be a significant determinant of the ability of the community to attract the immigrant into its social boundaries.

A macro-unit test of the small-groups finding that social interaction varies with group size is provided by Stuart Dodd in the fourth reading. Dodd tested the thesis that the amount of interaction is negatively related to size by means of a controlled experiment using six towns which varied in population from 1,300 to 325,000. The findings confirm the general thesis and are suggestive for further exploration of behavioral consequences of size of place.

The Influence of Siblings and Friends on Fertility[*][1]

Robert G. Potter, Jr., and John F. Kantner

This report examines the relationships between the family sizes of couples in the Indianapolis sample and those of their siblings and friends. In a previous article[2] the influence of another "primary group," the family of origin, was investigated with generally negative results so far as the present sample is concerned. However there are both theoretical and methodological reasons for expecting closer fertility relationships in connection with contemporary "primary" groups. Indeed, as it turns out, fertility of friends provides the closest correlate of planned family size uncovered by the Indianapolis Study of Fertility.

Before considering these matters, however, it is appropriate to summarize the experience of one of the authors with a related set of items. The Indianapolis Study included among its original hypotheses the following two: the relevance of "childhood situations" and the relevance of "conformity to group patterns" to both fertility and fertility planning. Information about the primary groups and their fertility represents only part of the data collected to test these hypotheses.

CHILDHOOD SITUATIONS

To test the hypothesis that childhood experiences influence fertility, several types of information were collected about the family of origin in addition to its size. These may be classified as those dealing with (1) the affectional tone of the home (e.g., happiness of children, happiness of parents) and the difficulties encountered by the parents in raising their children,[3] (2) the extent to which parents actively encouraged their children to have families of their own, and (3) the structural characteristics of the family of origin (e.g., marital history of parents, ordinal position

[*] Robert G. Potter, Jr., and John F. Kantner, "Social and Psychological Factors Affecting Fertility, XXVIII. The Influence of Siblings and Friends on Fertility," *The Milbank Memorial Fund Quarterly*, XXXIII (July, 1955), 246–67.

[1] This is the twenty-eighth of a series of reports on a study conducted by the Committee on Social and Psychological Factors Affecting Fertility, sponsored by the Milbank Memorial Fund with grants from the Carnegie Corporation of New York. The Committee consists of Lowell J. Reed, Chairman; Daniel Katz; E. Lowell Kelly; C. V. Kiser; Frank Lorimer; Frank W. Notestein; Frederick Osborn; S. A. Switzer; Warren S. Thompson; and P. K. Whelpton.

[2] J. F. Kantner and R. G. Potter, "Social and Psychological Factors Affecting Fertility, XXIV. The Relationship of Family Size in Two Successive Generations," *The Milbank Memorial Fund Quarterly*, XXXII, No. 3 (July, 1954), 294–311. (Reprint pp. 1069–1086.)

[3] E. F. Borgatta and C. F. Westoff have used these items in a scale which they call "happiness of family and childhood situations." *See* "Social and Psychological Factors Affecting Fertility, XXV. The Prediction of Total Fertility," *The Milbank Memorial Fund Quarterly*, XXXII, No. 4 (October, 1954), 408. (Reprint p. 1112.)

and number of siblings, occupation, and education of parents). Although there is much that is interesting in these data, no association between them and either fertility or fertility planning has been found. This negative result is especially true for the items relating to the assessment of childhood and parental encouragements to family formation (1 and 2 above). Regarding the structural characteristics, couples reared in broken homes or reared by persons other than their biological parents exhibit above-average fertility. Examined within socioeconomic categories, however, these differences tend to disappear.

Reasons for so many negative findings are not difficult to find. During the time that elapses between childhood and marriage, early experiences become entangled with a multitude of other influences, the disentangling of which poses formidable problems in a nonlongitudinal study. Even if full information were available on all significant intervening influences, the small size of the Indianapolis sample and the frequently skewed response distributions would tend to frustrate analysis. Other problems probably arise because childhood is recalled so selectively. This does not mean, however, that future research should ignore the childhood milieu. With the aid of more appropriate study designs certain early influences may yet appear as important determinants of fertility.

CONFORMITY TO GROUP PATTERNS

Among the hypotheses formulated at the outset of the Indianapolis Study was one that posited a relationship between conformity to group patterns and both fertility and contraceptive effectiveness. Over half of the items here probe for values pertinent to fertility (ideal number of children, best age to marry, best birth intervals, attitude toward childlessness, attitudes toward birth control clinics and birth control advertisements, etc.). A modal or median response has been ascertained for each value. However, the degree of deviation from these empirically established norms shows little relationship either to fertility or fertility planning. The result is also negative when conformity, measured by an interviewer rating scale, is treated as a personality trait.

Though adding little to our knowledge of fertility differentials, the responses to the "conformity" questions are of interest in their own right. For example, three-fourths of the wives said that for families "in moderate circumstances" two or three children are ideal. This holds rather uniformly in each of the various fertility-planning groups. Birth control ads in magazines and birth control clinics are favored by an overwhelming number of wives (only a little more than 5 per cent of the wives state that they are "opposed" to clinics or even indifferent about their value). Similarly, few wives approve of having children as late as age 40. The preferred period of reproduction for most respondents, then, falls short of a dozen years on the basis of their statements as to ideal age at marriage, ideal interval from marriage to first birth, and best age to complete the family. However, this preferred period of child-bearing is long enough on the average so that if the couples had followed the "ideal" birth interval of two years reported by most wives, they would have had substantially larger families than they did.

Thus far "conformity" has been approached in two ways. It has been treated as acceptance or nonacceptance of the majority position on various values pertinent to fertility and secondly as a generalized personality trait. In the present analysis "conformity" is viewed more narrowly as responsiveness to the fertility examples provided by relatives and friends. This type of responsiveness is investigated by examining the fertility correlations between couples and their primary groups.

PROPOSITIONS TO BE TESTED

Information is available on the family sizes of husband's siblings, wife's siblings, and wife's best friends. The remainder of this report is devoted to analyzing correlations between fertility values of the Indianapolis Study couples and these three groups. The analyses are set up to test three main propositions:

1. There is a positive relationship between one's own family size and the family size of one's married siblings (to be stated henceforth as the relationship between couple fertility and sibling fertility). This relationship is true for either husband's or wife's siblings.

2. The relationship between fertility of couples and fertility of friends is also direct and substantially stronger than the one above.

3. In the "efficient family planner" sample these relationships maintain their strength within socioeconomic status. However in the "inefficient family planner" sample, effectiveness of contraception decreases with decreasing socioeconomic status, giving a strong relationship between status

and family size. Hence in this sample the relationships hypothesized in (1) and (2) above should be reduced when socioeconomic status is held constant.

The "relatively fecund" couples are classified as "efficient family planners" or "inefficient family planners" according to their success at birth control.[4] The "efficient planners" all claim that they had their last pregnancy only when they stopped contraception for the purpose. The "inefficient planners" admit to one or more "unwanted pregnancies."[5]

---

[4] A description of the criteria for "relatively sterile" and "relatively fecund" is provided in P. K. Whelpton and Clyde V. Kiser, "Social and Psychological Factors Affecting Fertility, VIII. The Comparative Influence on Fertility of Contraception and Impairments of Fecundity," *The Milbank Memorial Fund Quarterly*, XXVI, No. 2 (April, 1948), 182–236. (Reprint pp. 303–358).

[5] More specifically, the "efficient planners" include those couples who had no pregnancies that were not deliberately planned by stopping contraception in order to conceive and those whose last pregnancy was deliberately planned by stopping contraception in order to conceive but who had one or more pregnancies under other circumstances. In previous reports in the Indianapolis series, these groups have been referred to as "Number and Spacing Planned" and "Number Planned" respectively. The "inefficient planners" are couples classified as least successful in planning family size because one or more pregnancies occurred after the last that was wanted. It is recognized that probably in some cases the "unwanted" pregnancy was "wanted" by the time it occurred. In previous reports this group has been designated as "Excess Fertility." An additional group of couples, the "Quasi-Planned" in earlier reports, who did not deliberately plan the last pregnancy, but who either wanted the last pregnancy or wanted another pregnancy, is excluded in the present analysis. A fuller discussion of these planning types is given in P. K. Whelpton and C. V. Kiser, "Social and Psychological Factors Affecting Fertility, VI. The Planning of Fertility,"

The three propositions above are directed toward couples who have completed their family building. This ideal condition is not quite met by the Indianapolis couples. Their marriage durations of 12–15 years mean that they probably have completed from 80 to 90 per cent of their eventual fertility.[6] In other respects, too, the sample is highly specialized. The couples are native-white Protestants, married during 1927–29 with neither spouse previously married, with husband under 40 and wife under 30 at the time of marriage, with city residence during most of the time since marriage, and with both husband and wife having at least a complete grammar school education.

To the authors' knowledge no previous tests have been made of the relatedness of family sizes among siblings or friends. Thus there is little guidance for expectations. The hypothesis that siblings and couples are directly related in their fertilities must be regarded as provisional. In the first place, the same couples show no relationship between their fertility and that of their

---

parents'.[7] This result disagrees with other studies which on large samples have reported correlations of about 0.20. It is taken by the authors to mean that in the Indianapolis Study an adverse sampling scheme attenuates 0.20 correlations into nonsignificance. Because of the eligibility criteria employed, the couples tend to represent middle-class urbanites proficient in the use of contraception. Their parents, not directly subject to these eligibility criteria, represent a wider range of income and residence. Thus the sample contains a certain proportion of urban middle-class couples with rural or low-income parents. In this group the generational contrast in fertility is likely to be widest; and the inclusion of this group naturally reduces the fertility relationship between generations. At the same time couples of another type who might help to strengthen the fertility relationship between generations are automatically excluded. These are the nonmobile sons and daughters of rural and low-income parents, who on account of their nonmobility are more apt to retain their parents' high fertility.

For the same reason the sampling design must be taken as adverse for the fertility relationship between couples and siblings. It is possible to get into the sample urban, middle-class couples paired with rural and low-income siblings; but impossible to get the pairing of a rural and low-income couple with similar siblings. However, the force of this type of bias may be lessened by the fact that so many siblings have participated in the respondents' upward mobility or their cityward migration. Also siblings, belonging to a more recent gen-

The Milbank Memorial Fund Quarterly, XXV, No. 1 (January, 1947), 63–111. (Reprint pp. 209–257). The "Quasi-Planned" are excluded on the basis of an analysis showing that this group is probably a mixture of two types: couples wanting the number of children they have and perhaps additional ones and couples properly belonging to the "Excess Fertility" category, but without any means of reliably separating the two types. (*See* R. G. Potter, *The Influence of Primary Groups on Fertility,* Unpublished Ph.D. dissertation, Dept. of Social Relations, Harvard University, 1955, Appendix A.)

[6] The source for this estimate is D. V. Glass and E. Grebenik, "The Trend and Pattern of Fertility in Great Britain," Part I: Report, Papers of the Royal Commission on Population, Vol. VI (London, H.M.S.O., 1954), Table 26.

---

[7] Kantner and Potter, *op. cit.,* pp. 302 and 308. (Reprint pp. 1077 and 1083.)

eration, have participated that much more in the secular trend toward more efficient birth control.

There is another reason for expecting a stronger bond between the fertilities of siblings than between fertilities of consecutive generations. A respondent may react negatively to his family of origin and desire a family of very different size for himself. For example, the authors found a slight tendency for couples from very large families of origin to have smaller families than couples reared in families of moderate size.[8] If it exists, a negative reaction of this type may tend to reduce the average relationship of parent-offspring fertility. Yet if this negative reaction is sufficiently shared by his brothers and sisters, it might actually contribute to the relatedness of their family sizes. Thus to some extent a factor that reduces a fertility relationship in the parents' case may at the same time enhance a relationship in the siblings' case.

However, a shared resolve to have small families cannot be achieved unless birth control is used with success. Accordingly any relationship between the fertility of couples and siblings should be stronger among "efficient planners" than among "inefficient planners," provided that socioeconomic status is held constant. Without such a control couples and siblings might be related in their fertility simply because, being of similar status, they tend to be similar in contraceptive efficiency.

The reasons for expecting a relationship between fertility of friends and couples are multiple and, on the whole, more compelling. Friends are

probably in a more strategic position than siblings or parents to influence ideals of family size. To be sure, couples exercise a right to choose their own family size. But their ideas are subject to influence regarding such matters as what size of family can be afforded on a certain income, what is a fair load on the wife, and many other pertinent values. Seemingly friends are in a good position to sway such ideas. The Warner school in sociology has stressed the clique's importance as a socializing agent in adult life. Then too, friends are often in closer contact with the couple than are siblings or parents. Several years of marriage may be required before the couple decide how many children they want. By this time the couple may be far removed from nearest relatives.

Yet one can easily overstress this idea that friends influence ideals of family size. In this report the term "friends" refers to three friends of the wife and presumably most of them are current friends. These friends may not be the most strategic ones, especially if the couple made their crucial fertility decisions years earlier.

Selective factors also play a part, perhaps a predominant one. Friends may be selected in a fashion that leads to related family sizes. For example, childless couples are apt to find that they have most in common with other childless couples and choose them as friends with disproportionate frequency. Small family size increases the chances that the wife will work for pay, usually with the work situation then bringing her into contact with other wives of low fertility. Over small areas housing tends to be homogeneous in rent and living space. This may reduce the chances that two

---

[8] Kantner and Potter, *op. cit.*, pp. 302 and 307. (Reprint pp. 1077 and 1082.)

couples similar in income but widely separated in family size will be neighbors.

There are several reasons, then, for expecting a relationship between the fertilities of couples and their friends. This fertility relationship should be stronger among "efficient family planners" provided that friends exercise an important influence upon the couples' family size ideals and provided that socioeconomic status is held constant. Without adequate family planning, family size ideals cannot be implemented and influence counts for less.

Expectation that the fertility relationships will be independent of socioeconomic status in the "efficient planner" sample and dependent in the "inefficient planner" sample follows from known relationships.[9] In the "efficient planner" sample socioeconomic status has a negligible relationship with couples' fertility, and it is hard to anticipate anything different for its relationships with fertility of siblings or friends.[10] In the

"inefficient planner" sample, because adequacy of birth control decreases steadily with decreasing socioeconomic status, there is a substantial relationship between socioeconomic status and fertility of couples. Moreover, it seems highly plausible that the statuses of siblings and friends are closely related to the couples' statuses. As a result the fertility relationships of this sample should depend tangibly on the tendency of couples, siblings, and friends to be alike in socioeconomic status and hence to be alike in contraceptive effectiveness and fertility.

SIBLINGS' AND COUPLES' FERTILITY

Siblings refer to "sociological" siblings rather than to "biological" siblings.[11] These are children reared in the same household with the respondent, though not necessarily born of the same parents. The ages of sociological siblings tend to be more closely grouped around those of the respondents. This tends to increase the homogeneity of childhood environments. It also means less variable marriage durations.

---

[9] The measure of socioeconomic status used here is the "Summary Index of S.E.S." which is based upon the husband's occupation, his annual earnings since marriage, rental, net worth, purchase price of car, education of husband and wife, and the Chapin Social Status Scale. For a full description of this index, *see* P. K. Whelpton and C. V. Kiser, "Social and Psychological Factors Affecting Fertility, IX. Fertility Planning and Fertility Rates by Socioeconomic Status," *The Milbank Memorial Fund Quarterly*, XXVII, No. 2 (April, 1949), 188–244. (Reprint pp. 359–415.)

[10] The "efficient planner" sample includes both the "Number and Spacing Planned" and the "Number Planned." When just the "Number and Spacing Planned" are considered, the correlation between socioeconomic status and couples' fertility rises to 0.16. See C. F. Westoff and C. V. Kiser, "Social and Psychological Factors Affecting Fertility, XXI. An Empirical Re-Examination and Intercorrelation of Selected Hy-

pothesis Factors," *The Milbank Memorial Fund Quarterly*, XXXI, No. 4 (October, 1953), 430. (Reprint pp. 953–968.)

[11] "Sociological" siblings are defined as

(a) Full and half brothers and sisters within 10 years of the age of the wife (husband) provided that they were not separated from the wife (husband) by death or other reason before they reached 3 years of age or the wife (husband) reached 6 years of age.

(b) Step and adopted brothers and sisters within 10 years of age who shared the home throughout the time the wife (husband) was under 6, or for 3 years while she (he) was 6–16 (or an equivalent combination).

(c) Other children meeting the re-

This second advantage is important because the chief problem connected with measuring fertility of siblings is their variable marriage durations. Obviously on the average more births can be expected of siblings married 20 years than of siblings married 5. But also on the average more births can be expected of four siblings each married 5 years than of one sibling married 20 years. One way of meeting these problems is to measure sibling fertility as a ratio, with the births of a sibling expressed as a ratio of the births expected of persons having his duration of marriage. This expected number of births is derived by using the fertility record of all siblings in the sample. The average number of births per sibling in the first, second, third, and so on year of marriage is calculated and then these averages are summed for those specific years which fall within the marriage duration of the particular sibling. Of course, if the respondent has more than one married sibling, a ratio of observed to expected births may be computed for each sibling and then averaged.[12]

Siblings and couples may be related in their fecundities, or physiological capacities to reproduce. It follows, then, that the presence of many siblings and couples whose fertility is determined only by fecundity would cloud the meaning of any relationships found between their fertilities. To minimize this problem, the "relatively sterile" couples have been excluded. The sample of siblings cannot be refined in the same way. As a substitute for direct refinement, siblings and associated couples are excluded if the married siblings in question have not had at least one birth. Such a procedure excludes some voluntarily childless siblings, but removes most of the extremely infecund siblings as well. Besides the elimination of couples without married siblings, this cuts sample size by approximately one-third.

Results for the "efficient planners" are first examined. Fertility of wife's siblings yields a correlation of 0.25 ($N = 230$) with fertility of couples. The corresponding correlation for fertility of husband's siblings is 0.22 ($N = 231$). Neither relationship gives evidence of nonlinearity.

Fertility distributions are typically skewed, with the lowest fertility values naturally stopping at zero but with the highest values free to spread

---

quirements of (2) and reared with the wife (husband) if the latter lived longest while 6–16 with nonrelatives (but not in an institution) or with other relatives than one or both parents.

[12] This measure is more easily described with symbols. For each year of marriage—first, second, third, and so on —an average number of live births per sibling is calculated from the experience of all married siblings. Denote these average fertilities as x_i, $i = 1, 2, 3, \ldots$. Analogously the live births observed for a given sibling may be denoted as f_{ij}, i, $j = 1, 2, 3, \ldots$ where i again stands for the ordinal year of marriage duration and j identifies the sibling. Then the measure of fertility for a respondent's siblings is simply

$$\sum_j (\sum_i f_{ij}) / \sum_j (\sum_i x_i)$$

where x and f are summed over the full length of marriage of each married sibling and these totals are then summed over the total number of married siblings which the respondent has. One additional remark should be made. Instead of the x_i, coders of the Indianapolis Study used as their expected fertilities $y_i = 10 \ (x_i/x_{10})$. Their final measure of the fertility of a respondent's siblings is

$$\{\sum_j (\sum_i f_i) / \sum_j (\sum_i y_i)\} \div x_{10/10}$$

This formula may be simplified by cancelling terms to obtain the formula cited above. Thus:

$$\frac{\sum_j (\sum_i f_i)}{10 \sum_j (\sum_i x_1/x_{10})} \times \frac{10}{x_{10}} = \frac{\sum_j (\sum_i f_i)}{\sum_j (\sum_j x_i)}$$

out. By employing square roots instead of the original fertility values, distributions are obtained which come much closer to the assumptions usually made in significance tests. Under these conditions the fertility correlations between couples and husbands' siblings and between couples and wives' siblings are 0.15 and 0.25 respectively, with a correlation of approximately 0.15 needed to reject, at a 0.95 confidence level, the hypothesis that the two sets of fertility are unrelated.

As anticipated, relationships are not reduced when socioeconomic status is held constant. Among the "efficient planners" much the same fertility is exhibited in the various socioeconomic strata; and the same is true for siblings. The two lowest strata ($N = 40$) are exceptions since their couples show a sharp increase in family size. However, it may be doubted whether this is an authentic rise in size of planned family. The separation between "efficient" and "inefficient" family planners becomes very uncertain in these lowest strata. Accordingly they are left out of the analysis summarized in Table 1.

Among "inefficient planners" the relationships between sibling fertility and couple fertility remain very low

but do not vanish. Coefficients of 0.15 are evinced both in the cases of the wife's siblings and her husband's. Such coefficients put the relationships on the border of 0.05 significance. Both relationships appear to be linear.

However, both relationships collapse when socioeconomic status is held constant (see Table 2). Very probably siblings and couples are closely related in their socioeconomic statuses and the 0.43 correlation which couples exhibit between their family sizes and their socioeconomic status is repeated among siblings.

FRIENDS' AND COUPLES' FERTILITY

Much stronger relationships are found between the fertilities of couples and friends than between the couples and siblings discussed above. In both the "efficient planner" and "inefficient planner" samples the correlation is approximately 0.40. Before considering these relationships in detail, something should be said about measurement.

In the next paragraphs the term "friends" refers to three married friends of the wife. No restrictions were imposed on the wife concerning her choice of married friends. Thus

TABLE 1. Coefficients of Correlation[a] Between Fertility of Efficient Family Planners and the Siblings of Husband or Wife

Partial controls (1)	" Sociological siblings " of wife (N=200)[b] (2)	" Sociological siblings " of husband (N=202)[b] (3)
No control	0.21	0.11
Socioeconomic status	0.21	0.12

[a] Fertility values are converted into their square roots.
[b] Excluded are the two lowest socioeconomic status divisions. Needed to reject $p = 0$ with 0.95 confidence when $N=200$ is a correlation coefficient of about 0.15.

TABLE 2. Coefficients of Correlation[a] Between Fertility of Inefficient Family Planners and the Siblings of Husband or Wife

Partial controls (1)	"Sociological siblings" of wife (N=206) (2)	"Sociological siblings" of husband (N=210) (3)
No control	0.15	0.15
Socioeconomic status	0.05	0.10

[a] Fertility values are converted into their square roots. Needed to reject $p=0$ with 0.95 confidence when $N=200$ is a correlation coefficient of about 0.15.

a friend might be a next door neighbor or a distant childhood chum with whom she has kept in touch by mail. But it seems reasonable to assume currentness of contact and geographical proximity in most cases. Also, a friend may be married a longer or shorter time than the wife, with her family size naturally affected. However to the extent that friendship cliques are age-graded, the marriage durations should tend to be homogeneous.

The wives' fertility is measured in terms of live births; their friends' fertility in terms of living children. Had the latter measure also been applied to the wives, the correlations between fertility of wives and friends more likely would have been higher rather than lower than the ones to be examined. To the extent that selective factors operate in these correlations, they operate in terms of living children, not live births. However, the issue almost certainly is a secondary one, since a comparison of the wives' distributions of live births and living children shows them to be very similar.[13]

One further remark about measure-

ment should be made. The fertilities of the wife's friends were not reported individually in the study. Only a single figure giving the total number of living children of the three friends was required. If the wife reported on only two friends, their total fertility was multiplied by 1.5. If she reported on only one friend, her answer was not used. As expected the reports usually relate to three friends. This means that an extreme family size of one friend tends to be averaged toward a more median value by the fertilities of the other two friends. Undoubtedly this feature raises the fertility correlation between friends and couples over what it would be if wives reported on only one friend. Chances are greatly diminished that wife and friends both will have extreme family sizes. This is important because when these extremes are opposite, they contribute relatively huge deviations to the standard error of estimate.

Among "efficient planners" the fertility correlation between wives and their friends is 0.37 $(N = 337)$. Again fertility values are converted into their square roots in order to obtain better shaped distributions. The relationship shows no evidence of non-

[13] P. K. Whelpton and C. V. Kiser, "Social and Psychological Factors Affecting Fertility, VI. The Planning of Fertility," *The Milbank Memorial Fund Quar-terly*, XXV, No. 1 (January, 1947), 63. (Reprint, p. 232.)

TABLE 3. Coefficients of Correlation Between Fertility of Couples and Average Fertility of Wives' Three Friends, by Family Planning Status of Couples[a]

Partial controls (1)	Efficient family planners (N=297)[b] (2)	Inefficient family planners (N=268)[b] (3)
No controls	0.38	0.40
Socioeconomic status	0.38	0.31

[a] All fertility values are converted into their square roots.
[b] Excluded are the two divisions of lowest socioeconomic status (N=40). Needed to reject p=0 at a 0.95 level of confidence when N=260 is a correlation coefficient of about 0.13.

linearity. As expected, it is not reduced when socioeconomic status is held constant (Table 3).

Of special interest is whether among the "efficient planners" childless wives select other childless wives as friends more often than do wives with children. This cannot be answered directly. Information on the fertility of wife's three friends is restricted to a single figure stating their total number of children. However, if three friends total two or fewer children, then one or more of them are without children. Proportions of such cases can be calculated and then compared for wives with 0, 1, 2, and 3 or more children. The results, starting with childless wives, are 40 per cent, 22 per cent, 8 per cent, and 12 per cent—this for sample sizes of 88, 77, 106, and 66. The evidence is clear that among the "efficient planners" childless wives report friends without children more often than do wives with children.

Among "inefficient planners" the fertilities of wives and their friends show a correlation of 0.40 ($N = 268$). Again the relationship appears to be linear, and it manifests no signs of attenuation among wives with large or small families.

A coefficient of 0.40 puts it a shade above the corresponding correlation in the "efficient planner" subsample. The slight edge is specious, however. The two coefficients cannot be compared directly with each other, since in the "inefficient planner" sample the variance of couples' fertility is 38 per cent greater than the variance of the couples' fertility in the "efficient planner" sample. If the coefficient in the "inefficient planner" sample had a standard error of estimate no larger than the standard error of estimate in the "efficient planner" sample, the "inefficient planner" coefficient would be nearer 0.60 than 0.40. No special assumptions are required for this calculation.[14]

The families of "inefficient planners" increase in size as one descends

---

[14] Let the subscripts e and i distinguish whether a statistic belongs to the "efficient planner" or "inefficient planner" sample. No arbitrariness is introduced if $s_e{}^2$ is assigned a value of 1. Then $s_i{}^2 = 1.38$. r_e is 0.37. Its square, $r_e{}^2$, will be defined as $1 - s_z{}^2/s_e{}^2$ which means that $0.14 = 1 - s_z{}^2$ or that $s_z{}^2 = 0.86$. Now suppose that $s_z{}^2$ takes the same value of 0.86 in the "inefficient planner" sample with its $s_i{}^2 = 1.38$. Then hypothetical $r_i{}^2 = 1 - 0.86/1.38$ or approximately 0.38, the square root of which gives r_i as approximately 0.62.

the socioeconomic scale. The tendency is marked enough to give a correlation of −0.43 between socioeconomic status of wives and their fertility. Wives and friends are closely related in their statuses so that there is even a correlation of −0.30 between fertility of friends and wives' socioeconomic status. Thus the fertility tie between wives and friends depends partly on a similarity of socioeconomic status together with the tendency of fertility to increase as socioeconomic status decreases. The degree of this dependence turns out to be about 40 per cent. When socioeconomic status is held constant, the correlation between fertilities drops from 0.40 to 0.31. This means a reduction to $0.31^2/0.40^2$ or 0.60 in the proportion of fertility variation originally accounted for.

Part of the reason why the fertility relationship depends on socioeconomic status is that effectiveness of contraception is directly associated with socioeconomic status. This can be demonstrated quite directly. The number of pregnancies unwanted by husband and the number of pregnancies unwanted by wife are recorded. The correlation between these unwanted pregnancies and the couples' fertility is 0.55. That is, about 35 per cent of the fertility variation of the "inefficient planners" can be accounted for in terms of unwanted pregnancies. Moreover, number of unwanted pregnancies is to a substantial extent inversely correlated with socioeconomic status, the correlation being −0.30. In summary, the relationship between fertility of wives and fertility of wives' friends drops about 40 per cent when socioeconomic status is held constant. Part of the reason for this dependence is the familiar fact that socioeconomic status is closely related

to effectiveness of contraception and this in turn accounts for an important fraction of the variation in family size.

ROLE OF QUALIFYING FACTORS

The influence of a primary group on fertility is not automatic. The types of social relationships between couples and members of a particular primary group vary enormously. Undoubtedly this variation affects the likelihood that a primary group will influence the size of family preferred by the couples. To test this supposition in relation to friends, the couples may be variously classified according to their relationships with their friends. Each set of subgroupings which results from such a classification then is examined for evidence of differing levels of influence. That is, fertility correlations between wives and wives' friends are calculated in each subgroup and their rank order compared with expectation.

This extension of the analysis actually has been carried out. Relationships have been classified along such dimensions as: feeling of luckiness about friends, frequency of contact with friends, residential mobility, perception of own finances as compared with friends', social mobility of couples, and others. The analysis has been restricted to "efficient planners" since inadequate family planning could only obscure the comparisons.

Results have proved negative. Three factors may have contributed to this outcome. The classifications of social relationship are few and crude. This is not surprising, since the data were not collected with this type of

TABLE 4. Among "Efficient Planners" Percentages Having More Children Than Wife's Friends, by Husband's and Wife's Perception of Their Income Situation as Compared With Their Friends'

Perception of economic situation (1)	Pertaining to husband's perception Percentage having more children than wife's friends (2)	Sample size (3)	Pertaining to wife's perception Percentage having more children than wife's friends (4)	Sample size (5)
Perceive having less to spend than friends	46	111	44	112
Perceive having about the same to spend	36	146	38	161
Perceive having more to spend than friends	35	80	33	64
Total	40	337	39	337

classification in mind. Nor has it been possible in any classification to hold constant more than one factor. Ideally the bearing of differing kinds of social relationship is investigated only when some control has been achieved over such aspects as frequency of contact, uniformity of family size among friends, and the presence or absence among friends of extreme family sizes. Finally, there is no justification for expecting qualities of social relationship to give differing fertility correlations between couples and their friends, unless the influencing of family size ideals by friends is an important component in these correlations. It may be that these correlations depend on selective factors. If so, a negative outcome is virtually inevitable.

One result merits specific notice. Husbands and wives are asked, "During most of your married life have you had as much to spend as most of your friends?" The answers are fairly evenly divided among "having less," "the same," and "more money to spend."

One characteristic of couples per-

ceiving that they have less money to spend than do their friends is a feeling of economic insecurity.[15] This makes sense since friends afford the readiest benchmark of economic adequacy. But this specific group of couples also has a distinctively high proportion of wives having more children than the average for their three friends. This is surprising because of the association between low fertility and low economic security.[16]

Probably this association is overshadowed by another. Among couples of similar income, those who see themselves with more children can honestly say that they have less money to spend on many things, especially of a recreational nature. In corroboration, Table 4 indicates that spouses who perceive having less to spend are

[15] Economic security is measured here by the "summary index of economic security" used in C. V. Kiser and P. K. Whelpton, "Social and Psychological Factors Affecting Fertility, XI. The Interrelation of Fertility, Fertility Planning, and Feeling of Economic Security," *The Milbank Memorial Fund Quarterly*, XXIX, No. 1 (January, 1951), 112–114. (Reprint pp. 538–540.)
[16] *Ibid.* (Reprint pp. 195 ff.)

selected toward having a higher fertility than their friends.

SUMMARY

The relationships between the couples' fertility and the fertilities of husbands' or wives' siblings are very weak. In the sample of "efficient family planners" they barely reach statistical significance. Among "inefficient family planners" they do not exist independently of socioeconomic status. Relationships equal to those found could be expected between any two groups having statuses as closely related as those of the couples and their siblings.

A much stronger bond exists between fertility of couples and fertility of wives' three friends. A correlation coefficient of 0.37 is met in the "efficient planner" subsample and is maintained within socioeconomic strata. This apparently linear relationship holds up well at both extremes of couple fertility. Childless wives, more often than wives with children, report as friends women without living children. Wives having three or more children report friends of higher fertility than do wives with two children.

Unexpectedly the fertility correlation between couples and wives' friends is just as high in the "inefficient planner" sample, standing at about 0.40. One reason for this surprising result is mechanical: the family sizes of couples are 38 per cent more variable in the "inefficient planner" sample than in the "efficient planner" sample. The relationship also depends partly on the fact that couples and friends tend to be similar in socioeconomic status and therefore in effectiveness at birth control. The amount of variation in couple fertility which can be accounted for in terms of fertility of wives' friends is reduced 40 per cent when socioeconomic status is held constant.

INTERPRETATION

Probably even in an unrestricted sample the correlation between fertility of couples and fertility of their siblings would be low. It seems unlikely that siblings wield much influence upon each other's ideals of family size. Nor do shared reactions to a family of upbringing seem to be the basis for a substantial fertility relationship. Then too, the awkward way in which sibling fertility had to be measured contributes toward weaker relationships. To allow for differing marriage durations, sibling fertility must be measured as a ratio of observed to expected fertility. Unfortunately these ratios are sensitive to a number of factors, as the following example shows. Think of a couple who want two children, have them in the first two years of marriage, but stop there. If their fertility is measured at the end of this second year, their rating will be well above two other types of couple who also stop at two children: namely the couples who space their two children more widely and secondly the couples who have their two children in the first two years of marriage but whose fertility is not measured until several years of marriage have elapsed. Naturally this looseness between measured fertility and actual completed size of family tends to attenuate fertility relationships.

The fact remains, however, that in the "efficient planner" sample the fertility relationships between fertility of couples and that of siblings reach statistical significance while the relationships involving parents do not.[17] For interpretation little can be done except to repeat a rationale given earlier. It is improbable that the difference arises solely because siblings wield greater influence upon family size ideals than parents. Some fraction of the couples have reacted negatively to the size of their families of upbringing. These negative reactions tend to weaken the fertility relationship between generations. But if these negative reactions are sufficiently shared by brothers and sisters, then they should enhance, not reduce, the fertility relationship between siblings.

This supposition gathers support from the contrasting results in the "efficient planner" and "inefficient planner" subsamples. If the fertility relationship between couples and siblings depends primarily on shared reactions to families of origin, then it should diminish among couples whose birth control is so inadequate that they cannot implement their common goals. When socioeconomic status is held constant, the relationship actually does dwindle among the "inefficient planners."

Seemingly the fertility relationship between couples and wives' friends has a multiple basis. Friends are in a strategic position to influence family size ideals. Couples of similar fertility are apt to find more in common and to seek each other out as friends. Principles of nonpurposive selection may also operate. Couples of like fertility are led into unintentional association by similar housing needs and common activities, with propin-

quity then favoring the formations of friendships.

From the data at hand, it is impossible to say which principle contributes the most. One cannot decide whether influences upon family size ideals play a primary or secondary role in the over-all relationship. Nevertheless there are several reasons for believing that the principles of purposive and nonpurposive selection together have an important, if not predominant, role.

1. The main reason for suspecting that selection plays a large part in the relationship of couples' fertility and friends' fertility is the persistence of the relationship in the "inefficient planner" sample. To be sure, it shrinks when proper account is taken of the wider variation in fertility and of the partial dependence of the relationship on socioeconomic status. Nevertheless a sharper shrinkage would be expected if the relationship depended heavily upon wives being influenced by their friends. Such influences forfeit much of their power among couples unable to practice efficient birth control.

2. Evidence has been provided that childless wives tend to have childless wives as friends. It is a little farfetched to think of a newly married wife coming into the company of several childless wives and then being "influenced" to remain childless herself. It is much easier to think of wives coming together on the basis of common interests that are partly conditioned by the absence of children.

3. Finally there is the consideration that "friends" in this report doubtless refers in the main but not necessarily to three *current* friends of the wife. Current friends may not be the crucial ones from the standpoint of influencing fertility. This

---

[17] Kantner and Potter, *op. cit.*, p. 302. (Reprint p. 1077.)

would be especially true for couples who made their basic fertility decisions much earlier.

RECOMMENDATION FOR FUTURE STUDIES

How best may the study of primary group influence upon fertility be advanced? The present report has examined fertility correlations between respondents and their siblings and friends. These correlations are difficult to interpret. For example, how much does the relationship between fertility of siblings and couples depend on mutually influenced ideals of family size and how much upon shared reactions to families of upbringing? It is no easier to tell whether the relationship between fertility of friends and couples rests on friends influencing size preferences or on the tendency of persons with similar family sizes to meet and choose each other as friends. Because of this difficulty, merely duplicating studies like the present one on other samples is not enough.

More direct studies are needed of the ways in which primary groups influence fertility. Before such studies can proceed very far, however, more must be known about family size ideals and their processes. A couple may take years to reach the final and effective decision as to how many children they want. The processes by which vague, tentative ideas about family size grow into firm, highly rationalized goals ought to contain many regularities. Hitherto these regularities have not been studied systematically. Suited for such study would be a panel design, permitting trends to be followed over time. The sample of couples should cover a range of marriage durations, so that these trends may be checked against hypotheses for various marriage points.

Ideals of family size have a long time reference. Not only are they changing through time, but also the influences playing upon them are changing. Therefore subtle means are required to isolate the influence of any one group. The most successful measures may be indirect ones—e.g., asking for examples of "successful families" from among the respondent's relatives or near acquaintances. Special situations may provide the largest yields in terms of results. Among these situations might be spouses in disagreement over their family plans or spouses exposed to conflicting advice. In general, there seems to be an important area of study here, but a very difficult one. Considerable ingenuity will be demanded.

Role Satisfactions and Length of Life in a Closed Population*

Francis C. Madigan

Clinical studies of psychosomatic illness have shown that pathological physical conditions can be caused by purely psychic states. However, despite the central position of role analysis in contemporary sociological thought, no projective, quantitative test has been made of the relationships between role satisfactions and mortality.[1] Such a study would be feasible and valuable: Its value would be in submitting to rigorous test the long-held belief that "square pegs in round holes" are less healthy, as evidenced by their less favorable mortality rates. The results might require important readjustments in our thinking about the effects of social conditions upon health.

The research reported here was no such rigorous test of this relation. It was rather an *ex post facto* mortality-rate study of an order of Catholic priests, without using hypotheses of the effects of role satisfactions upon health. The results, however, suggest the hypothesis that when high role

satisfactions are experienced over a long period, they tend to prolong life when other factors are held constant.

METHODOLOGY

SUBJECTS OF STUDY. The population studied was a large American subdivision of an order of Roman Catholic priests. This subdivision (hereinafter called "the order") has its headquarters in a large city of the Northeastern United States, while its main field of operations covers two of the Middle Atlantic states. It also maintains two foreign missions, one in the Far East and the other in several island groups of the Pacific. Although both native and foreign-born persons, and white and nonwhite racial strains are included in the membership, nonwhite members were eliminated from this study to obtain a more homogeneous universe. (Foreign-born whites were retained inasmuch as they made up less than 5 per cent of the total.)

This population must be distinguished from religious Brothers and Sisters of Catholic teaching orders. The subjects of the present investigation are all male and include no teaching Brothers.[2] "Priest" is defined

* Francis C. Madigan, "Role Satisfactions and Length of Life in a Closed Population," *American Journal of Sociology*, LXVII (May, 1962), 604–649. Copyright 1962 by The University of Chicago.

[1] Studies have attempted to relate mortality differentials, illnesses, and response to pain to such variables as social and environmental factors, ethnic origin, emotions, life stresses, and sex differences. In particular, cardiovascular diseases, rheumatoid arthritis, peptic ulcers, ulcerative colitis, diarrhea, and constipation have been studied as dependent variables.

[2] In a previous study, "Are Sex Mortality Differentials Biologically Caused?" *The Milbank Memorial Fund Quarterly*, XXXV (April, 1957), 202–223, I investigated the death rates of 10,000 religious Brothers and 32,000 Sisters of Catholic teaching orders. Brothers pronounce religious vows but

here as a person already ordained to the priesthood, or as a seminarian studying to receive such ordination.

THE DATA. During 1953–57, the author spent eight months residing in eight religious houses of this order, observing at close hand the manner of life of the priests and engaging in frequent discussions with members of the order.

The statistical data of the study were drawn from the order's records. These consist of annual printed catalogs, containing (together with other information such as present occupation) each member's birth date, date of entrance into the order, and his date of death or termination of membership (if either of these had occurred). (The precise date of withdrawal from the order is available from files in the superior's office.)

The techniques used to compile these catalogs proved to be very satisfactory. The person in charge of compiling data for the order is highly competent and great care is exercised to avoid mistakes. In addition, members are urged to examine each year's catalog and to report any mistakes they may find. An extensive check on the consistency of the dates reported in the 1954 and the 1957 catalogs, made by the author, revealed no discrepancies. It is reasonable to conclude that the records are highly ac-

---

are not ordained, nor do they study for ordination. In contradistinction to my earlier study, which involved a national sample embracing both men and women of *many different* religious orders, the present study deals with men only (priests) of *one particular* religious order. Religious priests differ from diocesan priests by the pronouncement of religious vows which incorporate them into some particular religious order. Both religious and diocesan priests are ordained, but only the former belong to a religious order.

curate (error from all sources is estimated at less than 0.001).

LIFE STRESSES OBSERVED IN THE ORDER. Physical and nervous strains experienced during 1953–57 derived principally from the results of military service, from the after-effects of war experiences in enemy-occupied territories, from missionary service, and from travel, diet, and stresses inherent in the life of the order. The following descriptive material shows that members of the order underwent most of the chief strains experienced by male members of the general population, in addition to strains experienced because of their membership in the order.

Approximately 10 per cent of the ordained priests (excluding those caught in enemy-occupied territories by the outbreak of the war) had served as military chaplains during World War II. Three men were seriously wounded, two of them remaining permanently crippled. Eleven to fourteen priests have been chaplains each year since 1952, some serving for 10 years or more. Three of these "peacetime" chaplains have died at less than 49 years of age, one in a military accident. These facts and the accounts of the overworked regime of a Catholic chaplain given by these men leave little doubt that military service in this capacity sets up strains which curtail length of life.

During World War II, 110 priests (approximately 9 per cent of the 1955 white membership) were in Japanese interment camps or lived with guerrillas in the mountains. This percentage is much higher than that found in the adult male general population, less than 2 per cent of whom were war prisoners or with guerrilla forces. In both cases, members of the order experienced serious malnutrition and tensions. Six died or were killed during the war, and eight more died in the 7 years between V-J Day and the beginning of the period of observation of this study. Of these, four had not yet reached their thirty-ninth birthday. The after-effects of the war undoubtedly tended to shorten the later life of some of the missionaries who had survived into the period of observation, although for others, good medical care after the war may have eventually offset their war experiences. Sixty-one of these priests returned to the missions after one or more years of recuperation in the United States. Twenty-nine have remained in the United States, and the remaining six have died.

In 1957, a typical year, 184 American priests were employed in the order's two foreign missions. About two-thirds of these had not served in these missions during the war. Peacetime mission service, however, probably also tends to shorten life. Residence in any foreign culture, but especially in that of an underdeveloped mission country, is notably associated with frustrations. Moreover, conditions of sanitation, epidemiology, medical practice, heat, and dampness in these missions are vastly different and less healthful than those of the mother country. Equivalent strains are not found in an equally large proportion of the general population.

Unlike religious Brothers, the work of ordained priests requires frequent travel, so that travel accidents during the period of study claimed the lives of two priests. Such accidents probably are equally common among men of the general public.

Aside from hospital and military chaplains and parish priests (7.4 per cent of the membership in 1955), members of the order lead very seden-

tary lives. On the other hand, 57.0 per cent of the adult male general population in 1950 were employed in such active occupations as farming, manual labor, skilled and semiskilled factory jobs, and mechanical repair work.[3]

The writer observed, and verified his observation, that most priests of the order give up regular exercise shortly after ordination (which is generally at about 30 to 35 years of age). The majority, certainly more than 60 per cent, quickly become from five to more than forty pounds overweight by standard age-height tables; about 33 per cent are at least 10 per cent above average weight, taking age and height into account. On the other hand, only about 20 per cent of the male general population are 10 per cent above average weight.[4]

Typical meals contain high concentrations of cholesterol-producing foods such as meat fats, butter, cream, and eggs. This diet is important when joined to the lack of exercise and the high incidence of overweight condition reported, because recent medical research has associated precisely these three factors (high cholesterol levels, lack of exercise, and overweight) with high incidences of atherosclerosis, coronary occlusion, and other cardio-

---

[3] *United States Census of Population: 1950*, Vol. II, *Characteristics of the Population*, Part I, *U.S. Summary*, chap. c, pp. 1-261–1-266.

[4] Society of Actuaries, "Build and Blood Pressure Study, 1959," cited in the *Statistical Bulletin* (Metropolitan Life Insurance Co.), XLI (January, 1960), 4–7. This investigation covered several million people. Authority for the statement about the incidence of overweight in the order rests principally upon my observations and a sample investigation which I conducted, asking members their weight and height and comparing the responses with standard tables.

vascular diseases. In addition, during the period of study priests who had been more than eight years in the order typically smoked from one-half to more than one pack of cigarettes a day, which by common standards classifies them as moderate to heavy smokers.[5] Such smoking aggravates certain types of circulatory disorders and probably also affects the lungs.

In addition to the stresses shared with the general population, these men experienced the stresses inherent in the order: these were derived from the religious life in general and from the mode of this life particular to the order.

Observance of the three vows of poverty, chastity, and obedience constitute the essence of religious life in any Catholic order. These vows, as sources of stress, seem to be without equivalents in the great majority of the general population.[6]

The vow of chastity forbids marriage and the deliberate enjoyment of venereal pleasure in thought or act. For healthy young men this self-dedication obviously is stressful. The

chief stress arising from this vow for mature religious persons, however, seems to be an inner loneliness which reflects the absence of those intimate ties of affection which bind together members of a conjugal family. Family affections and interests undoubtedly contribute much to mental health. Their absence probably lowers resistance to the effects of nervous and mental strains.

Obedience is the most stressful vow. The emotional struggles a man undergoes, not just in performing externally an enjoined course of action, but in submitting his judgment in important matters to that of his superiors in matters of great personal interest to him, can generate protracted hardships. The strains connected with obedience do not seem to decrease but to grow with age.

The Rule of the order requires approximately 3½ hours of daily prayer, including an hour of meditation. Attentive prayer demands real effort, and in some cases imprudently forcing a tired imagination generates nervous ailments. However, while the hours of prayer may increase the physical and nervous strains of daily life in the order, from another point of view they contribute to the mental health of members resulting from the peace of mind which they engender.

Catholics, and members of the order, too, regard the particular order as an intellectual elite and expect a high standard of excellence of performance from its members. These expectations occasion strains. Similar strains (although in most cases less arduous) may be experienced by professionals, executives, and entertainment personnel of the general public, but the proportion of persons so involved in the order is much higher (100 per cent) than in the general

---

[5] See William Haenszel, Michael B. Shimkin, and Herman P. Miller, *Tobacco Smoking Patterns in the United States* (Washington, D.C.: Government Printing Office, 1956), p. 6. The smoking rates of members of the order seem considerably in excess of the white male general population in which 21.5 per cent never smoked, and only 28.6 and 13.3 per cent, respectively, regularly smoked (at the time of the survey) one-half to one pack of cigarettes, and more than one pack daily. An additional 10.7 per cent had smoked regularly in the past but no longer did, while 4.0 per cent stated that they smoked only occasionally (*ibid.*, p. 36).

[6] In my earlier study (*op. cit.*), I unintentionally gave some readers the impression that the religious life is not stressful. In fact, observance of the three vows seems connected with considerable stresses, as is the observance of any principles of action.

public (approximately 18 per cent).[7]

Fifteen years of study after high school (or thirteen after college), broken by a teaching assignment from the eighth to the tenth years, are designed to prepare members who can, at least by extra diligence, uphold the order's reputation for intellectual achievement. The material covered is voluminous and difficult, and extremely searching oral examinations at the end of each scholastic year screen out candidates who lack the necessary talent.[8] A poor showing in any oral examination after the fourth year of study makes the person ineligible in later life for higher administrative posts and for specialization in philosophy or theology, while it also makes him a less likely choice for specialization in the secular branches of knowledge. Two of the oral examinations are particular hazards of the course; they cover, respectively, three and seven years of study, and come at the end of the seventh and fourteenth years of study.

This training period is for many priests a severe grind and the source of very many nervous strains which build up in cumulative fashion the further one has progressed through the period. Moreover, many priests also pursue one or more secular graduate degrees after they have completed their regular training program; this adds from one to six years of study with accompanying strains to an already long period of intensive preparation.

Afterward, the member feels that to live up to expectations, he must operate on a high level of performance, especially in public activities like preaching or writing. Although many exceptionally gifted men have been attracted to the order because of its reputation, still the majority are, while fairly keen, not unusually bright or brilliant. Often such members can satisfy expectations only by devoting more time to particular commitments than is rationally expendable in view of other duties.

Some solve the resulting dilemma of finding time to do other duties well by cutting down on sleep and going for weeks or even months on from four to six hours of sleep instead of the usual seven. Others solve it by curtailing or omitting some duties. Others lower their standards of performance. None of these solutions is very satisfactory from the standpoint of the individual's mental and physical health.

The typical member is a teacher in an educational institution of the order.[9] His class load is heavier than is common among teachers in comparable nondenominational universities, colleges, or schools. He also generally directs at least one extra-class student activity such as the school newspaper or the dramatics guild. Such extra-class activities require large expenditures of time and energy, and excellence of product is expected. Further, in boarding schools or colleges, the priests supply most of the corridor prefects—a time-consuming assignment almost inevitably associated with substantial losses of sleep at night. Finally, many priests devote much time each week to pastoral activities with students such as formal and informal counseling, hearing

---

[7] *United States Census of Population: 1950, op. cit.*, pp. 1-261–1-262.

[8] There are no regular oral examinations from the eighth through the tenth year of training.

[9] "Teacher" is used here in the broad sense to cover professors and instructors in both colleges and graduate schools as well as teachers in high schools.

sacramental confessions, and preaching. Strains from these and the following activities can be classified as "occupational" stresses. Thus it appears that the average priest of the order seems much more overworked than an average member of the general population. The priests also have less opportunities for relaxation.

Members are widely sought out as confessors, particularly by persons with difficult or troublesome problems. This, in addition to week-end parish assignments and confessional work with students, causes priests of the order to carry a heavy load of other people's troubles. Such work is tiring and sometimes discouraging. Even the physical inactivity of sitting three to four hours in a confessional box while sharply attending to what penitents say is fatiguing.

Extracollegiate work involves regular week-end parish help and special-occasion assignments or commitments. The latter include articles for journals, lectures before learned societies, conferences and "retreats" (periods of prayer of three to eight days, involving four or five talks per day, much confessional work, and considerable counseling by the priest conducting the retreat), parish missions (popular retreats of three days), sermons, and popular talks. Retreats require a great deal of preparation; thus teaching priests can only give them during vacation periods. Retreats thus cut into periods of relaxation.

Week-end parish assignments are rather common throughout the year. They are often to a distant parish in the suburbs or in the country. The priest is usually expected to hear confessions for three to five hours on Saturday afternoon and evening and to preach and say two masses on Sun-

day morning. When he arrives home on Sunday afternoon, he is tired and he may still have to prepare his Monday classes. Week-end work prevents Saturday and Sunday relaxation such as religious Brothers and secular teachers enjoy, while classwork during the week prevents relaxation on a weekday such as diocesan priests can enjoy. About one-fourth of the ordained priests may have parish assignments on any particular week end.

Few of the ordained members take the two-week vacation in the summer to which they are entitled. They are too busy with retreats, with teaching in summer school, and with other occupations to take the time off. On the other hand, members of the general population are much more likely to relax on Sundays and to take two weeks of annual vacation from work.

Several conclusions concerning life stresses in the order during the period of study can be made: First, a greater incidence of deaths from cardiovascular-renal causes than in the general population should be expected among members of the order because of their high cholesterol diet, their greater lack of exercise, and their more prevalently overweight condition. Cardiovascular-renal diseases currently account for more than 50 per cent of the deaths of American white males of ages 40–64;[10] therefore, mortality

10 Metropolitan Life Insurance Company, "International Variations in Mortality," *Statistical Bulletin*, XXXVIII (October, 1957), 3; "Mortality Remains at Elevated Level," *ibid.*, XLII (July, 1961), 9; and United States Department of Health, Education, and Welfare, "Mortality from Selected Causes by Marital Status: United States, 1949–51," *Vital Statistics—Special Reports*, XXXIX, No. 7 (May, 1956), 377; "Death Rates by Age, Race, and Sex: United States, 1900–1953—All Causes," *ibid.*, XLIII, No. 1 (January, 1956), 14; "Death Rates by Age, Race, and Sex:

rates in the order should be notably inflated by less favorable cardiovascular-renal mortality.

Second, average life stresses in the order appear to exceed those of the general population by at least the amount (and probably by more) that the strains upon physicians in general practice (as opposed to specialists and physicians holding public office) surpass those of the general population. Since after age 35 the mortality rates of general practitioners are less favorable than those of the general population,[11] when other factors are controlled one would also expect the mortality rates of priests of the order to be less favorable, after age 35, than those of the general population.

RESEARCH HYPOTHESIS. On the basis of the preceding observations, the following hypothesis was made: priests of the order would have shorter life expectations than persons of the general population. This hy-

pothesis was supported by the only two mortality-rate studies on priests readily available at the time of research.[12] Each of these studies showed a mortality rate in excess of the rates of comparable general populations.

ANALYSIS OF THE DATA. The period of study was from January 1, 1953, to December 31, 1957; the population enumerated at the midpoint of this period of observation, June 30, 1955, comprised 1,247 persons with 6,235 person-years of exposure to risk of death. All deaths occurring during the period were related to appropriate five-year age groups of this population. The age-specific central death rates thus computed were converted into life-table mortality rates by the Reed-Merrell tables.[13] An abridged five-year life table, based upon the *observed* rates (because it was desirable to compute the standard error of life expectancies) was constructed, and expectations of life of priests of the order were compared with expectations of the general population to test

---

United States, 1900–1953—Major Cardiovascular-Renal Diseases," *ibid.*, XLIII, No. 13 (July, 1956), 214.

[11] Frank G. Dickinson and Leonard W. Martin, "Physician Mortality, 1949–1951," *Journal of the American Medical Association*, CLXII (December 15, 1956), 1462–1468; J. N. Morris, J. A. Heady, and R. G. Barley, "Coronary Heart Disease in Medical Practitioners," *British Medical Journal* (March, 1952), No. 1, p. 503; J. N. Morris and J. A. Heady, "Mortality in Relation to the Physical Activity of Work," *British Journal of Industrial Medicine*, X (October, 1953), 245–254; Louis I. Dublin and Mortimer Spiegelman, "The Longevity and Mortality of American Physicians, 1938–1942," *Journal of the American Medical Association*, CXXXIV (August 9, 1947), 1211–1215; L. I. Dublin, M. Spiegelman, and R. G. Leland, "Longevity and Mortality of Physicians," *Postgraduate Medicine*, II (September, 1947), 188; and L. I. Dublin and M. Spiegelman, "Mortality of Medical Specialists, 1938–1942," *Journal of the American Medical Association*, CXXXVII (August, 1948), 1519–1524.

[12] The first study covers all priests in England and Wales for 1931. The second study relates to one American province of a particular religious order for 1941–51 (see Office of the Registrar-General, *The Registrar-General's Decennial Supplement, England and Wales, 1931*, Part IIa, *Occupational Mortality* (London: H.M. Stationery Office, 1938), No. 341, p. 137; No. 771, p. 206; and No. 341, p. 319; and Reverend Edwin Foley, C.S.S.R., "A Life Table for Redemptorist Priests of the Baltimore Province, 1941–51" (unpublished study, Sociology Department of Catholic University of America, Washington, D.C., 1951).

[13] These death rates seemed sufficiently stable for the purposes of the research. Computations of the standard error were based upon Edwin B. Wilson, "The Standard Deviation of Sampling for Life Expectancy," *Journal of the American Statistical Association*, XXXIII (1938), 705–708.

the study hypothesis. The observed mortality rates were then graduated by difference equations and graphic techniques into five-year and one-year graduated rates for purposes of study, but the statistical analysis was based upon the observed rates.

RESULTS

The hypothesis was not sustained by the data. The central death rates and life-table mortality rates of the priests were consistently much more favorable than corresponding rates for white males of the American general population.

Table 1 shows that the standardized death rate for priests (based upon age-specific central death rates) was 28.2 per cent less than the 1953 rate of white males of the general population (hereinafter called simply the general population), while it was 21.3 per cent less than the standardized rate of married white males of the general population for 1949–51. These are large differences which are accountable for neither by sampling variation ($P < 0.001$ in both cases) nor by the base years of comparison. Differences in the base years might explain as much as 2 per cent of the difference of the white males' rate and as much as 3 per cent of the married white males' rate, but hardly more. All these base years belong to the first half of the same decade; moreover, the difference between the life-table mortality rates of white males of the general population for ages 15–74 for the years 1953 and 1955 was only 1.3 per cent (0.59523 and 0.58764, respectively).[14]

---

[14] These figures were derived from "Abridged Life Tables: United States,

TABLE 1. Standardized Death Rates per 100,000 Persons of Observed Priests, 1953–57, of United States White Males, 1953, and of United States Married White Males, 1949–51

Standardized death rate,[a] priests, ages 15–84, 1953–57 :	
Based on observed rates	858.6[b]
Based on graduated rates	879.6
Standardized death rate, white males, ages 15–84, 1953	1,100.8[b]
Percentage excess of rate for white males over rate for observed priest	28.2
Standardized death rate,[c] priests, ages 20–74, 1953–57 :	
Based on observed rates	669.2[b]
Based on graduated rates	682.0
Standardized death rate, married white males, ages 20–74, 1949–51	811.6[b]
Percentage excess of rate of married white males over rate of observed priests	21.3

[a] Based upon a standard million of the white male population of the United States, 1940.

[b] Differences between priests' and white males' rates and priests' and married white males' rates are significant beyond 0.001.

[c] Based upon the native white male population of the United States, 1940, rounded to the nearest thousand.

Source for age-specific rates of United States white males, 1953: National Office of Vital Statistics, *Vital Statistics—Special Reports*, Vol. XLIII, No. 1 (January, 1956). For United States married white males, 1949–51: *Vital Statistics— Special Reports*, Vol. XXXIX, No. 7 (May 8, 1956).

The more favorable mortality experience of these priests is revealed in greater detail in Table 2. The

---

1954," *Vital Statistics—Special Reports, National Summaries*, XLIV, No. 2 (May, 1956), 40, and "Abridged Life Tables: United States, 1955," *ibid.*, XLVI, No. 9 (July, 1957), 268. (The first source, on the page cited, gives data for 1953 as well as for 1954 and other years.)

TABLE 2. Selected Life-Table Functions of Observed Priests 1953-57, Ages 15 and Above, by Five-Year Age Groups, and Comparable Functions of United States White Males, 1955

Age	Probability of dying during interval priests[a] Graduated	Observed	United States males	United States rate, priest rate Per cent excess	Expectation of life[b] Priests	United States males
15–19	0.0034	0.0000	0.0064	—	58.0	54.8
20–24	0.0035	0.0055	0.0089	61.8	53.0	50.1
25–29	0.0038	0.0058	0.0080	37.9	48.3	45.6
30–34	0.0044	0.0000	0.0088	—	43.5	40.9
35–39	0.0055	0.0063	0.0130	106.3	38.5	36.3
40–44	0.0076	0.0068	0.0207	204.4	33.8	31.7
45–49	0.0149	0.0387	0.0348	−10.1	29.0	27.3
50–54	0.0333	0.0318	0.0558	75.5	25.0	23.2
55–59	0.0676	0.0290	0.0841	190.0	20.8	19.4
60–64	0.1180	0.0904	0.1272	40.7	16.3	16.0
65–69	0.1908	0.2867	0.1876	−34.6	12.6	12.9
70–74	0.2731	0.1338	0.2555	91.0	11.7	10.3
75–79	0.3550	0.4590	0.3615	−21.2	8.1	8.0
80–84	0.3869	0.3639	0.4988	37.1	7.8	6.1
85–89	0.4590	0.3995	—	—	6.1	4.8
90	1.0000	1.0000	1.0000	—	—	—

[a] Life-table functions for priests are based on *observed* rates since it was desired to compute standard errors. Graduated rates were obtained by means of graphic techniques and difference equations.
[b] The standard error of priests' expectation of life at age 15 was 0.020, at 45 it was 0.020, and at 60 it was 0.021. At each of these three ages, the priests' expectation of life differed significantly from that of white males of the general population beyond 0.001.
Source of data on white males: National Office of Vital Statistics, *Vital Statistics—Special Reports*, XLVI, No. 9 (July 2, 1957).

priests enjoyed their greatest advantage from the fifteenth to the forty-fourth year of life when their overall mortality rate was but 38 per cent that of the general population. They maintained a substantial advantage, however, from 45 to 74 years of age, during which period their mortality rate was only 86 per cent of that of the general population. Each of these differences is significant beyond the 0.001 level. In the age group 75–84, there was little to choose between the two populations, the priests' rate being 96 per cent that of the general population. The number exposed to risk among the priests was relatively small at these advanced ages so that sampling variability may account for the high mortality rate between ages 75–79 and for the comparatively low rate at 80–84 years of age.

The order's low death rates were particularly notable in the age groups 50–54 and 55–59. It appears that a lower incidence of deaths caused by cardiovascular-renal diseases occurs in the order than in the general population at these ages—despite stress conditions in the order favorable to a high incidence at these years. The relatively high mortality rate at ages 65–69 may reflect the eventual occurrence of delayed cardiovascular-renal deaths during the later period of life.

Expectations of life were also greater in the order. At 15 years of age its priests enjoyed a 3.2 year advantage over the general population, at 45 an advantage of 1.7 years, and at 60 an advantage of 0.3 of a year. All these differences from expectations of the general population were significant beyond 0.001.

These findings were so at variance with the research hypothesis as to call for reexamination of the assumptions and background data upon which the hypothesis had been based.

After careful reconsideration of the material, the author confirmed his opinion that life stresses typically experienced in the order substantially exceed those of the general population. The suggested explanation of the results is that the typically high degree of role satisfactions experienced by priests of the order had more than offset the curtailing effects upon length of life caused by the excessive life stresses they undergo.

Clearly this explanation can be *only* tentative, inasmuch as the hypothesis was neither formulated before collection of the data nor tested by it. As a hypothesis, however, it seems worthy of examination, especially in studies of other sample populations. The rationale for this hypothesis can be briefly stated as follows: Members

of the order typically enjoy very high role satisfactions. Ordained priests value their status and role as a priest very highly, finding in the priesthood a lasting source of satisfaction and pleasure. The seminarians also greatly esteem their status as candidates for the priesthood and look forward eagerly to the time when they will be ordained. Membership in this particular religious order is a further important source of role satisfactions because both members and the Catholic laity consider the order as an especially select group making eminent contributions to Catholic life, scholarship, and culture.

As in lay organizations, small informal friendship groups arise among members of the order, based upon personal qualities and similarities of interests, assignments, and time schedules. In the order, however, these cliques usually lack intense ingroup feelings and exclusiveness. One can therefore generalize more easily about such roles in the order than about clique roles in lay society: First, although not all priests belong to a small group, such persons do not feel isolated or without friends; second, the membership role in such groups is generally supportive. There is little tendency to undervalue a member, hence members generally find strength and satisfaction in their friendship-group roles.

While not every member is fully satisfied with his particular work, few are left for long in jobs they find exceptionally frustrating or incompatible with personal capacities and aspirations. Every position carries considerable authority and responsibility and most positions are made more interesting for the holder by the opportunities for religious ministrations. The member's self-image is almost invariably that of a person whose life has purpose and meaning for himself, and value for others.

Finally, the life of prayer, familiarity with God, and good works which are involved in the role of religious priest build up a feeling of moral security. This rather secure "moral stance" may be associated with a much lower emotional stress (e.g., worries about one's religious duties and other moral issues) than would be the lot of many members of the general population.

ADDITIONAL HYPOTHESES

Several additional hypotheses may explain the fact that death rates in the order were so much lower than had been expected:

1. The benefits of regularity of life in the order may more than offset its strains.

2. Members of the order do not compete for jobs in the same sense that typical laymen do, and therefore have a security which the average layman does not possess.

3. The order screens out unhealthy persons—obviously reducing mortality in the earlier years of religious life —and admits only the more intelligent, which may be associated with more physical vigor, hence accounting for greater longevity.

4. Many young men who might wish to be priests may be deterred from entering the seminary because of an extra-strong need for sexual satisfaction. Hamilton blames the shorter life of males upon the heightened metabolism caused by testicular secretions in the system.[15] Hence

---

[15] James B. Hamilton, "A Relationship of Maleness to Shortness of Lifespan and to Certain Pathological Condi-

lowering the representation of over-sexed men in a group might increase that group's expectation of life.

5. The high level of role satisfactions prevalent in the order may more than counterbalance the effects of its stressful way of life.

PROBABLE USEFULNESS OF HYPOTHESES AS BASES OF RESEARCH

HYPOTHESIS 4. Inasmuch as a quantitative test of physical virility can scarcely be made in this group, this hypothesis is useless. Moreover, recent research casts doubt on the theory that the action of the male hormones shortens life. There appears to be no lack of virility in the sense of qualities of manliness in the priests included in this study. They enjoy, in fact, a reputation for being unusually "manly" men.

HYPOTHESIS 3. The effect of screening out unhealthy candidates usually ends within approximately five years, according to insurance companies.[16] Inasmuch as more than 90 per cent of the members enter the order before their twenty-fourth birthday, such selection can hardly explain the lower age-specific death rates at 30 years of age and above. Whether selection of persons with

---

tions," *Journal of Gerontology*, III, No. 4 (Suppl. 7) ; and "The Role of Testicular Secretions ... and the Short Lifespan Associated with Maleness," *Recent Progress in Hormone Research: Proceedings of the Laurentian Hormone Conference*, III (1948), 257–324.

[16] J. Buchanan, "The Theory of Selection: Its History and Development," *Transactions of the Faculty of Actuaries* (Scotland), XII (January, 1926), 43; and L. I. Dublin and M. Spiegelman, *Length of Life* (New York: Ronald Press Co., 1949), pp. 287–289.

above-average intelligence affects the death rates is problematic.

HYPOTHESIS 1. It is hard to see how regularity—in eating meals, performing certain duties, and so forth—can greatly affect length of life. In addition, the regularity of regime in a religious order can be exaggerated (e.g., as noted elsewhere in this paper, members under pressures of work may find it difficult to get to bed on time and thus disrupt regular and sufficient amounts of sleep).

HYPOTHESIS 2. Worries about his family's security because of business competition possibly curtail the length of life of the average layman. Religious priests of the order studied undergo only remotely analogous stresses because they are personally secure in regard to the economic necessities of life and have no families of procreation. Does this difference underlie the divergences observed in the death rates? Probably not, because many strains which the religious priest undergoes are not shared by the layman. However, this second hypothesis can be tested together with hypothesis 5—and it would be useful to do so—by studying a population of businessmen *only*.

HYPOTHESIS 5. If role satisfactions counterbalanced strains of life in the order and in effect lengthened the average lifetime, why did not role satisfactions extend length of life in the two other groups of priests previously cited?

The British data of 1930–32 did not encompass a homogeneous population but rather embraced a wide cross-section of priests belonging both to diverse religious orders and to the diocesan clergy.[17] Diocesan priests do

not belong to any religious order; hence there is not standardization of living conditions from parish rectory to parish rectory. Thus the degree of role satisfactions experienced may have fluctuated considerably from priest to priest. Role satisfactions may have reached a lower average than those reported in this paper. In addition, in 1930–32 greater dangers of infection attended the parish priest's regular visits to the sick, and sulfa and antibiotic drugs were not yet available.

The 1941–51 study of religious priests was concerned with a small population in an order other than that observed by the author. Particular conditions in that order at that time may have been conducive to high levels of mortality. Moreover, the population studied was so small that an unusual mortality experience may be reflected, based merely upon sampling variation. The four war years may have affected the rates unfavorably, too, if chaplains killed or injured in military service were included in the data.

Linking high role satisfactions to greater longevity thus seems a more useful hypothesis than the others in explaining the results of the present study and thus warrants testing in further research. If formulated as "When other factors are controlled, length of life varies directly with degree of role satisfactions experienced," it can be generalized and tested on different categories of people. Role satisfactions can be varied from high to low by double sampling, and the death rates examined for concomitant variation.

Present medical knowledge suggests that the hypothesis will prove correct. Further research may demonstrate a strong association between role satisfactions, health, and a longer

---

[17] See studies cited in *n.* 12.

life, and thus open a new chapter in medical sociology. For these reasons the hypothesis seems particularly promising and challenging.

Institutional Completeness of Ethnic Communities and the Personal Relations of Immigrants[*][†]

Raymond Breton

INTRODUCTION

Many researchers, in attempting to explain the integration of immigrants, have stressed the factors pertaining to the social background, the motivation, and the primary group affiliations of the immigrant.[2] In the present study the view was adopted that some of the most crucial factors bearing on the absorption of immigrants would be found in the social organization of the communities which the immigrant contacts in the receiving country. There are three communities which are relevant: the community of his ethnicity, the native (i.e., receiving) community, and the other ethnic communities.

It was also felt that the integration of the immigrant should not be seen from a purely assimilationist point of view in which integration is said to

* Raymond Breton, "Institutional Completeness of Ethnic Communities and the Personal Relations of Immigrants," *American Journal of Sociology*, LXX (September, 1964), 141–146. Copyright 1964 by The University of Chicago.

† The material for this article has been taken from the writer's unpublished dissertation, "Ethnic Communities and the Personal Relations of Immigrants" (Baltimore: Johns Hopkins University, 1961). I wish to thank Professors James S. Coleman and Arthur Stinchcombe for their most helpful assistance throughout the study.

This study was originally carried out at the Social Research Group in Montreal. It was sponsored by La Fédération des Oeuvres de Charité in Montreal and The Canadian Department of Citizenship and Immigration. Their assistance is gratefully acknowledged.

2 See, e.g., C. W. Mills *et al.*, *The Puerto Rican Journey* (New York: Harper & Bros., 1950); W. L. Warner *et al.*, *The Social System of American Ethnic Groups* (New Haven, Conn.: Yale University Press, 1945); S. N. Eisenstadt, "Social Mobility and Intergroup Leadership," *Transactions of the Second World Congress of Sociology*, II (1954), 218–230; and his *The Absorption of Immigrants* (New York: Free Press of Glencoe, Inc., 1955); and L. G. Reepolds, *The British Immigrant* (Toronto: Oxford University Press, 1935).

have taken place when the immigrant is absorbed in the receiving society. Integration was rather conceived of as taking place in any one of the communities mentioned above or in two or three directions at the same time. That is, an immigrant can establish a network of social affiliations extending beyond the boundaries of any one community. Finally, it is also possible for the immigrant to be unintegrated.

It is argued that the direction of the immigrant's integration will to a large extent result from the forces of attraction (positive or negative) stemming from the various communities. These forces are generated by the social organization of the communities. In the present paper the influence of the institutional completeness of the immigrant's own ethnic community on the direction of his social integration is examined. In other words, I will examine the extent to which the institutional completeness of the ethnic community is related to its capacity to attract the immigrant within its social boundaries.

INSTITUTIONAL COMPLETENESS OF THE ETHNIC GROUP

Ethnic communities can vary enormously in their social organization. At one extreme, there is the community which consists essentially in a network of interpersonal relations: members of a certain ethnic group seek each other's companionship; friendship groups and cliques are formed. But beyond this informal network, no formal organization may exist. The immigrant who is a member of such a group will establish all his institutional affiliations in the native community since his ethnic group has little or no organization of its own.

Most ethnic groups probably were at one time—and some still are—of this informal type. Many, however, have developed a more formal structure and contain organizations of various sorts: religious, educational, political, recreational, national, and even professional. Some have organized welfare and mutual aid societies. Some operate their own radio station or publish their own newspapers and periodicals. The community may also sustain a number of commercial and service organizations. Finally, it may have its own churches and sometimes its own schools. Between the two extremes much variation can be observed in the amount and complexity of community organization; the degree of institutional completeness in fact shows variations from one ethnic group to another.

Institutional completeness would be at its extreme whenever the ethnic community could perform all the services required by its members. Members would never have to make use of native institutions for the satisfaction of any of their needs, such as education, work, food and clothing, medical care, or social assistance. Of course, in contemporary North American cities very few, if any, ethnic communities showing full institutional completeness can be found.

DIRECTION OF PERSONAL AFFILIATIONS

When the immigrant is transplanted from one country to another, he has to reconstruct his interpersonal "field." He will rebuild in a new community a network of personal affiliations.[3] Such a reconstruction is accomplished through his activities to satisfy his immediate needs: making a living, learning the new language, participating in social life, going to church. To satisfy these needs he will use a certain institutional setup; he will introduce himself into a social group. Which one? The native community? His own ethnic community? Another immigrant community of an ethnicity different from his own? Will he integrate himself primarily in one of these communities, or will he split his affiliations among them?

In the present paper two questions will be discussed: (1) Does the interpersonal integration of the immigrant in fact take place in different directions? In other words, to what extent are immigrants integrated in the native, their own, or another immigrant community? (2) To what extent does the institutional completeness of the ethnic community determine the direction of the interpersonal integration of the immigrant?

DATA AND METHODS

The analysis of the effect of the community characteristics on the direction of integration was carried out through a comparison of the personal relations of immigrants from thirty different ethnic groups. The findings are based on data from interviews with 230 male immigrants in Montreal, Canada, 163 of whom were reinterviewed fourteen months later.[4]

---

[3] S. N. Eisenstadt, "The Process of Absorption of New Immigrants in Israel," *Human Relations*, V (1952), 222–231.

[4] The first wave was done during April, May, and June, 1958; the second during July, August, and September, 1959.

In drawing the sample, no restriction was put either on the length of residence in Canada or on the ethnicity of the immigrant.

The sample was drawn in two stages. The first stage was an area sample in which thirteen census tracts were randomly selected. The census tracts in which the number of immigrants was extremely small had first been eliminated. Of the 18,415 households in the thirteen census tracts, 75 per cent were visited in order to enumerate their foreign-born population. From this enumeration was drawn a list of 1,689 male immigrants 18 years of age or older who had been at least 15 years of age when they came to Canada. In the second stage, a sample of 350 was drawn at random from the list.

Questionnaires were then administered in personal interviews. Approximately 14 per cent refused to be interviewed; others were not interviewed because they were "never at home," because no one was found to conduct the interview in their own language, or because they had moved during the four to five months between the enumeration and the interviewing. Losses in this last category probably constitute the most serious bias in the sample. Finally, some of the returns of those interviewed had to be rejected because of their poor quality.

The measure used to rate the ethnic communities according to their degree of institutional completeness is constructed from information on the number of churches, welfare organizations, newspapers, and periodicals in each ethnic community. Because all spheres of social activity are not covered it is possible only to approximate the level of institutional completeness of each ethnic group. However, the error is probably consistent for all ethnic groups and consequently does not affect their ranking along that dimension, particularly in view of the fact that the ranking is a very gross one: "Low" or "High."[5]

The direction of the affiliations of the immigrant was determined by the ethnic character of the person with whom he was in contact. The respondent was first asked whether during the week preceding the interview he had visited any people in their homes or had received any visitor himself. He was also asked whether he went to the movies, theater, night clubs, dance halls, taverns, bowling alleys, or other similar places; whether he attended concerts, sporting events, or other entertainments of some sort; and if he did, whether he went alone or with other people. Finally, he was asked if he met socially some of his coworkers, if he had any. Information was obtained on the national origin and

---

[5] Ethnic communities classified as "high" in institutional completeness are Greek, German, French, Hungarian, Italian, Lithuanian, Polish, Russian, Ukrainian. Those classified as "low" are Albanian, American, Austrian, Belgian, Bulgarian, Czechoslovak, Danish, Dutch, English, Indian, Irish, Latvian, Portuguese, Romanian, Scotch, Spanish, Swedish, Swiss, South African, Yugoslavian, West Indian.

In referring to degree of institutional completeness, what is meant is the *relative degree*, not the absolute degree. First of all, not all the organizations are included. The schools, for example, are left out and—what is even more important—so are voluntary associations, which are not only numerous but also very significant in the social life of any ethnic community. However, it seems reasonable to assume that the distribution of these associations among the various groups would be about the same as the distribution of the organizations presented above. Second, there are probably minor errors in the above list. Some ethnic groups may have a welfare organization, for example, which was not listed in the sources used.

birthplace of each person met (identified by first name or some other symbol). Then the respondents were classified, according to the proportion of the people met who were from each group, as having a *majority* or a *minority* of their personal relations in their own ethnic group, among other immigrants, or among members of the receiving community.[6]

ATTACHMENTS TO NATIVE AND TO ETHNIC COMMUNITIES

Most immigrants become absorbed into the new social system in the sense that they establish some personal attachment to it. But in which direction? Table 1 presents data bearing on the extent to which immigrants are interpersonally integrated inside or outside their own ethnic community.

The relations of the immigrants with their ethnic group seem quite strong as far as social ties are concerned. Indeed, nearly 60 per cent have a majority of their personal ties with members of that group, and comparatively few—approximately 20 per cent—have most of their relations with members of the native community.

If we examine the changes that take place as the immigrant spends more time in his new society, we find that the idea of the immigrant segregated from the native community fits more closely, although far from

---

[6] No attention is given here to the difference between those with affiliations in two or three communities and those whose affiliations are concentrated in a single one. Consideration of such differences would be revealing as regards both patterns of change over time and the social and psychological impact of the ethnic homogeneity or heterogeneity of affiliations on the immigrant personality and behavior.

TABLE 1. Ethnic Composition of Interpersonal Relations for Total Sample
and by Length of Residence in Receiving Country

		Years of residence		
Interpersonal relations	*Total* (N=173)ᵃ	*0–6* (N=73)	*7–12* (N=57)	*13+* (N=43)
Proportion with majority of their personal relations:				
In own ethnic group	0.59	0.70	0.58	0.42
In another ethnic group	0.14	0.15	0.07	0.21
With members of native group	0.19	0.10	0.25	0.28
In none of the above groups	0.08	0.05	0.10	0.09

ᵃ Respondents with no personal relations and those who did not give the necessary information are excluded.

perfectly, the situation of the recent immigration. But this situation changes more and more as the number of years spent in the receiving society increases. It is partly true that at one time the immigrant is drawn into the ethnic subsystem, but it does not take too long before he begins to break these ties and to form new attachments outside his ethnic community. Indeed, it is after six years in the host country that the ties with the native community show a substantial increase.

INSTITUTIONAL COMPLETENESS OF THE ETHNIC COMMUNITY

The presence of formal organizations in the ethnic community sets out forces that have the effect of keeping the social relations of the immigrants within its boundaries. It tends to minimize out-group contacts. This is what Table 2 shows. The communities showing the highest degree of institutional completeness have a much greater proportion of their members with most of their personal relations within the ethnic group: 89 per cent of the members of highly institutionalized communities, as compared with 21 per cent of those from ethnic groups with few or no formal organizations. The relationship between institutional completeness and in-group relations is about the same when the groups themselves, rather than the individual immigrants, are classified on these dimensions (Part B of Table 2).[7]

The institutions of an ethnic community are the origin of much social life in which the people of that community get involved and as a consequence become tied together in a cohesive interpersonal network. We

---

[7] In order to test the relationship between institutional completeness and the composition of personal relations, several factors were held constant: the size of the group, its residential concentration, the proportion of professionals in the group, the similarity and difference of the language of the group with those of the natives (English and French), the proportion in the group who are ignorant of the native languages, years of residence in Canada, and occupational status. The relationship held under all these controls. The strength of the relationship was reduced by as much as one-third in only one case: when the proportion ignorant of the native languages was held constant.

TABLE 2.   Institutional Completeness and In-Group Relations

	Degree of institutional completeness of ethnic group		
	Low	Medium	High
A. Proportion of *individuals* with majority of relations within ethnic group	0.21	0.54	0.89
Number of individuals	(62)	(28)	(83)
B. No. of *ethnic groups* with majority of all relations within group	5 out of 21	4 out of 5	4 out of 4

may note, incidentally, that the same result would obtain in the case of ethnic organizations whose stated purpose is to help the immigrant to "adjust" to the conditions of life and cultural habits in the country of adoption. Through such organizations immigrants may become partly acculturated; but at the same time they would become more strongly integrated into an interpersonal network of their own group. In other words, the existence of an institution in the group would tend to have the observed effect on the cohesiveness of the ethnic group irrespective of its orientation toward the native and its own national culture.

SOCIAL ORGANIZATION OR INDIVIDUAL PARTICIPATION?

Do the institutions of an ethnic community affect the social relations only of those who use them, or do they generate a social life that extends beyond the realm of the participants? Table 3 shows that the presence of churches in a community is related to more in-group relations even among those who do not attend the ethnic church.

The number of ethnic publications also affects the composition of interpersonal networks, but only among nonreaders (Table 4). The nonreaders are much more likely to associate within their ethnic group if the latter has several publications rather than a single one ($d = 0.31$), but the difference in the case of readers is not only much weaker, but in the opposite direction ($d = 0.09$). This is perhaps due to the difference in the distribution of the members of each category of ethnic groups in terms of education, language read, or other relevant attributes. The size of the sample, however, does not allow a more detailed analysis.

There is further evidence in Table 4 concerning the effect of publications in the ethnic community on in-group relations. This is found by comparing the difference between readers and nonreaders of ethnic publications in communities having only one publication with the corresponding difference for communities having more than one publication. These differences are 0.48 and 0.08, respectively. If the immigrant is a member of a community with many publications, it does not seem to make much difference whether he reads them himself or not. If, on the other hand, there is only one publication, then it seems impor-

TABLE 3.   In-Group Relations, by Number of Churches in Ethnic Community and Church Attendance[a]

	Number of churches in community				
	1 or 2			3 or more	
	None	Non-national attendance	National attendance	Non-national attendance	National attendance
Proportion of respondents with majority of relations within ethnic group	0.12	0.62	0.85	0.82	0.98
N[b]	—	—	—	—	—

[a] a (effect of number of churches) = 0.16, $P(a \leq 0) < 0.05$; b (effect of attendance at a national church) = 0.19, $P(b \leq 0) < 0.02$.

[b] Respondents from communities without churches are not considered in the calculation of the index. This measure of the effect of an independent attribute X on a dichotomized dependent attribute Y is the mean of the percentage difference in each pair of comparisons when controlling for other independent attributes. The sampling variance of this statistic is obtained by summing the variances of each percentage difference and dividing by the square of the number of paired comparisons through which these differences were obtained. This estimate of the variance and a table of the standardized cumulative normal distribution are used to find the level of significance. For the basis of this statistic see James S. Coleman, *Introduction to Mathematical Sociology* (New York: Free Press of Glencoe, 1964).

TABLE 4.   In-Group Relations, by Number of Publications in Community and Reading of Publications[a]

	Number of publications in community				
	1 only			2 or more	
	None	Not read every month	Read at least every month	Not read every month	Read at least every month
Proportion of respondents with majority of relations within ethnic group	0.35	0.43	0.91	0.74	0.82
N[b]	—	—	—	—	—

[a] a (effect of number of publications) = 0.11, $P(a \leq 0) = 0.27$; b (effect of reading of publications) = 0.28, $P(b \leq 0) < 0.01$.

[b] Respondents from communities with no newspapers and periodicals are not considered in the calculation of the index.

tant that he be directly exposed to its influence if it is to affect the composition of his personal relations. We may note also that the respondents from communities with no publications at all are the most likely to associate outside their ethnic group.

Through what processes does the

institutional completeness of the community affect the composition of the interpersonal networks of the members of an ethnic group? There are at least four such processes that we can speculate about:

Substitution.—The ethnic group succeeds in holding its members' allegiance by preventing their contact with the native community. This is achieved by a process of substitution whereby ethnic institutions rather than those of the native community take hold in the immigrant's social life. Immigrants have to find jobs; if they belong to a religion, they will want to go to church; being members of an occupational group, they may wish to join a work association; like other members of a modern society, they will read newspapers, listen to the radio, and watch television; they will send their children to school, etc. The immigrant and his family establish a wide range of institutional attachments, inevitably or nearly so, through the performance of their work. If these attachments are established within the native community, they will constitute channels for the formation of personal relationships with the members of that community.

If, however, the ethnic group develops its own institutions and forms its own associations, it will in this way control to a large extent the interpersonal integration of at least those of its members who become participants in the ethnic instead of the native organization.

Indeed, the findings presented in Table 3 show that, to the extent that there is actual substitution, that is to say, to the extent that individual immigrants do attend ethnic religious institutions instead of others, the expected effect on the composition of interpersonal ties is observed. But this effect through the process of substitution is fairly weak. In fact, if we take as a measure of this substitution effect the average difference between those who attend a national church and the others (the value of "B" in Table 3), we find that it accounts for less than one-fifth of the total variation in the composition of personal ties. If there is at least one church in the community, a large proportion of the immigrant's personal relations are contained within the social boundaries of the community. The increment in that proportion stemming from the individual's actual attendance at the ethnic church is not very large.

Extension within the community of the personal networks of the participants in institutions.—The immigrants who belong to ethnic organizations value highly their nationality and, as we have seen, form associations within it. The organizations sustain and perhaps increase this group of "attached" individuals, who in turn nourish the national sentiments of nonparticipants and include them among their associates. Since we do not know if the nonmembers have among their personal relations other individuals who are members, we can only suggest that this may be one of the processes taking place.

Organizations and associations in a community also raise new issues or activate old ones for public debate.—The arousal of public interest in the life of the group probably results in greater cohesiveness of the group. For instance, the group may become united in some action against outside elements such as over an immigration bill which would be detrimental to this particular group, or the expropriation of houses which would force a large number of families of that ethnic group to move away, or again the attempts of a non-national parish to have the national church closed down in order to increase its own membership.

Of course, issues which divide subgroups within the ethnic community will also have the effect of keeping the personal relations within the ethnic boundaries. The attachments of the members of each subgroup will be strengthened. To the extent that they become polarized on the issues facing their group, association with individuals who are not members of the ethnic group will be less appealing, unless they could become allies in the conflict. An important controversy among Italians, for example, will make Italians associate among themselves in cliques fighting each other.[8]

Leaders of organizations actively attempt to maintain or enlarge the clientele.—This is particularly true if the rate of immigration is decreasing, and because of this the survival of some of the organizations comes to be in danger. An illustration of this is found, for example, in Wittke's history of the German press in America. He notes that "at various times efforts were made to organize German press clubs on a local, state, or national basis." He reports that in 1863, "a number of German publishers and editors met at Reading, Pennsylvania, to work out plans to solve the problem of the rising cost of paper during the Civil War. The agenda was expanded to include a discussion of ways and means to keep the German press alive by supporting German Sunday Schools, reading clubs, and libraries, and by insisting that German be taught in the schools. From this meeting stemmed an organization."[9] After about twenty-five years, the organization died.

This example suggests that some ethnic organizations are dependent on other ethnic organizations for their survival and expansion. In the case quoted above, there was even a direct attempt to create new organizations in the ethnic community for the purpose of keeping alive a particular one. Such direct attempts, however, may occur only when the leaders (in this case the publishers) have some personal interest in the survival of the organization. But this is perhaps only a question of degree in the sense that leaders always have some personal interest in the survival of the organizations for which they are responsible.

TYPE AND NUMBER OF INSTITUTIONS

EFFECT OF DIFFERENT TYPES OF INSTITUTIONS

Of the three types of institutions included in the index of institutional completeness—churches, welfare organizations, and newspapers and periodicals—religious institutions have the greatest effect in keeping the immigrant's personal associations within the boundaries of the ethnic community. This is shown in Table 5 where the effect of the other types of institutions is controlled. In both cases, the presence and number of religious institutions explain about the same proportion of the variation in the dependent phenomenon (40 per cent and 45 per cent).[10]

---

8 On the unifying role of social conflict see G. Simmel, *Conflict* (New York: Free Press of Glencoe, Inc., 1955), pp. 13 ff.

9 C. Wittke, *The German-Language Press in America* (Lexington: University of Kentucky Press, 1957), pp. 215–216.

10 The number of cases in certain cross-classifications did not allow an

TABLE 5.   Churches, Welfare Organizations, Publications, and Extent of In-Group Relations

	Number of churches in community							
	2 or less	3 or more		2 or less		3 or more		
	Welfare organizations				Publications			
	None	Some	None	Some	None	Some	None	Some
Proportion of individuals with majority of relations within ethnic group	0.26	0.54	0.75	0.95	0.23	0.67	0.73	0.98
N	(61)	(48)	(4)	(60)	(70)	(39)	(11)	(53)

Note: a (effect of welfare organizations on in-group relations) $=0.24$. $P(a \leq 0) \simeq 0.05$; b^1 (effect of churches holding welfare organizations constant) $=0.45$, $P(b_1 \leq 0) < 0.01$: b^2 (effect of churches holding publications constant) $=0.40$, $P(b_2 \leq 0) < 0.01$; c (effect of publications) $=0.35$, $P(c \leq 0) < 0.01$.

The weight of the religious institutions can be attributed to the dominant role they hold in the community. Churches are very frequently the center of a number of activities; associations are formed and collective activities are organized under their influence and support. Also, the national sentiments of the immigrant find support in having experiences in church very similar to those in the country of origin—the language is the same; the images used in preaching are the same; the saints worshipped are also those the immigrant has known from early childhood. Moreover, religious leaders frequently become advocates and preachers of a national ideology, providing a *raison d'être* for the ethnic community and a motivation for identification with it.

Publications have the second most important effect on the immigrant's interpersonal network. The presence of publications in the ethnic community explains 35 per cent of the variation in the proportion of ingroup relations.[11]

Newspapers have a role in promoting the national ideology and keeping alive the national symbols and values, national heroes, and their historical achievements. Moreover, they interpret many of the events occurring in the country of adoption in terms of the survival or interests of the ethnic community. It is the very business of the national periodical or newspaper to be concerned with the events and personalities of the ethnic group.

Finally, the effect of the presence of welfare organizations is the least. It explains only 24 per cent of the variation. This, we presume, is due to the fact that these organizations are not concerned with the national interests of the community. They deal with people in need of food, shelter, clothing, or medical attention. They have to support "human" feelings rather than "national" feelings;

___

identical break for each type of organization. It was done as a check, and the results were in the same direction.

[11] The estimate of the effect of the presence of publications remains the same when it is computed while holding constant the presence of welfare organizations.

nevertheless, the existence of such organizations points to the presence of an active elite in the community which perhaps has its influence on the community's cohesiveness through channels other than the welfare organizations themselves. Also, their existence has a negative effect on contact with the host community: immigrants in need who address themselves to ethnic organizations miss a chance of contact with the "native" community.

VARIATION WITH INCREASING NUMBER OF FORMAL ORGANIZATIONS

What most differentiates one community from another in its capacity to control the social integration of its members is not so much its having many formal organizations as having some as opposed to none at all. This is shown in Table 6 where the extent of in-group relations is presented for im-

TABLE 6. Various Community Organizations and Extent of In-Group Relations

	Proportion of individuals and number of ethnic groups with majority of in-group relations				
	Individual			Group	
Community organization	Proportion	d^{a}	N	Number	Total
Number of churches:					
2 or more	0.80		(108)	7	8
		0.13			
1 only	0.67		(15)	4	6
		0.55[b]			
None	0.12		(50)	2	16
Number of welfare organizations:					
2 or more	0.58		(36)	3	4
		−0.28[b]			
1 only	0.86		(72)	3	5
		−0.57[b]			
None	0.29		(65)	7	21
Number of newspapers and periodicals:					
2 or more	0.93		(62)	3	3
		0.26[b]			
1 only	0.67		(30)	3	5
		0.37[b]			
None	0.30		(81)	7	22

[a] Difference between the proportion in the first column and the proportion immediately below it in the same column. The variance of the differences was estimated by using the method suggested by Leo Goodman in " Modifications of the Dorn-Stouffer-Tibbitts Method for Testing the Significance of Comparisons in Sociological Data," *American Journal of Sociology,* LXVI (January, 1961), 355–363.
[b] This difference is significant at least at the 0.01 level.

migrants whose group has no organization of a certain type, for those whose group has one organization of that type, and finally, for those who belong to groups with two or more such organizations.

All comparisons show that it is the existence of the first organization which makes the greatest difference. Second, third, or further additions have an effect on the extent of in-group relations, but much smaller than the effect of the first organization, or in the opposite direction. A drastic expansion occurs in the ethnic interpersonal network when the ethnic community ceases to be an informal system and acquires some first elements of a formal structure. This expansion continues as the formal structure develops but in increments smaller than the initial one.

CHANGE IN COMPOSITION OF INTERPERSONAL NETWORKS

If the ethnic community to which he belongs determines to a certain degree the composition of an immigrant's interpersonal network, it should also show some effect on the rate at which the immigrant changes his personal associates as well as on the kind of people he includes among, and abandons from, his personal relations.

Changes took place in both directions: some immigrants associated more within their ethnic group, some less. Of those who were not members of an ethnic interpersonal network at the time of the first interview, 22 per cent were included in one a year after; on the other hand, 17 per cent of those who associated mostly in their ethnic group had become interperson-

ally integrated in the native group.[12]

The changes in the composition of the immigrants' personal relations were then approximately as likely to be in the direction of the ethnic community as in that of the native community. This fact is of crucial importance for this study indeed; it serves to validate the scheme used in the analysis. It supports the idea that the integration of immigrants cannot really be studied without taking into account the fact that it can be achieved in at least two directions, that is, within the native or within the ethnic community; and that the integration can take place as frequently in one as in the other direction. Integration within the ethnic community cannot be ignored under the assumption that it is relatively unimportant or that it occurs relatively unfrequently.[13]

The degree of institutional completeness of an immigrant's ethnic community is one of the main factors

---

[12] If there had been no panel dropouts, the proportions changing in each direction would probably not have been different. Indeed, if we compare those who changed address with those who did not, under the assumption that the dropouts were mostly movers, we find that the movers were more likely to change the composition of their personal ties than the nonmovers during the period between the two panel waves, but in both directions: among those who had mostly in-group relationships at the time of the first panel wave, 13 per cent more of movers than of nonmovers had changed to a majority of out-group contacts by the time of the second wave; among those with a majority of out-group contacts, 11 per cent more of movers than of nonmovers changed to a majority of in-group relationships.

[13] There are two other possibilities: the immigrant may become interpersonally integrated in another immigrant group of an ethnicity different from his own, or he may remain an isolate. These alternatives will be examined elsewhere.

TABLE 7. Institutional Completeness and Change in Ethnic Composition of Personal Relations

Proportion of relations within ethnic group	High degree of institutional completeness			Low degree of institutional completeness		
	Wave II			Wave II		
	Minority	Majority	N	Minority	Majority	N
Wave I:						
Minority	0.71	0.29	17	0.82	0.18	34
Majority	0.15	0.85	60	0.14	0.86	7
No personal relations	0.38	0.62[a]	13	0.80	0.20[a]	10

[a] d $(0.62-0.20)=0.42$ is significant at the 0.03 level.

determining the direction of the change in the composition of his personal relations. As Table 7 shows, the immigrant who is a member of an institutionalized ethnic community is more likely to have shifted to a high proportion of in-group relations than the one who belongs to a less institutionalized one (29 per cent as compared to 18 per cent).

Also, Table 7 shows that the immigrants who had no personal relations at the time of the first interview and acquired some between the interviews acquired different kinds of associates depending on the degree of institutional completeness of their ethnic group. If the immigrant is a member of a group with organizations of its own, he is three times more likely to have acquired associates within his own group than if he is a part of a group with a more informal social organization (62 per cent as against 20 per cent).

The degree of institutional completeness and the magnitude of the ethnic interpersonal network are interdependent phenomena. It can be argued that the existence of an informal structure in an ethnic community is a prerequisite for the appearance of formal organizations. But it is also true that once a formal structure has developed it has the effect of reinforcing the cohesiveness of already existing networks and of expanding these networks. This expansion is achieved mostly by attracting within the ethnic community the new immigrants. A community with a high degree of institutional completeness has a greater absorbing capacity than those with a more informal social organization. The present findings on the changes in the composition of personal relations show the difference between the two types of ethnic communities in their ability to exert influence on the direction of the interpersonal integration of the immigrant.

On the other hand, the ethnic community does not seem to have much effect in preventing some of its members from establishing relations outside its boundaries. The proportion who had most of their relations within their own ethnic group and who now have most of them outside of it is the same for members of communities with either formal or informal social organization. The proportions, however, are based on a very small number of cases.

CONCLUSION

Having found that the institutional completeness of the ethnic community is an important factor in the direction of the social integration of immigrants, it is interesting to speculate about the determinants of this property of an ethnic community. There seem to be at least three sets of factors related to the formation of a public for ethnic organizations.

First, the ethnic group may possess some differentiating social or cultural attribute which can set it apart from the native community. Language, color, and religion are prominent among these features; but other traits and customs of a group can bring about the same result. The more different the people of a certain ethnicity are from the members of the native community, the easier it will be for them to develop their own institutions to satisfy their needs.

In the present study, it was found that a difference in language was associated with a high degree of institutional completeness. It was also found among ethnic groups with a different language that the higher the proportion in the ethnic group who are ignorant of the native languages (French and English), the higher the degree of institutional completeness of the group.[14]

The differentiating characteristics of an ethnic group constitute the basis for the formation of a clientele or a public for ethnic organizations. The mobility potential of the immigrant is reduced by such factors; he is more confined to his ethnic group. This is particularly true—or perhaps only true—when the differentiating features are negatively evaluated by the native community.

The second set of factors related to the degree of institutional completeness has to do with the level of resources among the members of the ethnic group. If a large proportion of the members of an ethnic group have few resources of their own, as indicated for instance in rural origin and lack of occupational skills, then there is in this ethnic group an important "clientele" to support welfare and mutual benefit organizations. Such a situation is likely to incite a "social entrepreneur" within the ethnic group to try to organize something for the new immigrants in need, seeing there an interesting opportunity for himself. His rewards would be either monetary profit, prestige in the community, more members for his church, or more buyers for his newspaper. In the present study, a strong positive relationship was in fact found between the proportion of manual workers in an ethnic group and the degree of institutional completeness of that group.[15]

A third set of factors relates to the pattern of migration. The number of immigrants of a given ethnicity and the rate at which they arrive are rele-

---

[14] Institutional completeness is high in one group out of eight whose language is also spoken by the native community and in twelve out of twenty-two whose language is different. Also, it is high in six of the thirteen groups with less than 20 per cent ignorant of the native languages and in six of the seven groups with 20 per cent or more not knowing these languages. (No data were available for two of the ethnic groups with a language other than French or English.)

[15] Of thirteen ethnic groups with less than 50 per cent of their workers in manual occupations, two are high on institutional completeness. Of the fourteen with 50 per cent or more of their workers in manual occupations, seven have a high degree of institutional completeness. (No occupational information was available for three of the ethnic groups.)

vant factors in the formation of an ethnic public. Perhaps a more important factor is whether the migration is an individual or a group phenomenon. Immigration during certain periods of time or for a given ethnic group can be the result of discrete decisions by individuals experiencing similar conditions in their country of origin; but it can also be a more or less organized group response, ranging from the migration of a group (such as a sect) under a leader to the pattern in which a migratory chain is established over a few years within a kinship network or a village and funds are collected in the new country to pay the passage of others from the native village or city.[16] Such factors provide very different sets of conditions for the development of ethnic institutions.

Ethnic communities are formed, grow, and disappear; they go through a life cycle.[17] They probably begin

either as simple aggregates of individuals, as amorphous informal groups, or as fairly well-structured informal groups. This group can constitute a public for ethnic organizations, a set of opportunities for social entrepreneurs. The organizations established by these entrepreneurs will maintain themselves as long as a public exists to use their services, or as long as the ethnic identity of the organization is important for the members of the ethnic group. The very existence of such organizations, as the findings of this paper show, act to strengthen this identity. But other mechanisms also operate, such as the fact that the leaders of the organizations have a vested interest in these organizations and will attempt in various ways to strengthen the ethnic identity so as to keep their public as large as possible.

If the rate of migration is low or nil, the ethnic public will progressively decrease, because even a high degree of institutional completeness will not prevent some integration into the native community. With time—and it may be quite long—the ethnic organizations will themselves disappear or lose their ethnic identity, completing the life cycle of the community.

---

[16] See W. Peterson, "A General Typology of Migration," *American Sociological Review*, XXIII (1958), 256–266; and C. A. Price, "Immigration and Group Settlement," in W. D. Borrie, *The Cultural Integration of Immigrants* (New York: UNESCO, 1959).

[17] The community life-cycle approach to the study of the integration and acculturation of immigrants is well represented by W. I. Thomas and F. Znaniecki, *The Polish Peasant in Europe and America* (Boston, 1920); and E. A. Galitzi, "A Study of Assimilation among the Roumanians in the United States"

(unpublished Ph.D. dissertation, Columbia University, 1929).

A Power of Town Size Predicts an Internal Interacting[*][†]

A Controlled Experiment Relating the Amount of an Interaction to the Number of Potential Interactors

Stuart C. Dodd

THE DIMENSIONAL MODEL HYPOTHESIZED

The research reported here sought an answer to the question: How may the amount of a mass interaction in a community depend on its size?

It is commonly said that there is more interaction for the average person in cities than in villages. Life in the city is said to be more exciting, to move faster, to be more varied. Life in smaller communities is thought to have fewer interperson stimulations and respondings (whatever their satisfying quality). In small communities one is likely to speak with, deal with, see, hear about, or otherwise attend to fewer persons per day, whether directly or by symbolic mediation, than does the average metropolitan. Can such common-sense generalizations be exactly formulated and measured and used as predictive rules under specified and observable preconditions? Will some dimensional formula describe the general curve relating the quantity of any interacting to the size of the given population? Then if other factors are constant, can the volume of interacting in specified ways be predicted statistically as a function of the number of interactions?

If these questions can be answered affirmatively by experiments, as we believe they can be, a further basic question for sociologists emerges. We ask whether from indices measuring the amounts of specified kinds of interaction between people estimates could be derived for the total amount of interacting of all kinds in a community.[2]

Could the total volume of social behavior in communities become measurable at least relatively between communities? For we believe from our interactance formula (3)[3] or princi-

* Stuart C. Dodd, "A Power of Town Size Predicts an Internal Interacting," *Social Forces*, XXXVI (December, 1957), 132–137.

† This research was supported in part by the United States Air Force under contract AF 33 (038)–27522, monitored by the Human Resources Research Institute (now Officer Education Research Laboratory, Air Force Personnel and Training Center), Air Research and Development Command, Maxwell Air Force Base, Alabama. Permission is granted for reproduction, translation, publication, and distribution in part and in whole by or for the United States Government. For exploratory computations the author is indebted to Melvin L. DeFleur, and to Marilyn Loranger for the final computations reproduced here.

2 This is a bit like expecting a general price level to be determined from observed prices of representative commodities, each commodity price in turn being an average of many selling-and-buying interacts.

3 This and following numbers in parentheses relate to the author's references appended to this article.

ple of demographic gravitation and from our more inclusive transact model (5) that the total quantity of interaction among persons in communities should be estimable. These estimates should improve accordingly as researchers could measure the number of representative interacts and the number of interactors while holding constant the context of the transact, i.e., controlling the factors of time, space, values, and other standardizable circumstances.

An opportunity to begin answering such questions was given to the Washington Public Opinion Laboratory by Project Revere. This was a contract research from the Air Force to develop principles for airborne leaflet operations. Such leaflet operations provided an almost ideal laboratory for controlled experiments testing mathematical models for interaction. The form of communicative interaction tested was the all-or-none spreading of a message on a leaflet among a population. This message diffusion was measured by the percentage of the population knowing that the leaflet requested each finder to pass one on and to mail back a stub. The public's fuller response, called "compliance," was observed here by the number of leaflet stubs (postage-free tracer postcards) which were either passed on to someone else or torn off a leaflet, filled out, and mailed back to the Laboratory. The stimulation of the public to interact thus with each other and with the research role-actors was well under the researcher's control. The public's response was easily measured, clearly identified as due to our stimulation and only to that, and in clearly controllable context.

As trial answers, or hypotheses, about the basic question of the de-

pendence of interacting upon the number of interactors, we chose on the basis of incompletely controlled pretests (4) a "power of the population" as a simple model to test. (See Eqs. 1 and 2.) This is a dimensional family of curves which says that the amount of some homogeneous kind of interacting between people is expected to be proportional to some power of the number of people (when, as usual, the context is either held constant at specified levels or varies without correlation to that interacting).

This hypothesis is expressible in general as:

$$\left[B_0 \overset{\text{hyp.}}{=} P^p \right] \qquad \text{(Eq. 1)}$$

the dimensional formula for full self-interaction p times within a population, P, or in more detail, specific to the local situation, as:

$$B_0 \overset{\text{hyp.}}{=} aP^p + b \qquad \text{(Eq. 2)}$$

the statistical formula for the same internal interaction.

As always, the dimensional formula denoted by square brackets specifying the exponent parameter only states the *shape* of curve or most generalized aspect of the relation between the independent and dependent variables, whereas the statistical formula also states the local accident of the *slope* and *location* of the curve by specifying its coefficient parameter, a, fixing the units, and by specifying its addend parameter, b, fixing the origin point.

When this exponent, p, is negative, the formula is called a generalized hyperbola (if in continuous form), or a generalized harmonic series (if in discrete data). The harmonic series are the inverse natural numbers, $1/1$, $1/2$, $1/3$, $1/4 \ldots 1/N$, and these are "generalized" when the exponent is other than unity.

This power of a population model has two variables with two forms for the dependent variable. The independent variable, which was varied in controlled amounts by the researcher, was the population, P, of the community. Thus we chose six communities, as shown in Table 1, varying in size in a roughly geometric series from around a thousand population to over three-hundred thousand. The dependent variable was the public's reaction to the leaflets in either (a) picking one up off the ground, filling it out, and mailing it in, or (b) passing one on to someone else to mail in. The former was called physical diffusion, and the latter was called social diffusion. Both behaviors involved interaction between the research role-actors and the reactors who mailed leaflets back as requested. But the social diffusion involved further interaction among givers and receivers of leaflets.

In relating both physical and social diffusion to the context factor of population size by this model, at least one social precondition is hypothesized, i.e., taken as a mathematical assumption in deriving the formula, Eq. 2, which states the model exactly. The model assumes *equal opportunities* for all persons. Equal *opportunities* mean that in respect to this act everyone had an equal probability of getting a leaflet. It implies that the population was not composed of subpopulations which might have very unequal likelihood of getting at least one leaflet per person.

In summary, the model here, Eq. 2, expresses in mathematical language of a dependent variable equated to a power of an independent variable the following social hypothesis: *The transact of diffusing any message (or any other form of one-way, all-or-none interacting) is expected to vary with the size of the population when weighted by the exponent (which may measure the proportion of actual interactors in that population of potential interactors), provided that the other factors of a transact are either constant or uncorrelated with the diffusing.* This is our "population power" hypothesis of interaction stating in prose what Eq. 2 states in algebraic symbols. It implies that insofar as these operationally defined and culture-transcending variables are related to each other, fully and solely, by the two preconditions hypothesized, in just so far the results specified by Eq. 2 can be expected to recur always and everywhere.

THE EXPERIMENT TESTING THE MODEL

A testing of this population-power model was made in Project Revere somewhat as a by-product of other tests. Six communities were found, as exhibited in Table 1, which had received airborne drops of our standard

TABLE 1. Diffusion and Population in Six Towns

Town	Population	Diffusion ("social and physical") (= % pop. mailing back)	
		Expected	Observed
Poulsbo	1,304	13.1	10.3
Okanogan	2,013	9.58	7.3
Raymond	4,150	6.24	6.1
Ellensburg	8,430	4.65	4.0
Everett	34,600	3.48	3.9
Birmingham	325,994	3.14	3.1

$r_{eo} = 0.99$; $p\,(\chi^2) > 0.05$.

leaflets and whose sizes represented roughly the following six points on a power scale: 10^3 (2^0, 2^1, 2^2, 2^3, —, 2^5, —, —,$^{28.5}$). With the population factor thus varying, the amount of each community's response by physical and by social diffusion was measured by the percentage of the population in each town mailing back one leaflet which the mailer had either picked up or received from someone else.

A plane spread the dramatized leaflet calling on each citizen to be a modern Paul Revere and help spread a trial message such as could save lives in a bombing emergency. The leaflets were scattered over each town's area at a ratio of one leaflet per capita, from about 500 feet altitude. The timing was on a Wednesday noon in good weather. Every inhabitant who went outdoors or lived in a household where some other normal member went outdoors had about an equal physical opportunity of finding a leaflet near his doorstep or of having one brought to him.

Toward control of the six factors of a transact other than the population size, the following approximations to constancy or controlled variation from town to town can be recorded:

THE ACTS FACTOR. The kind of interacts in getting, giving, and sending postcards back were the same for every town. The diffusing of the message was solely from leaflets and interperson contacts as all information about the leaflets by radio, newspaper, and wire services had been effectively sealed off in those communities during the 69 hours of the experiment.

THE TIME FACTOR. The time of day and day of week for the leaflet drop and the 69-hour interval to Saturday morning for mailbacks to be received were the same for all six towns.

THE SPACE FACTOR. The distance from people to available leaflets varied negligibly and randomly over a few yards from their doorsteps in every town. The density of people per unit area increased with town size, but this effect of space on the leaflet interacting, if any, would be correlated with and reflected in the dependence of the interacting upon town size—which is the variable at issue. (The reader should note that in expecting interacting to vary as a function of the population size no implication is intended that this is purely due to more bodies being present. The number of people is simply an index of whatever varies with that number of people—their interests and habits, their knowledge and possessions or anything else the amount of which is measurable in whole communities by counting heads.)

THE VALUES FACTOR. The value systems or motivations appealed to by the "Paul Revere" leaflet message and civil defense implications were common to the United States in 1953 and probably fairly much the same from town to town however much individuals varied in response to that appeal.

THE RESIDUAL FACTORS. These were uncontrolled and left to chance to average up somewhat alike from town to town. We avoided choosing any towns with unusual features unrelated to their size. From our other studies including analyses of 14 demographic and ecological indices the only variable we found which might disturb the comparability of the six towns was the Negro-white difference in Birmingham. Negroes mailed back less than whites, so Birmingham's mail-

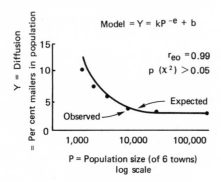

FIG. 1. How Diffusion Waned with Population

backs were slightly less than they would have been if it were an all-white town like the other five. This bias was too small, however, to alter the fit of the model in Fig. 1 by much more than one unit in the third decimal place of the correlation coefficient.

The facts observed in this controlled experiment on diffusion by town size are tabulated in Table 1 and graphed in Fig. 1. The data are fitted excellently by a "die-away" or negative power curve. *The relative interacting, whether physical or social, varied inversely with a power of the population.*[4] The absolute number of persons diffused or complying increased as town size increased—but increased at a slower and slower rate.

For the total interacting, combining both physical and social diffusion, the population power model fitted the data very closely. The correlation coefficient between the total diffusion data and the model ($= B_h$ or P^p), Eq. 1, was 0.989. The best-fitting exponent was 0.9, the intercept, b, in

Eq. 2 was Birmingham's diffusion (3.1 per cent), and the curve was fitted by anchoring it on the Birmingham end as the most reliable point. The small discrepancies of the observed total diffusing from this model were not statistically significant as $p(\chi^2) > 0.2$. In short, the hypothesis that this form of interaction among individuals in a town would vary with a negative power of the population or inversely to town size was clearly confirmed in this testing. The model fitted the total interaction data closely and surely under the specified conditions. But, of course, this must be reobserved by other scientists in further tests with more than six points on the curve before the general hypothesis can be considered fully confirmed.

INTERPRETATIONS OF THE FINDINGS

What may be the interpretation(s) or explanation(s) of the power relation observed here between town size and message diffusing? What rationale or mechanism may produce it? If its preconditions can be specified and tested in isolation, it should become possible in the future to predict a given town's interaction of some kind from knowledge of its population size and actuarial experience with that kind of interaction.

The precondition we see as most plausible and universal to any culture and period might be called our "relative interstimulation" or "shrinking share" hypothesis.[5] By this explana-

---

[4] The physical and social diffusion when plotted separately showed closely parallel curves but with less excellent fit to the model.

[5] Just as an excellent fit to the hyperbola does not preclude the six-point data from fitting other curves (and requires more discriminating experimental designs to decide), so our offer-

tory hypothesis we expect that the total interstimulation of all kinds in a town will increase by more than any increase of the population as the town enlarges. The interstimulations mean that the acts of one person constitute a stimulus to which another person responds. The number of possible single interstimulations of one kind between persons, P in number, is proportional to P^2. As suggested by the sociomatrix cross-classifying every person in a row against every person in a column, the maximum number of pair permutations[6] would be P^2 (allowing self-stimulations in the main diagonal cells). But this would be a ceiling since, as towns get larger, it becomes physically impossible for everyone to interact daily with everyone else individually. Therefore, as towns get larger the pair interactions may be expected to be proportional to a power of the population larger than the first power yet smaller than the second power or square. The total pair interactions of all kinds then will vary with the P^{1+q} power of the population where the q in the exponent is less than 1. Then on dividing by the population to get the total per capita pair interacting the expectable formula is P^q (i.e., $P^{1+q}/P^1 = P^q$).

Now the per capita reaction of the population of each town to the leaflet when dropped at a constant ratio of one leaflet per person might be expected within any one culture and period to be constant ($= a$) if they reacted to the leaflets only.

But now consider their reacting to a constant leaflet stimulation in the context of their joint reacting to it and to all the rest of the stimulation of all kinds playing on them and demanding their attention. This relative part that per capita leaflet reacting is of all per capita reacting seems measurable as their ratio. This is the ratio of a constant over a population-to-a-fractional-power. This is a negative fractional power of the town populations (i.e., $a/P^q = aP^{-q} = aP^{p-1}$ in relative terms). Multiplying by the population, P^1, to reexpress this in absolute terms of number of people gives our model, Eq. 2, where $b = 0$. (i.e., $aP^{p-1} \cdot P^1 = aP^p$).

This was exactly what was observed. The per capita compliance of mailbacks varied as a negative fractional power of the town's population as shown in the dropping curves in Fig. 1. This negative fraction as found by best fitting technics was -0.9 for the total diffusion (including both physical diffusion and social diffusion) as graphed in Fig. 1. *This means that the per capita reacting to the leaflets wanes as the towns enlarge because that reacting becomes a shrinking share of the townsmen's total behavior in any one day.*

This also means that on multiplying by the population, the absolute total reaction of each town to the leaflets varies as a positive fractional power (which is the complement of the negative fraction in the exponent above). In less technical language, it means that as town size enlarges the total absolute leaflet response in-

---

ing one behavioral interpretation or explanatory subhypothesis does not preclude other consistent but differently formulated interpretations. Thus Simon's probabilistic formulation for rank-size curves of population might be adapted to provide a more analytic interpretation for our shrinking shares of interstimulations. See Herbert Simons, "On a Class of Skew Distribution Functions," *Biom.*, XLII, Parts III and IV (Dec., 1955).

6 The number of permutations is here double the number of pair combinations and means that one counts A's initiating an interact with B as a different interact from B's initiating it with A.

creases but at a diminishing rate. Of course this translating the per capita leaflet response into the total leaflet response agrees exactly with what was observed since it is but a shift of units. The positive complementary fractional exponent was $+0.1$ for total diffusion $(= P^{-0.9} \cdot P^1 = P^{+0.1})$.

The hypothesis in this study of compliance in six towns was a very general dimensional one which expected leaflet interacting to vary as some power of the population, and per capita leaflet interacting to vary as a negative fractional power (i.e., as P^{-q}). Beyond this the hypothesis did not specify the size of the exponent nor the size of any other parameters such as the coefficient a or addent b in Eq. 2. These were left to be found as the best-fitting parameters in the given data. But as further research narrows the model down, we should learn to what extent these exponents, coefficients, and addends (determining respectively the shape, slope, and location of the curve relative to its coordinates) vary with the particular behavior, or the particular actors, period or place, value system, or other circumstances.

As the exponents converge around some central point in a frequency distribution of best-fitted exponents from many researches, this central exponent may prove a useful index. For it may indicate the relative amount, as between towns, of internal interacting of all kinds. It may eventually become a means of estimating the total interactivity of individuals or tempo of social life in each community. But first many exploratory studies are needed applying constant stimulation to towns of varying size with all else constant to see what exponents relate the interaction tested to the town size.

This shrinking-share mechanism which is proposed to explain the facts is a special case of our "counteractance" model or system of hypotheses (6, 7). This counteractance model attempts a unifying explanation of all cases of generalized hyperbolic curves of behavior, i.e., where the dependent transact varies inversely with some power of one of its factors. The inverse factor is seen as an index of some counteracting or competitive force that resists or cancels out part of the transact at issue. In our present research the compliance or percentage of people mailing a leaflet stub back was the transact or dependent behavior-in-context that was at issue in the series of six towns. The larger the town's population, the more the total amount of competitive interstimulation that is generated. This, we hypothesize, counteracts or reduces the per capita rate of complying responses to the constant leaflet stimulation.

A tenet of dimensional analysis is that the basic dimensions are sufficiently homogeneous (even though manifested in a great diversity of indices) that many confirmed generalizations or laws can be built up in dimensional terms from single representative indices. Thus here from the single particular index of mailing in leaflets we seek to generalize on how the amount of any one kind of interacting depends on the number of interactors, all else being constant. Our hypothesis is not limited to responding to leaflets nor to the situation and culture of the United States during the cold war in 1953. Our hypothesis is deliberately stated in terms general to any all-or-none communicating act that may be done by many people, not more than once each, under conditions approximating equal opportunity, where the varying size of population in a series of towns that are otherwise alike is expected to generate a counteractive effect or competition reducing the per capita act at issue in a hyperbolic curve. This hypothesis can be tested by other investigators in diverse situations using a variety of indices of many kinds of behavior.

For dimensional models seek maximal generality in each of the six major factors of a transact. Thus a dimensional model specifies the form of varying of certain variables and preconditions which are *otherwise* expected to be:

1. General to any *acts* of the form specified regardless of the kind of behavior;
2. Invariant with the *actors* on the average among any sorts of people;
3. Permanent in *time* regardless of any historic period;
4. Universal in *space* transcending differences in regional cultures;
5. Important in *values* systems recording what men want most; and
6. Constant in residual *circumstances* which we usually attempt to describe for a first approximation in probabilistic terms.

It is because the shrinking-share hypothesis (which is as yet untested within this inverse power of a population model, P^{-q}) seems to us to be highly general in all six dimensions that we propose it in preference to alternative explanatory hypotheses until further controlled experiments will confirm whichever explanatory hypothesis best fits the facts.

AUTHOR'S REFERENCES[7]

1. *Dimensions of Society* (New York: The Macmillan Company, 1942).
2. *Systematic Social Science* (offset edition; Seattle: University of Washington Bookstore, 1947).
3. "The Interactance Hypothesis: a gravity model fitting physical masses and human groups," *American Sociological Review*, XV, No. 2 (April, 1950).
4. Mimeographs in Project Revere, U: 52–160, 172; U: 51–39, p. 13.
5. "The Transact Model—a predictive and testable theory of social action," *Sociometry* (December, 1955).
6. "Formulas for Spreading Opinions —a report of controlled experiments on leaflet messages in Project Revere," *Public Opinion Quarterly*, XXII (Winter, 1958–59).
7. "The Counteractance Model—for a resistive part of a whole interaction," *American Journal of Sociology*, LXIII (November, 1957).

---

[7] All references are publications of S. C. Dodd, author of this article.

4

The family offers one of the most important units relating demographic and social factors. Yet, as various scholars have pointed out, the family has not been as intensively investigated by social demographers as its obvious advantages for such studies would suggest it should be. In seeking to explain this neglect Kingsley Davis has pointed out that demographers frequently have little theoretical knowledge of the family as a social system, while sociologists who do possess such knowledge

MARRIAGE

AND THE

FAMILY

have been ignorant of demographic data or methods that would help to test theoretical propositions.[1] Glick has also observed that demographers working with family data have typically been more preoccupied with problems of collecting and adjusting such data than with seeking to answer fundamental questions.[2]

It should be recognized, too, that there is no single analytical framework employed by sociologists in the study of the family. Further, demographic data and techniques are more useful to some approaches than others. Christensen, in the

[1] Kingsley Davis, "The Sociology of Demographic Behavior," in *Sociology Today*, eds. Robert K. Merton, Leonard Broom, and Leonard S. Cottrell, Jr. (New York: Basic Books, Inc., Publishers, 1959), pp. 309–333.

[2] Paul C. Glick, "Demographic Analysis of Family Data," in *Handbook of Marriage and the Family*, ed. Harold T. Christensen (Chicago: Rand McNally & Co., 1964), pp. 300–334, esp. p. 331.

Handbook of Marriage and the Family,[3] discusses five basic theoretical frames of reference: institutional, structural-functional, interactional, situational, and developmental. Demographic methods and data have probably been most frequently employed in developmental studies, which emphasize the various cycles or stages of the nuclear family from formation, through marriage, to dissolution through death, divorce, or separation.

The institutional and structural-functional approaches to the family are distinguished primarily by the emphasis accorded change over time. The institutional approach is more concerned with the place and functioning of the family system within a broader social context of other institutional systems, and how its status and functions change over time. The structural-functional approach places greater attention on the internal structure and workings of the family, the means by which it performs basic social functions, and the reciprocal relationships with other social systems at a given time and place in history. Both approaches, however, conceptualize the family as a social system possessing an identifiable structure and performing certain functions through patterned interaction of the family members.

The particular importance of the family to the social demographer is that the way in which the family system operates to perform such functions as reproduction, maintenance of its members, socialization, and status allocation has important demographic consequences. Most reproduction takes place within the family system, and what is perceived as the fertility of a demographic system represents the aggregate of events occurring within, and shaped by, a number of individual family systems. The social and cultural factors that enter into a decision to employ contraceptive devices are of evident import to the demographer seeking to understand and predict fluctuations in the birth rate. Changes in the birth rate that cannot be attributed to changes in population structure often provide clues to significant changes in the working of the family system.

The adequacy of the maintenance function of the family system may be reflected in mortality rates. It is meaningful to ask why a nation such as the United States which enjoys great wealth and an advanced level of medical technology has an infant mortality rate significantly higher than many other nations. To what extent does the functioning of the family enter into such a demographic phenomena? Or a relatively high suicide rate? Or a high mortality rate from automobile accidents?

Migration is usually directly affected by events occurring within the family system and often involves the geographic movement of entire

[3] Harold T. Christensen, "Development of the Family Field of Study," in *Handbook of Marriage and the Family*, ed. Harold T. Christensen (Chicago: Rand McNally & Co., 1964), pp. 3–32.

family units. Family values and beliefs concerning the appropriate behavior of children after they reach maturity may be decisive in the determination of whether, and if so, when and how far they are likely to migrate.

Although most social demographic studies of the family have been primarily concerned with how operations of the family social system influence demographic structure and processes, it should be constantly kept in mind that the influences are reciprocal. Growing public recognition of the consequences of high or low fertility will sooner or later be reflected in family decisions regarding the number of children. Lowering mortality, especially infant mortality, also has effects upon the size of the family system. The increasing number of aged persons in our society has affected the family system, among other institutional systems, as increasing numbers of families have been faced with common problems meeting the needs of aged members under situational circumstances poorly suited to that purpose.

Similarly, it is not difficult to show ways in which change in the age-sex composition of a society or the volume of migration may have a number of significant consequences for individual families.

The reading selections included here provide only a brief sampling of the possible relationships between the family system and the demographic system. In the first paper, "Intra-Family Communication and Fertility Planning in Puerto Rico," the authors deal with the question of how communication between husband and wife is related to the practice of fertility control. The research is specifically cast within the framework of one of the theories in the sociology of the family. This permits testing and generalizing within specified theoretical limits. While other frameworks might suggest additional factors, the results indicate that the Puerto Rican families in which the husband and wife communicated most freely were most likely to use birth control methods.

Do changes in family structure affect mortality? Two related papers report on the effects of the death of a spouse on the life expectation of the surviving spouse. Folklore has it that after the death of a husband or wife, the survivor often "loses the will to live" and shortly thereafter dies also. The two studies from British data seek to test such a proposition and find evidence that mortality rates among the widowed shortly after widowhood differ from those of control groups. Unanswered are some interesting questions on how life expectation is reduced.

Eugene Litwak explores some family determinants and consequences of migration in the fourth selection. Contrary to certain theoretical propositions, he found from a study in Buffalo, New York, that the extended family system did not deter the migration of its members, nor did migration destroy the emotional ties of migrant members to their families.

In the final selection, Glen Elder and Charles Bowerman look into the effect of family size and sex composition on child-rearing patterns. Paternal involvement and external control were hypothesized to be more characteristic of child-rearing patterns in large as compared with small families and in families composed of boys rather than girls. The results indicate that class status of the family must also be considered and the theoretical generalizations are recast within this social structural framework.

Intra-Family Communication and Fertility Planning in Puerto Rico[*]

Reuben Hill, Kurt Back, and J. Mayone Stycos

As is well known, Puerto Rico has a population density that is among the highest in the world. While the Commonwealth is rapidly controlling its death rate, a fact which further increases its population, it has to date made only minor adjustments in reducing its phenomenally high birth rate.

By 1951, at the beginning of the present research, demographic studies in Puerto Rico[1] had highlighted the following:

1. The average *ideal family size* in all strata of the population was *three* children.
2. Religious objections to birth control were minimal despite the high nominal affiliation with the Catholic Church.
3. Yet the average *number of children born* to Puerto Rican mothers was six children, which reflects a birth rate virtually the same in 1950 as in 1900, when the death rate was several times what it is now.

To the family sociologist, the problem looked like a consequence of poor family organization. The goals of small family size were more or less present, the means for controlling fertility were at least superficially known,[2] and the usual resistances of

---

* Reuben Hill, Kurt Back, and J. Mayone Stycos, "Intra-Family Communication and Fertility Planning in Puerto Rico," *Rural Sociology*, XX (September–December, 1955), 258–271.

[1] The most comprehensive of these was Paul K. Hatt's *Backgrounds of Human Fertility in Puerto Rico* (Princeton, N.J.: Princeton University Press, 1952).

[2] See J. Mayone Stycos, "Patterns of Birth Control in Puerto Rico," *Eugenics Quarterly*, I (September, 1954).

religious teachings were minimal; therefore, it would seem to be a problem in family relations. This assumption was the basis for the research which was undertaken and is partially reported here.

In planning the research, the research team was conscious of several important needs: The unit of study and observation should be one that would provide optimal returns. The theoretical design should be one which would make sense out of the many propositions forthcoming from discussions with colleagues. The lack of an encompassing theory had been a deficiency in the otherwise monumental Indianapolis study of the social and psychological factors affecting fertility.[3] An appropriate theoretical design could be expected to give focus and organization to the explorations and would set limits to the subsequent analysis of the data collected. Finally, the research should be planned for carrying out in three stages—exploration, quantitative verification, and validation through controlled experiments.

This paper is a description of how these questions were resolved and a brief account of some findings from the second stage of the project, the quantitative verification phase. The data presented here relate to the focal area of intrafamily communication as it affects use of birth control.

---

[3] See the series of articles in the *Milbank Memorial Fund Quarterly*, 1943 through 1955, under the general title, "Social and Psychological Factors Affecting Fertility." Despite 23 precisely stated hypotheses in this study, there is lacking a conceptual system which might render theoretically relevant the findings of the study. As a consequence, it is difficult to make these findings accretive to existing social and psychological theories about human behavior.

CRITERIA FOR SELECTING THE UNIT OF STUDY AND OBSERVATION

The units of observation and analysis for demographic studies of human fertility and its control have varied greatly; counties, states, provinces, countries, and whole societies have been used, sometimes stratified by income, occupation, education, and residence for purposes of studying differential fertility. Medically oriented researchers have usually focused on mothers, treating the woman as the biological unit of study, which fits their conception of the problem as a special instance of maternal health. The Indianapolis researchers appear to have focused on wives, although they obviously treated the wives as reporting agents for their families. Husbands were also interviewed in that study, but the data from husbands and wives were rarely joined to construct family behavior measures. Unemployed to this moment by any research team are reference groups and nuclear families as units of study.

In the exploratory phase of the research, four criteria were proposed for the selection of a study and observational unit in fertility control:

1. The unit should be the entity of planning, choice making, and action. The assumption is that fertility planning is *group* rather than individual planning.
2. The unit should be capable of serving as a referent in some conceptual system of theory, if findings are to become part of accretive theory.
3. The unit must be accessible for empirical observation and investigation.
4. Ideally, the unit of study should also be the unit of medical and educational services in matters of fertility control.

Of the possible units considered—individuals, marriage pairs, family groups, reference groups, communities, regions—only one met all the above criteria satisfactorily, namely, the *nuclear family of procreation*. The husband and wife are the major actors in family planning and action, but their offspring exercise significant influence at later stages of the family cycle. Husband and wife are really acting as agents of the *family group* in their thinking and planning. They are more than a companionate pair: they are a family, in the process of becoming, and they think in those terms.

CHOICE OF A CONCEPTUAL SYSTEM

The nuclear family having been chosen as the unit of study and observation, it was necessary to choose from among the many approaches to the study of the family that conceptual system under which the nuclear family could be utilized most fruitfully as a planning and decision-making association. There are at least six alternatives from which to choose, each with its own distinctive definition of the family, its favorite key concepts, and its body of theory:

1. The institutional-historical approach, developed and interpreted by Carle C. Zimmerman.
2. The learning theory approach of the child psychologists, represented by Robert Sears and associates.
3. The situationist approach of James H. S. Bossard and associates.
4. The structure-function approach of the social anthropologists and some Harvard-trained sociologists.
5. The household economics approach of the consumption economists, in which management of time, money, and energy is the focus of attention.
6. The "family as an interactive system" approach of E. W. Burgess, the late Willard Waller, and others.

The choice seemed to lie between the structure-function and the interactive system approach, both of which have much to contribute to the research problem at hand. The interactional frame of reference for studying small groups was chosen, since it lends itself especially well to the study of the family as a planning and decision-making association. Its key concepts constitute a kit of mental tools which are uncommonly useful in studying the dynamics of human fertility. Some of the component concepts of the system are (1) status and interstatus relations, which become the bases for authority patterns and initiative-taking; (2) role, role conceptions, role taking, role playing, and role organization, with parents and children viewed in role-playing and role-taking terms, respectively; and (3) processes of communication, consultation, conflict, compromise, and consensus.

Interactional-role analysis is broad enough to capture and order the central processes involved in group planning and problem solving which are to be observed in a study of fertility dynamics. This is a large order, for included, among others, are the processes of goal setting, choice among means, and allocation of accountability and responsibility for actions taken—as well as the built-in processes of evaluation of the successes and failures of the plan. Such evaluation problems must be fed back as matters for group solution and reorganization.

Finally, the interactional approach provides more than tools for observation. It provides a body of theory which can be drawn upon in the formulation of diagnostic study questions. From family-interaction theory come propositions which may be used as guideposts in the quest for the social-psychological antecedents of success in fertility planning and control. Note that these antecedents are different in quality from the psychological and socioeconomic correlates of fertility in the Indianapolis study. They pertain to the dynamic quality of interaction systems and are oriented to intragroup processes rather than to the psychological traits, characteristics, and status categories captured by the Indianapolis group.[4]

FOCI SUGGESTED BY FAMILY INTERACTIONAL FRAMEWORK

When the family-interaction conceptual framework is used as a microscope for observation, the family can be seen in its most intimate internal operations. If one were permitted free and constant observation, he would find that the family, primarily the marriage pair to be sure, is concerned intermittently with what Robert B. Reed has called negative and positive control of procreation.[5] Decisions are reached and actions agreed upon. Failures are discussed and actions taken to correct them. The process remains at the agenda level of discussion for the effective period of childbearing unless cut short by sterilization of one of the actors; and even this will be a consequence of husband-wife interaction.

By means of this perception of the

family as the decision-making unit of society with respect to the control of family size, family-interaction theory tells us that the family's effectiveness as a planning unit will be a function of the efficiency of its communication system. A profitable study-focus, then, would be the processes of communication and the factors thought to be related to communication. Conditions favoring communication and impediments to communication which thwart goal setting, discussion, consensus, and decision making would receive major attention.

In a preliminary study by two of the present authors, in 1951–53, questions were designed to explore this dimension of family life and were tried out, with highly provocative results.[6] From the findings of this ini-

---

[4] P. K. Whelpton and Clyde V. Kiser (eds.), *Social and Psychological Factors Affecting Fertility* (New York: Milbank Memorial Fund, 1950), II, 147–149.

[5] *Ibid.*, pp. 270–276, a paper by Robert B. Reed, "The Interrelationship of Marital Adjustment, Fertility Control and Size of Family."

[6] Major details of these first 2 years of work are to be found in the report by J. Mayone Stycos, *Family and Fertility in the Lower Class of Puerto Rico* (New York: Columbia University Press, 1955), and the typescript by David Landy, "Child Rearing Patterns in a Puerto Rican Lower Class Community." The methodology, the hypotheses, and some of the research findings from the exploratory phase have also appeared in:

Millard Hansen, "The Family in Puerto Rico Project," in *Approaches to Problems of High Fertility in Agrarian Societies* (New York: Milbank Memorial Fund, 1952), pp. 50–61.

J. Mayone Stycos, "Family and Fertility in Puerto Rico," *American Sociological Review*, XVII (Oct., 1952), 236–246.

———, "La Dinámica del Control de la Natalidad en la Clase Baja de Puerto Rico," *Revista Mexicana de Sociologia*, XV (Jan.–Apr., 1953), 37–65.

———, "La Psicología Social del Control Poblacional," *Memorias de la Septima Convencion de Trabajo Social en Puerto Rico* (San Juan, P.R., 1955).

———and Reuben Hill, "The Prospects of Birth Control in Puerto Rico," *Annals of the American Academy of Political and Social Sciences*, CCLXXXV (Jan., 1953), 137–145.

tial exploratory study, hypotheses were formulated for the quantitative verification study of 888 families during 1953–54.[7] The present paper presents some of the diagnostic study questions from family interaction theory which were used as guideposts in exploring the processes of communication and the impediments to communication as they relate to fertility planning and control. The paper concludes with some findings which pertain to the issues raised by the study questions and come from three sample surveys undertaken in the island, 1951–54.

Findings will be drawn partially from intensive semistructured interviews with 72 lower-class husbands and wives, partially from 3,000 short interviews with patients in public health clinics and hospitals throughout the island, and largely from the sample of 888 families studied in more detail. All three groups are of the lower educational class. The sample of 888 families was drawn from units meeting the following criteria: husband and wife living together, married 5 to 20 years, of proven fertility, and having less than six grades of education. All these couples faced problems of fertility control, since they still had several reproductive years ahead of them. The sample was stratified by rural-urban residence, length of marriage, and history of birth control use —"never users," "quitters," "current users," and "sterilized."

Figure 1 illustrates the range of materials which are available from the

---

[7] For a statement of the hypotheses employed in the quantitative verification phase of the research, see especially the paper presented to the American Sociological Society by the present authors in September, 1954, "Family Structure and Fertility in Puerto Rico," *Social Problems*, III (Oct., 1955).

study of 888 families. This analytical model permits emphasis upon parts, as in the present paper, while specifying the interrelationship with the whole. The final report, in book form, will tie the parts together and emphasize the whole.

As can be seen in the figure, the analytical procedures consist of interrelating independent, intervening, and dependent variables singly and by blocks. The demographic factors (Block A) of residence, education, occupation, type of marital union, religious affiliation, and rental value of domicile become meaningful in the schema when they are translated into the influence brought to bear by their corresponding reference groups on the formation and maintenance of general values. (The intercorrelations between combinations of reference groups and values held are high enough to warrant this inference.) Once the influences of the demographic factors through reference groups are identified as largely located in the motivational system of families, it is possible to relate the general and specific value systems (Blocks B and D) and the general and specific action systems (Blocks C and E) to the actions taken to limit family size (Block F). The expected interrelationships between the large blocks of variables are specified crudely by the size of the bars connecting them. The present paper focuses on the interrelationships between certain family action possibilities (listed in Block C) and effective family planning (shown as Block F). Efficient family organization is not enough by itself to bring about effective family planning; it is hypothesized that *general motivations to take action*—the *combination* of the ideal of small family size, knowledge about the means of control, and effi-

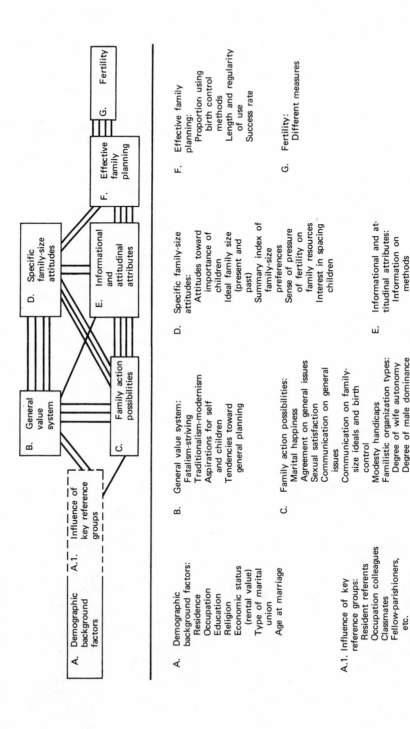

FIG. 1. Schema Specifying the Hypothetical Interrelationships of Selected Antecedent, Intervening, and Consequent Variables in Fertility Planning

A. Demographic background factors:
Residence
Occupation
Education
Religion
Economic status (rental value)
Type of marital union
Age at marriage

A.1. Influence of key reference groups:
Resident referents
Occupation colleagues
Classmates
Fellow-parishioners, etc.
Extent of social participation
Patrons of birth control clinics

B. General value system:
Fatalism-striving
Traditionalism-modernism
Aspirations for self and children
Tendencies toward general planning

C. Family action possibilities:
Marital happiness
Agreement on general issues
Sexual satisfaction
Communication on general issues
Communication on family-size ideals and birth control
Modesty handicaps
Familistic organization types:
Degree of wife autonomy
Degree of male dominance
Extent of prohibitions exercised by husband
Family readiness for action on birth control

D. Specific family-size attitudes:
Attitudes toward importance of children
Ideal family size (present and past)
Summary index of family-size preferences
Sense of pressure of fertility on family resources
Interest in spacing children

E. Informational and at-titudinal attributes:
Information on methods
Attitudes toward birth control
Extent of agreement on birth control

F. Effective family planning:
Proportion using birth control methods
Length and regularity of use
Success rate

G. Fertility:
Different measures

cient family organization—make up the "path" which families must follow to reach the goal of ideal family size.

INTRA-FAMILY COMMUNICATION

The diagnostic questions divide logically into those concerned with the processes and modes of communication and those highlighting the barriers to communication.

I. *Processes of Communication:*
  A. Adequacy of communication:
    1. On what basic issues do spouses communicate well, and on what topics do they communicate poorly?
    2. On how many basic issues is there communication and agreement?
    3. How accurately can the husband describe the wife's attitudes about sex, contraception, childbirth, and number of children desired? Conversely, how accurately can the wife describe her husband's position on these matters?
    4. How much actual goal setting, crystallization of family ideals, and discussion of modes of implementing these ideals has occurred?
  B. Modes of communication:
    1. What modes of communication are used in arriving at decisions on matters relating to fertility?—Highly rational?—Unidirectional discussion?—Equalitarian with much consultation?
    2. How does the division of areas of accountability and responsibility between spouses affect initiative in raising problems for discussion and achieving agreement on actions taken?
  C. History of communication in the marriage:
    1. What situations in the past have been provocative of discussion of family planning and/or the decision to have another child?
    2. When did husband and wife first talk about how many children they wanted?—Before the first child?—After subsequent children—Never?
    3. How long after one of the spouses feels he (she) has had enough children do the spouses share that perception?
    4. What is the threshold of tolerance or difference on fertility matters which has to be exceeded before discussion will be precipitated? How painful must the objective situation become before communication occurs?
II. *Impediments to Communication:*
  A. Female modesty barriers to communication:
    1. How much does the modesty of the wife inhibit her in seeking information about birth control from her husband and others?
    2. How much does modesty of the wife reduce the communication between husband and wife on general matters?
    3. How much does modesty of the wife render her a passive participant in family planning and decision making, waiting upon the husband for taking the initiative in restricting family size?
  B. Status difference between husband and wife statuses as barriers:
    1. How much does the wife's respect for her husband's position inhibit her in raising questions about the family size and birth control matters?
    2. How much does the husband's culturally defined dominance in the home prevent discussing matters of sex and birth control for purposes of planning with his wife?

It is not possible to relate the

answers to all of the diagnostic study questions in this paper. Accordingly, a selection has been made from among them which most clearly demonstrates the place of intra-family communication in fertility planning.

BARRIERS TO COMMUNICATION

From the exploratory study of seventy-two families, the cleavages which make communication difficult have been identified. The differential statuses of male and female are expressed in ideologies which invidiously define the women as weak, naïve, and pure, and the men as strong, shrewd, and inherently evil. These ideologies are expressed in differential child-rearing practices and in different role expectations for the sexes before marriage. Girls internalize patterns of modesty, low sexual drives, and subservience to males. Boys internalize the patterns of high sex curiosity, strong sexual drives, and assertiveness with respect to women. To maintain this character structure the sexes are segregated in work and play, although exceptions are everywhere seen in the island with the inauguration of coeducation in the schools. There are, however, few opportunities for boys and girls to develop companionship patterns before marriage. Boys run with boys, and girls share their thoughts primarily with their own sex. Courtships are carried out under supervision of chaperons, which minimizes the opportunity for developing patterns of give-and-take discussion before marriage.[8]

Once married, two important bar-

---

[8] See Reuben Hill, "Impediments to Freedom of Mate Selection in Puerto Rico," *Journal of Home Economics*, XLVII, No. 3 (March, 1955).

riers to communication are manifested —respect for the husband and modesty of the wife. The first is an important norm of husband-wife and father-child relations. A certain degree of formality is supposed to characterize the relations between wife and husband which would be threatened by discussion of intimate topics of interpersonal relations. One lower-class woman expressed the position poignantly:

> ...I never discuss such things with my husband. I feel too much respect for him.

Men, in turn, are hesitant to open up discussion on matters which they have not heard discussed by their own parents. They want to believe that their wives are innocent and too modest to talk about matters of sex and childbirth. Said one husband in this connection:

> ...to my wife, me talk about these things? Look, man, I couldn't even try. I am not accustomed to talking about these things with women.

Modesty operates as a barrier to communication between husband and wife on topics which to an outsider would appear far removed from the tabooed areas of sex and childbirth. In a tabulation of the answers of 150 mothers from the sample of 888 families, the amount of communication between husband and wife on crucial marital issues appears small even for such neutral matters as child discipline and the husband's work, about a fourth never talking about these areas of family life (Table 1). In general, the more intimate the area, the more attenuated the discussion between husband and wife, with almost half never talking about birth control or sexual relations.

Another piece of evidence of the

TABLE 1. Extent of Discussion Between Husband and Wife of Key Marital Issues, as Reported by 150 Wives[a] in Puerto Rico

Topic	Frequency of discussion during marriage			All respondents
	Never	Occasionally	Frequently	
		Percentage distribution of respondents		
Husband's work	23.0	42.0	35.0	100.0
Discipline of children	25.0	47.0	28.0	100.0
Religion	35.0	48.0	17.0	100.0
Future plans	35.0	46.0	19.0	100.0
Birth control	47.0	35.0	18.0	100 0
Sexual relations	53.0	34.0	13.0	100.0

[a] A subsample of 888 wives interviewed.

same order is the finding for 3,000 families that more than a third of the wives had never talked with their husbands about the number of children they desired. This reticence to talk about family size was greatest among the couples married over twenty years —about 50 per cent of this group had never discussed family-size ideals, compared with 30 per cent for the couples married less than five years.[9] One would think that the longer a couple had been married and exposed to the necessity of talking about family problems, the more likely they would have talked. The evidence is clearly in the other direction, even when differences in education between the two generations of couples are held constant, which suggests the possibility that the older couples have been more tongue-tied by the norms of respect and modesty.

It has been possible to quantify the phenomenon of female modesty by

scaling the wife's answers to questions about the extent of embarrassment felt in facing certain familiar situations such as hearing off-color jokes, being examined by a physician, speaking about menstruation to her husband, informing her daughter about sexual matters, and undressing before her husband. Table 2 provides the data from which the modesty scale was constructed—the preliminary tabulations for 150 of the 888 families. It can be seen that embarrassment rises rapidly; for the different aspects of the test, the percentage who would feel "much embarrassment" varies from 15 to 56 per cent. Even the situation least likely to embarrass the respondents (talking with the husband about sex) would cause "much" or "some" embarrassment to 37 per cent of them. The modesty situation may be aggravated by the tendency of husbands to overestimate the amount of embarrassment felt by wives on these issues. In 53 per cent of the families, the husband overestimated his wife's modesty—as judged by her own statements— whereas in only 28 per cent of the cases did he underestimate it.

---

9 For further discussion of this finding, see J. Mayone Stycos, Kurt Back, and Reuben Hill, "Problems of Communication between Husband and Wife on Matters Relating to Family Limitation," *Human Relations* (June, 1956).

TABLE 2.   Extent of Embarrassment Women Say They Would Feel in Certain Situations, as Reported by 150 Wives[a] in Puerto Rico

Situation	Extent of embarrassment that would be felt			All respondents
	Much	Some	None	
	Percentage distribution of respondents			
Telling children about sex	56.0	18.0	26.0	100.0
Being examined by a physician	53.0	15.0	32.0	100.0
Having to listen to off-color jokes	32.0	20.0	48.0	100.0
Discussing menstrual period with husband	24.0	20.0	56.0	100.0
Undressing in front of husband	16.0	33.0	51.0	100.0
Talking with husband about sex	15.0	22.0	63.0	100.0

[a] A subsample of 888 wives interviewed. From these data a modesty scale was constructed.

A seven-point modesty scale was constructed from the data in Table 2. When scale scores were cross-classified by communication on birth control matters, an appreciable relationship was found—the more modest the wife, the less the communication between husband and wife. The median modesty score for wives who had never talked with the husband on birth control matters was 3.70 as compared with 3.30 for wives who had.

In summary, then, there appear to be a number of areas of husband-wife relationships which are not open for free give-and-take discussion. Status differences between husband and wife, the taboos on discussion of sex, and the modesty of women in general combine to make many Puerto Rican couples reticent when facing problems of goal setting with respect to family size, of mutuality in sex relations, of seeking the means for fertility control, and of putting these means to work. There follows now a discussion of the consequences of inadequate communication for fertility control. In this analysis, still more refined measures of effectiveness of communication are used to test the hypotheses.

CONSEQUENCES OF POOR INTERSPOUSAL COMMUNICATION

Table 3 shows the relationship between interspousal communication on the general issues of marriage and two expressions of fertility control: (1) "ever use" and (2) length of use (proportion of time in which birth control was used during marriage). "Users" have higher communication scores than "non-users," and long-term users have higher scores than short-term users. In both comparisons, the tetrachoric correlations are significant at or below the 5-per-cent level.

A more specific type of communication with respect to fertility control is discussion between husband and wife about methods of birth control, a first essential step in family planning. In Table 4, communication on birth control matters has been cross-classified with fertility control. In even more striking fashion than in Table 3, the proportion using birth control increases with improved communication. The tetrachoric correlations are statistically significant.

A third index of communication

TABLE 3. Relation of Fertility Control and Interspousal Communication on General Marital Issues, 888 Families in Puerto Rico

Communication on general marital issues Scores	Classification by fertility control practice				All respondents
	"Never users"	"Users"[a]	Short-term users[b]	Long-term users[b]	
	Percentage distribution of families				
Low (0–2)	48.2	27.4	29.3	24.4	35.4
High (3–5)	51.8	72.6	70.7	75.6	64.6
All	100.0	100.0	100.0	100.0	100.0

Tetrachoric $r=0.32$.
Tetrachoric $r=0.13$.
[a] Users of nonsurgical and surgical methods of birth control.
[b] Users of nonsurgical methods only.

TABLE 4. Relation of Fertility Control and Interspousal Communication on Birth Control, 888 Families in Puerto Rico

Communication on birth control	Classification by fertility control practice				All respondents
	"Never users"	"Users"[a]	Short-term users"[b]	Long-term users[b]	
	Percentage distribution of families				
Have discussed	51.8	83.4	81.4	85.8	71.6
Have not disscussed	48.2	16.6	18.6	14.2	28.4
All	100.0	100.0	100.0	100.0	100.0

Tetrachoric $r=0.52$.
Tetrachoric $r=0.12$.
[a] Users of nonsurgical and surgical methods of birth control.
[b] Users of nonsurgical methods only.

adequacy has been constructed by matching the husband's statements about his wife's attitudes with the wife's answers about her own attitudes. This is a most rigorous test of adequacy of communication, since it concerns the major criterion of effective "interspousal" communication—the ability to understand and predict the spouse's wants. According to folk theory, children are more perceptive of the attitudes of parents than vice versa, wives more perceptive of husbands than vice versa, and servants more perceptive of their employers than vice versa, because subordinate individuals listen more carefully and are more sensitive to nonverbal cues as attitude indicators than are superordinated individuals. The use here of perception of spouse's attitudes as a test of adequacy of communication provides a test of this folk theory.

A comparison of the totals in Tables 5 and 6 shows that the folk theory concerning superior perception by

TABLE 5. Relation of Fertility Control and Wife's Perception of Husband's Attitudes on Family Size and Birth Control, 318 Families in Puerto Rico[a]

Wife's perception of husband's attitudes	"Never users"	"Users"	Short-term users	Long-term users	All respondents
	Classification by fertility control practice				
			Percentage distribution of families		
Husband's desire for more children:					
Wife correct	60.5	76.9	66.3	76.6	73.0
Wife incorrect	39.5	23.1	33.7	23.4	27.0
	100.0	100.0	100.0	100.0	100.0
	Tetrachoric $r=0.30$.		Tetrachoric $r=0.17$.		
Husband's intensity of desire for children:					
Wife correct	46.1	55.1	60.0	50.6	53.0
Wife incorrect	53.9	44.9	40.0	49.4	47.0
	100.0	100.0	100.0	100.0	100.0
	Tetrachoric $r=0.15$.		Tetrachoric $r=-0.15$.		
Husband's attitudes on justification for birth control:					
Wife correct	23.1	43.4	38.7	48.3	40.7
Wife incorrect	76.9	56.6	61.3	51.7	59.3
	100.0	100.0	100.0	100.0	100.0
	Tetrachoric $r=0.23$.		Tetrachoric $r=0.15$.		

[a] A randomly drawn subsample of the master sample of 888 families.

wives in subordinate positions is not upheld for the Puerto Rican sample. The husbands' record in perceiving accurately their wives' attitudes is actually higher for two of the three attitudes measured—the desire for more children and the intensity with which they are desired. The husbands were correct in 84.6 per cent of the families on the first attitude, as compared with 73 per cent accuracy by the wives. On the intensity question, 59.6 per cent of the husbands had correct answers, as compared with 53 per cent of the wives.[10] As to empathy

theory is that men in this patriarchal society of Puerto Rico are on the receiving end of information from wives and children but they do not reciprocate by giving of their own thoughts. Like the benevolent despots of old, they wish *to be informed* but they do not wish *to be understood,* and are consequently close-mouthed to preserve the formal distance between them and their subordinates. Further analysis of the interconnections between communication on birth control and accuracy of perception of spouses' attitudes revealed that the husband's *view* of whether or not birth control discussion really had taken place was predictive of higher empathy among spouses, whereas the wife's report on the matter was not. In families, then, where the husband said communication had in fact occurred, both husband and wife were more accurate in perceiving the other's attitudes, whether the wife agreed with his assertion or not.

10 The writers' best *post hoc* explanation for this reversal of the folk

with respect to attitudes on birth control, husbands and wives were tied; only 40 per cent of each group had correct answers, perhaps a reflection of lower intercommunication in this area of family life.

In Table 5, accuracy of perception by the wife of the husband's attitudes on three family items is cross-classified with fertility control behavior. The findings are very much as expected: Where birth control has been practiced, wives show higher empathy —i.e., the wife is more accurate in estimating her husband's desire for more children, the intensity of this desire, and his evaluation of situations justifying birth control. The tetra-

choric correlations of all three of these items with history of "ever use" of birth control methods are statistically significant.

Length of use is similarly correlated with correct perceptions of husband's position—except on the intensity of wishing more children, which is more closely related to short-term than to long-term use. The tetrachoric correlations are modest but statistically significant.

Table 6 provides similar information on the record of the husbands in predicting their wives' attitudes, as this in turn predicts types of fertility-control behavior. Although the husbands' empathy is higher than their

TABLE 6. Fertility Control by Husband's Perception of Wife's Attitudes on Family Size and Birth Control, 318 Families in Puerto Rico[a]

Husband's perception of wife's attitudes	Classification by fertility control practice				
	"Never users"	"Users"	Short-term users	Long-term users	All respondents
	Percentage distribution of families				
Wife's desire for more children:					
Husband correct	80.3	86.0	89.0	87.0	84.6
Husband incorrect	19.7	14.0	11.0	13.0	15.4
	100.0	100.0	100.0	100.0	100.0
	Tetrachoric $r=0.20$.		Tetrachoric $r=0.05$.		
Wife's intensity of desire for children:					
Husband correct	56.7	60.7	71.0	57.1	59.6
Husband incorrect	43.3	39.3	29.0	42.9	40.4
	100.0	100 0	100.0	100.0	100.0
	Tetrachoric $r=0.05$.		Tetrachoric $r=-0.22$.		
Wife's attitudes on justification for birth control:					
Husband correct	42.9	39.2	42.1	35.7	40.0
Husband incorrect	57.1	60.8	57.9	64.3	60.0
	100.0	100.0	100.0	100.0	100.0
	Tetrachoric $r=0.07$.		Tetrachoric $r=-0.12$.		

[a] A randomly drawn subsample of the master sample of 888 families.

wives', Table 6 does not reveal the close correspondence between empathy of husbands and family fertility control that Table 5 revealed for wives' empathy and fertility control. Failure to use birth control is predicted by only one item from the husbands' table, namely, the desire for more children. Length of use is *negatively* related to the husband's empathy, as

of family size control. Sterilization as a solution to the problem of population pressure within families is widespread in Puerto Rico,[11] and is the best-known method on the island. Its popularity among all classes is due in part to the lack of popularity of the less drastic mechanical and chemical methods which offend the sensitivities of modest or prudish women, and

TABLE. 7. Relation of Fertility Control Methods Used and Husband's Perception of Wife's Attitudes on Family Size, 318 Families in Puerto Rico[a]

Husband's perception of wife's attitudes	Methods of fertility control used		All respondents
	Nonsurgical	Sterilization	
	percentage distribution of families		
Wife's desire for more children :			
Husband correct	88.1	80.0	86.0
Husband incorrect	11.9	20.0	14.0
	100.0	100.0	100.0
	Tetrachoric $r = 0.20$		
Wife's intensity of desire for children :			
Husband correct	65.0	49.2	60.7
Husband incorrect	35.0	50.8	39.3
	100.0	100.0	100.0
	Tetrachoric $r = 0.26$		

[a] A randomly drawn subsample of the master sample of 888 families.

measured by his perception of his wife's intensity of desire for more children and his success in predicting his wife's position on the use of birth control. This runs counter to expectations, since the short-term users were thought to be those who would have incorrectly perceived their wives' positions on these matters.

The data also show a close relationship between husband empathy and the choice of nonsurgical birth control methods over sterilization as a means

which are considered by many males to interfere with pleasure.

Data for the 888 families suggest that sterilized mothers have many of

[11] The survey of 3,000 families found sterilization in 7.1 per cent of the couples married less than 5 years, 25 per cent in the group married 5–9 years, 28.7 per cent among those married 10–14 years, 27 per cent in the group married 15–19 years, and 17.9 per cent in the group married more than 20 years. See J. Mayone Stycos, "Female Sterilization in Puerto Rico," *Eugenics Quarterly*, I (June, 1954), 5.

the same characteristics as women who have never used other birth control methods at all; indeed, nearly 50 per cent moved directly to sterilization from the category of "never users." Most of the remainder used birth control methods irregularly, or on a short-term basis before being sterilized. Less than 10 per cent were regular and long-term users before being operated on.

In Table 7 there is a statistically significant association between the man's incorrect perception of his wife's attitudes about having more children and the use of sterilization as the family's solution to family size control. For both attitude measures the tetrachoric correlations are significant at the 5-per-cent level. This suggests that sterilization, like failure to use contraceptives at all, is a concomitant of faulty communication between husband and wife. Further analyses along this line are being carried out.

SUMMARY

As strangers to the social demography of Puerto Rico, the authors faced a number of problems when the family and fertility project was launched. A number of choices had to be made: the selection of a suitable unit of observation, the choice of a conceptual system appropriate to the problem, and the utilization of this system for constructing diagnostic study questions.

One section of the study, developed directly from propositions in family-interaction theory, centered on the consequences—for successful family planning—of effective "interspousal" communication and empathy in inter-personal relations. The hypotheses were confirmed for the most part, though reversed in two instances. The preliminary findings are summarized below:

1. Communication between spouses is low in Puerto Rico, not only on tabooed topics of sex and birth control but also on number of children desired, future plans, discipline of children, and husband's work.

2. Modesty among women is negatively associated with communication on birth control matters.

3. Modesty among women and wifely respect for the husband, combined with overestimation of his wife's modesty by the husband, conspire to impede discussion on a wide variety of topics crucial to effective family planning.

4. The higher the "interspousal" communication scores on the general issues of marriage, the higher the proportion of families using birth control methods and using them on a long-term basis.

5. Communication on birth control matters is closely related to use of birth control methods and to their long-term use.

6. Accuracy of perception—by the husband of his wife's attitudes toward family size, and by the wife of her husband's attitudes—is associated with prior history of adequate "interspousal" communication.

7. Husbands were more frequently correct in perceiving their wives' attitudes than vice versa, a finding which reverses the theory that subordinates are more perceptive than superordinates.

8. Accuracy of perception by the wife of her husband's attitudes concerning family size and birth control is associated significantly with a history of using birth control methods and with their long-term use.

9. Accuracy of perception by the husband of his wife's attitudes toward family size and birth control is not uniformly associated with the use of birth control and is negatively associated with its

long-term use. This is contrary to the expected relationship.

10. Accuracy of perception by the husband of his wife's family-size attitudes is significantly asso-

ciated with the choice of non-surgical methods of birth control over sterilization as the means of fertility control used by the family.

The Mortality of Widowers[*]

Michael Young, Bernard Benjamin, and Chris Wallis

Durkheim was the first well-known sociologist to stress the connection between widowhood and a particular kind of death, that due to suicide. "The suicides occurring at the crisis of widowhood ... are really due to domestic anomy resulting from the death of husband or wife. A family catastrophe occurs which affects the survivor. He is not adapted to the new situation in which he finds himself and accordingly offers less resistance to suicide."[1] Sainsbury showed that suicides (causing over 5,000 deaths a year, not far off the number who die in road accidents) were commoner among the widowed than the single, and that the rate was lowest among the married.[2] The Bethnal Green studies drew attention to the general psychological effects of bereavement.

Marris wrote of the anguish felt by young widows, from which they only gradually recovered,[3] and Townsend of the sense of desolation felt by older widowed people of both sexes.[4] These studies suggested that the shock of widowhood might weaken the resistance to other causes of death, and not just to suicides. We report here a beginning in the exploration of this suggestion.

THE INQUIRY

The death-rates for widowed people in every age-group are known to be higher than for married people. What has not been known so far is the "duration effect" of being widowed— we know how old widowed people were when they died, but not for how long they had been widowed. For our purpose an inquiry into "duration effect" was clearly essential. Since a large field study was beyond the resources

* Michael Young, Bernard Benjamin, and Chris Wallis, "The Mortality of Widowers," The Lancet, No. 7305 (August 31, 1963), 454–456.

1 E. Durkheim, Suicide (London, 1952), p. 259.

2 P. Sainsbury, Suicide in London (London, 1955), p. 81.

3 P. Marris, Widows and Their Families (London, 1958), pp. 55, 65.

4 P. Townsend, The Family Life of Old People (London, 1957), p. 180.

of the Institute of Community Studies, the opportunity to explore this question in collaboration with the General Register Office was welcomed. We had to concentrate on widowers. Widows had to be ruled out because the death certificates of men do not identify their spouses in a way that makes it possible to follow them up. Our procedure was to pick a sample of widowers who figured on the death certificates of their wives.

It was difficult to choose the age-group to investigate. The figures already published show that the excess mortality of widowed over married people is greatest for younger people below the age of thirty-four.[5] Another way of putting the point is to say that widowerhood seems to accelerate ageing most in the younger age-groups, attaching to the widowed the mortality risk of married people several years older. Perhaps younger people are especially vulnerable, because spouses often die very suddenly at these ages, many from accidents, so that the shock is greater. This suggested that an inquiry into younger people might be the most fruitful. Against this was the telling point that, for any given size of sample, the numbers of deaths would be larger for older groups. In the end expense was decisive.

The cohort chosen was of 4,486 widowers of 55 years and older whose wives died in 1957. To allow for seasonal fluctuations, half of the group comprised those whose wives died in January, 1957, and the other half those whose wives died in July, 1957. The cohort has so far been followed up for five years, and all deaths of widowers have been noted. Mortality-

---

[5] *Registrar General's Statistical Review for England and Wales for 1958*, part III, commentary, 55.

rates were calculated for the first six months and second six months of duration of widowerhood, and for each year of duration thereafter, for each quinary age-group at widowerhood. These rates were arrived at by dividing the deaths by the mean number of widowers at risk during the interval. The rates for the widowers were then expressed as a ratio to the rate, for the same attained age, for married men at the corresponding ages. The results are shown in the accompanying table. The average ratios, weighted for reliability, are given in the last line of the table.

All death entries of married women in the first half of the volume of such entries for January and all those in the second half of the volume for July were extracted. This secured a geographical as well as a seasonal balance. The surviving spouses were subsequently traced through the National Health Service Central Register.

RESULTS

Out of the ratios set out in the table, the only ones that are significantly and consistently greater than unity are for those dying within six months of being widowed. There are three points to be made about the six months' ratios.

First, if we ignore age differences we have:

Actual deaths 214
Expected deaths (based
   on married men's
   mortality) .... 148 ± 12
Excess 66
$$t = 5.5 \quad p < 0.0001$$

Second, taking the age-groups separately, the ratios are significantly above unity for age groups 60–64,

70–74, 75–79, and 80–84. Third, all the age-groups have *positive* deviations from unity. If there is no real excess mortality these positive and negative deviations would be equally likely and the chance of getting eight positive deviations together would be $(\frac{1}{2})^8 = 0.004$, which is very small. If we look at the ratios for the later deviations (taking all ages together) we find that none of these is statistically significantly different from unity.

The conclusion is that the excess mortality in the first six months is almost certainly real. In other words, widowerhood appears to bring in its wake a sudden increment in mortality-rates of something like 40 per cent in the first six months. This increase is eventually followed by a fall back to the level for married men in general.

SHORT-TERM AND LONG-TERM MORTALITY

We naturally do not know for certain what happens to mortality-rates subsequently. All that is clear is that the widowers' rates cannot remain at the low level they reach after four years. If they remained the same as for married men, the over-all ratio of widowers' mortality to that of married men would, having regard to the duration structure of all widowers in the general population, be about 1.05 at most ages. But the observed ratio is above 1.4. If this figure is reliable there must be a further differential rise in mortality at later durations of widowerhood.

On the other hand, the over-all ratio of 1.4 may be inflated for two reasons. The first is that the average age of widowers in any age group is older than the average age of married men in the same age group.[6] There is a difference of about a year in average age. But this does not go very far—not more than one quarter of the way—towards explaining the 40 per cent mortality excess. The second reason is that widowers may be under-enumerated in the census or over-recorded among the deaths.[7] But such information as there is does not suggest this can possibly explain more than a very small part of the 40 per cent excess mortality. It therefore seems that there must be a rise in mortality at later duration of widowerhood.

This could come about, for example, as a result of the progressive selective remarriage of the fittest men. The annual remarriage rates of widowers in 1961 were as follows:

Age	Annual remarriage-rate per thousand
45–49	100.1
50–54	72.3
55–59	57.7
60–64	44.3
65–69	25.4
70–74	16.7
75–	4.2

If the widowers who remarried were so healthy that we may consider them as withdrawn only from the denominator of the death rate for widowers and added only to the denominator of the married men's death rate, then at ages 55–59, for example, this would in five years create a widower/married mortality

---

[6] *Registrar General's Statistical Review for England and Wales for 1959*, p. 166.

[7] Great Britain, General Register Office, 1951, *Census of England and Wales*; general report, chap. ii.

TABLE 1. Mortality-Rates of Widowers in England and Wales by Duration of Widowerhood and Ratio to Married Men's Mortality at Same Attained Age

Age at widowerhood	No. of widowers	—		Duration of widowerhood (yr.)					
				0—	¹/₂—	1—	2—	3—	4—
55–59	559	No. of deaths	(a)	6	12	13	15	10	13
		Mean widowers' death-rate	(b)	0.0216	0.0443	0.0243	0.0288	0.0197	0.0262
		Married men rate (at attained age)	(c)	0.0172	0.0182	0.0196	0.0216	0.0236	0.0255
		(b)÷(c)	(d)	1.3	2.4	1.2	1.3	0.83	1.0
60–64	694		(a)	16	10	18	18	30	23
			(b)	0.0467	0.0297	0.0273	0.0281	0.0486	0.0389
			(c)	0.0274	0.0289	0.0312	0.0342	0.0372	0.0403
			(d)	1.7	1.0	0.88	0.82	1.3	0.97
65–69	827		(a)	25	18	41	52	47	40
			(b)	0.0163	0.0454	0.0537	0.0725	0.0704	0.0632
			(c)	0.0429	0.0450	0.0481	0.0523	0.0566	0.0608
			(d)	1.4	1.0	1.1	1.4	1.3	1.0
70–74	921		(a)	41	25	82	71	65	52
			(b)	0.0910	0.0576	0.101	0.0962	0.0970	0.0850
			(c)	0.0641	0.0665	0.0701	0.0749	0.0798	0.0846
			(d)	1.4	0.87	1.4	1.3	1.2	1.0
75–79	818		(a)	54	39	74	66	75	57
			(b)	0.137	0.105	0.108	0.107	0.137	0.118
			(c)	0.0902	0.0965	0.106	0.119	0.131	0.144
			(d)	1.5	1.1	1.0	0.90	1.0	0.82
80–84	503		(a)	49	42	62	62	47	48
			(b)	0.205	0.194	0.163	0.194	0.177	0.221
			(c)	0.154	0.161	0.173	0.188	0.203	0.218
			(d)	1.3	1.2	0.94	1.0	0.87	1.0
85–89	139		(a)	18	14	22	20	15	13
			(b)	0.277	0.246	0.229	0.267	0.263	0.295
			(c)	0.230	0.237	0.247	0.261	0.275	0.289
			(d)	1.2	1.0	0.93	1.0	0.96	1.0
90+	25		(a)	5	7	2	2	2	2
			(b)	0.434	0.824	0.167	0.200	0.250	0.333
			(c)	0.296					
			(d)	1.4					
Total	4486		(a)	214	167	314	306	291	248
Weighted average of ratio (d) at ages between 55 and 89[a]				1.39	1.06	1.04	1.04	1.04	0.94

[a] Weights are reciprocals of variance of ratios shown at (d).

differential of the order of 30 per cent. At ages 70–74 the differential thus created would, however, be only 10 per cent, so that at older ages where the observed 40 per cent mortality differential persists, selection on remarriage cannot be by any means the full explanation. Moreover, selection cannot serve to explain the similar mortality differential observed for widows, since their chances of remarriage are much less than the chances of widowers. Some further light will be thrown on all this in 1967 if we are still alive and if funds are available to enable us to have another look at our cohort.

DISCUSSION

The results show that there is a problem to investigate; they do not in themselves either confirm or deny the suggested explanation put forward at the beginning of this paper. The sudden short-run increase could conceivably also be due to other possible influences such as:

HOMOGAMY. It is known that there is a tendency for the fit to marry the fit, and the unfit the unfit. Downes has, for instance, found a marital disease association, in a study on couples over 45 years of age, for hypertensive vascular disease and for arthritis.[8] But although homogamy might have a small influence, it could hardly produce such a large increment as quickly as seems to happen.

COMMON INFECTION. Both spouses may die from the same infectious disease. Ciocco, in his study of the causes of death among a sample of 2,571 husbands and wives who died in Washington County, Maryland, found significant tendencies for spouses both to die of tuberculosis, influenza, pneumonia, heart diseases, and can-

cer.[9] Mutual infection could obviously arise, at any rate with the first three of these.

JOINT UNFAVORABLE ENVIRONMENT. Kraus and Lilienfeld suggested that the unfavorable environment which brought about the death of one spouse might do the same for the other.[10] Death in a common accident, where the husband survives a little longer than the wife, is a particularly obvious example.

LOSS OF CARE. Widowers may become malnourished when they no longer have wives to look after them. They may also go to their doctor and take their medicine less diligently when they no longer have someone to prod them—although the reverse is also possible. Widowers may consult their doctors more often and expose themselves to more infections and other hazards as a consequence. Having to adapt to a changed social role as the result of losing a spouse may itself impair resistance to disease.

All these are possible influences. But we still consider that the first suggestion we made about the "desolation effect" of being widowed, may be at least a good part of the explanation. The grief, precipitated by the death, is almost certainly associated with changes in the function of the endocrine and central nervous systems. Tears, slowed movements and constipation cannot be the only bodily effects, and whatever may be the other effects they could scarcely fail to have secondary consequences for resistance to various illnesses.

Only further study will make it possible to attach "weights" to these

---

[8] J. Downes, *The Milbank Memorial Fund Quarterly*, XXV (1947), 334.

[9] A. Ciocco, *Human Biology*, XII (1940), 508.

[10] A. S. Kraus and A. M. Lilienfeld, *Journal of Chronic Diseases*, X (1959), 207.

various possible influences. Further cohort studies of the kind described here would be helpful. But perhaps the most useful course from now on would be to pay special attention to the immediate physical "causes" of death. The Registrar General has recently given some information about the "causes" of death in widowed people. This shows that tuberculosis of the respiratory system, syphilis, cancer (especially buccal cavity, larynx, and testis for widowers, cervix uteri for widows), diabetes, iron-deficiency anæmia, vascular lesions of the central nervous system, degenerative and hypertensive heart-disease, cirrhosis of liver, diseases of pancreas, and suicide are particularly responsible for the higher mortality of the widowed as compared with the married.

A first step would be to analyze the groups divided by duration of widowerhood according to the diseases responsible for death and according to age to see if there were any pattern. But it would obviously be better to design a field inquiry of a kind which might be undertaken, say, by the College of General Practitioners. Detailed records of widowers who did not die immediately, as well as of those who did, should make it possible to sort out the influence of the factors listed above, as well as others, such as the presence of children, and perhaps point the way to more effective "treatment" of bereaved people.

The Mortality of Widows Shortly after Widowhood*

Peter R. Cox and John R. Ford

In a recent article, Young, Benjamin, and Wallis[1] discussed what they called the "duration effect" of being widowed—i.e., the extent to which mortality differs, during the

* Peter R. Cox and John R. Ford, "The Mortality of Widows Shortly after Widowhood," *The Lancet*, No. 7325 (January 18, 1964), 163–164.
[1] M. Young, B. Benjamin, C. Wallis, *The Lancet* (Aug. 31, 1963), 454.

first few months after the death of the spouse, from that of marriage partners generally. For reasons connected with the form of their investigation they were obliged to concentrate their attention upon widowers aged 55 and over.

A search through the files of the Government Actuary's department revealed that a durational mortality

TABLE 1. Actual Deaths in the Five Years Following Widowhood Compared with Expected Deaths

Attained age	First year		Second year		Third year		Fourth year		Fifth year	
	Expected	Actual	Expected	Actual	Expected	Actual	Expected	Actual	Expected	Actual
Under 40	66	67	56	58	46	43	37	40	30	27
40–44	45	52	42	49	37	36	34	20	30	31
45–49	67	74	62	65	58	68	54	47	51	38
50–54	100	92	94	93	88	96	83	83	75	76
55–59	155	159	148	152	144	159	138	129	135	121
60–64	217	197	217	239	214	221	209	215	205	190
65–68	201	202	209	238	217	211	221	197	219	219

For technical reasons, the experience at age 69 is omitted from the table.

investigation was made in 1933, in relation to widows, in connection with the first Decennial Review of the working of the national Contributory Pensions System. The results were not published, but the records are still available. They relate to all those women (60,000 in number) who were awarded widows' pensions of 10s. a week during the calendar year 1927 (they were all under age 70), and show particulars of every death, remarriage, and other cessation of pension that occurred among them during the five years following the dates of their awards. Particulars are given separately for each calendar year of birth of widow.

The numbers of deaths recorded in each of the five years are shown in Table 1. They are compared with the numbers expected according to the mortality experience, not of married women, but of the same widows during the first five years of widowhood taken as a whole.

These figures clearly do not exhibit any strongly marked durational effect. For all ages taken together, however, the comparison is as shown in Table 2.

When a variety of statistical tests is applied to them, in total and for individual ages and durations, the figures in these two tables suggest that the mortality of widows is probably not exactly the same in each of the five years, and in particular that it is higher than average in the second year after widowhood. Young et al.[1] found a significant excess in the mortality of widowers (as compared with the mortality of married men) only in the first six months.

TABLE 2. Deaths Following Widowhood (All Ages)

—	Expected	Actual	Ratio of actual to expected
First year	851	843	0.99
Second year	828	894	1.08
Third year	804	834	1.04
Fourth year	776	731	0.94
Fifth year	745	702	0.94
Total	4004	4004	1.00

It seems likely that there is at least a mild "duration effect" in the widows' data. This was not apparent immediately after the husband's death: For some reason it was delayed and weighed most heavily on the second year of widowhood.

We have examined carefully the tabulating instructions for the compilation of the statistical records (using punched cards) and it seems to us that, if these instructions were fully complied with, all deaths must have been recorded in the year in which they actually occurred. Late notification of deaths was probably not therefore responsible for the apparent delay. There is, however, another possible explanation: A widow who died shortly after her husband may not have applied for a pension. We do not know how soon after widowhood a widow might have applied or what delays may have occurred—the mortality record commences only at the date as from which the pension was awarded. It is possible, however, in those cases, for instance, where the widow was already ill, or felt her husband's death so keenly that it affected her vitality, that she may not have immediately applied for the benefit. If this were so, then a part of the very short-term effect on women of widowhood may be missing from our experience. This possibility, coupled with the likelihood that the "duration effect" was still felt in the second and perhaps even in the third year, suggests that it may have been more lasting than for widowers.

The discovery of Young *et al.* that, for durations of between six months and five years since bereavement, the mortality of widowers differed little from that of married men led them to conclude that at later durations the mortality of widowers would rise again in relation to that of married men, as widowers have considerably the higher mortality. We have attempted to answer this question in relation to widows but feel that the evidence available to us is insufficiently precise for any definite conclusion. It does appear that the mortality over the period 1927–32 of those awarded Contributory Pensions was broadly similar to that of all widows in the population in 1930–32, and this is not surprising, since nearly all of them qualified for the State pension. This mortality was thus higher than that of married women, though four or five years after widowhood it was only marginally higher. The difference between the mortality of widows and that of married women in 1930–32 was, however, much less pronounced than the difference in mortality for the corresponding male groups today; and we do not feel certain that it can properly be concluded that, for widows, the relative fall in mortality four or five years after bereavement necessarily implies a corresponding rise later.

Geographic Mobility and Extended Family Cohesion*

Eugene Litwak

This is the second of two companion papers, both of which seek to demonstrate that *modified* extended family relations are consistent with democratic industrial society.[1] These papers, then, attempt to modify Parson's hypothesis that the isolated nuclear family is the only type which is functional for such a society.[2] Because Parsons so clearly relates his hypothesis to a more general theory of class and business organization there is considerable value in keeping his point of view in the forefront of discussion, for its modification under such circumstances provides rich intellectual dividends.

Parsons assumes only one kind of extended family relational pattern, the "classical" type exemplified in the Polish and Irish peasant families.[3] There is some evidence, however, for the existence of a modified[4] extended family that is theoretically more relevant and empirically more predictive than either of the two alternatives posed by Parsons' hypothesis—the isolated nuclear family and the classical extended family.[5] The present inquiry supplements the earlier paper by demonstrating that modified extended family relations can be maintained despite differential geographical mobility. The first part of this paper examines the assumptions underlying Parsons' point of view as well as the modification suggested herein. In the second part empirical evidence is presented to show that extended family identification can be maintained despite geographical mobility.

GEOGRAPHICAL MOBILITY AND EXTENDED FAMILY ANOMY

There are at least three arguments which support the view that extended family relations are not consistent

---

* Eugene Litwak, "Geographic Mobility and Extended Family Cohesion," *American Sociological Review*, XXV (June, 1960), 386–394.

[1] The first paper is Eugene Litwak, "Occupational Mobility and Extended Family Cohesion," *American Sociological Review*, XXV (February, 1960), 9–21.

[2] Talcott Parsons, "The Social Structure of the Family," in *The Family: Its Function and Destiny*, ed. Ruth N. Ashen (New York: Harper & Row, Publishers, Inc., 1949), pp. 191–192.

[3] These families were marked by geographical propinquity, occupational integration, strict authority of extended family over nuclear family, and stress on extended rather than nuclear family relations.

[4] The modified extended family differs from past extended families in that it does not require geographical propin-

quity, occupational nepotism, or integration, and there are no strict authority relations, but equalitarian ones. Family relations differ from those of the isolated nuclear family in that significant aid is provided to nuclear families, although this aid has to do with standard of living (housing, illness, leisure pursuits) rather than occupational appointments or promotions.

[5] The counter hypothesis advanced in this paper is a modification of Parsons' position in that it accepts his analysis that the classical extended family is disfunctional for contemporary society, but it rejects his view that the isolated

with geographical mobility: (1) individuals who are strongly attached to their extended families will be reluctant to move even if better jobs are available elsewhere; (2) it is unlikely that identification with extended family will be retained where only one nuclear family moves while the rest of the extended family remains behind; and (3) it is financially more difficult to move a large family and locate jobs for many individuals simultaneously.

The first and third of these propositions suggest that individuals with extended family ties are unlikely to move. The second proposition suggests that if they do move individuals are unlikely to retain their extended family identification with those who remain behind. These arguments can be buttressed by the more general analysis of Homans, who points out that contact is one of the four major prerequisites for primary group cohesion.[6] Since these are familiar arguments they need not be elaborated.

GEOGRAPHICAL MOBILITY AND EXTENDED FAMILY COHESION

In this analysis, major attention is given to propositions which are contrary to those stated above, namely, the following: (1) individuals who are part of a modified extended family grouping are in a better position to move because the latter legitimizes such moves, and as a consequence provides economic, social, and psychological support; (2) extended family

nuclear family is the only theoretically meaningful alternative.

[6] George C. Homans, *The Human Group* (New York: Harcourt, Brace & World, Inc., 1950), p. 36.

relations can be maintained over great geographical distances because modern advances in communication techniques have minimized the socially disruptive effects of geographic distance; and (3) financial difficulties of moving extended families in a bureaucratic industrialized society are minimized because family coalescence takes place when the family is at its peak earning capacity and when it is least likely to disrupt the industrial organization.

1. MODIFIED EXTENDED FAMILIES AID GEOGRAPHICAL MOBILITY. Implicit in the argument that extended family relations lead to a reluctance to move is the view that extended families cannot legitimize geographical mobility. If it can be demonstrated that in current society the contrary is the case, then it can also be shown that such families have far greater facilities than the isolated nuclear family for encouraging spatial movement.

Past instances of legitimation of such movement by the extended family help to clarify the point. In situations of economic or political catastrophe (the Irish potato famine or the Russian pogroms), the extended family encouraged mobility. Given this type of situation, the extended family had at least two advantages over the isolated nuclear family. First, its greater numbers permitted easier accumulation of capital to finance the trip of any given nuclear family. This led to a push-and-pull kind of migration, with the migrant sending money to help those who had remained behind. Secondly, because of its close ties and size the extended family had superior lines of communication. Thus the migrant became a communication outpost for those who remained behind, providing information on jobs, housing, local social customs, and language. Those who had migrated earlier also could aid the newcomer at the most difficult point of migration.[7]

In a mature industrial society there is great institutional pressure on the extended family to legitimate differential geographical mobility among its nuclear family members. This pressure derives from the fact that the extended family can never fully control the economic destiny of its nuclear sub-parts. Although the extended family provides important aid, the major source of economic support for the nuclear family must come from its own occupational success, which is based much more on merit than nepotism. As a consequence, if the extended family wants to see its member nuclear families become successful, it must accept one of the chief prerequisites to occupational success—geographical mobility.[8]

In other words, it is postulated that a semi-independent relation links the nuclear family to the extended family. Because the extended family cannot offer a complete guarantee of occupational success it legitimates the

moves of nuclear family members. On the other hand, receiving as it does significant aid in achieving many of its goals, the nuclear family retains its extended family connections despite geographical distance.

2. EXTENDED FAMILY IDENTIFICATION IS RETAINED DESPITE BREAKS IN FACE-TO-FACE CONTACT. There are two reasons why extended families can provide important supplements to nuclear family goal achievement despite geographical distance and therefore two reasons why extended family identification can be maintained despite breaks in face-to-face contact.[9] As noted above, the rapid development of techniques of communication has made it relatively easy for family members to keep contact despite great distances. Nor does distance, in a money economy, prevent or seriously hinder such aids to family members as help in times of illness, emergency loans or gifts, home purchase, and the like—all at long range.

3. GEOGRAPHICAL COALESCENCE TAKES PLACE AT PEAKS OF EARNING POWER. Although the extended family encourages mobility when it is occupationally rewarding, it does not do so when such moves no longer bring rewards. Given the character of large-

---

[7] Of the large literature on this point, see e.g., Walter Firey, *Land Use in Central Boston* (Cambridge: Harvard University Press, 1947), pp. 184–186.

[8] C. Wright Mills, C. Senior, and R. K. Goldsen in the *Puerto Rican Journey* (New York: Harper, 1950), p. 51, provide some indirect evidence on legitimation when they point out that the Puerto Rican migrant rarely moves out of a sense of economic necessity but because of a desire for economic betterment. They also show that these migrants rely on extended family communications before migrating (pp. 53–55). These facts illustrate that for the lowest income strata of migrants there has been a legitimation of geographical mobility for maximizing goals. This would seem to be doubly true of the middle-class migrant since he is economically better off to start with.

[9] In addition to these assumptions, two more general ones should be made. First, it is assumed (in counter-distinction to W. F. Ogburn, for example, in "The Changing Functions of the Family," *Selected Studies in Marriage and the Family* (New York: Henry Holt, 1953), pp. 74–75, that extended families have not lost their functions. See Litwak, *op. cit.* Secondly, it is assumed that extensive family activity does not lead to occupational nepotism (*ibid.*); but Parsons' hypothesis states that extended family structures will collapse, or nepotism will destroy the industrial order.

scale organizations, there are regular occasions when geographical mobility is not linked to occupational rewards, for example, when the individual is at the peak of his career. The career in the large organization is one in which the individual moves up until he reaches a position from which he can no longer advance; here he remains until he retires. Careers of bureaucrats are rarely downward. Two aspects of this situation are particularly important in the present context: (1) once a person has advanced as far as he can occupationally his working efficiency is no longer tied to geographic moves; and (2) it is at this point that the nuclear family is in the best economic position to support moves of extended family. At this period of his life, the careerist can seek a position near his extended family if he can find a job which matches his present one. Or he can encourage retired parents to settle near him. In short, it is suggested that when the extended family does coalesce it does not lead to undue financial strain (trying to locate jobs for many people simultaneously), nor is it likely to mean an irrational distribution of labor since it involves either retired people or job exchanges between people on the same occupational level.

FINDINGS

In order to test alternative propositions about the relationship between family structure and geographical mobility, data from a survey of 920 white married women living in the Buffalo, New York, urban area were analyzed. The sample is biased in the direction of white, younger, middle-class, native-born individuals and as such is not represen-

tative of the total population.[10] However, the bias is a useful one since this is the very group which should most likely illustrate Parsons' hypothesis.[11] If it can be shown that his hypothesis does not hold for this group, then it is unlikely to hold for any division of the society.

1. MOBILITY REDUCES EXTENDED FAMILY FACE-TO-FACE CONTACT. The common basis for the opposing views —that geographical mobility is or is not antithetical to extended family relations—should be made explicit so that it is not mistaken for the main issue. Both positions are in agreement that geographical mobility generally reduces extended family face-to-face contact. Of the respondents in this study, 52 per cent with relatives living in the city received one or more family visits a week. In contrast, only 4 per cent of those with no such nearby relatives received visits this frequently.

---

[10] The field study was conducted in the Buffalo area between June and October, 1952. For details of the study and the sampling, see Glenn H. Beyer, Thomas W. Mackesey, and James E. Montgomery, *Houses Are for People: A Study of Home Buyer Motivations* (Ithaca: Cornell University Housing Research Center, 1955). Some special features of the sample should be noted here. The sample cannot be considered to be a random one. Being a study designed to investigate housing, five or six different sampling procedures based on neighborhood and housing design were used. The varied nature of the sample complicates the problem of the appropriate statistical test. Therefore the argument must rest heavily on its theoretical plausibility and its consistency with other relevant studies. However, if the assumptions of a random area sample are made, and the sign and Wilcoxon signed-ranks tests are used, then all major findings are significant at the 0.05 level and beyond. The signs for these tests were always taken from the most complex table in which the given variables appeared.

[11] Parsons, *op. cit.*, pp. 180–181.

2. BREAKS IN FACE-TO-FACE CONTACT DO NOT REDUCE EXTENDED FAMILY IDENTIFICATION. Central to the argument advanced in this paper is the view that geographical distance between relatives does not necessarily lead to a loss of extended family identification. In order to measure family orientation, all individuals were asked to respond to the following statements: (1) "Generally I like the whole family to spend evenings together." (2) "I want a house where family members can spend time together." (3) "I want a location which would make it easy for relatives to get together." (4) "I want a house with enough room for our parents to feel free to move in." These items formed a Guttman scale pattern.[12] Individuals who answered items 3 or 4 positively[13] were considered to be oriented toward the extended family. Those who answered items 1 or 2, but not 3 or 4, positively were considered to be nuclear family oriented. Those who answered none[14] of the questions positively were classified as nonfamily oriented.

In order to measure the effects of distance between relatives on family identification, all respondents were divided into two categories, those who had relatives living in town and those who did not. The data presented in Table 1 indicate that geographical

TABLE 1. Geographical Distance Does Not Lead to a Loss of Extended Family Identification

	Percentage extended family oriented	Percentage nuclear family oriented	Percentage nonfamily oriented	Total
Relatives living in town	20	52	28	100 (648)[a]
Relatives living out of town	22	58	20	100 (272)

[a] In this and the following tables the figures in parentheses indicate the population base for a given percentage. For tests of significance in these tables, see Footnote 10.

distance does not mean a loss of identity. Those who are geographically distant from their relatives are as likely as those who live nearby to retain their extended family identifi-

---

12 Although these items were dichotomized to form a Guttman scale pattern, it is not argued that they meet all of the requirements for such a scale. See Eugene Litwak, *Primary Group Instruments of Social Control in Industrial Society: The Extended Family and the Neighborhood* (Unpublished Ph.D. thesis, Columbia University, 1958), pp. 43–47.

13 The fact that only 4 per cent of the population answered item 4 positively means that item 3 defines extended family orientation for most of the population. In this connection, no assumption

is made that this operational definition exhausts the meaning of extended family orientation; it is only assumed that it will correlate highly with any other measures of extended family orientation.

14 Because some people may have interpreted "family" to mean only extended family it is possible that in this nonfamily oriented group there are some people who are nuclear family oriented. This plus the fact that the items were dichotomized to maximize their scaling properties suggests that little reliance should be placed on the absolute percentage of people exhibiting each value position but only on their differential distribution in various groups.

TABLE 2. Migrants Are Not Less Extended Family Identified Than Non-migrants

	Percentage extended family oriented	Percentage nuclear family oriented	Percentage nonfamily oriented	Total
Spent major part of first 20 years in the city	18	51	31	100 (504)
Spent major part of first 20 years out of the city	23	56	21	100 (416)

cation (22 and 20 per cent, respectively).

Table 1 very likely underestimates the relationship between mobility and extended family identification, since there may have been many individuals who either moved to the community because their relatives lived there or encouraged relatives to come later. In such cases family identification would have been maintained initially despite geographical distance. To deal with this question, all respondents again were divided, this time between those who spent their first 20 years in the city under study and those who were raised elsewhere. If the latter are considered to be migrants, it can be seen from Table 2 that the migrants (23 per cent) are more likely than the nonmigrants (18 per cent) to be identified with their extended families.

3. CLOSE IDENTIFICATION WITH EX-
TENDED FAMILY DOES NOT PREVENT
NUCLEAR FAMILIES FROM MOVING
AWAY. Are people who are close to their extended families likely to leave them in order to advance themselves occupationally? To measure the likelihood of persons moving from the community for occupational reasons, the respondents were asked the following question: "Is there a good chance that your husband might take

a job out of town?" Those who answered "yes" were classified as potential migrants. To test the likelihood of leaving their relatives, only respondents with relatives in town were examined. It can be seen from Table 3 that those individuals more closely identified with the extended family also were more likely to leave the city

TABLE 3. Strong Identification with Relatives Does Not Prevent People from Taking Jobs Elsewhere

	Among those with relatives in the city the percentage saying good chance husband will take job out of town
Extended family orientation	23 (128)
Nuclear family orientation	18 (336)
Nonfamily orientation	14 (184)

and presumably their nearby relatives (23 and 14 per cent, respectively). The same point can be made for the general population if the figures from Tables 1 and 2 are calculated to show how likely family oriented persons are to be migrants. Table 4 presents results which are consistent with Table 3. People are likely to move, then, even when they are strongly

TABLE 4. People Identified with Extended Family Are as Likely or More Likely to be Migrants Than Others

	Percentage raised out of town	Percentage having no relatives in the city
Extended family oriented	51 (187)	32 (187)
Nuclear family oriented	47 (493)	31 (493)
Nonfamily oriented	37 (240)	23 (240)

identified with their families, and once having moved away from them, they are likely to retain their family identity.

4. BUREAUCRATIC CAREER AND EXTENDED FAMILY MOBILITY. The analysis is thus far consistent with the view that in modern bureaucratic society extended family relations can retain their viability despite differential rates of geographic mobility. To be fully consistent, however, it should be shown that extended family movement is related to career development in the way anticipated by the foregoing discussion. For it was pointed out that it is only when the individual is on the upswing of his career that mobility will be encouraged, while it will be discouraged when he reaches the peak.

In order to measure career stages individuals were asked: "Within the next 10 years, do you expect the head of the household will be making: (a) a great deal more than now; (b) somewhat more than now; (c) same as now; (d) other, e.g., retired, don't know, etc." Those who said that they expected to earn "a great deal more" income were assumed to be on the upswing of their careers, those who named "somewhat more" were

assumed to be fast approaching the peak, while all others were assumed to have reached the peak or plateau of their careers.[15] Table 5 confirms the

TABLE 5. Those on the Upswing of Their Career Are Likely to be Migrants

		Percentage without relatives living in the city
	Within the next ten years	
Upswing of career	Expect to make a great deal more than now	39 (183)
Medium point	Expect to make somewhat more than now	29 (603)
Peak of career or plateau	Expect to make the same or less than now	16 (134)

view that bureaucratic development is congenial to family movement when people are upwardly mobile: 39 per cent of those on the upswing were migrants, while only 16 per cent of those who had reached their career plateaus were migrants.

Two additional bits of evidence supplement this point. First, if the hypothesis advanced in this paper is correct, the individuals who are both extended-family oriented and rising in their careers should be most mobile because they have the advantage of aid from their extended families. Comparatively speaking, extended family identity should not lead to mobility when individuals have reached the career plateau. Table 6 suggests that this is the case. When individuals are moving ahead occupationally,

---

15 Since 95 per cent of the sample subjects were 45 or younger, and since the study was conducted during a period of great prosperity, virtually no one said he expected to earn less than now.

TABLE 6. Extended Family Identification Is Likely to Encourage Geographical Mobility When Individuals Are on the Upswing of Their Careers

		Percentage having no relatives in the city		
	Within the next ten years	Extended family oriented	Nuclear family oriented	Nonfamily oriented
Upswing of career	Expect to make a great deal more than now	47 (49)[a]	40 (107)	22 (27)
Medium point of career	Expect to make somewhat more than now	30 (112)	31 (322)	27 (169)
Peak or plateau of career	Expect to make the same or less than now	12 (26)	22 (63)	11 (45)

[a] This cell reads as follows: 47 per cent of the 49 people who are extended family oriented and who expect to make a great deal more in the future have no relatives in the city.

those who are psychologically close to their families are much more mobile than those who dissociate themselves from their families (47 and 22 per cent, respectively, are mobile). In contrast, among people at the career peak, the extended family oriented are no more mobile than the nonfamily oriented (12 and 11 per cent, respectively).

The second bit of evidence which supports the view that extended family aid encourages mobility on the upswing of the career and discourages it otherwise involves the direction of the move. Individuals who have reached the career plateau *might possibly* still move if such moves meant bringing them closer to their extended family. To investigate this possibility, respondents were asked: "Compared to your last house is your present house closer, the same, or farther away from your family?" Table 7 shows that where individuals are climbing the ladder they are as likely,

TABLE 7. Extended Family Identification Is Likely to Encourage Moves[a] Away from the Extended Family When People Are on the Upswing of Their Careers

	Percentage whose last move carried them farther from their families		
	Extended family oriented	Nuclear family oriented	Nonfamily oriented
Expect to make a great deal more in 10 years	53 (49)[b]	37 (67)	48 (27)
Expect to make somewhat more	52 (112)	56 (322)	59 (169)
Expect to make the same or less	38 (26)	62 (63)	53 (45)

[a] Those with relatives in the city were classified together with those without relatives, since the same statistical pattern occurred in each case.

[b] This figure reads 53 per cent of 49 people who were extended family oriented and who expected to earn a great deal more in the next ten years moved farther away from their families.

if not more likely, to move away from their relatives when they are identified with their extended families as when they are not (53 per cent as compared to 37 and 48 per cent). However, where individuals have reached the occupational plateau, those who are identified with their extended families are less likely to move away from them (38 per cent as compared to 62 and 53 per cent).

In short, the evidence presented here indicates that the career strongly influences the extent and the direction of geographical mobility in a manner consistent with the view that extended family relations are viable in contemporary bureaucratic society.

5. BUREAUCRATIC AND NONBUREAUCRATIC CAREERS. This index of career, however, does not necessarily imply a *bureaucratic* career. Earlier discussions often assume that careers take place in a bureaucratic context. Therefore, the findings of this study should be further differentiated in terms of bureaucratic and nonbureaucratic occupations. In order to isolate the nonbureaucratic career, working-class persons whose fathers were also from a working-class occupational group were segregated from the rest of the population. Nonmanual middle-class and upper-class individuals are more likely to follow bureaucratic careers, involving standard promotional steps associated with geographical mobility.[16]

In contrast, these features do not

necessarily mark occupational advancement among manual workers. In this group occupational success may mean the achievement of plant seniority or the opening of a small business.[17] In such cases success is negatively related to future geographic mobility. As a consequence, a manual worker who envisions an upswing in his career may encourage family members to settle nearby because future

---

cross classified to provide four occupational categories: (1) upper-class husbands whose parents were upper class; (2) husbands whose parents were from a higher occupational group; (3) husbands whose parents were from a lower occupational group; (4) working-class husbands whose parents were working class. Two groups were eliminated: all individuals of farm background; and middle-class individuals of middle-class parentage (excluded because of the small number of cases). The stationary upper-class group is considered to approximate most closely the bureaucratic occupations while the stationary manual groups are assumed to be the polar opposite. Here "upper class" does not refer to an old-line "aristocracy" but to a professional-managerial occupational grouping. By definition, all people in administrative positions in large-scale organizations and professionals are included in the upper class or upwardly mobile occupational groups. There remains the question of whether or not they constitute a sufficiently large number within the over-all classification to give a distinct direction. Gold and Slater in a study based upon a random sample of the Detroit area point out that in the one category roughly similar in age and occupation to the "upper class" in this investigation, 74 per cent of the individuals were members of a bureaucratic organization. Martin Gold and Carol Slater, "Office, Factory, Store—and Family: A Study of Integration Setting," *American Sociological Review*, XXIII (February, 1958), 66, 69.

[17] See, e.g., Seymour Martin Lipset and Reinhard Bendix, "Social Mobility and Occupational Career Patterns," in *Class, Status and Power*, eds. Bendix and Lipset (New York: Free Press of Glencoe, Inc., 1953), pp. 457–459.

---

[16] On the basis of the U.S. Census's occupational categories, the husband and the husband's father were classified into: (1) professional, technical, and kindred, and managers, officials, and proprietors; (2) clerical and kindred workers, and sales workers; or (3) all others except farmers or farm help. Husbands' and husbands' fathers' occupations were

TABLE 8. Only Among Upper- and Middle-Class Bureaucratic Occupations Do Career Lines Play a Role

		Percentage having no relatives in the city			
	Within the next ten years	*Stationary upper class*[a]	*Upwardly mobile*	*Downwardly mobile*	*Stationary manual workers*
Upswing of career	Expect to make a great deal more than now	43 (76)[b]	39 (72)	40 (25)	10 (10)
Medium point of career	Expect to make somewhat more than now	42 (146)	39 (183)	26 (99)	11 (176)
Peak or plateau of career	Expect to make the same or less than now	23 (26)	13 (32)	28 (18)	12 (58)

[a] For a definition of occupational classification, see footnote 16.
[b] This cell should read as follows : 43 per cent of the 76 people who were stationary upper class and who had high expectations of future economic improvement had no relatives in the city.

success is closely linked to present location. Thus, it is expected that occupational advance has far different meanings for members of the working class and for the middle- and upper-class persons.

In Table 8 it can be seen that the only instances of upswings in careers leading to geographic mobility occur among members of the upper class (43 per cent of those who are on the upswing have no relatives in the community compared to 23 per cent of those who have achieved a plateau). For members of the stationary working class, occupational advancement is least likely, comparatively speaking, to result in geographical mobility (10 per cent of those on the upswing and 12 per cent of those on the plateau have relatives in the city).

Table 8 more than any other should indicate the limitations of the present hypothesis. The latter cannot claim to explain any major features of current American society but only the be-

havior of members of that group which is often thought to be prototypical of future American society—those belonging to bureaucratic occupations. It is assumed here that future societies will in fact become increasingly bureaucratized. Since Parsons' analysis is largely concerned with this same group,[18] it is maintained that this study provides evidence contrary to his hypothesis.

6. THE EXTENDED FAMILY AND EMOTIONAL, SOCIAL, AND ECONOMIC AID. Extended families have a unique function in providing aid to those who are moving. This is based partly on the fact that family membership is defined in terms of blood ties and therefore is least pervious to changes in social contact, and partly on the fact that the individual receives his earliest and most crucial socialization with people who eventually become extended family members. The indi-

[18] Parsons, *op. cit.*, pp. 180–181.

TABLE 9.   The Extended Family Meets the Needs of Recent Movers[a]

	Percentage receiving frequent family visits[b]	*Percentage belonging to more than one club*[c]	*Percentage knowing five or more neighbors*[d]	*Total population*
	Respondents having no relatives in the city			
Newcomers	22	25	38	110
Long-term residents	16	51	63	166
Difference	08	−26	−25	
	Respondents having relatives in the city			
Newcomers	54	44	41	163
Long-term residents	49	43	60	485
Difference	05	01	−19	

[a] The respondents were divided between the newcomers or those people who had lived in their houses nine months or less and the long-term residents or all others.

[b] When no relatives in the city a frequent visit is defined as one or more family visits a month—either invited or noninvited. When relatives live in the city a frequent visit is defined as one or more family visits a week.

[c] This is the closest approximation to the average number of clubs to which the population belonged.

[d] This is the closest approximation to the average number of neighbors the respondents knew well enough to call on.

vidual might find voluntary associations of lesser help than family aid because new personal contacts must be established when one moves, and old contacts tend to have no continuing meaning when geographical contact is broken. Aid from neighbors has somewhat the same character. This point emerges clearly when newcomers to a neighborhood are compared with long-term residents in terms of the average amount of social participation in various areas of life. Table 9 shows that family contacts are as likely, if not more likely, to occur among newcomers than among long-term residents. In contrast, neighborhood and club affiliations are likely to increase the longer individuals live in the neighborhood.[19] This

[19] The striking differences between respondents with relatives live in the

suggests the unique function of the extended family during the moving crisis.

SECONDARY EVIDENCE

The evidence presented above consistently documents the position that extended family relations are not antithetical to geographical mobility in bureaucratic industrialized society. In fact, at times such relationships actually encourage mobility. The limits of the sample, however, place severe restrictions on the general application of these data. It is of some im-

city and those without nearby relatives, shown in Table 9, are discussed in an unpublished paper by Eugene Litwak, "Voluntary Associations and Primary Group Development in Industrial Society."

portance, therefore, to seek in other researches supportive evidence for extended family viability.

First, as a necessary but not sufficient condition, it should be shown that extended family relations are fairly extensive in American society today. In recent years, four studies that provide data on extended family visiting have been carried out, respectively, in Los Angeles, Detroit, San Francisco, and Buffalo. Three of these indicate that close to 50 per cent of the residents made one or more such visits a week. And three of the four investigations, on the basis of comparisons of family, neighbors, friends, and voluntary associations, conclude that the family relationships were either the most frequent or the most vital. These findings, as limited as they are, strongly suggest that extended family relations are extensive.[20]

What is of even greater interest is that these studies indicate that middle-class white persons share this viability with others and that these relations are highly important ones. Thus Sussman, in a study of middle-class white Protestant families, shows that 80 per cent of the family relationships studied involved giving aid, and in 70 per cent of the cases respondents felt that the recipients would suffer loss of status if the aid were not continued. Moreover, this aid had much more to do with standard of living than with locating jobs or helping people to advance in them through nepotism.[21] This investigation was supplemented by a study by Bell and Boat which indicates that 76 per cent of the low-income and 84 per cent of the high-income subjects could count on extended family aid in cases of illness lasting a month or longer; they also report that 90 per cent of the respondents indicated that at least one member of the extended family was a close friend.[22] Studies on working class families,[23] Puerto Rican families,[24] Negro families,[25] and Italian families[26] indicate that extended family relations in these cases are viable and warm.

Although these relations are of a far different character from the middle-class family contact discussed in this paper,[27] the studies of working-class and ethnic groups do provide insight into the extension and warmth of extended family relations in all strata of contemporary society. They do not by themselves refute Parsons' formulation because he assumes that extended family relations are declining, not that they have disappeared. However, they buttress the alterna-

---

20 Morris Axelrod, "Urban Structure and Social Participation," *American Sociological Review*, XXI (February, 1956), 13–18; Wendell Bell and Marion D. Boat, "Urban Neighborhoods and Informal Social Relations," *American Journal of Sociology*, LXII (January, 1957), 391–398; Scott Greer, "Urbanism Reconsidered," *American Sociological Review*, XXI (February, 1956), 22; Litwak, *Primary Group Instruments . . .*, *op. cit.*, p. 82.

21 Marvin B. Sussman, "The Help Pattern in Middle Class Family," *American Sociological Review*, XVIII (February, 1953), 22–28 *passim.*

22 Bell and Boat, *op. cit.*, p. 396.

23 Michael Young and Peter Willmott, *Family and Kinship in East London* (London: Routledge and Kegan Paul, 1957), pp. 159–166.

24 Mills, Senior, and Goldsen, *op. cit.*, pp. 115, 117.

25 E. Franklin Frazier, "The Impact of Urban Civilization Upon Negro Family Life," in *Cities and Societies: The Revised Reader in Urban Sociology*, eds. P. K. Hatt and A. S. Reiss, Jr. (New York: Free Press of Glencoe, Inc., 1957), pp. 495–496.

26 Firey, *op. cit.*, pp. 184–186.

27 Cf. Litwak, "Occupational Mobility and Extended Family Cohesion," *op. cit.*

tive hypothesis advanced here since they do suggest a basic prerequisite of that hypothesis, namely, that extended family relations are viable in contemporary urban society.

CONCLUSIONS

It is argued, then, that these relations can retain their social significance under industrial bureaucratic pressures for geographical mobility. Evidence has been presented that is inconsistent with Parsons' hypothesis. Two theoretical points support this contrary view: first, that the extended family relationship which does not demand geographical propinquity (not examined by Parsons) is a significant form of social behavior; second, that theoretically the most efficient organization combines the ability of large-scale bureaucracy to handle uniform situations with the primary group's ability to deal with idiosyncratic situations. These two theoretical points suggest that there is both a need and a capacity of extended families to exist in modern society.

The data presented here (and in the earlier companion paper) demonstrate that persons separated from their families retained their extended family orientation; those with close family identification were as likely, if not more likely, to leave their family for occupational reasons; those on the upswing of their careers were apt to move away from their families and to receive family support; those

on the career plateau were not likely to move or to move toward their family; that considerations of this kind hold only for bureaucratic occupations; and that the modified extended family seems to be uniquely suited to provide succor during periods of movement. These findings suggest interesting questions for future research. With respect to the family system, there is a need to isolate the mechanisms by which the nuclear family retains its semi-independence while receiving aid from the extended family.[28] It is also important to specify in greater detail the limits of the modified extended family organization in terms of time (does it extend over two or three generations?) and social distance (is it limited, for example, to parents and married children or siblings?). Concerning the occupational system, it is important to identify the type of bureaucratic structure which permits the family to be linked with occupations without affecting productivity.[29] For the analysis of class structure, the question arises as to how likely it is that extended family relations become significant factors blurring class identification without reducing occupational mobility.

---

[28] Cf. Eugene Litwak, "The Use of Extended Family Groups in the Achievement of Social Goals: Some Policy Implications," *Social Problems*, VII (Winter, 1959–60), 177–187.

[29] Cf. Litwak, "Occupational Mobility and Extended Family Cohesion," *op. cit.*; and *Primary Group Instruments...*, *op. cit.*, pp. 6–30.

Family Structure and Child-Rearing Patterns: The Effect of Family Size and Sex Composition*

Glen H. Elder, Jr., and Charles E. Bowerman

Half a century ago, Simmel stressed the importance of numbers in group life.[1] As the size of a group

* Glen H. Elder, Jr., and Charles E. Bowerman, "Family Structure and Child-Rearing Patterns: The Effect of Family Size and Sex Composition," *American Sociological Review*, XXVIII (December, 1963), 891–905.

[1] In some prefatory remarks to his treatise, "On the Significance of Numbers for Social Life," Simmel points to the heart of the research problem we consider in this paper. "It will immediately be conceded on the basis of everyday experiences, that a group upon reaching a certain size must develop forms and organs which serve its maintenance and promotion, but which a smaller group does not need. On the other hand, it will also be admitted that smaller groups have qualities, including types of interaction among their members, which inevitably disappear when the groups grow larger." *The Sociology of George Simmel*, translated and edited by Kurt H. Wolff, p. 87. Two important laboratory studies of interaction in groups varying in size are the following: A. Paul Hare, "A Study of Interaction and Consensus in Different Sized Groups," *American Sociological Review*, XVII (June, 1952), 261–267, and Philip E. Slater, "Contrasting Correlates of Group Size," *Sociometry*, XXI (June, 1958), 129–139. For recent reviews of correlates of group size, see Edgar Borgatta, "Small Group Research: A Trend Report and Bibliography," *Current Sociology*, IX (1960), No. 3; A. Paul Hare, *Handbook of Small Group Research* (New York: The Free Press of Glencoe, Inc., 1962), pp. 224–231; and Robert F. Bales, A. Paul Hare, and Edgar F. Borgatta, "Structure and Dynamics of Small Groups, A Review of Four Variables," in *Review of Sociology*, ed. Joseph P. Gittler (New York: John Wiley and Sons, Inc., 1957).

increases, members are less likely to maintain a distinct identity, the number of possible relationships increases sharply, leadership becomes more differentiated, isolates and coalitions form, and consensus in decision-making grows more difficult. Many of the effects of group size were investigated by Bossard and Boll in regard to patterns of authority, affection, and personality development in large families.[2] Others have shown very little interest in family size as a variable in family and socialization research, a lack of interest surprising in view of the number of small-group studies employing group size as an independent variable.[3]

In response to this need and to the theoretical significance of the effects of family size on child-rearing practices, we will test a set of hypotheses pertaining to the effects of the number and sex ratio of children in a

[2] See James H. S. Bossard, *Parent and Child* (Philadelphia: University of Pennsylvania Press, 1953), and James H. S. Bossard and Eleanor S. Boll, *The Large Family System* (Philadelphia: University of Pennsylvania Press, 1956).

[3] Rosen comments: "Considering the sociologist's traditional and continuing concern with group size as an independent variable (from Simmel and Durkheim to the recent experimental studies of small groups), there have been suprisingly few studies of the influence of group size upon the nature of interaction in the family." Bernard Rosen, "Family Structure and Achievement Motivation," *American Sociological Review*, XXVI (August, 1961), 346.

family on two aspects of child-rearing: (1) the involvement of the father in rearing children, and (2) the differential use of certain practices and training techniques which represent methods of external rather than indirect control.

Methods of external behavior control are employed by parents to terminate or direct a child's behavior, i.e., autocratic control, physical punishment, shouting and criticizing. The effectiveness of these measures depends on parental action since they do not engage the child's own mechanism of self-control; they represent an *imposed* system of controls, designed to elicit *obedience* and discourage the transgression of rules of conduct. In contrast, indirect methods, such as parental explanation and reasoning, work through the child's cognition and sense of right and wrong behavior to *induce* appropriate behavior regulation.

Since external methods attempt to arrest undesirable behavior without appealing to the child's understanding, there is often conflict between parent and child. Indirect or "psychological" methods of behavior regulation aim at reducing or eliminating motivational differences between parent and child, and eliciting compliance. It is true that parents who reason also use external techniques, such as the withdrawal of privileges, but other research has indicated two relatively distinct syndromes of discipline techniques: external methods such as physical punishment and symbolic methods such as reasoning.[4]

In the following analysis, we move beyond the question of how child rearing varies in families of different

size to examine the effects of the sex of children on the patterns of child training observed in small and large families.[5] If, for example, fathers are generally more active in child rearing in the large family, to what extent does the number of boys and girls in the family influence this tendency? From teachers' ratings of 128 five- and six-year-old children, each of whom had one sibling, Koch found that boys were rated as more active, expressive of anger, quarrelsome, revengeful, given to teasing, extrapunitive, insistent on their rights, exhibitionistic, and cooperative with teachers and peers. Girls, on the other hand, were rated as more tenacious of purpose, responsible, obedient, and affectionate than boys.[6] These results suggest that boys with brothers and no sisters are apt to be more rigorously controlled by father than boys with sisters and no brothers.

Research that we shall discuss shortly indicates that family size,

---

[4] Charles E. Bowerman and Glen H. Elder, Jr., *The Adolescent and His Family*, chap. vii, in preparation.

[5] Birth order and the spacing of children are two other important structural properties of the family not examined in this paper because of space restrictions.

[6] Helen L. Koch, "Some Personality Correlates of Sex, Sibling Position and Sex of Siblings Among Five and Six Year Old Children," *Genetic Psychology Monographs*, LII (1955), 3–50. See also Orville Brim, "Family Structure and Sex Role Learning by Children: A Further Analysis of Helen Koch's Data," *Sociometry*, XXI (March, 1958), 1–16. Similar sex differences in grade school children's evaluation of their peers were obtained in a study conducted by Tuddenham. R. D. Tuddenham, "Studies in Reputation: I. Sex and Grade Differences in School Children's Evaluations of their Peers; II. The Diagnosis of Social Adjustment," *Psychological Monographs*, LXVI, No. 333 (1952). Sharp differentiation of sex roles is clearly documented in Landy's careful analysis of child rearing in a lower-class rural Puerto Rican village. David Landy, *Tropical Childhood* (Chapel Hill: University of North Carolina Press, 1959).

paternal involvement in child rearing, and the use of external behavior control are correlates of social class. In addition, available data suggest that paternal involvement and the use of external control methods vary with the sex of child. Social class and sex will therefore be controlled in the presentation of our hypotheses and in the subsequent analysis. It is true, of course, that the relation of social class to child-rearing patterns is an important research problem, but it has received much more attention than the one dealt with in this paper.

THE SAMPLE

Our data were drawn from a larger research project on adolescence in the Institute for Research in Social Science at the University of North Carolina. The principal objective of the larger study was to investigate types of parent-peer attitudinal orientations among adolescents, to analyze the social contexts and factors associated with basic patterns of orientation and to evaluate possible consequences of these patterns. Almost half the sample was obtained through public and parochial schools in central Ohio, while the remainder was obtained in public schools in central North Carolina. This sample included all adolescents in grades seven through twelve who were in school when a structured questionnaire was administered by teachers in the classroom in April and May of 1960.

For the present study, we drew a 40 per cent random sample of the seventh-grade white Protestant students from unbroken homes, living mainly in urban areas, from the larger sample. We restricted the sample to children of one grade to insure the exclusion of subjects' siblings; only one report on each family and on each parent is included in the analysis.[7] We selected seventh graders because our interest is in child-rearing practices used more commonly on children of this age than on older youths.

HYPOTHESES

THE INVOLVEMENT OF FATHER IN CHILD REARING. In an analysis of the large family system, Bossard hypothesized that "the larger the family group becomes, the more internal organization and dominance of some one or two persons appear," and as family size increases, "the stronger the position of the father as its directive symbol becomes."[8] Increasing centralization of leadership as a function of increasing size of group has been observed in a large number of task-oriented *ad hoc* groups in small group experiments.[9] Accordingly, we hypothesize that (1) *the probability of paternal involvement in the control and discipline of children increases as family size increases.*

Because of shared interests and other sex-linked factors, fathers tend to do more things with their sons than with their daughters. In a sample of 85 fathers with children ranging from

---

[7] Various restrictions and data processing problems made it necessary to limit our analysis to a 40 per cent sample of seventh graders. The 1,261 members of the sample are distributed as follows: middle-class boys (294) and girls (332); lower-class boys (287) and girls (348).

[8] Bossard, *op. cit.*, pp. 108–110.

[9] See A. Paul Hare, *Handbook of Small Group Research*, pp. 227–230. Hare suggests that "the development of leadership is possibly in part an alternative to an actual reduction in size" (p. 230).

new-born to 17 years of age, Tasch found that from the age of six there is an increasing tendency for fathers to engage in more activities with their sons than with their daughters.[10] Adolescent boys are much more likely to want to do things with and be with their fathers rather than their mothers.[11]

Results from a study of parental roles in child rearing indicate that working-class fathers are much less likely to see child rearing as part of their responsibility than are middle-class fathers.[12] These results suggest that fathers in the middle class are more likely than those in the working class to take leadership responsibility in child rearing. Thus, we hypothesize that (2) *paternal involvement in child rearing is most frequent when all of the children in the family are boys.* The hypothesized relationship should be strongest in large middle-class families.

DIFFERENTIAL USE OF CHILD-REARING PRACTICES. Since an increase in the size of a family heightens the complexity of intragroup relations and poses new problems in the fulfillment of individual and family needs, it is reasonable to assume that different methods of rule transmission and behavior control are employed. For instance, the time and patience needed to explain rules are no doubt less

available to parents with large families.[13] As family size increases, parents may increasingly rely on strong behavior control, requiring the child to assume a passive role, and adolescents in large families may be less apt to feel that parental control has decreased over the past several years. And as family size increases, parental expressions of praise, approval, comfort and acceptance are likely to decrease in frequency per child.

External control is also more likely to be utilized by lower-class parents than by middle-class parents. Bernstein's research on social class differences in linguistic form indicates that lower-class parents are much less likely to use reasoning or offer explanations to their adolescent sons and daughters than middle-class parents.[14] Physical discipline, such as spanking and slapping, are used more frequently by lower-class parents.[15] Several other studies have shown that middle- and lower-class parents desire somewhat different qualities in their children beyond such core values as honesty.[16] While middle-class parents

---

10 Ruth J. Tasch, "The Role of the Father in the Family," *Journal of Experimental Education,* XX (June, 1952), 319–361.

11 Glen H. Elder, Jr., "Family Structure and the Transmission of Values and Norms in the Process of Child Rearing" (unpublished Ph.D. dissertation, University of North Carolina, 1961), chap. x.

12 Melvin L. Kohn and Eleanor E. Carroll, "Social Class and the Allocation of Parental Responsibilities," *Sociometry,* XXIII (December, 1960), 372–392.

13 See, for instance, Lee Rainwater, *And the Poor Get Children* (Chicago, Ill.: Quadrangle Books, 1960).

14 See two insightful research papers by Basil Bernstein on qualitative differences in cognitive expression between English middle- and lower-class parents and children. "Some Sociological Determinants of Perception," *The British Journal of Sociology,* IX (June, 1958), 158–174; and "A Public Language: Some Sociological Implications of Linguistic Form," *The British Journal of Sociology,* X (December, 1959), 311–326.

15 Bowerman and Elder, *op. cit.*

16 Melvin L. Kohn, "Social Class and Parental Values," *American Journal of Sociology,* LXIV (January, 1959), 337–351: and "Social Class and Parent-Child Relationships: An Interpretation," *American Journal of Sociology,* LXIX (January, 1963), 471–480; and Lee Rainwater, Richard P. Coleman, and Gerald Handel, *Workingman's Wife: Her Personality World and Life Style* (New York: Oceana Publications, 1959), p. 94;

prefer their children to be curious, responsible and autonomous; lower-class parents tend to favor qualities such as obedience and respectability. Thus it seems that the organizational requirements and frustrations of a large family should *reinforce* the external control orientation of lower-class parents. If so, the relation between family size and parental control should be strongest among lower-class families. In order to examine this possibility, social class, as measured by father's occupation, will be systematically controlled throughout the analysis.[17]

Gerhard Lenski, *The Religious Factor* (New York: Random House, 1961), p. 201; Urie Bronfenbrenner, "Socialization and Social Class Through Time and Space," in *Readings in Social Psychology*, eds. Eleanor E. Maccoby, Theodore M. Newcomb, and Eugene L. Hartley (New York: Henry Holt, 1958); and Alex Inkeles, "Industrial Man: The Relation of Status to Experience, Perception, and Value," *American Journal of Sociology*, LXVI (July, 1960), 1–31.

[17] To place our respondents and their families in social class categories, we assigned father's occupation to the occupational categories used by the U. S. Bureau of Census. Since farmers, farm managers, and farm laborers are not assigned a social class, they were removed from the larger sample, our sample was drawn from this nonfarm sample and is therefore composed chiefly of adolescents in families residing either in urban or rural nonfarm areas.

Social class	U.S. census occupation categories
Middle	Professional, technical, and kindred workers, managers, officials, and proprietors except farm, clerical and kindred workers, sales workers.
Lower	Craftsmen, foremen, and kindred workers, operative and kindred workers, service workers, laborers except farm and mine.

On the utility of occupation as a single measure of social class, see Joseph H. Kahl and James H. Davis, "A Comparison of Indexes of Socio-economic Status," *American Sociological Review*, XX (June, 1955), 317–325.

These expectations may be reduced to one predictive statement: (3) *Family size will be positively related to parental use of external behavior-control methods in child rearing.* Indicators of an external behavior-control orientation are the relative infrequency of adolescent independence in personal decision making, relaxation of parental control over time, parental explanations, and symbolic techniques of discipline. The relation between family size and external control should be strongest in lower-class families.

The sex of the child is likely to affect these relationships. Previous research has indicated that fathers are more likely to discipline their sons than they are their daughters,[18] while mothers are more likely than fathers to discipline daughters. One might also expect parental control, parental explanations of rules, and techniques of discipline to vary with the sex composition of the family. Since boys tend to be more assertive, aggressive, active, and argumentative than girls, physical discipline, shouting, and nagging may be more prevalent in families with several sons.[19]

A family that includes both sons and daughters provides parents with two sets of experiences, one introduced by the peer activities of sons, and the other by the girls' activities. For example, the onset of puberty is likely to heighten parental awareness of their daughters' sexuality. These factors, plus the intransigence and dislike of parental direction characteristic of youth of this age, suggest that a girl with brothers may behave differently

[18] Andrew Henry, "Sibling Structure and Perception of the Disciplinary Roles of Parents," *Sociometry*, XX (March, 1957), 67–74; and Bowerman and Elder, *The Adolescent and His Family*, in preparation.

[19] Koch, *op. cit.*

and be perceived differently by parents than a girl with sisters only. While Tuma and Livson found a slight tendency for girls to be more accepting of authority than boys, we would expect girls in mixed-sex families to hold unfavorable attitudes toward parental control and thereby encourage greater behavioral regulation.[20]

These aspects of the possible effects of sex composition suggest the following hypotheses: (4) *Boys who have brothers and no sisters, in contrast to boys with sisters, are more likely to experience external behavior-control methods.* (5) *Girls who have brothers are more apt, than girls with sisters and no brothers, to experience external behavior-control methods.* External behavior-control methods are indicated by the use of physical discipline and negative verbal methods such as yelling and ridicule.

Differences in the value orientations of middle- and lower-class persons, such as those delineated by Miller and Reissman,[21] suggest that the hypothesized relationship for girls should be strongest in lower-class families. Since the number of child-rearing problems presumably increases as the number of children in the family increases, the sharpest differences in the direction predicted with respect to girls should occur in the large lower-class family.

Social class differences are less easily predicted for boys. In our society as well as in others there is greater pressure toward nurturance, obedience and responsibility in girls and self-reliance and achievement in boys.[22] Lower-class fathers may therefore stress obedience and responsibility less in rearing their sons than in rearing their daughters.[23] Thus, sex-composition effects on the rearing of boys, especially by their fathers, are more likely to be evident among middle-class families.

RESULTS

THE INVOLVEMENT OF FATHER IN CHILD REARING. To test whether family size has any effect on paternal involvement in child rearing, we shall examine variations in parental roles in formulating rules of conduct, setting up and maintaining a policy of discipline, and in administering discipline (see hypothesis 1). The relation between paternal role and family size with social class and sex of adolescent controlled is shown in Table 1. The data indicate that fathers are a little more likely to be dominant in rearing children as family size increases.[24]

---

[20] Elias Tuma and Norman Livson, "Family Socioeconomic Status and Adolescent Attitude Toward Authority," *Child Development*, XXXI (June, 1960), 387–399.

[21] S. M. Miller and Frank Reissman, "The Working Class Subculture: A New View," *Social Problems*, IX (Summer, 1961), 86–97. See also William F. Whyte, "A Slum Sex Code," *American Journal of Sociology*, XLIX (July, 1943), 24–31; and Walter B. Miller, "Lower-Class Culture as a Generating Milieu of Gang Delinquency," *Journal of Social Issues*, XIV (1958), 5–19.

[22] Herbert Barry, III, Margaret K. Bacon, and Irvin L. Child, "A Cross-Cultural Survey of Some Sex Differences in Socialization," *Journal of Abnormal and Social Psychology*, LV (November, 1957), 327–332.

[23] See Martin Gold, "Social Class, Family Structure, and Identity Processes Related to Juvenile Delinquency," paper read at American Psychological Association, New York, September, 1961.

[24] We have used in this analysis an asymmetric measure of association, dyx, developed by Robert Somers, "A New Asymmetric Measure of Association for Ordinal Variables," *American Sociological Review*, XXVII (December, 1962), 799–811.

TABLE 1. Parental Roles in Child Rearing as Reported by Seventh-Grade Children, by Family Size, Sex of Adolescent, and Social Class

Sex	Social class	Size of family	N[a]	Father usually or more often makes final decisions on rule policy, per cent	Father usually or more often makes final dicisions on discipline policy, per cent	Father disciplines more often than mother, per cent
		1–2	130	24	29	34
	MC	3	90	31	20	40
		4 or more	74	31	34	39
		dyx	—	+0.051	+0.010	+0.042
Boys						
		1–2	134	19	25	31
	LC	3	93	20	21	31
		4 or more	105	29	26	25
		dyx	—	+0.066	+0.001	−0.044
		1–2	122	15	14	18
	MC	3	98	14	11	19
		4 or more	67	29	20	28
		dyx	—	+0.074	+0.035	+0.070
Girls						
		1–2	127	12	12	12
	LC	3	107	16	18	10
		4 or more	114	20	20	21
		dyx	—	+0.057	+0.059	+0.060

a Percentages in this table and Tables 2 and 3 are based on the number of adolescents in each family-size category. Although the total number of cases varies slightly for each table due to nonresponse, this variation is not great enough to require inclusion of the base numbers in each cell.

Parental leadership in establishing rules of conduct was measured by asking each child the following question: "When your parents disagree with each other about what you should be allowed to do, which parent usually makes the final decision or has the

In the initial analysis of family-size effects, we used five size categories ranging from one to five or more children. We found very small percentage differences between the one- and two-child family and between the four- and five-child family, with the largest differences among the two-, three- and four-child families. Thus, we decided to group respondents in the three size categories shown in Table 1.

greatest influence in making the decision?" (1) Father, usually; (2) father, more often; (3) about equally; (4) mother, more often; (5) mother, usually. In Table 1, we see that the frequency with which paternal leadership in this area is reported tends to increase as family size increases, although percentage differences between small and large families, as well as the coefficients, reveal that the association is not very strong.

Since shared decision making is the modal pattern regardless of family size, it is useful to examine the ratios of adolescents checking father as dominant over those reporting mother as dominant in the final decision making: middle-class boys, 1.2, 1.8, 1.8; lower-class boys, 0.6, 0.7, 1.7; middle-class girls, 0.9, 2.5, 1.4; and lower-class girls, 0.4, 0.6, 0.8. Boys are more likely than girls to describe fathers as dominant, though the direction of the relation with family size is the same in all subgroups. Class differences within each family size category are relatively small with middle-class fathers more likely to be dominant in this area than lower-class fathers.

In regard to decision making on discipline policy, the question was: "When your parents disagree about your punishment, which parent usually makes the final decision?" The response categories were the same as those listed for the previous item. The percentages of youths indicating father as dominant in this area are shown in Table 1; the relation with family size is in the same direction as for the first question. Again, the shared arrangement is the modal pattern regardless of family size. The ratios of reported father-dominance over mother-dominance show a gradual increase from small to large family for boys and girls. Only among lower-class boys do we find practically no relation between leadership on discipline policy and family size.

The administration of discipline presents a picture similar to policy-making on discipline. In response to the question, "Which parent disciplines, punishes, or corrects you *more often?*," we find that middle-class boys and girls are more likely to report father as chief disciplinarian if they have three or more siblings in the family than if they have fewer. The frequency with which paternal discipline is reported is negatively related to size of family for lower-class boys;

among lower-class girls, the relationship is positive.

The discipline item, like the previous two, includes a response indicating *shared* administration of discipline, but this is usually not the modal pattern. The ratio of girls checking father as disciplinarian over those reporting mother increases from small to large families: middle-class, 0.4, 0.6, 1.1, and lower-class, 0.3, 0.3, 0.6. For boys, the ratios are: middle-class, 1.3, 1.6, 2.4, and lower-class, 1.3, 1.3, 0.8. These ratios and the percentages in Table 1 indicate that sons in large lower-class families are *less likely* to see father as the chief disciplinarian than they are in small lower-class families. Daughters of lower-class fathers, on the other hand, are slightly more apt to report father as the principal disciplinarian when there are four or more children. A satisfactory explanation of this difference is difficult to obtain with the data at hand. While Kohn and Carroll observe that working-class fathers were reluctant to participate in child-rearing matters, they do not discern differential involvement by the sex of the child.[25] Perhaps this difference in paternal involvement becomes more evident as the children become older (the Kohn and Carroll sample included boys and girls in the fifth grade).

To summarize: Father is reported as being more likely to make decisions on child-rearing matters and act as chief disciplinarian as family size increases, except when the respondent is a lower-class boy. In accordance with hypothesis 1, paternal involvement is more likely in large families. Eleven of the twelve relationships shown in Table 1 are in the direction predicted, though in most cases the

---

[25] Kohn and Carroll, *op. cit.*, p. 385.

degree of association is not strong. Results are weakest for lower-class boys, with only one relationship at least moderate in strength and in the predicted direction.

DIFFERENTIAL USE OF CHILD-REARING PRACTICES

PARENTAL CONTROL AND EXPLANA-

TIONS. We hypothesized that parental control is likely to increase as family size increases, and that parental explanation of rules is negatively related to family size (see hypothesis 3). Table 2 presents the relation between family size and (1) parental power in the child-rearing relationship, (2) the persistence of parental control over time, and (3) infrequent parental explanations of rules. These three

TABLE 2. Parental Control, Persistence in Control Over Time, and Frequency of Explanations in Child Rearing, by Family Size, Sex, and Social Class of Seventh-Grade Youths

Sex	Social class	Size of family	N	Parent is autocratic or authoritarian in control,[a] per cent		Parent has not relaxed his control over past few years, per cent		Parent infrequently explains rules of conduct, per cent	
				Mother	Father	Mother	Father	Mother	Father
Boys	MC	1–2	130	28	34	18	18	25	24
		3	90	30	45	12	21	36	42
		4 or more	74	37	43	20	28	33	39
		dyx	—	+0.059	+0.080	+0.009	+0.074	+0.071	+0.122
	LC	1–2	134	27	41	20	24	37	38
		3	93	35	42	29	31	34	37
		4 or more	105	35	44	26	35	41	45
		dyx	—	+0.059	+0.019	+0.048	+0.081	+0.022	+0.048
Girls	MC	1–2	122	16	22	8	13	19	21
		3	98	16	21	10	10	11	21
		4 or more	67	23	35	21	28	24	24
		dyx	—	+0.033	+0.066	+0.065	+0.070	+0.012	+0.014
	LC	1–2	127	27	38	12	18	23	33
		3	107	29	33	11	19	19	36
		4 or more	114	37	54	27	30	33	47
		dyx	—	+0.067	+0.102	+0.102	+0.083	+0.068	+0.090

[a] Each respondent was asked two similarly worded questions: "In general, how are decisions made between you and your (mother/father)?"

Autocratic	1—My (mother/father) just tells me what to do.
Authoritarian	2—(She/he) listens to me, but makes the decision (herself/himself).
Democratic	3—I have considerable opportunity to make my own decisions, but (she/he) has the final word.
Equalitarian	4—My opinions are as important as my (mother's/father's) in deciding what I should do,
Permissive	5—I can make my own decision, but (she/he) would like me to consider (her/his) opinion.
Laissez-faire	6—I can do what I want regardless of what (she/he) thinks.
Ignoring	7—(She/he) doesn't care what I do.

variables are related to family size in the direction predicted in all 24 comparisons, with the majority indicating a moderate degree of association. The strongest relationships are evident among middle-class boys and lower-class girls. As family size increases, adolescents in these two subgroups are more likely to report being dominated by their parents and having been given relatively few explanations of rules and policy. Let us examine the effects of family size on each variable in more detail.

In a recent study, it was found that parents are more likely to be autocratic in families with three or more children than in small families.[26] With the more detailed breakdown of family size given here, we note that parents who have four or more children are more likely to be dominant than parents with three children in the home, particularly in the case of girls. Parents of lower-class girls are more likely than middle-class parents to be dominant, especially in larger families.

The number of children in the family has relatively little effect on the reported dominance of fathers of lower-class boys. As in the case of discipline administration (see Table 1), father-son relations in the lower-class family do not support our hypothesis regarding family size effects on paternal involvement and control. In contrast, the lower-class girl in the large family is more likely to experience paternal involvement in child-rearing matters and autocratic or authoritarian control from both parents.

A child may feel that his parents currently give him more, less, or about the same amount of freedom in self-direction, compared to the extent of his independence a few years ago. We measured perceived stability of adolescent status in the family with the question, "Does your (mother/father) let you have more freedom to make your own decisions and to do what you want to do than (she/he) did two or three years ago?" A change in status is reflected by the responses, (1) "much more," and (2) "a little more," while no increase in independence is indicated by (3) "about the same," (4) "a little less," or (5) "much less."

Children in large families are more likely than those in small families to report no increase in independence over the last few years (Table 2). All eight relations between family size and perceived stability of parental control are in the expected direction. The relation between stability of control and family size is stronger among girls than among boys, and for paternal than for maternal control. The only social class difference appears among girls; the likelihood of no perceived relaxation of control increases more sharply with family size among lower-class girls. Whether their evaluation is valid or not, parental control during the transition from grade school to junior high is likely to be a source of conflict. Earlier research has indicated that reports of no increase in freedom were most common among youths who described their parents as autocratic or authoritarian, and were strongly associated with feelings of discontent and unhappiness.[27]

Similar results were obtained for parental explanations. We asked each

[26] Glen H. Elder, Jr., "Structural Variations in the Child Rearing Relationship," *Sociometry*, XXV (September, 1962), 252–256.

[27] Elder, "Family Structure and the Transmission of Values and Norms in the Process of Child Rearing," *op. cit.*, chap. vii.

child whether his parents explain the reason for rules that are not understood. *Infrequent* explanations are indicated by three responses—"never," "once in a while," and "sometimes," while "usually" and "yes, always" indicate *frequent* explanations. The relation between family size and reported frequency of parental explanation is relatively strong for both parents among middle-class boys and lower-class girls. Thus, the data on parental explanations provide some support for hypothesis 3: parental control is more likely as family size increases, especially among families of middle-class boys and lower-class girls. Of all youths in this study, middle-class girls are least likely to be exposed to this kind of regulation in each size of family.

For the most part, family size has relatively little effect on the training tactics of middle-class parents with respect to their daughters. Compared to boys in either social class and to their lower-class counterparts, middle-class girls are more likely to be included in decision making of personal relevance and to be given explanations of rules not thoroughly understood, whether or not they are members of large families. In contrast, lower-class parents appear to be particularly influenced by a large family in rearing their daughters. Though the probability of parental control and incommunicativeness is higher in the small lower-class family than in the middle-class family of comparable size, it tends to increase as family size increases. We will interpret these results more fully after we examine the effects of family size on techniques of discipline.

TECHNIQUES OF DISCIPLINE. Emphasis on external behavior control may also be manifested in the types of discipline parents employ. If this approach to the rearing of children is more common as family size increases, we would expect parents in large families to be more likely to use physical punishment, ridicule, shouts, reprimands, and nagging, and less likely to offer praise, approval, and encouragement.

Hypothesis 3, which states in part that as family size increases, parents tend to use physical techniques of discipline more and verbal methods such as reasoning less, is supported in 17 out of 24 comparisons (Table 3), and some of the differences are quite large. We find strongest support for the hypothesis in relation to the use of praise, etc., while negative verbal methods show few consistent effects of family size. Among families of lower-class girls, all six relationships are relatively strong, while very little support for the hypothesis appears among lower-class boys, and the middle-class families are intermediate.

Family-size effects are particularly strong with respect to the frequency with which lower-class girls report physical discipline. A comparison of large and small families shows that a girl in a large lower-class family is twice as likely to report being disciplined in this manner as is her counterpart in a small family. Parallel to previous comparisons, family size has much less effect on the reported physical disciplining of middle-class girls, particularly by fathers. As for boys, the effect of family size on the frequency of physical discipline by father is greatest among those in middle-class families.

Data on the use of scoldings and criticism show relatively little variation by family size except for small differences for middle-class boys and lower-class girls.

Verbal rewards of one kind or

TABLE 3. Techniques of Discipline, by Family Size, Sex, and Social Class of Seventh-Grade Youths[a]

Sex	Social class	Size of family	N	Physical discipline[b] used at least once in a while, per cent		Negative verbal[c] methods used at least once in a while, per cent		Symbolic rewards[d] used frequently or more often, per cent	
				Mother	Father	Mother	Father	Mother	Father
Boys	MC	1–2	130	43	31	32	26	43	43
		3	90	30	37	29	27	36	32
		4 or more	74	42	50	40	35	36	26
		dyx	—	−0.007	+0.121	+0.038	+0.053	−0.054	−0.121
	LC	1–2	134	40	45	41	37	37	28
		3	93	42	36	27	36	33	29
		4 or more	105	43	51	39	34	30	26
		dyx	—	+0.020	+0.041	−0.024	−0.023	−0.049	−0.006
Girls	MC	1–2	122	18	18	30	21	62	55
		3	98	26	16	26	25	63	56
		4 or more	67	27	23	26	20	43	43
		dyx	—	+0.070	+0.021	−0.029	−0.008	−0.099	−0.064
	LC	1–2	127	22	16	26	26	47	47
		3	107	38	31	36	35	47	37
		4 or more	114	44	38	33	31	32	24
		dyx	—	+0.199	+0.156	+0.052	+0.040	−0.104	−0.159

[a] Note that the predicted direction of the relation between family size and symbolic rewards is negative.

[b] Frequency of physical punishment was obtained by asking: "How often does your (mother/father) discipline or punish you by spanking, slapping, or striking you?" (1) very often, (2) frequently, (3) once in a while, (4) very seldom, and (5) never.

[c] Frequency of negative verbal methods was obtained by asking: "How often does your (mother/father) discipline or punish you by nagging, yelling, scolding, criticizing, or making fun of you?" (1) very often, (2) frequently, (3) once in a while, (4) very seldom, and (5) never.

[d] Frequency of symbolic reward was obtained by asking: "How often does your (mother/father) ever give you praise, encouragement, or approval for what you do?" (1) very often, (2) frequently, (3) once in a while, (4) very seldom, (5) never.

another are consistently reported less often as family size increases. This finding parallels the results obtained by several studies of the effects of size on the emotional dimension of group life.[28] Primary attachments are less possible as the group gains in size, while problems of regulation, control, and task achievement come to the fore. Evidence of a similar process in our

sample is seen in the tendency for various forms of external control to increase as family size increases.

Up to this point, our analysis has generally confirmed three of the six hypotheses presented earlier—one pertaining to the involvement of father in child rearing, and two concerning the prevalence of external control methods—and by controlling sex and social class, we specified conditions under which these expectations were

28 Hare, *op. cit.*, p. 227.

most likely to be confirmed. Note, however, that the relations observed between family size and the various dependent variables are surprisingly weak. We shall comment on this outcome in our concluding discussion. Let us briefly review some of the results obtained up to this point.

Fathers in large families are generally more apt to be active in child rearing than are fathers of fewer children. The major exceptions are lower-class fathers of boys. These fathers are slightly *less apt* to assume disciplinary responsibilities in the large family. Lower-class girls, on the other hand, are *more likely* to be disciplined by father in the large rather than small family.

While the father generally tends to take a more active role in child rearing as the demands of a large family require it, we have observed that as family size increases, middle-class parents of boys and lower-class parents of girls are more likely than other parents to be autocratic or authoritarian, to maintain a similar degree of control over the adolescent over a period of time, to explain their rules infrequently, to seldom express praise, encouragement and approval in response to good behavior, and to use physical discipline and negative verbal methods. In short, *parental behavior-control orientation is most strongly related to family size among middle-class families for boys and among lower-class families for girls.*

Since all indications are that lower-class girls experience more restraint, paternal direction, and punitive discipline than lower-class boys, in large as well as in small families, it seems likely that family size and frequency of external control are most strongly associated in families with only one daughter. In what follows, we examine briefly the extent to which sex composition influences paternal involvement and behavior-control strategy in large and small families.

SEX COMPOSITION EFFECTS

If the behavior of boys is perceived by peers, teachers and parents as different in many aspects from the behavior of girls, it is probable that parents rear a son in an "all male" family quite differently than they would if he had sisters. They no doubt tend to be more rigorous in setting behavior limits. Likewise, we suspect that one boy in an otherwise "all female" family tends to alter the way his parents rear his sisters. Since bossiness, assertiveness, hyperactivity, and quarrelsomeness appear to be characteristics more typical of boys than girls, it follows that if the activities of adolescents are to be kept under a reasonable degree of control, paternal involvement in child rearing should increase more or less directly as the proportion of male children in the family increases. The presence of a male child in the family should also induce a high rate of paternal participation because of the requirements of sex-role socialization. For these reasons, we should expect a father to take a more active role in rearing a child when he has one or more sons.

Here we are focusing on the social system requirements of the family in regard to paternal involvement. Obviously, fathers may take an active part in child rearing for many other reasons. Our expectations were formalized on hypotheses 2 and 4, summarized as follows: *Fathers are most likely to be active in rearing boys when the family is large and includes only male offspring, and in rearing girls when the family is large and includes at least one boy. An external control orientation is similarly most likely to prevail in families with male offspring.*

If father tends to assume a more active role in rearing children in families that include one or more boys, then we would expect fathers to be more likely to be perceived as making final decisions in regard to boys who have brothers and in regard to girls who have at least one brother. The utilization of external controls is most apt to be manifested in two ways (according to the data we have examined thus far): autocratic or authoritarian parental control and physical methods of discipline.

Possible variations in sex-composition effects by family size and social class are complex and thus difficult to predict. The results obtained up to this point suggest, however, that our predictions concerning girls and boys in mixed-sex families are most likely to hold for lower-class girls and middle-class boys in large families. For the purposes of this analysis, we shall assess sex composition effects only in families of two or more children.[29]

Our data on paternal involvement in rearing boys and girls in same-sex and mixed-sex families of large and small sizes support our predictions only in the large family. Boys from large families are somewhat more likely to perceive father as dominant in making decisions on behavior rules and discipline when they have siblings only of the same sex. For girls, pater-

nal involvement is slightly more common in mixed than in same-sex families. The percentage differences in these comparisons are extremely small and worth noting only as differences in the expected direction.

The data on family-size effects suggest that the involvement of middle-class fathers should respond differently than that of lower-class fathers to the number of sons and daughters in the family. With social class controlled, several meaningful variations in the previous results appear. First, we find that paternal dominance in deciding on rule and discipline policy for boys is practically unrelated to sex composition in the lower-class family but is strongly related to sex composition in large middle-class families. Differences in the small middle-class family are small and contrary to our predictions.

Second, comparing social class differences in paternal control, we find that middle-class girls are slightly more apt to perceive father as the authority figure when they have no brothers, while the reverse is true of lower-class girls. The difference is 5.8 per cent for the small family and −8.7 per cent for the large family. Thus, *lower-class girls in large families are even more likely to be under the direction of their fathers when they have brothers.* A corresponding set of comparisons on rule policy shows essentially no class variation.

In conclusion, we find that social class specifies the conditions under which differences in paternal activity in child rearing are greatest and least. As hypothesized, sex composition affects paternal involvement most for boys in large middle-class families and girls in large lower-class families. For the most part, the data on

---

[29] In Table 4 a positive percentage difference indicates that the percentage in the same-sex subgroup is larger than the percentage in the mixed-sex subgroup. Thus differences in the expected direction are positive for boys and negative for girls.

TABLE 4. Variations in Parental Role Patterns and Child-Rearing Practices by Sex Composition of Small and Large Families, as Reported by White Seventh-Grade Students[a]

Parental role patterns and child-rearing practices	Sex composition of family	Boys: positive differences are those in the predicted direction		Girls: negative differences are those in the predicted direction	
		Two-child family	Three or more child family	Two-child family	Three or more child family
		(127)	(78)	(67)	(49)
Father makes	Same sex	19.7	34.6	15.0	16.4
final decision		(106)	(268)	(103)	(330)
on rule policy	Mixed	21.6	25.4	13.6	19.1
	Per cent diff.	−1.9	+9.2	+1.4	−2.7
		(99)	(80)	(67)	(46)
Father makes	Same sex	26.3	32.5	16.4	15.3
final decision		(104)	(264)	(111)	(320)
on discipline policy	Mixed	30.8	26.1	11.7	17.2
	Per cent diff.	−4.5	+6.4	+4.7	+1.9
		(133)	(83)	(69)	(50)
Mother is autocratic	Same sex	29.4	38.4	20.3	18.1
or authoritarian		(106)	(267)	(103)	(309)
	Mixed	29.2	32.6	25.3	30.7
	Per cent diff.	+0.2	+5.0	−5.0	−12.6
		(132)	(85)	(58)	(50)
Father is autocratic	Same sex	38.7	42.5	37.8	22.1
or authoritarian		(108)	(269)	(108)	(314)
	Mixed	39.0	43.9	33.3	40.7
	Per cent diff.	−0.3	−1.4	+4.5	−18.6
		(100)	(86)	(73)	(50)
Mother uses physical	Same sex	36.0	34.9	32.9	24.0
punishment at least		(107)	(269)	(114)	(334)
once in a while	Mixed	36.4	29.7	25.4	32.0
	Per cent diff.	−0.4	+5.2	+7.5	−8.0
		(100)	(86)	(73)	(50)
Father uses physical	Same sex	39.0	46.5	12.3	14.0
punishment at least		(108)	(270)	(114)	(334)
once in a while	Mixed	37.0	42.6	17.5	29.9
	Per cent diff.	+2.0	+3.9	−5.2	−15.9

[a] One-child families have been excluded from this analysis.

parental roles in making discipline policy show less sharp and consistent differences than the results on parental roles in establishing rules of conduct. One possible explanation for this is that mother is more likely to discipline boys *and* girls of this age than is father.[30]

Known social class differences in

---

[30] Kohn and Carroll, *op. cit.*, pp. 372–392, and Bowerman and Elder, *op. cit.*

paternal influence and in the socialization of boys and girls are relevant to these results. Research has indicated that fathers are less likely to exert leadership in the lower-class family than in the middle-class family.[31] A recent study reports class differences in the control parents exercise over their daughters relative to their sons, with lower-class mothers and especially fathers tending to be more controlling and generally more restrictive than middle-class parents.[32]

Our data on behavior control support our predictions most consistently in the large family. Both mother and father are much more likely to be highly controlling of daughter's behavior if she has one or more brothers (see Table 4). No comparable differences exist for parent-son decision making.

Sex composition has the greatest effect on maternal control in the large lower-class family. For instance, boys with brothers rather than boys with sisters are more likely to report that mothers are dominant in the large rather than in the small family. (The family-size percentage differences are 3.8 for boys with sisters and 10.5 for boys with brothers.) Girls with at least one brother as against those with sisters are also more likely to describe mother as dominant in the large rather than small family. (The family-size percentage differences are 18.2 and −7.1.) In such a context behavior control needs are great, female respectability within the family is valued, and "obedience" values are salient.

31 Bowerman and Elder, *op. cit.*, and Robert O. Blood and Donald M. Wolfe, *Husbands and Wives* (New York: The Free Press of Glencoe, Inc., 1960).
32 Elder, "Structural Variations in the Child Rearing Relationship," *op. cit.*, p. 248.

Similar results appear for paternal control of girls with social class controlled, while no variations are evident among boys. The number of boys in the family seems to have little effect on the degree of control fathers exercise over their sons' behavior. In sharp contrast with this outcome is the −25.1 percentage difference between lower-class girls with autocratic or authoritarian fathers and no brothers, and those with brothers. *Lower-class girls who have brothers are more than twice as likely to report father as autocratic or authoritarian as are girls in "all girl" families.* Much smaller differences, though in the same direction, appear in similar comparisons of middle-class girls and their families.

Sex-composition effects on the use of physical punishment, by and large, follow a pattern similar to that described above. All of the percentage differences are in the direction predicted and are greater among girls than among boys. Large percentage differences on parental discipline appear only among youth from large lower-class families. Girls with brothers and no sisters are more likely than girls with sisters to report that father or mother occasionally uses physical punishment. Among boys, the strongest effect is likewise manifested in large families, but in those of middle-class status. Both findings are in the expected direction. Clearly, sex composition has little effect on parental role patterns in the small family, and this minimal effect is especially evident in policy-making pertaining to the rearing of boys.

Turning to the effects of sex composition on the use of *behavior control techniques,* the two outstanding results pertain to the large lower-class family. Without question, the strongest effect of sex composition is manifested in the rearing of girls in this type of family. Girls from large families with one or more brothers are much more likely than girls without brothers to report that their parents are autocratic or authoritarian in behavior control and use physical punishment at least "once in a while." Boys from "all male" families are much more apt than boys with sisters to perceive mother as dominant and to report that both mother and father occasionally use physical punishment.

DISCUSSION

Family-size and sex-composition effects on paternal involvement in child rearing and on child-rearing methods are heavily contingent on the sex of the child and on his family's class status. Generally, family size affects paternal involvement most strongly among middle-class boys and lower-class girls. Sex-composition effects are greatest in the rearing of girls in large lower-class families. As family size increases, these girls are more likely to perceive father as prominent in making child-rearing decisions, to see parents as less communicative and more controlling, and to report that parents use physical punishment occasionally and praise infrequently. These tendencies are stronger when there are one or more boys in the family. Family size and sex composition apparently have less effect on the rearing of middle-class girls.

Among middle-class boys, the likelihood of paternal dominance in child-rearing matters, paternal stability of control, incommunicativeness, and the father's occasional use of physical punishment increases as family size increases. The sex composition of the family appears to have little effect on

child rearing in these families regardless of the number of children. Although fathers are more likely to be dominant in large families, the number of boys in the family seems to make no difference in child rearing.

The picture changes markedly among lower-class boys and their families. Although behavior control techniques of an external nature are for the most part not affected by size of family, external control techniques are used more frequently in the large family *when all children in the family are boys.* In such cases, lower-class fathers are much more apt to control their sons' activities firmly as well as to punish them physically when they disobey.

A number of factors might account for the sharp variations in family-size and sex-composition effects by social class. First of all, middle- and lower-class parents have different goals. As Kohn and Carroll point out, "to middle-class parents, it is of primary importance that a child be able to decide for himself how to act, and that he have personal resources to act on these decisions—to working-class parents, on the other hand, it is of primary importance that the child act reputably, that he not transgress proper rules."[33] Our data lend plausibility to this description. Practices that encourage the child to understand and adopt rules of conduct and to develop the ability to govern himself accordingly are more commonly used by middle-class parents. Methods such as physical punishment, which inhibit self-reliance and which curtail disapproved behavior without facilitating the learning of parental values and norms, tend to be favored more by parents of lower-class status.

-----

[33] Kohn and Carroll, *op. cit.*, p. 388.

Another factor may be differential socialization of girls by middle- and lower-class parents. We suggest that lower-class parents are more concerned about maintaining their daughters' respectability than about delegating much responsibility to them. This orientation is reinforced and made more imperative in a large family composed of both boys and girls. A morality concern is less relevant to the masculine interests of boys and hence may partially explain why family size has a greater effect on the rearing of lower-class girls. The greater likelihood of paternal involvement in making policy decisions concerning girls in lower-class families may be similarly explained. Lower-class fathers with an interest in their daughters' welfare may be persuaded to assume a more active role in controlling their daughters' experiences in peer relationships.

In a recent study of the correlates of adolescent leadership and responsibility, Bronfenbrenner found that boys who received insufficient discipline and love in the home were least likely to receive high ratings on leadership and responsibility in school, while girls who were over-controlled in the home were unlikely to receive favorable ratings on either dimension.[34] This is particularly suggestive when we consider the attitudes and responsibilities of lower-class girls in large families. Since parental control and punitive discipline are most common in this type of family, these girls may feel rebellious toward adult

authority.[35] This type of home may, in fact, produce daughters who are anything but obedient and responsible. Greater paternal activity in handling disciplinary problems is another factor that may encourage this tendency; Bronfenbrenner notes that adolescents seemed to be more dependable when the same-sex parent was principal disciplinarian. Restrictive and punitive control on girls in large lower-class families may, when combined with their relatively small chances of social advancement by means of education beyond high school, encourage early departure from school, early entry into the labor market, and early marriage as available means of escape.

One of the more important results of this study is that neither family size nor sex composition explains even a moderately large portion of the variation in the perceived parental behaviors we have examined in this paper.[36] The effects they do have are

---

[34] Urie Bronfenbrenner, "Some Familial Antecedents of Responsibility and Leadership in Adolescents" in *Leadership and Interpersonal Behavior*, eds. Luigi Petrullo and Bernard Bass (New York: Holt, Rinehart, and Winston, 1961), pp. 239–271.

[35] Nye found that adolescents have better relations with their parents in small than in large families. Ivan Nye, "Adolescent-Parent Adjustment: Age, Sex, Sibling, Number, Broken Homes and Employed Mothers as Variables," *Marriage and Family Living*, XIV (November, 1952), 327–332.

[36] The relatively weak effects of family size are puzzling when we note that measured intelligence, achievement motivation, and educational aspirations of youth tend to be appreciably lower among youth from large families, particularly those of lower-class status. Earlier research on the educational and occupational goals of adolescents indicated that family-size effects on the goal-orientations of parents and adolescents are stronger, especially among lower-class families. See Glen H. Elder, Jr., *Adolescent Achievement and Mobility Aspirations* (Chapel Hill: Institute for Research in Social Science, 1962), chap. iii. For an analysis of the relation between family size and measured intelligence see John Nisbet, "Family Environment and Intelligence" in *Education, Economy, and Society*, eds. A. H.

highly contingent upon the sex and social class of the child.

It is quite possible that family size has its greatest effect on the rearing of preschool children. When a majority of the children in a large family are not of school age, the caretaking and training problems facing mother are most pressing. In their Boston study, Sears, Maccoby, and Levin explored some of the child-rearing correlates of birth order and family

size; however, their analysis was severely limited by the size of their sample.[37] Their data indicate that mothers were apt to be more restrictive in large families. Since a large number of children is generally more common among low-income families, further research on the effects of family size is likely to enhance our understanding of the culturally deprived child.

Halsey, Jean Floud, and C. Arnold Anderson (New York: The Free Press of Glencoe, Inc., 1961), pp. 273–287. On family size in relation to achievement motivation see Bernard C. Rosen, "Family Structure and Achievement Motivation," *American Sociological Review*, XXVI (August, 1961), 574–585.

[37] Robert R. Sears, Eleanor E. Maccoby, and Harry Levin, *Patterns of Child Rearing* (Evanston, Ill.: Row-Peterson, 1957), pp. 407–419.

5

Most social scientists would agree that religion is one of the more influential institutions in society and that religious affiliation is one of the more important social characteristics in differentiating human behavior. Indeed, several generations of sociologists have been interested in the influence of religion on a wide range of human behavior, including demographic behavior, and in very recent years the scientific study of religion has increased dramatically.

RELIGIOUS

INSTITUTIONS

The demographic perspective has numerous points of contact with religious factors. A current topic of interest is the relationship between religious beliefs and family size. Since there is an absence of religious information in the United States Census, data on fertility differentials by religious affiliation have been gathered by sample surveys. Such surveys have been numerous, not only in the United States but in other parts of the world and with people of widely varying religious beliefs.[1] The most notable United States fertility studies—the Indianapolis Study,[2] the Growth of the American Family Study,[3] and the

[1] United Nations, *The Determinants and Consequences of Population Trends* (New York: United Nations Department of Social Affairs, Population Division, 1953), pp. 71–97.

[2] Pascal K. Whelpton and Clyde V. Kiser (eds.), *Social and Psychological Factors Affecting Fertility* (New York: Milbank Memorial Fund), 5 vols., 1946–58.

[3] Ronald Freedman, Pascal K. Whelpton, and Arthur A. Campbell, *Family Planning, Sterility and Population Growth* (New York: McGraw-Hill Book Company, 1959); and Pascal K. Whelpton, Arthur A. Campbell, and John

Family Growth in Metropolitan America Study[4]—have provided consistent evidence of differences in family size for Protestants and Catholics. Indeed, the latter of these studies concluded that religion is now the most significant factor differentiating family size in the United States.

Numerous other studies have been concerned with age-sex and socioeconomic status differentials in religious participation. Two general foci of these studies have been differentials in church attendance and in religious group affiliation.[5] A clear-cut relationship has been reported between socioeconomic position and membership in the various Protestant denominations. Not only is the church one attends related to socioeconomic status factors, so is the frequency of attendance.

Other social demographers have investigated such problems as the effect of migration on church attendance and intermarriage patterns between members of different religious bodies. The emphasis on the scientific study of religion, with its concern for methodological and conceptual refinement, may open new vistas for research. However, the fullest applications of social demographic research methods on religious influence undoubtedly await the inclusion of a question on religion in the census.

The sociology of religion has numerous points of contact with studies in various disciplines. It is not surprising that this area of sociology has no unified theoretical system that can serve as a basis for deductive generalizations concerning the relationships between religion and the demographic system. There are, however, several general frames of reference, some of which are more amenable to social demographic research than others.

Perhaps the major frame of reference in the sociology of religion is functional analysis—a ubiquitous perspective that emphasizes certain integrative links and the manifest and latent connections between religion and other social structural units. Cultural comparisons of religion, including the famous Protestant Ethic study of Weber, con-

E. Patterson, *Fertility and Family Planning in the United States* (Princeton: Princeton University Press, 1966).

[4] Charles F. Westoff, Robert G. Potter, Jr., Philip C. Sagi, and Elliot G. Mishler, *Family Growth in Metropolitan America* (Princeton: Princeton University Press, 1961); and Charles F. Westoff, Robert G. Potter, Jr., and Philip C. Sagi, *The Third Child* (Princeton: Princeton University Press, 1963).

[5] See, for example, Harold A. Phelps and David Henderson, "Religion," chap. xiv in *Population in Its Human Aspects* (New York: Appleton-Century-Crofts, 1958); and the work by B. A. Lazerwitz, "A Comparison of Major United States Religious Groups," *Journal of the American Statistical Association*, LVI (1961), 568–579; "Some Factors Associated With Variations in Church Attendance," *Journal for the Scientific Study of Religion*, II (1962), 74–84; "National Data on Participation Rates Among Residential Belts in the United States," *American Sociological Review*, XXVII (1962), 691–696.

stitute another major frame of reference. Then there are numerous studies that trace the process of institutionalization in religion and the allied conceptual task of analyzing typologies of religious organizations. The church-sect continuum is one of the better known of these typologies. Other research falls under the general rubric of religion and society, including studies of religion and stratification, ethics and moral behavior, intergroup prejudice, and so forth. Although this list of frames of reference is by no means exhaustive nor the entries mutually exclusive, it does provide the social demographer with a working perspective of possible points of theoretical and conceptual overlap.[6]

The reading selections included here provide a cross-sectional view of different types of relationships between religion and the demographic system. The first two selections discuss different ways religion affects fertility. The first reading by Charles F. Westoff and Raymond H. Potvin focuses on a structural issue by investigating the consequences that attending a Catholic institution of higher education has upon the number of children desired by Catholic women. This line of inquiry develops from previous observations that Catholic women with higher education appear to want and have larger families than do Catholic women with less education. Is this an institutional effect or a consequence of selectivity for other factors such as individual religiosity? The results afford an insightful view of the reciprocal influence of institutional and socialization factors in relation to fertility attitude stability and change.

The second selection by Gordon F. De Jong focuses on a dimension of individual religiosity of Protestants as related to the fertility attitudes of residents of the Southern Appalachian region of the United States. While the well-known generalization of Protestant-Catholic-Jewish fertility differentials was inapplicable because of the very few members of the latter two groups living in Appalachia, the degree to which individuals held fundamentalistic religious beliefs was an important correlate of attitudes about fertility and family planning. It appears that the internalization of the tenets of fundamentalistic religion has consequences for demographic behavior.

In the third selection Poplin investigates the relationship between religion and mortality. Do members of various religious groups have different mortality rates which cannot be explained by traditional demographic factors? The findings suggest that this is the case, and the author discusses some possible reasons, based on the different belief systems.

Migration, sociologically conceived, involves the breaking of social

[6] For a more thorough discussion see Louis Schneider, "Problems in the Sociology of Religion," chap. xx in *Handbook of Modern Sociology*, ed. Robert E. L. Faris (Chicago: Rand McNally & Co., 1964).

and psychological ties in one community and reestablishing them in another. Factors in the reestablishment of religious group ties in a new community are a topic of interest not only to the clergy but to the social scientist. Involved are such theoretically significant issues as individual adjustment, group cohesion, and organizational structure. But what if an entire religious group, such as a sect, migrates from one place to another? What is the influence of migration on the ideal-typical model of a sect as a stationary, cohesive body of "intimate personal fellowship"? Hammond, in the reading "The Migrating Sect: An Illustration From Early Norwegian Immigration," finds that migrating sects are frequently disorganized and suggests some possible reasons for this finding. His research illustrates the relationship between demographic process and organizational structure.

Higher Education, Religion and Women's Family-Size Orientations*†

Charles F. Westoff and Raymond H. Potvin

This study began as an inquiry into the culture of Catholic women's colleges in an attempt to describe the formal and informal mechanisms through which such institutions promote or sustain a norm of high fertility. We had recently finished the

* Charles F. Westoff and Raymond H. Potvin, "Higher Education, Religion and Women's Family-Size Orientations," *American Sociological Review*, XXXI, 4 (August, 1966), 489–496.

† The data for this study were collected under a research grant of the Ford Foundation, supplemented by the Council on Human Relations of Princeton University. The analysis made use of computer facilities at Princeton supported in part by National Science Foundation Grant NSF-GP 579. Acknowledgments are due to many people who helped in the collection and processing of data, and especially to Boris Karashkevych who supervised the data-collection phase of the study. We are also grateful to the Population Council for the post-doctoral fellowship to R. H. Potvin, permitting him to spend a year at the Office of Population Research, Princeton University.

analysis of a second round of interviews in a longitudinal study of fertility[1] which had supported our earlier observations that Catholic women educated in Catholic colleges and universities are one of the highest fertility groups in contemporary America. The impression emerged of a numerically important and perhaps socially dominant group of middle- and upper-middle-class Catholics of predominantly Irish background, highly religious, educated in Catholic schools and colleges, who have internalized a family-size norms of four to six children, a goal moreover that reflects desired family size and deliberate planning rather than any simple consequence of birth control doctrine. Although not all of the components of this cluster were neatly disentangled, the experience of Catholic higher education seemed to have an independent and strong significance for fertility and family-size goals. In fact, Catholics educated in Catholic schools who did not attend college appeared to want and have smaller families, while a negative relationship between fertility and amount of education prevailed not only for non-Catholics but also for Catholics educated in nonsectarian schools and colleges.

The next question we posed was the familiar input-output problem of the connections between Catholic higher education and fertility. Is the effect produced by the experience of four years in an institution which presumably promotes values consistent with high fertility and reinforces such values through association with like-minded women? Or is it more a matter of selectivity for fertility values and

[1] Charles F. Westoff, Robert G. Potter, Jr., and Philip C. Sagi, *The Third Child* (Princeton: Princeton University Press, 1963).

other factors like religiosity which are related to fertility? Are women who are more religious attracted to such colleges and could the effect we were imputing to the college experience be mainly a reflection of the relationship between religiousness and fertility? Attempts to reconstruct the religiousness of early home environment in order to evaluate the selectivity hypothesis suggested that both factors operate independently. However, the problems of reconstructing such influence—in addition to the emergence of some new evidence compiled to explore this very hypothesis —led us to reconsider the entire research strategy. In brief, our conclusion was that the question of whether or not higher education has any effect on fertility values cannot be answered from existing evidence and is obviously a consideration logically prior to any inquiry into the mechanisms of the process.

HYPOTHESES

The object of the inquiry was now formulated to test, within the context of religious differentials, a series of hypotheses about the effects of different types of higher education on the family-size preference (number of children desired) of women of various religions.

The hypotheses about the effects of higher education were derived from the position that a nonsectarian education would have a secularizing influence on any religiously supported or conditioned fertility values, whereas education in church-related institutions would sustain a norm of high fertility when it already existed or would promote it when it did not. More specifically, higher education is conceived to open up areas of interests competitive with familial interests unless such experience is in a context which integrates education with reli-gio-familial values. The hypotheses called for the following particular outcomes:

(1) Protestant and Jewish women —and even more so women with no religious preference—in nonsectarian schools were expected to state pref-erences for the smallest families. Jews and Protestants were expected to show a slight decline in average number of children desired after four years of college.

(2) Protestant women in Protes-tant institutions were expected to prefer more children than those of the same religion in nonsectarian schools and to experience no reduction in family-size preferences during the college experience.

(3) Protestant women are also to be found in Catholic colleges; despite their numerical insignificance, they offer an interesting theoretical oppor-tunity to observe the "effects" of Catholic education on non-Catholics. These Protestant women were ex-pected to prefer fewer children than Catholic women but more than other Protestant women; their family-size preferences were expected to increase as a result of the Catholic college experience.

(4) Catholic women were expected to register preferences for the largest families, with education in Catholic institutions, and particularly colleges, associated directly with family-size preferences. Our primary interest is the effects of higher education—both nonsectarian and Catholic—on the fer-tility values of Catholic college women. We hypothesized that the number of children desired by Catholic women in nonsectarian colleges who attended

nonsectarian high schools would de-cline over the four years like those of women of other religions and that those who had attended Catholic high schools would experience the greater decline during nonsectarian college.[2] We expected further that the number of children desired by Catholic women in Catholic colleges who were gradu-ated from nonsectarian secondary schools would increase over the four years and that the number wanted by those who were graduated from Catholic high schools would remain unchanged. The theory is that the Catholic college would operate to maintain an established high-fertility norm and to promote such a norm if it does not exist, whereas the non-sectarian college would have only a slight effect on preferences already in line with the normative system of the society and a depressive effect on pref-erences which diverge in the direc-tion of high fertility.

SOME METHODOLOGICAL CONSIDERATIONS

A few words are necessary about the methodology of this study.[3] The classical procedure calls for a straight-forward longitudinal study, taking a sample of women in different types of colleges who would be surveyed at the beginning and at the end of their

---

[2] We also subdivided each of the four combinations of Catholic and non-sectarian high school and college into Catholic and nonsectarian elementary school attendance; since this distinction produced only slight modifications in expected directions, it is not employed herein.

[3] For a review of many of the methodological problems intrinsic to this type of research design, see Allen H. Barton, *Studying the Effects of College Education* (New Haven: Hazen Founda-tion, 1959).

college experience, and a control group of women of the same ages who were not in college. For practical reasons this design was compromised in two ways: we relied upon the synthetic cohort technique in comparing first- and fourth-year students,[4] and we did not employ a control group.

The absence of a control group is justified by the fact that our hypotheses call for different patterns of "change" in the two classes in different kinds of institutions. The absence of a control would be particularly problematic if, for example, we were testing a hypothesis that family-size preferences would decline as a consequence of higher education. The question would then arise of whether they declined among women generally between the ages of 17–18 and 21–22. But our hypotheses assert that the number of children desired will change in different ways depending upon religion, type of institution and, in some cases, type of secondary education. This system of comparative hypotheses reduces the importance of a control group.[5]

Another major problem complicating the assumption that today's seniors represent today's freshmen three years later is the fact of selective attrition. Students drop out of college for academic reasons, for marriage and for numerous other personal reasons that may result in the senior class being a quite biased residue of the freshman class.[6] Although such attrition is probably associated with actual fertility, it is not obvious that it selects women with initially different family-size preferences. The main safeguards against the possibility of drawing erroneous inferences because of this bias of selective attrition are to compare the results for the two classes in institutions of little attrition with the results for the rest, and in all institutions to make the comparisons within certain sub-groups (such as women whose mothers had attended college) where the attrition rates would be low. In the final analysis, only a longitudinal study will solve these problems.[7]

THE SAMPLE

Many studies of the effects of higher education on values have been

---

[4] Since it was impractical to contact the freshmen students early in the year, we do not actually have observations of their fertility values prior to *any* exposure to college. Our assumption is that fertility attitudes are not likely to change radically in the few months prior to our measurement.

[5] A more difficult problem and one that makes the synthetic cohort approach particularly vulnerable is its susceptibility to changes in the society at large which may affect first- and fourth-year students differently. This is an especially thorny question because of the recent well-publicized deliberations of the Catholic Church on the subject of family limitation. Our implicit assumption is that first- and fourth-year students are equally affected (if at all); in any event our hypotheses demand different outcomes in Catholic and non-sectarian colleges, relative to type of secondary school training. It is our impression, based on some admittedly

unsystematic group interviews with Catholic college women on several campuses that, although they were aware of the discussion in theological circles, they were doubtful that any radical change would be forthcoming.

[6] Transfer students at both first- and fourth-year levels—who pose a similar problem methodologically—were excluded from the analysis. However the freshman classes do contain varying proportions of students who will transfer later; this diminishes the purity of the comparison.

[7] The women who were freshmen when this study began will be seniors in 1966–67; we have collected their names in the hope of actually following them up.

based on nonrandom samples of institutions. We felt it was important to avoid this source of bias by drawing a probability sample of schools. The population we aimed to represent is defined generally as first-year and fourth-year women in four-year institutions of higher education throughout the United States. Partly in order to increase the homogeneity of the population and partly for theoretical reasons, various types of institutions were eliminated: junior colleges, theological schools, professional and art schools, colleges with enrollments under 300, and miscellaneous other categories.[8] The purified universe remaining comprises 683 schools which are best described as four-year universities, liberal arts colleges, and teacher's colleges, with full-time undergraduate female enrollments of at least 300 students.

Since our theoretical interests are concentrated on the connections of Catholic higher education with fertility values, we stratified the sample to secure an adequate number of such institutions. Catholic institutions admitting women comprise about 20 per cent of the total population of institutions. Since we wished to compare the "effects" on family-size preference of education in the two types of institutions we decided to draw an equal number of each, with the one modification of including some Protestant denominational schools.

The remaining forms of stratification imposed on the sample were

intended simply to insure the proper representation of characteristics such as women's colleges and co-educational schools,[9] region of the country, and number of women enrolled. The number of schools we aimed to include was 48; the number cooperating was 45. The final sample of institutions is described in Table 1.

Ideally we were interested in including all freshmen and senior women, but we compromised in two ways. Although we did maintain the ideal in all 24 Catholic institutions and in 13 of the 21 non-Catholic schools, the enrollments in the remaining 8 institutions were so large that we employed varying sampling ratios. The second compromise was unavoidable— some students are not motivated sufficiently to complete questionnaires. The sources of nonresponse are persons absent from school, as well as those present but disinterested. The individual response rate for all institutions and classes combined was 72 per cent which, after eliminating ineligible returns, provided us with nearly 15,000 persons in the sample

TABLE 1. Number of Institutions in the Sample by Type

Nonsectarian, co-educational	15
Nonsectarian, women only	3
Protestant, co-educational	3
Catholic, co-educational	8
Catholic, women only	16
Total	45

---

[8] The other categories include institutions for men only, technical and semiprofessional schools, and Negro colleges. A Negro Catholic college had been included in the Catholic sample, and a Negro nonsectarian school for comparative purposes; since these are very small samples we have excluded them from the present report.

[9] Among Catholic schools, 72 per cent of women are enrolled in women's institutions while among non-Catholic schools only 8 per cent are in women's colleges. In itself this contrast suggests differences in the two types of educational experience.

TABLE 2. Distribution of Colleges by Average Number of Children Desired by First- and Fourth-Year Women

Average number of children desired	Non-Catholic colleges[1]		Catholic colleges	
	First-year	Fourth-year	First-year	Fourth-year
3.0–3.4	—	6	—	—
3.5–3.9	19	13	—	—
4.0–4.4	—	1	—	—
4.5–4.9	2	1	1	5
5.0–5.4	—	—	7	7
5.5–5.9	—	—	13	11
6.0–6.4	—	—	3	1
Total	21	21	24	24

[1] Includes 18 nonsectarian and 3 Protestant schools.

who completed self-administered questionnaires.[10]

In some institutions these questionnaires were administered in a classroom or auditorium either by us or by an interested faculty member or person in the administration. In others, primarily the large schools, they were mailed to the students to be returned to us. In all instances strict confidentiality of response was stressed.

RESULTS

Analysis of the number of children desired by women in each of the 45 institutions revealed little difference between small and large schools, or between co-educational and women's colleges, but a sharp difference between women in nonsectarian and Catholic institutions. Table 2 presents

the distribution of the means for Catholic and nonsectarian (including the three Protestant) colleges. There is a striking contrast between the two categories and considerable homogeneity within each category. One of the nonsectarian institutions with average family-size preferences overlapping the distribution of Catholic schools is composed predominantly of Mormon students; they resemble the Catholics in many ways.[11]

This analysis does not distinguish the religion of the women in these institutions; although women in the Catholic schools belong mainly to that religion, the religious composition of the nonsectarian schools is heterogeneous. The point of the analysis is primarily to examine the homogeneity of the schools prior to grouping certain types together.

Our central hypotheses relate to the differences expected in family-size preferences among women of various religious groups and between first- and fourth-year students of each major religious preference in the different types of educational institutions. Since the synthetic cohort technique is particularly vulnerable to interpretive problems stemming from selective attrition, we compared freshman-senior differentials in average number of children desired for each of the 45 schools individually. No difference in pattern was observed within categories between institutions with high or low rates of attrition. We further controlled for education of mother on the assumption that less attrition exists for women with college-educated mothers. Again no dif-

---

10 The response rates varied considerably among the nonsectarian schools; Catholic schools contributed the highest response rates probably because they are smaller and more centrally organized.

---

11 The data on Mormons are not included in this paper because they are limited to one nonsectarian institution and no data are available for Mormons in sectarian institutions.

ference in pattern was observed.[12]

Given the nature of our research design and the complicating factor of selective entrance into different types of institutions, our analysis will present three basic comparisons: (1) among the various religious categories; (2) between freshmen and seniors for each religious category in each type of institution; and (3) between freshmen of the same religious preference in different types of institutions to assess the differential selectivity of high and low fertility oriented women.

The tabulations presented in Table 3 confirm the hypothesized rank order of religion and family-size preference. Women with no religious preference and Protestant and Jewish women in nonsectarian schools prefer the "smallest" families, followed by Protestant women in Protestant and Catholic schools who express preferences for slightly larger families as first-year students but not as seniors. Catholic women who have had some Catholic education, at either secondary or college level, want larger families; the highest potential fertility (5.6 children) is indicated by the Catholic women who have attended both Catholic high schools and colleges.[13] Almost two-thirds of the first-year students in this group say they would like to have five or more children and ten per cent say they want nine or more children.

Such responses cannot be disregarded as the immature sentiments of late adolescents because the proportion wanting these large families remains quite high among seniors—who are in their early twenties. Admittedly unmarried women just graduating from college have not yet faced the realistic demands of raising a family; perhaps they will modify such attitudes after the arrival of the first few children. Nevertheless, evidence from other studies[14] shows that married Catholic women with similar Catholic education who already have children still want and have considerably larger families than other Catholic women.

Quite aside from Catholics, the entire pattern of variations in family-size preference of college women of different religions in the present study is quite consistent with all we know about group variations in actual fertility among married women. From comparisons with other studies, it appears that the average number of children desired by women in the present sample is no more than 20 per cent above what it would be after some 5 to 10 years of marriage, during which time it would be affected by reactions to childbearing and children, husband's attitudes, economic considerations, and the like.

---

[12] The data are presented in detail in the parent study. See Westoff and Potvin, *op. cit.*

[13] About 95 per cent of this group also attended a Catholic elementary school.

[14] See Charles F. Westoff, *et al., Family Growth in Metropolitan America* (Princeton: Princeton University Press, 1961), and *The Third Child, op. cit.* See also Pascal K. Whelpton, Arthur A. Campbell, and John E. Patterson, *Fertility and Family Planning in the United States* (Princeton: Princeton University Press, 1966), pp. 87, 99; Pascal K. Whelpton and Patience Lauriat, "College Study Report—1956," *Population Bulletin*, XII (1956); Ronald Freedman, Lolagene C. Coombs, and Larry Bumpass, "Stability and Change in Expectations About Family Size: A Longitudinal Study," *Demography*, II (1965), 250–275. An investigation of alumnae of a Catholic college has demonstrated the persistence of high fertility values over several decades (Philip C. Sagi and Walter F. Zenner, "Family Size Among Alumnae of a Catholic Women's College," paper presented at the 1965 meetings of the Population Association of America).

TABLE 3. Number of Children Desired by Religion, Class Year, and Type of College

Religion of woman	Type of college[a]	Class year	Less than 2	2	3	4	5	6 or more	Total	Mean	Standard deviation	Number of women
None	NS	Total	9	24	32	22	7	6	100	3.2	1.7	423
		1	11	24	32	18	8	8	100	3.2	1.8	226
		4	5	26	32	27	7	3	100	3.1	1.3	197
Jewish	NS	Total	1	18	41	30	6	3	100	3.4	1.2	864
		1	1	18	40	30	7	4	100	3.4	1.2	529
		4	2	18	43	31	5	2	100	3.2	0.9	335
Protestant	NS	Total	1	18	35	34	6	6	100	3.5	1.3	5518
		1	1	17	34	34	7	7	100	3.5	1.3	3682
		4	1	19	36	33	5	5	100	3.4	1.1	1836
Protestant	P	Total	1	14	31	39	8	7	100	3.7	1.4	814
		1	1	14	27	40	9	9	100	3.8	1.5	613
		4	1	13	43	34	5	4	100	3.4	1.0	201
Protestant	C	Total	1	17	34	32	6	9	100	3.6	1.4	102
		1	1	14	35	32	7	10	100	3.7	1.5	81
		4	—	24	33	33	5	5	100	3.3	1.0	21
Catholic:												
NSHS	NS	Total	1	10	22	35	13	19	100	4.2	1.7	960
		1	2	11	23	32	14	19	100	4.2	1.7	590
		4	1	10	22	41	11	15	100	4.1	1.4	370
NSHS	C	Total	1	5	12	34	15	32	100	4.9	2.0	1193
		1	1	6	13	32	15	33	100	4.9	2.1	772
		4	—	4	11	38	16	32	100	4.9	1.9	421
CHS	NS	Total	—	4	14	34	15	32	100	5.0	2.0	396
		1	—	3	12	33	17	35	100	5.2	2.0	258
		4	1	6	20	38	13	22	100	4.3	1.4	138
CHS	C	Total	—	2	7	26	18	46	100	5.6	2.2	4154
		1	—	2	7	25	18	47	100	5.7	2.2	2670
		4	—	2	7	28	20	43	100	5.4	1.9	1484

[a] NS—nonsectarian; C—Catholic; P—Protestant; HS—high school.

Our present concern, however, is whether higher education has the effects on family-size preference that we have hypothesized. Among women with no religious preference and among Protestant and Jewish women, in nonsectarian institutions, there is a slight "drop" of 0.1 and 0.2 in the average number of children desired. Although the differences are statistically significant between the classes for Jews and Protestants,[15] they are very slight and could be attributed to differences in age. Although this decrease is predicted by our theory, its magnitude is too small to permit inferring any college influence.

[15] According to the critical ratio test, the differences are significant at the 0.05 level.

Contrary to our hypothesis, the Protestant groups in Protestant and Catholic colleges also "experience" declines in their average family-size preference.[16] The declines are larger than for the preceding group perhaps because these students enter college with slightly higher preferences. For Protestants the experience of a denominational college does not appear to differ from that of a nonsectarian one.

The association of higher education with the family-size preferences of Catholic women presents a more complex picture. As expected, women in nonsectarian colleges "experience" a decline in the number of children desired. However the 0.1 differential for women from nonsectarian high schools is not statistically significant and only the "change" (of 0.9) among the graduates of Catholic high schools is impressive; this supports our hypothesis about the secularizing effect of a nonsectarian college on women who enter with high-fertility orientations. Nonetheless this secularizing effect goes just so far, bringing those women in line with their religious counterparts who attended nonsectarian high schools but not with the non-Catholic students. Although there is some evidence of selectivity, the "change" is nevertheless substantial in comparison with the other groups.

We had also expected a Catholic college education to promote attitudes favorable to high fertility among women from nonsectarian high schools and to maintain these attitudes among women from Catholic high schools. The first hypothesis is certainly refuted—no change appears in our data. In the case of the Catholic col-lege students from Catholic high schools the hypothesis is also refuted, since there is a statistically significant "decline" (of 0.3) in the number of children desired.[17] Again the magnitude of this difference is so slight that it might be due to the age factor rather than to the college itself. Furthermore, seniors still express preferences for 5.4 children (more than any other group) and it appears more realistic to conclude that high-fertility orientations are maintained and that the Catholic college may counteract influences that would otherwise prevail. A more conservative interpretation is that the college has no effect at all. However, the apparent effect of a nonsectarian college experi-ence on the family-size preferences of Catholic high school graduates encour-ages the interpretation that the Catho-lic college maintains the initial values and counteracts potentially competing influences.

The evidence in Table 3 also shows that selectivity is a more important factor than the college experience it-self in explaining the family-size pref-erence of Catholics in different types of colleges. Freshmen from non-sectarian high schools who enrolled in nonsectarian colleges desire 0.7 fewer children than those who enrolled in Catholic colleges; and for freshmen from Catholic high schools the com-parable differential is 0.6. These sta-tistically significant differences are larger than any freshmen-senior dif-ferential except that for women from Catholic high schools who are now in nonsectarian institutions. Further-more, except for the case just men-tioned, these differentials due to selec-tivity are not eliminated by a com-mon college experience. Although the common experience appears to exert

---

[16] The difference is significant at the 0.01 level for Protestants in Protestant colleges.

[17] $p < 0.01$.

little influence on the average number of children desired, it may have an effect on the extent of consensus. In each of the 9 comparisons in Table 3, the variance of the distribution among seniors is less than among freshmen. Whether this is due to selective attrition or to the shared experiences over the college years can only be determined conclusively by a longitudinal study.

SUMMARY AND CONCLUSIONS

In effect some of our hypotheses are sustained and others are not. Our expectations about religious differences are largely confirmed. In connection with education, seniors reporting no religion, Jews, Protestants, and Catholics from nonsectarian high schools in nonsectarian colleges desire slightly fewer children than freshmen but this is as likely to be a consequence of aging as of the college experience itself. Protestants in Protestant and Catholic colleges show a somewhat larger but not substantial decline. Nevertheless it is sufficient to bring them in line with their religious counterparts in nonsectarian colleges. The most pronounced change is experienced by Catholic women from Catholic high schools who enrolled in a nonsectarian college; this supports the hypothesis that this type of institution exercises a definite secularizing effect upon Catholic women who arrive with high-fertility attitudes. Our data for women in Catholic colleges suggest that, in spite of a slight decline for women from Catholic high schools, the over-all effect (if any) of that type of institution is to maintain the high family-size preferences of its students. In any

case, our data from nearly 15,000 first- and fourth-year women in a probability sample of 45 institutions of higher education throughout the country suggest that selectivity rather than the college experience itself is the main explanation of differentials in family-size preference among college women.

In order to reduce the vulnerability of our inferences to the unknown biases of selective attrition, and to increase general confidence in the assumption that these comparisons are not distorted by differences between the college classes in social factors relevant to fertility, we imposed an elaborate set of statistical controls[18] in the comparisons. This detailed analysis in no way modifies our conclusions. Despite the assumptions and theories connecting family-size and family-planning attitudes with higher education, our evidence indicates that, with the one noted exception, American women in their fourth year of college prefer only slightly fewer children on the average than women in their first year. This could be as much a function of maturation as of the college experience. Although the methodological limitations of the present study may qualify the conclusions, it appears then that the well-known generalization of Jacob[19] (from a review of numerous studies) that higher education has little effect on a whole range of basic

---

[18] In addition to the religion of the student and the type of college (and high school for Catholics) the distribution of number of children desired in each class was compared within each of the following controls: education of parents, occupational class of father, nationality background of parents, religion and religiousness of parents and friends, the woman's religious practices and her religious self-image.

[19] Philip E. Jacob, *Changing Values in College* (New York: Harper & Row, Publishers, 1957).

values covering social, political, economic, intellectual, and religious areas should be extended to include values in the area of family size.

We began this study primarily to determine whether the higher fertility of Catholic women educated in Catholic colleges is in any sense a consequence of that education conceived as both formal and informal processes. Again, with the same methodological qualifications, the answer seems to be negative; the explanation of the difference appears to be mainly the selectivity of women with higher fertility orientations into Catholic colleges. The nature of this selectivity, analyzed elsewhere,[20] is primarily but not exclusively religiousness.

Based partly on the implications of the findings of this study as well as previous work in this area, we have developed a theory of the origins and stability of family-size ideals. In brief, it asserts that a normative range of family size (e.g., two to four children) is internalized by the girl during the period of late childhood and early adolescence (say 8 to 13) in much the same way as a child learns other values and styles of interaction. Of particular relevance in the formulation of these family-size norms is the number of siblings within the girl's own family, within the families of her playmates, and within other reference groups to which she is exposed.[21] Determinants of this early

context in which socialization to the norms of family size takes place are religious, ethnic and class memberships; these vary in the extent to which they carry direct substantive significance for the numerical values of the normative range. Certain distinct types such as the Irish-Catholic middle-class subculture fall in this category. Although other ethnic subcultures may also carry overtones for fertility values, perhaps the majority of the present population has no group identification imposing distinctive subcultural prescriptions on family-size norms; for them there is simply a fairly elastic range of two to four children defined as normative in the national culture.[22]

The stability of the normative range formulated in childhood and thus its predictability for later years depends on the extent of continuity or consistency of the individual's reference groups. Discontinuities implied by second-generation status, rural-urban migration, social mobility (or exposure to different types of education for Catholics), and other possible changes including those posed by marriage are all theoretically relevant for the stability of the normative range.

These speculations are all in some respects testable; some have been corroborated in our larger study. Nevertheless the need for a longitudinal study remains abundantly clear.

---

[20] Westoff and Potvin, *op. cit.*

[21] See Otis Dudley Duncan, *et al.*, "Marital Fertility and Size of Family of Orientation," *Demography*, II (1965), 508–515.

[22] See Ronald Freedman, "Social Values About Family Size in the United States," *Population Conference* (Vienna: International Union for the Scientific Study of Population, 1959), pp. 173–183.

Religious Fundamentalism, Socio-Economic Status, and Fertility Attitudes in the Southern Appalachians

Gordon F. De Jong*

RESUMEN

One of the notable demographic phenomena of our lifetime has been the postwar upsurge in the national birth rate. Although the consequences of this trend are many, certainly one has been the re-emphasis of fertility as the key variable in understanding and predicting national population change. This emphasis spotlights the demographer's interest in fertility research.

An excellent point of departure for fertility research is the analytical framework developed by Davis and Blake.[1] Among other things, this framework points up the conclusive importance of such "intermediate variables" as factors affecting exposure to intercourse and conception. However, with increasing proportions of the population effectively controlling the size of their families, investigations of peoples' attitudes and values concerning fertility take on added salience. This study focuses on factors which differentiate attitudes

about fertility in the predominantly rural Southern Appalachian Mountain Region.[2]

BACKGROUND

Several studies, notably the Indianapolis Study,[3] the Growth of American Families Study,[4] and the Prince-

---

* Gordon F. De Jong, "Religious Fundamentalism, Socio-Economic Status, and Fertility Attitudes in the Southern Appalachians," *Demography*, II (1965), 540–548.

[1] Kingsley Davis and Judith Blake, "Social Structure and Fertility: An Analytic Framework," *Economic Development and Cultural Change*, IV (April, 1956), 211–235.

[2] Interest in the Southern Appalachians stems, in large measure, from a population-economy imbalance which has been a topic of academic as well as administrative concern. In no small measure this problem relates to the fact that the people of the Southern Appalachians have had one of the highest reproduction rates of any major region of the United States during the present century. As recently as 1940, Appalachian fertility rates were 50–60 per cent higher than fertility rates for the nation. By 1960, however, the birth rates for the region as a whole had declined to national rates, although there was considerable difference between rural and urban fertility patterns.

While fertility in metropolitan America has received considerable attention, few studies have focused on fertility attitudes in predominantly rural areas, especially a "problem" area such as the Southern Appalachians.

[3] Pascal K. Whelpton and Clyde V. Kiser (eds.), *Social and Psychological Factors Affecting Fertility*, vols. I–V (New York: Milbank Memorial Fund, 1946–58).

[4] Ronald Freedman, Pascal K. Whelpton, and Arthur A. Campbell, *Family Planning, Sterility and Population Growth* (New York: McGraw-Hill Book Company, 1959).

ton Study,[5] have provided systematic analyses of factors differentiating fertility—both actual fertility and attitudes related to fertility. From these and other research efforts has emerged a general mosaic of factors which reappear with regularity.[6] Two of these factors are religion and socioeconomic status.[7]

The general theoretical relationships between religion, socioeconomic status, and fertility are well known. For religion, Catholics tend to have high fertility norms, Jews at the other extreme, and Protestants in an intermediate position. However, the Protestant-Jewish fertility differences are largely a function of socioeconomic status.[8] High socioeconomic status usually has been associated with low fertility norms and high rationality in family planning, while low socioeconomic status has been associated with high fertility norms and low rationality in family planning.

In applying this theoretical perspective to the Southern Appalachians, one immediately encounters a problem. There are very few Catholics or Jews in the Appalachians. In fact,

less than 3 per cent of a recent sample survey identified with these two religious groups.[9] In this case the fertility patterns of Catholics and Jews are obviously an inapplicable theoretical basis for research. Is religion, then, a significant factor in differentiating fertility attitudes and values of Appalachian residents, and, if so, what dimension of religious orientation? Further, if a religious dimension is important, how will it relate to fertility attitudes when other variables such as socioeconomic status are taken into account? This research provides some basis for answering these questions.

Following the general Weberian thesis, differing religious orientations would be expected to have an effect on fertility.[10] And a 1957 U.S. Bureau of the Census national survey indicated rather striking fertility differences for women of various Protestant denominations.[11] In fact, the fertility rate for Baptists was higher than that for Catholics. However, fertility issues are not so much a matter of church doctrine in Protestant denominations as they are in the Catholic church. Accordingly, fer-

[5] Charles F. Westoff, Robert G. Potter, Jr., Philip C. Sagi, and Elliot G. Mishler, *Family Growth in Metropolitan America* (Princeton: Princeton University Press, 1961).

[6] For an excellent summary of fertility research including an extensive bibliography, see "The Sociology of Human Fertility," *Current Sociology*, vols. X and XI, 1961–62.

[7] Ronald Freedman, "American Studies of Family Planning and Fertility: A Review of Major Trends and Issues," in *Research in Family Planning*, ed. Clyde V. Kiser (Princeton: Princeton University Press, 1962), pp. 211–227.

[8] Ronald Freedman, Pascal K. Whelpton, and John W. Smit, "Socioeconomic Factors in Religious Differentials in Fertility," *American Sociological Review*, XXVI (August, 1961), 608–614.

[9] The data presented were obtained from a 1958 sample survey of the Southern Appalachian Region financed by a grant from the Ford Foundation.

[10] While Weber's primary analysis concerned the impact of religious institutions on economic institutions, he clearly noted the influence of religion on other major institutions of society. Cf. Max Weber, *The Protestant Ethic and the Spirit of Capitalism*, trans. Talcott Parsons (New York: Charles Scribner's Sons, 1958), pp. 13–17, 168–249. Also see Gerhard Lenski, *The Religious Factor* (Garden City, N.Y.: Doubleday & Company, Inc., 1963), pp. 2–12.

[11] United States Bureau of the Census, *Statistical Abstract of the United States, 1958* (Washington: Government Printing Office, 1958), Table 40, based on a survey in March, 1957.

tility differences among Protestant denominations are not explainable primarily in terms of church doctrine as in Protestant-Catholic fertility differences. It would appear important, then, to relate fertility correlates of Protestants to a dimension of religious orientation rather than denominational affiliation.[12]

APPROACH TO THE PROBLEM

The people of the Southern Appalachians traditionally have been characterized as having fundamentalistic religious beliefs. Although this popular image may have been exaggerated from time to time, a recent study found that it was still an important aspect of the attitude and value structure of many Appalachian residents.[13] From this it was reasoned that, if any dimension of Protestant religious orientation was significantly related to

fertility attitudes, it would be the fundamentalism dimension.

The logic of this relationship stems from consequences of fundamentalistic religious beliefs. A salient feature of fundamentalism is the literal interpretation of the Bible. Perhaps the best-known biblical references to fertility emphasize the command to "be fruitful and multiply." The fundamentalist is also likely to act on the assumption that life proceeds according to the will of God. The attempt to regulate conception interferes with God's plan, and this is viewed with condemnation as a secular trend.[14] Hypothetically, then, a very fundamentalist religious orientation would be associated with attitudinal responses which support high fertility, while a nonfundamentalist religious orientation would be associated with attitudinal responses which support low fertility.[15]

SOURCE OF DATA AND PROCEDURE

The data for this study were collected as part of a broad survey of social and economic characteristics and attitudes of Southern Appalachian Mountain residents which was conducted in 1958.[16] The survey uni-

---

[12] To date, attempts to relate fertility norms and behavior to various dimensions of Protestant religious orientation have not proved very successful. Freedman and Whelpton, for example, reported that indications of religious interest and activity were not of great importance in explaining fertility variation. Likewise, the analysis by Westoff and associates indicated minimal variation associated with items concerning religious activities and "religiosity" for Protestants. Cf. Ronald Freedman and Pascal K. Whelpton, "Fertility Planning and Fertility Rates by Religious Interest and Denomination," *Milbank Memorial Fund Quarterly,* XVIII (July, 1950), 294–343, and Westoff, Potter, Sagi, and Mishler, *op. cit.,* pp. 194–221 and 320–336.

[13] Thomas R. Ford, "The Passing of Provincialism," in *The Southern Appalachian Region: A Survey,* ed. Thomas R. Ford (Lexington: University of Kentucky Press, 1962), pp. 9–34; Thomas R. Ford, "Status, Residence, and Fundamentalistic Religious Beliefs in the Southern Appalachians," *Social Forces,* XXXIX (October, 1960), 41–49.

[14] Viewing birth control as a secular trend is, of course, not a new idea. See, for example, Frederick L. Hoffman, "The Decline in the Birth Rate," *North American Review,* CLXXXIX (May, 1909), 677–687, and Frederick S. Crum, "The Decadence of Native American Stock," *American Statistical Association Journal,* XIV (September, 1914), 215–222.

[15] For evidence for the relationship between attitudes about fertility and actual fertility patterns, see, for example, the matched sample data in Freedman, Whelpton, and Smit, *op. cit.,* p. 610.

[16] For a full description of the area included in the survey and sample procedure, see Gordon F. De Jong, *Human Fertility in the Southern Appalachian*

verse was defined as the households located in one hundred ninety counties of a region containing parts of seven states: Alabama, Georgia, Kentucky, North Carolina, Tennessee, Virgina, and West Virginia. A stratified two-stage area sample was used in the selection of respondent households, the strata representing standard metropolitan areas, nonmetropolitan urban places, and rural areas. Schedules were administered through personal interview to some 1,466 respondents, of whom 49 per cent were from rural, 19 per cent from urban, and 32 per cent from metropolitan area households. Not included in the present analysis were Catholic, Jewish, and nonwhite responses which constituted less than 7 per cent of the total sample.[17]

To provide a measure of fundamentalist orientation, responses to a number of relevant belief and attitude questions were analyzed for scalability.[18] Dichotomized responses to six questionnaire items yielded a Guttman scale with a coefficient of reproducibility of 0.92. The scale included six items: (1) attitude toward gambling, (2) attitude toward drinking, (3) view on religious doctrine (ultimate reliance upon biblical authority), (4) view on the importance of "calling" for the ministry, (5) attitude toward card playing, and (6) view

on the coming of the end of the world. Individual scale scores were grouped into four categories on the basis of common response patterns.

Socioeconomic status was measured by an index composed of income, occupation, education, household equipment, and the respondent's perception of social class identification. Four groupings were made, from lower to upper status, on the basis of the distribution of scores.[19]

Measures of fertility attitudes included questions on the ideal family size for the average, the economically "well-off," and the economically "not well-off" young couple beginning married life today. Additional questions concerned birth control practices for married people and the ideal age of marriage for a girl and a boy.

FINDINGS

From Table 1 it is clear that fertility attitudes of Southern Appalachian respondents are markedly differentiated by religious fundamentalism as well as by socioeconomic status. In all cases differences are in the hypothesized direction. That is, a very (highly) fundamentalist religious orientation is associated with attitudinal responses which support high fertility, while high socioeconomic status is associated with attitudinal responses which support low fertility. For instance, the mean ideal family size for the average young couple today was 3.40 for very fundamental respondents compared with 2.83 for not very fundamental respondents. Similarly, low socioeconomic status respondents reported a mean ideal of 3.47 children compared with 2.79 for

Region: Some Demographic and Sociological Aspects (unpublished Ph.D. dissertation, University of Kentucky, 1963).

[17] There were fifty-four nonwhites, forty-one Catholics and Jews, and thirty-seven others for whom information was not complete.

[18] A detailed description of the development of the scale is provided in Ralph E. Lamar, *Fundamentalism and Selected Social Factors in the Southern Appalachian Region* (unpublished Master's thesis, University of Kentucky, 1962), pp. 28–30, 88–97.

[19] Ford, "Status, Residence, and Fundamentalistic Religious Beliefs...," *op. cit.*

respondents with high socioeconomic status.

Some rather interesting points can be noted about the various attitudinal items. As would be expected, the mean number of children considered ideal for the economically well-off couple was greater than for the not well-off couple in all religious fundamentalism and socioeconomic status categories. But, for each question, a consistent differential was noted between successive status and fundamentalism categories. Interestingly, the differentials were less marked under the posited adverse economic condition (where a young couple was not well-off). This was the only question which yielded more than one statistically insignificant difference between pairs of means, although even here the differences were in the predicted direction.

It might be observed in passing that, by national standards, a majority of Appalachian families would not be considered well-off economically. Nevertheless, fertility is still above the national average in many areas,[20] even though the statements about ideal family size for a not well-off couple were rather low (mean of 1.74). This incongruity may indicate the difference between a generalized fertility ideal and actual fertility. But it may also indicate possible national and Appalachian differences in the conception of what constitutes an economically not well-off couple.

Another line of questioning concerned attitudes about ideal age of marriage. These responses were of interest not only because age of mar-

riage establishes general limits to childbearing but also because early marriages may be indicative of dispositions toward large families.[21] An approximate two-year differential was observed between the mean ideal age of marriage for a boy and girl for all socioeconomic status and religious fundamentalism categories. However, of more interest here is the marked differential between successive status and fundamentalism categories.

Responses to the question on birth control practices for married people again show a striking differential by socioeconomic status and religious fundamentalism categories. Nearly 42 per cent of the respondents in very fundamental and low socioeconomic status categories compared with only 4 per cent in the not very fundamental and high socioeconomic status categories felt that birth control practices for married people were "always wrong." For the total sample, a surprising 25.4 per cent of the respondents expressed unqualified disapproval of birth control practices—surprising, that is, when compared with Freedman's national sample where only 1 per cent of Protestants and 13 per cent of Catholics express unqualified disapproval.[22] In many ways, the fundamental religious beliefs held by a sizable proportion of Protestant Appalachian respondents have consequences for fertility attitude differential which are quite like the perspective of Catholics. While the difference between ideal and actual fertility is unknown, the fairly sizable percentage of respondents expressing reservation about birth control practices sheds light on the high fertility

---

[20] Thomas R. Ford and Gordon F. De Jong, "The Decline of Fertility in the Southern Appalachian Mountain Region," *Social Forces*, XLIII (October, 1963), 89–96.

[21] Westoff, Potter, Sagi, and Mishler, *op. cit.*, p. 284.
[22] Freedman, Whelpton, and Smit, *op. cit.*, p. 610.

TABLE 1. Selected Fertility Attitudes of Southern Appalachian Region Respondents by Religious Fundamentalism and Socioeconomic Status

Fertility attitudes	All respondents	Religious fundamentalism				Socioeconomic status			
		Very	Consider-ably	Some-what	Not very	Lower	Lower middle	Upper middle	Upper
Number of cases	1334	249	565	313	207	382	457	332	163
Mean ideal number of children for average young couple today	3.15	3.40	3.24	3.03	2.83	3.47	3.07*	3.07	2.79
Mean ideal number of children for "well-off" young couple today	4.55	4.93	4.70	4.33	4.03	5.04	4.47*	4.36	4.02
Mean ideal number of children for "not well-off" young couple today	1.74	1.96*	1.80	1.61*	1.51	2.09	1.63*	1.61*	1.50
Mean ideal age for girl to marry	20.3	19.6	20.1	20.6	21.4	19.7	20.1	20.9	21.3
Mean ideal age for boy to marry	22.5	21.8	22.3	22.8	23.5	21.8	22.3	23.1	23.7
Opinion on birth control practices for married people Percent expressing:									
Always wrong	25.4%	42.1%	28.2%	12.6%	4.3%	41.4%	33.4%	12.1%	4.4%
Sometimes wrong	43.3	39.3	45.7	48.5	35.6	45.0	43.4	47.6	34.8
Never wrong	31.3	18.6	26.0	39.9	60.1	13.6	23.2	40.3	60.8
Total	100.0	100.0	100.0	100.0	100.0	100.0	100.0	100.0	100.0

* Not significantly different statistically at < 0.05 level, using the t test.

patterns which continue in some areas of the Southern Appalachians.

In general, then, the results support the reasoning that religious fundamentalism as well as socioeconomic status is related to fertility attitudes of Southern Appalachian respondents. A question remains, however: Is religious fundamentalism significantly related to fertility attitudes independent of other variables such as socioeconomic status? In other words, do lower socioeconomic status and a very fundamentalistic religious belief system refer to much the same dimension when related to attitudes about fertility?

To provide a basis for answering this line of questioning, a multiple

gious fundamentalism indicates the association between fundamentalism and given fertility attitudinal responses with the influence of socioeconomic status statistically controlled.

In an effort to ascertain more precisely the relative importance of religious fundamentalism, age of respondent was added as an independent variable.[23] In this context, age of respondent may be an important variable in indicating fertility attitudinal change through time.

Based on the partial correlation coefficients, religious fundamentalism continues to be significantly related to fertility attitudes even when socioeconomic status and age are taken into

TABLE 2. Multiple and Partial Coefficients of Correlation for Religious Fundamentalism, Socioeconomic Status, Age, and Selected Fertility Attitudes, Southern Appalachian Region

Fertility attitudes	Partial correlations			Multiple correlation
	Religious	Socio-economic	Age	
Ideal number of children for average young couple today	0.100	−0.098	0.183	0.276
Ideal number of children for "well-off" young couple today	0.112	−0.122	0.140	0.276
Ideal number of children for "not well-off" young couple today	0.058*	−0.098	0.140	0.220
Ideal age for girl to marry	−0.191	0.223	0.148	0.395
Ideal age for boy to marry	−0.134	0.222	0.095	0.343
Opinon on birth control practices for married people	0.261	−0.179	0.151	0.441

* Only coefficient of correlation *not* statistically significant at < 0.05 level.

correlation analysis was employed. This statistical technique provides a basis for assessing the importance of a given independent variable with other independent variables statistically controlled. Thus, for example, a partial correlation coefficient for reli-

account (see Table 2). Fundamentalism was most notable in explaining the statistical variation for the ques-

---

[23] In order to be consistent with religious fundamentalism and socio-economic status, age of respondent was grouped into four categories.

TABLE 3. Multiple and Partial Coefficients of Correlation for Religious Fundamentalism, Socioeconomic Status, Age, and Selected Fertility Attitudes, by Residence, Southern Appalachian Region

	Rural				Nonmetropolitan urban				Standard metropolitan areas			
	Partial correlations				Partial correlations				Partial correlations			
Fertility attitudes	Religious fundamentalism	Socioeconomic status	Age	Multiple correlations	Religious fundamentalism	Socioeconomic status	Age	Multiple correlations	Religious fundamentalism	Socioeconomic status	Age	Multiple correlations
			N=692				N=249				N=309	
Ideal number of children for average young couple today	0.051	−0.079*	0.187**	0.232**	0.044	0.003	0.067	0.085	0.126*	−0.057	0.265**	0.315**
Ideal number of children for "well-off" young couple today	0.042	−0.116**	0.167**	0.235**	0.086	−0.110	0.127	0.237	0.187**	−0.028	0.089	0.241**
Ideal number of children for "not well-off" young couple today	0.041	−0.041	0.157**	0.182**	−0.055	−0.053	0.091	0.120	0.032	−0.090	0.147**	0.195**
Ideal age for girl to marry	−0.166**	0.159**	0.104**	0.280**	−0.135*	0.161*	0.113	0.277**	−0.128*	0.185**	0.196**	0.347**
Ideal age for boy to marry	−0.100**	0.132**	0.061	0.201**	−0.025	0.209**	0.066	0.242**	−0.134**	0.189**	0.141**	0.332**
Opinion on birth control practices for married people	0.195**	−0.129**	0.187**	0.347**	0.344**	−0.030	0.132	0.410**	0.239**	−0.300**	0.101*	0.492**

* Statistically significant at the < 0.05 level.
** Statistically significant at the < 0.01 level.

tion concerning birth control practices. Nevertheless, on other items, the partial correlation coefficients for fundamentalism usually approximated those for socioeconomic status. Of the fertility questions considered, socioeconomic status was somewhat more important in explaining response variation for ideal age of marriage. Age of respondent appeared as a rather significant factor, particularly in response variation for ideal family size questions.

Over-all, religious fundamentalism, socioeconomic status, and age accounted for a statistically significant but relatively small part of Southern Appalachian fertility attitude variation. This was true despite the exclusion of such demographically important groups as Catholics, Jews, and nonwhites. Multiple correlation coefficients ranged from a high of 0.44 on the question concerning the use of birth control methods, to a low of 0.22 on the question of ideal family size for an economically not well-off couple. At best, then, about 20 per cent $[(0.44)^2]$ of the statistical variation was explained.

Up to this point, the analysis has considered the entire Southern Appalachian Region as a unit. As has been pointed out, however, the region is far from homogeneous.[24] There are some rather marked differences between rural and urban areas, and thus one would expect rural-urban differences in the association of the independent variables with fertility attitudes.

The total sample was divided on the basis of rural, nonmetropolitan urban, and metropolitan residence. For each of these subsamples, mul-

tiple and partial correlation coefficients were computed between religious fundamentalism, socioeconomic status, and age (the independent variables), and fertility attitudinal responses (the dependent variables).

A most striking feature of this phase of the analysis is the almost complete absence of statistically significant partial correlations in nonmetropolitan urban areas (see Table 3). Whereas fundamentalism, status, and age were all significantly related to fertility attitudes for the entire Appalachian survey population, only 4 of 18 partial correlation coefficients for these nonmetropolitan urban areas were statistically significant. In part, this may be influenced by the smaller number of urban respondents compared with metropolitan and rural respondents included in the sample. Also important may be the relatively small proportion of urban respondents grouped in the extreme religious fundamentalism and socioeconomic status categories. But this finding suggests that factors which differentiate fertility attitudes in metropolitan and rural areas may not be the same as those in small cities and towns.

For rural and metropolitan areas, fundamentalism, status, and age were significantly related to fertility attitudes. The influence of age was particularly notable for questions concerning ideal family size—a fact which may be indicative of changing values, particularly among young people of the Southern Appalachians. On the other hand, socioeconomic status was not significantly related to questions on ideal family size for metropolitan area respondents. At the attitudinal level, this supports the general findings of a decline in the inverse relationship between socioeconomic status and family size.

24 This point is repeatedly made throughout Ford (ed.), *The Southern Appalachian Region: A Survey, op. cit.*

Fundamentalism, it is interesting to note, was significantly related to more fertility items for the metropolitan than the rural subsample. This might be presumed a rather unexpected finding since rural Appalachia is considered the citadel of fundamentalistic religious beliefs. The marked groupings of rural respondents toward the very fundamental end of the scale offer one explanation for the low number of statistically significant correlations. On the other hand, Goldberg's research indicating fertility differences between indigenous urbanites and urbanites with farm background suggests a hypothesized explanation for the larger number of statistically significant correlations for metropolitan areas.[25] Metropolitan areas have received a sizable influx of rural Appalachian migrants during the past twenty years.[26] It is plausible that the religious orientation as well as the fertility attitudes of these migrants has

been different from that of indigenous residents, and that these differences have tended to enhance the number of statistically significant relationships between fundamentalism and fertility attitudes. Indeed, this may be an example of the rural to urban (instead of urban to rural) diffusion of a cultural trait which has demographic as well as sociological consequences.

This analysis has empasized the relationship between a measure of religious fundamentalism and fertility attitudes and how this relationship was affected when other selected variables were taken into account. In general, fundamentalism was found to be significantly related to fertility attitudes of Southern Appalachian respondents, even when socioeconomic status, age, and residence were statistically controlled. A notable exception was for nonmetropolitan urban respondents. While fundamentalism is a dimension of Protestant religious orientation which seldom has been considered in fertility research, the generalization of these results to other populations must be done with extraordinary care. Nevertheless, for this segment of the national population, religious fundamentalism appears as an important factor in differentiating attitudes and values related to fertility.

[25] David Goldberg, "The Fertility of Two Generation Urbanites," *Population Studies*, XII (March, 1959), 214–222, and David Goldberg, "Another Look at the Indianapolis Fertility Data," *Milbank Memorial Fund Quarterly*, XXVII (January, 1960), 23–36.

[26] James S. Brown and George A. Hillery, Jr., "The Great Migration, 1940–1960," in Ford (ed.), *The Southern Appalachian Region . . .*, op. cit.

Religion and Rates of Mortality Among Total Populations

Dennis E. Poplin

During recent years numerous studies have focused upon religion as an independent variable influencing rates of fertility. In most cases, the findings have been rather consistent. Although there are exceptions, it appears that Roman Catholic families have higher rates of fertility than do Protestant or Jewish families.[1]

At a time when demographers have been gaining significant insight into fertility, they have almost completely ignored the other vital process, mortality, and only Madigan has suggested that religion might have an influence upon rates of death.[2] The reasons for this lack of concern with mortality are probably twofold. First, high rates of fertility have constituted the problematical aspect of the world "population explosion" and have thus captured the interest of professional persons and laymen alike. Secondly, mortality as a vital process is only partly influenced by cultural and social variables. All men must die sooner or later. About the most that sociocultural systems may do is determine whether this will be "sooner" or "later."

It is the purpose of this paper to shed light on mortality as a *socially and culturally influenced process* and, in specific, to examine the influence of selected religious organizations on rates of mortality among populations exposed to the teachings of these organizations. If it can be shown that church membership does influence length of life, then a significant step forward will have been made in understanding demographic behavior.

---

[1] For recent evidence see Ronald Freedman, Pascal K. Whelpton, and Arthur A. Campbell, *Family Planning, Sterility and Population Growth* (New York: McGraw-Hill Book Company, 1958); Gerhard Lenski, *The Religious Factor: A Sociologist's Inquiry* (Garden City: Anchor Books, 1959); Charles F. Westoff, Robert G. Potter, Jr., Phillip C. Sagi, and Elliot G. Mishler, *Family Growth in Metropolitan America* (Princeton: Princeton University Press, 1961); Charles F. Westoff, Robert G. Potter, Jr., and Phillip C. Sagi, *The Third Child: A Study in the Prediction of Fertility* (Princeton: Princeton University Press, 1963); and Albert J. Mayer and Sue Marx, "Social Change, Religion, and Birth Rates," *American Journal of Sociology,* LXII (January, 1957), 383–390. The survey conducted by the U.S. Bureau of the Census in 1957 found Catholic fertility rates to be lower than the rates for certain Protestant denominations, and the present writer has found that Catholic fertility rates are lower than those for selected Lutheran and Latter-Day Saints populations. See U.S. Bureau of the Census, *Statistical Abstract of the United States: 1957* (Washington, D.C.: U.S. Government Printing Office, 1958), Table 40, and Dennis E. Poplin, *Religion and the Vital Processes: An Analysis of County Data for Catholics, Lutherans, and Latter-Day Saints* (unpublished Ph.D. Dissertation, University of Kentucky, 1956), pp. 105–152.

[2] See Francis C. Madigan, "Role Satisfaction and Length of Life in a Closed Population," *American Journal of Sociology,* LXXVII (May, 1962), 640–649.

RELIGION AND RATES OF MORTALITY

There are several ways in which religion could potentially affect rates of mortality. Among other things, some religious groups have value systems pertaining to bodily care and hygiene, the nonuse of tobacco and alcohol and, in general, an emphasis upon "healthful living." This research focuses upon three religious organizations: The Roman Catholic Church, The Church of Jesus Christ of Latter-Day Saints ("Mormon"), and a constellation of Lutheran denominations.[3] One of these organizations, the Church of Jesus Christ of Latter-Day Saints, has a set of value orientations which could quite clearly influence mortality rates among its members. As far as can be determined, the Roman Catholic Church and the Lutheran churches do not.

There are two specific sets of beliefs which could potentially affect the mortality experiences of LDS (Latter-Day Saints) Church members. The first is the positive emphasis which the LDS Church places upon bodily care and preservation. Quite early in its history, leaders of this religious group counselled their followers that "complete living requires a sound body. The sound mind in the sound body is the first requisite of any person who desires to live happily and serve well."[4] This pronounce-ment is a key to understanding many aspects of contemporary LDS social philosophy and goes far in explaining the emphasis which LDS persons put on good health.

The second set of values which could have an impact upon the mortality rates of LDS persons enjoins the church member to avoid completely the use of alcohol, tea, tobacco, and coffee:

> That inasmuch as man drinketh wine or strong drink among you, behold it is not good, neither meet in the sight of your Father.
> And again, strong drinks are not for the belly, but for the washing of your bodies.
> And again, tobacco is not for the body, neither for the belly and is not good for man, but as a herb for bruises and all sick cattle, to be used with judgement and skill.[5]

Inasmuch as modern medical research seems increasingly to suggest an inverse association between the excessive use of tobacco and alcohol and longevity,[6] this constitutes another

---

3 It was necessary to combine several Lutheran denominations in order to find counties in which Lutheranism was clearly predominant. Chief among these were the American Lutheran Church, the Lutheran Church in America, and the Lutheran Church—Missouri Synod.

4 Cited in Thomas F. O'Dea, *The Mormons*, 1st Phoenix ed. (Chicago: University of Chicago Press, 1964), p. 144. The original reference is to John A. Widstoe, *Rational Theology* (Salt Lake City: Church of Jesus Christ of Latter-Day Saints, 1915), p. 56.

5 These statements, collectively known as "The Word of Wisdom," appear in the *Doctrine and Covenants of the Church of Jesus Christ of Latter-Day Saints* (Salt Lake City: Church of Jesus Christ of Latter-Day Saints, 1951), Sec. 89.

6 In regard to smoking see U.S. Public Health Service, *Smoking and Health: Report of the Advisory Committee of the Surgeon General of the Public Health Service* (Washington, D.C.: Public Health Service Publication No. 1103). Among conditions affecting health which seem to be associated with, or aggravated by, excessive consumption of alcoholic beverages are (1) selected diseases of the heart, kidneys, liver, and stomach, (2) certain conditions of malnutrition and under-nourishment, and (3) fatal or debilitating automobile and other types of accidents. For a convenient and reasonably objective summary of findings relating to the influence of alcohol upon health and longevity see Dr. L. Weston Oaks, *The Word of Wisdom and You*

value orientation which could potentially influence mortality rates among LDS persons. Because of the presence of these two value orientations in LDS social philosophy, the hypothesis has been advanced that *after other major factors which might influence mortality have been controlled, mortality rates will be significantly, but inversely, related to the percentage of LDS persons found in each county in which the LDS church predominates. The rates will be consistently lower than the rates found in the Catholic and Lutheran counties.*

The LDS Church, of course, is not alone in its active concern for health and physical well-being of its members. Similar value systems characterize the Seventh Day Adventists, Christian Scientists, Theosophists, and several other religious organizations. However, an extensive examination of the literature has not revealed any such active concern on the part of the Catholic and Lutheran churches. Apparently some members of these religious organizations smoke, drink, and largely ignore matters of health while others do not. The fact that the other major denominations do not have a similar value system led one writer to say that the Word of Wisdom "is one of the distinguishing traits of the Latter-Day Saints."[7] It has also led the present writer to hypothesize that *after other major factors which might influence mortality have been controlled, there will be no consistent association between mortality rates and the percentage of the total population*

belonging to the dominant faith in the Catholic and Lutheran counties: rates of mortality will vary independently of the religious composition of these counties.

METHODOLOGY

The study units used to test these hypotheses are populations exposed to the relevant religious organizations rather than individual members of the Roman Catholic, Lutheran, or Latter-Day Saints churches. To be more specific, by using the 1952 report on *Churches and Church Membership in the United States*,[8] the researcher identified counties which had the following characteristics: (1) at least 60 per cent of all *church members* in the county belonged to the dominant religious organization, i.e., Catholic, Lutheran, or LDS;[9] and (2) the percentage of the *total population* belonging to the dominant religious organization varied between 25 per cent and 100 per cent. Thus, some counties were "high" in the percentage of their total population belonging to the dominant faith while others were "low." All told, the researcher identified forty-

---

(Salt Lake City: Bookcraft, Inc., 1958), pp. 91–154. Especially helpful is the extensive bibliography provided by the author, pp. 154–156.

[7] Leonard J. Arrington, *Great Basin Kingdom: An Economic History of the Latter-Day Saints* (Cambridge: Harvard University Press, 1958), p. 250.

[8] National Council of Churches of Christ in the U.S.A., *Churches and Church Membership in the United States: 1952* (New York: National Council of Churches, 1956), esp. Series C. It is regrettable that this paper is somewhat "historical" due to the lack of more recent data on church membership by county. For comments on the accuracy of the above report see Dennis E. Poplin, *op. cit.*, pp. 78–88.

[9] This criterion has the purpose of controlling for the potential influence of other religious bodies on the rates of mortality. Actually, the percentage is greater in most of the counties. In specific, six counties fall into the 60.0 to 69.9 per cent category, eighteen into the 70.0 to 79.9 per cent category, twenty-seven into the 80.0 to 89.9 per cent category and twenty-nine into the 90.0 to 100.0 per cent category.

two Catholic counties, twenty-three LDS counties, and sixteen Lutheran counties which met these standards.[10]

The fundamental methodological problem posed by this research was to control other factors influencing the mortality rate for each county to a degree that church membership alone might be the major factor affecting the size of the rate. The significant variables controlled and the way in which control was actually exercised are now discussed.

PLACE OF RESIDENCE. Rural or urban residence has been shown to be a significant factor affecting rates of mortality.[11] Place of residence has been taken into account in this research by dividing the counties into "metropolitan" and "nonmetropolitan" groups. The metropolitan counties had, as of 1950, at least one urban center with a population of 10,000 or more.[12] The nonmetropolitan counties had no such urban center.[13]

AGE, SEX, AND RACE. Age, sex, and racial composition can obviously have a significant impact upon the mortality rates which characterize a population. These variables were controlled by working only with the white population and by indirect standardization of the mortality rates for age and sex.[14]

SOCIOECONOMIC VARIABLES. Several studies have suggested that occupation, education, and income are inversely associated with rates of mortality.[15] Control has been exercised over these variables by means of tabular analysis (see below). In each case, the cutting points place 50 per

---

10 The Roman Catholic counties were located in California, New Mexico, Louisiana, Massachusetts, Maine, and New Hampshire; the Lutheran counties in Minnesota and North Dakota, and the LDS counties in Utah.

11 Cf., J. Lambert Molyneaux, "Differential Mortality in Texas," *American Sociological Review*, X (February, 1945), 23–24; Homer L. Hitt and Alvin L. Bertrand, "Rural-urban Differences in Mortality," and C. A. McMahan, "Rural-urban Differences in Longevity," both in T. Lynn Smith and C. A. McMahan, *The Sociology of Urban Life* (New York: The Dryden Press, 1951), pp. 267–280 and 281–289. Bogue summarizes by stating that "persons living in urban areas have death rates that are roughly 20 to 25 per cent higher, on the average, than the rates for rural areas." Donald J. Bogue, *The Population of the United States* (New York: The Free Press of Glencoe, Inc., 1959), p. 193.

12 There is, of course, no commonly accepted way to classify entire counties as rural or urban. It was thought, however, that if a county had an urban center of 10,000 or more, most of its popu-

lation would be exposed to urban values and ways of thinking, even though they might be engaged in farm occupations. For supporting evidence see Jack P. Gibbs and Kingsley Davis, "Conventional versus Metropolitan Data in the International Study of Urbanization," *American Sociological Review*, XXIII (October, 1958), 504–514.

13 Four groups of study counties are considered below, Catholic nonmetropolitan, Lutheran nonmetropolitan, LDS nonmetropolitan, and Catholic metropolitan. It was impossible to find enough counties which were metropolitan *and* Lutheran or metropolitan *and* LDS to include in this research.

14 For discussions of standardization see A. J. Jaffe, *Handbook of Statistical Methods for Demographers* (Washington, D.C.: U.S. Government Printing Office, 1960); George W. Barclay, *Techniques of Population Analysis* (New York: John Wiley and Sons, 1958); and Hugh H. Wolfenden, *Population Statistics and Their Compilation* (Chicago: University of Chicago Press, rev. ed., 1964). The specific technique used in this paper is discussed in Poplin, *op. cit.*, pp. 224–230.

15 Cf., Metropolitan Life Insurance Co., "Mortality and Social Class," *Statistical Bulletin*, XL (October, 1959); and Lillian Guralnick, "Mortality by Occupation and Industry among Men 20 to 62 Years of Age: United States, 1950," *Vital Statistics—Special Reports*, LIII, No. 2 (September, 1962), 59–70.

cent of the relevant counties in the   cent in the "low status" category.
"high status" category and 50 per

TABLE 1.   Mortality Rates[a] by Percentage Belonging to the Dominant
Faith and Socioeconomic Status[b]; Catholic, Lutheran and LDS Study
Counties: 1950

Religion, residence type, of dominant faith[c]	Per cent white collar		Per cent attended college		Median income		
	Low	High	Low	High	Low	High	All
LDS nonmetropolitan							
High	9.3	9.5	10.4	9.1	9.8	9.2	9.4
Low	10.3	9.3	10.0	8.7	10.1	9.4	9.5
All	9.7	9.4	10.1	9.0	9.9	9.2	9.5
Catholic nonmetropolitan							
High	9.6	9.5	8.9	10.6	9.5	9.5	9.5
Low	9.0	9.6	9.3	9.6	9.7	9.4	9.5
All	9.5	9.5	9.0	10.0	9.5	9.5	9.5
Catholic metropolitan							
High	10.4	9.4	10.3	9.3	9.8	9.6	9.6
Low	8.2	10.0	10.9	9.4	11.1	9.5	9.7
All	9.8	9.6	10.5	9.3	10.5	9.5	9.7
Lutheran nonmetropolitan							
High	7.7	8.6	7.6	9.2	7.7	8.2	8.0
Low	8.4	9.5	8.4	9.5	9.7	8.2	9.1
All	7.9	9.2	7.8	9.4	8.7	8.2	8.6

[a] Standardized for age, sex, and race. The standard population for these data is the total white population, both male and female, found in the United States as of 1950.

[b] All data on socioeconomic status are from the *U.S. Census of Population: 1950*. The category "white collar occupations" refers to the percentage of the total labor force, both male and female, which was engaged in (1) professional, technical, and kindred occupations, (2) clerical and kindred occupations, (3) managerial, official, and kindred occupations, and (4) sales occupations. The economic status of the population has been measured by median *family* income, while "per cent attended college" includes all persons 25 years of age and over who had one to three years of college education plus those who had four or more years of such education. It was impossible to keep the cutting points constant from study group to study group due to the great variability in educational and economic levels, and in occupational composition between regions within the United States.

[c] The cutting points between "high" and "low" are as follows: Latter-Day Saints nonmetropolitan. 70.0 per cent; Catholic nonmetropolitan, 60.0 per cent; Catholic metropolitan, 45.0 per cent; and Lutheran nonmetropolitan, 60.0 per cent. In all cases these cutting points place 50 per cent of the counties in the "high" category and 50 per cent in the "low" category. During the course of the research the writer also experimented with other cutting points. The choice of cutting points proved to have little influence on the findings.

SOURCES: Standardized death rates calculated from data contained in U. S. Public Health Service, *Vital Statistics of the United States: 1949* (Part II, Table 1), *1950* (Vol. II, Table 6.08 and Vol. III, Table 12), and *1951* (Vol. I, Table 17). Data on white collar occupations, per cent attended college, and median family income processed from U. S. Bureau of the Census, *U. S. Census of Population: 1950*, Vol. II, *Characteristics of the population* (Washington, D. C.: U. S. Government Printing Office, 1953), Tables 42 and 45. All data on church membership are from the National Council of Churches of Christ in the U. S. A., *Churches and Church Membership in the United States: 1952* (New York: National Council of Churches, 1956), Series C.

FINDINGS

The data designed to shed light on the above hypotheses are contained in Table 1. This table may be examined from several perspectives.

COMPARATIVE LEVELS OF MORTALITY. Perhaps the first question of interest concerns comparative levels of mortality in the Catholic, Lutheran, and Latter-Day Saints counties. Seemingly, one finding stands out above all others: Rates of mortality are considerably lower in the Lutheran counties than in the Catholic or LDS counties. The age-sex standardized death rate for all Lutheran counties (i.e., the "all" column in Table 1) is 8.6 per 1,000 and in only one cell of Table 1 is the rate higher than the 1950 U. S. crude death rate of 9.5 per 1,000. Similarly, one cannot fail but take notice of death rates of below 8.0 per 1,000 which are found in several of the Lutheran cells. This immediately suggests the possibility that membership in the Lutheran churches is associated with low mortality rates and increased length of life.

At the same time, the standardized death rates for all countries in which the Catholic or LDS groups were dominant closely parallel the U. S. norm. For both the LDS nonmetropolitan and the Catholic nonmetropolitan counties the rate is 9.5 per 1,000. For the Catholic metropolitan counties the rate is 0.2 per 1,000 higher, a difference of probably no consequence. However, it must also be noted that there is considerable variation in the death rates from cell to cell within each study group. In the LDS counties, for example, the lowest standardized death rate is 8.7 per 1,000 and the highest 10.4 per 1,000. The variation in the Catholic metro-

politan counties is even more noticeable with the lowest rate being 8.2 per 1,000 and the highest rate being 11.1 per 1,000. Somewhat less variation is found in the rates for the Catholic nonmetropolitan counties.

MORTALITY, RELIGION, AND SOCIOECONOMIC STATUS. As pointed out before, several studies have indicated an inverse association between socioeconomic status and rates of mortality. This relationship appears for all measures of socioeconomic status in the LDS and Catholic metropolitan study counties, but breaks down in the Lutheran nonmetropolitan and Catholic metropolitan counties.

To be more precise, mortality rates are noticeably lower in the LDS and Catholic metropolitan counties which are high in socioeconomic status than they are in counties which are low in terms of the same variables. On the other hand, there is no consistent relationship between rates of mortality and socioeconomic status in the Catholic nonmetropolitan counties. In the case of occupation and income, the rates are identical in the "high" and "low" counties while on the variable of college attendance the rate is noticeably higher in the high status counties. The Lutheran counties display yet a third pattern. In these counties a direct association is found between the mortality rates and occupation and education, but an inverse association between mortality and median income.

RELIGION AND RATES OF MORTALITY. The relationship between church membership and rates of mortality is more complex. However, the over-all picture may be stated quite simply: Membership in the Catholic and Latter-Day Saints churches obviously has no consistent impact upon rates of mortality while, at the same time, the Lutheran churches may be influencing rates of mortality among populations exposed to these organizations.

It should be noted that in the LDS counties rates of mortality are inversely associated with church membership in three cases and directly associated with church membership in three cases. Thus, on an over-all basis there is virtually no difference in the death rates for the "high LDS" counties as compared to the "low LDS" counties. Furthermore, there is no consistent pattern of variation between high and low status counties. The death rate is lower in those counties with a combination of a high percentage of the population belonging to the LDS Church and low median incomes and a low percentage in white collar occupations but higher in those "high LDS" counties in which a low percentage of the total population has attended college. In short, it cannot even be concluded that membership in the LDS Church has an effect upon rates of mortality under certain conditions, e.g., low socioeconomic status.

Much of the same is true for both sets of Catholic counties. In some cases the mortality rates are higher in those counties in which a high percentage of the total population belongs to the Catholic Church while in other cases they are lower. Again, there is no consistent pattern of variation between high and low status counties. Sometimes an inverse association is found in counties of high socioeconomic status while at other times it is found in the low status counties. In short, there is no consistent association between rates of mortality and the percentage of the population belonging to the dominant faith in either of these groups of study counties.

The picture is entirely different in the counties in which the Lutheran churches predominate. In every case except one the rates of mortality are lower in those counties in which a high percentage of the population belongs to the dominant faith. Furthermore, in several cases, the differences are quite noticeable. On an over-all basis, there is a difference of 1.1 per 1,000 in the mortality rates between those Lutheran counties in which a high percentage of the population belongs to the dominant faith and those in which a low percentage do so.

CONCLUSIONS

The data presented above cannot be considered substantial enough to warrant the complete rejection or acceptance of the hypotheses. However, in the absence of other data, the following conclusions seem germane.

1. First, the hypothesis that populations exposed to the teachings of the LDS Church will have low mortality rates must be rejected. Rates of mortality are not noticeably below the U.S. norm in the LDS counties and there is no consistent association between the percentage of the total population belonging to the LDS Church and rates of mortality. It is, of course, still possible that persons who adhere strictly to LDS doctrine do have low mortality rates. It must be remembered that the above data include persons of all degrees of religious commitment, and even persons who are not affiliated with the church in any direct way. This can be considered an advantage or a limitation of this research, depending upon one's

perspective. On the one hand, it is important that demographers assess the effects of various institutions on total populations, since it is such populations which set demographic trends. On the other hand, scientific hypotheses can sometimes be best tested by focusing upon "pure" samples. Perhaps more could be learned about LDS influences on mortality by studying a group of persons who adhere rigidly to LDS rules concerning smoking and drinking and to the LDS emphasis upon good health.

2. Secondly, the hypothesis that the Catholic Church has no influence upon the mortality rates of persons exposed to this organization has been substantiated. The evidence above suggests that exposure to the teachings of the Roman Catholic Church leads to neither higher nor lower rates of mortality.

3. The populations exposed to the teachings of the Lutheran churches constitute an entirely different problem. In short, it can only be concluded that Lutheranism may well have some influence upon rates of mortality. Time and again the rates of mortality were lower in those counties in which a high percentage of the population was exposed to the teachings of these churches.

It would be ideal, of course, if the pattern of association found in the Lutheran counties could be explained. There are several possibilities. First, it may be that Lutheran persons, for one reason or another, adhere to health practices which might increase length of life. Perhaps persons of this faith do smoke or drink less than the average American, adhere to good dietary practices, enlist the help of physicians when needed and, in general, look after their health. Secondly, it is possible that membership in the Lutheran churches has an effect upon mortality similar to that described by Madigan who contended that Catholic Priests have a long life expectancy because of general satisfaction with their life situation.[16] Finally, it is highly possible that a third variable is intervening between Lutheranism and rates of mortality. Presumably this variable would be directly associated with high rates of membership in the Lutheran churches and inversely associated with low mortality rates. One such variable could be the Scandinavian origins of Lutherans in the geographical areas under investigation, that is, Minnesota and North Dakota. Although it seems highly unlikely that the hypothesized inverse association between Scandinavian ethnicity and rates of mortality is biologically induced, it is entirely possible that it reflects social and cultural factors in the Scandinavian heritage which could potentially influence length of life.

These suggested explanations of the inverse association between Lutheranism and mortality must, of course, be considered highly tentative. The fact is that this research does not definitely establish whether any causally significant relationship exists at all, let alone offer an empirically grounded explanation for it. Hopefully, additional research will serve to confirm, modify, or even reject the findings of the present research and throw further light on the hypothesized interplay between religion and mortality.

---

[16] Francis C. Madigan, *op. cit.*, pp. 640–49.

The Migrating Sect: An Illustration from Early Norwegian Immigration*

Phillip E. Hammond

Considerable attention has been given to the origins and development of radical religious groups. The sociological literature, from Weber and Troeltsch onward, is full of suggestions and analyses as to why and how sects emerge, behave, and tend to become something else. Exploration of still another aspect of some sects, however—their migration and subsequent life in new societies—provides additional understanding of the theory of these groups. The present paper suggests a way of expanding the view of "stationary" sects to include the migrating sect and illustrates the case with an early segment from Norwegian American immigration.

AN ILLUSTRATION

Nineteenth-century Norway provides a classic example of church-sect relations. Along with economic and political rebellion and reform, two similar sects emerged. First were the followers of H. N. Hauge, sometimes called "Saints," who agitated for lay preachers, personal salvation, and faith by good works.[1] The second group, the Quakers, appealed to the same people as did the Haugeans.

Unlike the latter, however, Quakers operated outside the framework of Lutheranism and therefore underwent even more persecution.[2]

In 1825 a group of Quakers and Haugeans sailed to the United States.[3] Called the Sloopers, after their type of ship, these fifty-three people were the first Norwegian immigrant party of any size. Their main motivation apparently was to escape religious persecution. A New York newspaper at the time wrote of them:

> They belong to a religion called the Saints; corresponding in many points to the principles of the Friends. We understand furthermore that they sought an asylum in this favored land from religious persecution and that they will

---

* Phillip E. Hammond, "The Migrating Sect: An Illustration from Early Norwegian Immigration," *Social Forces*, XLI (March, 1963), 275–283.
[1] C. T. Jonassen, "The Protestant Ethic and the Spirit of Capitalism in Norway," *American Sociological Review*, XII (December, 1947).

[2] H. J. Cadbury, "The Norwegian Quakers of 1825," *Norwegian American Historical Association Studies and Records*, I (1926), 60–95. Hereafter this Association will be abbreviated as NAHA.

[3] Early Norwegian immigration is discussed in many sources. See R. B. Anderson, *First Chapter of Norwegian Immigration* (Minneapolis: private, 1896); O. M. Norlie, *History of Norwegian People in America* (Minneapolis: Augsberg, 1925); J. M. Rohne, *Norwegian American Lutheranism up to 1872* (New York: The Macmillan Company, 1926); G. T. Flom, *A History of Norwegian Immigration to the United States* (Iowa City: private, 1909); C. C. Qualey, *Norwegian Settlement in the United States* (Northfield, Minnesota: NAHA, 1938); and the most systematic, T. C. Blegen, *Norwegian Migration to America*, 2 vols. (Northfield, Minnesota: NAHA, 1931 and 1940). Unless otherwise cited, this latter account is followed.

shortly be succeeded by a much larger body of emigrants.[4]

Elsewhere we are told that religious services were held during the voyage by a Haugean lay preacher;[5] we know that Lars Larson, an active Quaker leader and organizer in Norway, was the leader of the Sloopers; and records show that, under Larson and with the legal and financial help of New York Quakers, these earliest immigrants first settled on farms in upper New York State. It is safe, therefore, to impute a sectarian motivation to the first Norwegian Americans.[6]

In Kendall, New York, for nine years, and later in the Fox River Valley, Illinois, however, these sectarian immigrants behaved in seemingly unsectlike manner. Little evidence points to harmony and unity; ample evidence attests to the situation one historian describes as "chaos and confusion."[7]

Even contemporary observers remarked about Fox River's disorganization. One disillusioned immigrant (who arrived several years after the Sloopers) wrote from there in 1839:

> When all these people get together in one community you can easily imagine what goes on in these American forests. There isn't a church within a hundred miles, and we are thrown into the midst of the worst heathendom.[8]

A tourist of various Norwegian settlements in 1841 (for by now many had immigrated and settled not only in Illinois but also Wisconsin) noted that in one, "The colonists . . . are satisfied and live a quiet, happy life in good understanding with one another." But in Fox River:

> They all have a good deal of land. . . . They live well. [but] For the most part they are . . . indifferent to the common good, and quarrelsome among themselves. Religion means nothing to them whatsoever; they have abandoned its principles completely.[9]

And in the late 1840's another Norwegian tourist observed that, compared with Americans, religious conditions among his countrymen were not good. "I have never before seen such a bitter and fault-finding spirit as among them."[10]

Surely these are characteristics unlike the ideal-typical sect. Whereas the sect is cohesive, these immigrants were divisive; whereas the former exhibits a strong commitment from members, many of the latter were proselytized by other religions or defected altogether. The sect is frequently led by someone with great personal magnetism or charisma; the leadership in Kendall and Fox River changed repeatedly.

At the time of their migration the earliest Norwegian Americans were clearly sectarians, yet within a few years they had lost their ideological unity. Nor is this an isolated historical accident as shown by other similar instances.

The Doukhobors who migrated

---

[4] Quoted in Cadbury, *op. cit.*, pp. 80–81.

[5] Norlie, *op. cit.*, p. 193.

[6] Norwegian newspapers at the time made note of the departure of "Quakers." "There can be no doubt that . . . the two influences largely coalesced and that one or both of them had affected the sloopers." Cadbury, *op. cit.*, pp. 80–81.

[7] Anderson, *op. cit.*, p. 398.

[8] "The Disillusionment of an Immigrant," ed. and trans. G. J. Malmin, *NAHA Studies and Records*, III (1928), 1–2.

[9] T. C. Blegen, *Land of Their Choice* (Minneapolis: University of Minnesota, 1955), pp. 80–81. This volume is a collection of letters to Norway by immigrants.

[10] Blegen, *Norwegian Migration* I, *op. cit.*, pp. 346–347.

from Russia to British Columbia at the end of the nineteenth century provide another case.

> [In Russia] under real and imagined threats to existence, life was organized in various closely knit units, to which the individual was tied with bonds of belief and custom . . . yet that the bonds were not permanent nor the life in the communities completely satisfactory has been demonstrated in startling fashion by continued schisms and defections. . . . The historical fact is that the communities have disintegrated. In Russia they split several times on issues of principle as well as on disputes over leadership. In Canada they have dwindled by the defection of individuals until no communities in the former sense remain. . . . [This] was shown in the first years in Canada, with the splitting-off of independents, and is now shown in . . . the formation of the many new groupings. . . .[11]

Another example is found in Eric Janson's Bishop Hill, Illinois, colony. The Swedish Janson was anti-Lutheran. He and his followers founded their "socialistic, theocratic" community in 1846. The colony lasted only until 1862. "Beginning with religious convictions which enabled them to overcome appalling hardships, they lost them more quickly than any other community holding similar views. Religious dissension rapidly distributed members among various faiths, few adhering to Janson's Pietism."[12]

THE PROBLEM

How is this apparently common phenomenon to be explained? Does it simply reflect the hardships of migration? Or, granted the hardships, is sectarianism, the very motive for migrating, actually another barrier to successful migration?

If the answer were "simply" hardships, then presumably migrating sects would have no harder time than other migrants. But as indicated above, among Norwegians at least, those with sectarian motives did evidence more disorganization than other early settlers.[13] If, on the other hand, sectarianism is a barrier to organization in the new land, then an analysis of sects should reveal the sources of that barrier.

The many theorists of sects have been in agreement on a number of attributes of sects. In contrast to the church, they have said, the sect is small and cohesive, appeals to the lower classes and/or dissenters, and makes membership voluntary but exacting. It is suspicious of rival ideologies while its members aspire toward inward perfection and aim at direct personal fellowship one with another. Other forms of social life, e.g., the State, are minimized; members are cooperative, their commitment being to each other and to the sect.[14]

In time, however, sects tend to modify their organization, their membership, their values. The second gen-

---

[11] H. B. Hawthorn (ed.), *The Doukhobors of British Columbia* (Vancouver: University of British Columbia, 1955), pp. 24–25.
[12] Mark Holloway, *Heavens on Earth: Utopian Communities in America, 1680–1880* (London: Turnstile Press, 1951), pp. 164–168. Francis' account of the Mennonites who went from Russia to Manitoba is still another example. E. K. Francis, *In Search of Utopia: The Mennonites In Manitoba* (New York:

The Free Press of Glencoe, Inc., 1955). See esp. Chap. 4 on "Disruptions of the Social Fabric."
[13] See also below, fn. 48.
[14] Cf. Ernst Troeltsch, *The Social Teaching of the Christian Churches*, 2 vols., trans. Olive Wyon (New York: The Macmillan Company, 1931), pp. 331 ff, and other statements that have added to the list. See note below.

eration, the desire for new converts, the need for trained leadership, etc., all conspire to change them into "established sects," "denominations," or "churches."[15] Only under certain circumstances does the sect remain sectarian. It may develop a clandestine organization, or "an alternative development in the past has been for the sect to migrate and seek an environment where it could live according to its own standards."[16]

From these statements the expectation would seem to be that the migrating sect either (a) retains its cohesion, its ideological unity, in the new environment, or else (b) migration having little effect, it continues to modify in the direction of a "church." In fact, however (to the extent the Sloopers, the Doukhobors, the Jansonists, are representative), the migrating sect does neither. Rather, in the years immediately following its migration, it shows a marked tendency toward disorganization and ideological disunity.

The following discussion attempts to identify the features of sects that make them vulnerable to disorganization when they migrate. Those features are then illustrated by the experience of the Norwegians during their first two decades in America.

THE MIGRATING SECT

The oft-noted "cohesion" of the sect can best be understood as involving three attributes. It rests first upon its members' *consensus on and conformity to a unique set of values and beliefs.*[17] Second, the sect, though perhaps more autonomous than many groups, is nevertheless *dependent* on the wider society for meeting many of its (especially subsistence) needs. And third, because the sect has many of its needs met externally, it can be, and is, characterized by a low level of *collective interdependence* or complementarity.[18]

When it is said, therefore, that sects "have a totalitarian rather than a segmental hold over their members,"[19] the statement is to be understood as identifying the attachment sectarians feel as a result primarily of their value-consensus. The hold, in other words, stems more from ideological unity rather than mutual need. The wider society from which its members come still surrounds it. And unless the sect meets its subsistence problems internally—is a society unto itself, is autonomous rather than dependent—by default it loses to the larger society, the neighborhood, the market, etc., some hold over its members.

---

[15] See, e.g., H. R. Niebuhr, *Social Sources of Denominationalism* (New York: Meridian Books, 1957), pp. 17–21; L. Pope, *Millhands and Preachers* (New Haven, Conn.: Yale University Press, 1942), pp. 117–140; L. Von Wiese and H. Becker, *Systematic Sociology* (New York: John Wiley & Sons, Inc., 1932), pp. 624–628; J. M. Yinger, *Religion in the Struggle for Power* (Durham: Duke University, 1946); Bryan R. Wilson, "An Analysis of Sect Development," *American Sociological Review*, XXIV (February, 1959), pp. 1–15.

[16] Wilson, *op. cit.*, p. 8.

[17] This value-consensus has also been called "normative integration" and "culturally induced cohesion." See Ronald Freedman, *et al.*, *Principles of Sociology* (Rev. Ed.) (New York: Henry Holt, 1956), chap. v; and R. K. Merton, *Social Theory and Social Structure* (Rev. Ed.) (New York: The Free Press of Glencoe, Inc., 1957), p. 316.

[18] Freedman *et al.* label this "function integration," *op. cit.*, chap. vi; Merton calls this "organizationally induced cohesion." The group property of autonomy-dependence is also discussed by Merton, *op. cit.*, p. 322.

[19] Wilson, *op. cit.*, p. 4.

Troeltsch noted the segmental nature of a sect's cohesion:

> The very life of the sect... depends on actual personal service and cooperation; as an independent member each individual has his part within the fellowship.... *It is, however, naturally a somewhat limited form of fellowship,* and the expenditure of so much effort in the maintenance and exercise of this particular kind of fellowship produces a certain indifference towards other forms of fellowship which are based upon secular interests.[20]

However, although the sect may disparage the "fellowships based upon secular interests," it cannot eliminate them. Unless it migrates....

To migrate in a body would seem to require a high degree of value-consensus. Commitment to the sect ideology must be great if members are to pull up roots, leave relatives and jobs, and join others, trusting in the righteousness of their venture. In fact, selection (by self or others) would likely be on the *basis* of ideological commitment and similarity. The migrating sect embarks, then, as an intensely loyal and cohesive body.

But in migrating and isolating itself, the sect takes on an array of subsistence problems which previously were met by individuals' independent arrangements with the larger society. Now the sect must turn inward for the solution to these problems.[21] Building homes, establishing farms or factories, locating new markets, finding or developing schools, and providing protection—these become crucial and must be met if the group is to continue.

However, value-consensus may not be a substitute for patterns of coordination and interdependence. Problems and disputes, e.g., over land and its use, are bound to arise. These will thrust upon the sect tasks its ideology has disparaged and its leaders are unprepared to handle. Leaders, then, may cease to lead; loyalty to the group may weaken.

During this time, moreover, these people retain a sectarian outlook. That is, issues arising from whatever source will likely be defined in ideological terms. And as issues arise and become religiously cloaked, the tendency for schism and defection will be great. Value-consensus thus decreases, and ideological or religious heterogeneity takes its place.

Analysis of sectarianism suggests, therefore, that an intense cohesion based primarily on value-consensus is not only insufficient to hold a migrating sect together, but, paradoxically, may even facilitate the sect's disorganization in two ways.[22] First, by minimizing the importance of subsistence problems, problems that are inevitable in the migration setting, makes less likely their solution. And second, by moving sectarians to define problems in ideological terms leads to schism and defection.

---

20 Troeltsch, *op. cit.*, p. 339. Italics added.

21 Cf. Wilson's observation that migration has "consequences for the sect organization and promotes communistic arrangements," *op. cit.*, p. 8. See below, fn. 35.

22 Linton earlier identified a similar situation: "The value of a high degree of culture integration to a society must always be relative to the society's environment. In a stable environment, the greater the degree of culture integration the better. However... increased efficiency which comes with a heightened degree of [culture] integration is balanced by a corresponding loss of the ability to alter the culture rapidly and with a minimum of discomfort to the society's members." *The Study of Man* (New York: Appleton-Century-Crofts, 1936), p. 364 (student's ed.).

More specifically the analysis of sectarianism suggests that the migrating sect will evidence the following:

(1) recruitment of migrants on the basis of ideological similarity rather than on the basis of complementary skills or collective interdependence,

(2) dissatisfaction and disputes over "economic (subsistence) arrangements" during the first years in a new environment,

(3) frequent change of leaders as now one and now another seems best to exemplify the values of the sect and/or best able to solve the subsistence problems, and

(4) frequent defections and rifts which, whatever their *source*, will likely be manifested as *religious* defection and *religious* rifts.

A CASE IN POINT

If early Norwegian immigration was sectarian, and if the above theoretical analysis is correct, then the "chaos and confusion" of the Norwegians' first decades in America can be interpreted, at least in part, as a sectarian response to migration. The disorganization at Kendall and Fox River will be seen not only as a result of difficult conditions in a new environment. It will also be seen as a result of a particular sectarian set of social arrangements for responding to those conditions.

For the first Norwegian-Americans, then, were not a group held together both by an ideological unity and by a collective interdependence. They were a group of persons similarly motivated to emigrate, similarly antagonistic to a state church, and with similar goals they hoped to achieve in a new land, but unused, unprepared, and unable *collectively* to solve subsistence problems forced on them by migration.

The first chapter of Norwegian immigration, in its retelling, contains evidence to support such a point of view. The fact, for example, has already been noted that the Sloopers were both Quakers and Haugeans. Since Larson was the organizer, it is perhaps safe to infer that Quakers instigated the venture. But, there not being enough Quakers, the passenger list was apparently filled out not by persons whose *skills* complemented the emigrants' skills, but by persons whose *ideology* most nearly conformed to that of the Quakers. Already the emphasis on similarity of values to the neglect of collective interdependence has a restrictive effect on their subsequent life in America.

The story of what happened immediately after this emigration of 1825 can be briefly retold in terms of land, leaders, and loyalty to the sect ideology.

LAND. In 1825 most of the fifty-three Sloopers settled in Kendall, New York, on land arranged for them by a scout, Cleng Peerson, the year before. At first life was difficult, several died, and all were discouraged. The Scandinavian consul in New York wrote to his government at the time:

> An unverified rumor has reached me that the immigrants have expressed dissatisfaction with their undertaking; that they have not realized the advantages which, before their departure from Norway, had been presented to them as certain to result from this strange emigration.[23]

Within a few years, however, a contemporary diarist could write that, "Well-to-do neighbors assisted them ... and by their own industry they at last got their land in such condition

---

[23] Blegen, *Norwegian Migration* II, *op. cit.*, p. 628.

that they could earn a living from it, and live better than in their own native land."[24] In the eleven years following the arrival of the Sloopers, a few more Norwegians immigrated. Most of these people settled in Kendall also, and one of them had made, within four years, a $500 profit on land he improved.

Nevertheless, in 1834 and 1835 almost all of the Kendall colony went westward to Illinois, settling in the Fox River valley, again on land that had first been scouted and arranged by Cleng Peerson. The Slooper leader, Lars Larson, did not go, and he might well have had this event in mind when he wrote to a Norwegian Quaker in 1838 that "As I learn to know human nature, I realize that men are continually restless, unless their hearts are where they ought to be. They think of nothing more important than this present life."[25]

Fox River was a center from which other settlements, some unsuccessful, originated. One of these, Shelby County, Missouri, "began to disintegrate" after a few years.[26] Other early Fox River sectarians later moved to Wisconsin, Iowa, Utah, Minnesota, and Texas.[27] From their initial difficulty, then, through the next few decades marked often by success, the Sloopers evidenced considerable dissatisfaction with their economic (land) arrangements. Significant though were the ideological overtones of Larson, who regretted his countrymen's concern for the "present life" to the neglect of their spiritual values.

LEADERSHIP. Just as the first Norwegian Americans seem to have moved from place to place, so too did they change leaders with some frequency. Lars Larson, the Quaker leader in Norway, is known to have organized the Slooper party and led them as far as upper New York State. However, while most of the party settled in Kendall, Larson, his family, and one other went to Rochester some miles away.[28] Furthermore, as already noted, when the others moved on to Fox River, Larson stayed behind.

Leadership now was Cleng Peerson's. He seems to have had great personal magnetism, for he reappears throughout the first thirty years of Norwegian-American history as guide, settler, colonizer, and rescuer. It was he who explored and located Fox River, returning to Kendall to lead the others west. His companion at the outset of this exploration, a devout Quaker, instead of continuing west with Peerson, stopped in Michigan. Later this companion said that Peerson was "proud and essentially an adventurer." He accused Peerson of marrying for money.[29]

It was during the difficult years in

---

[24] Ole Rynning, "True Account of America," trans. T. C. Blegen, *NAHA Travel and Description Series,* I (1926), 74.

[25] Blegen, *Land of Their Choice, op. cit.,* p. 30.

[26] Blegen, *Norwegian Migration* I, *op. cit.,* p. 113.

[27] In 1836 and 1837 four more boatloads arrived in America, many going to Fox River. These people were Haugeans or at least dissident Lutherans. In another ten years, Norwegian immigration seemed to be devoid of specifically religious overtones. Events after 1836 necessarily involved some who were not, strictly speaking, sectarian. The important point, however, is that much of the movement out of Fox River to new lands did involve some of the original sectarian settlers.

[28] Blegen points out that Larson, a carpenter and not a farmer like the other Sloopers, naturally went to Rochester where boatbuilding flourished as it did not around Kendall. Vol. I, *op. cit.,* p. 54. Though reasonable, this explanation minimizes the fact that Larson was the *leader* yet ceased to lead once on the new land.

[29] Anderson, *op. cit.,* pp. 181–182.

Kendall that Peerson apparently took charge. In 1826 he wrote a letter, signed also by seven others, to the communistic Harmony Society in Pennsylvania. In it he requested a loan of $1600 to buy land for the site of a lumber mill.[30] This failing, Peerson collected money from wealthy Americans to aid his destitute settlers. A letter several years later indicated that:

> This did not meet with everybody's approval, partly because... [Peerson] had spoken on behalf of all Norwegians without asking their permission, partly because he had shown some favoritism in his distribution of means.[31]

One of the first settlers in Fox River wrote that it was he, not Peerson, who was responsible for Norwegians in Fox River.[32] It has been suggested that Peerson prevented this man from getting the New York land he wanted.[33]

It should be pointed out that the mercurial Peerson had as many defenders as he had detractors.[34] Yet that he antagonized others there can be no doubt. His command was periodic; he held sway over some people some of the time; he had greater plans than he carried out. For example, a letter of 1838 from Fox River asserts that "His endeavor was . . . and still is to unite all Norwegians into one community owning all its property in common."[35] He had appealed for help from a communistic group in 1826. He established at least one community (not known to be communistic, however) which failed within a few years.[36] He bought land in Fox River but never settled on it. And in 1847, Peerson joined a communistic sect in Illinois. Shortly thereafter, "robbed of all he possessed, and sick in body and mind," he left it.[37] In 1849 he journeyed from Fox River to Texas, returning the next year endeavoring to interest Norwegians in settling there. He left with a small party, never to return to Fox River, obviously no longer its leader.

Other persons, e.g., Bjorn Anderson, Elling Eielsen, Ole Rynning, served as leaders momentarily or for a portion of the immigrants. In some instances they enhanced the social organization and consensus of the Fox River people. But this restoration affected at most only some of the community, much of it remaining religiously heterogeneous.[38]

---

[30] M. S. DePillis, "Still More Light on the Kendall Colony: A Unique Sleeper Letter," *NAHA Studies and Records*, XX (1959), 24–31.

[31] Quoted in Blegen, *Land, op. cit.*, pp. 42–43.

[32] "Johannes Nordboe and Norwegian Immigration," ed. A. O. Johnson, *NAHA Studies and Records*, XIII (1934), 36.

[33] Anderson, *op. cit.*, p. 138.

[34] Much of the information about Peerson is contained in T. C. Blegen, "Cleng Peerson and Norwegian Immigration," *Mississippi Valley Historical Review*, VII (March, 1921), 303–331.

[35] Quoted in Blegen, *Land, op. cit.*, p. 42. See above, fn. 21.

[36] An incident indicative of the volatility of Peerson's followers is told of this Missouri community. After establishing it in 1837, Peerson returned to Norway to recruit more members. On coming back, Peerson led them, not through the Great Lakes but via the Ohio River. "(His) reason for going by way of the Ohio River was that the two persons... who came with him to Missouri in 1837... had gone back... (to Fox River) dissatisfied, and Cleng feared that if he went by way of the Fox River settlement, his recruits might be persuaded not to proceed with him." Anderson, *op. cit.*, p. 187.

[37] Blegen, *Norwegian Migration* I, *op. cit.*, p. 193.

[38] Even those whom Eielsen gathered around him suffered many schisms for the next few decades. See Rohne, *op. cit.*, chap. v.

LOYALTY. No aspect of early Norwegian immigrants is more puzzling than their susceptibility to various religious ideologies. For many at Fox River at least, the tenets of a sectarianism had once been vital. During the first years at Fox River such men as Ole Olson Hetletvedt, Bjorn Hatlestad, Jorgen Pedersen, Ole Heier, and Hans Balder were active and prominent lay preachers. They "testify to the power of the Haugean ferment and the fervency of religious feeling among the pioneers."[39] Yet by 1839 a Wisconsin pioneer, in requesting an ordained Lutheran pastor from Norway, could mention that "The Fox River colony . . . represented such various religious views that it would not accept a Lutheran minister."[40] Anderson says that "Some of the Norwegians there were Quakers, others Baptists, others Presbyterians, others Methodists, others Lutherans, others Mormons, and some were free thinkers, all in inextricable disorder."[41]

Many became Mormons, including at least two of the original Sloopers and the elected Haugean lay leader of Fox River. One contemporary in 1845 estimated that eighty of the Fox River settlers had accepted Mormonism.[42] Ole Heier was more fickle; he became a Mormon preacher, then joined the Close Communion Baptists. One of his acquaintances insisted that Ole belonged to seven different churches.[43] Hans Balder became a Baptist preacher, converting at least a handful of other Fox River people. By the time he left for Minnesota Balder was a militant freethinker.[44]

An ordained Lutheran, sent from Norway to Wisconsin to minister to the immigrants, wrote of his visit to the Illinois settlement:

> I had no expectation of accomplishing anything in a religious way in a colony in which I had heard that the confusion was great. . . . Our dear countrymen, baptized and confirmed in the faith of our fathers, are here divided into seven or eight different sects.[45]

A "Handbook for Emigrants" published in Norway in 1847 urged all to go to Wisconsin. Iowa, it declared, was too far away, lacked woods, and was unhealthful; in Illinois there were heavy state debts, and "religious conditions were disturbed."[46]

[39] Blegen, *Norwegian Migration* I, *op. cit.*, p. 249.

[40] *Ibid.*, p. 122.

[41] Anderson, *op. cit.*, p. 398. Schisms apparently began among the Sloopers in Kendall, New York. Norlie mentions that "Even the Quakers in the party found it difficult to agree as to whether they should be Orthodox, Hicksite, Willburite, or Primitive," *op. cit.*, p. 190. Larson and Iverson were Orthodox; Johnson, a Hicksite. In a letter of 1837 Larson's wife makes cryptic mention of this split: "The dissension among the Friends is the same now as before. Those who have left have shown the world a very poor example." Quoted in Blegen, *Land, op. cit.*, p. 30. It is possible that the schism referred to by Martha Larson was involved in the decision by some of the Kendall people to resettle in Illinois. Although some who left for Fox River were Quakers, most seem to have been Haugeans.

[42] Cited in Mulder, "Norwegian Forerunners Among the Early Mormons," *NAHA Studies and Records*, XIX (1956), 50. The Norwegians even became embroiled in Mormon schisms. They pledged themselves first to the deviationist, Strang; but then "there was a falling away," and the projected tabernacle and "gathering place for the Scandinavian people" never flourished. *Ibid.*, pp. 52–58.

[43] Anderson, *op. cit.*, pp. 399–400.

[44] P. Stiansen, *History of the Norwegian Baptists in America*, The Norwegian Baptist Conference of America and the American Baptist Publication Society, 1939, pp. 21–28. For his Baptist preaching, Balder reports, "The minds of my country-men were now aroused against me."

[45] Quoted in *ibid.*, pp. 29–30.

[46] Cited in Blegen, *Norwegian Migration* I, *op. cit.*, p. 256.

EXPLAINING THE DISORGANIZATION

The "disturbance" was in Fox River, and many have taken pains to show why. The disorganized first decades in New York and Illinois, so contrary to expectations about sectarians, have been attributed to epidemics, the fact that settlement was on prairie rather than woodland, and the shortage of land which forced later immigrants to move on. These factors no doubt enter in, yet it should be noted that: (1) ample evidence suggests that when epidemics hit Fox River, they ravaged other mid-west valleys as well,[47] (2) many other Norwegian settlements were also prairie and not woodland, and (3) Fox River did continue to grow, although not as rapidly as later communities; furthermore, some of its earliest settlers who owned land were among those who moved on.

More pertinent is the explanation supplied by several writers—a state church, the bond of union in Norway, was absent in America.[48] But even this explanation can be buttressed if the Norwegian experience is analyzed further in terms of its sectarian character, both before and after migrating. If this is done, the social disorganization of early Norwegian immigration is better understood and may serve as an illustration of the behavior of migrating sects generally.

CONCLUSION

First, the emigrants apparently gave little thought to the subsistence problems that would be forced upon them collectively once they broke their individual ties in Norway. Thus, in filling out the roster with non-Quakers, Haugeans, rather than persons with complementary skills, were chosen. In one sense, of course, the Slooper party ceased then to be a *sect* although most if not all of their motivation remained *sectarian*. The important point for this analysis, however, is that, without sectarian impetus, the Sloopers might have made economically more feasible arrangements for their migration.

Second, the Norwegian sectarians had considerable misgivings about their subsistence arrangements. This is seen by: (1) their initial choice of land which was appropriate to most of them but not the leader, (2) vague indications that some, but not all, of them flirted periodically with the idea of communal living, and (3) their frequent moves from land to land despite apparent success in farming. Although

---

[47] K. Gjerset and L. Hektoen, "Health Conditions and the Practice of Medicine Among Early Norwegian Settlers, 1825–1865," *NAHA Studies and Records*, I (1926), 1–59.

[48] Rohne, *op. cit.*, p. 26; Blegen, *Norwegian Migration* I, *op. cit.*, p. 249. Anderson, after devoting many pages to liken the Sloopers to the Mayflower, attempts to resolve the paradox by saying that a considerable number of the early Norwegian immigrants were not really avowed sectarians, *op. cit.*, p. 396. However, a clear indication of the role played by sectarianism in the disorganization at Fox River emerges when the latter is contrasted with Muskego and Koshkonong Norwegian settlements of 1839 and 1840. Within four years of its founding, Koshkonong, apparently devoid of sectarian influence, was supporting an ordained Lutheran clergyman from the State Church. Muskego, with only some sectarian overtones, had

a moderate amount of religious unrest, more than Koshkonong but less than Fox River. For example, where dozens at Fox River became Mormon, only a handful from Muskego did so. See Rohne, *op. cit.*, pp. 48, 64–89; and Soren Bache, *A Chronicle of Old Muskego*, trans. C. Clausen and A. Elviksen (Northfield, Minnesota: NAHA, 1951), p. 140.

evidence is scant, it seems reasonable to impute to them an initial unconcern for how well land would meet present and future requirements, followed by discrepancy between the actual utility of new land and the utility the sectarians came to expect.

Third, leadership during the first two decades was ineffective and amorphous. Once having landed in America only one serious candidate emerged during the period, and this was more the role of innovator and antagonist than organizer and administrator. The man credited with organizing and guiding the first group from Norway did not even settle with his followers. All others who developed followings in Fox River were religious leaders who functioned more to divide the community than unite it.

And fourth, rather than retain their ideological unity, the earliest Norwegian Americans began dividing religiously almost from the first. Of the Quakers who eventually got to Fox River only one is known to have remained a Quaker. Others remained in New York State or defected to other ideologies. Haugeanism remained strong in Fox River, but many of its adherents became Mormons, Baptists, etc.

These features portray a situation very unlike the ideal-typical sect, a cohesive body of "direct personal fellowship." They suggest that such cohesion, based primarily on value-consensus, is not only insufficient to hold a migrating sect together; it may even contribute to the sect's disorganization in two ways. First, by minimizing the importance of subsistence problems, problems that are inevitable in the migration setting, it makes less likely their solution. And second, by moving sectarians to define problems in ideological terms, it leads to schism and defection. The disorganization frequently noted in migrating sects is explained, then, not only by such environmental factors as epidemics or land shortage (although obviously they cannot be left out), but also by the sects' response to their environment. And that response is limited, even prior to migration, by the nature of sectarianism.

The Decline in Religious Participation of Migrants*

J. J. Mol

There is considerable evidence that migration often has a negative effect on religious interest in general and church going in particular.

Speaking about Catholic migrants in the Belgian province of Limburg, Dr. Beda Claes, o.f.m., has the following statistics: "As long as they remained in Italy, 55–67 per cent of men and 69–79 per cent of women went to mass regularly. Here 17–27 per cent of men and 25–35 per cent of women practice their religion regularly."[1] The Polish immigrants also become less active but not to the same extent: "In the country of origin 74–88 per cent of men and 83–95 per cent of women went to mass each Sunday. Here 49–65 per cent of men and 61–75 per cent of women go regularly."[2]

In France the situation seems to be no different. As mentioned by Girard and Stoetzel, the Polish and Italian immigrants do not feel at home in the French Church and tend to drift away from the Church unless a priest of their own nationality is present.[3]

Similar evidence is available from studies of Dutch immigrants in Australia and New Zealand. Although only 18.1 per cent of the Dutch emigrants who left the Netherlands for Australia from 1948–June 1961 stated to have "no religion" at their departure, 26.9 per cent of those born in the Netherlands at the June 1961 Australian census said that they had no religion, or gave no reply.[4] The most likely source for the increase is the Hervormd emigrants, many of whom are already nominal adherents in the Netherlands. Their home church advises them to join the Presbyterian Church of Australia, but although 25.7 per cent ($N = 29,480$) are Hervormd when they leave the Netherlands, only 14.4 per cent ($N = 14,680$) of the Dutch-born population at the 1961 Australian census stated to belong to the Presbyterian Church.

---

* J. J. Mol, "The Decline in Religious Participation of Migrants," *International Migration*, III (1965), 137–142.

[1] The Rev. Dr. Beda Claes, o.f.m., *De Sociale Integratie van de Italiaanse en Poolse immigranten in Belgisch-Limburg* (Hasselt: Heideland, 1962), p. 228.

[2] *Ibid.*, p. 230.

[3] Alain Girard et Jean Stoetzel, *Français et Immigrés* (Presses Universitaires de France, 1953), pp. 84, 198, 402 and 404.

[4] Those who gave no reply (in the relevant column of the schedule it is stated that "there is no penalty for failure to answer this question") are generally regarded as having no religious affiliation. However, there is another reason why the percentages are not strictly comparable: they refer to a different universe. Of the 114,585 persons who left for Australia from 1948–1961 several thousands may have returned or may have moved on to other countries. Of the 102,083 persons born in the Netherlands according to the 1961 census many may have arrived in Australia before 1948 or may have entered from other countries. Still it is unlikely that their movements have had sufficient, if any, effect on the denominational distribution. The effect is certainly not significant enough to explain a 8.8 per cent increase.

TABLE 1. Religious Affiliation of Dutch Immigrants Before and After They Left the Netherlands

Religious affiliation in Holland	Religious affiliation in New Zealand					
	Catholic	Presbyterian	Reformed	Other	None	Total
Katholiek	149 (89%)	2 (1%)	—	2 (1%)	14 (9%)	167 (100%)
Hervormd	1 (1%)	63 (60%)	9 (8%)	7 (7%)	25 (24%)	105 (100%)
Gereformeerd	2 (5%)	6 (15%)	27 (68%)	2 (5%)	3 (7%)	40 (100%)
Other	—	5 (19%)	—	18 (69%)	3 (12%)	26 (100%)
None	—	2 (3%)	—	3 (5%)	54 (92%)	59 (100%)
Total	152	78	36	32	99	397

There is also a drop of 4.2 per cent (from 44.6 per cent ($N=51,131$) to 40.4 per cent ($N=41,241$) in the Catholic figures, but this is much smaller than the Hervormd-Presbyterian decrease of 11.1 per cent. It is true that some of these immigrants change to the typical Anglo-Saxon denominations, which are practically nonexistent in the Netherlands. But here too the percentages are rather small (2.8 per cent of the Dutch-born stated to belong to the Church of England at the 1961 census, 2.6 per cent to the Methodist Church), and the conclusion that in the course of migration particularly the Protestant Dutch migrants in Australia have swelled the no-religion and no-reply categories is a plausible one.

Supporting evidence for the interpretation of the Australian figure comes from an empirical study which the author undertook in Christchurch, New Zealand,[5] of a random sample of 397 adult Dutch immigrants. Fifty-nine (14.9 per cent) said that in the Netherlands they had no religion. However ninety-nine (24.9 per cent) stated that now they had no religious affiliation. As can be seen in Table 1 the majority of the addition in this category came from the Hervormd Kerk, the former Reformed or Presbyterian State Church. All but one of the twenty-five who used to think of themselves as Hervormd were nominal members in the Netherlands. Also some of those who were Katholiek and Gereformeerd (a strictly Calvinist denomination which split off from the Hervormd Kerk in the nineteenth century for theological reasons) contributed to the no-religion category, but to a much lesser extent.

Church attendance also tended to decrease, as Table 2 shows. It is interesting to compare these findings with a Western Australian study made by John Eric Gough.[6] Although Gough did not attempt to get a representative sample of the entire population of a certain area, used a mailed questionnaire with a 46 per cent return of usable responses and has different categories, there are a few findings in his Table A8 regarding religious affiliations in the Nether-

---

[5] This study ("Changes in Religious Behaviour of Dutch Immigrants") has recently been published by the REMP as Supplement No. 8, July 1965.

[6] John Eric Gough, *The role of Church membership in the assimilation and adjustment of immigrants* (unpublished M.A. thesis, Uni. of Western Australia, 1963).

TABLE 2. Comparison of Changes in Affiliation and Church Attendance of the Various Denominations

	Denominations in the Netherlands		
	Katholiek (N=167)	Gereformeerd (N=40)	Hervormd (N=105)
Percentage of those who now state to have no religion	8	7^1/$_2$	24
Percentage of those who have joined other denominations	2^1/$_2$	25	16
Percentage of those who continue to attend regularly (nearly always or usually)	77	60	15
Percentage of those who continue to attend irregularly (never or hardly ever, occasionally)	1	—	14
Percentage of those who improve churchgoing	2^1/$_2$	5	11
Percentage of those who change to lesser churchgoing	9	2^1/$_2$	20
Total percentage	100	100	100

lands and in Australia which are comparable.

In Gough's study, too, the category with the greatest gains are the "nonaffiliates" (our category "no religion"). Although twenty-two of the 164 migrants who were nonaffiliates in the Netherlands joined religious denominations in Western Australia (mainly "Apostolic" and "Nonethnic Protestant"), a much larger number (forty-nine) swelled their ranks from primarily the Hervormd Kerk (twenty-two) and the Katholiek Kerk (nineteen). The percentage loss of Katholieken to the nonaffiliates was 7 per cent of Gough's study; in the Christchurch study it was 9 per cent. The percentage loss of Hervormden to the nonaffiliates was 16 per cent in Gough's study; in the Christchurch study it was 24 per cent.

Other evidence regarding the decline in religious participation of migrants comes from the U.S.A. In his Detroit study Gerhard Lenski points to the fact that the decrease in religious participation applies not only to immigration from other countries, but to intrasocietal migration as well.

Speaking about the 1958 Detroit study he says: "Among first-generation immigrants from abroad and first-generation migrants from the south, there was a net loss to the churches of 24 per cent."[7] Lenski's figures are all the more remarkable in that he found that "among second and third generation immigrants the net loss dropped to a mere 3 or 4 per cent" and that "when the Southern-born were excluded, the churches enjoyed a net gain of more than 5 per cent among fourth-, or more, generation Americans."[8]

To again switch for evidence to other migrants and another country: Clifford S. Hill did some research on the church attendance of West Indian migrants in the Greater London area. His figures "reveal that in the County of London 2,563 or 4 per cent of the total immigrant population attend churches in the areas where they have settled. Comparing this with the figure of 69 per cent for the West Indies, it may be seen that 94 per

[7] Gerhard Lenski, *The Religious Factor* (New York: Doubleday and Company, Inc., 1961), p. 42.
[8] *Ibid.*

cent of the immigrants who used to attend churches in the West Indies have ceased to do so since coming to London."[9]

Is there no evidence to the contrary? In other words can we find instances of increase in religious interest of immigrants? There are a number of reasons why one could expect it. If, as is generally accepted, immigrants feel lost and rootless in a new country, one would expect those institutions to be at a premium which provide a meaningful interpretation of existence. And quite apart from the spiritual possibilities, one would expect the institutional and social aspects to appeal, particularly when the churches through their foreign language program recreate a bit of old country in the new.

If the immigrants are not primarily interested in theology and liturgy one would still expect them to seek the social outlets of the churches both for their own satisfaction and (at a more advanced stage of the integration process) for the contacts with the native population.

Whatever evidence of increase there is seems to be of an impressionistic nature. It is quite likely that there are some sources which give statistical evidence of this possibility. I would feel very obliged if those readers who know of other sources, not mentioned here, could write me.

What one often finds, particularly in the American historical writings, is a description of the vitality of the churches as a result of immigrant participation.

Marcus Lee Hansen wrote: " . . . (The) laymen who before emigration had had only a casual connection with the church entered with enthusiasm into problems of congregational finance and orthodoxy."[10]

Oscar Handlin said: "In the American environment, so new and dangerous, these people (the dissenters) felt more need than ever for the support of their faith."[11]

Even when there is not only historical, but also statistical evidence of immigrant religious participation, there usually is nothing known of the previous behavior patterns of these same immigrants. This for instance is true for the 104 newcomers in Grodka and Hennes' Study Sample of Immigrants. Sponsored by Church World Service in the U.S.A.,[12] 62.5 per cent of these immigrants had adjusted well to the expectations of church attendance according to the sponsors. It can indeed be speculated that these church-sponsored newcomers attended church better than in the home country, but there is no evidence for it. The basis for this speculation is that almost all these newcomers came from Europe where church attendance is generally much lower, particularly in those countries where there is or was a State Church.

But similar speculation would be rather precarious if one would apply it to the figures which Clarence Senior mentions for Puerto Ricans. He says: "A 1959 survey of Puerto Ricans in the New Haven area showed that while 93 per cent reported church membership, only 26 per cent attended regularly. Findings in New York City showed 25 per cent of the Catholics were regular in attendance,

9 Clifford S. Hill, *West Indian Migrants and the London Churches* (London: Oxford University Press, 1963), pp. 22–23.

10 Marcus Lee Hansen, *The Immigrant in American History* (Boston, 1940), p. 83.
11 Oscar Handlin, *The Uprooted* (Boston, 1940), p. 83.
12 Sonia Grodka and Gerhard Hennes, *Homeless No More* (New York: National Council of Churches of Christ in the U.S.A., 1960), p. 57.

as compared with 50 per cent of the Protestants."[13] Although the Catholic attendance appears to be below and the Protestant attendance above the American average, these differences are likely to reflect the Catholic majority and Protestant minority situation in Puerto Rico and one can therefore only speak about increase or decrease of religious participation when one has reliable figures of church attendance in Puerto Rico.

So far our concern has been with varying forms of statistical evidence of decrease and increase in religious affiliation and participation. The statistical evidence is insufficient for a comprehensive explanatory analysis which takes both decrease and increase into account. And still there is sufficient material to make at least an attempt.

1. The cases of increase appear to be confined to the U.S.A., where both Catholic and Protestant church attendance is higher than in almost any other western country. We can expect that the progressive adjustment of the immigrant to the new country also includes the gradual adoption of more religious activity. This was all the more true in the past when the foreign language church was a home away from home which often became the "nucleus around which the majority of (immigrant) organizations (were) formed and the center of organized social activities."[14]

2. The cases of decrease can partially be explained in that the available churches (see the French example), instead of being "a home away from home," were foreign institutions to which the immigrant felt less compelled to adjust. The occupational and language demands, on the other hand, were much more directly related to his bread and butter.

3. The cases of decrease can also at least partially be explained by emigration from countries with relatively high religious interest to countries with a predominantly low religious pulse (e.g. from the West Indies to the Greater London area).

4. Also the immigrants often go to the more industrialized countries where the standard of living is higher, but where the churches are socially more on the periphery as compared with the rural areas. This is also true for intrasocietal migration.

5. Still even "over-conformity" could not even begin to explain why the Detroit immigrants, the West Indian immigrants in London, the Dutch in Australia and New Zealand appear to affiliate or participate less than the native population.[15]

6. The specific religious situation in either the country of departure or the country of adoption has of necessity an important bearing in the decrease or increase of religious affiliation and participation. Still the existing religious patterns in stable societies may through traditional conformity hide the functional erosion of the religious institutions. Migration can therefore be looked upon as one of the few ways to measure this erosion. "... (Migration) often functions as a clearing-house for pseudo-codes. The less vital religion is for

---

[13] Clarence Senior, *Strangers Then Neighbors* (New York: Freedom Books, 1961), p. 73.

[14] See Samuel Koenig, *Immigrant Settlements in Connecticut: Their Growth and Characteristics* (Hartford, Connecticut, 1938), p. 56.

[15] The percentage of the total population in the 1961 Australian census which had no religion or gave no reply was 10.9 per cent. Of the Dutch-born, the percentage was 26.9 per cent. The percentage of the total population in the 1961 New Zealand census which had no religion or objected to stating it was 9.1 per cent. Of the Dutch migrants in Christchurch the percentage stating that they had no religion was 24.9 per cent. Of course, it is true that in both countries many so-called Anglicans are virtually identical with those who say to have no religion.

the self-identity of the immigrant, the easier it will be for him to forget all about it."[16] The motivations of migrants may have much to do with the lure and excitement of the cities, the desire for a higher standard of living, the escape from personal frustrations. As religion does seldom occupy a central part in these motivations, it is also unlikely that it will figure prominently as a focus for the rearrangement of new habits and norms necessitated by the move.

7. However neither the prevailing religious situations in the countries of emigration or immigration, nor the secular motivations, can fully explain why some denominations, such as the Dutch Reformed, suffer far more decrease (see Table 1) than the Dutch Catholics in the same country. Here we have to look at the capacity of denomination in the country of emigration to inculcate loyalty norms. A particular denomination may be cohesive—that is, members do what is expected of them and return loyalty to the organization for the desire of being accepted by the church. In such a case apostasy in the new country seems to be minimized. But on the other hand, a denomination may show all the characteristics of what Durkheim called "anomie," a lack of control by the group over its members, and piecemeal and shallow contacts between members. In such a case we seem to have the phenomenon of the downward spiral, observed by Homans.[17] The already low religious involvement of the emigrant becomes even lower in the new country.

---

[16] J. J. Mol, *Churches and Immigrants* (The Hague: Research Group for European Migration Problem, 1961), p. 56.

[17] See his description of Hilltown as an example of social disintegration in George C. Homans, *The Human Group* (New York: Harcourt, Brace & World, Inc., 1950), p. 334.

A basic function of all societies is the production of goods and services needed by their members. The patterns of activities and relationships developed in the production of these goods and services constitute their economic institutions. In primitive societies economic institutions may be relatively simple, with most of the production tasks performed by the family. Modern industrial-commercial societies, on the other hand, are characterized by awesomely complex economic

6

ECONOMIC
INSTITUTIONS

systems involving many hundreds of interrelated organizations staffed by workers in highly specialized roles.

Neither sociologists nor demographers have studied economic institutions as thoroughly as their importance warrants. This neglect can be attributed in part to the existence of economics as an older social-science discipline with a staked-out territory upon which sociologists have been reluctant to encroach. It has also been suggested that a major factor separating the fields of economics and sociology was a "revolt" on the part of sociologists against the permeation of the intellectual atmosphere by economic thinking.[1]

Economists have long considered demographic factors in the analysis of economic systems, but as Joseph Spengler has noted:

Although students of economics, together with students of statistical and actuarial methods,

[1] Talcott Parsons and Neil J. Smelser, *Economy and Society—A Study in the Integration of Economic and Social Theory* (London: Routledge & Kegan Paul, Ltd., 1956), p. 18.

were perhaps the first to give considerable attention to questions of population, they did not explore effectively the data available for the analysis of interrelations between economic and demographic movements.... [It] is only within more recent decades that careful consideration began to be given to these points.[2]

Spengler, in the work from which the above quotation is taken, has outlined systematically the major connections between economics and demography, defining an area of analysis that might be termed "economic demography." No similar set of relations between economic sociology and demography has been developed, owing in part to the immature state of development of the former field. Smelser has distinguished between economic sociology and economics on the basis of the analytic frameworks employed by the two disciplines.[3] In his view, "Economic sociology is the application of the general frame of reference, variables, and explanatory models of sociology to that complex of activities concerned with the production, distribution, exchange, and consumption of scarce goods and services."[4] Most recent studies in economic sociology in the United States have been conducted under such headings as industrial sociology, the sociology of occupations, and the sociology of complex organizations. Although Smelser, in the cited work, does not deal with the relationships between economic sociology and demography, Wilbert Moore in an earlier discussion of the sociology of economic organization viewed demography, as a field "on the borderline between economics and sociology."[5] Demography was seen to intersect economic analysis at two principal points: the supply of labor and the demand for goods. Population variables influencing this supply and demand are influenced by social institutions. Economics, sociology, and demography have all given attention to various aspects of the labor force.

The most thorough review of the relations between demographic variables and economic variables that are of interest to both economists and sociologists is provided in *The Determinants and Consequences of Population Trends*, published by the Population Division of the United Nations in 1953. This important source of information for social demographers summarizes some of the major ways in which population variables influence economic variables as well as the ways in which economic processes influence population growth and composition.

[2] Joseph J. Spengler, "Economics and Demography," in *The Study of Population*, eds. Hauser and Duncan (Chicago: The University of Chicago Press, 1959), pp. 793, 797.

[3] Neil J. Smelser, *The Sociology of Economic Life* (Englewood Cliffs, New Jersey: Prentice-Hall, Inc., 1963).

[4] *Ibid.*, p. 32.

[5] Wilbert E. Moore, "Sociology of Economic Organization," in *Twentieth Century Sociology*, eds. Georges Gurvitch and Wilbert E. Moore (New York: The Philosophical Library, 1945), p. 453.

In the first selection, Richard A. Easterlin examines the effects of population growth on economic development. Some economic theories hold that high rates of population growth retard development; others point to positive effects of high population growth rates. Easterlin's analysis indicates that the two variables are not simply related in such a manner as to permit a clear-cut resolution of the issue, for population growth and economic development are always accompanied by changes in political, social, and educational institutions which influence the relationship.

In the second reading, David Heer examines a reciprocal relationship. How does economic development affect fertility? Again, conflicting theories support differing effects. Heer hypothesizes that the direct effect of economic development is to increase fertility. However, other changes that generally accompany economic development, such as a rise in the educational level and a reduction in infant and childhood mortality, serve to reduce fertility. Developing nations that wish to reduce fertility levels, Heer suggests, should support health and education programs along with other programs designed to raise the economic level.

Much less interest has been shown in the relationship of economic factors with mortality than with either fertility or migration. It is well-known, of course, that countries with more advanced economies have lower death rates than developing countries, partly because of the greater accessibility of modern health and medical technology in the former. Numerous studies have also demonstrated differences in mortality rates by occupational groups and social classes, but usually with little consideration of the relationship of such categories to the embracing economic system.

Joseph J. Spengler discusses some of the economic effects of migration in the third reading. The major consequences of migration are classified into those stemming from changes in population size and those resulting from changes in the population composition. However, Spengler believes that the psychological changes of migrants may also have salubrious effects on the economies of those areas into which they move. "Immigration," he observes, "increased the drive, the willingness to work, and the ambitions that animated America's labor force."

In the final selection, Chester Hunt examines the influence of urbanization and industrialization upon the sex composition of the urban population. In the United States, industrialization provided relatively more jobs for women in the cities, leading to selective migration of females to the city. This selectivity has also occurred in the Philippines, even though it is much less industrialized. But it has not occurred in the highly industrialized nation of Japan. Japanese cultural norms governing the occupational roles open to women apparently are responsible for the divergence from a pattern of low urban sex ratios found in most industrialized countries of the Western world.

Effects of Population Growth on the Economic Development of Developing Countries*

Richard A. Easterlin

As a distinctive era, modern economic development dates from the eighteenth century. It may be defined as a rapid and sustained rise in real output per head of the population and accompanying shifts in technological, economic, and demographic characteristic of a society. Together with the more recent concepts of social and political development, it forms the phenomenon which historians designate "modernization," embracing innovation in numerous aspects of individual behavior and social organization.

From the viewpoint of the economic system as a whole, the central feature of modern economic growth is an immense and continuous rise in the yield from human economic activity, that is, in the productivity of labor. The fundamental basis for such productivity growth has been technological innovation on a widespread and continuous scale. This has been accompanied by a marked rise in capital investment per worker and by a vast improvement in the "quality" of labor, that is, in such conditions as the nutrition, health, and education of the labor force.

The question of the effect of population growth on economic development thus centers on the issue of its productivity impact, either directly or through its concurrent influence on other productivity factors such as technological change, capital investment, health, and education. The majority view today, at least with regard to the developing nations, those under discussion here, is that rapid population growth impedes economic development. There is, however, some dissent from this position, for there are arguments on the other side.

* Richard A. Easterlin, "Effects of Population Growth on the Economic Development of Developing Countries," *Annals of The American Academy of Political and Social Science*, 371 (January, 1967), 98–108.

Nor is the evidence of history un-equivocal. The present paper attempts to sketch the state of existing knowl-edge. It first summarizes briefly some of the leading theoretical views, pro and con, and then touches on the lessons of experience. To cover such a large subject in brief compass re-quires a highly selective treatment, and the over-all impression conveyed inevitably reflects the author's per-sonal judgments.[1]

THEORY

UNFAVORABLE EFFECTS. The most common reasoning, the Malthusian analysis, is rooted in the law of di-minishing returns. One's first thought might be that the growth in total output is unaffected by the growth of population, in which case a rise in the rate of population growth would entail a corresponding reduction in

---

[1] For a valuable and more extended recent discussion of many of the issues under consideration here, the reader is referred to two summary papers pre-sented at the 1965 World Population Conference by Simon Kuznets: "Demo-graphic Aspects of Modern Economic Growth: Background Paper," United Nations Doc. WPC/WP/389 (hereafter cited as "Background Paper"), and "Demographic Aspects of Modern Eco-nomic Growth: Moderator's Statement." A short summary of the pertinent ses-sion at the Conference is given by C. Gotchac in *Population*, XX, No. 6 (No-vember–December, 1965), 1100–1106. An influential study, stressing the adverse effects of population growth, is Ansley J. Coale and Edgar M. Hoover, *Popu-lation Growth and Economic Develop-ment in Low-Income Countries* (Prince-ton, N.J.: Princeton University Press, 1961). For a valuable survey of the literature prior to the early 1950s, cf. United Nations, *The Determinants and Consequences of Population Trends* (New York: United Nations, 1953), chap. xiii (hereafter, "Determinants and Consequences").

the growth of output per head of the population. Such a simplified view obviously overlooks the fact that, with due allowance for the lag between birth and labor force entry, popula-tion growth implies growth in the labor supply and thus in productive capacity. It does not follow, however, that the growth in output would be proportionate to the increase in labor supply. Labor is but one of the inputs in the production process; only if the others were increased in the same proportion as labor would it seem reasonable to expect output to grow correspondingly. If they are not, and if production methods remain un-changed, then one would expect out-put to grow less than proportionately to labor. To put it differently, if tech-nology is assumed fixed, then popula-tion growth coupled with slower or zero growth in one or more other productive agents implies that there will be progressively less materials, equipment, and/or natural resources per worker, and, hence, that output per worker will tend to diminish.

In this reasoning, the fixity of natural resources, particularly land, is most often emphasized, and the in-ference is drawn that agricultural productivity, and thus food supplies per capita, will become progressively less. Of course, if the new workers provided by population growth simply increase the under- or unemployed and do not add to the actual labor input in the economy, then the productivity of employed labor will be unaffected. However, since the same total output must be shared among progressively greater numbers, output per head of the total population would still decline.

A recent variant of this analysis concerns itself with the relation, not of natural resources to population, but of reproducible capital—structures, equipment, and inventories—to population. In this analysis, the stock of reproducible capital is taken as normally growing, rather than constant, at a rate varying with the proportion of national income invested. If population and labor force were constant, then capital per worker and hence output per worker would normally grow over time. Population and labor force *growth* would imply a reduction in the increase of capital per worker —part of the addition to capital being required simply to keep the stock of capital per worker constant—and a consequent slowing down of the growth of output per worker. This analysis thus sees high population growth not necessarily as reducing the *level* of output per head but as lowering the rate of increase—the higher the rate of population increase, the greater the reduction in the growth of output per head. This line of reasoning is often used in discussions of development plans in less developed countries, where the proportion of national income invested is a strategic planning variable, often taken as determined by the plan. High population growth is seen as using up limited additions to capital resources on "unproductive" investment such as housing, as well as diverting government revenues that might have been used for the purpose of capital formation to "current" expenditures on items such as education and health.

Typically, of course, the proportion of national income invested depends not only on government capital formation but on private saving and investing decisions. The question naturally arises whether population growth may affect such decisions and thereby additionally influence the growth of capital, both total and per worker.

The view most often advanced stresses the adverse consequences of high fertility on the age structure of the population and through this on savings rates. High fertility tends to produce a population with a relatively large proportion of persons below working age, and thus a situation where the number of dependents per worker is relatively high. This dependency burden creates pressures on the household to spend currently for consumption rather than save. The lower rate of private saving in turn keeps down private investment. Of course, high fertility, the initiating factor in this analysis, does not necessarily imply high total increase of the population, since it may be coupled with either low or high mortality. The point is made, however, that a reduction of fertility (which would imply a reduction in population growth) would tend to raise savings and capital formation.

In sum, the present conditions of rapid population growth in less developed nations are seen as creating pressures on limited natural resources, as reducing private and public capital formation, and diverting additions to capital resources to merely maintaining rather than increasing the stock of capital per worker. In consequence, the growth of output per employed worker is retarded and/or under- and unemployment grow. Output per head of the total population grows at a reduced rate or actually declines in absolute level.[2]

---

[2] The present discussion omits the theory of the "low-level equilibrium trap." Cf. Harvey Leibenstein, *Economic Backwardness and Economic Growth* (New York: John Wiley & Sons, Inc., 1957) and Richard R. Nelson, "A Theory of the Low-Level Equilibrium Trap in Underdeveloped Economies," *American*

Concern with such problems is manifest in the replies received from the governments of some developing countries to a United Nations inquiry on problems resulting from the interaction of economic development and population changes. An excerpt from Ceylon's reply provides an illustration:

> ... unless there is some prospect of a slowing down in the rate of population growth and relative stability in at least the long run, it is difficult to envisage substantial benefits from planning and development. It is not so much the size of the population in an absolute sense; but rather the rate of increase that tends to frustrate attempts to step up the rate of investment and to increase income per head. Apart from the difficult process of cutting present levels of consumption, the source for increasing the volume of investment is the "ploughing back" of portions of future increases in incomes. This task is handicapped if these increases have instead to be devoted each year to sustaining a larger population.
> ... Population growth has obviously an impact on the magnitude of the economic, social and financial problems which we have to solve. For instance, the Government's current expending on food subsidies, education and health is now considerably higher than it would have been if our population had increased at a slower rate. The same applies to our import requirements and the scarcity of foreign exchange.[3]

FAVORABLE EFFECTS. The most common argument for the positive impact of population growth on economic development is that relating to economies of scale and specialization. Within a productive establishment, there tends to be at any given time an optimum scale of operation, large in some industries, small in others. If the population is small, then the domestic market will not be able to support the most efficient level of operation in some industries. Extending one's view from an establishment in a given industry to the economy as a whole brings into view additional productivity gains associated with increased size. George Stigler has put it as follows:

> The large economy can practice specialization in innumerable ways not open to the small (closed) economy. The labor force can specialize in more sharply defined functions. ... The business sector can have enterprises specializing in collecting oil prices, in repairing old machinery, in printing calendars, in advertising industrial equipment. The transport system can be large enough to allow innumerable specialized forms of transport, such as pipelines, particular types of chemical containers, and the like.[4]

The view is prominent among economists that economies of size are significant in accounting for the high productivity of the United States economy.

It does not follow, however, that any given nation must have a population large enough to realize all or even most of such gains, if it is willing to

---

Economic Review, XLVI, No. 5 (December, 1956), 894–908. The assumptions of this analysis have been shown by Simon Kuznets to be highly unrealistic ("Background Paper," *op. cit.*, pp. 8–9).

[3] United Nations, "Inquiry Among Governments on Problems Resulting from the Interaction of Economic Development and Population Changes," United Nations Doc. E/3895/Rev. 1 (24 November 1964), pp. 19–20.

[4] Conference on Research in Income and Wealth, *Output, Input and Productivity Measurement*, Studies in Income and Wealth, Vol. XXV (Princeton, N.J.: Princeton University Press, 1961), p. 61.

participate in international trade. Through specialization in particular branches of economic activity and exchange with other nations, it is possible for a nation to achieve high levels of economic development. This is one important argument for customs unions and free trade areas among smaller less developed nations today. It also helps explain how among the richest nations today are some with small populations—Switzerland, Norway, Finland, Denmark, Israel, and New Zealand all have populations around five million or less. But to recognize this is not to gainsay that increasing population size within a given geographic area widens the alternatives available for productivity gains.

A second view makes the point that accelerated population growth in less developed areas today is a reflection of sweeping reductions in the death rate, and that the health advances that have made this possible have themselves expanded productive capacity and promoted attitudes favorable to economic development. Thus, a major survey of the world social situation points out:

> Medical services and medical advances are often pace-makers of social change. Penicillin (and the whole range of antibiotics which followed its discovery) and DDT (and the other insecticides) have already transformed the lives of millions, not only by benefiting the individual directly, but also by increasing capacities and changing the attitudes of whole communities.[5]

---

[5] United Nations, *Preliminary Report on the World Social Situation* (New York: United Nations, 1952), p. 22. Cf. also Rashi Fein, "Health Program and Economic Development," in The *Economics of Health and Medical Care*, Proceedings of the Conference on the Economics of Health and Medical Care,

A concrete example of the impact on economic productivity of the health advances which have at the same time raised population growth is offered later in the report:

> ...disease is a considerable factor in the incapacity of people to feed themselves. In Mymensingh, a district in East Pakistan, malaria control not only diminished infant mortality ("more mouths to feed") but increased the production of rice by 15 per cent—from the same acreage ("more and better hands to work") without any improvement in methods of cultivation or the variety of rice. This increase was due to the fact that whereas in the past three out of every five landworkers had been sick of the fever at the critical seasons of planting and harvesting, five out of five were available for the manual operations when the malaria had been controlled. In other areas, removal of a seasonal malaria has made it possible to grow a second crop. In still others, hundreds of thousands of acres of fertile land, which had been abandoned because of malaria, have been recovered for cultivation. People who are sick, ailing and incapacitated by disease lack the energy, initiative and enterprise needed to adopt new methods and improve their means of food production and so increase the yields from existing acreages.[6]

It should be noted that in this argument, the line of causation is not from high population growth to improved productivity. Rather, high population growth *and* improved productivity both arise from the same source—the reduction in mortality and associated improvement in health. It could be argued that if the mortality

---

May 10–12, 1962, sponsored by the Bureau of Public Health Economics and the Department of Economics of the University of Michigan (1964), pp. 271–82.

[6] *Ibid.*, p. 36.

reduction were accompanied by a fertility reduction, so that population growth did not accelerate, then the productivity increase would be higher, for the positive effects of better "quality" workers would not be partially offset by the tendency toward diminishing returns produced by a greater quantity of workers. Thus, while this analysis does, on the one hand, point up a dubious aspect of the usual Malthusian argument as it bears on the present situation in less developed areas—the assumption that the quality of labor is unchanged—it does not deny that the stimulus to increased numbers as such is adverse.

Another argument, however, is based directly on accelerated population growth—or at least natural increase—as the cause. The key element in this analysis is the impact of the pressure of increased family size on individual motivation. It may be illustrated by comparison with the Malthusian approach. Assume in a population initially with a zero growth rate that a substantial cut occurs in the infant mortality rate owing, say, to new public health measures. The effect will be to raise dependency and, with a lag, the labor supply. The Malthusian view reasons that, assuming no change in production methods or other productive factors, the employment of this extra labor will reduce output per worker and consumption per head of the population.

At this point, a question might be asked whether human beings are likely to be totally oblivious to the implications of the growth in dependency for their consumption levels. Clearly the rise in dependency creates a threat both to the maintenance of existing consumption levels and to future improvements therein. Will individuals passively accept this consequence? Or may the threat posed by this "population pressure" provide the motivation for changes in behavior? At least two broad alternatives to passive acceptance come to mind. One, stressed in Kingsley Davis' presidential address to the Population Association of America, is a change in demographic behavior, a reduction in fertility or rise in outmigration. Looking back at western European experience over the past century and a half, Davis asserts:

> Although generally overlooked because of our preoccupation with the contraceptive issue, the fact is that every country in northwest Europe reacted to its persistent excess of births over deaths with virtually the entire range of possible responses. Regardless of nationality, language, and religion, each industrializing nation tended to postpone marriage, to increase celibacy, to resort to abortion, to practice contraception in some form, and to emigrate overseas.[7]

The stimulus to this, in Davis' view, is the decline in mortality and sustained natural increase to which it gave rise:

> Mortality decline impinged on the individual by enlarging his family. Unless something were done to offset this effect, it gave him, as a child, more siblings with whom to share whatever derived from his parents as well as more likelihood of reckoning with his parents for a longer period of life; and, as an adult, it gave him a more fragmented and more delayed share of the patrimony with which to get married and found his own family, while at the same time it saddled him, in founding that family, with the task of pro-

---

[7] Kingsley Davis, "The Theory of Change and Response in Modern Demographic History," *Population Index*, XXIX, No. 4 (October 1963), 350–51. [See also Chap. 2 of this book.]

viding for more children—for rearing them, educating them, endowing their marriages, etc.,—in a manner assuring them a status no lower than his.[8]

The second alternative is a change in productive behavior, for example, the adoption of new production methods or increased saving to utilize more capital in production. To this, it may be objected that, at a given time, individuals are likely to be employing the best methods available to them. While this is a standard assumption of economic theory, a recent article by Harvey Leibenstein (not itself dealing with the question of population growth) points out that "the simple fact is that neither individuals nor firms work as hard, nor do they search for information as effectively, as they could."[9] Population pressure arising from mortality reduction may provide the spur to work harder, search out information, increase capital formation, and try new methods. Two recent exponents of this view have been Colin Clark and Ester Boserup.[10] The latter argues that what are typically regarded as more advanced agricultural techniques have actually required more labor per unit output, that is, the sacrifice of leisure. His-

torically, therefore, populations which have been aware of the availability of more advanced methods have often resisted their adoption until growth raised population density to a point of compelling the adoption of such methods in order to maintain consumption levels. With this shift may come better work habits and other changes facilitating sustained economic growth.

It is clear that this line of reasoning does not lead inexorably to the conclusion that economic development may be promoted by the pressure arising from accelerated population growth. The nature of the changes in behavior, if any, clearly depends on many conditions—the education of those involved, the supply of information, and institutional conditions which may impede change along some lines and favor it in other directions. But it does raise a valid issue which is often neglected in discussions of this subject: the impact of population pressure on individual motivation. To the proponent of this view, government planners who view population growth as excessive are perhaps assuming to themselves undue responsibility and influence in the promotion of economic growth, and are failing to allow for the possible significance for the growth process of widespread individual initiative and enterprise, which population growth may spur.

A final positive effect turns on the age distribution of the population. To the extent that the age structure is skewed towards children, the numerical proportion of young to old is raised. If the young are viewed as more amenable to the adoption of new forms of behavior, then a young population, such as characterizes less developed areas, may be more favora-

---

[8] *Ibid.*, p. 352.

[9] Harvey Leibenstein, "Allocative Efficiency vs. 'X-Efficiency,'" *American Economic Review*, LVI, No. 3 (June 1966), 407.

[10] Ester Boserup, *The Conditions of Agricultural Growth: The Economics of Agrarian Change under Population Pressure* (Chicago: Aldine, 1965); and Colin Clark, "The First Stages of Economic Growth," United Nations Doc. WPC/WP/347, paper prepared for 1965 World Population Conference. For references to similar ideas in the earlier literature, cf. United Nations, *Determinants and Consequences . . ., op. cit.*, p. 230.

ble for economic development.[11] Younger persons are, of course, those who predominate in migration—a type of adjustment essential to economic growth. There is also some evidence that young persons may be more likely to be innovators.[12] An extension of this type of reasoning is involved in what Harvey Leibenstein has termed the "quality replacement rate."[13] Following a suggestion of Nathan Keyfitz, Leibenstein argues that if those entering the labor force are more favorably equipped than those leaving, in attitudes, capacities, motivation, and the like, then in a population whose age structure favors the young, the replacement of those with less favorable capacities by those with more will occur more rapidly. For example, if the educational system is steadily raising years of schooling, then the replacement of less by better educated persons in the work force will occur more rapidly if the age distribution is characterized by a higher proportion of young to old. This effect is not necessarily connected with high population growth rates, for a "young" age distribution may occur in connection with low population growth rates if both fertility and mortality are high. Most less developed nations today have relatively young populations (and thus the above positive effect is applicable) though they differ substantially in population growth rates. Leibenstein goes on to point out, however, that if population growth is high, the strain

thereby created on a limited government budget for educational purposes may compel a sacrifice of quality for quantity in the education of the young, and a consequent offset to the replacement effect.

THE RECORD

Although the theoretical possibilities include both favorable and unfavorable effects, it is possible that one or a group of factors on either the positive or negative side may be so overwhelming in the size of its effect that it dominates actual experience. The history of the past two centuries embraces countries exhibiting a variety of population growth patterns both in time and space. Unfortunately, relatively little has been done to analyze systematically the implications of these for economic development. However, it is at least possible to ask, to the extent data are available, whether variations in population growth rates show any consistent relation to growth of product per capita. This question is no more than a start, for it fails to allow for variations among nations or through time in other growth-affecting factors which may obscure the actual relationship between population and economic growth. However, if the effect of population growth is very strong relative to these other factors, then it might be expected to show up even in such a simple two-variable comparison.

For the less developed countries of the world, reliable population estimates prior to the twentieth century are generally not available. Durand's recent examination of the available evidence since 1750 suggests that a discernible rise in growth rates did occur, though it was highly uneven in

---

[11] Cf. Kuznets, "Background Paper . . . ," *op. cit.*, p. 15.

[12] Everett M. Rogers, *Diffusion of Innovations* (New York: Free Press of Glencoe, Inc., 1962), pp. 172–74.

[13] "The Impact of Population Growth on 'Noneconomic' Determinants of Economic Growth," United Nations Doc. WPC/WP/95, paper prepared for the 1965 World Population Conference.

TABLE 1. Frequency Distribution of Developing Nations by Growth Rate of Real Per Capita Income Cross-Classified by Growth Rate of Population, 1957–1958 to 1963–1964

Rate of population (growth per cent per year)	Rate of growth of real per capita income (per cent per year)							
	Total	Less than zero	0 to 0.9	1.0 to 1.9	2.0 to 2.9	3.0 to 3.9	4.0 to 4.9	5.0 and over
Total	37	3	4	12	12	2	2	2
3.5 and over	2	1	0	0	0	0	1	0
3.0–3.4	10	0	2	3	4	0	1	0
2.5–2.9	11	1	2	5	1	1	0	1
2.0–2.4	8	0	0	3	5	0	0	0
1.5–1.9	4	1	0	0	2	1	0	0
Less than 1.5	2	0	0	1	0	0	0	1

Notes: The countries included are non-Communist ones in Africa, Asia, and Latin America (except for Israel, Japan, and the Union of South Africa) with populations of around two million or more, for which data were available. In a few cases data for one of the two variables were not available for the specified period, and the nearest overlapping period was used.

Sources: Per capita income: A. I. D. Statistics and Reports Division, "Estimated Annual Growth Rates of Developed and Less Developed Countries" (♯R. C. W-138, Mimeo.). Population: United Nations, *1964 Demographic Yearbook* (New York: United Nations, 1965).

time and space.[14] It is fairly clear, however, that in this century, and particularly since around 1940, growth has been noticeably greater than in the past and generally accelerating. Unfortunately, estimates of per capita income even for this century are generally not available, except for very recent years, and experience has shown that short periods are not necessarily reliable indicators of secular tendencies. For what they are worth, the data for the period since 1957–1958, when population growth rates in most of these countries are among the highest ever experienced, show that per capita income has generally increased (see Table 1). Moreover, if India, where long-term estimates are available, is representa- tive, it is likely that in a number of cases these rates of economic growth are noticeably higher than earlier in this century.[15] Thus, accelerating population growth in recent years has not generally precluded positive per capita income growth, and has perhaps even been accompanied by accelerated income growth.

What of the now-developed nations? It is, perhaps, of some interest to look back into their history, when they were closer to the situation of today's less developed areas. The evidence is not as complete as one might wish, but it appears correct to say that virtually every one of these nations (other than those undergoing new settlement) went through a

14 John D. Durand, "World Population Estimates, 1750–2000," United Nations Doc. WPC/WP/289, paper prepared for 1965 World Population Conference.

15 M. Mukherjee, "A Preliminary Study of the Growth of National Income in India, 1857–1957," in International Association for Research in Income and Wealth, *Asian Studies in Income and Wealth* (New York: Asia Publishing House, 1965), pp. 71–103.

phase in which the population growth rate was noticeably above both prior and present levels, as mortality declined while fertility remained high.[16] The timing of this period in relation to the trend in the growth rate of per capita income cannot at present be firmly established, but it seems to have come early in, and perhaps in some cases before, the period of modern economic development, as economic historians would commonly date it.

To return to the data for today's less developed nations, is there evidence of a consistent relation between growth rates of population and of per capita income? That is, even if per capita income growth is in most cases positive, do those nations with low growth of per capita income usually exhibit high population growth and vice versa? Table 1 summarizes the data for thirty-seven less developed countries, those with populations under two million having been omitted. It is clear from the table that these is little evidence of any significant association, positive or negative, between the income and population growth rates. A similar comparison by Simon Kuznets for eleven now-developed countries for which data were available for about a half-century prior to World War I yielded the same conclusion.[17] Of course, in

the comparison for the current period, if the present experience of the now-developed nations were added, one would find that there was some indication that countries with higher growth rates of per capita income tended to have lower population growth rates. But if the less developed nations were added to the pre-World War I comparison, the reverse conclusion would obtain—those with higher per capita income growth rates tended to have higher population growth rates.[18]

On the whole, then, simple empirical comparisons between economic and population growth rates are inconclusive. Cases of high per capita income growth are associated with both high and low population growth, and the same is true for cases of low per capita income growth. None of this means that per capita income growth would have been the same if population growth rates had been markedly higher or lower. But the effect of population growth, whether positive or negative, is not so great relative to other growth determinants as to stand out in a simple comparison. This cautions against preoccupation with the effect of population growth on economic development to the exclusion of other determinants. At a minimum, the evidence, as far as it has been touched on here, suggests that in the past two centuries accelerated population growth has not typically prevented growth in per capita income, let alone compelled a decline.

---

[16] D. V. Glass and D. E. C. Eversley (eds.), *Population in History* (Chicago: Aldine, 1965); D. V. Glass and E. Grebenik, "World Population, 1800–1950," in *The Cambridge Economic History of Europe*, Vol. VI: *The Industrial Revolutions and After: Incomes, Population and Technological Change*, eds. H. J. Habakkuk and M. Postan, Part I (Cambridge: Cambridge University Press, 1965), pp. 56–138.

[17] Simon Kuznets, "Quantitative Aspects of the Economic Growth of Nations," Part I: "Levels and Variability

of Rates of Growth," *Economic Development and Cultural Change*, V, No. 1 (October 1956), 30.

[18] Jean Bourgeois-Pichat, "Population Growth and Development," *International Conciliation*, No. 556 (January 1966), p. 15.

CONCLUDING OBSERVATIONS

The theories and evidence surveyed here do not, it seems, add up to any clear-cut generalization as to the effect of population growth on economic development in today's less developed areas. Indeed, it may well be that no single generalization is appropriate for countries differing as widely in growth rates, densities, and income levels as do these areas. Clearly there is need for more basic research on the actual experience of nations, currently and in the past.

It should be stressed that the basic conclusion is the unsatisfactory state of present scientific knowledge, no more than that. It would not be correct to infer from this that the present population situation in a number of less developed areas provides no cause for concern. It is a fact that in many areas population growth rates have risen at a rate and to levels unprecedented in past experience. It is plausible that these large and abrupt changes may create such widespread pressures and needs as virtually to overwhelm both individual and collective capacities to cope with them. And it is a sobering fact that in some less developed areas, primarily in parts of Asia, there now exists a combination of higher population growth rates, higher population densities, and lower income levels than appears to have prevailed in any of the now-developed nations in their early phases of development. While it is possible that a high population growth rate may be one important stimulus to abandoning traditional modes of behavior and spurring innovation, one may wonder how high the rate need go.

At the same time one must be wary of viewing the present population situation in less developed areas as an isolated occurrence in otherwise static societies, without any parallel whatsoever in historical experience. Along with the rapid mortality decline and consequent surge in population growth, drastic changes are occurring, too, in economic, political, and social institutions, and in educational systems.[19] Many less developed societies are currently exhibiting characteristics which, in broad outline, are like those which appeared in the early phases of modernization in Europe, its overseas descendants, and Japan. The current surge in population growth may thus be symptomatic of the further diffusion of modernization to today's less developed areas, of a social transformation which in the past has brought with it, in due course, modern economic growth.

Finally, one should note that recognition of the inadequate state of knowledge does not necessarily call into question the principal population-policy action usually advocated for less developed areas, namely, promotion of measures encouraging fertility reduction. Quite aside from the issue of effects on economic development, there is ample basis for advocating such programs. It is recognized that an increase in reliable information and widening of alternative open to individuals in general contribute to greater welfare. The need for such measures in the area of family planning, where open discussion is rare, is manifest. There is, moreover, evidence that many parents in less developed areas have more children than they desire or consider ideal.[20] The present discus-

---

[19] A valuable survey of some of these developments is given in United Nations, *1963 Report on the World Social Situation* (New York: United Nations, 1963).

[20] Ronald Freedman, "Norms for Family Size in Underdeveloped Areas,"

sion implies only that policies for fertility reduction should stress voluntary decisions on the part of the individuals concerned rather than compulsion, and should be conceived in the context of a much wider program for social, economic, and politi-

cal development, that is, of a program strengthening modernization generally. Indeed, it is only in such a context that these measures are likely to be successful.[21]

Proceedings of the Royal Society, B, CLIX (1963), 222.

---

[21] Cf. Ronald Freedman, "The Transition from High to Low Fertility: Challenge to Demographers," *Population Index*, XXXI, No. 4 (October 1965), 417–30.

Economic Development and Fertility

David M. Heer

ECONOMIC DEVELOPMENT AND FERTILITY

Two different schools of population theorists have developed contrasting views concerning the effect of economic development on fertility. The first school has contended that economic development has an inhibiting effect on fertility. This view has been perhaps the predominant view in recent years. The viewpoint is expressed most succinctly in the theory of the demographic transition, which has been set forth by Warren S. Thompson, C. P. Blacker, Kingsley Davis, Frank Notestein, and others.[1] Accord-

ing to this theory, a nation manifests characteristic types of demographic process dependent on its stage of industrialization and, by implication, depending on its level of economic development.

For example, Warren Thompson and Kingsley Davis divide the nations of the world into three classes. Class I nations are highly industrialized, have low fertility and mortality, and show little or no population growth. Class II nations are beginning the

---

* David M. Heer, "Economic Development and Fertility," *Demography*, III (1966), 423–44.
[1] See Warren S. Thompson, *Population and Peace in the Pacific* (Chicago: University of Chicago Press, 1946), pp.

22–35; C. P. Blacker, "Stages in Population Growth," *Eugenics Review*, XXXIX, No. 3 (October, 1947), 88–102; Kingsley Davis, *Human Society* (New York: The Macmillan Company, 1949), pp. 603–8; and Frank W. Notestein, "The Economics of Population and Food Supplies," in *Proceedings of the Eighth International Conference of Agricultural Economists* (London: Oxford University Press, 1953), pp. 15–31.

process of industrialization, have declining but still high fertility, rapidly declining mortality, and, in net balance, a high rate of population growth. Class III nations are not yet industrialized, have both high fertility and high mortality, and at most only a moderate degree of population growth.

The theory of the demographic transition, which was popularized soon after World War II, is congruent with the generally inverse association between fertility level and degree of industrialization among nations today. The theory is also congruent with the fact that currently the nations which are now industrialized all have lower fertility than they did before industrialization.

Additional evidence supporting the viewpoint that economic development results in reduced fertility is the general pattern of association between fertility and social class. In most nations during recent years, the social classes having the highest incomes have had lower fertility than those with lower incomes.[2] From this phenomenon one can argue that, as the income of the lower classes rises in the future to approach the present level of the higher classes, their future fertility will conform to the current fertility of the higher classes.

On the other hand, a second school of thought has contended that economic development promotes fertility. Malthus was perhaps the foremost representative of this viewpoint. Malthus believed that an increase in the demand for labor increased the proportion of persons marrying and re-

duced the average age at marriage. Furthermore, this change in marriage pattern led in turn to an increase in fertility.[3] Malthus himself lived during the middle of the Industrial Revolution in England. Presumably, therefore, his views were colored by what he conceived to be recent trends in fertility in his own country. The later critics of Malthus considered Malthus' views on the relation between fertility and economic development to be erroneous and generally attributed the large acceleration in population growth which accompanied the Industrial Revolution to be due exclusively to lowered mortality.

However, recently several historical demographers have produced evidence indicating that fertility may well have increased during England's period of industrial development in the early nineteenth century[4] and that a similar increase may have occurred in the Netherlands during its period of commercial development in the late seventeenth and early eighteenth centuries.[5]

In later years support for the school of thought linking fertility increase to economic development has been supplied by studies showing the association of birth and marriage rates with business cycles.[6] For example,

---

[2] For a bibliography of various studies on this topic, see Ronald Freedman, *The Sociology of Human Fertility* (Oxford: Basil Blackwell, 1963), pp. 95–97.

[3] Thomas R. Malthus, *An Essay on Population* (New York: E. P. Dutton & Co., Inc., 1914), I, 167, 277–78; II, 27–28, 132, 140, 230–31.

[4] J. T. Krause, "Some Implications of Recent Work in Historical Demography," *Comparative Studies in Society and History*, I, No. 2 (January, 1957), 164–88; H. J. Habakkuk, "English Population in the Eighteenth Century," *Economic History Review*, VI, No. 2 (December, 1953), 117–33.

[5] William Petersen, "The Demographic Transition in the Netherlands," *American Sociological Review*, XXV, No. 3 (June, 1966), 334–47.

[6] In citing studies whose conclusions can be interpreted as lending support to

Galbraith and Thomas showed that for the United States during the time period 1919–37 not only marriages but births of each order were affected by business cycles. With an appropriate time-lag, marriages and births of each parity increased when business conditions improved and declined when business fell off.[7] Dudley Kirk did an analysis for Germany during the 1920s and arrived at similar conclusions.[8] Other researchers have worked with data from other countries, and in all cases the results have shown the positive correlation between birth and marriage rates and the height of the business cycle.[9]

Further evidence that economic development promotes fertility comes from other types of studies. For example, Richard Easterlin, in a recent study, has considered not only the influence of general business conditions but also the effect on fertility of the relative demand for labor from young persons of reproductive age versus older persons past reproductive age. Specifically, Easterlin hypothesizes that one of the prime factors sustaining the American baby boom of the 1950s was the very high wage and salary level of persons 20–29 years old during this decade. He explains the high income level of this age group by two factors. First, the number of persons in this age group was exceptionally low because of the small number of babies born during the depression. Therefore, during the 1950s the supply of new entrants to the labor force was abnormally reduced during a period when demand for labor was high. Secondly, the group entering the labor force in the 1950s was exceptionally well educated in comparison with older age groups and thus had a competitive advantage in employment during a time period in which educational qualifications became increasingly important.[10]

Another recent study lending support to the conclusion that a high economic level promotes fertility was conducted by W. Stys. Stys has shown that, for Polish peasant women born during the latter half of the nineteenth century, average completed family size varied directly with size of farm. For example, among landless peasants the average number of births per mother was 3.9. However, on farms of more than seven hectares the average number was 9.1. The difference in fertility by size of farm was mostly the result of differences in the mother's age at marriage. However, in addition, there was some tendency for births per year of marriage to be slightly higher among women living on the larger farms than on the smaller.[11]

A very recent study by Gordon De Jong also contains results from which one may infer that an increase in economic status leads to an increase in

the Malthusian theory of a direct relation between economic development and fertility, I do not wish to imply that the authors of the studies necessarily themselves subscribe in whole or in part to Malthus' views in this regard.

[7] Virginia Galbraith and Dorothy S. Thomas, "Birth Rates and the Interwar Business Cycles," *Journal of the American Statistical Association*, XXXVI (December, 1941), 465–76.

[8] Dudley Kirk, "The Relation of Employment Levels to Births in Germany," *Milbank Memorial Fund Quarterly*, XXVIII (April, 1942), 126–38.

[9] For further bibliography on this topic, see Freedman, *op. cit.*, p. 108.

[10] Richard Easterlin, *The American Baby Boom in Historical Perspective* (New York: National Bureau of Economic Research, 1962).

[11] W. Stys, "The Influence of Economic Conditions on the Fertility of Peasant Women," *Population Studies*, XI, No. 2 (November, 1957), 136–48.

fertility. De Jong queried respondents in the Southern Appalachian region of the United States, one of the most economically deprived regions of the nation. Theree questions were asked: (1) the ideal number of children for the average young couple today; (2) the ideal number of children for a "well-off" young couple today; and (3) the ideal number of children for a "not well-off" couple today. The respondents in the study believed that the ideal number of children for the "not well-off" couple should be only 1.5; for the average couple, 2.79; and for the "well-off" couple, 4.02. Similar results were obtained for the respondents of each social class separately.[12] One may draw the implication from De Jong's results that respondents of each social class would increase their fertility as their economic circumstances improved and would reduce it if their economic circumstances declined.

STATEMENT OF HYPOTHESIS

It is obvious that these two contrasting views concerning the effect of economic development on fertility demand reconciliation. Until recently, however, few persons have addressed themselves to an attempt to reconcile the facts which have led theorists to believe that economic development impedes fertility with the other facts which tend to an opposite conclusion.

Recently the writer was engaged in a study of fertility in Latin America. One of the findings from that study is quite relevant to the present discussion. In a paper on the correlates of areal differences in Latin-American fertility, authored by the present writer and Elsa S. Turner, we described what were for us some very interesting findings concerning the relation between fertility, economic level, and change in economic level.[13]

Making use of the child-woman ratio, we measured the fertility of 318 local areas in eighteen Latin American nations which had a census around the year 1950. We correlated the child-woman ratio with eight other variables, six of which measured various correlates of level of economic development. These six variables were the local and national proportions urban, local and national proportions literate, and local and national proportions of the labor force in agriculture. A multiple-regression analysis revealed that, taken together, the six variables correlated with level of economic development were inversely related to fertility.

We then looked at the differences between actual fertility in each local area and that predicted by the correlates of economic development. In examining these differences between actual and predicted fertility, we were struck by the fact that the areas with higher than expected fertility seemed to cluster in nations which had experienced unusually high advances in per capita economic level; those areas with lower than predicted fertility, on the other hand, appeared to be largely in nations whose recent increase in income per person had been slow.

A more rigorous test confirmed this conjecture. Latin American nations

---

[12] Gordon De Jong, "Religious Fundamentalism, Socio-economic Status, and Fertility Attitudes in the Southern Appalachians," *Demography*, II (1965), 540–48.

[13] David M. Heer and Elsa S. Turner, "Areal Differences in Latin American Fertility," *Population Studies*, Vol. XVIII, No. 3 (March, 1965).

with higher-than-predicted fertility tended to have had greater increases in the per capita production of electric power and in per capita income than nations with lower-than-predicated fertility.

We concluded,

> In summary, we feel that the results we have obtained are such that serious consideration must be given the hypothesis that a rapid increase in the level of economic development tends, *ceteris paribus*, to lead to higher fertility. Of course the other factors are never equal. What appears to happen can be stated as follows. An increase in the level of economic development leads to an increase in fertility as married couples become more optimistic concerning their future economic status. On the other hand, the increase in the level of economic development then sets in motion other forces such as increased knowledge and use of birth control and increases in net economic cost of children, which tend to reduce fertility. In the long run, the forces depressing fertility tend to be stronger than the forces increasing fertility unless the increase in per capita income continues at a high rate. Thus many, if not most, nations exhibit the classic pattern of fertility decline with advancing industrialization.

At the time this statement was written, we were unaware of two studies, by then just recently published, which have a major bearing on the correctness of the conclusion then advanced. Both of these studies have related national differences in fertility to contemporaneous national differences in per capita income and other variables. Both studies have come to the conclusion that, controlling for other variables, fertility is directly rather than inversely associated with per capita income.

The first of these studies was performed by Robert Weintraub.[14] For a sample of thirty nations, including both developed and underdeveloped nations, he obtained the partial regression and correlation coefficients of the 1953–54 crude birth rate on the following three variables: mean per capita income; 1953–54; proportion of all population on farms; and 1953–54 mean infant mortality rate. In his sample the coefficient of partial correlation between the crude birth rate and per capita income was .25. On the other hand, the coefficient of partial correlation between the birth rate and the proportion of farm population was .11, and the partial correlation between the birth rate and infant mortality was .78. The matrix of zero-order coefficients was not published.

The second study, by Irma Adelman, was concerned with the regression of several independent variables on the fertility of women in each of seven five-year age groups.[15] Her independent variables were per capita income, an index of education, the per cent of labor force employed outside of agriculture, and population density. Adelman tested a multiplicative model of the form $Y = a(x_1^{b_1})(x_2^{b_2}) \ldots (x_n^{b_n})$ and therefore established regression equations relating the natural log of her fertility measure with the natural logs of her independent variables. The 37 nations included in her study were not given equal weights; instead, differential weights were given to each nation depending on the presumed accuracy

---

[14] Robert Weintraub, "The Birth Rate and Economic Development: An Empirical Study," *Econometrica*, XL, No. 4 (October, 1962), 812–17.

[15] Irma Adelman, "An Econometric Analysis of Population Growth," *American Economic Review*, LIII, No. 3 (June, 1963), 314–39.

of its statistical data. Weights for the European nations were in general 4 times larger than weights for the nations with the poorest statistical systems, such as El Salvador and the Dominican Republic. Adelman showed that for each of seven age groups the regression coefficient (B coefficient) of per capita income on fertility was positive. On the other hand, the regression coefficients of the other three variables on fertility were all negative for each age group.

Adelman's study does not present values for either partial correlation coefficients or standardized regression (Beta) coefficients. Hence, statements as to which variables showed the highest association with fertility cannot be made precisely. However, Adelman does present the standard error for each of her regression coefficients. Dividing each regression coefficient by its standard error, one can compute a t ratio. Using this t ratio as an approximate measure of the magnitude of partial association between each independent variable and fertility for each age group, we find that Adelman's index of education is the variable most strongly associated with fertility at each age. In general, population density is the second most important variable. Per capita income and per cent of the labor force outside agriculture are the least important; the former variable is important only in the two youngest age groups (15–19 years and 20–24 years) and the latter only in the two oldest age groups (40–44 years and 45–49 years). Like Weintraub's study, Adelman's study does not show the matrix of zero-order correlation coefficients.

From Weintraub's and Adelman's studies, we now have considerable evidence for the hypothesis that the direct effect of economic development is to increase rather than decrease the level of fertility. If this hypothesis is true, the historical fact that fertility over the long run has declined in all present-day industrial societies as their income advanced must then be explained by an inverse association between fertility and other social factors which tend to be positively associated with income. Many such factors thought to be inversely related to fertility have been previously advanced.[16]

Among these many factors is the level of education. We may suppose that an increase in economic level usually results in an increase in educational level and that the increase in educational level has in turn two consequences inimical to high fertility. Perhaps the most important of these consequences is an increased flow of communications of all types.[17]

Coinciding with this increased flow of communications of all types will probably be an increase in communications specifically concerned with the technology and consequences of birth control practices. Assuming that in any society there are at least some women who have already had as many children as they wish, the more women who have knowledge of birth control consequences and procedures, the more widespread will be the practice of birth control and the lower will be that society's fertility.

Second, an increase in the level of

---

16 For an excellent review of these factors see Ronald Freedman, "The Sociology of Human Fertility," *Current Sociology*, Vol. X-XI, No. 2 (1961–62). For a comprehensive series of zero-order correlation coefficients between many such variables and the fertility level, see *Population Bulletin of the United Nations*, No. 7, 1963 (New York: United Nations, 1965), pp. 134–51.

17 Wilbur Schramm, *Mass Media and National Development* (Stanford: Stanford University Press, 1964), pp. 20–57.

education will usually mean an increase in the proportion of adolescents and young adults attending school. This will probably mean a rise in the average age at marriage, which in turn will probably lead to a reduction in fertility. Hence, holding constant that level of the nation's economic well-being, we should expect the level of education to vary inversely with fertility. Adelman's study tends to support this line of reasoning. Her index of education, which combined a measure of literacy with a measure of newspaper circulation per capita, was inversely related to fertility after controls for her other variables had been instituted.

A third factor that we may consider is the nation's mortality level for infants and children. One may suppose that a usual consequence of increase in a nation's economic level is a decline in its mortality level for young ages. Adelman has, in fact, shown a very high negative association between a nation's per capita income and its infant mortality level. The level of infant and childhood mortality may affect the fertility level in four different ways.

First, reduction in the level of infant and childhood mortality will increase the economic cost of supporting a family under conditions of constant fertility and hence may serve as a stimulus to fertility reduction. The economic cost of supporting a family depends on the number of economically dependent children in each family per economically productive adult. Given constant fertility, the lower the national level of infant and childhood mortality, the larger will be the number of children in each family surviving to adulthood. On the other hand, reductions in mortality at young ages are also usually accompanied by

reductions in mortality at older ages. Therefore, a general reduction in mortality at all ages would not necessarily increase the number of children per productive adult. However, in the usual case a general reduction in mortality produces a greater decline in the mortality rates at younger than at older ages. For example, the United Nations estimates that, for a stable population with a gross reproduction rate of 2.5, when the expectation of life at birth is 20 years, the ratio of population 15–59 years to that under 15 years is 1.78, whereas, when the expectation of life at birth is 70 years, this ratio is reduced to 1.20.[18] Thus it can be shown that a decline in infant and childhood mortality, even though accompanied by a decline in mortality at older ages, does lead to an increase in the number of children per productive adult and hence to an increase in the cost of child support.

Second, on a more biological level, a high rate of infant mortality should also lead to increased fertility in any society where a substantial proportion of mothers breast-feed their children. If a child survives and is breast-fed by his mother, during the period of the mother's lactation her fecundity is greatly reduced and her chance of conceiving a second child therefore declines. On the other hand, if a child dies and the mother ceases to lactate, high fecundity soon returns and her chance of having an early conception is increased.[19]

In an oral communication, Dr. Laila Sh. El Hamamsy, the anthropologist

[18] United Nations, Department of Economic and Social Affairs, *The Aging of Populations and Its Economic and Social Implications* (New York: United Nations, 1956), pp. 26–27.

[19] Robert G. Potter, Jr., "Birth Intervals: Structure and Change," *Population Studies*, XVII, No. 2 (November, 1963), 155–66.

who heads the Social Research Center of the American University in Cairo, Egypt, has advanced a third reason why high infant and childhood mortality should be positively correlated with elevated fertility. In her view, a high death rate among infants and children causes parents to refrain from investing large amounts of emotional energy in any of their children. They do this because the pain of bereavement, if a child should die, would be directly proportional to the amount of energy that they have invested in that child. However, the more emotional energy one puts into any one child, the less emotional energy is left over for other children. Therefore, the investment of large amounts of energy in any one child should lead one to wish to have fewer children. Thus reduced rates of infant and childhood mortality, by encouraging intensive emotional investment in each child, should promote fertility reduction.

Finally, a high rate of infant and childhood mortality may cause women to bear a number of children which, on the average, will produce more children surviving to adulthood than the women would wish to have. A very low rate of infant and childhood mortality would have no such effect. In a society where the average level of childhood mortality is high, the variance in the proportion of children in each family who die will also be high. In such a situation, each couple will probably wish to assure the survival of a given minimum number of children. If each family wishes to assure a minimum number of children surviving to adulthood, the high variance in the proportion of children in each family who will die will cause the average number of children who actually survive to adulthood to be considerably higher than the average

number of children surviving to adulthood which couples would ideally desire. On the other hand, under conditions of very low infant and childhood mortality, women can virtually assume that all children will survive to maturity. Hence, the number of children women bear is almost identical to the number they wish to see survive to adulthood, and the average number who actually survive to adulthood is no larger than the average number which couples would ideally desire.

Weintraub's study, showing a positive partial association between infant mortality and the birth rate, lends support to these several lines of reasoning concluding that high infant mortality leads to high fertility.

There are, of course, other institutional changes usually accompanying economic development which may also have adverse effects on fertility. One change that has recently received emphasis is the increased reliance of the elderly on pensions from governments and business corporations rather than on sustenance from other members of their kin. Under a system in which the elderly must rely on sustenance from their kin, there is a strong tendency to have sufficient children so that at least one son will be alive at the time when the couple has reached old age.[20] Under an impersonal system of old age insurance, on the other hand, this motivation for children is lacking.

Another change that may frequently accompany economic development and is possibly inimical to high fertility is an increased rate of social mobility. Most studies of the influence

---

[20] William A. Morrison, "Attitudes of Males toward Family Planning in a Western Indian Village," *Milbank Memorial Fund Quarterly*, XXXIV, No. 3 (July, 1956), 262–86.

of social mobility on fertility have focused on the individual level and have attempted to find out whether socially mobile persons have lower fertility than nonmobile persons. However, this level of analysis is irrelevant to the question of the influence on fertility of societal differences in social mobility.[21]

This is so because a change in the level of social mobility in a society might have the effect of influencing fertility both among the mobile and nonmobile segments of a population. On the societal level we may suppose that a high level of social mobility may be associated with a fading of traditional and hereditary ranking procedures and hence, in compensation, may lead to an increased use of conspicuous consumption as a means of demonstrating high status. An increase in conspicuous consumption in turn would necessitate a diversion of funds from other types of consumption—including the consumption expenditures of raising a large family.[22] J.A. Banks has previously noted the association between the high standard of living considered necessary by the middle class of England in the late Victorian period and its success in reducing the number of its children.[23]

Still another institutional change often accompanying economic development and detrimental to a high fertility level may be an increase in the net economic cost of children relative to that of other consumer commodities which parents might buy in place of children. The net economic cost of children is, by the economist's definition, equal to the gross expenditures involved in child-bearing minus the productive return which the children themselves bring into the family. As the economic well-being of a society rises, child labor becomes less frequent and hence, other factors remaining equal, the net economic cost of children rises. It has been frequently suggested that an increase in the net economic cost of children relative to other commodities which parents might buy in their stead is a cause of fertility decline.[24]

The present analysis is focused on a more refined testing of the general theory just outlined than is possible from previously published data. According to this theory, the direct effect of an increase in the level of economic well-being in a society is an increase in fertility, but various indirect effects of an increase in economic well-being have such adverse consequences for fertility that, taking into account both direct and indirect effects, an increase in economic level decreases fertility. One may therefore predict that the zero-order association between economic well-being and fertility is inverse but the partial association, holding constant the indirect effects of changes in economic well-being, is positive.

---

[21] The use of individual data where aggregate data are appropriate is known as the atomistic fallacy. For a fuller discussion of this error in reasoning, see Matilda White Riley, *Sociological Research*. Vol. I. *A Case Approach* (New York: Harcourt, Brace & World, Inc., 1963), 706–7.

[22] Professor Jean Morsa has previously emphasized that a high rate of social mobility in a society may cause a reduction of fertility even among non-mobile persons. See Ronald Freedman, "The Sociology of Human Fertility," *Current Sociology*, XX–XXI, No. 2 (1961–62), 60.

[23] J. A. Banks, *Prosperity and Parenthood* (London: Routledge & Kegan Paul, Ltd., 1954).

[24] See, for example, Gary S. Becker, "An Economic Analysis of Fertility," in *Demographic and Economic Change in Developed Countries* (Princeton: Princeton University Press, 1960), 209–40.

It may be further hypothesized that an increase in the level of economic well-being produces an increase in the educational level and a decrease in the level of infant and childhood mortality. One may therefore predict that, holding other relevant variables constant, the partial association between the level of economic well-being and the level of education is positive and the partial association between economic well-being and infant and childhood mortality negative.

One may further hypothesize that a high level of education and a low level of infant and childhood mortality are necessary conditions for low fertility. It may therefore be predicted that the partial association between educational level and fertility should be negative and the partial association between infant and childhood mortality and fertility should be positive.

The theory also states that an increase in economic well-being also may produce an increased reliance on governments and other impersonal organizations rather than on kin units for sustenance of the elderly, increased social mobility, and increases in the net economic cost of children relative to other consumer commodities.

Each of these changes is supposed to have an adverse effect on fertility. However, since these other possible changes accompanying increased economic development are not easily measured, a test of this part of the theory will not be attempted in the present paper.

TEST OF THE HYPOTHESIS

Like the studies done by Weintraub and Adelman, the present study is based on a cross-sectional analysis of all nations in the world for which relevant data are available. In the present study, forty-one nations are included, a somewhat larger number than the thirty-seven included in Adelman's study or the thirty included by Weintraub. The data of the present study, in common with those of Weintraub and Adelman, refer to the early years of the 1950 decade. Almost without exception, data are taken from official publications of the United Nations.

Fertility is measured by the general fertility rate for males (number of births divided by the male population 15–54 years old) for the year 1953.[25] This somewhat unconventional measure of fertility was considered more appropriate than either the birth rate or one of the commonly used measures of female fertility. In comparison with the general fertility rate for males, the crude birth rate suffers because its denominator includes more than that portion of the population capable of conceiving a child. In the present sample of nations, a measure of male fertility is preferable to a measure of female fertility because certain of the nations, in particular the U.S.S.R., had a very large excess of women over men in the reproductive ages. In such a situation the level of male fertility is probably a more accurate indicator of what

---

[25] The sources for number of births were the *United Nations Demographic Yearbook, 1954,* and *United Nations Demographic Yearbook, 1961.* The figures for Colombia are for baptized births only; the figures for Ecuador exclude live births dying within twenty-four hours of birth; the figures for Peru and Venezuela exclude births to jungle Indians; and the figures for the Belgian Congo are a weighted average of figures for white and native populations.
Data on the male population 15–54 years old were obtained from *United Nations Demographic Yearbook, 1960.*

the fertility level would be, given a normal sex ratio, than is a measure of female fertility.

Level of economic development is measured by estimated average income per capita of the population in the age group 15–64 years of age.[26] It will be remembered that both Weintraub and Adelman measured economic well-being by income per capita of the total population. However, the change in denominator was made because, among two nations with equal average income per wage-earner, the country with the lowest fertility will have the highest income per capita of the total population. Hence, if one uses income per capita of the total population as the index of economic well-being, one creates an automatic tendency for high income to be statistically associated with low fertility.

Level of education is measured by newspaper circulation per thousand of the population 15 years old and over in either 1952, 1953, or 1954.[27] It may be remembered that Adelman's index of education was an average of a measure of literacy and a measure of

newspaper circulation per capita. According to the writer's hypothesis, literacy is only relevant insofar as it is associated either with communication flow or with school attendance among young adults. Because of the writer's presumption that literacy would reflect neither of these variables as well as newspaper circulation, he decided not to use the Adelman index. The decision to divide newspaper circulation by the population 15 years old and over rather than by the total population of all ages was made because it was assumed that very few newspaper subscribers were under 15 years of age and that only communication flow in the group 15 years old and over would have any effect on fertility. The operational measure of infant and childhood mortality was simply the mortality of infants under 1;[28] mortality at older ages of childhood correlates so highly with infant mortality that it can be ignored.[29]

The writer decided to include two additional variables as control variables. The first of these is population density in 1953.[30] The decision to include population density was made for two reasons. First, in Adelman's study this variable was shown to have an important partial association with fertility. Second, a recent study by Grauman shows population density to be inversely associated with fertility in several areas of the world.[31]

---

[26] Figures on per capita net national product for all countries except Hungary and the U.S.S.R. were obtained from "Per-capita National Product of 55 Countries—1952–54," *United Nations Statistical Papers*, Series E, No. 4 (New York, 1957). Figures for Hungary and the U.S.S.R. were obtained from Simon Kuznets, *Six Lectures on Economic Growth* (New York: The Free Press of Glencoe, Inc., 1959), p. 20.

Data on the proportion of the total population 15–64 years of age were obtained from *United Nations Demographic Yearbook, 1960.*

[27] Newspaper circulation per capita of total population was obtained from the 1953, 1954, and 1955 editions of *United Nations Demographic Yearbook.* Data on the proportion of the total population 15 years old and over, not always for the same year as for newspaper circulation per capita, were obtained from *United Nations Demographic Yearbook, 1960.*

[28] Source of the figures was *United Nations Demographic Yearbook, 1962.* Figures for the Belgian Congo were a weighted average for the white and indigenous population.

[29] Oral communication from Professor Ansley J. Coale, director, Office of Population Research, Princeton University.

[30] Source was *United Nations Demographic Yearbook, 1954.*

[31] John V. Grauman, "Fertility and Population Density: A Macrodemographic Approach" (paper presented at the

The second control variable was the percentage increase in per capita energy consumption from 1937 to 1953.[32] Basically this variable was considered to be a good index of the magnitude of recent change in the level of economic development. This variable was considered of possible importance for two reasons. In the first place, it was presumed that the indirect effects of an increase in economic well-being which were conducive to fertility reduction took place somewhat later in time than the increase in economic well-being itself. Measures were available for two of these indirect effects, that is, newspaper circulation and infant mortality. However, no measures were available for the remaining indirect effects of economic development which were assumed to be conducive to fertility reduction. Nations for which the increase in level of economic development was high were thus assumed to be nations for which the unmeasured indirect effects of economic development conducive to reduced fertility were still of low magnitude. Hence, nations which had a relatively large recent increase in level of economic development were presumed to manifest, *ceteris paribus*, a relatively high level of fertility.

Recent change in level of economic development was also thought to be important for a second reason. It was considered possible that many persons in a rapidly developing country might not yet have developed a taste for the newer type of consumption articles available to them because of their new wealth. Rather than spend their money on new consumer articles to which they were not accustomed, they might wish to expand their consumption of the more-familiar articles. This expansion in consumption of the more-familiar items might include the "consumption" of an additional quantity of children.

Adelman's study excluded a measure of infant and childhood mortality. Weintraub's study excluded any measure of literacy or any communication flow. This study, by including both of these measures (each of which has been previously shown to be important), enables a comparison of the relative importance of these two variables with respect to fertility. The present study excludes a measure of the proportion of the total population engaged in agricultural pursuits. This decision was taken because both Weintraub's and Adelman's study showed that the partial association of this variable with fertility was small. As in Adelman's study and in contrast to Weintraub's, in the present analysis population density is included as one of the variables.

In the current study, all forty-one nations are given equal weight. Adelman's study gave much greater weights to nations with good statistical systems. Although the present writer recognizes that the statistics for many nations may be prone to error, he decided against Adelman's procedure on the ground that such a procedure introduces another possibility for error which would be avoided if each nation were given equal weight. Specifically, the countries with available data already overrepresent

1965 meeting of the Population Association of America; an abstract of this paper appears in *Population Index*, XXXI, No. 3 [July, 1965], 263).

[32] Source for most nations was *United Nations Statistical Yearbook, 1956*. Source of data for Jamaica and West Germany was *United Nations Statistical Yearbook, 1955*. Data for Belgium and Luxembourg were given only for the combination of the two nations. Both Belgium and Luxembourg were assigned the value for the combination of the two nations.

TABLE 1. Values for Each Variable, Each Nation, Circa 1953

Nation	Male fertility (births per 1,000 males aged 15–54) X_1	Net national product per capita aged 15–64 (in dollars) X_2	Newspaper circulation per 1,000 persons aged 15 and over X_3	Infant mortality (infant deaths per 1000 births) X_4	Population density (persons per square kilometer) X_5	Percentage increase in per capita energy consumption, 1937–1953 X_6
Argentina	84.2	708	144	63.4	6.6	31
Australia	80.6	1,489	578	23.3	1.1	49
Austria	58.5	561	278	49.9	83.0	66
Belgian Congo	140.6	127	3	148.0	5.2	200
Belgium	58.9	1,189	487	41.9	287.7	−9
Canada	104.1	2,144	360	35.6	1.5	47
Ceylon	136.8	194	63	71.2	126.4	50
Chile	133.1	613	126	112.4	8.7	31
Colombia	157.5	460	99	111.0	10.6	150
Denmark	66.3	1,172	515	27.2	101.5	25
Dominican Republic	165.8	304	43	74.2	48.3	200
Ecuador	191.8	278	87	115.8	12.8	200
Egypt	159.2	204	40	145.8	22.0	62
Finland	83.0	1,069	387	34.2	12.3	41
France	68.2	1,131	311	41.9	78.0	4
West Germany	59.0	752	340	46.4	197.8	−5
Greece	64.6	334	97	45.3	59.2	50
Guatemala	201.2	289	47	102.8	28.1	100
Honduras	168.8	271	34	64.0	13.3	−12
Hungary	78.5	407	167	70.8	103.1	114
Iceland	109.3	1,329	663	19.0	1.5	43
Ireland	79.7	679	333	39.4	42.0	3
Italy	63.7	474	145	58.4	158.0	32
Jamaica	138.2	310	63	64.1	135.6	188
Japan	81.1	313	536	48.9	234.5	4
Luxembourg	52.8	1,264	555	42.3	116.4	−9
Malaya	176.2	581	89	83.4	42.7	−5
Mexico	184.4	401	82	95.2	14.3	48
Netherlands	81.6	805	355	22.2	312.2	24
New Zealand	95.5	1,656	515	25.7	7.6	35
Norway	67.8	1,140	529	22.0	10.4	37
Peru	148.2	227	72	98.2	7.0	131
Portugal	85.7	313	90	95.5	92.8	33
Puerto Rico	145.0	813	120	62.8	247.7	237
Sweden	55.4	1,448	642	18.7	15.9	48
Switzerland	61.4	1,519	393	29.8	118.1	31
Thailand	120.2	140	7	64.9	38.0	300
United Kingdom	57.6	1,178	796	27.6	208.4	9
United States	91.8	2,959	494	27.8	17.1	35
U. S. S. R.	100.0	766	322	68.0	8.5	92
Venezuela	176.0	975	112	67.9	6.2	337

the economically developed nations which tend to have the best statistical reporting. Therefore, any further differential weighting of nations with good statistics would further bias the sample as representative of the universe of nation states during the 1950 decade.

The study seeks to test both an additive model concerning the determinants of fertility in the form of $Y = a + b_1x_1 + b_2x_2 + \ldots + b_nx_n$ and a multiplicative model of the form $Y = a\ (x_1^{b_1})\ (x_2^{b_2})\ (x_3^{b_3}) \ldots (x_n^{b_n})$. It will be remembered that Weintraub's study used the former model and Adelman's study the latter. On the basis of preliminary work with her data, Adelman found the multiplicative equation to give a better fit than the additive. However, one could not legitimately conclude from her analysis which type of equation would best fit the present data.

An important part of the current study is the examination of the adequacy of prediction for individual nations. Data of this sort were not presented previously by either Weintraub or Adelman. The analysis of the residuals from the regression equation gives one the opportunity of examining what additional factors may also be important in determining cross-national differences in fertility.

RESULTS

The values of each variable for each nation are presented in Table 1.

The matrix of zero-order coefficients is presented in Table 2. Part A presents the matrix for the actual values of each variable (appropriate for the additive model); Part B for the natural logs of these values (appropriate for the multiplicative model).

TABLE 2. Matrix of Zero-Order Correlation Coefficients

	X_2	X_3	X_4	X_5	X_6
A. For the additive model					
X_1	−0.4417	−0.6851	0.7051	−0.3794	0.5467
X_2	—	0.7111	−0.6642	−0.0607	−0.3207
X_3	—	—	−0.7761	0.2150	−0.5160
X_4	—	—	—	−0.2795	0.4109
X_5	—	—	—	—	−0.1993
B. For the multiplicative model					
X_1	−0.5270	−0.6617	0.6801	−0.3654	0.5547
X_2	—	0.8460	−0.7735	−0.1380	−0.4151
X_3	—	—	−0.7747	0.0868	−0.5760
X_4	—	—	—	−0.0192	0.4323
X_5	—	—	—	—	−0.2214

X_1 = Births per 1,000 males 15 to 54 years old
X_2 = Net national product per capita aged 15 to 64 years old
X_3 = Newspaper circulation per 1,000 aged 15 and over
X_4 = Infant deaths per 1,000 births
X_5 = Persons per square kilometer
X_6 = Percentage increase in per capita energy consumption, 1937–1953

TABLE 3. Results of the Multiple Regression Analysis with Male Fertility as the Dependent Variable

Variable	Partial correlation coefficient	T ratio for partial correlation coefficient (35 d. f.)	Standardized regression coefficient (B coefficient)	Regression coefficient (B coefficient)
A. For the additive model				
X_2	0.1020	0.6065	0.0996	0.0075
X_3	−0.2384	−1.4520	−0.2811	−0.0579
X_4	0.3690	2.3490	0.4153	0.5511
X_5	−0.2131	−1.2907	−0.1504	−0.0791
X_6	0.3082	1.9169	0.2329	12.2787
	$R_{1.23456} = .7911$		$F_{(5,35)} = 11.7104$	
	$R^2_{1.23456} = .6259$			
B. For the multiplicative model				
X_2	0.0371	0.2197	0.0487	0.0262
X_3	−0.1440	−0.8609	−0.2005	−0.0678
X_4	0.4240	2.7695	0.4748	0.3443
X_5	−0.3995	−2.5785	−0.2901	−0.0788
X_6	0.2447	1.4928	0.1900	0.1875
	$R_{1.23456} = .8008$		$F_{(5,35)} = 12.5107$	
	$R^2_{1.23456} = .6412$			

X_2 = Net national product per capita aged 15 to 64 years old
X_3 = Newspaper circulation per 1,000 aged 15 and over
X_4 = Infant deaths per 1,000 births
X_5 = Persons per square kilometer
X_6 = Percentage increase in per capita energy consumption, 1937–1953

The results of the multiple regression and correlation analysis with fertility as the dependent variable are presented in Parts A and B of Table 3. Part A contains the results for the additive model and Part B for the multiplicative. Table 3 presents the following types of data: (1) partial correlation coefficients; (2) values of t corresponding to each partial correlation coefficient; (3) standardized regression coefficients (Beta-coefficients); (4) regression coefficients (B coefficients); (5) the value of the multiple correlation coefficient; (6) the value of the square of the multiple correlation coefficient; and (7) the value of F for the multiple correlation coefficient.[33]

---

[33] For the purpose of determining which of several independent variables has the highest association with the dependent variable, an examination of the relative magnitude of either the partial correlation coefficient or of the standardized regression coefficient is ap-

TABLE 4. Results of the Multiple Regression Analysis with Net National Product Per Capita Aged 15 to 64 Years Old as the Dependent Variable

Variable	Partial correlation coefficient	T ratio for partial correlation coefficient (35 d. f.)	Standardized regression coefficient (B coefficient)	Regression coefficient (B coefficient)
A. For the additive model				
X_1	0.1020	0.6065	0.1044	1.3876
X_3	0.4412	2.9083	0.5327	1.4575
X_4	−0.3450	−2.1744	−0.3975	−7.0092
X_5	−0.3382	−2.1263	−0.2444	−1.7084
X_6	0.0151	0.0893	0.0117	8.1819
	$R_{2.13456} = .7796$ $R^2_{2.13456} = .6078$		$F_{(5,35)} = 10.8488$	
B. For the multiplicative model				
X_1	0.0371	0.2197	0.0282	0.0526
X_3	0.6495	5.0539	0.6884	0.4335
X_4	−0.3327	−2.0875	−0.2837	−0.3829
X_5	−0.3298	−2.0666	−0.1822	−0.0922
X_6	0.0812	0.4817	0.0480	0.0881
	$R_{2.13456} = .8200$ $R^2_{2.13456} = .7921$		$F_{(5,35)} = 26.6726$	

X_1 = Births per 1,000 males 15 to 54 years old
X_3 = Newspaper circulation per 1,000 aged 15 and over
X_4 = Infant deaths per 1,000 births
X_5 = Persons per square kilometer
X_6 = Percentage increase in per capita energy consumption, 1937–1953

propriate. The square of the partial correlation coefficient is equal to the incremental variance explained by the given independent variable divided by the variance left unexplained by the previous variables. The standardized regression coefficient is equal to the change in the dependent variable associated with a unit change in a given independent variable when both independent and dependent variables are expressed in the form of standard scores. Usually, but not invariably, the rank order of the several partial correlation coefficients will be identical to the rank order of their corresponding standardized regression coefficients.

Table 4 presents the results of the multiple regression and correlation analysis for each of the two models with economic development as the dependent variable....

We should now like to discuss these results with reference to how well they support the hypothesis of this study. Multiple regression and correlation analysis, of course, does not by itself reveal anything concerning causation. To make causal inferences, one needs to have knowledge not only of statistical association but, in addition, one has to be able, on the basis of outside information, to decide to what extent a given association between two variables is a spurious result of a third variable or variables and whether a given association beteen variable A and variable B occurs because variable A causes variable B, variable B causes variable A, or both variable A and variable B are mutually interacting.

According to the present theory, the direct and indirect effects of economic development, taken together, cause fertility to decline with an increase in economic development. This part of the causal hypothesis receives support in the zero-order correlation of −.448 between fertility and economic development (−.525 correlation among the natural logs). Logically, one could say that the association results solely from the fact that high fertility impedes economic development. However, it is probable that few economists would care to take this position. If only a small part of the association between fertility and economic development is due to the effect of fertility on development, then the validity of the theory is supported.

The present theory further predicts that the direct effect of level of economic development on fertility is positive. This part of the theory receives support from the results of the multiple and partial correlation analysis. However, the partial associations in both the additive and multiplicative models (e.g., partial correlation coefficient of .102 in the additive model and .037 in the multiplicative) are slight, and the values of t for the partial correlation coefficients are below the level of statistical significance.

Nevertheless, there is reason to believe that the direct effect of economic level on fertility is stronger than the partial association would indicate. This results from the fact that high fertility probably has a long-run adverse influence on economic development, a point which has been strongly stressed by Coale and Hoover and other leading demographer-economists.[34] If the influence of fertility on the level of economic development is to produce a negative association between the two variables and in fact we find a positive association, then there are grounds for believing that the positive effect of economic level on fertility is greater than that suggested by the partial association between the two variables.

Finally, the theory predicts that economic development is the cause of several factors which tend to reduce fertility levels. I specifically attempted to test the hypothesis that economic development caused a rise in educational level and a decline in infant mortality and that each of these two effects tended to reduce fertility. From Table 2 we see that there are indeed strong zero-order associations between economic level and newspaper circulation and between economic level and infant mortality. From Table 4 we see that the partial associations between economic level and these two variables are also high, and we therefore have some reason to believe that the associations are not spurious. . . .

The present data do not prove the author's theory of the relationship between economic development and fertility. On the other hand, none of the present data serve to refute that theory. Further research on small

---

[34] Ansley J. Coale and Edgar M. Hoover, *Population Growth and Economic Development in Low-Income Countries* (Princeton, N.J.: Princeton University Press, 1958).

areas within nations may serve to test the theory further....

DISCUSSION

If true, the results presented here may have several very important policy implications. First, they show that it may be unwise to rely on uncontrolled economic development to reduce fertility. The present results imply that economic development, if it is to be effective in reducing fertility, must be accompanied by certain changes in social structure. The results imply that these changes in social structure usually do in some degree accompany industrialization. However, for policy-makers, perhaps the most important point to be made is that among nations with equal levels of economic development there are variations in the health and educational levels of the population, and these variations are determinative of variations in fertility. This fact would imply that a national government, committed to a reduction in the nation's level of fertility as a means to further economic development, should also make sure that the national budget includes relatively large sums for health and education expenditures.

According to the results presented here, the educational level may be of some importance in determining the level of fertility. The writer has hypothesized that the major part of the effect of education on fertility may be due to its increasing the flow of communications concerning birth control through the society. A question unanswered by this study is whether a society through special organized effort can strongly increase the flow of communications about birth control despite the fact that the level of general communications flow is very low. The birth control campaigns in several nations where the educational level is inconsiderable may soon answer this question.

The finding that levels of infant and childhood mortality may be highly determinative of the fertility level is very relevant to the current controversy concerning the present worth of public health programs in underdeveloped nations. Two of the most vociferous exponents of the view that public health programs impede economic development are William and Paul Paddock. In a chapter of their book *Hungry Nations*, entitled "The Fallacy of Public Health Programs— You Can't Afford the Luxury," they state:

> When faced realistically, nevertheless, it will be recognized that public health actually damages the economy of a backward nation and definitely delays, if it does not eliminate, hope for a rise in living standards until population control is effectively organized.... If product remains constant, then each year the standard of living, the amount of food available per person, is reduced as the number of mouths increases.
>
> And the cause of population expansion is not a rise in birth rates; it is a decrease in death rates.
>
> Herein is the fallacy of public health programs; they decrease death rates without curtailing birth rates.[39]

The Paddocks' arguments is very persuasive as far as it goes. Nevertheless, it ignores any possible dependence of birth rates on death rates. If the reduction of infant and childhood mortality is in fact a condition for the eventual reduction of fertility, then

---

[39] William and Paul Paddock, *Hungry Nations* (Boston: Little Brown & Co., 1964), 128–29.

the Paddocks' argument is invalidated. The findings of this study would tend to indicate that the vigorous support of public health programs is of strong aid in achieving a rapid reduction in fertility, even if such vigorous support means a temporary increase in the rate of population growth.[40] Hopefully, however, strong public health programs, coupled with a simultaneous strongly organized effort to institute measures of birth control, would minimize the duration and magnitude of the period of high population growth.

[40] For a statement of similar view, see Harvey Leibenstein, *Economic Backwardness and Economic Growth* (New York: John Wiley & Sons, 1957), pp. 250–52.

However, further research on this topic is obviously needed. There is no reason why the effect of infant and childhood mortality levels on the success of fertility control programs cannot be studied experimentally in those nations which presently provide only weak health programs for their populace. Four possible types of program are created if presence or absence of an organized birth control effort is cross-classified by presence or absence of a program for the improvement of infant and child health. An excellent experimental design would result if magnitude of fertility decline were to be compared in areas assigned at random to each one of these four possible programs.

The Economic Effects of Migration

Joseph J. Spengler*

"No phenomena are causal; all phenomena are contingent."
> Karl Pearson: THE GRAMMAR OF SCIENCE, 3rd ed., p. 174.

"It is only possible in actual cases to give uncertain conjectures as to the future. This is partly because only some of the existing conditions are known, and partly because new surprising conditions may emerge."
> F. Zeuthen: ECONOMIC THEORY AND METHOD, p. 219.

Because of shortage of time I shall have to confine my discussion to the economic theory of migration. I shall not be able to present much empirical information. This omission is not an uncompensated shortcoming, however. For it is seldom possible that the researcher can specify and quantify with precision enough of the relevant variables to permit his deducing just

* Joseph J. Spengler, "The Economic Effects of Migration," in *Selected Studies of Migration Since World War II.* (New York: Milbank Memorial Fund, 1958), pp. 172–92.

what have been the economically significant effects of given migratory movements. Furthermore, if allowance is made for the mobility-reducing effect of international barriers (e.g., language, transport cost, ignorance or uncertainty respecting prospects, etc.), much of the analysis is applicable to internal migration.

Migratory movements may be divided into two categories, movements which are comparatively regular and continuous, and movements which, being the result of war, territorial partition, etc., are both nonrecurrent and relatively massive. Illustrative of the former type has been migration from Europe to the Western Hemisphere since 1800. Illustrative of the latter type are the movements which took place during or immediately after the first and second world wars, and after the partition of British India into India and Pakistan.[1] I shall concern myself almost entirely with effects of

essentially regular and continuous movements. Nonrecurrent movements give rise to many problems and effects which are associated with particular movements and situations rather than with migratory movements in general.

The economic effects of migration are variously classifiable. I shall examine most of them under two broad headings, aggregative effects and substitutive or compositional effects. Under each of these headings I shall touch also upon effects which, although not specifically aggregative or substitutional, are related to such effects. In my analysis I shall usually suppose the economies under discussion to be relatively free of constraints, since there is not time to consider the impact of each of the important constraints that might be introduced. Before turning to the economic effects proper, notice must be taken of (a) demographic effects of migration which give rise to economic effects, and of (b) the effect of migration upon the migrant himself.

I

The demographic effects of migration whence economic effects flow are principally of two sorts, modification of absolute rate of population

---

[1] E.g., see G. Frumkin, *Population Changes in Europe Since 1939* (New York, 1951); J. B. Schechtman, *European Population Transfers* (New York, 1946); *Population Transfers in Asia* (New York, 1949); E. M. Kulischer, *Europe on the Move* (New York, 1948); W. S. and E. S. Woytinsky, *World Population and Production* (New York, 1953), pp. 95–104. Perhaps the most carefully studied of these nonrecurrent movements is that into Western Germany after 1945. According to H. C. Wallich, the influx of immigrants, most of them refugees, into Western Germany produced a variety of effects, some favorable and some unfavorable. The refugees were enterprising, willing to work, and disposed to compete, with the result that the German economy became more competitive and its labor force more industrious than it otherwise would have been. The coming of the refugees greatly increased social and industrial capital requirements, the bulk of which had to be supplied out of current savings. Expansion of plant capacity was somewhat facilitated by the fact that the presence of the refugees held down the wage level (though less than had been anticipated), thereby

augmenting profits and savings. Even so, the use of so much of the Nation's savings to equip the immigrants made capital equipment per capita in the resident population lower than it otherwise would have been and affected per capita output and income similarly. This effect was not offset by effects consequent upon a broadening of domestic markets. Such increase in import requirements as was occasioned by the immigrants was more than offset, however, by the contribution immigrants made to the production of exports and of substitutes for products that had formerly been imported. See Wallich, *Mainsprings of the German Revival* (New Haven, 1955), chap. ix. See also F. Edding, *The Refugees as a Burden, a Stimulus and a Challenge to the West German Economy* (The Hague, 1951).

growth and change in age composition. Immigration operates, at least in the shorter run, to increase the absolute rate of growth of population and the labor force, and emigration, to reduce it. The absolute rate of growth of net national product is affected accordingly, it being given that the employed fraction of the labor force is not significantly affected.

While it is generally admitted that net migration affects a population's absolute rate of growth, at least in the short run, opinion appears to differ somewhat respecting the probable effects of net migration upon age composition. My comment is limited to effects that may be regarded as typical, since, in theory, one may conceive of a wide range of migration movements, with many of which atypical effects are associated. Initially, net migration tends to modify the size of the labor force more than that of the population, since usually a disproportionately large fraction of the migrants are of working age. Thus net immigration tends to increase somewhat the relative number of persons of working age and in a country's labor force, with the magnitude of the effect dependent in part upon the net-immigration/population ratio.[2] In the

longer run, however, net migration of the continuous sort is not likely to affect significantly the age composition of countries either of immigration or of emigration.[3] Only if net immigration increases sufficiently, will the immigrant-receiving country's age composition be affected enough to increase significantly the ratio of its labor force to its population. If net immigration declines continuously, the fraction of the immigrant population of working age eventually will fall below that of the native population. As a rule, one cannot safely generalize much respecting the effect of migration upon a country's age structure in the absence of knowledge of the age, size, sex, and time dimensions of the migratory movement under consideration.

II

Any analysis of the economic effects of migration must take into account, as O. A. Brownson long ago observed, the possible effects of the migratory

---

[2] For example, in the United States between 1870 and 1910, increase in the number of foreign born contributed about 7.9 million of the 52 million increase in population and about 5 million of the 25 million increase in the labor force. See S. Kuznets and E. Rubin, *Immigration and the Foreign Born* (NBER Occasional Paper 46, New York, 1954), pp. 44 ff.; also E. P. Hutchinson, *Immigrants and Their Children* (New York, 1956), pp. 14–18. After 1945 estimates were made in France of the kind and volume of net immigration required to give France's population the kind of age composition considered desirable. See A. Sauvy, "Evaluation des besoins de l'immigration française," *Population*, I (1946), 91–98; and

"Besoins et possibilités de l'immigration française," *Ibid.*, V (1950), 209–28, 417–34; Paul Vincent, "Vieillissement de la population, retraites et immigration," *Ibid.*, I (1946), 212–44. See also United Nations, *The Determinants and Consequences of Population Trends* (New York, 1953), pp. 136–41, 146–49. For an econometric approach see Julius Isaac, *The Effect of Migration on the Economy of Sending and Receiving Countries* (The Hague, 1953).

[3] See United Nations, *The Aging of Populations and Its Economic and Social Implications* (New York, 1956), pp. 22, 47–49; *The Population of South America, 1950–1980* (New York, 1955), pp. 109–39; and "Some Quantitative Aspects Of The Aging of Western Populations," *Population Bulletin*, No. 1 (1951), pp. 42–57. The first two of these are in St/Soa/Series A. See also P. K. Whelpton, *Forecasts of the Population of the United States, 1945–1975* (Washington, 1947), p. 36; A. Sauvy, *Théorie Générale de la Population*, I, (Paris, 1952), 99–105.

process upon the migrant himself. I do not here refer to the fact that migration sometimes tends to select individuals with relatively great drive, capacity, cultural attainment, etc., or to the fact that the migrant may find himself in a preferred social situation after migration. I refer rather to the fact that the act and experience of migrating may modify the aspirations, propensities, etc., of the migrant. If a cake of custom has encrusted him, it is likely to be broken. He escapes ambition-suppressing ties which have bound him to an extended family, to a village, to a particular occupation, or to a particular way of doing things. In consequence his potential productive capacity increases. Witness the success of those Chinese who left China for foreign parts and there eventually engaged in trade, industry, etc. Or the improvement in the methods of production pursued by British migrants after they settled in Australia.

III

I turn now to what I have called the aggregative effects of net migration. These arise principally from changes in the size of a country's population as distinguished from changes in its composition. It is to be noted, however, that sometimes changes in composition eventually generate changes that closely resemble those describable as aggregative. I shall consider these effects primarily from the standpoint of a country of immigration, and, for the present, disregard the fact that migratory movements are cyclical in character. Moreover, I shall confine my discussion to effects that are contingently predictable, ignoring residual and less predictable effects seemingly consequent upon increases in size of population. For such conse-

quences, while of concern to historians bent upon tracing the actual course of an economy's past development, seldom fit nicely into explanatory models.

1. Immigration may operate in several ways to set in motion forces making for increase in output per worker. (a) If the immigrants introduce a culture that is technologically and otherwise superior to that of the resident population, output per head will rise in time.[4] (b) If immigration, by increasing the size of the population, enlarges a country's markets and thus augments division of labor and industrial differentiation sufficiently to offset increases in various costs (e.g., raw materials), it will eventually make possible greater output per head. It will have a similar effect if it greatly improves entrepreneurial expectations and thereby markedly stimulates productive investment.[5] If, however, the required

---

[4] This has happened in various parts of the world in which immigrants have introduced a superior culture. It is through the immigration of individuals possessed of superior skills, etc., that output per head may be increased in backward countries. E.g. see T. H. Silcock's essay in Thomas Brinley, (ed.): *International Migration* (London: Macmillan & Co. Ltd., 1958).

[5] E.g., see A. A. Young, "Increasing Returns And Economic Progress," *Economic Journal*, XXXVIII (1928), 527–42; also P. N. Rosenstein-Rodan, "Problems Of Industrialisation Of Eastern and South-Eastern Europe," *ibid.*, LIII (1943), 202–11; H. W. Arndt, "External Economies In Economic Growth," *Economic Record*, XXXI (1955), 192–214. It is essential that all costs be taken into account; otherwise both conventional income and "welfare" are exaggerated. In practice, costs tend to be underestimated. See M. Fleming, "External Economies and the Doctrine of Balanced Growth," *Economic Journal*, LXV (1955), 241–56, for a critique of a thesis somewhat similar to Young's. Immigration would tend to produce such effect in Canada, Australia, Argentina, and similarly situated countries E.g., see

increase in division of labor does not take place, and if the increase in population is not accompanied by a proportionate increase in agents of production utilized by the labor force, output per head will fall. Furthermore, even if these agents increase proportionately, output per head will be less than it would have been, given such increase together with no increase in numbers.

2. Net immigration may operate in several ways to increase the absolute rate at which an immigrant-receiving country forms capital. First, insofar as it accelerates population growth and intensifies the expectation of entrepreneurs that their markets will expand, it tends to extend entrepreneurial time horizons, to stimulate induced and autonomous investment, and probably to step up the rate at which input-saving innovations are introduced. While such is likely to be the outcome in a private enterprise economy, it is less likely to be so in a mixed or centrally planned economy in which the parameters of prospective population growth would be somewhat differently interpreted.

Net immigration, secondly, entails an increase in an immigrant-receiving country's investment, since otherwise output per worker would fall either absolutely or below expected levels, and it might even prove impossible to employ the entire increment to the labor force. Immigrants, it is true, may bring with them claims that are convertible into productive resources, but these claims are offset at least in part by immigrant remittances. Im-

Mable Timlin, *Does Canada Need More People?* (Toronto, 1957); F. Bastos De Avila, *L'immigration au Bresil* (Rio De Janeiro, 1956). See also W. M. Corden, "The Economic Limits To Population Increase," *Economic Record,* XXXI (1955), 242–60.

migration may also stimulate an inflow of foreign capital, but rarely in sufficient volume to provide, directly and indirectly, for equipping the immigrants. Finally, immigration spares a country some of the cost of producing its population, but this saving constitutes a true gain only so long as a country's population is of infra-optimum size, optimum being defined in terms of some index that is to be raised to a sufficiently stable maximum value.[6] Even when a country's population is of infra-optimum size, capital is essential to equip the immigrant and also provide him with a sufficient amount of social capital. Almost invariably, therefore, a portion of the capital required to equip immigrants must be supplied through domestic saving.[7] Either the *ex ante* rate at

[6] E.g., suppose the index is net national product per worker. This index would be of maximum value if average output per worker coincided with marginal output per worker. But this coincidence would be unstable, since it would entail zero return to the owners of reproductive capital utilized jointly with labor, with the result that the stock of such capital would diminish. Stability therefore is contingent upon this stock's being maintained and growth of per capita income upon the stock's being increased.

[7] See Sauvy, *op. cit.,* I, chap. xxiii. One can only estimate the effect of immigration on the basis of given assumptions. One might, for example, postulate two populations, each growing at the same rate, with their age compositions remaining similar, but with one deriving half of its annual growth from immigration. Then, given assumptions regarding the cost of producing population domestically, the alternative use value of resources thus employed, capital investment per head, etc., one might project these two populations for 30 or 40 years and arrive at an estimate of the amount of invested capital that net immigration, as compared with natural increase, had made available, together with its time-pattern. Recently, D. C. MacGregor estimated the cost of equipping an increment of 1,000 Canadians (repre-

which capital is formed domestically must rise, or capital that might have been used to improve the facilities of the domestic population must be diverted to equipping the immigrants. Should neither of these courses (or a combination of them) be followed, the coming of the immigrants would be accompanied, if government policy permitted it, by an increase in *ex ante* offsets to saving which was not matched by a corresponding increase in *ex ante* savings. Price inflation would result, with the amount depending principally upon the extent to which agents of production initially were underemployed or unemployed, and upon the degree to which the increase in demand for agents of production was incident upon those in relatively short supply.[8] Should immi-

gration stimulate an increase in the rate of investment, however, the real rate would rise even more than had been anticipated, since conventional depreciation charges tend to exceed necessary replacement outlays and this excess expands when the rate of investment accelerates.[9]

Superficial comparison of the immigration history of America and Australia, for the period 1850–1914, suggests that, when a country is in early stages of economic and demographic development, heavy immigration may, by somewhat reducing labor scarcity, prevent the establishment of institutions which at the time are unfavorable to economic development. Immigration retarded the development of trade unionism in the United States, thus facilitating investment in mass-production methods (that depreciated craft skills) and thereby giving a modern structure to the American economy. In Australia, on the contrary, the volume of immigration remained small and labor continued to be scarce. For this and other reasons the trade union movement early became relatively strong, investment in enterprise was less than it otherwise might have been, and the economy was less flexible than it would have been, given much heavier immigration.

Immigration operated, in the situation just described, to give rise to inflation by increasing aggregate demand. It may also produce inflation by increasing costs, and under such

---

sentative of the population at large) at $12–13 million. Public capital and consumer's capital approximated $4.3 million each, and industrial capital, $4.5 million. This study will appear in a forthcoming number of the *Canadian Journal of Economics and Political Science*. The cost of equipping an increment of 1,000 immigrants would differ somewhat, since its composition would not be the same as that of a cross-section of 1,000 Canadians. On remittances, etc., see J. Isaac, *Economics of Migration* (New York, 1947), chap. vii; A. Winsemius, *Economische Aspecten der Internationale Migratie* (Haarlem, 1939), Pars. 16–19, 22; J. Bourgeois-Pichat, "Migration et balance des comptes," *Population*, IV (1949), 417–32.

[8] In any particular case the movement of prices will also be affected by capital movements, changes in industrial structure, and other circumstances, only some of which may be functionally connected with an influx of immigrants. On Canada's experience in 1900–1913 see G. M. Meier, "Economic Development And The Transfer Mechanism; Canada, 1895–1913," *Canadian Journal of Economics And Political Science*, XIX (1953), 1–19; D. C. Corbett, *Canada's Immigration Policy* (Toronto, 1957), 127–42; J. C. Ingram, "Growth In Capacity And Canada's Balance of

Payments," *American Economic Review*, XLVII (1957), 93–104. See also N. G. Butlin's paper, in Hugh J. G. Aitkin, (ed.): *The State and Economic Growth*, forthcoming in 1958 under auspices of the Social Science Research Council.

[9] E.g., see E. D. Domar, *Essays in the Theory of Economic Growth* (New York, 1957), chap. vii.

conditions that little if any capital may be formed. Such inflation will result if a society insists on paying inferior immigrant workers at the same rate as more skilled workers, or if it seeks to maintain wages at a higher real level than is compatible with the comparatively full employment of both the resident labor force and the incoming immigrant workers. If the wage is too high, unemployment results. When unemployment results, the government resorts to deficit spending to set the unemployed to work. Prices rise, with the result that the standard money wage must be increased. Again unemployment increases and again there is recourse to deficit spending. Eventually entrepreneurs come to expect increases in money costs, with the result that they increase prices in anticipation of increases in costs. Inflation, already self-perpetuating, accelerates. The pattern described will continue so long as the government insists on maintaining a too-high wage level. Illustrative of the inflation described is that experienced in Israel.[10]

3. It is quite possible, should an economy be technologically or otherwise dynamic, that the population growth resulting from net immigration might render the labor force somewhat more flexible through time and thus enable it more readily to adapt itself to changes in occupational requirements flowing from technological and related changes. Seasonal immigration may also be considered under this head. When a country is able to draw on foreign sources for a part of its seasonal labor supply, it

may, to that extent, avert having a portion of its labor force engaged in part-time employment in which the average annual income is relatively low. In consequence, this country's average income is somewhat higher than it otherwise would have been. It may, of course, be said that seasonal unemployment is being exported. Yet, since the seasonal immigrant freely chooses his role, it may be inferred that it is preferable to any alternative available to him.[11]

4. Migration, by affecting the magnitude and/or the composition of a country's gross national product, affects both the absolute and the relative importance of a country's external trade, at least in the relatively short run. Immigration tends to enlarge the absolute volume of external trade; emigration tends, at least in the short run, to make it smaller than it otherwise would have been. Immigration is likely, at least in later stages of an economy's development, to reduce the relative, but not the absolute, importance of external trade. It does this by facilitating the domestic production of some of the goods that formerly were imported, thus occasioning a relative diversion of resources from export industries to those serving the domestic market. Emigration has a similar effect insofar as it makes a country's dependence upon imported raw materials less than it otherwise would have been. Should 10 million Britons emigrate, for example, Britain's import requirements would be reduced in greater proportion than its

---

10 See A. P. Lerner's paper, based on Israel's experience, in Thomas, ed., *op. cit.*; also my paper in I. L. Webber, (ed.), *Aging: a Current Appraisal* (Gainesville, 1956), pp. 112–15.

11 In the fiscal year ending June 30, 1956, 431,985 agricultural workers, mostly Mexican nationals, were admitted into the United States. Seasonal immigration is often condemned. E.g., see Eleanor M. Hadley, "Immigration," in *Law and Contemporary Problems*, ed. M. G. Shimm, XXI, No. 2 (1956).

population or its gross output. These observations relate to the relatively short run. What happens in the much longer run depends in some measure upon whether or not migration eventually stimulates (as it did in the Atlantic Community) population growth in countries of emigration as well as in countries of immigration. It depends also, as is implied above, upon the extent to which migration diminishes the degree to which countries of immigration differ from countries of emigration in respect of relative endowment of primary factors of production. For, as this difference declines, the *relative* importance of external trade diminishes, unless international specialization is greatly increased through the development, initially in the immigrant-receiving countries, of sufficiently trade-fostering economies of scale.[12]

Inasmuch as international trade is a substitute, at least within limits, for the international migration of labor and other factors of production, it has been suggested that industrial workers residing in densely populated countries (e.g., United Kingdom) had better remain there and produce goods for export to (say) Canada and Aust-

ralia than emigrate to these countries and engage in either industrial or raw-material production.[13] Even if the necessary preconditions were present, this solution, though acceptable to a densely populated country, would not be acceptable to such underpeopled lands as Canada and Australia. For these countries are interested, as are similarly peopled countries with fairly good resource bases, in achieving populations and domestic markets sufficiently large to make realizable most of the economies of division of labor and industrial and occupational differentiation. The countries in question would therefore not be disposed to facilitate the establishment of the preconditions referred to above.

The money value of a country's external trade reflects, among other things, its terms of trade. These terms, in turn, are sensitive to a variety of circumstances, the effects of some of which are not easily isolated. Among the circumstances which, other conditions being given, may change the terms of trade one must include migration. Emigration tends to improve a country's terms of trade, and immigration to worsen them. For emigration usually makes a country's exports, together with its import requirements, less than they otherwise would have been whilst immigration usually makes a country's absolute volume of exports, together with its import requirements,

---

12 I have said "diminishes" above, since the most probable effect of migration is "diminution" of relevant intercountry differences. The above argument runs in relatively static terms. Yet, as Romney Robinson has shown, international trade, while consequent upon the existence of comparative advantage, also affects the conditions upon which comparative advantage rests at any time. Trade may, therefore, produce changes that either intensify or reduce the effect produced by migration per se. See Robinson, "Factor Proportions and Comparative Advantage," *Quarterly Journal of Economics*, LXX (1956), 169–92, 346–63. See also Helen Makower, *Activity Analyses and the Theory of Economic Equilibrium* (London, 1957), chap. ix and appendix.

13 See P. A. Samuelson, "International Trade and The Equalization of Factor Prices," *Economic Journal*, LVIII (1948), 163–84. The underlying problem has since been treated by a number of writers, some of whom are cited by Robinson, *op. cit.* On difficulties associated with the smallness of the population of New Zealand, see H. Bernardelli, "New Zealand And Asiatic Migration," *Population Studies*, VI (1952), 39–54.

greater than they otherwise would have been. Several possible exceptions are to be noted, however. If a country's emigrants set themselves up in industries competitive with export industries of the mother country, and carry on these activities under circumstances more favorable than those encountered in the home country, the prices of the mother country's exports may in time be sufficiently depressed to worsen its terms of trade. If immigration makes for industrial diversification and for diminution in a country's dependence upon foreign markets, it may make that country less sensitive to adverse changes in its external economic relations.[14]

5. Regarding the impact of migration upon functional distribution, detailed generalization is not possible. Immigration tends to increase the relative prices commanded by suppliers of land and natural resources; emigration produces a contrary effect, and this may be further accentuated if the emigrants engage abroad in the production of foodstuffs and raw materials. Immigration tends to increase the return on various forms of capital, and emigration to reduce it, though in the shorter run the financing of emigration may temporarily increase the return commanded by some forms of capital in the country of emigration. Immigration tends to make the *average* return to labor lower than it otherwise would have been, unless the

influx of immigrants sets in motion forces making for increasing return (see point 1 above), as was the case in Australia before 1914, or gives rise to a sufficient amount of productive investment (see point 2 above) that would not otherwise have taken place. Emigration tends to increase the *average* return to labor in the country of emigration unless the departure of emigrants sufficiently depresses longer-run business expectations and the rate of investment to offset the improvement initially occasioned in the ratio of productive wealth to the labor force.

6. Immigration seems to have produced several effects in the United States which, however, are likely to be encountered only when immigration continues on a scale too vast to be probable in the contemporary world. First, immigration increased the drive, the willingness to work, and the ambitions that animated America's labor force. For the ethnic and the cultural characteristics of the immigrants changed, as they came increasingly from the more easterly and southerly parts of Europe. Relatively recent arrivals tended to enter the lower reaches of the occupational pyramid whence, however, many hoped to rise to higher reaches, or to advance their children there. Those in the comparatively upper reaches were thus always subject to considerable competitive pressure from below, with the result that the level of performance in most reaches was better than it otherwise would have been. Second, the heavy influx of immigrants, few of whom were committed to an aristocratic or a highly differentiated pattern of consumption of the kind affected by the well-to-do in Europe, strengthened the thing-mindedness already present in American culture, facilitated the

---

[14] Brinley Thomas touches upon migration and the terms of trade in his *Migration and Economic Growth* (Cambridge, 1954). See also W. W. Rostow, *The Process of Economic Growth* (New York, 1952), chaps. viii and ix. It is not customary, in discussions of the terms of trade, to separate out migration and estimate its influence. The direction of this influence may be arrived at through the use of a model of the sort implicit in the discussion in the text above.

standardization of American tastes, and thus fostered the development of consumption patterns compatible with the mass production of consumer goods.[15]

Turning now to the impact of emigration upon emigrant countries, we may first note the advantages. (a) If, as in Puerto Rico or Southern Italy, capital is not being formed fast enough to give employment to the growing labor force, emigration may serve to reduce the labor force and therewith the relative amount of unemployment. However, in the event that natality and natural increase are high in the country of emigration, it may be preferable to invest in the emigrant-sending country the capital that would otherwise be used to set immigrants to work in the immigrant-receiving country. For such expenditure might accelerate the transformation of the emigrant-sending country's economy and thus reduce natality. (b) If a country's emigrants settle in regions that sufficiently complement the emigrant-sending country, international division of labor increases, together with specialization and industrial differentiation in the emigrant-sending country. Income levels rise in both the emigrant-sending and the immigrant-receiving areas, with the result that population growth is stimulated (e.g., in the Atlantic Community). If, however, the immigrant-receiving countries become competitive with the emigrant-sending countries, the latter may, in time, be adversely affected.[16] (c) Emigration may

even encourage investment when, by reducing the supply of manpower and elevating wages, it makes for the introduction of labor-saving machinery (e.g., the introduction of tractors into agricultural Europe since the 1930s). Such stimulus is of limited importance, however, inasmuch as this type of investment forms a relatively small fraction of total investment.

Emigration is not likely to produce markedly adverse effects in countries of emigration that are already well populated. Flexibility may be reduced somewhat, but the age structure is not likely to be significantly affected. Markets may be contracted somewhat, but this contraction may be offset by improvements in the population-resource ratio and in the balance of payments. In the event that emigration reduces the rate of population growth appreciably, savings and investment per head may rise. A well-populated country experiencing considerable emigration would be confronted principally by the problem of adjusting its economy to a lower rate of population growth. A thinly populated country, however, would almost certainly experience quite adverse economic effects as a result of continuous emigration.

IV

Migration produces compositional changes, or substitutive effects, when the composition of the migrant stream differs either from that of the country of immigration or from that of the country of emigration. In consequence, changes may be produced either in the level of employment, or

---

[15] See Ruth Mack's perceptive "Trends In American Consumption and the Aspiration to Consume," *American Economic Review*, May, 1956, XLVI (2), pp. 55–68, esp. pp. 58–62.
[16] See Brinley Thomas, *Migration and Economic Growth*; also Papers of

the Royal Commission on Population, III (London, 1950), pp. 5–21. See also James Duesenberry, "Some Aspects of The Theory of Economic Development," *Explorations In Entrepreneurial History*, III, No. 2 (1950), pp. 96–102.

in the factor-price structure of the countries affected.

1. Migration from country A to country B may increase the amount of employment to be had in the two countries considered as a unit, much as migration from one region to another within a country may produce such effect. Migration would not have this effect, of course, if interoccupational mobility of labor were great enough *and* if the proportion in which labor might be combined with complementary agents of production were sufficiently variable; for then full employment would always be attainable within a country. In the past, economists usually have supposed that these conditions were present, even in countries where industries and processes were few in number. In recent years, however, economists have questioned these assumptions, particularly the second, and have concluded that unemployment may be caused not only by imperfections in the wage or price structure, but also by a dearth of productive agents complementary to labor, given existing technology and/ or the structure of demand. Suppose that such is the case in country A, but not in country B where, either because capital is plentiful or because factor-combinableness is sufficiently variable, a greater amount of labor may be employed jointly with the existing stock of productive factors. Then migration from A to B will diminish unemployment in A and increase jobs in B. In consequence per capita income will rise in A and aggregate income in B. Output per worker in the occupations entered by immigrants into B will tend to fall appreciably unless they are combined with first-order capital theretofore idle and the income elasticity of demand for their output is sufficiently high. Illustrative of the migration here under consideration is that from Puerto Rico (or Southern Italy) to the United States.

In the preceding paragraph capital has been treated as the employment-limiting factor in country A. If, however, the labor force in country A were subdivided into categories a and a', category a might be discovered to be the limitational factor: there might be too few workers in this category to permit full employment of those in a'. If a surplus of a workers lived in country B, then, abstracting from the effects associated with magnitude of capital supply, some a' workers might emigrate from country A to country B, or some a workers might emigrate from country B to country A.[17]

_____

[17] By abstracting from the role of capital in this paragraph the solution has been unduly simplified. The net effect of migration along the lines set down in the preceding paragraph would be determinable only if one could estimate, besides the primary effect, the secondary influences of the movement and the extent to which expansion in B would affect the demand for labor in A and thus serve to offset adverse secondary consequences of emigration. Concerning the theory underlying the above argument see R. S. Eckhaus, "The Factor Proportions Problems In Underdeveloped Areas," *American Economic Review*, XLV (1955), 539–65; also Joan Robinson, *The Accumulation of Capital* (London, 1956), pp. 78–80. According to Hilde Wander, a shortage of skilled workers accentuated unemployment in Western Europe in the late 1940s. See her *The Importance of Emigration for the Solution of Population Problems in Western Europe* (The Hague, 1951).

Emigration is presently relieving population pressure in Puerto Rico. Between 1946–1947 and 1955–1956 net emigration approximated 434,000, and population growth, 163,000, with total population rising from 2,104,000 to 2,267,000. During this same period the number of persons employed rose from 572,000 in 1946–1947 to 604,000 in 1950–1951, gradually fell to 539,000 in 1954–1955, and then rose to 558,000 in 1955–1956. The decline in total employment after 1952 is primarily the result

2. Migration sets up a chain of substitutive and complementary effects in countries of immigration and emigration. These effects worsen the comparative economic situation of some elements in the population and improve that of others. These effects may be felt even in regions not much affected directly by immigration or emigration. In a dynamic and mobile society these effects are relatively short run in character, tending to disappear as the composition of the population of foreign origin or parentage approaches that of the population of native parentage. These effects, though of diminishing relative importance, are partly renewed so long as immigration continues. But, as noted, they gradually disappear, under the impact of social capillarity, when immigration declines.

The immigrants of working age who enter a country must market their labor or services. These services are substitutable for (i.e., competitive with) those offered by some members of the resident labor force, and complementary to (i.e., cooperant with) those offered by other members of this labor force.[18] Members of the

resident labor force who are subject to the rivalry of immigrant workers tend to experience a decline in their relative wage or salary rates whereas those whose relationship with immigrant workers is one of complementarity tend to experience an increase in their relative rates. Thus, for two or three decades preceding 1914, immigration into the United States prevented the wages of unskilled workers from rising even though average income and the real wages of skilled workers were rising.[19] Should wage rates not be sufficiently flexible to permit adjustment of the wage structure to the coming of the immigrants, some unemployment tends to develop in occupations favored by the immigrants, with the result that the gains of the beneficiaries of complementarity are less than they otherwise would have been.

The effects just described will be most pronounced in the areas in which immigrants initially settle. They may be felt in other regions, however, being propagated principally through adjustments in the wage, salary, and price structure and through responses to these adjustments. There will be some tendency for those adversely affected to migrate elsewhere, and for the ranks of those benefited to be augmented by migrants from other regions. Unless the volume of foreign immigration is relatively large, however, absorption of foreign workers will not give rise to conspicuous manifestations. For a relatively large num-

---

of a decrease in the number of persons employed in agriculture and in the home needlework industry. I am indebted to Dr. Felipe S. Viscasillas for information relating to 1946–1956. For detailed information see Departmento Del Trabajo, *Informe Especial Número 15 Sobre El Grupo Trabajador: Empleo Pleno Y Sub-Empleo En Puerto Rico: 1953 A 1956.* San Juan, 1957.

[18] For the sake of expositive convenience, we have classified the relationships as either substitutive or complementary. In reality, the relationship is one of degree. The relationship between a given immigrant worker and a given resident worker may be predominantly substitutive or predominantly complementary (or cooperant). Similarly, the relationship between a given immigrant worker and a nonhuman factor of production (e.g., land, capital) may be pre-

dominantly substitutive or predominantly complementary. This last relationship will not here be explored, since it has already been noticed in section III; it trends to be predominantly complementary. For a fuller discussion see my paper in Thomas, ed., *op. cit.*

[19] E.g., see A. C. Pigou, *The Economics of Welfare* (4th ed., London, 1932), pp. 658–61.

ber of jobs remain concentrated in a relatively small number of places, in most of which there is considerable wage disparity, and virtually all of which are subject to various sorts of change unconnected with immigration. For example, the relationship between immigrant and Negro workers has always been essentially one of rivalry. Yet, while this relationship has checked the movement of immigrants into the South and has somewhat affected the direction and volume of Negro migration out of the South, it has not been sufficiently strong to prevent Negroes and immigrants from settling in the same cities. What amounts to an aggregative influence, reenforced here and there by Negro-immigrant complementarity, has swamped Negro-immigrant rivalry; for jobs are principally to be had by both Negroes and immigrants in the relatively small number of counties in which industry and commerce are concentrated.[20]

V

In my previous discussion I have sought to identify, isolate, and assess the nature of particular effects of migration. When, however, one views migration as a process continuing through time, one must view it, just as one must view other population movements, as a part of the longer-run economic growth process. For, even if migration is set in motion by essentially noneconomic changes, it produces economic effects and thus makes the extent and the course of economic growth, if not the actual sequence of economic events, different than they otherwise would have been. Migration

is thus related (to phrase it loosely) "causally" and "effectually" to a number of the elements that enter into the process of economic growth.

Because international migration is part of the process of economic growth, its course is subject to fluctuation even as is that of economic growth, particularly when, as in the nineteenth century, migration is subject to few constraints or stimuli of governmental origin. For, except in periods when men seek to escape persecution for their religious or political beliefs, migration is primarily a form of behavior designed to improve the economic and/or the social situation of the migrant and his family (if he has one). The potential migrant tends to move when he estimates the margin of advantage of a prospective foreign socioeconomic situation over that of his present situation to be sufficiently great to warrant movement. The magnitude of this margin, as of his estimate of it, is affected by fluctuations, in both his own country and the prospective country of immigration, in economic conditions, prospects, and opportunities for employment. These fluctuations may also affect his assessment of the probable costs of migrating and of his capacity to meet these costs. Such fluctuations, as has been noted, are somewhat influenced by migration. For example, migration may accelerate or decelerate economic movements already underway; or it may give rise to subsequent movements, as when net immigration, by augmenting the return on capital, stimulates the influx of foreign capital, the inflow of which, in turn, may stimulate further immigration.

The pattern of fluctuation to which immigration and emigration are subject tends to change as economies evolve and circumstances affecting

---

[20] On the circumstances producing population concentration see Walter Isard, *Location and Space-Economy* (New York, 1956).

migration undergo modification. Emigration tends to fall off as a result of changes in countries of emigration; e.g., decline in absolute rate of natural increase, especially in rural regions; increase in rate of domestic investment; increase in industrialization and urbanization; increase in volume of exports. Similarly, changes in countries of immigration may conduce to immigration; e.g., decline in rate of natural increase; increase in rates of investment, industrialization, and urbanization; possibly the selective restriction of imports.[21] Nonrecurring and irregularly recurring events also temporarily affect the propensity to emigrate, when these events worsen the domestic prospects of potential migrants (e.g., the Suez fiasco in the United Kingdom; the present incidence of British social security costs).

The studies of Thomas and Kuznets reveal something of the cyclical nature of immigration into the United States prior to 1914, but they do not suggest that a quite similar pattern characterized the movement of migrants to other major countries of immigration. Immigration into the United States was dominated by something like twenty-year movements. The pattern of American immigration changed somewhat in that, after 1870, "push" conditions, although still important in parts of Europe, affected immigration into the United States less than did "pull" conditions. After 1870, Thomas finds, the inflow of immigrants from "industrial" countries lagged behind

coal output and railway construction while that of immigrants from "agricultural" countries virtually coincided with the movement of capital investment. "Building activity ... always lagged after inflow of population (except in the seventies)." Variation in emigration from the United Kingdom to the United States was significantly and positively associated with variation in the ratio of British capital exports to total British investment. "Outstanding waves of immigration coincided with minor secular upswings in the rate of economic growth of the United States." The "periodic inflows of population" occasioned or intensified "minor secular swings in induced investment."[22] Kuznets and Rubin report that, before 1914, "the twenty-year swings" in net immigration "tended to *follow* those in gross national product per worker and to *precede* those in the constant dollar volume of residential construction" They suggest also that, so long as migration is free, as it was in America, the foreign labor supply may be regarded "as a sort of stabilizing reservoir."[23]

---

[21] Some of these factors have been discussed by Thomas, *op. cit.*; I. Svennilson, *Growth and Stagnation in the European Economy* (Geneva, 1954), chap. iv; Dorothy S. Thomas, *Social and Economic Aspects of Swedish Population Movements, 1750–1933* (New York, 1941).

[22] Brinley Thomas, *op. cit.*, chaps. vii, viii, x, xi. In the forthcoming Proceedings of the 1957 Conference, Western Economic Association (Salt Lake City), some relations between American immigration and investment are treated by D. A. Baerucopf in "A Note On Long Cycle Analysis."

[23] See *op. cit.*, pp. 5–6, 30–36. On French experience respecting the stabilizing influence of migration, see my *France Faces Depopulation* (Durham, 1938), pp. 201 ff. The inference Kuznets and Rubin draw regarding the stabilizing effect of migration is somewhat open to question. It is valid to infer that the departure of foreign-born workers tends to ease the pressure of unemployment during the downswing and to make the volume of unemployment, at the beginning of the upturn, smaller than it otherwise would have been, thereby reducing the amplitude of the cycle. If,

It is not to be inferred that temporal relationships of the sort described need always obtain. Suppose that m and k are complements. Then, if m increases in country A in consequence of migration thereto from country B, k will increase in A, so long at least as the supply of k is at all elastic, as it would be if k might migrate from B to A. Under the circumstances m precedes k; yet k might also precede m. It is possible, furthermore, that, even though m typically precedes k, k might be made to precede m; such would be the outcome if those who controlled the movement of k, anticipating an increase of m in A, would move k into A even before the increase in m occurred. For example, growth of population normally precedes residential construction; yet builders, if they can satisfactorily finance construction, may build in advance of the very increase in population (or labor force) that will occupy this construction. It may be possible, by categorizing capital and ascertaining the conditions under which each category is supplied, and by proceeding similarly with a potential immigrant labor force, to estimate under what circumstances capital is very likely to precede immigration, and under what circumstances capital is likely to lag after immigration. Stu-

dies of sequences observed in the past, together with the rationale underlying these sequences, may facilitate the making of such estimates. It is only after studies of this sort, however, that one may predict with considerable confidence what sequences are to be expected in the future. In the absence of such studies one could not infer that the sequences or pattern observed before 1914 would continue to prevail, even under conditions of free migration. They cannot all be expected to prevail, of course, in the present-day world in which migration is frequently assisted and always subject to variable quantitative controls at the hands of both emigrant and immigrant countries.

While it is possible to determine what elements are complements to migrants, and while it may be possible to determine which of these elements tend, in their movements, to follow those of migrants, it is not possible to forecast with much precision the manner in which migration will fluctuate, within the limits set by quotas, etc. For, as noted, the movement of migrants is greatly influenced by some of the movements that make up the economic-growth process, and the specific manner in which these movements are likely to fluctuate in the proximate future is not inferable from our knowledge of present conditions and potential novelties. Accordingly, whatever be a country's policy regarding migration, it is most effectively administered when the economy is kept flexible and capable of readily adjusting to variations of the sort to which migration is subject....

however, immigration greatly increases on the upswing, this influx makes the upswing greater than it otherwise would have been. Such has been the experience, in fact, of countries undergoing heavy, city-bound, internal migration. The research carried on in conjunction with this study has been facilitated by a grant from the Ford Foundation.

Female Occupational Roles and Urban Sex Ratios in the United States, Japan, and the Philippines[*]

Chester L. Hunt

This paper is an attempt to test the hypothesis that industrialization promotes a demand for female labor in the nonagricultural sectors of the economy which in turn is reflected in low (fewer men than women) urban sex ratios. The Philippines was selected as a country in the initial stage of industrialization, Japan as a country in the intermediate stage, and the United States as a country in the advanced stage.[1] If this hypothesis were substantiated one would expect high urban sex ratios in the Philippines, intermediate urban sex ratios in Japan and low urban sex ratios in the United States.

The situation in the United States as described by Landis would seem to bear out the hypothesis:

> The urban migration is selective in the feminine direction. Generally speaking, so far as the American culture pattern is concerned, the migration from farm to town and city involves more women than men. The urban community attracts women in part, because they are more interested in the superficial attractions of urban life than are men, but primarily, no doubt, because most of the occupations open to women are found in town and city. Farming is primarily a male occupation.... Massachusetts, the most urban state in the nation in 1940, had the ratio of only 95 men to 100 women.[2]

More recent data indicate the trends described by Landis have continued. The 1960 census reported 60 million men in urban areas as compared to 64 million women and an urban sex ratio of 94 compared to a rural sex ratio of 104.[3]

PHILIPPINE SEX RATIOS

Since the Philippines is a country in which industrialization has barely gotten underway one would expect the opposite type of urban sex ratio. Earlier reports supported this assumption:

> Manila is the only Philippine city at present for which an analysis is possible.... Now if there were no unusual events or migration occurring, one would expect that the city would be composed of nearly equal numbers of males and females in every age group.

---

[*] Chester L. Hunt, "Female Occupational Roles and Urban Sex Ratios in the United States, Japan, and the Philippines," *Social Forces*, XLIII (March, 1965), 407–17.

[1] For the purpose of this paper the most significant measure of industrialization is the proportion in agricultural and related (forestry and fisheries) employment. Philippine agricultural employment accounts for approximately 63 per cent of the labor force, Japanese for 32 per cent and the United States for 6 per cent. Percentages are calculated from data in Table 2.

[2] Paul H. Landis, *Population Problems: A Cultural Interpretation* (New York: American Book Company, 1948), p. 257.

[3] *Census of the United States, 1960.*

However, in 1948, for the age group of 25 to 34, there are 88,622 males and 83,746 females in Manila—a difference of 4,786. This suggests that migrants to Manila are usually young men. It seems likely that the same pattern would also be true for other Philippine cities, although there are no data available at present.[4]

Coller's statement was written before results of the 1948 census were fully available, and more complete data bear out his position. Thus, Manila had a sex ratio of 101.6 males per 100 females. The next largest group of municipalities, those between 100,000 and 200,000 population, had a sex ratio of 103.8. For the Philippines as a whole the sex ratio in 1948 was practically equal: 9,651,000 males to 9,583,000 females.[5]

Many reasons could be adduced for the minority position of women in Philippine cities. Perhaps most important were the relative lack of occupational opportunities and the tradition that women remain in the home. In the past, occupational opportunities for women have been mainly in housework. There was a steady demand for domestic helpers which kept several labor agencies busy recruiting women from the provinces. This recruitment of household help did stimulate a constant movement of young women to Manila and other urban centers, but by itself, was hardly equal to the opportunities available to male workers. Nor was female labor unwanted on the farm. Unlike some western countries, Filipino women are not excluded from agricultural work and their labor in the fields is highly valued in rural areas.

Not only were women inhibited from moving to the city alone, but the wife did not necessarily accompany her husband when he secured work in another area. Filipino family ties seem to be so strong that the family can remain intact even when husband and wife are living in different communities. Manila in 1948 had 39,633 married men whose wives were not living with them in the city.[6] This means that approximately one fourth of the married men in Manila at the time had moved to the city and left their wives in their former community. Another explanation of the male predominance is found in the fact that Manila had about 40 per cent of the Chinese population in the Philippines[7] and that this was a group with a high proportion of males.

RECENT CHANGES IN PHILIPPINE SEX RATIOS

The most recent data, however, reveal a striking change in the Philippine sex ratio. A 1957 sampling type of survey found that the sex ratio in urban areas was 97.7 as compared to 102.6 in rural areas.[8] The 1960 census

---

[4] Chester L. Hunt and Richard W. Coller, *et al.*; *Sociology in the Philippine Setting* (Manila: Alemar's, 1954), p. 312.

[5] *Census of the Philippines, Summary of Population and Agriculture* (Manila: Bureau of Census and Statistics, 1954), pp. 30 and 67.

[6] *Journal of Philippine Statistics*, V (September 1952), Table 7, p. 17.

[7] George Henry Weightman, "A Preliminary Ecological Description of the Chinese Community in Manila," *Philippine Sociological Review*, III (November 1955), 24.

[8] Includes metropolitan Manila and suburbs, chartered cities, provincial capitals and *poblaciones* (towns in which government buildings of a municipality are located). Figures are taken from data in "The PSSH Survey Results," *The Statistical Reporter*, I (April 1957), 33.

indicated that the Manila sex ratio had dropped to 88.8 although the sex ratio of the Phillippines as a whole was 101.8[9]

This rather drastic shift in sex ratios is probably most directly due to an advance in industrialization between 1948 and 1960 which accelerated certain developments that had long been apparent to observers of sex-linked conduct in the Philippines. This industrialization is minor compared to that of the United States or Japan but did open up a number of opportunities for industrial employment which seem to have been filled largely by women.

There are a number of causes for this industrial development, including the fact that postwar reconstruction had been pretty well completed by this time and that at least some of the necessary facilities for a business "take-off" were present. Other factors would include the adoption of a protectionist policy favoring industrialization, the increased tempo of international trade and the effects of the American aid program.

Many industrial firms have found that female operatives are less bored by routine work and more willing to accept detailed supervision than male workers. In some of the Manila factories, the wage workers are overwhelmingly female. The result is that the expansion of industrial and related employment has offered proportionately more opportunity to female than to male workers. Between 1948 and 1957, the proportion of females employed in manufacturing and mining nearly tripled and the proportion in trade and services more than doubled. At the same time, the pro-

portion of males in mining and manufacturing made only a slight increase and the proportion in trade and services showed a slight drop.

Both the absolute numbers and the proportion of women listed as employed in agriculture decreased sharply while the reverse was true in other categories. The absolute number of men employed in agriculture and other primarily rural occupations increased, while their percentage representation dropped only slightly. In both manufacturing and mining and in trade and services, there was an absolute increase in the number of male employees but in the latter, this increase was so small that the percentage of male workers in this category showed a drop while in the former, it showed only a slight percentage increase. On an over-all basis, the number of women in primarily urban industrial occupations is estimated to have increased by 1,054,000 and the number of men by only 508,000—a difference large enough to have attracted a considerably greater number of women to the city.[10]

Changes in occupational distribution by sex are also related to changes in educational patterns. In recent years, such occupations as nursing, secretarial work and teaching have become predominantly female. One result of this change is a greater female participation as students in the institutions of higher education. The traditional pattern in which girls drop out of school at an early age to get married is changing to one in which the young women attend college in order to qualify for an occupation by which they can help to support

[9] *Census of the Philippines 1960*, unpublished data obtained from Bureau of Census and Statistics, Manila.

[10] Figures computed from data in *Population Growth and Manpower in The Philippines* (New York: United Nations Department of Economics and Social Affairs, 1960), p. 19.

a family. In the school year 1958–59, females made up 48 per cent of total college enrollment compared to 38 per cent in the United States and 20 per cent in Japan.[11] As in other countries, most colleges are found in urban areas. In the Philippines, this is likely to mean Manila since in 1960, 140,-953 out of a total of 232,117 college students were enrolled in Manila schools.[12] A growing female college attendance is thus one of the influences bringing women to the city.

It is probably also true that the Manila Chinese population has less of an effect on the sex ratio than in previous years. As immigration is restricted and the Chinese group becomes one more largely represented by those born in the Philippines, the sex ratio comes closer to equality. In 1918, the sex ratio was one woman to thirteen men; in 1939, it was 1 to 4 and in 1948, 1 to 2.1.[13] Although no figures are available since that date, one would assume that the trend has continued toward a more nearly equal Chinese sex ratio.

THE JAPANESE URBAN SEX RATIO

As a nation midway between the United States and the Philippines in the industrialization process the hy-pothesis would indicate an urban sex ratio midway between the two countries. Actually Japan has a comparatively high urban sex ratio and its women show the least tendency to head for the cities of any of the three countries. War-time casualties affected Japanese manpower to such an extent that the national sex ratio is low and therefore direct comparisons of urban sex ratios with other countries are misleading. The proportion of women, however, is greater in the rural districts than in the cities. Thus the statistics for "densely inhabited" areas show that the sex ratio is 97.7, while in the remainder of the nation the sex ratio is 95.4. For Japan as a whole the sex ratio is 96.4.[14]

The statement that women are underrepresented in the cities will come as a surprise to those who have observed the large numbers of young women laborers in textile mills and other types of light industry. Factories of this type often relied on female labor to the extent that it was necessary to build large dormitories to house female employees. This utilization of young single women was the result of a cultural adjustment which, while it made available this type of occupational opportunity, sharply curtailed other forms of employment. Young women were given an education which made them literate but did not fit them to compete with males. They worked for wages until marriage but as wives they often returned to rural districts and their labor was an unpaid contribution to a family enterprise—usually agricultural in nature.

One indication of the survival of this pattern is found in the sexual

[11] Statistical Bulletin of the Research and Evaluation Division, Bureau of Public Schools (Manila 1959), Table 7, p. 16. Japanese percentage based on data in *1% Sample, 1960 Census of Japan* (Tokyo: Bureau of Statistics Office of the Prime Minister), p. 359. U.S. percentage computed from data for 1961 from the U.S. Office of Education and Statistics reported in *World Almanac for 1963*, p. 539.

[12] *Journal of Philippine Statistics*, XIII (October–December 1960), p. 47.

[13] Data for 1948 computed from data in *Census of the Philippines, op. cit.*, p. 67. Other figures taken from

Victor Purcell, *Chinese in Southeast Asia* (London: Oxford University Press, 1950), pp. 575–77.

[14] *1% Sample Tabulation, op. cit.*, pp. 26 and 31.

distribution of unpaid family workers. In 1958 some 29.7 per cent of a total of 12,680,000 unpaid family workers were males as contrasted to 70.3 per cent female workers. The proportion of female workers has been farily constant in recent years and increased about 1 per cent between 1953 and 1958.[15]

The work plan of many Japanese factories is carefully designed to insure that girls should look on their jobs as a temporary prelude to marriage rather than an introduction into a lifelong career as a wage worker. Lewis makes the following analysis of the Japanese factories described by Abegglen:

> It can be seen from this description that these girls do not have a long-term commitment to the industrial labor force. Their period of participation in the labor force is a temporary brief interlude in their life pattern, the interval between school and marriage, after which they can be expected to assume the more traditional roles of mother and housekeeper. It is also evident that the men in this factory hold the more permanent and prestigeful positions. They perform the jobs of foreman, silk specialist, and mechanic. In addition there is a young boy who acts as messenger and handyman. It is notable that this boy is learning the trade, and has thus assumed a long-range commitment to the labor force. These positions contrast noticeably with the routine operation of the looms which is the only job held by the girls. These girls are paid largely in food, clothing, and the necessities of life rather than in money or wages, which is further evidence that their work situation does not

encourage a primarily industrial orientation.[16]

While the proportion of women laborers in industry has been rising in recent years, it is still not large and many women workers are restricted to unskilled work or honorific functions such as serving tea. A recent article by Japanese sociologists summarizes the situation as follows:

> Although the women have entered professional and technical work in increasing numbers, they are concentrated largely in the teaching profession at the lower levels and as technicians, largely midwives and nurses, in the medical field. As a group, women are still concentrated in lower occupations requiring less skill—agriculture, retail trade, manufacturing, and domestic service. . . . By and large, the Japanese people (including women) still conceive of an adult woman's place as in the home and in a position subordinate to that of her husband.[17]

Although Japanese women share in the generally high literacy rate, their role in higher education is extremely

[15] Bureau of Statistics, Office of the Prime Minister, Japan, Figures of Labor Force Survey Concerning the Population 15 Years Old and Over: January 1953–December 1958 (1959), pp. 38–41.

[16] David M. Lewis, *The Acceptance of Work-Related Values by Young Rural Japanese*, 1963, unpublished dissertation, Michigan State University, pp. 20–21. Analysis is based on factory description in James C. Abegglen, *The Japanese Factory: Aspects of Its Social Organization* (New York: The Free Press of Glencoe, Inc., 1958), pp. 73–74. For discussion of the composition of Japanese labor force see "The Indigenous Components in the Modern Japanese Economy," Henry Rosovsky and Kazushi Ohkawa, *Economic Development and Cultural Change* 9 (April 1961), pp. 476–501.

[17] Edna Cooper Masuoka, Jitsuichi Matsuoka, and Nozomu Kawamura, "Role Conflicts in the Family," *Social Forces*, XLI (October 1962), 5. Supporting data are found in an opinion survey: Robert J. Smith, Charles E. Ramsey, Gelia Castillo, "Parental Authority and Job Choice: Sex Differences in Three Cultures," *American Journal of Sociology*, XLIX (September 1963), 143–50.

TABLE 1. Females as a Per Cent of Total Labor Force by Occupation for United States, Japan, and Philippines

Occupation Year	United States[a] 1960		Japan[b] 1960		Philippines[c] 1958	
	Number	Per cent Female	Number	Per cent Female	Number	Per cent Female
Professional and technical	7,232,410	38.1	2,136,800	35.4	249,870	49.7
Management	5,409,543	14.4	1,016,600	4.3	249,870	48.6
Clerical	9,306,896	67.6	4,555,800	36.9	174,909	24.2
Sales	4,638,985	35.8	4,613,200	41.6	508,069	61.1
Agriculture, forestry, fishing	3,950,491	9.1	14,252,400	51.7	5,255,599	25.7
Manual labor[d]	23,746,463	15.2	14,276,900	25.4	1,324,311	41.1
Service	7,170,784	62.9	2,827,400	59.4	533,056	59.3
Miscellaneous	—	—	11,400	59.6	—	—
Total	64,639,247	32.8	43,690,500	39.1	8,295,684	33.9

[a] Source: U. S. Census of Population. 1960, General Social and Economic Characteristics, Final Report PC (1)-1C, U. S. Department of Commerce, p. 1–216, Table 87.
[b] Source: 1960 Population Census of Japan, Bureau of Statistics, Office of the Prime Minister, p. 290.
[c] Source: Table 12, PSSH Bulletin Series No. 5, Labor Force Nov. 58, Manila; Bureau of the Census.
[d] Composite of: 1) Mining, quarry and related, 2) Operating transport occupations, 3) Craftsmen, factory operatives, 4) Manual workers and laborers not elsewhere classified.

limited. Not only are women a small minority of the total students in higher educational institutions but most women who do continue beyond the secondary school pursue only junior college work. This is strikingly borne out by the figures for school attendance of those 20 years of age or over. Men in this age bracket in 1957 amounted to 241,000 and women to only 29,000; a ratio of a little over 8 to 1.[18] In the 18 and 19 year age bracket the comparative totals are 342,000 men and 109,000 women or a ratio of about 3.1 to 1. The presence of a small number of women in Japanese universities proves that barriers against feminine entry are not insurmountable but their limited num-

18 Estimate of Population by Age, 1957, Bureau of Statistics, Office of the Prime Minister, Report of School Statistics, Ministry of Education, cited in *Education in Japan* (Tokyo: Ministry of Education, 1961), p. 88.

bers indicate that Japanese women have only begun to pursue the type of educational opportunities which are taken for granted in several other countries.

COMPARATIVE OCCUPATIONAL DISTRIBUTION. Many of the differences in feminine roles in the three countries are shown in Table 1. Women comprise more than half of the workers in agriculture and kindred occupations in Japan, about one fourth in the Philippines and less than ten per cent in the United States. American women are most prominent in the clerical force with Filipino women in last place, in sales the position is reversed. In management and in professional and technical occupations, Filipino women are far more active than women in the other two countries. The feminine proportion of the total number of gainfully employed workers shows little variation running from

32.6 per cent in the United States to 39.1 per cent in Japan.

Certain peculiarities of the national cultures have affected this occupational distribution. In the Philippines pharmacy has become practically an all-female occupation while the drive of men for white collar positions has prevented many clerical jobs from being taken over by women. Similarly the role of women as family treasurer has promoted an interest in finance and trade which has given Filipino women a heavy predominance in this category. In the United States women have had available a variety of occupations at the intermediate status level which allows them to make a fairly substantial contribution to the family income with a minimum of competition with male wage earners, a situation which has not been true in either the Philippines or Japan.

INDUSTRIALIZATION AND FEMALE URBANIZATION

There is no doubt that a comparison of urban sex ratios and feminine occupational patterns in the three countries destroys the thesis that there is a direct and inevitable relationship between industrialization and the type of female emancipation which promotes urban migration. The Philippines as the least industrialized country would be expected to show the least indication of a feminine drift to the cities, with this movement greater in Japan and reaching its peak in the United States. Actually, as measured by the comparison between urban sex ratio and total sex ratio (Table 2), the Philippines shows the greatest trend toward a female urban drift, followed closely by the United States with Japan showing a lower proportion of women in the cities than in the country as a whole.

CHART 1. The Feminine Role in the United States, Japan, and the Philippines

Japan	Philippines	America
Strong status subordination	Status subordination	Status equality
Occupational subordination	Occupational equality	Supplementary occupational role
Only " token " representation ih higher education	Educational equality	Higher education less attractive to woman
Later marriage	Later marriage	Early marriage
Servants and relatives becoming less available for child care and housework	Child care and housework by servants and relatives	Child care and housework by both parents

TABLE 2. Urban-Rural Sex Ratios

Country	Urban	Rural	Total	Urban ratio as per cent Total ratio
United States	94.0	104.0	97.1	96.8
Philippines	97.7	102.4	101.8	95.9
Japan	97.7	95.4	96.4	101.3

Sources: U.S. Census 1960; Japanese 1% Tabulation of 1960 Census; Philippine Survey of Households, 1957; unpublished data from 1960 Philippine Census.

This lack of a direct relationship does not mean that industrialization is without effect on the feminine role. Rather it suggests that the reaction to industrialization is made through cultural channels which influence the sexual distribution of labor. The differences in feminine roles listed in Chart 1 indicate some of the factors which affect the participation of women in the industrialization process.

These role characteristics reflect the type of interaction which has taken place between the family and industrial society in various cultures. The interaction however is not completely in the expected direction. Status equality does not always lead to occupational equality although extreme status subordination does seem to support occupational subordination. Later marriage would appear to favor the entry of women into the labor market but early marriage in the United States has accompanied a trend toward rising female industrial employment. The presence of servants in the home may aid the careers of middle-class women in underdeveloped areas but, in the course of industrialization, the servants themselves are drawn into industrial employment. Education appears to be the factor most definitely related to female occupational patterns. The small number of Japanese women in the institutions of higher education effectively limits their advance to high positions, while the greater educational achievement of Filipino and American women corresponds with their position in the occupational structure.

Japan has been exposed to a rapid industrial development and one might assume that the demand for workers would draw female labor to the cities in the same fashion in which this has occurred in the United States. Apparently, however, the strong tradition of complete subordination of women has been sufficient to deflect most of the pressures of industrialization. The working wife is still comparatively rare in Japan, only 17.4 per cent in 1957 as compared to 32 per cent in the United States.[19] In

Japan female labor has been used to release men from farming along with the entry of a small number of unmarried girls in the unskilled industrial occupations. A declining birth rate and a growing demand for labor may force a readjustment in this situation, but as yet the traditional pattern of sexual roles has proved surprisingly resistant to the inroads of industrialization.

The United States, with the most industrialization and probably the greatest acceptance of sexual equality, would seem best adapted to female emancipation. The urban sex ratios indicate that American women have been drawn into the occupational complex of an industrialized society but their participation has been structured toward intermediate status roles. They show only a minor participation in professional, technical and managerial activities and make up a surprisingly small part of the industrial labor force. Similarly they attend higher educational institutions at little more than half the masculine rate and make hardly more than a token contribution to such professions as law and medicine.

The fragility of the American family may actually heighten "familistic" orientation among American women while the very richness of American industrial society may deflect feminine ambitions from the higher levels of achievement. The establishment of a home is the task of the young couple involved, with little assistance from the total family group. Mate seeking, especially, is an individual matter which arouses intense anxiety and stresses the idea that the

---

[19] Japanese data from *Ibid.*, p. 5, U.S. data from Women's Bureau, *Hand-book on Women Workers*, Bulletin 275 (1960), p. 234. Cited in Clifford Kirkpatrick, *The Family* (New York: Ronald Press, 1963), p. 133.

nubile female should find a husband while at the peak of her physical charms. The result is that the mean age of marriage is 20 for American women compared to 24 for Japanese and 22.6 for Filipino.[20] After marriage the American woman has little hope for household help from either servants or relatives although the husband often acts as part-time maid. The nature of her family orientation works against peak occupational aspiration while the substantial financial returns from comparatively low-level occupations enable her to bring home an adequate supplement to the family income. The result is that the American woman's economic activities are supplementary to those of her husband rather than being either subordinate or competitive.

THE FILIPINO WOMAN AS A DEVIANT CASE

Differences between the feminine occupation patterns and urban sex ratios of Japan and the United States are in the expected directions. Since the United States has a smaller percentage of the population engaged in

[20] U.S. Figure from *Vital Statistics of the United States 1959*, Section 2 (Washington, D.C.: 1961). Japanese figures from data in T. Fukutake, *Population of Post War Japan* (Tokyo: Yuhikaku, 1961), p. 46. Philippine mean computed from data in Table 8, *Vital Statistics Report 1960*, Bureau of the Census, Manila. Impressionistic observation suggests that the urbanized middle class population has a still higher age at marriage. This is supported by a survey of a Manila housing development, whose residents were government employees, which indicated a mean age at marriage for women married between 1950 and 1953 of 25.5 years. Amos Hawley, "Fertility in an Urban Population in the Philippines," *The Philippine Statistician*, II, No. 4, pp. 270–71.

agricultural employment and has given women generally higher status it is not surprising that American women have entered a variety of occupations and that American cities should have low sex ratios. The Philippine pattern cannot be explained on this basis. Here is a traditional society with many restrictions on female activities and with relatively little industrialization in which the relation between urban and rural sex ratios is closer to the United States than to Japan. Indeed, in matters of higher education and professional careers Philippine middle class women appear to be more emancipated than American women of similar status.

FEMALE STATUS IN RELATION TO OCCUPATIONAL ROLE. From the standpoint of status equality the Filipino woman appears closer to the Japanese than to the American pattern. The Spanish Catholic influence has encumbered her freedom by rigid concepts of modesty, handicapped her defense of family prerogatives by the absolute denial of divorce and in general emphasized the subordinate role of women in a society where the prestige figure is the patriarchical male. This pattern of feminine subordination, however, contrasts sharply not only with the more recent American emphasis but also with the pre-Spanish pattern. Evidence of the pre-Spanish period is fragmentary but seems to support the acceptance of female equality:

> The Filipino woman although she passed to the control of her husband was treated as an equal; she retained her maiden name, shared his honors and disposed freely of the property she had brought.[21]

[21] Encarnacion Alzona, *Social and Economic Status of the Filipino Woman*

This combination of patterns has brought the Filipino woman to a point where, although denied some of the adventurous freedom of the male, she may be even better prepared for economic competition. The acceptance of the boredom of routine work may be seen as part of the acceptance of "patient suffering" which is said to characterize the Filipino female to a greater extent than the male.[22] Her responsible role in the household means that the wife is charged with practical affairs while the husband is concerned to a greater extent with ritualistic activity which maintains prestige.

After noting that women in a province he was studying were far more active than men in manufacturing and commerce, Stoodley makes the following observation:

> ... [the] male has a strong "quality" orientations. He sees the society as a system of permanent positions having increments of power and allocations of prerequisites ... the position of rice farmer has neither power nor prerequisites but it is traditionally respectable. It has not become evident ... that "business" jobs have either power or prerequisites and furthermore in terms of the influential Spanish attitude they are hardly respectable.... Women, through their activities in the extended family group and their duties as family treasurers, have tended to develop orientations which Parsons, Bales, and Shils enumerate as affectivity, specificity, particularism, and performance. The attributes of specificity and performance here contrast nicely with the emphasis

of the male head on quality and diffuseness.[23]

The extended family system which appears to bind women to family duties may in practice operate to facilitate their entry into gainful employment. The daughters have the same obligation to help parents and younger siblings as do the sons. This often causes the young woman to postpone marriage until she has been able to pay off a mortgage or finance the education of a younger sibling. Since marriages are still usually "arranged" by family negotiation,[24] middle class girls do not have the tendency for early entry into matrimony which limits both the vocational and the educational activities of American women. Filipino family ties are so strong that they persist even when one or more members of the family are absent from the household. Grandparents, uncles, aunts and older siblings (usually aided by servants) can and do act as parent surrogates. The Filipino mother is not necessarily responsible for the physical care of her children and may even leave the home for long periods of study abroad without feeling that she is disrupting the family.[25]

ASPIRATION LEVELS AND LIMITED INDUSTRIALIZATION The present state of economic development leaves a large

---

from 1665 to 1932 (Manila: University of the Philippines Press, 1934), p. 16.

[22] Jaime Bulatao, "Philippine Values: The Manileno's Mainsprings," *Philippine Studies*, X (January 1962), 75–76.

[23] Bartlett H. Stoodley, "Some Aspects of Tagalog Family Structure," *American Anthropologist*, LIX (April 1957), 247–48.

[24] Richard Coller, "A Sample of Courtship and Marriage Attitudes Held by U.P. Students," *Philippine Sociological Review*, II (October 1954), 31–45.

[25] Fulbright awards for study in the United States in 1962 were given to 18 Filipino women and 12 Filipino men. *Exchange News* (3rd Quarter, 1962), (Manila: U.S. Educational Foundation), pp. 24–25.

TABLE 3. Filipino High School Seniors, Opinions as to Which Sex Should Hold the Job[a]

	Boys' responses			Girls' responses		
	Mainly or only men	Equally men and women	Mainly or only women	Mainly or only men	Equally men and women	Mainly or only women
		Per cent			Per cent	
Beautician	2	21	77	1	26	73
College professor	33	76	1	13	87	—
Corporation executive	79	19	2	73	24	3
Doctor	36	64	—	20	80	—
Government clerk	39	59	2	24	72	2
Lawyer	54	44	2	40	60	—
Movie artist	3	95	2	2	95	3
Nurse	2	11	87	2	12	86
Elementary school teacher	1	68	31	—	77	23
Private secretary	7	40	53	5	42	53
Storekeeper	16	64	20	7	79	14
Skilled factory worker	69	30	1	63	36	1
Unskilled factory worker	44	39	17	42	47	11

[a] Gelia T. Castillo, "Occupational Roles as Perceived by Filipino Adolescents," *Philippine Sociological Review*, IX (January–April 1961), 4 (adapted).

proportion of the population in subsistence agriculture but is peculiarly suited to encourage maximum status aspirations in urbanized women. Paradoxically this high aspiration level may be partially attributed to the limited degree of industrialization. Prior to 1948 the economy was so overwhelmingly of an agricultural nature that there was little opportunity for either sex in the urban areas. Economic growth between 1948 and 1960 did add a significant number of employment opportunities in urban areas but available positions are still far short of the demand.

Indeed the young woman whose family is above the subsistence level faces a situation in which opportunity is open to her at all levels without being assured at any. The Filipino woman might not be able to get a minor clerical, teaching, or industrial job but she has equal opportunity with men in a career as a physician, lawyer, or college professor and would be even more apt to be in a situation in which a small business enterprise might be expanded. Table 3, indicating "sex typing" of jobs by Filipino high school students, gives one indication of the acceptance of women in high-status urbanized occupations. A majority of male high school students view the position of college professor or physician as appropriate for either sex and 44 per cent take this viewpoint of lawyers.

The limited nature of Philippine industrialization means that even though the Filipino women participate in urbanized occupations they are still restricted in the opportunities available. Thus women comprise over 40 per cent of the nonagricultural manual laborers in the Philippines, but this category still employs only 19 per cent of the total Philippine women workers. Conversely women comprise only about 25 per cent of the agricultural workers, yet nearly half of the total women workers are employed in agriculture. In other words, women comprise a high proportion of the urbanized occupations but these are still a relatively small porportion of the Philippine economy.

On the other hand, even the relatively underdeveloped nature of the Philippine economy does not completely distort this picture. A larger proportion of the gainfully employed Filipino women are found in management than in either the United States or in Japan. Likewise, the proportion of Filipino women employed in sales exceeds that of American women and is nearly as great as the Japanese.

Industrialization has not proceeded to the place where most Filipino women can leave the farm. Competition for employment at intermediate levels is still severe, but most of the top posts are as open to women as to

TABLE 4. Per Cent Male and Female in Urban Residence in Selected Countries[a]

Country	Per cent urban	Per cent male urban	Per cent female urban
Most highly urbanized countries (over 65 per cent)			
United Kingdom	80	79.4	80.4
Israel	77.6	77.5	78.3
Sweden	72.8	71.9	74.4
United States	69.9	68.8	70.9
Canada	69.6	68.2	71.1
Next highest level of urbanization (50 to 64.4 per cent)			
New Zealand	64.4	62.6	66.6
Japan	63.5	63.9	63.2
Finland	55.9	53.7	58
Mexico	50.7	49.4	52
Early stages of urbanization (25 to 40 per cent)			
Iraq	39.2	40.3	38.1
Hungary	39.7	39.3	40.1
United Arab Republic	37.7	38.2	37.3
Philippines	35.3	34.7	35.9
Bulgaria	33.6	33.6	33.5
Iran	31.4	31.8	31
Dominican Republic	30.5	28.5	32.5
Turkey	28.8	30.6	26.9
Korea	28	27.9	26.9

[a] Based on data in Table 9 "Urban and Rural Population by Sex," *Demographic Year Book 1962* (New York: United Nations), pp. 304–15.

men. The result is that the Filipino woman's work is not confined to a subordinate role as is largely the case with the Japanese woman, nor has she developed the supplementary type of activity characterizing the American woman. Rather, she is entering the labor market as a full-fledged competitor of the male even while she gives ritualistic assent to male superiority. The Filipino woman is thus in a good position to take advantage of opportunities in an expanding society and a comparatively small degree of industrialization has brought about a considerable shift in the urban sex ratio.

URBAN SEX RATIO IN OTHER COUNTRIES. Table 4 offers some comparative data from other countries. The countries are selected on the basis that their proportion of urbanization indicates some degree of similarity in industrialization development. It will be noted that the countries listed in the first category with the United States all show a low urban sex ratio. In the next category, all the countries except Japan show a low urban sex ratio. Within the third category, four countries indicate a low sex ratio and six countries show a high sex ratio. A low sex ratio is defined as one in which there is lower percentage of men than women and a high sex ratio as the reverse.

While the data are incomplete this table supports the belief that a low sex ratio is apt to accompany urbanization. The Japanese case, though, indicates that this is not an inevitable result of urbanization and that a pattern of female subordination with a tendency toward rural residence may accompany rapid industrialization. The case of the Philippines and other countries in this category indicate

that an urban drift of women may or may not be a feature of the early stages of industrial development, depending upon the cultural roles allocated to women.

An adequate understanding of the processes which repel or attract women to city life would require an intensive analysis of several countries. The observations on the Philippines, the United States, and Japan are offered as a partial description of the process of feminine urbanization in these particular countries.

CONCLUSIONS

To test the hypothesis that industrialization is directly related to female occupational roles, a comparison was made of urban sex ratios in Japan, the United States, and the Philippines. The hypothesis was not confirmed, although the most highly industrialized area, the United States, had a predominantly feminine urban sex ratio. This is not true of Japan which is also highly industrialized, while, in recent years, it is true of the Philippines which is still a predominantly agricultural economy.

Detailed examination of the occupational and educational activity of women in these countries suggests that while some degree of industrialization is required in order to provide nonagricultural opportunities, other factors are more effective in determining occupational roles and the extent of the drift toward urbanization. The Japanese family system has maintained feminine subordination in spite of a growing industrialization with a consequent demand for urban labor. In the United States an advanced stage of industrialization combined with a commitment to sex equality has led to a development of the feminine occupational role along supplemental rather than equalitarian lines. In the Philippines a minor move toward industrialization has provided more opportunity for women than for men reflecting a concept of the feminine role peculiarly favorable to urban occupational careers in spite of a formal commitment to male dominance.

There is no more timely nor timeless topic than the relations between population factors and political institutions. Timely because of the great current concern with such issues as: how population growth affects the economic development of nations and their political subdivisions, the social and political consequences of international and internal migration, and the extent to which government can exercise control over population growth and distribution without violating indi-

7

POLITICAL

INSTITUTIONS

vidual rights. Timeless because many of the issues that we view as contemporary have received the attention of political administrators and scholars throughout recorded history. As E. P. Hutchinson has observed, "... concern with population questions seems to be as old as organized human society; and the history of population thought can be traced from quite early times down to the present."[1] And we can anticipate that many of these questions, because of their very nature, will be considered on into the indefinite future.

Some of the current political dilemmas implicit in population growth appear in various ancient writings. Early philosophers of India and China, for example, saw a large population as a source of national strength but also recognized the imbalance between population and economic resources as a problem of political concern. Nearly 2500 years ago Confucian scholars held that it was a responsibility of the government to maintain a balance

[1] E. P. Hutchinson, *The Population Debate* (Boston: Houghton Mifflin Company, 1967), p. 5.

between population and resources by moving people from overpopulated to underpopulated areas.[2]

The idea of an optimum population balance maintained by government action was also advanced by Plato and Aristotle in their conceptions of the ideal city-state. Although Plato's main reason for limiting population size was the equitable distribution of property, Aristotle specifically recognized that a population growth in excess of land requirements would be a source of civil discord and, consequently, an impediment to effective government.[3]

The political importance attached to population by the seventeenth-century founders of modern demography is evident in the name "political arithmetic" by which the new discipline was first known.[4] Political considerations also motivated the institution of modern national censuses, of which that of the United States was one of the earliest. Although initiated as a means of determining the number of legislative representatives to be apportioned to the various states, the United States census of population has become an indispensable instrument of the government for planning and evaluating national policies.

Despite their obvious influence on political behavior, demographic factors have rarely received explicit consideration in recent studies by either political scientists or political sociologists. In general, European political scientists have given greater attention to the political effects of population factors than have political scientists in the United States.[5] The reasons for this difference probably reside in the types of problems chosen for study as well as the analytical approaches used in studying them. At least one large segment of American political scientists has been primarily concerned with the influence of psychological factors and group interaction on political behavior rather than with the influences of so-called macrosystem variables which have more often attracted the attention of European political scientists.

It is difficult to distinguish between "behavioral" political science and political sociology in the United States on the basis of either phenomena studied or methods of analysis. Perhaps the major distinction is that political sociology tends to analyze political behavior within the framework of a broader social system which both limits and directs such behavior.[6]

[2] *The Determinants and Consequences of Population Trends* (New York: United Nations, Department of Social Affairs, Population Division, 1953), p. 21.

[3] Hutchinson, *op. cit.*, pp. 11–13.

[4] Frank Lorimer, "The Development of Demography," in *The Study of Population*, eds. Philip M. Hauser and Otis Dudley Duncan (Chicago: The University of Chicago Press, 1959), pp. 124–31.

[5] See, for example, references to demography and population in *Contemporary Political Science, A Survey of Methods, Research and Training* (Paris: UNESCO, 1950).

[6] Scott Greer and Peter Orleans, "Political Sociology," in *Handbook of Modern*

As summarized by Scott Greer and Peter Orleans in the *Handbook of Modern Sociology*,[7] current studies in political sociology are primarily concerned with three areas of interest. One is the study of "consensus," which includes the broad questions of shared definitions, roles in political behavior, and political norms. Voting studies constitute a large block of political consensus research. So do studies of political ecology such as geographic distribution of political ideologies and studies of physical and sociopolitical segregation. A second area of interest in political sociology is political representation and participation. The behavior of governmental representatives, factors in public political participation, and the influence of pressure groups and the elites are indicative of significant issues here. A third area includes questions of public order, private order, and the government. Most manifest are the behavioral influences of formal legislation. However, internal organization and interorganizational relations may exert behavioral pressures that fall outside the domain of formal legislation. One example is the many direct and indirect influences of government on economic development.

Social demographers have contributed most notably to research in two of these current areas of interest in political sociology: (1) in delineating factors in political consensus, and (2) in exploring determinants and, to a lesser extent, consequences of governmental policies. Several studies have concerned the general issue of "population and world politics." In general these investigations have pointed to population as a major determinant in such issues as international competition for political power between the free and Communist blocs and between have and have-not nations.

It should be reiterated that demographic factors can be viewed in either a determinant or consequent role when related to political phenomena. For example, population issues are often considered as causes of world political tensions; however, this is only one perspective.

"It would be over-simple, of course, always to see population as the cause of other happenings, political and economic, for often cause and effect run the other way. Wars, depressions, and national policies have profound effects upon fertility, mortality, and migration, the three factors responsible for population trends. To do this topic justice, one must trace not only the ways in which population affects world power and world politics, but also the ways in which the major trends of our time affect the world's population."[8]

Perhaps the largest number of politically related social demography studies have focused on national population policies. Almost every nation

Sociology, ed. Robert E. L. Faris (Chicago: Rand McNally & Co., 1964), p. 808.

[7] Greer and Orleans, *op. cit.,* pp. 808–51.

[8] Katherine Organski and A. F. K. Organski, *Population and World Power* (New York: Alfred A. Knopf, 1961), p. 4.

of the world now has an immigration policy, and many nations have policies concerning fertility. The development of the United States immigration policy is a fascinating analysis of kaleidoscopic socio-political factors ranging from pressure groups to prejudice to political practicalities. Today the most topical demographic policy issue is fertility. The high birth rates in many nations of the world have occasioned increased governmental concern, especially in those nations which appreciate the hampering effects that high fertility has on efforts to raise living standards. As a result, policies and programs for fertility control are increasing. In these concerns social demographers have made some notable contributions in applied as well as analytical endeavors.

A somewhat related sociodemographic interest has been the influence of population factors on governmental forms. Although sketchy, this research is suggestive of interesting new investigative pursuits into such issues as the political consequences of population decline, rapid population increase, and dramatic shifts in population composition.

The reading selections that follow illustrate various relationships between demography and political and governmental institutions. In the first reading, "Demographic Science and the Redirection of Population Policy," Judith Blake analyzes the social and demographic assumptions of the two major approaches of most national policies in attempting to make birth rates consonant with low mortality rates. The first approach sees decreases in family size as the long-range result of complete socio-economic development which, in turn, leads to a desire for fewer children. The second approach overlooks the institutionalization of reproduction entirely and assumes that education and communication concerning birth control will eventually reduce births to a level in keeping with low mortality. The dilemma of these two approaches revolves around the developmental importance of *both* change in family size desires *and* actualities. Based on theoretical and empirical propositions in sociology and demography, Dr. Blake discusses other possible strategies for population policy.

The second reading also focuses on population policy, but this time concerns abortion. In his article, "The Demographic Significance of Legal Abortion in Eastern Europe," Christopher Tietze investigates what effect the policies of legalization of abortion has had on post-World-War-II birth rates in these economically redeveloping nations.

Lawrence Fuch's paper, "Some Political Aspects of Immigration," illustrates a completely different and seldom-investigated relationship between demography and political behavior: the influence of a demographic process on political participation and political style. The specific focus is on the extent to which the historic American policy of welcoming immigrants has influenced two aspects of American political life: (1) ideological unity, and (2) group pluralism. The author discusses the consequences of contemporary developments such as changes in the immigration policy.

The companion reading by Harry Sharp investigates the effect of migration on the primary and most direct mechanism of consensus and cleavage in a democratic polity—voting. In a nation as residentially mobile as the United States, this paper poses a most significant question: Is migration a factor in non-voting?

The selection by Philip Hauser provides a macroscopic view of world political consensus. As suggested by the title, "Demographic Dimensions of World Politics," the paper investigates trends in demographic structure and process and their implications for the conflict between the free world and the Communist bloc. Of particular interest are the generalizations about world politics which emerge from this paper.

The last reading in this section concerns "Forms of Government and Socioeconomic Characteristics of Suburbs." In investigating whether population structure affects political structure, Professors Schnore and Alford look at three major suburban governmental forms: commission, mayor-council, and council-manager. The findings suggest that certain demographic factors may be important limiting conditions on political structural units.

Demographic Science and the Redirection of Population Policy*

Judith Blake

In recent years informed laymen as well as professional demographers have become increasingly convinced that poor but densely settled countries must achieve a successful demographic revolution and a rapid one. Although consensus on this goal is nearing unanimity, persons equally committed to it are frequently in disagreement about how it is to be

* Judith Blake, "Demographic Science and the Redirection of Public Policy," *Journal of Chronic Diseases*, XVIII (November, 1965), 1181–1200.

achieved. In fact, policy aimed at reducing rates of population growth in developing countries has become bipolarized. One group tends to say that decreases in family size will occur only as an end-product of advanced economic and social development which, in due time, will lead to a desire for fewer children. The other group is inclined to bypass the institutional setting of reproduction entirely and to assume that education and communication respecting birth control will eventually reduce births to a level consonant with low mortality. Yet these approaches do not appear to be adequate either in fact or in theory when taken alone, or even in some combination. Consequently additional strategies designed to solve the dilemma of population growth are needed. This can be seen by examining each position and the objections to it.

The development school of thought emphasizes that motives for a transition from high to low birth rates such as occurred in presently industrial countries were contingent not only on declines in mortality, but also on changes in the social and economic organization that previously had led individuals to desire numerous births. Without such changes (and in spite of mortality declines) individuals would have continued to attach independent importance to institutionalized roles, activities, and goals that directly or indirectly provided the motivational underpinning for many offspring. Hence, it is claimed, changes similar to the industrial and urban revolutions of the Western world must occur in developing countries if their family structures are to alter and a wish for drastically curtailed reproduction is to evolve. Policy must therefore be directed at accelerating overall social and economic development

which, in turn, will indirectly affect the family and reproduction. The most that can be expected by way of directly reducing family size is to spread birth control knowledge and means among crucial groups (such as educated urban elites) where desires for smaller families may already exist.

This position is, however, clearly open to objections of both a scientific and practical nature. For instance, it can be argued that social structures are far less tightly integrated than the theory just outlined presupposes. Since all societies have visible lines of cleavage, strain, and vulnerability, important social changes can occur without a complete socioeconomic revolution. Particular sectors of the population such as the young, the females, the peasants, or the outcasts may be so chronically dissatisfied that they are eager to experiment if the opportunity arises. In actual fact, many developing countries have undergone enormous, if piecemeal, changes in recent years. These changes have typically been accelerated by the importation of technical knowledge and assistance, the rapidity and influence of which should not be underestimated.[1] We therefore hesitate, on purely empirical grounds, to assume that these societies do not have their own internal sources of motivation for change, and that these cannot be stimulated to an unprecedented degree by close contact and cooperation with more modern societies.[2] From a prac-

---

[1] For a discussion of the multiphasic theory of demographic change, see K. Davis, "The Theory of Change and Response in Modern Demographic History," *Population Index*, XXIX (1963), 345.

[2] See for example, K. Davis, "Fertility Control and the Demographic Transition in India," in *The Interrelations of Demographic, Economic and Social Problems in Selected Underdevel-*

tical standpoint, the objections to exclusive reliance on the "development approach" center on the appalling dilemma it poses. If birth rates will not decline markedly prior to industrialization and modernization, what will happen if the latter are effectively slowed down, as seems to be the case, by the very malady they are supposed to cure—population growth itself? A shift back to higher levels of mortality is of course the answer, and it is one that few people are willing to accept without a struggle.

Many thoughtful persons have therefore been led to advocate demographic strategies that are more directly geared to affecting reproduction. Unfortunately, so little systematic thought and analysis have been devoted to the presuppositions involved and the possible alternatives available, that this more direct population policy has fallen into what appears to be an intuitively "obvious" course of action. The assumption is made that high birth rates in developing countries are today primarily a result of unwanted births. On this assumption, population policy in developing countries has recently taken the form of an intensive planned parenthood campaign for contraceptive education and distribution. Such policy seems to have gone beyond a modification of the sociological and economic assumptions of the "development" approach to the pole of ignoring them altogether. It is therefore hardly surprising that this extreme course of action is not leading to marked reductions in birth rates and rates of population growth among the illiterate

rural masses that predominate in developing countries.[3] In fact, because family size desires are so substantial in these countries, primary reliance on inhibiting the births that are in excess of these desires may have little effect on birth rates under conditions of relatively high mortality, and no effect on present population growth rates if mortality declines. This dilemma requires some systematic consideration.

In countries like India mortality is declining enough to provide a high rate of demographic increase—as far as we know, over 2 per cent annually. But even so, mortality remains shockingly high, and improvements may be sporadic. Although surveys show that Indians normally desire three to five children, it is still true that in India many births are required to guarantee this result. Presumably Indian parents want their children to survive at least through their own reproductive periods. This dependency of birth-reducing motives on confidence in mortality improvements is widely recognized as a principal reason for the lack of success to date of family planning programs.[4]

---

[3] D. J. Bogue, "Some Tentative Recommendations for a 'Socially Correct' Family Planning Communication and Motivation Program in India," in *Research in Family Planning*, ed. C. V. Kiser (Princeton, N.J.: Princeton University Press, 1962), p. 503.

[4] See, for example, *ibid.*, p. 528. Although the direction of the relationship is not made clear, Edwin D. Driver presents for Central India some suggestive data on births and child mortality. He shows that the larger the number of births in a family the larger the proportion of children who have died. Doubtless some of this association is due to the independent effect of high fertility on child mortality as well as to the fact that large families will have older children who may have lived out a normal adult

---

oped Areas, Milbank Memorial Fund (New York, 1954), p. 65.

But even if continuously spectacular improvements in mortality were to be made and births were proportionately reduced, population growth rates would remain high unless the *desired size of the planned families* was itself greatly curtailed. Developing peoples may not wish to have an unlimited number of offspring, but survey data gathered so far do not turn up excessively modest family-size desires either. For example, available data on ideal family size in India show that the mass of the people on the average prefer about four (presumably surviving) children.[5] But high proportions (30–45 per cent) either refuse to answer the question or are not asked it, often because they do not wish even to consider limiting births. The averages may therefore have a downward bias, although a countervailing tendency for subfecund couples to refuse to

answer may also exist. In Latin America, the four—child preference has also been found in a large study of Santiago, Chile; and in Taiwan, Freedman and his colleagues have found four children to be the ideal.[6] In all these cases, such an average typically means that close to 60 per cent of the respondents consider four *or more* children to be ideal. To be sure, these desires represent a wish for a family of only moderate size, and in general the ideals are lower than the actual numbers of births, but for reducing population growth under conditions of low mortality the desires are not low enough. They are on the whole somewhat higher than the actual family size of the overseas European countries (the United States, Canada, Australia, and New Zealand) and these countries have been experiencing population growth rates which, if continued, will result in a doubling of their populations every 30–40 years. Family-size aspirations such as those among peoples who characteristically marry and reproduce even earlier than overseas Europeans, will, if realized in practice, result in higher rates of population growth (at comparable mortality levels), because the mean length of a generation is shorter, thereby allowing more generations to be squeezed into a given unit of time.

Can family planning programs solve this dilemma by introducing not only

---

span for India and then died. The ages at death were not recorded. See, E. D. Driver, *Differential Fertility in Central India* (Princeton, N.J.: Princeton University Press, 1963) chap. vi. For a discussion of the "realization lag" respecting mortality see H. Leibenstein, *Economic Backwardness and Economic Growth* (New York: John Wiley & Sons, Inc., 1957), p. 166.

[5] See, for example, Driver, *op. cit.* In this study 30 per cent of the couples had no interest at all limiting the size of their families. This percentage ranged from 23 per cent for couples where the wife was under 25, to 38 per cent where she was 45 or more. The data on ideal family size were only obtained from the couples interested in limiting. See also, United Nations, *The Mysore Population Study*, chaps. ix to xii; United Nations, Population Studies No. 34, 1961; V. M. Dandekar and K. Dandekar, *Survey of Fertility and Mortality in Poona District* (Poona: Gokhale Institute, 1953), chap. vii; close to one half of respondents in both urban and rural districts answered in terms of "any number" or that they "could not say."

[6] L. Tabah and P. Samuel, "Preliminary Findings of a Survey on Fertility and Attitudes Toward Family Planning in Santiago, Chile," Kiser, *op. cit.*, p. 289. Out of 1,970 respondents only 12 did not answer, and 14 said "an unlimited number." See also R. Freedman, *et al.*, "Fertility Trends in Taiwan: Tradition and Change," *Population Studies*, XVI (1963), 232.

contraceptive means but more modest family-size desires? In answer we can only say that to date we have no compelling reason to believe that developing peoples will ever be merely propagandized "educated" into wanting really small families—slightly more than two children on the average —regardless of the level of mortality. It does not seem as if their desires for larger families will succumb to flipcharts, flannelboards, message movies, group leaders, or "explanations" about the "advantages" of few children. As we shall see, this expectation is so discontinuous with our existing knowledge of the institutionalization of reproduction as to be virtually incongruous.

Have we then exhausted the alternatives available for reducing population growth by means of direct policy? The answer is, I think, that we have not yet begun to explore them. But if we are to bring them to light, we must review what is already known of reproductive motivation through research concerning family-size declines and present levels in industrial countries. In doing so we shall find that an analysis in terms of the social and economic factors affecting reproduction does not necessarily only result in indirect choices for population policy such as economic development. This type of analysis is just as capable of generating possibilities for direct action regarding family size.

HISTORICAL PERSPECTIVES
ON FAMILY SIZE

Concomitant with improved mortality, the desire for smaller families among Western industrializing peoples appears to have resulted from a complex of factors (among them urbanization, increased opportunities for social mobility, separation of work from residence, compulsory education, child labor laws) that diminished the economic utility of offspring (as income producers and security in old age) leaving simply their noneconomic utility for parents to take into account. This complex not only decreased the range of utilities but augmented the costs of children, both direct and indirect. Parents had to undergo increased direct costs such as those for compulsory education, food, recreation, and space in crowded urban circumstances. They also suffered an extension of indirect or opportunity costs since expanding economies offered them unprecedented opportunities for upward mobility and investment, and a modern, urban, middle-class way of life opened up virtually unlimited nondomestic avenues of recreation and interest.[7] This account amounts to a delineation of how modernizing and urbanizing soci-

[7] This highly generalized statement of the elements in declining family-size goals may be found in Leibenstein, *op. cit.*, chap. x. Other statements of the same basic ideal by sociologists and demographers have usually been in terms of particular features of modernization—urbanization, educational levels, social mobility, etc.—and have seldom attempted to differentiate clearly among utilities, direct costs, and opportunity costs. See for example, F. W. Notestein, "The Economics of Population and Food Supplies," *Proc. 8th Int. Conf. Agricultural Economists* (London: Oxford University Press, 1953); and F. W. Notestein, "Population—the Long View," in *Food for the World*, ed. T. W. Schultz (Chicago: University of Chicago Press, 1945). For recent efforts to document the important role played by opportunity costs, see J. A. Banks, *Prosperity and Parenthood* (London: Routledge & Kegan Paul, Ltd., 1954); K. Davis, *Population Index*, XXIX (1963), 345; and K. Davis, "Population," *Scientific American*, CCIX (September, 1963), p. 63.

eties affected the family and its articulations with socioeconomic structure, and how couples reacted by altering the number of their "hostages to fortune."[8]

In utilizing this outline of Western experience for clues as to the determinants of very modest family-size ideals, we must, however, be wary of two potential fallacies: the *particularistic fallacy* and the *economic fallacy*. The particularistic fallacy occurs when one turns one's attention entirely to the associations between particular variables — urbanization, education, social mobility—and declining family-size goals, instead of utilizing the associations to trace out the basic and more general mechanisms involved. Thus our real concern seems to be with factors making children less and less useful to parents and increasingly expensive (both directly and indirectly). The exact nature of these factors will necessarily vary between historical periods and among societies, although we may expect to find some recognizable patterns and repetitions. But we must be sensitized to search for this common element of decreased utilities and increased costs in a wide diversity of events. Otherwise, we are operating in demography as epidemiologists did prior to bacteriology—we mistake the vector for the agent.[9]

On the other hand, although the framework of utilities and costs outlined above is reasonable as far as it goes, it becomes very limited in its applicability if we are led to assume that the *noneconomic* utilities of offspring are somehow not very important or meaningful, as is implied when we say that children have become mere "items of consumption." If we fall into this line of reasoning, then we are expecting the theory to explain some of the most social aspects of human motivation, without giving these aspects independent status in the formulation. Thus, as the theory is stated in the "economic development" school of thought, the family plays an almost completely passive role in the formulation. It is assumed throughout that the family is acted upon and that it only indirectly affects individual calculation regarding familial investment. Yet one can readily point out that the family has powerful sources of resistance to its own demise. Socialization is not simply "a function" that the family "performs" for "the society"; it is a primary mechanism of indoctrination and control. Individuals who are socialized in families will be likely to want families themselves, to enforce norms and sanctions regarding families, and to take pleasure in acting out familial roles. This means that the family complex is itself a goal—the utilities represented by children are not merely economic or affectional but socially structured in a powerful manner. Moreover, societies with long familial traditions have powerful sanctioning and ideological systems which

---

[8] The theory also accounts for other related adjustments such as delayed marriage and nonmarriage but these need not concern us here. The phrase "hostages to fortune" is Francis Bacon's, from *Essays or Counsels, Civil and Moral* (1625).

[9] This in effect has been one of the principal criticisms of so-called "demographic transition theory," namely that it represents a more or less unweighted and nonspecific collection of associations between broad social trends and fertility (as well as mortality) with little attempt to assess common factors and their actual connection with fertility. See L. Van Nort and B. P. Karon, "Demographic Transition Re-examined," *American Sociological Review*, XX (1955), 523.

help to keep parents from being discouraged by direct reproductive costs, or distracted by indirect ones. It is hardly surprising therefore that in its purely economic form the theory led social scientists to extreme conclusions. The idea arose that the desire for children was on the way to disappearing altogether from Western societies, and this expectation made the subsequent "baby boom" a source of never-to-be-forgotten embarrassment.

Unfortunately, the lesson of the reproductive renaissance seems to have concluded with the rediscovery that social institutions like the family are adaptive to change and hence (without direct intervention) are neither transformed readily nor obliterated rapidly. The relevance of family-size declines up to the "baby boom" is not extended to an analysis of possibilities for further declines in family size—that is, from moderate to small numbers of offspring. This disjuncture is due primarily to the inability of the theory, when stated in purely economic terms, to deal with variability within the moderate to small family range. Such variation is categorized as short-term fluctuation, and no long-term institutional determinants of small families are postulated.[10] This truncating of the theory is, moreover, buttressed by the fact that long-term and widespread institutional influences leading to small families may well not actually exist in any major societies today. Even if this is the case, it does not argue against the scientific and practical advantages of extending the theory to logical closure. In fact, even if it appears that modern industrial societies typically generate desires for a moderate, rather than a small family, this very fact should give us some insights into the types of factors that to date *prevent* families from stabilizing at few children. Let us examine then one of the principal existing differences in fertility among modernized countries —the family-size differential between Western Europeans and overseas countries (the so-called "frontier" countries).

FAMILY SIZE VARIATIONS AMONG MODERNIZED PEOPLES—WESTERN EUROPE AND THE OVERSEAS COUNTRIES

For some years the overseas or "frontier" countries (the United States, Canada, Australia, and New Zealand) have been exhibiting a noticeable difference from Western Europe in family-sized ideals and desires, as well as in actual family size itself. Table 1 indicates that with the possible exception of the Netherlands, Western Europeans for whom we have data consider two to three children "ideal," whereas respondents in the frontier countries are more inclined to place their ideals at three

---

10 For example, H. Leibenstein, *op. cit.*, p. 169, only discusses the theory with reference to the demographic revolution up to the point of achieving some undefined level of relatively low fertility. He says, "This point refers to the stage of which per capita output is quite high, considerably beyond the subsistence level, and where the economy has overcome the major obstacles to sustained growth. Usually, this is a point at which the gap between mortality and fertility rates closes gradually.

In this situation the business cycle is likely to be a significant determinant of economic and social phenomena. Since we are not concerned, in this essay, with short-time fluctuations we shall not enter into an analysis of fertility determinants under such circumstances."

TABLE 1. Ideal Number of Children. Selected Western European and Overseas European Countries at Various Survey Dates, 1936–1960

Country	Date	Average ideal number of children	Per cent saying 4+
Austria	1960[a]	2.0	4.0
Belgium	1952[b]	2.64	25.0
Finland	1953[b]	2.84	22.0
France	1944[b]	3.17	34.0
	1945[b]	2.92	24.0
	1946[b]	2.70	20.0
	1947[b]	2.77	23.0
	1947[b]	2.88	23.0
	1959–60[a]	2.77	16.9
Italy	1951[b]	2.80	19.0
Netherlands	1947[b]	3.66	46.0
	1960[a]	3.3	38.7
Norway	1960[a]	3.1	25.0
Switzerland	1960[a]	2.9	22.4
Great Britain	1938[b]	2.94	25.0
	1939[b]	2.96	29.0
	1944[b]	3.00	33.0
	1947[b]	2.84	25.0
	1952[b]	2.84	26.0
	1960[a]	2.8	23.2
Sweden	1947[b]	2.79	22.0
West Germany	1950[b]	2.21	11.0
	1953[b]	2.28	11.0
	1958[c]	2.6	12.0
Australia	1947[b]	3.79	64.0
Canada	1945[b]	4.06	60.0
	1947[b]	3.91	55.0
	1960[a]	4.2	70.1
United States	1936[b]	3.17	34.0
	1941[b]	3.42	41.0
	1945[b]	3.61	49.0
	1947[b]	3.37	43.0
	1949[b]	3.91	63.0
	1953[b]	3.33	41.0
	1960[a]	3.6	50.6

[a] D. V. Glass: "Family limitation in Europe: a survey of recent studies," in *Research in Family Planning*, ed, C. V. Kiser, (Princeton, N. J.: Princeton University Press, 1962), p. 244.

[b] J. Stoetzel: "Les attitudes et la conjuncture demographique: la dimension ideale de la famille," *Proceedings of the World Population Conference, 1954* (Papers), VI, 1019. United Nations, New York, 1955.

[c] R. Freedman, G. Baumert and M. Bolte: "Expected Family Size and Family Size Values in West Germany," *Population Studies* XIII (1959), 141.

TABLE 2. Recent Gross Reproduction Rates for Western European Countries

	1955	1956	1957	1958	1959	1960	1961
Western European							
With rising rates							
Austria	1.08	1.17	1.20	1.23	1.26	1.28	—
Belgium	1.16	1.18	1.19	1.22	1.26	1.24	—
West Germany	1.03	1.08	1.12	1.12	1.16	1.17	—
Netherlands	1.48	1.48	1.50	1.51	1.54	1.52	1.58
Norway	1.33	1.37	1.37	1.38	1.39	1.38	—
Switzerland	1.10	1.12	1.14	1.14	1.15	—	—
England and Wales	1.08	1.15	1.19	1.22	1.23	1.29	—
With stable rates[a]							
Denmark	1.24	1.26	1.24	1.23	1.21	1.24	—
France	1.31	1.30	1.32	1.31	1.34	1.33	—
Sweden	1.09	1.10	1.11	1.08	1.08	1.06	—
With falling rates							
Finland	1.42	1.37	1.38	1.29	1.31	1.29	—
Overseas European							
Australia	1.59	1.61	1.66	1.67	1.68	1.68	1.73
Canada	1.86	1.87	1.91	1.89	1.92	1.90	1.87
New Zealand	1.82	1.84	1.89	1.93	1.95	1.97	2.03
United States (whites)	1.67	1.72	1.76	1.73	1.73	1.72	—

Source: *Population Index*, XXIX (1963), 196.
[a] This category also used for cases of no discernible trend.

to four offspring. Moreover, the difference in proportions replying in terms of four or more children between the two sets of countries is quite striking.

Turning to recent trends in actual family size we must rely on a series of age-adjusted birth rates (in this case we have used gross reproduction rates (GRR) to document the trends since the fifties (Table 2)). It is not yet possible to bring together recent cohort data on family size for a large number of the countries in question. The over-all contrast between the frontier and European countries constitutes about a one-child difference in favor of the overseas group (remembering that the GRR refers to girls only and that the differentials must therefore be roughly doubled).

This difference between period data from the two sets of countries seems to be a continuation of earlier trends that were beginning to show up in marriage cohort data from censuses around 1950 (Table 3).

Are there dissimilarities between the two sets of countries that may lead to long-term stabilization of the family-sized differential? If this is the case, Western Europe may contain significant clues to the institutionalization of the small family as a way of life. Indeed, Freedman has suggested that analysis of the institutional settings for this difference may provide just such guidance.[11] Still,

[11] See R. Freedman, *et al.*, "Expected Family Size and Family Size Values in West Germany," *Population Studies*, XIII (1959), 136, 142; R.

TABLE 3. Number of Live Births Per 100 Marriages Existing at Census Data by Duration of Marriage—Around 1950

	Census year	Number of years after marriage			
		0–4	5–9	10–14	15–19
Western European Countries					
Lower than overseas European					
Belgium	1947	69	146	182	—
France	1946	84	169	211	231
West Germany	1950	73	137	178	214
Great Britain	1946	57	134	182	209
Norway	1950	81	174	217	240
Switzerland	1950	81	182	221	237
Higher than overseas European					
Finland	1950	106	210	274	320
Netherlands	1947	72	200	275	322
Overseas European Countries					
Australia	1947	66	164	225	271
United States	1950	79	168	220	253

Source: United Nations: *Recent Trends in Fertility in Industrialized Countries*, p. 60. ST/SOA/Series A/27. New York, 1958.

Belgium: Includes families headed by a widow or widower, but excludes divorced couples.

France: First marriages only. Includes marriages where the woman was widowed or divorced at the age of 45 or over. All children born alive to the woman, including children born before marriage.

W. Germany: Federal Republic of Germany excluding Berlin. Including stillbirths. Excludes marriages where the couple was separated, e.g., the husband was missing or a prisoner of war.

Gt. Britain: First marriages only. Excludes marriages where the woman was 45 or over at marriage. Includes marriages where the woman was widowed or divorced at 45 or over. All children born alive to the woman (including children born before marriage). Adjusted for understatement of childlessness.

Norway: Excluding marriages where the woman was aged 45 or over at marriage.

Switzerland: All legitimate and legitimized children born alive.

Netherlands: First marriages only.

Australia: Excluding marriages where the couple was permanently separated, legally or otherwise.

U. S. A.: White women married once and husband present who were aged 15–49 at date of census.

before we embark on such a mammoth undertaking, let us consider how reasonable it is to assume that the differential is at all stable. It is initially sufficient to deal with one set of countries alone. If these promise to be unstable, there is no need to go further. We shall start with Western Europe because it offers the nearest hope for clues to small family desires.

First, to judge from actual period data (see Table 2 on GRR) fertility is rising somewhat among the European countries that previously experienced the very lowest rates, and it appears to be stabilizing among others like Denmark.[12] Second, the average "ideal" number of children given by Europeans (like the ideals given by

---

Freedman, "American Studies of Family Planning and Fertility: a Review of Major Trends and Issues," Kiser, *op. cit.*, pp. 216, 226.

[12] See, for example, the discussion by R. Pressat, "Tendences recentes de la fecondité en Europe occidentale," *International Population Union Conference*, Paper No. 93 (mimeo), 1961.

TABLE 4. Mean Number of Children Expected and Desired, by Occupation and Education of Head of Family. West Germany, 1958

	Mean number of children expected	Mean number of children desired (good conditions)
Occupation of family head		
Professional	2.5 (37)	2.9 (37)
Businessman	2.1 (167)	2.7 (176)
White collar workers	2.1 (305)	2.7 (314)
Officials	2.1 (136)	2.7 (145)
Skilled laborers	2.1 (581)	2.6 (598)
Unskilled laborers	2.3 (304)	2.8 (887)
Education of family head		
Elementary school	2.2 (1429)	2.7 (1491)
Secondary school, or high school without *abitur*	2.0 (220)	2.7 (228)
High school with *abitur*, or university	2.3 (59)	2.9 (62)

Source: R. Freedman, G. Baumert, and M. Bolte: "Expected family size and family size values in West Germany," *Population Studies*, XIII (1959), 145.

Americans) is typically in excess of actual behavior or of expectations. This excess is particularly marked when the question refers to the number desired under better financial or living conditions if these were available. Finally, both ideal and actual family size in some European countries have been showing either a U-shaped or a direct linear relationship with socioeconomic status.

THE DISCREPANCY BETWEEN FERTILITY IDEALS AND EXPECTATIONS OR BEHAVIOR. The discrepancy among modernized peoples between the number of children they say they consider "ideal" and the number they personally intend to have, or in fact do have, has been noted in the literature for many years. In his 1954 summary of existing European survey data on "ideal" family size, Stoetzel was struck by the discrepancy between actual European fertility in the reporting countries and "ideal" fertility.[13] A recent study in West Germany that found the same type of excess of ideals over actualities was fortunately designed so that an explicit analysis of the differences in reply to three related questions was possible. These were (1) the number of children actually expected, (2) the "ideal" size of the average family in Germany, and (3) the number of children personally desired "if financial and other conditions of life were very good." German respondents expected fewer children than they considered ideal for "average Germans," and they desired for themselves (under good conditions) more children than they thought the average German family should have, and hence

---

[13] J. Stoetzel, "Les attitudes et la conjuncture demographique: la dimension idéale de la famille," *Proceedings of the World Population Conference 1954* (Papers) VI, p. 1019. United Nations, New York, 1955.

more than they expected.[14] The German study is particularly valuable in presenting these data by socioeconomic indicators (Table 4). At all nonfarm occupational levels there is a discrepancy between expected and desired family size. Although the professional class desires the most children, the discrepancy for them is the smallest because they expect the most as well. On the other hand, most other nonmanual workers desire over 25 per cent more children than they expect to have. The stability of this gap for most of the population comes out clearly when we look at the data broken down by educational level.

These data suggest that among Western European populations that have been experiencing very low fertility since the Second World War or before, there is what we might call a latent child hunger that would be satisfied under more favorable financial and living conditions. Moreover, it is of interest that in desiring or idealizing more children than they expect to have, Western Europeans are similar to Americans.[15] The Euro-

peans apparently do not have some stabilized low fertility ideology that their recent behavior expresses. Let us now test the idea that Europeans would desire and have larger families under what they conceive to be better conditions by looking at European ideal and actual family-size data according to socioeconomic indicators. If the hypothesis has any validity we should find that the better situated Europeans both idealize and are beginning to have larger families than less fortunate groups.

DIFFERENTIAL "IDEAL" AND ACTUAL FERTILITY AMONG WEST EUROPEANS. As far back as the late 1940s and early 1950s when systematic data on ideal family size in selected European countries begin, there have been noticeable exceptions to the inverse relationship between these ideals and socioeconomic status. Table 5 shows that many of the highest socioeconomic groups express a family-size ideal of around three children. Among different educational levels and nonfarm occupations, the data indicate a positive association between social advantage and family-size goals. On the economic variable, Sweden and France evince a direct relationship with familial ideals, and Britain and Germany a U-shaped one—the middle-income groups have the lowest reproductive ideals. It seems possible that West Europeans of the upper strata have for many years desired a family of relatively modest size. In fact, some upper-status European groups come close to idealizing the same number of children as was found for

---

14 R. Freedman, *op. cit.*, 141. The differences between the expected number and the number desired under good conditions are not accounted for merely by the fact that couples expecting to be childless actually desired some children. For example, the percentage expecting three or more children was 31.9, but 49.5 per cent would have desired that many if conditions were good.

15 For a discussion of the Growth of American Families Study data on this topic, see R. Freedman, P. K. Whelpton and A. A. Campbell, *Family Planning, Sterility and Population Growth* (New York: McGraw-Hill Book Company, 1959), p. 220. Also, similar findings have been reported for the Detroit Area Study and for the Indianapolis Study. See R. Freedman, *et al.*, "Ideals about Family Size in the Detroit Metropolitan Area, 1954," *Milbank Memorial Fund*

Quarterly, XXXIII (1955), 187; L. Pratt and P. K. Whelpton, "Social and Psychological Factors Affecting Fertility," *Milbank Memorial Fund Quarterly*, XXXIV (1956), 1245.

TABLE 5. Ideal Family Size by Economic, Occupational, and Educational Levels, Selected European Countries, 1939–1958

Country	Date	Economic level			
		Impoverished	Poor	Middle class	Rich
West Germany	1950	2.18	2.20	2.14	2.33
	1953	2.34	2.30	2.21	2.35
	1958	2.8	2.6	2.4–2.5	2.6
France	1944	—2.92—		—3.72—	
	1946	2.54	—2.77—		3.15
	1947	2.70	—2.90—		3.27
United Kingdom	1939	3.00	—2.90—		3.07
	1947	2.92	2.79	2.93	2.89
	1952	3.10	2.79	2.81	2.92
Sweden	1947	2.72	—2.89—		3.41

	Date	Occupational level						
		Farmers	Farm laborers	Laborers	Clerical	Officials	Industry-commerce staff	Free pro-fessions
West Germany	1950	2.88	2.20	2.03	2.11	2.37	2.23	2.08
	1953	2.71	2.44	2.17	2.23	2.49	2.31	2.44
	1958	—2.9 —		2.5–2.6	2.6	2.6	2.6	2.8
Belgium	1952	—3.45—		2.25	2.44		2.69	2.80
Finland	1953	3.10	2.65	2.71	—2.98—		—3.15—	
France	1944	—3.74—		2.70	—2.80—		—2.95—	
	1945	—3.15—		2.60	—3.03—		2.78	3.34
	1947	—3.33—		2.67	—2.79—		2.94	3.32
	1947	—3.09—		2.73	—2.76—		2.87	3.47

		Educational level		
		Primary	Secondary	Higher
West Germany	1950	2.26	2.18	2.22
	1953	2.26	2.31	2.42
	1958	2.6	2.5	2.7
Finland	1953	2.75	3.16	3.24
France	1947	2.77	3.15	3.35

Sources: J. Stoetzel, "Les attitudes et la conjuncture demographique: la dimension ideale de la famille," *Proceedings of the World Population Conference*, VI (Papers, 1954), 1019. United Nations, New York, 1955.

Data for West Germany, 1958, from R. Freedman, G. Baumert, and M. Bolte. "Expected family size values in West Germany," *Population Studies*, XIII (1959), 145.

Americans of all classes in the Growth of American Families Study—3.3 (minimum) or 3.5 (maximum).[16]

The pertinence of these differentials in reproductive ideals is sug-

[16] The average minimum and maximum figures come from using the lower and upper limits of answers giving a range of children—i.e. "2 or 3" or "3 or 4." See R. Freedman *et al.*, *Family Planning, Sterility and Population Growth, op. cit.*, pp. 220, 266.

gested by the recent trends in *actual* fertility for selected European countries (where we have data), which show the same types of variation with status indicators. Special studies in Great Britain, Sweden, and the Netherlands indicate that the family size of the better educated is "clearly above the average rates for these countries."[17] In Britain, Norway, and the Netherlands, the professional class no longer has the lowest fertility. The latter is found among civil servants and other white collar employees.[18]

It thus seems unlikely to us that Europeans are on the road to permanent adjustment of family size at approximately two children. Like Americans they typically desire at least two, and there is an apparent backlog of motivation for more under better circumstances. That this desire is meaningful seems to be illustrated both by the very recent upturn in period rates and by the larger families desired and achieved among higher socioeconomic groups.

Hence the one-child difference between European and frontier countries may be due not to some fundamental differences in reproductive or social and economic goals, but to the fact that Europeans have, during the past 25 years, experienced a heavier dose of the cost factors involved in reproduction than the overseas countries. Although Europeans operated within the same modern context as other industrialized people (that is, they were subject to the modern costs

of child rearing, plus the need to maintain their own positions and assure themselves of security later in life), they underwent a relatively long period of deprivation during which the realization of these goals was very difficult. No one factor can necessarily be said to be crucial. But differences in per capita income between Western Europe and the overseas countries have long been unfavorable to Europe, and Europe suffered the principal direct devastations of war and its aftermath. Moreover, it is more densely settled. There are apparently fewer opportunities for social mobility, and more clogging and insufficiency of channels of mobility such as education.[19] It hardly seems

---

[17] G. Z. Johnson, "Differential Fertility in European Countries," in *Demographic and Economic Change in Developed Countries* (National Bureau of Economic Research, Princeton, N.J.: Princeton University Press, 1960), p. 53.

[18] *Ibid.*, p. 59; and D. H. Wrong, "Class Fertility Differentials in England and Wales," *Milbank Memorial Fund Quarterly*, XXXVIII (1960), 37.

[19] The difficulty of constructing international indicators of living levels is widely recognized, but per capita income is highly correlated with other well-known indicators such as those suggested by the United Nations (*Expert Report on International Definition and Measurement of Standards and Levels of Living*, United Nations, 1954). For a recent discussion of historical and present differences between the frontier and North West European countries in per capita income see L. J. Zimmerman, "The Distribution in World Income," in *Essays on Unbalanced Growth*, ed. E. de Vries, (Gravenhage Mouton, 1962). It is of some interest that in recent years the disparity in per capita income between Europe and the other countries is lessening because of increasing rates of growth in Europe and relative slowness in North America. For discussion of this point see Zimmerman, *op. cit.* Information on trends in intergenerational occupational mobility in the United States may be found in several works: B. Barber, *Social Stratification* (New York: Harcourt, Brace & World, Inc., 1957), chap. xvi; E. Chinery, "Social Mobility Trends in the United States," *American Sociological Review*, XX (1955), 180; J. A. Kahl, *The American Class Structure* (New York: Holt, Rinehart & Winston, Inc., 1957), chap. ix; G. Lenski, "Trends in Intergenerational Mobility in the United States," *American Sociological Review*, XXIII (1958), 514; W. Petersen, "Is America Still the Land of

surprising in terms of existing theory that the frontier peoples should feel more carefree about having an extra child or two than do Europeans, since they have enjoyed unprecedented wealth, a halcyon period of suburbanization, high rates of social mobility, and a great expansion of educational opportunity.

Opportunity?" *Commentary* (November 1953), p. 477; N. Rogoff, *Recent Trends in Occupational Mobility* (New York: The Free Press of Glencoe, Inc., 1953); G. Sjoberg, "Are Social Classes in America Becoming More Rigid?" *American Sociological Review*, XVI (December, 1951); W. L. Warner and J. Ablegglan, *Occupational Mobility in American Business and Industry*, 1928–1952 (Minneapolis: University of Minnesota Press, 1955). For comparison of occupational mobility in Europe and the United States, see S. M. Lipset and R. Bendix, *Social Mobility in Industrial Society* (Berkeley: University of California, 1959), chap. ii. Using a manual/nonmanual breakdown, the authors find that total vertical mobility for nonfarm sons is approximately the same in the United States, and Germany, Sweden, France, and Switzerland. However their conclusion that "... total mobility in these countries is practically the same" seems to be an overstatement, because they fail to take into account the higher agricultural proportions in the European countries they discuss. For example, in the early 1950s France had over a quarter of its population still engaged in agricultural pursuits, Sweden and Germany more than 20 per cent, and Switzerland over 15 per cent J. F. Dewhurst, *et al.*, *Europe's Needs and Resources* (New York: Twentieth Century Fund, 1961), chap. iii. The United States, on the other hand, had less than 13 per cent in agriculture in 1950. Moreover, for our purposes the manual/nonmanual breakdown on an intergenerational basis is too crude an indicator of differential opportunity, since chances for mobility in nonmanual careers are fully as important as is opportunity to cross the blue collar line intergenerationally. In this connection, see C. A. Anderson, "The Social Status of University Students in Relation to Type of Economy: an International Comparison," in *Transactions of the Third World Congress of Sociology*, V (1956), 51.

POPULATION POLICY AND THE SMALL FAMILY PATTERN

Nowhere in the world to date, therefore, has modernization alone had an abiding and drastically downward effect on family-size desires. Peoples of the wealthy overseas countries have sustained a prolonged boom in births not merely because of intrinsic demographic factors (age structure, shifts in age at marriage, or changes in the age patterning of childbearing), but because they have come close to realizing their wishes for families of three to four children. Europeans seem clearly to be attempting to bridge the gap between their desires for a moderate-size family and their modest achievements of the last quarter of a century. Yet it is certainly true that the modern world exacts the high direct and indirect costs for reproduction that have been attributed to it.

Why do adults buck the pressures against childbearing to the extent that they do? To understand this paradox it seems necessary to return to the noneconomic utilities of children as powerful forces outweighing the impact of direct and indirect costs. Although it cannot be denied that modernization has brought about many changes in family organization, the complex of roles and goals we call the family is still a major focus of individuals' expectations and activities. This means, by definition, that children are high on the list of adult utilities. Offspring are not simply outlets (and inlets) for affection, they are the instrumentalities for achieving virtually prescribed social statuses ("mother" and "father"), the almost exclusive avenues for feminine creativity and achievement, and the least common denominator for community participation—to give but a few examples.[20] Parents (and potential parents) are thus motivated to create and respond to seemingly superficial arguments for an extra child or two. Childhood mortality risks, desires for a boy, for a girl, for companionship for the youngest—such reasons prevail because parental motivation is already socially structured toward having children. This structuring blunts the sense of deprivation in things foregone (the indirect costs of additional offspring). It even permits the rationalization of direct costs, particularly if the latter are the sort that the children rather than the parents suffer—outgrown and worn clothing, educational limitations, crooked teeth, congenital defects that have a high probability of occurring—the list is not difficult to lengthen. That parental rationalization does not carry the day in modern societies is testimony to the strong social pressures for "doing a good job" at parenthood, and the aforementioned difficulty of finding outside sources of relief from the costs of this privileged status.

This analysis clearly begs the further question of why individuals are still so oriented toward achieving familial statuses in such a seemingly nonfamilial world. One suggested answer is that the family as a social group has certain attributes uniquely suited to the individual's needs in a

modern, urban, mobile society.[21] This view is certainly stimulating as far as it goes, but to understand the family's unique powers we must pay some attention to the types of control mechanisms that channel the quest for satisfactions in the direction of children (and not something else) and families (and not some other social groupings). In a sense, the answer has already been suggested. A strong parental orientation is readily perpetuated through a prolonged period of youthful socialization. Beyond this, the *de facto* primacy of the family provides mechanisms for excluding viable alternative affiliations and satisfactions. Implementation of such alternatives—even popular discussion of them—is ridiculed, or at the worst branded "immoral." Insofar as such alternatives are thrown open for consideration at all, it is typically with reference to clearly disadvantaged or despised choices (celibacy, prostitution, homosexuality, the 'Don Juan' complex), descriptions of which make traditional family roles seem over-

---

[20] A systematic account of the noneconomic utilities of children would be well worth considering. For instance, they allegedly prevent marital boredom and premature aging and "stodginess," as providing couples with a "common interest" and topics of conversation with their own parents. The further one extends the list, the more one becomes aware of how explicitly the marital institution is structured in terms of reproduction.

[21] For instance, Freedman says, "...I suggest that with all its loss of functions, the family in a highly mobile, specialized society continues to have a unique set of core functions. It is, in the first place, the only continuing primary group that a man takes with him in his travels in space and in society. It is the unit which specializes in nonspecialized relationships in a highly specialized society. It is, therefore, the only social unit which can provide dependably the emotional support and stable orientation man needs in a kaleidoscopic, mobile, specialized world. ...The family performs a correlated and equally important function in serving as the center which organizes the impersonal socialized services of the economy and the society for consumption on a personal basis by its members. This important function increases the family's strength as a source of nonspecialized orientation and emotional support. See "Comment" on G. Z. Johnson, *op. cit.*, p. 74.

poweringly advantageous by contrast. The family thus seems to be uniquely well-suited to modern life in part because functional rivals (competing roles, satisfactions, and activities) are effectively relegated to the sidelines.

It seems therefore that a stabilized reduction in the family-size desires of both prosperous and poor countries will require a significant lessening of involvement in familial roles. Otherwise, policy is bucking a motivational syndrome that has a built-in "righting reflex" in the face of antinatalist blows. The family complex may bow to depression, stoop to war, and shrink into an urban apartment, but until nonfamilial roles begin to offer significant competition to familial ones as avenues for adult satisfaction, the family will probably continue to amaze us with its procreative powers.

Yet policy directed at reducing rates of population growth has to date failed to come to grips with this predicament. It has either enjoined institutional changes, such as economic development that are once-removed from the family, or it has taken off toward purely technical and instrumental considerations respecting birth control. In neither case is there direct manipulation of family structure itself—planned efforts at deflecting the family's socializing function, reducing the noneconomic utilities of offspring, or introducing nonfamilial distractions and opportunity costs into people's lives. In neither case is there genuine leadership out of the demographic dilemma posed by declining mortality.

The question may well be raised, however, as to whether we have other than purely theoretical reasons for believing that direct policy affecting family structure would also affect family-size desires and their implementation. For example, would deflection from important familial roles lead individuals to desire smaller families? A full answer to such a question will require a wide variety of research endeavors. But, fortunately, demographers and sociologists have already devoted fairly intensive study to this problem in their research on female labor force participation and family size.

FAMILY SIZE AND WORKING WIVES

From the standpoint of the theory discussed in this paper, the employment of women outside the home constitutes one of the most likely sources of a desire for small families. Such employment will often entail satisfactions alternative to children (companionship, recreation, stimulation, and creative activity), or the means to such satisfactions in the form of financial remuneration. Foregoing employment will frequently be experienced as a cost—one of the costs of having children. Thus employment is a means of introducing into women's lives the subjective awareness of opportunity costs involved in childbearing—an awareness that traditional feminine roles and activities are well-designed to circumvent.

In actual fact, female labor force participation has long been known to bear none of the most impressive relationships to family size of any variable—typically in Western countries it has been equaled or exceeded in strength only by Catholic–non-Catholic religious affiliation. An inverse relationship between the labor force participation of married women and their family size has been suggested by census data for Western Europe and the United States for many years.[22]

Recently, Collver and Langlois found a high negative association of fertility with women's participation in work (other than domestic service). For twenty countries of varying modernization levels (having data available) the Pearsonian correlation was −0.60. The regression equation shows that the number of children per 1000 women declined by seven for each 1 per cent increase in the work participation rate.[23] Jaffe and Azumi contrasted the smaller families of both Puerto Rican and Japanese wives employed outside the home with the families of wives not in the labor force or engaged in cottage industry. Among Puerto Rican women it was possible to control for women's educational levels and the relationship still was maintained.[24]

Furthermore, family—size ideals, desires, and expectations have also been related to women's work behavior. In a number of American studies it was discovered that the longer the work experience of fecund wives since marriage (holding constant age of wife or duration of marriage or both) the smaller the family size expected.[25] The difference in desired or expected family size between wives who have had no work experience and those having "much" (5 years or more) is about one child—a difference as great as is typically found between Catholics and non-Catholics, and usually greater than any other single dif-

---

[22] These data for married women during the 1930s and 1940s have been summarized by the United Nations (U.N. Population Division: *The Determinants and Consequences of Population Trends*, p. 88). Population Studies No. 17 (ST/SOA/Ser. A 17) New York, 1953.

[23] A. Collver and E. Langlois, "The Female Labor Force in Metropolitan Areas; an International Comparison," *Economic Development and Cultural Change*, X (1962), 381.

[24] A. J. Jaffe and K. Azumi, "The Birth Rate and Cottage Industries in Underdeveloped Countries," *Economic Development and Cultural Change*, IX (1960), 52. The authors say, "What implications can be drawn from these findings? First, it is clear that cottage industries are not an unmixed blessing, even if it can be proven—which is doubtful—that they are economically advisable. By maintaining high fertility levels together with relatively low levels of worker productivity they simply help perpetuate a system of rapid population

growth together with a rate of economic growth which at best barely manages to keep abreast of population growth. Traditional forms of social and family relationships are maintained (one of the important elements involved in sustaining traditionally high fertility levels) and no or little progress is made toward transforming the entire socioeconomic structure into that of a rapidly growing modern economy.... From the population viewpoint, perhaps the most desirable industries to be introduced into an underdeveloped country would be those using large quantities of female labor away from home, in modern factories, stores, offices, etc. If enough women were so occupied the birth rate would be lowered considerably." See also, A. J. Jaffe, *People, Jobs and Economic Development* (New York: Free Press of Glencoe, Inc., 1959), chap. x. The same type of relationship between women working and family size is suggested by data from a survey on fertility and attitudes toward family formation in Santiago, Chile. See L. Tabah and P. Samuel, *op. cit.*

[25] L. V. Pratt and P. K. Whelpton, *op. cit.*, 1254; and J. C. Ridley, "Number of Children Expected in Relation to Nonfamilial Activities of Wife," *Milbank Memorial Fund Quarterly*, XXXVII (1959), 277; R. Freedman, D. Goldberg and D. Sleisinger, "Current Fertility Expectations of Married Couples in the United States," *Population Index*, XXIX (1963), 377.

ference.[26] A recent study in West Germany revealed a similar association.[27]

Although this association between married women working and family size is generally acknowledged to be one of the strongest, most persistent over time and space, and most theoretically reasonable, questions must be raised about the nature of the causal relationship. It seems clear by now that the relationship is not due simply to the fact that involuntarily infecund or subfecund wives are more inclined or able to work. The association holds among fecund wives. However, from none of these studies is it clear whether the small-family ideal is solely a *result* of labor force participation by women (a result of their becoming socialized to earning their own living, a nondomestic way of life, etc.), or whether the *intention* of working precedes the desire for small families (or coincides with it in youth), before either family experience or intensive work experience is undergone. Fortunately, data now being analyzed at the University of California, Berkeley, allow us to examine this very point, because the sample was drawn from high school and college students who were asked about both their work intentions after marriage and about their family-size ideals.[28] As may be seen from Table 6,

whether girls intend to work for any prolonged period of time outside the home after marriage exerts approximately as important an influence on their family-size desires as does their religious affiliation—probably the other single most important influence we will be able to show. The importance of most socioeconomic variables other than religious affiliation is relatively slight.

These data should serve to illustrate that already existing research on one of the possible means of reducing the noneconomic utilities of children, and increasing the opportunity costs in childbearing, shows considerable promise for reducing family size. From the standpoint of population growth, the potential influence of policy designed to deflect women from family participation lies not only in the direction of reducing family-size desires, but of lengthening the period between generations through later marriage and delayed childbearing. Further, policy designed to increase feminine labor outside the home will often involve few direct governmental outlays, but rather merely the abolition of legal restrictions and informal barriers. Even actual investment in such policy (for example, in-service training for women) would have social and economic functions, rather than solely helping to reduce family size. Finally, work in factories and other organized situations outside the home makes women readily (and inexpensively) accessible to all types of educational influences, including (in

26 *Ibid.*, 384. The 1955 and 1962 studies have shown that the difference between the religious groups contrasts with increased length of wifely work experience. In the 1962 study, wives with at least five years experience evinced a Catholic–non-Catholic difference of 0.6 in expected family size, those with no such experience since marriage showed a difference of 1.2–double the other figure.

27 R. Freedman, *et al.*, *Population Studies*, XIII (1959), 145.

28 The data are from the Gallup Youth Study, 1961. Their analysis is part of a project being conducted by the

author and Kingsley Davis at International Population and Urban Research Institute on family formation attitudes in the United States. This project utilizes survey data from a variety of agencies. I wish to thank Glen Elder for allowing us to make use of some of his tabulations.

TABLE 6. Mean Number of Children Desired and Percentage Distribution of Children Desired, by Work Intentions After Marriage and Selected Social and Economic Characteristics (Gallup Study of High School and College Students, 1961. White Females Only)

Selected characteristics	Mean number desired	Percentage distribution—desired number of children				Number
		0–1	2–4	5+	Total	
Work intentions after marriage						
Does not intend to work	4.1	2.2	67.8	30.0	100	270
Intends to work:						
Until family	3.8	1.3	79.9	18.8	100	149
1–2 years	3.7	0.8	82.0	17.2	100	239
3 years	3.5	1.6	79.5	18.9	100	127
4 years	3.4	2.1	87.5	10.4	100	48
5 or more years	3.3	6.9	81.0	12.1	100	173
Occupation of household head						
Professional and business	3.6	2.2	81.0	16.8	100	417
Clerical and sales	3.8	1.4	75.0	23.6	100	148
Skilled	3.8	4.4	69.6	26.0	100	135
Semi-skilled and service	3.7	1.8	81.8	16.4	100	171
Laborers (nonfarm)	3.5	0.0	84.6	15.4	100	26
Farmers/farm laborers	4.3	5.1	70.9	24.0	100	64
Education of household head						
<8 yr	3.5	1.8	85.5	12.7	100	55
8–11 yr	3.6	3.4	77.7	18.9	100	238
12 yr H.S. graduate	3.7	3.0	74.7	22.3	100	305
Some college	3.9	0.6	77.7	21.7	100	152
College graduate	3.4	3.1	80.1	16.8	100	131
Professional, etc.	3.6	2.7	78.5	18.8	100	149
Religious affiliation						
Catholic	4.3	1.6	61.3	37.1	100	248
Protestant	3.5	3.0	81.8	15.2	100	664
Jewish	3.3	0.0	94.0	6.0	100	50
None	3.4	4.8	83.3	11.9	100	42
Region of country						
East	3.7	1.7	76.0	22.3	100	346
Midwest	3.8	3.5	73.9	22.6	100	310
South	3.5	3.6	79.6	16.8	100	225
West	3.5	1.3	86.7	12.0	100	158
Age						
14–15	3.8	0.7	75.7	23.6	100	148
16–17	3.7	2.7	76.9	20.4	100	333
18–19	3.5	3.5	78.9	17.6	100	142
20–21	3.6	3.0	78.8	18.2	100	363
22–23	3.7	1.1	79.1	19.8	100	91
Grade						
H.S. sophomore	3.6	2.8	78.1	19.1	100	320
H.S. senior	3.7	2.6	76.2	21.2	100	302
College junior	3.7	2.0	80.7	17.3	100	249
College senior	3.5	3.3	88.9	7.8	100	234

developing countries) those that will help them to reduce infant and child mortality as well as undesired fertility.

In view of the advantages just cited, it is surprising that a country like India (where impressive amounts are being invested in family planning campaigns) is not taking advantage of this structural means of influencing family-size motivation. If anything, the cumulative effect of governmental policy has been one of discouraging rather than encouraging the employment of females. While trends in long-term employment of women in India are difficult to evaluate, there does seem to have been a decided decrease in the proportion of all women classified as working in census reports during the first half of the century.[29]

---

[29] A recent study of female employment in India claims that "the number of working females declined from 43 million in 1911 to 40.7 million in 1951, while the female population during the period increased from 149.9 million in 1911 to 173.4 million in 1951." In other words, there was a decrease of about 2.3 million working females as against an increase of 23.5 million in the female population (*Women in Employment, 1901–1956*, p. 10. A Joint Study by the Labour Bureau, Simla, and the Labour and Employment Division, Planning Commission, Government of India, August 1958). See also, Labour Bureau, Ministry of Labour Government of India: *Economic and Social Status of Women Workers in India* (Delhi: Ganga Printing Press, 1953), p. 12; P. Sengupta, *Women Workers of India* (Bombay: Asia Publishing House, 1960), p. 26; G. R. Gokhale, *Summary of Workmen's Records,* The Millowners Association, Bombay, 1941; and *The Bombay Cotton Mill Worker,* The Millowners Association, 1957, as quoted in R. C. James, "Discrimination Against Women in Bombay Textiles," *Industry Labour Relations Review,* XV (January, 1962), 211.

SUMMARY

To date efforts at curtailing population growth in developing countries have been bipolarized into the "economic development" approach on the one hand, and the family planning approach on the other. The first sees decreases in family size as the long-range resultant of a complete socio-economic overhauling which, in turn, leads to a desire for fewer children. The second overlooks the institutionalization of reproduction entirely and assumes that education and communication regarding birth control will eventually reduce births to a level in keeping with low mortality. Neither approach seems to be practical taken alone, nor do they even appear to be adequate in combination. Population growth is clearly impeding economic development in many poor countries, rather than itself being reduced through the modernization process. Family planning programs are not lowering birth rates among the mass of the people in such countries, and their failure is understandable in view of their superficiality. We are thus led to ask whether additional types of direct action for reducing family size cannot be incorporated into population policy.

In answer, we have taken the position that the limitation of alternatives is more a function of insufficient thought and analysis than actual circumscription of choice. For example, theory and research accounting for declining family size in Western societies is as relevant for direct action concerning reproduction as it is for indirect action respecting family size (such as economic development). It is instructive to analyze the present-day preference in industrial societies for approximately *three* children from the standpoint of the institutional barriers to further declines. We then see that the purely economic assumptions concerning the utility of children discount too readily the importance to individuals of the noneconomic benefits involved in reproduction. These far exceed simple affectional or companionship elements, since they are built into the achievement of familial statuses and the success of marriage. When one analyzes further why modern, urban, mobile individuals are so familially oriented, one cannot discount the advantages of the family group in a modern world. But one must also take into account the strong social controls which isolate individuals from alternative roles and satisfactions and, hence, bolster their intense feelings of dependency on the family, and *a fortiori* on having children.

It would thus appear that policies expressly related to family roles, and opportunities for legitimate alternative satisfactions and activities, constitute the crux of future reduction in family size because they directly assault the motivational framework of reproduction. Moreover, many of these policies for influencing the family do not depend on prior economic development, they can be implemented concomitantly with modernization strategies. Regardless of the level of development, policy can undermine the utilities found in offspring (thereby allowing a sense of increased costs to prevail) and can structure itself in terms of crucial existing foci of change in the society. We have used female labor force participation as an example because it met both of these criteria—a lessening of family involvement on the part of a disadvantaged (and hence potentially revolutionary) group. Numerous additional facets of policy come to mind, one such being rigidly compulsory education of children which would remove them as potential economic utilities (even as household help on anything but a token level), all the while effectively putting intellectual barriers between them and the past generation. Regardless of the specific paths taken by population policy, its designers cannot afford to overlook the lesson already available to them in the substantial family-size desires and actualities to be found in presently industrial countries. Modernization and birth control alone will clearly not bring family size into line with modern levels of mortality unless this reproductive institution is itself modified to make the small family a way of life.*

* *Acknowledgments:* Research for this paper was conducted at International Population and Urban Research, Institute of International Studies, University of California, Berkeley, under a grant from The Equitable Life Assurance Society. The author wishes to thank Kingsley Davis for his criticism and suggestions.

The Demographic Significance of Legal Abortion in Eastern Europe*

Christopher Tietze

Induced abortion, performed legally by qualified physicians in public institutions, has in recent years become an important demographic factor in most countries of Eastern Europe. The report which I shall present, based on published and unpublished data from official sources, obtained in part during recent visits to East Germany,[1] Poland, Hungary, and Czechoslovakia, and in part by correspondence, contains some new data for the period 1960–62 not previously brought to the attention of American demographers.

Following the example of the U.S.S.R. in 1955, all countries of Eastern Europe, except Albania and East Germany, adopted legislation permitting interruption of pregnancy at the request of the pregnant woman or on very broadly interpreted social indications. The stated aims of this legislation, according to the preamble of the decree of the Presidium of the Supreme Soviet of November 23, 1955, are to "permit the limitation of the harm caused to the health of women by abortions carried out outside of hospitals" and to "give women the possibility of deciding by themselves the question of motherhood."[2]

Contrary to the stereotype of monolithic uniformity, a substantial degree of variation prevails between the countries which have adopted the new legislation. The U.S.S.R., Bulgaria, and Hungary provide for abortion at the request of the pregnant woman. In Poland, the law of 1956 required a "difficult social situation" as an acceptable reason for the interruption of pregnancy and made the physician responsible for its determination. Since early 1960, however, an oral declaration by the pregnant woman suffices to establish her "difficult social situation."

In Czechoslovakia, the law allows abortion for reasons "worthy of special consideration," among which the Ministry of Health lists the following: (1) advanced age of the woman, (2) three or more living children, (3) death or disability of the husband, (4) disruption of the family, (5) predominant economic responsibility of the woman for the support of the family or the child, and (6) a difficult situation arising from the pregnancy of an unmarried woman. In Yugoslavia, interruption of pregnancy may be authorized if the birth of the child "would result in a serious personal, familial, or economic situation for the pregnant woman which cannot be averted in any other way."

As a rule, abortions for medical

* Christopher Tietze, "The Demographic Significance of Legal Abortion in Eastern Europe," *Demography*, I (1964), 119–25.

[1] C. Tietze and H. Lehfeldt, "Legal Abortion in Eastern Europe," *Journal of the American Medical Association*, CLXXV (April 1, 1961), 1149–54.

[2] M. G. Fild, "The Re-legalization of Abortion in Soviet Russia," *New England Journal of Medicine*, CCLV (August 30, 1956), 421–27.

TABLE 1. Abortions and Live Births: Hungary, 1946–62; Bulgaria, 1953–61;
Czechoslovakia, 1953–62; Poland, 1955–62; and Yugoslavia, 1959–60
(In 1,000s)

Country and year	Legal abortions	Other abortions[a]	Live births	Abortions and live births
Hungary				
1949	1.6	31.6	190.4	223.6
1950	1.7	34.3	195.6	231.6
1951	1.7	36.1	190.6	228.4
1952	1.7	42.0	185.8	229.5
1953	2.8	39.9	206.9	249.6
1954	16.3	42.0	223.3	281.6
1955	35.4	43.1	210.4	288.9
1956	82.5	41.1	192.8	316.4
1957	123.4	39.5	167.2	330.1
1958	145.6	37.4	158.4	341.4
1959	152.4	35.3	151.2	338.9
1960	162.2	33.8	146.5	342.5
1961	170.0	33.7	140.4	344.1
1962	163.7	33.9	130.1	327.7
Bulgaria				
1953	1.1	16.3	153.2	170.6
1954	1.1	17.5	149.9	168.5
1955	—(19.1)—		151.0	170.1
1956	—(40.0)—		147.9	187.9
1957	31.7	14.5	141.0	187.2
1958	38.1	17.4	138.3	193.8
1959	45.6	18.2	136.9	200.7
1960	54.8	19.3	140.1	214.2
1961	68.8	19.9	137.9	226.6
Czechoslovakia				
1953	1.5	29.1	271.7	302.3
1954	2.8	30.6	266.7	300.1
1955	2.1	33.0	265.2	300.3
1956	3.1	31.0	262.0	296.1
1957	7.3	30.2	252.7	290.2
1958	61.4	27.7	235.0	324.1
1959	79.1	26.4	217.0	322.5
1960	88.3	26.3	216.9	331.5
1961	94.3	26.0	218.0	338.3
1962	89.8	26.0	217.2	333.0
Poland				
1955	1.4	101.6	793.0	896.0
1956	18.9	101.9	779.8	900.6
1957	36.4	85.4	782.3	904.1
1958	44.2	82.2	755.5	881.9
1959	79.0	82.9	722.9	884.8
1960	150.4	73.4	665.8	889.6
1961	143.8	72.8	620.9	837.5
1962	140.4	70.3	594.8	805.5
Yugoslavia				
1959	54.5	57.3	426.0	537.8
1960	84.9	62.1	430.2	577.2

[a] Hospital admissions.

TABLE 2. Abortions and Live Births Per 1,000 Population: Hungary, 1949–62; Bulgaria, 1953–61; Czechoslovakia, 1953–62; Poland, 1955–62; and Yugoslavia, 1959–60

Country and year	Legal abortions	Other abortions[a]	Live births	Abortions and live births
Hungary				
1949	0.2	3.4	20.6	24.2
1950	0.2	3.7	20.9	24.8
1951	0.2	3.8	20.2	25.2
1952	0.2	4.4	19.5	24.1
1953	0.3	4.2	21.5	26.0
1954	1.7	4.3	23.0	29.0
1955	3.6	4.4	21.4	29.4
1956	8.3	4.2	19.5	32.0
1957	12.5	4.0	17.0	33.5
1958	14.7	3.8	16.0	34.5
1959	15.3	3.5	15.2	34.0
1960	16.2	3.4	14.6	34.2
1961	17.0	3.4	14.0	34.4
1962	16.3	3.4	12.9	32.6
Bulgaria				
1953	0.1	2.2	20.9	23.2
1954	0.2	2.4	20.2	22.8
1955	$-\left(\begin{matrix}2.5\\5.3\end{matrix}\right)-$		20.1	22.6
1956			19.5	24.8
1957	4.1	1.9	18.4	24.4
1958	4.9	2.3	17.9	25.1
1959	5.8	2.3	17.6	25.7
1960	7.0	2.5	17.8	27.3
1961	8.7	2.5	17.4	28.6
Czechoslovakia				
1953	0.1	2.3	21.2	23.6
1954	0.2	2.4	20.6	23.4
1955	0.2	2.5	20.3	23.0
1956	0.2	2.3	19.8	22.3
1957	0.5	2.3	18.9	21.7
1958	4.6	2.1	17.4	24.1
1959	5.8	1.9	16.0	23.7
1960	6.5	1.9	15.9	24.3
1961	6.8	1.9	15.8	24.5
1962	6.5	1.9	15.7	24.1
Poland				
1955	0.1	3.7	29.1	32.9
1956	0.7	3.7	28.0	32.4
1957	1.3	3.0	27.6	31.9
1958	1.5	2.9	26.2	30.6
1959	2.7	2.8	24.7	30.2
1960	5.1	2.5	22.4	30.0
1961	4.8	2.4	20.7	27.9
1962	4.6	2.3	19.6	26.5
Yugoslavia				
1959	3.0	3.1	23.1	29.2
1960	4.6	3.3	23.1	31.0

[a] Hospital admissions.

TABLE 3. Abortions and Live Births Per 1,000 Population: Budapest and Remainder of Hungary, 1959 and 1960

Year and area	Legal abortions	Other abortions[a]	Live births	Abortions and live births
1959				
Budapest City	26.5	5.0	9.2	40.7
Pest County	7.7	1.4	14.8	23.9
Greater Budapest	20.8	3.9	10.9	35.6
Remainder of country	13.4	3.4	16.7	33.5
All Hungary	15.3	3.5	15.2	34.0
1960				
Budapest City	27.3	4.8	8.8	40.9
Pest County	8.7	1.3	14.3	24.3
Greater Budapest	21.7	3.7	10.4	35.8
Remainder of country	14.3	3.3	16.1	33.7
All Hungary	16.2	3.4	14.6	34.2

[a] Hospital admissions.

reasons are performed free of charge, while those done on request or on "social indications" must be paid for by the applicant. The charges cover only a part of the costs of the operation and hospitalization. In Czechoslovakia, fees for abortion on social indication were abolished in 1960. Abortion is forbidden after the twelfth week of pregnancy, except on medical grounds. It is also forbidden if the applicant had undergone an induced abortion during the preceding 6 months. Interruption of pregnancy by an unauthorized person or under unauthorized circumstances (e.g., in a doctor's office) is a punishable offense, but the woman who induces an abortion on herself, or on whom it is performed, does not face prosecution.

Table 1 shows available statistics on the numbers of legal abortions in five countries, while Table 2 presents the same information in terms of crude rates per 1,000 population.

In addition to the numbers and rates of legal abortions, Tables 1, 2, and 3 also contain data on other cases of abortion treated in hospitals. This category includes spontaneous abortions as well as cases of illegal abortion induced outside the hospital and subsequently admitted because of fever or other complications.

The third column in Tables 1, 2, and 3 shows the number of live births as registered, i.e., of live-born infants rather than of pregnancies ending in the birth of one or more live babies. Data on stillbirths have been omitted from the three tables. Since the number of stillbirths is roughly equal in Eastern Europe to the number of multiple pregnancies, the sum total of legal abortions, other hospitalized abortions, and live births, shown in the last column, is a close approximation to the total of known pregnancies.

In Hungary, strong efforts were made in 1952 and 1953 to enforce existing laws against illegal abortion. These efforts led to an increase in births in 1953 and 1954. At about the same time, medical boards for the authorization of therapeutic abortions were established. The growing numbers of legal abortions from 1953 on indicate the progressive liberalization of the policies of these boards. After the decree of June 3, 1956, had established the principle of abortion on demand, the number of legal abortions increased rapidly until in 1961 it reached 170,000, exceeding the number of live births by more than one-fifth.[3,4] A drop of 4 per cent in the number of abortions was reported in 1962.[5]

In Bulgaria, comprehensive statistics on abortion by type are not available for 1956, when the new law was enacted, or for 1955. However, the trends are well established by the data available for the years preceding and following this hiatus.[6,7]

In Czechoslovakia, legislation legalizing abortion for nonmedical reasons was preceded by almost two years of public discussion. Moderate increases in therapeutic abortions in 1956 and 1957 reflect the changing attitude of the medical profession. Promulgation of a new abortion law in December 1957 was followed by a steep rise in legal abortions in 1958, continuing at a decelerating pace until 1961.[7] The trend was reversed in 1962 with a drop of 89,400, 5 per cent below the figure for the preceding year.[8,9]

In the latest year for which information is available, the rate of legal abortions was highest in Hungary (16.3 per 1,000 population), followed by Bulgaria (8.7 per 1,000), Czechoslovakia (6.5 per 1,000), Poland[10] and Yugoslavia[11] (less than 5 per 1,000). No data are available for the U.S.S.R. and Rumania.

Table 3 illustrates the urban-rural differential on the incidence of legal abortions and of other hospitalized abortions in Hungary in 1959 and 1960. In both years and for both types of abortions, legal and other, the reported incidence for the city of Budapest was much higher than for the country as a whole. Pest County, which surrounds Budapest City, is for the most part suburban in character. The two areas together constitute the Budapest metropolitan area or Greater Budapest. It is perfectly obvious that many women in Pest County are aborted or hospitalized in the central city. The abortion rates for Greater Budapest are still very high, but the rate of known pregnancies is well in line with the corresponding rate for the remainder of Hungary.[12]

What has been the effect of the

[3] I. Hirschler, "Die Abortsituation in der Volksrepublik Ungarn," *Internationale Abortsituation, Abortbekämpfung, Antikonzeption*, ed. K. H. Mehlan (Leipzig: Thieme, 1961), pp. 114–22.

[4] E. Szabady, "Magyarország népesedési helyzete; a családtervezés gazdasági, társadalmi és egészségügyi vonatkozasai," *Demográfia*, (1962), pp. 325–32.

[5] G. Acsádi, Personal communication.

[6] I. Starkaleff, B. Papasoff, and G. Stoimenoff, "Die Abortsituation in der Vokskrepublik Bulgarien," *Internationale Abortsituation, Abortbekämp-*

fung, Antikonzeption ed. K. H. Mehlan (Leipzig: Thieme, 1961), pp. 26–31.

[7] K. H. Mehlan, Personal communication.

[8] M. Vojta, "Die Abortsituation in der Tschechoslowakischen Sozialistischen Republik," *Internationale Abortsituation, Abortbekämpfung Antikonzeption*, ed. K. H. Mehlan (Leipzig: Thieme, 1961), pp. 107–13.

[9] V. Srb and M. Kučera, "Potratovost v Československu v letech 1958–1962," *Demografie*, V, (1963), 289–307.

[10] Towarzystwo Świadomego Macierzyństwa and J. Lensinski, Personal communication.

[11] A. Mojic, "Pobačaj kao epidemioloski problem," *Ginekologija i opstetricija*, I (1961), 65–70.

[12] Hungary, Központi Statisztikai Hivatal, *Magyarország népesedése 1960* (Budapest, 1962), p. 63.

legalization of abortion on the birth rate, on illegal abortions, total induced abortions, and total pregnancies? Let us first consider natality. The upper panel of Table 4 shows the crude birth rates per 1,000 population

TABLE 4. Birth Rate Per 1,000 Population and Birth Rate Index (1950–54=100): Selected Countries, 1950–62

Country	1950–54	1955	1956	1957	1958	1959	1960	1961	1962
Eastern Europe									
Albania	38.9	44.5	41.9	39.1	41.8	41.9	43.4	41.2	—
Bulgaria	21.7	20.1	19.5	18.4	17.9	17.6	17.8	17.4	—
Czechoslovakia	22.0	20.3	19.8	18.9	17.4	16.0	15.9	15.8	15.7
Germany (East[a])	16.6	16.3	15.9	15.6	15.6	16.9	17.0	17.4	17.5
Hungary	21.1	21.4	19.5	17.0	16.0	15.2	14.6	14.0	12.9
Poland	30.1	29.1	28.0	27.6	26.2	24.7	22.4	20.7	19.6
Rumania	24.9	25.6	24.2	22.9	21.6	20.2	19.1	17.5	17.5
USSA	26.4	25.7	25.2	25.4	25.3	25.0	24.9	23.9	22.5
Yugoslavia	28.8	26.8	25.9	23.7	23.8	23.0	23.1	22.6	22.2
Western Europe									
Belgium	16.7	16.8	16.8	17.0	17.1	17.4	16.9	17.0	16.8
Denmark	17.9	17.3	17.2	16.8	16.5	16.3	16.6	16.6	16.9
France	19.5	18.6	18.5	18.5	18.2	18.4	18.0	18.2	17.7
Germany (West)	16.1	16.0	16.5	17.0	17.0	17.6	17.6	18.3	18.1
Italy	18.4	18.1	18.1	18.1	17.9	18.4	18.5	18.8	19.0
Netherlands	22.1	21.3	21.2	21.2	21.1	21.3	20.8	21.2	20.8
Sweden	15.5	14.8	14.8	14.5	14.2	14.1	13.7	13.9	14.1
Switzerland	17.3	17.1	17.4	17.7	17.6	17.7	17.6	18.1	18.7
UK	15.9	15.5	16.1	16.5	16.8	16.9	17.5	17.9	18.3
Eastern Europe									
Albania	100	114	108	101	107	108	112	106	—
Bulgaria	100	93	90	85	82	81	82	80	—
Czechoslovakia	100	92	90	86	79	73	72	72	71
Germany (East[a])	100	98	96	94	94	102	102	105	105
Hungary	100	101	92	81	76	72	69	66	61
Poland	100	97	93	92	87	82	74	69	65
Rumania	100	103	97	92	87	81	77	70	70
USSR	100	97	95	96	96	95	94	91	85
Yugoslavia	100	93	90	82	83	80	80	78	77
Western Europe									
Belgium	100	101	101	102	102	104	101	102	101
Denmark	100	97	96	94	92	91	93	93	94
France	100	95	95	95	93	94	93	93	91
Germany (West)	100	99	102	106	106	109	109	114	112
Italy	100	98	98	98	97	100	101	102	92
Netherlands	100	96	96	96	95	96	94	96	94
Sweden	100	95	95	94	92	91	88	90	92
Switzerland	100	99	101	102	102	102	102	105	108
UK	100	97	101	104	106	106	110	112	115

[a] Includes East Berlin.

for nine countries in Eastern Europe, including seven countries with new legislation on abortion and two countries without such legislation (Albania and East Germany), and for nine countries in Western Europe.[13] In the lower panel these annual birth rates have been converted into index numbers, with the average for 1950–54 equaling 100.

By the early 1960s, the birth rate had declined markedly in each of the countries where abortion had been legalized, except in the U.S.S.R. Compared with the early 1950s, the decline ranged from one-fifth in Bulgaria to almost two-fifths in Hungary. Over the same period, a moderate increase of natality occurred in several of the Western countries listed in Table 4, as well as in the two Eastern countries which had not legalized abortion. Other countries in Western Europe experienced a decline in the birth rate but none by more than one-tenth. The differences in natality trends between the two groups of countries have been sufficiently striking, in my opinion, and the basic patterns of population structure, including its distribution by sex and age, as well as relative changes in per capita income and other indicators of social well-being over the past several years, sufficiently similar to justify the conclusion, without more rigorous analysis, that the legalization of abortion has had a depressant effect on the birth rate in most of the countries concerned.

The position of the U.S.S.R., which initiated the new legislation on abortion but experienced a smaller decline in the birth rate than any of the other

six countries with similar laws, requires special consideration. The Soviet authorities have not released any statistics on the number of legal abortions performed and my own repeated efforts to pry loose this information from the Russian representative at last year's regional meeting of the International Planned Parenthood Federation in Warsaw ended unsuccessfully. The question has been raised as to what extent the apparent permissiveness of the decree of 1955 is implemented in actual practice. The commentary preceding the decree notes that "the prevention of abortion may be secured through . . . measures of an educational and explanatory nature." This passage has been interpreted as indicating that physicians have been instructed to discourage abortions as much as possible and not to perform the operation unless the applicant insists. Informal pressure could have kept the number of legal abortions in the U.S.S.R. at a comparatively low level and thus contributed to the maintenance of the birth rate. If this hypothesis is accepted, one is left with the puzzling question why no statistics have been released.

Another explanation of the trend of the Soviet birth rate, which is compatible with a high incidence of abortion and, therefore, with official secrecy on the subject, rests on the progressive normalization over the past decade of the sex ratio among persons of reproductive age in the U.S.S.R.[14] This normalization may be assumed to have resulted in a high rate of family formation and thus to

---

[13] United Nations, Statistical Office, *Demographic Yearbook and Population and Vital Statistics Report,* various issues.

[14] J. W. Brackett, "Demographic Trends and Population Policy in the Soviet Union," *Dimensions of Soviet Economic Power* (Joint Economic Committee, Congress of the United States [Washington, D.C.: U.S. Government Printing Office, 1962]), pp. 487–589.

have masked a trend toward smaller families, an assumption which gains support from the high marriage rates of about 12 per 1,000 population, reported for the period 1956–60. If this second interpretation is accepted, as I am inclined to do until more information becomes available, the position of the U.S.S.R. ceases to be exceptional.

What has been the effect of legalization on the frequency of illegal abortions in the various countries? This question cannot be answered with certainty since the number of illegal abortions is not known for any country, either before the new legislation or at the present time. The reported numbers and rates of "other" abortions, limited to hospitalized cases, have declined moderately in Hungary, Czechoslovakia, and Poland, but not in Bulgaria. No firm conclusions can be drawn from these trends, since these figures include spontaneous abortions as well as illegal abortions requiring hospitalization. Moreover, neither the proportion reaching medical attention among all abortions, other than those legally performed in hospitals, nor the proportion hospitalized among those under medical care remains constant—especially not if the legal and social provisions relating to medical practice in general and to abortion in particular are undergoing major changes. However, the physicians with whom the problem was discussed during my recent visit in Eastern Europe were in agreement that the proportion of hospitalized abortion cases among those reaching medical attention has increased substantially over the past years, owing to restrictions on the private practice of medicine and—in the case of illegal abortion—because women need no longer fear prosecution.

The only solid facts on which to base an estimate of the trend of illegal abortions are the numbers and rates of legal abortions and of live births. In Hungary and Bulgaria, and to a lesser extent in Czechoslovakia, the reported increases in legal abortion have exceeded the corresponding declines in births. This finding lends support to the interpretation that the number of illegal abortions has declined, and may have declined substantially. Nevertheless, illegal abortion still occurs with sufficient frequency to be considered a serious public health problem.

In Poland, the reported increase in legal abortions has been smaller than the corresponding decline in births. While several factors may be involved in this apparent anomaly, incomplete reporting of legal abortions is definitely one of them. Fewer abortions were reported in 1961 and 1962 than in 1960, although the birth rate continued to decline sharply.

Since the over-all incidence of induced abortion is the sum total of legal abortions, which have increased rapidly, and of illegal abortions, which have probably declined, the resultant trend must be closer to the horizontal than either of its two components. Even the direction of the slope, up or down, is in doubt. I believe, however, because of the rapid decline in natality which has occurred in most countries of Eastern Europe, that increases in the total number and rate of induced abortions are far more likely than declines.

The total number of known pregnancies, approximated by the sum of reported abortions and of live births, shown in the last column of Tables 1, 2, and 3, has increased substantially in Hungary and less steeply in Bulgaria. The reported rate has been fairly constant in Czechoslovakia and has declined in Poland.

To the extent that the total of known pregnancies has increased, these increases are doubtless inflated, and may even be caused entirely, by the increasing hospitalization of illegal abortions. Since there have been declines in births following the legalization of abortion in Eastern Europe, presumably accompanied by proportional declines in spontaneous abortions, while the totals of induced abortions—legal plus illegal—have probably increased, it is very difficult to make a guess concerning the trend of total pregnancies and then to defend that guess. I shall not undertake this bootless task, but shall stop at this point with the feeling of well-earned frustration which is a recurrent experience to those who, like me, cannot keep away from the statistics of abortion.

Some Political Aspects of Immigration*

Lawrence H. Fuchs

The understanding of American politics rests upon two facts of American life: ideological unity and group pluralism. The purpose of this article will be to show the extent to which the historic American policy of welcoming immigrants has shaped the pluralistic character of American politics and briefly to explore contemporary developments and the implied changes which will be wrought by the present restrictive immigration policy. The impact of the immigration issue on voting behavior and the party system has, with some exceptions, not been large; but the political consequences of immigration itself have been deep and continuing. While each immigrant group, in its turn, has been quick to acquiesce in the basic tenets of the American creed, each has brought into the contest for political power its own brand or style of politics, and, more importantly, its own particular group claims. The very fact of ideological unity in the European sense has heightened the cohesiveness of nationality and ethnic-group expression in the maelstrom of American politics.

* Reprinted, by permission, from a symposium, *Immigration*, appearing in *Law and Contemporary Problems* (Vol. 21, No. 2, Spring 1956); published by the Duke University School of Law, Durham, N.C. Copyright, 1956, by Duke University.

I

IMMIGRANT GROUPS AND THE DEVELOPMENT OF THE AMERICAN PARTY SYSTEM[1]

Soon after the writing of the Constitution, astute politicians recognized the importance of the immigrant vote. Jefferson and his followers labored hard and successfully to capture the loyalties of the newcomers. No single factor did as much to destroy the Federalists as a political party as the hostility of its hard-core Yankee group to the newer immigrants. Only a few Federalists realized that survival as a major party depended upon drawing a circle ever larger to include new and diverse groups, that American politics must be coalition politics. Too late did Alexander Hamilton and others recognize the political impotence of the policy of exclusions responsible for the Alien and Sedition Acts. In a last ditch effort to capitalize on the growing number of immigrant voters, the Federalists of New York offered a sprightly campaign tune for the gubernatorial election of 1810:

> Come Dutch and Yankee, Irish, Scot,
> With intermixed relation;
> From whence we came, it matters not;
> We all make, now, one nation.

But the basic animus of Federalist spokesmen, such as Harrison Gray Otis of Massachusetts, and Uriah Tracy of Connecticut, toward the same Dutch, Irish, and Scot celebrated in song was made clear in the Hartford Convention of 1812. Blind to the realities of pluralistic politics to the last

gasp, the Convention urged a constitutional amendment to bar naturalized citizens from elective and civil office.

A. SCOTCH-IRISH. The Virginia Republicans who ruled the White House between 1800 and 1824 welcomed the support they received from the low-status immigrant groups. During the colonial period, Pennsylvania became the distribution center for one of the largest of these groups, the Scotch-Irish-Presbyterians. Not wanted by the Puritans of New England, they were driven to the frontier and, in turn, to democracy and a hatred of the British and Indians alike. These were natural recruits for a leveling party. For the first quarter of the nineteenth century (and beyond), the Scotch-Irish played a leading role in the development of the Jeffersonian Party, feeding it with votes and leaders, some of whom reached the White House (Jackson, Polk, Buchanan).

B. IRISH-CATHOLICS. Soon replacing the Scotch-Irish-Presbyterians as the core ethnic group of the Democratic Party were Irish-Catholic immigrants. No other group has shown the flair and skill and group cohesiveness which, for more than a century, has characterized the political behavior of Irish-Americans.

Between 1820 and 1920, over four and one-half million Irish immigrants came to the United States, the great bulk arriving between 1840 and 1890. The summer of 1845 was the first of a series of cold and damp Irish summers which caused one-fourth of the Irish countryside to succumb to disease. Nearly one million Irish immigrants arrived between 1851 and 1860. These became the unskilled, marginal workers of America. Lacking the means to go West, most of

---

[1] Throughout this article, the writer has relied heavily on data compiled by the Bureau of the Census and on published election returns.

them supplied the brawn so desperately needed in the industrial East. They worked in construction gangs, building aqueducts, canals, and railroads, and they worked in the mines and mills. The party of Jackson was congenial to their aspirations for a better life, and the political talents of the Irish were welcomed by it.

The customary explanation for the Irish genius in politics rests on the Irish bent for oratory, his entrepreneural aptitude, and his conviviality. Without denying any of these, a sounder interpretation would insist on the following primary factors: the majority of Irish immigrants came within a 40-year period when naturalization was easy and when routes to prestige and privilege outside of politics were closed to them. They had one commodity of high value—votes! In the run-down rookeries and shantytowns where they dwelled, their needs were great. A bargain was struck. For the votes of large Irish families, their own political leaders would minister to the sick and weary, get a few jobs, and buy some drinks. Irish political power lay in the deliverability of the Irish-Democratic vote. The Irish, who fought free Negro labor on the docks of New York, had no sympathy for abolition and the new political parties which promoted the cause of the Negro. Alone among the large ethnic groups, they clung to their Democratic moorings after the war. Inevitably, they rose to key positions of leadership and skillfully recruited the newer immigrant groups into the Democratic Party. They also had the singular advantages of speaking English, being familiar with the mechanics of government, and being here first. For a half-century after Appomattox, the Irish kept the Democratic Party alive.

C. GERMANS. German immigrants also made a unique contribution to the shaping of our party system. Nineteenth-century German political behavior must be broken into two periods. Before 1850, the vast majority of Germans appear to have been Democrats. The slavery issue plus the sudden rush of German immigration in the 1850s, however, brought about a new and significant alignment. The Kansas-Nebraska Act of 1854 turned many Germans from the Democrats and Douglas. German immigrants were drawn in ever larger numbers to the new parties of free soil and free men.

Between 1845 and the outbreak of the Civil War, 1,250,000 German refugees came to America. Many remained in New York City, perhaps 100,000 in all. Most of them, however, migrated westward, along the Erie Canal, to the Great Lakes, and on to the prairies. Cincinnati became a leading German-American city. Columbus, Cleveland, Dayton, and Toledo in Ohio developed sizable German communities. Hundreds of thousands settled on farms. By 1860, there were more than 130,000 Germans in Illinois. To Wisconsin, particularly in the eastern and north-central counties, came thousands of German homesteaders. For 100 years, German-Americans living in the Midwest have constituted one of the most vital ethnic core groups in the Republican Party.

One important factor, however, mitigated the attraction of the Republican Party for German immigrants. Nativist Whig elements in some areas were instrumental in the formation of the new party. When an amendment to the Massachusetts Constitution was voted which would deprive all citizens who had not been naturalized for more than two years of the right to hold office, German-Americans made the Massachusetts amendment a national issue. Republicans generally were blamed, although the Know-Nothing Party, in control in Massachusetts since 1855, was actually responsible for pushing the amendment through. Lincoln was forced to reply to German charges of nativism. Chase and Seward were obliged to reassure Germans publicly. Republican leaders intensified their efforts to woo Germans. Local prohibition laws were amended to permit the sale of cider, beer, and cheap wines. Promises of patronage and cheap land were made. State Republican Parties nominated Germans for office, and in the national convention in 1860, German-Americans won a plank which came out squarely against the Massachusetts amendment or any other curtailment of the rights of naturalized citizens. Lincoln, after the election, then drew his German followers closer to the party through a liberal use of patronage. Finally, Republican homestead, reconstruction, monetary, and civil service policies appealed to the rugged virtues of German agrarian Protestantism. The biggest German migrations were yet to come, and the arrival of 1,452,970 German immigrants between 1881 and 1890 probably assured Republican domination of national politics from 1869 to 1930 as much as any other single factor.

D. SCANDINAVIANS. The last of the great nineteenth-century immigrant groups were the Scandinavians. The Norwegians and Swedes were largest among these. Their role in shaping the American party system parallels that of the Germans, although quantitatively it is not nearly as important.

In 1850, the federal census revealed only 12,678 Norwegians in the United States. Twenty years later, the number had jumped to 114,243. By 1872, they were concentrated in southeastern Wisconsin, with lesser numbers in Chicago, northern Illinois, central Wisconsin, southeastern Minnesota, and northeastern Iowa.

Altogether, about two million Scandinavians arrived between 1820 and 1920, climaxed during the 1880s, when in 1882, 100,000 settlers arrived. To this day, Swedes are an important political group in Minnesota, Iowa, Michigan, Illinois, Nebraska, the Dakotas, and Wisconsin. Probably four-fifths of the Swedish immigrants settled on the land, where their descendants live today.

Earliest Norwegian immigrants tended to vote for Democratic or Free Soil candidates before the Civil War. Whigs were suspect because of snobbishness and nativism. Like the Germans, the swelling Scandinavian population moved into the Republican Party with ease in the years following the war. Like the Germans, they opposed slavery, wanted free homesteads, and were sedulously cultivated by Republican politicians. Between 1860 and 1873, seventeen Norwegian-American newspapers were born (under different auspices), and all but one supported Republican policies.[2]

II

NEW IMMIGRANTS VERSUS THE OLD

Scotch-Irish, Irish-Catholics, Germans, and Scandinavians—these were the four key ethnic groups in nine-

---

[2] See Arlow W. Andersen, *The Immigrant Takes His Stand* (1953), pp. 12–13.

teenth-century American politics, each forming a stable element in the long-run development of one of our major parties. In their day, they were all new immigrant groups, and all suffered discrimination at the hands of Yankees already here.

The mutual hostility of old and new immigrant groups has been a persistent theme in American life and politics. It has given rise to the formation of new political parties, such as the American and Know-Nothing parties in the mid-nineteenth century. It has shaped the politics of entire regions, such as Rhode Island and Massachusetts, where political battle between Republicans and Democrats is partially the formal expression of deeper conflicts between Yankee-Protestants and Irish-Catholics.[3] Clashes between old and new immigrant groups often show themselves in a struggle for local political power. One hundred years ago, the Yankees in New York City fought a losing battle to keep newcomer Irishmen from gaining the upper hand. Today, the Irish defend their political bastions against the mounting onslaughts of Italians and, to a lesser extent, Jews and Negroes.

III

NATIVISM IN AMERICAN POLITICS

Nativism—the fear of and hostility

---

[3] There exists in Massachusetts an almost perfect correlation between the Yankee-ness and Republican-ness of counties, regardless of their wealth. For example, the three most Protestant counties, Barnstable, Nantucket, and Dukes, are the most Republican counties, even though they are among the poorest in the state as measured by census figures for the median income of families and unrelated individuals.

toward new immigrant groups—has been sharply etched in the tradition of American politics. There have been four broad nativist phases. Originally, nativism was simply the antagonism of old immigrants for new. With the arrival of large-scale Irish-Catholic immigration, it became primarily anti-Catholic, not just antiforeign. Thus, it became possible for the Germans and Swedes, once recovered from the wounds inflicted by initial struggles with Yankees, to join their former Protestant foes in shaping the nativist pattern. The third phase of American nativism came in response to the twentieth-century migrations of Italians, Jews, and East Europeans, combined with the growth of the cities. This third phase was not just anti-Catholic, anti-Semitic, or even antiforeign; it was largely antiurban. The Irish, although by this time an old immigrant group, could not yet become a part of the nativist tradition because they were too closely identified with the newer immigrants. They not only had failed to achieve economic status, they also were Catholic, lived in the big cities, and, indeed, were the organizers of the new immigrant voting power. It is only in the fourth phase of American nativism—the anti-Communist phase —that the Irish begin to swim in the main stream of American nativism.

The most crucial phase of American nativism is the second one—the reaction to Irish-Catholicism. This is the phase which cut most deeply and affected the largest number of people. It is the only phase which brought forth a major political party—the Know-Nothing movement of the 1850s. By 1830, there were 150,000 Irish-Catholics in New York alone. Small nativist parties emerged there and elsewhere. They flourished independently in the North and South and produced newspapers in a dozen cities. Riots, bloodshed, and the burning of churches were common in New York and Philadelphia. Presidential politics were affected. Van Buren was accused of being a Catholic in the 1836 campaign, and Polk was attacked on the floor of Congress for pandering to the Catholic vote in 1844. When it appeared that the foreign vote was responsible for Polk's election, membership in nativist parties rose sharply. In 1845 and 1847, national conventions of the Native-American Party were held.

Probably more attention was paid to the foreign vote in 1852 than ever before in a presidential election. A nationwide outbreak of antiforeignism and anti-Catholicism was occasioned by the election of Franklin Pierce. The result was the Know-Nothing Party. No political party in American history ever achieved the status of a major party so swiftly. No other party ever fell so fast. The platform of the party was simple. Members were pledged to vote for native-born candidates, to work for a long period of probation before naturalization, and to oppose the Catholic Church.

Within five years after its organization in New York in 1850, every state and territory in the country had a Know-Nothing executive council. In Connecticut, the Know-Nothings absorbed the Whig remnants. In 1854, Know-Nothing governors were elected in Massachusetts and Pennsylvania. Every member of the Massachusetts Senate and 375 of the 379 representatives were Know-Nothings.[4] In 1855, the party elected

governors in Rhode Island, Connecticut, New Hampshire, California, and Kentucky. Five state legislatures were captured, and as many as one hundred congressmen-elect shared the Know-Nothing point of view. In the South, where the Know-Nothings took over what was left of the Whig Party, substantial victories were won in 1856 in Kentucky, Tennessee, and Louisiana. Millard Fillmore, the Know-Nothing candidate for President, received 874,534 votes, more than half from the South.

Within a year, however, the Know-Nothing Party was destroyed. It foundered on the slavery issue. To please its northern faction, it condemned the Kansas-Nebraska Act in its national platform of 1856. To placate southern elements, it demanded enforcement of the Fugitive Slave Act. Neither side would be mollified.

The deposit left by this second phase of American nativism has been very large, and has located in a variety of political and social movements. The American Protective Association, born in Clinton, Iowa, in 1887, was founded almost entirely on anti-Catholicism, having its greatest impact in the Protestant Bible belt. Reaching its peak in 1894, it claimed one million members, one hundred of whom were elected to the 54th Congress. Populist and Prohibition Party platforms absorbed much of the APA nativist program in 1892, but the issue of nativism was again obscured by larger questions—free silver and Bryanism.

A resurgence of nativism followed World War I. The new nativism was antiurban and anti-Semitic as well as anti-Catholic and flowered in the Ku Klux Klan, which, by 1925, had five million members in strongholds

---

[4] See John Carroll Noonan, *Nativism in Connecticut, 1829–1860* (1938), p. 191.

throughout the South and in Ohio and Indiana. Again, a deeper and more pervasive issue came along— the depression—to cut across and veil the nativist battle.

IV

TWENTIETH-CENTURY IMMIGRATION AND AMERICAN POLITICS

Four-fifths of the southern and eastern European immigration which came after 1880 stopped within the great urban triangle formed by St. Louis, Washington, and Boston, much of it remaining in New York City. The new immigrants went to the cities not so much because they were urban folk—many Jews from the villages of East Europe were not, nor were many Italians and Greeks—but because their own economic needs and the demands of industrialism made it so. The free homesteads were gone. Three and one-half million came from Poland and stayed; two and three-quarter million from Russia; four and one-half million from Italy.

The arrival of new migrations coupled with the increasing involvement of the United States in foreign affairs were responsible for the intensification of ethnic-group politics in the twentieth century and for the burgeoning of a fourth phase of American nativism.

Rarely, in the nineteenth century, did foreign policy issues play havoc with the stable party loyalties of our large ethnic groups. The Irish were tried by Cleveland's alleged friendship for Great Britain, and Republican inroads were made on the Irish vote in 1888. But the dominant issues in American politics between 1845 and the end of the century were domestic. Only since World War I have foreign policy issues disrupted the long-term party alignments of major ethnic groups.

Both World Wars were opposed by the Germans and the Irish. The seventy-year-old German association with the Republican Party was almost interrupted by the 1916 slogan, "He kept us out of war." But German-Americans recoiled from the Democratic Party once Wilson took us into battle against the fatherland. They bounced back slightly with the disappearance of foreign policy issues in the 1932 and 1936 campaigns, when poor and middle-income farmers, regardless of ethnic background, were drawn to the agricultural programs of the New Deal. With the emergence of foreign issues again in the late thirties, however, the Republican tendencies of German voters were intensified, a posture they maintained, with a somewhat larger number of exceptions than usual in 1948, through 1952.

Irish-Americans were no less hostile to Wilson's English war and the Versailles Treaty which followed than were the Germans. However, the virtual absence of foreign policy issues for 15 years following the 1920 election (it still made good sense for mayoralty candidates in Irish cities to run against the King of England and the World Court) made it possible for the Irish comfortably to remain good Democrats. With the advent of World War II, Irish support for Roosevelt fell off sharply, as a close look at Irish districts in the 1940 and 1944 election shows.

The hard core of American isolationism during the thirties and early forties came from German-Republicans and Irish-Democrats. With the ending of the war and the rise of the Stalinist menace, however, Irish-Catholics could no longer maintain an isolationist position. Isolationism was transformed into nationalism and revisionism. The latter meant repudiating the Wilson and Roosevelt policies of aiding Britain against Germany. It also meant placing the blame for mistakes in World War II and the success of postwar Communism. The new nationalism meant Asia first, repudiation of the UN, and talking tough with Moscow and our allies. To these appeals, the Irish were congenial. But these very appeals were weapons in the arsenal of Republican leaders—McCarthy, Nixon, Knowland—and were used successfully in the 1952 campaign to split the Irish vote as it has never been split before.

It is this new turn in American politics that has finally allowed the Irish to participate in the tradition of American nativism. The first nativist phase was directed against them because they were new. The second hit them because they were Catholic. They were on the receiving end in the third phase because they were identified with the twentieth-century immigrant groups. Only now that Americanism has been mistaken for anti-Communism do the Irish march in the nativist pattern. The Know-Nothingism of the 1950s, so closely associated with the names of two Irish-Catholics, McCarthy and McCarran, feeds on the American fear of foreign domination no less than anti-Catholic persecutions thrived on hallucinations of Papal rule or than the Alien and Sedition Acts of 1798 and the waves of anti-Bolshevik terror which followed World War I were born in fright of foreign dangers.

V

THE PLURALISM OF AMERICAN POLITICS

Negro-rights issues, ethnic-religious group clashes, and class divisions have all formed the bases of party alignments in American political history. Not all three come to the fore at the same time or with the same intensity. Often they cut across each other. Class conflict (in a Marxian sense) dominated colonial politics (e.g., Paxton's Boys, Bacon's Rebellion, and Shays' Rebellion) because of the relative religious and ethnic homogeneity of the population and because slavery was not yet a significant social factor. During and prior to the Jacksonian period, class and ethnic cleavages combined to yield status politics (e.g., the Whiskey Rebellion was sometimes called "The Scotch-Irish Rebellion"). In the years preceding the Civil War, sectional division based on the slavery struggle and ethnoreligious conflict based on the nativist crusade molded American party alignments. From Appomattox until World War I, domestic issues dominated the party battle; with some exceptions, class politics prevailed (e.g., the Haymarket riots, Populism, and Bryan's Cross of Gold Speech). During the late twenties and the early thirties, it was status politics again; the upward thrust for status of the sons and daughters of the twentieth-century immigration combined with the economic drives of low- and middle-income groups generally to make the Democratic Party the majority party for the first time in 80 years.

Following the end of large-scale immigration and the quiescence of Negro–rights issues in the early thirties, the further development of class politics was often prophesied. The rapid urbanization of American society, it was predicted, would obliterate sectional politics based on a region's dominant crop, and would, by nationalizing domestic issues, cause the relationship of a voter's position in the economic system to govern his political behavior. The assimilation of the last of the immigrants would speed the process.

The prophets have tended to be correct only in those elections in which foreign policy issues were of minor importance. In 1932 and 1936, there was a sharp division between income classes in the distribution of the presidential vote.[5] In 1948, when most voters outside of the South were concerned about domestic economic questions, and when "foreign policy played no great part in voters' thinking about the election,"[6] there were much greater differences in Democratic and Republican strength between income and occupational class groups than in 1940 and 1944.

In the early forties, foreign policy issues—questions of war and peace—were important to the voters. In those years, the interests of various large ethnoreligious groups wrecked any theory of class politics. Then, the prosperous voters of the nation were much closer to the poorest electors in their presidential preferences, be-

cause, for a simple example, many wealthy Jews (the Jews were 92 per cent Democratic) and Poles voted Democratic, while many poor Italians and Germans voted Republican. In 1948, the lower-income groups were much more Democratic than they had been in the previous election,[7] because the great issue of intervention versus isolation had been taken out of the political arena. Low-income Irishmen, who in 1944 felt obliged to express their dissatisfaction with the prolonged and enervating war they judged to be England's, in 1948 could go back to voting their pocketbooks.

By 1952, the bipartisan foreign policy had disintegrated. Foreign policy issues again dominated the presidential campaign. Ethnoreligious feeling, dormant in 1948, rose to a considerable temperature in 1952. Again, the gap in Democratic or Republican strength between the high- and low-income and occupational-prestige groups was closed.[8] For example, the difference in the percentage Republican vote between the professional and managerial groups, on one hand, and the skilled and semiskilled workers, on the other, was narrowed from 58 per cent in 1948 to merely 25 per cent in 1952. The Polish lathe operator who knew his economic interests when he saw them in 1948 did not find the Taft-Hartley issue so compelling when he had a chance to punish the per-

---

[5] See Ogburn and Hill, "Income Classes and the Roosevelt Vote in 1932," *Political Science Quarterly,* L (1935), 186. Ogburn and Hill limited this study to a correlation of the vote with rental levels in forty Illinois cities, including Chicago. Also see Ogburn and Coombs, "The Economic Factor in the Roosevelt Elections," *American Political Science Review,* XXXIV (1940), 719.

[6] Angus Campbell and Robert L. Kahn, *The People Elect a President,* (Ann Arbor, Michigan: Survey Research Center, University of Michigan, 1952), p. 57.

[7] See Elmo Roper, *N.Y. Herald Tribune* (June 19, 1949), p. 19, col. 4. Roper reported the figures for Boston, which he said were typical:

Per Cent Republican		
	1944	1948
Prosperous	57.4	61.6
Upper-middle income	50.4	45.4
Lower-middle income	35.4	27.3
Poor	32.2	17.3

[8] See Campbell, Curin, and Miller, "The Elector Switch in 1952," *Scientific American* (May, 1954), p. 34.

petrators of Yalta in 1952. The Irish-Catholic milkman who thought well of Harry Truman in 1948 could not forgive him four years later for his stubbornness in sticking with Secretary of State Acheson. The German wheat farmer who thought it better to vote for certain fixed prices under Truman than to gamble with Dewey in 1952 welcomed the chance to vote for a man who seemed to promise full parity and, at the same time, freely indulged in criticism of past Democratic foreign policies.

The urbanization of American society has not produced class politics mainly because America has been moving out into the rest of the world even more quickly than farmers have been moving to the city. And the hopes and fears of many of our ethnic groups soar in elections when foreign policy issues are at stake.

Two world wars and the menace of world Communism have intensified nationality and ethnic group cleavage as a basis for party division. What do these developments portend for changing party alignments? Incipient ethnic realignments were already noticed in 1952, when Irish-Catholic and Polish-Catholic voters switched more sharply from their Democratic affiliation than any other group.[9]

It has long been supposed, and, indeed, is still generally believed that the Republicans are more deeply divided on foreign policy issues than the Democrats. The reason for that belief is that for nearly one hundred years, the core ethnic groups in the Republican Party have been rural Yankees and rural Germans and Scandinavians. While the Yankees have generally endorsed participation in both world wars and in international organizations, the Germans and Swedes have not.

What has only recently been noticed is that the Democratic rank and file (party voters as distinguished from party leaders) have also been deeply divided on foreign policy issues. The Irish pull in one direction; the Jews, Italians (except in 1940), and Poles (until Yalta) pull in another.

The Republicans give the impression of greater division because German and Scandinavian voting strength is disproportionately represented by Senators from the Midwest (Bricker, Case, Dirksen, Hickenlooper, Langer, Martin, McCarthy, Mundt, Jenner, Schoeppel, Young, and Thye) and in the House by representatives from districts gerrymandered to favor rural (German-Scandinavian) voting strength. Irish voting power, on the other hand, is diluted in the big East Coast cities.[10] The Irish have concentrated on the organizational aspects of politics. While they have contributed the last nine Democratic National Committee chairmen, they have not exercised power in formulating Democratic foreign policies since the Spanish Civil War. Many Yankees have played key roles in making Democratic foreign policies (Acheson, Hull, Hopkins, Lovett, Marshall, Stim-

---

[9] Survey results show that although twice as many Catholics voted Democratic as voted Republican in 1948, Catholic voters split evenly in 1952. See Angus Campbell, Gerald Curin, and Warren E. Miller, *The Voter Decides* (Evanston, Ill.: Row, Peterson, 1954), p. 71.

[10] Democratic Senators from the East Coast states, since the war, have been straightforward internationalists. Democratic Irish-Catholic isolationists cannot be elected from the large East Coast states. At least four have been defeated since 1944. Two internationalists were elected, however—the late Brian McMahon (Conn.) and John F. Kennedy (Mass.).

son), however, and so have many Jews (Baruch, Cohen, Morgenthau, Rosenman) ; but not one Irish-Catholic.

The appearance of unity at the level of party leadership is deceptive, however; the split at the level of the party rank and file is, nonetheless, great. That is why Democratic presidential candidates are now threatened when foreign policy issues dominate a campaign. Even if Eisenhower carries out the main outlines of the Truman-Acheson foreign policy, the Republicans are less threatened in presidential elections as long as they can continue to do three things: first, adopt a *posture* of toughness toward the Communists and our allies (e.g., unleash Chiang Kai-shek, agonizing reappraisal, massive retaliation) ; second, rake over the coals of past Democratic behavior (e.g., Yalta, Communism in government, the Korean War) ; and third, throw an occasional bone to nationalist-isolationist sentiment among Republican Senate leaders (e.g., discard the Genocide Convention and the International Bill of Human Rights, appoint men such as McLeod and Hollister to administer international programs, endorse a watered-down version of the Bricker amendment). These actions will help to wean Irish- and Polish-Catholics from the Democratic Party and will also serve to comfort the doubts of German and Scandinavian voters.

What turn ethnic group alignments take in 1956 and in future elections depends on how foreign policy issues are debated. If the Democrats can succeed in keeping Yalta-type issues from dominating the campaign, they are likely to hold on to the Irish as a core ethnic group. If voters think Republican leaders are just as internationalist as the Democrats, and if domestic issues such as farm and labor problems primarily hold their attention, the Democrats will have a chance not only to gather the Irish closer to the bosom of the party, but to woo German and Scandinavian farmers along crop and class lines.

IV

THE FUTURE OF ETHNO-RELIGIOUS POLITICS

Although ethnoreligious group interest still plays a crucial role in shaping the pluralistic character of American parties, present immigration legislation will, as the years go by, considerably lessen its influence. Already one important development has resulted, in part, from the closing of immigration—the extinction of the old-style political boss. A battery of social changes has emerged to revolutionize the social function of the boss. The curtailing of immigration is just one factor—prosperity, education, the welfare state, population mobility, and mass media are others—but it is an important one. The last of the bosses —men who can deliver a bloc of immigrant votes for virtually any candidate —operate in areas which are most depressed and underprivileged. It is in the Negro, Mexican, Puerto Rican, and, to some extent, Italian neighborhoods where the old-style boss persists. The late Vito Marcantonio built his machine in the Puerto Rican slums of Manhattan's East Side. The recently dethroned George Parr, during the last 20 years, was able to deliver more than 90 per cent of the Mexican vote in Duval, Starr, and Webb Counties, Texas, to any candidate of his choice. But the Martin Lomosneys, Charles F. Murphys, and Frank Hagues are gone, if not forgotten.

Despite the disappearance of the

immigrant, one aspect of ethnoreligious politics that will undoubtedly survive for a long time concerns the political issues which divide our three great religious groups. While Protestant fundamentalists frown on gambling, many Jews and Catholics enjoy it. Bingo has recently been one of the hottest political issues in New York State. All members of the state Senate voting against its legalization were Republican Protestants. It is in the Protestant communities that the local option to enforce prohibition is exercised; never in Catholic towns and villages. Although Catholics and Jews are allied against many Protestants on gambling and liquor, it is the Protestants who join the Jews in opposing Catholics on the birth-control question.

The problem of the delicate relationship between Church and State usually finds Catholics at odds with Protestants and Jews. Two issues beginning to assume national significance are federal aid to education (including parochial schools) and the intrusion of religious teaching in public education. A bitter struggle developed in the 1954 election in New Jersey over the attempt of Governor Meyner to raise a twenty-five million dollar bond issue to build a state medical-dental school. Catholic authorities met the proposal as an attack on a projected medical school for Seton Hall, a Catholic university, and priests in Paterson and Passaic Counties successfully urged worshippers to vote against the measure when it was submitted to referendum.

Domestic political issues which divide our three major religious groups are not new. The point is that they will not disappear with the cessation of immigration and will not evaporate in the foreseeable future.

But the impact of such issues on national politics, with the exception of presidential elections in 1884 and 1928, has been slight. Under the federal system, issues which divide the religious groups will remain primarily local.

A major question still remains. How will the changing ethnic composition of our population affect major party alignments? We are still in a period when the shifting demography of our foreign-stock groups favors the Democrats, at least as alignments now stand. The total number of the foreign-stock[11] Italians, Poles, Greeks, Jews, Austrians, and Hungarians (all more Democratic in presidential elections) is still going up, while the total number of foreign-stock Germans, Swedes, and Irish is steadily going down. But the proportion of total foreign-stock Americans goes down precipitously each year. The census for 1950 showed only 25.7 per cent of the white American population classified as foreign-stock compared to 30 per cent just 20 years ago.

The present McCarran-Walter Act favors immigration which will tend, if present group loyalties obtain, to help the Republicans, because so few immigrants are allowed to enter from southern and eastern Europe as compared to northern and western Europe.[12] The evidence is overwhelming that recent English immigrants, Scandinavians, and non-Jewish Germans tend to adopt the Republican affilia-

---

[11] Foreign-stock means born abroad or one or more parent born abroad.

[12] Under the act, 154,657 aliens are permitted to enter each year: 125,165 from northern and western Europe, the rest from southern and eastern Europe. Proclamation No. 2980, 66 Stat. c. 36, 8 U.S.C. §1151 (1952). Actually, 63,649 northern and western Europeans were admitted in 1953, as compared with 18,582 southern and eastern Europeans.

tions of the high-status ethnic groups to which they belong.

The Democrats will fare only slightly better from emergency immigration legislation under current party alignments. Nonquota immigrants admitted in 1954 totaled 114,079. Of these, 34,456 were Mexican, 27,055 Canadian, 19,309 English, 15,501 Italian, and 42,935 German. The Mexicans were largely seasonal labor brought in to offset labor shortages in the Southwest. Of those Mexicans, French Canadians, and Italians who remain in the United States and become voting citizens (perhaps as little as one-third), a large majority will become Democrats as long as present alignments continue. A large number of immigrants from Germany are actually refugees from East European Communism arriving under the Refugee Relief Act of 1953.[13] Should, as may be expected, Yalta-type politics disappear, a large number of these will vote for Democratic candidates eight and twelve years from now.

The total number of immigrants— 208,171 in 1954—admitted under all current legislation is too small, however, to make much impact on the future of American politics. Some stimulation to ethnic- and nationality-group politics will result from the admission of Alaska and Hawaii as states. The total number of foreign-stock Asians is up to 350,000. To a very large extent, Japanese-Americans (the largest of the Asian groups) have been apolitical,[14] but the admission of Hawaii, where Japanese-Americans now constitute the core ethnic group of the Democratic Party, is likely to have a sharp effect on the voting habits of Japanese on the continent. In California, where 100,000 of them live, Japanese may become a pivotal force in politics. Asian-American involvement in American politics will grow rather than lessen as the Asian population expands and as the United States becomes more involved in Far Eastern affairs.

Two other potential sources of ethnic-group influence in politics remain to be discussed. Legal Puerto Rican migrations and illegal Mexican entrants now constitute two of the largest groups of newcomers to the United States. In 1953, 63,000 Puerto Ricans entered the United States. The number has been halved in the past two years, and some experts predict that migration will dwindle to a trickle by 1960. Nonetheless, Puerto-Rican Americans will be a sizable voting group within a decade and predominantly Democratic. Their influence will be local, however, especially in New York, since foreign policy will not involve them as a group. Mexican-Americans will also form an important local political force (Los Angeles is 16.5 per cent Mexican), but will not be influential in national politics.

Only a fundamental liberalization of our immigration laws will sustain the contribution which ethnoreligious group interests have made in shaping the American party system.[15] Liberalization is, in the immediate future, highly unlikely. The executive branch of the national government has con-

---

[13] 67 Stat. 400, 50 App. U.S.C. §1971 (Supp. 1955).
[14] See Forrest E. LaVioletts, "Americans of Japanese Ancestry" (unpublished Ph.D. thesis in University of Chicago Library, 1946).

[15] Whether that contribution has been a good or bad thing is not under consideration here. The normative aspects of the problem are discussed in the first chapter of the writer's book, *The Political Behavior of American Jews.*

sistently proposed the easing of our immigration statutes in recent years, but the Congress has just as consistently rebuffed it. The reason is that urban constituencies, by virtue of the fact that the president must win in the large urban states to prevail in the electoral college, can bring considerable pressure to bear on presidential candidates; but in Congress, urban voters are heavily discriminated against by overrepresentation of rural states in the Senate, and by gerrymandering and the seniority rule in the House.

Immigration policy is determined primarily by Congress, which is not as susceptible to pressure or blandishments from the executive in this matter as it sometimes is on critical foreign policy or financial legislation. The rural constituencies, so heavily overrepresented in Congress, comprise the old immigrant groups which oppose liberal immigration—Yankees, Germans, and Scandinavians in the rural Midwest, Yankees in rural New England, and Anglo-Saxons in the South. These are the groups which developed and nourished the tradition of nativism. Now they have been joined by the Irish. Only the Italians, Poles, and Jews, among the numerically important ethnic groups, support proposals for liberal immigration. These groups must be pandered to by presidential candidates, but they wield little influence in Congress.

Only reform of Congress (the end of gerrymandering by state legislatures and an end to seniority) coupled with constitutional reform (elect members of the House every four years concurrently with the president) might possibly get proposals for drastic revision of our restrictive immigration statutes through the House of Representatives. Since neither of these reforms is likely, the prospects appear to be dim.

Politics in America will be pluralistic for a long time. There are many factors working against class politics in addition to ethnoreligious diversity. But differences in ethnic-group interests will not, given present immigration legislation, play the large role in forming national party alignments in the last half of this century than they have in the past.

Migration and Voting Behavior in a Metropolitan Community*

Harry Sharp

The frequency with which urban residents vote varies considerably among different segments of the population. The degree to which this activity in the Detroit area is influenced by migrant status is the concern of the present report.

The data presented here are from interviews with a randomly selected cross-section of the adult population of the tracted area of greater Detroit. The interviews were taken in the spring of 1952 and 1954 as a part of the annual survey of the Detroit Area Study of the University of Michigan.[1] The voting behavior discussed below refers to that in the last national and local elections in which residents could have voted at the time they were interviewed. Only those persons who were eligible to vote in these elections are included in the tabulations.

Although social scientists have long been concerned with the problem of political inactivity, migrant status has not received a great deal of attention as a factor in the voting record of community residents. There is some data from previous research, however, which indicate that length of residence in a new area and the frequency of voting are directly related.[2] Unfortu-

nately, much of this research is restricted to quite small time periods (e.g., under or over two years' residence) and includes migrants not yet eligible to vote.

The Detroit data indicate that in this community the frequency of voting in national or local elections increases consistently and markedly with a greater length of residence (Table 1). For example, while only one out of every five eligible migrants who has lived in the area under five years voted in the last local election, there is a regular increase in voting with length of residence until three out of every five migrants in the community over thirty years are voters. As expected, natives are much more likely to vote than are recent arrivals. Migrants who have lived in greater Detroit for an extended period, however, are significantly more likely to vote than are natives. These general patterns are also seen when the likelihood of voting in the last national election, in both national and local elections, or in neither election is considered. Apparently, insofar as voting is an index of the degree to which different groups are molded into a cohesive communal social system, the "disorganizing" influence of migration diminishes with a great number of years in the new community.

* Harry Sharp, "Migration and Voting Behavior in a Metropolitan Community," *Public Opinion Quarterly*, XIX (Summer, 1955), 206–9.
[1] The Detroit Area Study is associated with the Survey Research Center of the Institute for Social Research of the University of Michigan.
[2] For example, see Ben A. Arneson, "Non-Voting in a Typical Ohio Community," *American Political Science Review*, XIX (November, 1925), 816–23; A. H. Birch and Peter Campbell, "Voting Behavior in a Lancashire Constituancy," *British Journal of Sociology*, I (September, 1950), 197–208.

TABLE 1. Distribution of Number of Years in the Detroit Area, Place of Longest Previous Residence and Rural-Urban Background by Frequency of Voting

	Frequency of voting				
Migrant status	*Voted in national election*	*Voted in local election*	*Voted in both elections*	*Voted in neither election*	*Number of sample cases*
Natives	77%	50%	48%	21%	435
Number of years in area					
Migrants					
5 years or less	50%	19%	35%	48%	123
5-10 years	63	32	36	32	142
10-20 years	68	39	39	29	199
20-30 years	70	49	49	22	224
30 years or more	85	60	60	15	240
Migrant's place of longest previous residence					
Michigan	68%	37%	35%	35%	162
Other North Central	70	39	38	29	166
South	61	42	40	36	218
Other U. S.	77	49	48	22	123
Non-U. S.	83	51	52	17	143
Rural-urban background					
Migrants					
Urban North	74%	39%	38%	24%	276
Urban South	70	48	47	27	81
Urban non-U. S.	80	50	51	20	80
Rural North	65	42	41	33	164
Rural South	56	38	35	41	141
Rural non-U. S.	89	51	56	11	70

Even within age, sex and socio-economic classes the relationship between length of residence and the frequency of voting is maintained.[3] It should be noted, however, that the tendency for migrants who have lived in the community for an extended period to vote more often than do natives is in large part a function of an age differential. Migrants in the area for long periods are considerably older, as a group, than are natives; and, as is known, voting and age tend to vary together. When only those

persons 40 years old or older are considered, native Detroiters are at least as frequent voters as are migrants who have been in Detroit over 30 years.

While it is probable that in some areas Negroes are relatively less likely to vote than are whites, recent data for Detroit indicate that Negroes in this community are voting at least as often as are whites.[4] Thus, the low

[3] For reasons of space, these tables are not included in this paper.

[4] Detroit Area Study, "Comparison of Election Behavior of Negroes with the Total Detroit Area Population," unpublished report of the Detroit Area Study, Survey Research Center, University of Michigan (hectographed), 1953.

frequency of voting on the part of recent migrants is *not* due to a high proportion of Negroes in this group.

Variations in the frequency of voting by place of longest previous residence are much smaller than those based on length of residence in the new community, as Table 1 points out. The comparatively low voting record of southern United States migrants to Detroit is usually matched by that of migrants from Michigan and the other states of the North Central region. Foreign migrants and those from United States regions other than the North Central or the South vote about as frequently as do native Detroiters.

While the "good" voting record of foreign migrants was expected,[5] the somewhat low voting frequency on the part of midwestern migrants was not anticipated. It is possible that migrants from these areas do not utilize the vote as a means of protecting their interests as much as do persons from more distant northern regions. Perhaps, through a greater familiarity with the community, migrants from the North Central states are able to employ other ways of expression with respect to the administration of governmental agencies. This is an area in which much more research is needed before well-founded hypotheses can be formulated.

As seen in Table 1, there is a tendency for rural experience to be associated with a reduction in the proportion of voters among Southern migrants. This relationship is present both for national and local elections.

---

[5] For example, see Gordon M. Connelly and Harry H. Field, "The Non-Voter—Who He Is, What He Thinks," *Public Opinion Quarterly*, VIII, No. 2 (1944), 175–87.

While rural migrants from northern United States regions voted in national elections slightly less frequently than did northern urban migrants, this was not the case for local elections. There is no evidence that a farm background is related to the frequency with which foreign migrants vote. In any event, length of residence in the Detroit area appears to be much more closely related to the frequency of voting than does farm background.

Migration is apparently associated with a low frequency of voting on the part of recent migrants to greater Detroit. Even when demographic and socioeconomic differences are taken into account, *the longer the length of residence in the community, the greater the likelihood of voting.* Southern migrants to the Detroit area and migrants from the North Central states are less likely to vote than are natives. Only for southern migrants, however, is a farm background associated with a lower frequency of voting. It should be stressed that both place of longest previous residence and rural-urban status are of secondary importance with respect to voting behavior. There is little basis here for predicting widespread political apathy as a result of a high rate of northernward or urbanward migration. Voting appears to indicate a level of involvement in and adjustment to the community which is much more closely associated with length of residence in the new area than with place and type of previous residence. It would seem that appeals for the purpose of "getting out the vote" might well be aimed towards recent arrivals in the community in addition to lower status groups, younger persons, and women.

Demographic Dimensions of World Politics*

Philip M. Hauser

Politics in general, as well as world politics, is a branch of engineering—social engineering—not of science. Yet the consideration of the demographic aspects of world politics is not an inappropriate subject for a scientific journal. It is the purpose of this article to point to ways in which the findings of the science of demography illuminate various aspects of the world political scene.

There are various ways in which this subject can be developed, but I have arbitrarily chosen to discuss population factors in relation to politics, broadly conceived, on the global and on the international levels, respectively. By "global" problems I mean those that concern the earth as a whole; by "international" problems I mean those that arise among the various political subdivisions of the globe.

GLOBAL CONSIDERATIONS

There is no world government charged with the task of achieving world order and performing other civil governmental functions for the earth as a whole. This, however, does not mean that there are no political problems of a global, as distinguished from an international, character. Some such global problems are in fact dealt with by the United Nations and its specialized agencies, which are, of course, organizations of individual sovereign nations rather than organs of world government. Examples of global problems—problems which transcend and cannot be contained within national boundaries—include health, weather, fallout, and the newly emergent problems of outer space. It is easy to demonstrate that the contemporary rate of world population growth also constitutes a global problem—one which would be of great concern to a world government if we had one, and one which is of increasing concern to various organs of the United Nations and the specialized agencies.

Although the first complete census of mankind has yet to be taken, it is possible to reconstruct, with reasonable accuracy, the history of world population growth. This history may be encapsulated in the following estimates of the population of the earth: at the end of the Neolithic period in Europe (8000 to 7000 B.C.)[1] 10 million; at the beginning of the Christian era, 200 to 300 million; at the beginning of the modern era (1650), 500 million; in 1950, 2.5 billion.

These four numbers constitute a measurement of one of the most dramatic aspects of man's existence on the globe, and they explain the purple language of the demographer in describing the changes in rates of popu-

* Philip M. Hauser, "Demographic Dimensions of World Politics," *Science*, 131 (June 3, 1960), 1641–47. Copyright 1960 by the American Association for the Advancement of Science.

[1] *Determinants and Consequences of Population Trends* (United Nations, New York, 1953), chap. ii.

lation growth during the modern era as a "demographic revolution" or "population explosion."[2]

The basis for the demographer's emotionally surcharged language may be summarized as follows.

1. The present population of the world could be produced from an initial population of two dozen individuals increasing at the rate of 0.02 per cent per year over a period of 100,000 years, and man has been on the earth for at least 200,000 to 1 million years.

2. The rate of population growth has increased enormously over the three centuries of the modern era (1650–1950), during which time it averaged about 0.5 per cent per year. Over this period the rate of growth increased from about 0.3 per cent per year between 1650 and 1750 to 0.9 per cent per year between 1900 and 1950. World population growth averaged 1 per cent per year between 1930 and 1940.

Now, a 1 per cent return per year, even compounded, would by our standards represent a meager return on investment. But it constitutes a fantastically rapid rate of population increase. One hundred persons multiplying at 1 per cent per year, not over the period of 200,000 to 1 million years of man's occupancy of this globe but merely for the 5000 years of human history, would have produced a contemporary population of 2.7 billion persons per square foot of land surface of the earth! Such an exercise in arithmetic, although admittedly dramatic and propagandistic, is also a conclusive way of demonstrating that a 1 per cent per year increase in

world population could not have taken place for very long in the past, nor can it continue for very long into the future.

The demographer's concern is not based only on considerations of the past. It is even more justified by postwar developments in population growth.

Since the end of World War II the rate of population increase has continued to accelerate and has reached a level of about 1.7 per cent per year. There is justification, indeed, for pointing to a new population explosion in the wake of World War II of a greater magnitude than that previously observed. At the rate of world population increase for the period 1800–1850, for example, the present population would double in 135 years; at the 1900–1950 rate, in 67 years; and at the postwar rate, in only 42 years.

Projection of the post-World War II rate of increase gives a population of one person per square foot of the land surface of the earth in less than 800 years. It gives a population of 50 billions (the highest estimate of the population-carrying capacity of the globe ever calculated by a responsible scholar) in less than 200 years! This estimate, by geochemist Harrison Brown,[3] is based on the assumptions that developments in the capturing of solar or nuclear energy will produce energy at a cost so low that it would be feasible to obtain all the "things" we need from rock, sea, and air, and that mankind would be content to subsist largely on food products from "algae farms and yeast factories!"

Moreover, the United Nations estimates of future world population indi-

---

2 See the objection to this phrase in "Statement by Roman Catholic Bishops of U.S. on Birth Control," *New York Times*, November 26, 1959.

3 H. Brown, *The Challenge of Man's Future* (New York: The Viking Press, Inc., 1954).

cate even further acceleration in the rate of world population growth during the remainder of this century. Between 1950 and 1975 the average annual percentage of increase, according to the United Nations "medium" assumptions, may be 2.1 per cent, and between 1975 and 2000, almost 2.6 per cent.[4] Such rates of increase would double the population about every 33 and 27 years, respectively.

It is considerations of this type that would make it necessary for a world government to exercise forethought and planning, which constitute rational decision making, in facing the future. This, of course, is the purpose of the projections. The figures do not show what the future population of the world will be—for the world could not support such populations. They do demonstrate that man, as a culture-building animal, has created an environment in which the rhythm of his own reproduction has been modified in such a manner as to point to crisis possibilities.

CRISIS POSSIBILITIES

The crisis possibilities are of several forms, each posing major world political problems. The first, we may note, is the ultimate crisis, which would result from the fact that the globe is finite[5] and that living space would be exhausted. Unless one is prepared to argue that future technological developments will enable man to colonize other globes,[6] it is

clear that present rates of population increase must come to a halt by reason of lack of space. No facts or hopes as to man's ability to increase his food production and to increase other types of goods and services can indefinitely increase man's *lebensraum* (or could do so even if we accept the absurd assumption that man, at terrific cost, could burrow into the earth, live in man-made layers above it, or live on the seas).

In the short run, let us say to 1975 or to 2000, world population will be confined to much more manageable numbers. The United Nations projects, on the basis of its medium assumptions, a world population of about 3.8 billion by 1975 and 6.3 billion by 2000.[7]

In the short run there is no problem of exhausting the space on the globe, nor is there reason to fear serious decreases in world per capita food supply, as is evidenced by projections of The Food and Agricultural Organization and others concerning foodstuffs.[8] But there is great reason to be pessimistic about the possibility of greatly increasing the average world level of living during the remainder of this century.

In 1950, world per capita income was estimated at $223.[9,10] In North

---

[4] *The Future Growth of World Population* (United Nations, New York, 1958).

[5] This fact is ignored by Roman Catholic bishops, see *New York Times*, November 26, 1959, and by the Pope, see "Pope Denounces Birth Limitation," *New York Times*, December 15, 1959.

[6] The impracticability of colonizing

other planets is considered by G. Hardin, *Journal of Heredity*, L (1959), p. 2.

[7] *Determinants and Consequences of Population Trends* (United Nations, New York, 1953), p. 23.

[8] W. H. Leonard, *Science Monthly*, LXXXV (1957), p. 113.

[9] "National and Per Capita Income of 70 Countries in 1949," *U.N. Statistical Papers, Series E. No. 1* (United Nations, New York, 1950).

[10] The calculations were made by using United Nations per capita income figures for each continent applied to revised United Nations estimates of 1950 population of continents to obtain revised aggregate income by continent and for the world, as shown in Table 1.

America, per capita income was $1100. Had each person on the globe enjoyed the North American level of living in 1950, as measured by per capita income, the aggregate world product in 1950 would have supported only 500 million persons, as contrasted with the actual world population of 2.5 billion. For average world income to have matched income in North America, aggregate income would have had to be increased about fivefold. To bring world per capita income by 1975 to the level enjoyed in North America in 1950 would require about a 7.5-fold increase of the 1950 level in 25 years. To do the same by 2000 would require a 12-fold increase in the 1950 world income within 50 years.

Even if the more modest income level of Europe ($380 per capita in 1950) were set as the target, great increases in productivity would be necessary, because of prospective rates of population increase, to raise average world income to the required level by 1975 or 2000. To achieve this goal by 1975, world income would have to be increased 2.5-fold over the 1950 level, and to achieve it by 2000, the required increase would be greater than fourfold. A decline in the rate of world population growth to that of the period 1800 to 1850—namely, to 0.5 per cent—would decrease by three-fourths and four-fifths, respectively, the projected world income requirements for attaining this goal by 1975 or 2000.

These considerations not only show the enormous difficulty of materially increasing the world level of living on the basis of present rates of population increase but indicate, also, the

weakness of the argument that a solution to the population problem is to be found in more equitable distribution of the world's food supply or of goods and services in general.[11] The equitable distribution of world income in 1950 would, to be sure, have raised the per capita income of Latin America by 31 per cent; of Africa, almost threefold, and of Asia, four- to fivefold, but it would still have produced a per capita income per annum of $223, only one-fifth that in North America and only three-fifths that in Europe (exclusive of the U.S.S.R.). The miserably low level of living of most of the world's population is attributable not so much to maldistribution as to low aggregate product, the result of the low productivity of most of the world's peoples.

These political problems of a global character may perhaps be better understood through consideration of their international aspects, special attention being given to the plight of the two-thirds of the world's population resident in the underdeveloped areas of the world, in Asia, Africa, and Latin America.

INTERNATIONAL CONSIDERATIONS

The short-run implications of present rates of world population growth are manifest in specific forms and in

---

A new world per capita figure of $223 was obtained, as compared with the published figure of $230.

[11] For the Communist position see F. Lorimer, "Population Policies and Politics in the Communist World," in *Population and World Politics*, ed., P. M. Hauser (New York: The Free Press of Grencoé, Inc., 1958); for the Catholic positions see "Pope Denounces Birth Limitation," *New York Times*, December 15, 1959; for the Socialist position, see J. D. Bernal, "Population Growth Is No Threat For a Free Society," *National Guardian*, December 7, 1959 (extract from J. D. Bernal, *Science in History*).

TABLE 1.   Population, Income, and Energy Consumed Per Capita, by Continent, about 1950. Source of Data, United Nations, Except Where Otherwise Indicated

Area	Total population number (thousands)	Per cent	Aggregate income Dollars[a] (millions)	Per cent	Per capita income ($)	Energy consumed per capita (kw-hr)[b]
World	2497	100.0	556	100.0	223	1676
Africa	199	8.0	15	2.7	75	686
North America	219	8.8	241	43.3	1100	10,074
South America	112	4.5	19	3.4	170	741
Asia	1380	55.3	69	12.4	50	286
Europe (exclusive of U. S. S. R.)	393	15.7	149	26.8	380	3117
U. S. S. R.	181	7.2	56	10.1	310	1873
Oceania	13	0.5	7	1.3	560	3543

[a] See footnotes 8 and 9.
[b] See footnote 33.

varying degrees of intensity among the various regional and national subdivisions of the globe. The distribution of the world's population and of the world's utilized resources, manifest in differentials in levels of living, is the result, of course, of millennia of human history. The demographic dimensions of international politics may best be comprehended against the background of differences among peoples in levels of living and the significance of these differences at this juncture in world history (Table 1).[9,12,13]

To note the extremes, North America in 1950, with about 16 per cent of the earth's land surface, contained less than 9 per cent of the world's

population but about 43 per cent of the world's income. Asia, in contrast, with about the same proportion of the world's land surface (18 per cent), had 55 per cent of the world's population but only 12 per cent of the world's income. Per capita income in Asia was at a level of about $50 per year as contrasted with a level of $1100 in North America. Despite the fact that such comparisons are subject to considerable error,[14] there is no doubt that a tremendous difference in per capita income existed, of a magnitude perhaps as great as 20 to 1.

The major factor underlying this difference is indicated by the contrast in the difference in nonhuman energy consumed in North America and Asia, respectively—over 10,000 kilowatt-hours per capita per year for the former in contrast to less than 300 for

12 W. S. Woytinsky and E. S. Woytinsky, *World Population and Production* (Twentieth Century Fund, New York, 1953).
13 S. Kuznets, "Regional Economic Trends and Levels of Living," in *Population and World Politics*, ed., P. M. Hauser (New York: The Free Press of Glencoe, Inc., 1958).

14 *Report on International Definition and Measurement of Standards and Levels of Living* (United Nations, New York, 1954).

TABLE 2. Estimated Population Increases, by Continent, 1900 to 2000[a]

Area	Population (million)					Average annual increase (per cent)[b]			
	1900	1925	1950	1975	2000	1900–1925	1925–1950	1950–1975	1975–2000
World	1550	1907	2497	3828	6267	0.9	1.2	2.1	2.6
Africa	120	147	199	303	517	0.9	1.4	2.1	2.8
Northern America	81	126	168	240	312	2.2	1.3	1.7	1.2
Latin America	63	99	163	303	592	2.3	2.6	3.4	3.8
Asia	857	1020	1380	2210	3870	0.8	1.4	2.4	3.0
Europe (including U. S. S. R.)	423	505	574	751	947	0.8	0.6	1.2	1.0
Oceania	6	10	13	21	29	2.3	1.4	2.4	1.6

[a] See footnote 4.
[b] Arithmetic mean of percentage of increase for 25-year periods.

the latter. The availability of nonhuman energy for the production of goods and services is perhaps the best single measurement available of differences in capital investment, know-how, and technology which account for the great differences in productivity and, consequently, in the size of the aggregate product available for distribution.

The other relatively underdeveloped continents of the world also had relatively low shares of world income as compared with their proportions of world population. Africa, with a per capita income of about $75 per year, and South America, with $170, were also well below not only the level for North America ($1100) but also the levels for Europe (exclusive of the U.S.S.R.) ($380), the U.S.S.R. ($310), and Oceania ($560). There is a high correlation among these areas between per capita income and amount of nonhuman energy consumed (Table 1).

These differences in levels of living, as it turns out, are in general inversely related to present and prospective rates of population increase. The populations of the relatively underdeveloped continents of the world are increasing at a more rapid rate than those of the economically advanced continents[4,15] (Table 2). Between 1950 and 1975, to use the medium projections of the United Nations, while the population of Northern America is increasing at an average annual rate of 1.7 per cent and that of Europe, at 1.2 per cent, that of Asia will be growing at an average annual rate of 2.4 per cent, that of Africa at 2.1 per cent, and that of Latin America at 3.4 per cent. Between 1975 and 2000, while the rate of increase for Northern America will average 1.2 per cent per year and that for Europe, 1.0 per cent, the rate for Asia will be 3.0 per

[15] Note the different definitions of area in Tables 1 and 2. In Table 2, which gives population projections to 1975 and 2000, "Northern America" includes only North America north of the Rio Grande; "Latin America" includes South America, Central America, and North America south of the Rio Grande. For the rough comparisons made, no adjustment of the data was necessary.

cent, that for Africa 2.8 per cent, and that for Latin America 3.8 per cent, a rate at which the population would double about every 18 years.

As I have indicated above, rapid increase in world population imposes a severe burden on efforts to raise levels of living. It is easy to demonstrate that the burden would become an impossible one for the economically underdeveloped areas should their rates of population increase follow the trends indicated in the United Nations projections.

For example, Asia, merely to maintain her present low level of living, must increase her aggregate product by 60 per cent between 1950 and 1975, and by an additional 75 per cent between 1975 and 2000. To raise her per capita income to the European level for 1950 while continuing to experience her rapid population growth, Asia would have to increase her 1950 aggregate income 12-fold by 1975 and 21-fold by 2000. Africa, to do the same, must increase her aggregate income 8-fold by 1975 and 13-fold by 2000, and Latin America would have to increase her aggregate income 4-fold by 1975 and 8-fold by 2000.[16]

To achieve a per capita income equal to that of Northern America in 1950 while experiencing the projected population growth, Asia would have to increase her aggregate income 35-fold by 1975 and 62-fold by 2000. Africa, to achieve a similar goal, would require 22-fold and 38-fold increases, respectively, in aggregate income, and Latin America, 12-fold and 23-fold increases.

These considerations provide additional justification for the use by the demographer of the phrase *population explosion;* and they certainly indicate the hopeless task which confronts the underdeveloped areas in their efforts to achieve higher levels of living while experiencing rapid population growth. The control of rates of population growth would unquestionably decrease the magnitude of the task of achieving higher levels of living in the underdeveloped areas, especially in those with populations that are large relative to resources.[17]

Increasingly large proportions of the population in the underdeveloped areas of the world are becoming concentrated in urban places. The continued acceleration in the rate of world urbanization during the first half of this century was mainly attributable to urbanization in the underdeveloped areas, which proceeded at a pace considerably above that in the developed areas.[18] I have had occasion to make projections of the urban population of the world and of Asia to 1975; these are presented in Table 3 as illustrative of what is in prospect in the underdeveloped areas of the globe.[19] For the rate of urbanization in Latin America and Africa is also accelerating.

---

[16] Calculations were based on revised data, as explained in footnote 10. For Latin America the calculations were based on a comparison of estimated aggregate income for "Latin America" in 1950, per capita income for "South America" being used.

[17] The "population problem" differs for areas with different ratios of population to resources; for example, see "Political and Economic Planning," *World Population and Resources* (Fairlawn, N.J.: Essential Books, 1955).

[18] P. M. Hauser, "World and Urbanization in Relation to Economic Development and Social Change," in *Urbanization in Asia and Far East* (UNESCO, Calcutta, 1957), p. 57, based on work of K. Davis and H. Hertz.

[19] P. M. Hauser, "Implications of Population Trends for Regional and Urban Planning in Asia," UNESCO Working Paper No. 2, U.N. Seminar on Regional Planning, Tokyo, Japan (1958).

TABLE 3. Summary of Projections of Urban Population for the World and for Asia, 1975[a]

Cities (category)	Population (millions) Projection for 1975			Estimate of increase in population 1950–1975 (millions)		Estimate of increase in population 1950–1975 (per cent)		Proportion of total population in cities Projection	
	Upper	Lower	1950	Upper	Lower	Upper	Lower	1975[b]	1950
The world									
100,000 and over	745	488	314	431	174	138	55	19	13
20,000 and over	1155	779	502	653	277	130	55	30	21
Asia									
100,000 and over	540	170	106	234	70	222	66	15	8
20,000 and over	544	283	170	374	113	220	66	25	13

[a] See footnote 19.
[b] Figures are based on the " upper " projection, which assumes urbanization of an increasing proportion of the population.

The projections for Asia indicate that in the 25 years between 1950 and 1975, in cities either of 100,000 and over or of 20,000 and over, urban population will increase by at least two-thirds and may perhaps triple. The lower projection is based on the assumption that the proportion of urban population in Asia will be the same in 1975 as it was in 1950. Under this assumption the projected increase would result from total population growth alone. But if it is assumed that the rate of urbanization in Asia will increase as it did between 1900 and 1950 while the total population continues to grow at the rate projected by the United Nations, then tripling of Asia's urban population is indicated.

Thus, while the nations of Asia are attempting to improve their miserable urban living conditions, their urban populations will continue to increase explosively—perhaps to triple within a period of less than one generation.

In the economically more advanced nations of the world, urbanization is both an antecedent and a consequent of technological advance and of a high level of living—a symbol of man's mastery over nature. In the underdeveloped nations, however, urbanization represents instead the transfer of rural poverty from an over-populated and unsettled countryside to a mass urban setting. In the economically underdeveloped areas of the world, urbanization is outpacing economic development and the city is more a symbol of mass misery and political instability than of man's conquest of nature.[18,20]

The prospect for individual nations, while variable, is in general the same —one of explosive growth. Between 1955 and 1975, according to the United Nations medium projections, the population of China will increase by 294 million persons and that of India, by 177 million.[4,21] That of

20 P. M. Hauser, ed., "Urbanization in Latin America" (UNESCO, New York: International Documents Service, 1961).
21 "The Population of South East

Pakistan will increase by 45 million persons, and that of Indonesia by 40 million, in these 20 years. Japan, although she has now greatly slowed down her rate of population growth, will, despite her already great population pressure, increase by an additional 27 million. To confine our attention to the Far East for the moment, smaller countries with the most explosive increases include South Korea, Taiwan, and Ceylon. Each of these nations is faced with a task of tremendous proportions merely to maintain her present level of living, let alone to greatly increase it while continuing to grow at the projected rates.

POLITICAL INSTABILITY

What will happen if the underdeveloped areas in Asia are frustrated in their efforts to attain a higher standard of living?

Warren S. Thompson devotes his latest book to providing an answer to this question.[22] The larger of these nations are not apt to remain hungry and frustrated without noting the relatively sparsely settled areas in their vicinities—the nations in the Southeast Asian peninsula, Burma, Thailand, and the newly formed free countries of Indochina, Laos, Cambodia, and Vietnam. (Vietminh, that is, North Vietnam, is already engulfed by Communist China.) Even parts of thinly settled Africa may be subject to the aggressive action of the larger

and hungrier nations as feelings of population pressure mount. Moreover, Communist China, the largest nation in the world by far, faced with the greatest absolute population increases to add to her already heavy burdens in striving for economic development, may not confine her attention only to the smaller nations within her reach. Her present actions relative to her boundaries with India and possible tensions over her boundaries with the U.S.S.R. contain explosive possibilities.

It is Thompson's conclusion that the larger nations in the Far East, including Japan, India, and Pakistan, as well as China, may resort to force to achieve access to additional resources under sufficient population pressure. The smaller countries may not be able to resort to force but are almost certain to require outside aid to prevent chaos. Furthermore, while neither Indonesia nor the Philippines is in a position to be aggressive or is easily accessible to aggressors, both, under mounting population pressures, are likely to continue to experience growing internal political instability.

Population pressure as a factor in political instability is not confined to the Far East. Populations of the Middle East and North Africa—the Muslim area (exclusive of Pakistan) —may increase from 119 million in 1955 to 192 million by 1975, an increase of 73 million or 61 per cent in 20 years.[4] As Irene Taeuber has noted, this is an area "where internal instabilities and conflicts of religious and ethnic groups create recurrent crises for the region and world." Taeuber observes that the immediate political instabilities in this area are attributable more to "diversities among the peoples and the nations than to population pressure or popu-

---

Asia (Including Ceylon and China: Taiwan) 1950–1980," *U.N. Rept. No. 3 on Future Population Estimates by Sex and Age* (United Nations, New York, 1958).

[22] W. S. Thompson, *Population and Progress in the Far East* (Chicago: University of Chicago Press, 1959).

lation growth."[23] But she points to the importance, in the decades that lie ahead, of economic advances to lessen tension in this region and to the barrier that rapid population growth may contribute to that development.

Latin America, although in large part still a sparsely settled area of the world, is already experiencing problems associated with rapid population growth which give promise of worsening. For Latin America, as has been reported above, is faced with a population increase of 86 per cent between 1950 and 1975 and of 95 per cent, almost a doubling, between 1975 and 2000.[4,24] Especially difficult in Latin America are the problems posed by accelerating rates of urbanization. Recent measurements of rate of urban growth in Latin America indicated that of 15 countries for which data were available, urban population in one, Venezuela, was increasing at 7 per cent per year, a rate which produces a doubling about every 10 years; even had growth rates which would double their population in less than 18 years; and only two (Chile and Bolivia) had rates of urban growth of less than 1 per cent per year.[20,25] Growth rates (total and urban) of the magnitude which Latin

America is experiencing are likely to add appreciably to the difficulty of raising living levels and are likely to worsen already existent political instabilities that threaten internal order and may affect world peace.

Finally, a fourth region of political instability to which the population factor is a contributing element, and one where it will be increasingly manifest, is sub-Saharan Africa.[23,26] Middle Africa is sparsely settled, but increasing knowledge about the area indicates high birth rates, decreasing death rates, and explosive growth. The United Nations projections indicate a population increase from 154 million in 1955 to about 202 million in 1975, or an increase of 31 per cent. The familiar syndrome of underdeveloped areas—malnutrition, disease, and urban and rural squalor on the one hand and aspirations for independence and economic development on the other—are now emergent in this most primitive continent of the globe. And here, as in the other underdeveloped areas, rapid population growth is likely to intensify political unrest.

In southern Africa another type of population problem is also a major element in a political problem that has grave implications for world order as well as for the stability of the Union of South Africa. This is the problem arising from the conflict between the indigenous people and European settlers manifest in apartheid. Rapid and differential rates of growth of native and European populations are likely to intensify rather than to allay conflict in southern Africa.

The tensions and political instabilities generated by explosive population growth in the economically under-

---

[23] I. B. Taeuber, "Population and Political Instabilities in Underdeveloped Areas," in *Population and World Politics*, ed., P. M. Hauser (New York: The Free Press of Glencoe, Inc., 1958).

[24] "The Population of Central America (Including Mexico), 1950–1980," *U.N. Rept. No. 1 on Future Population Estimates by Sex and Age* (United Nations, New York, 1954); "The Population of South America, 1950–1980," *U.N. Rept. No. 2 on Future Population Estimates by Sex and Age* (United Nations, New York, 1955).

[25] "Demographic Aspects of Urbanization in Latin America," UNESCO Seminar on Urbanization Problems in Latin America, Santiago, Chile (1959).

[26] *Social Implications of Industrialization in Africa South of the Sahara* (UNESCO, London, 1956).

developed nations have a special significance in the contemporary world, characterized by the bipolar conflict between the Free and Communist blocs and the efforts on the part of each to win the allegiance of the uncommitted nations of the world. This conflict has several demographic dimensions of importance.

THE FREE AND COMMUNIST BLOCS

The first of these dimensions is evident in the way in which population is distributed among the three political blocs into which the world is divided. For in 1955, each of these political groups—the free nations, the Communist nations, and the uncommitted nations—had approximately the same population. The Free and the Communist blocs, respectively, each have much to gain in the struggle to win the allegiance of the uncommitted third of the world's people. This titanic competition is focused primarily on South and Southeast Asia at the present time, because the bulk of the world's politically uncommitted population is located there.

In this war for men's minds, the competition between free-world and Communist ideologies, each of the contestants has powerful weapons. Apart from military power, which I will leave out on the assumption that a nuclear stalemate exists, the key weapons of the Communists, as is daily attested to by their propaganda, are the exploitation of the wide gap between the levels of living of the "have" and "have-not" nations and the attribution of blame for the misery of the "have-not" nations on the imperialistic and colonial practices of the "have" powers. Needless to say,

the fire of this propaganda is effectively fed by the frustration of the underdeveloped areas in their efforts to advance their levels of living, or in their efforts to win independence from imperial powers, where this is not yet accomplished.

The Communist bloc, with relatively little, but with increasing, surplus product, is attempting more and more to help the uncommitted nations in economic development. The U.S.S.R. may perhaps be departing from its postwar cold-war policy of trying to persuade uncommitted nations to accept its ideology by means either of internal coups or direct external aggression.

The chief weapon of the free nations, apart from the example of their free way of life, is, undoubtedly, the provision of assistance to the underdeveloped nations to help them achieve their economic goals.

Thus, the success or failure of underdeveloped areas to raise their levels of living has the most profound world political implications. The most important immediate international political question is the question of whether the free-world approach or the Communist approach is the more effective one for achieving economic development.

It is to be emphasized that this is not a rhetorical or hypothetical question. It is being answered by the course of events, the definitive test of achievement. It is being answered by what may be regarded as the most important experiments of all time—experiments under way in each of the three blocs of nations. A great race is on among the economically underprivileged nations to attain higher living levels—some by relatively free, and some by totalitarian and Communist methods. The contests involve nations within each of the great political blocs, for within each of them both economically advanced and underdeveloped areas are to be found.[27]

The greatest single race under way is undoubtedly the race between the leaders of the Free and Communist blocs, respectively—that is, the United States and the U.S.S.R. The U.S.S.R. has certainly served notice that, by its methods, it hopes to surpass the level of living attained by the United States, and in the not too distant future. Overshadowed only by the direct contest between the United States and the U.S.S.R. is the race between India and Communist China,[28] a race of special and direct immediate interest to the underdeveloped areas. For these mammoth nations, the two largest in the world, are bending every effort to achieve higher living standards—one through the Communist approach and the other by democratic methods. The outcome of this race will be of great interest not only to the underdeveloped nations in the uncommitted bloc but also to those in the Free bloc—the underdeveloped nations in Latin America as well as those committed to the Free bloc in Asia and in Africa.

The international political situation, then, as described above, gives a special significance to explosive population growth. For present and future rates of population growth may, indeed, prevent underdeveloped nations

from raising their levels of living. Simon Kuznets' examination of the evidence indicates that the gap between "have" and "have-not" nations is increasing rather than decreasing.[13] To the extent that underdeveloped nations are frustrated in their efforts to advance their living standards, they will, it may be presumed, be more open to the blandishments of the Communist bloc. Furthermore, if the underdeveloped Communist nations demonstrate that they can achieve more rapid economic progress than the underdeveloped free nations, the free way of life may well be doomed. Success or failure in this fateful contest may well hinge on the ability of the nations involved to decrease their rates of population growth.[29]

THE ALTERNATIVES

The "why" of the population increase, in an immediate sense, is readily identifiable. It is to be found in the great increase in "natural increase"—in the gap between fertility and mortality.[1] Quite apart from the precise timing of changes in the relations between mortality and fertility, it is clear that explosive growth can be dampened only by decreasing

---

[27] K. Davis, "Population and Power in the Free World," in *Population and World Politics*, ed., P. M. Hauser (New York: The Free Press of Glencoe, Inc., 1958).

[28] W. Lippmann, "China Is No. 1 Problem," *Chicago Sun-Times*, December 14, 1959; "To Live India Must Change Its Way of Life...," *Chicago Sun-Times*, December 15, 1959.

[29] Nor is population a factor in political instability only in the underdeveloped areas. There are many other demographic dimensions of world politics which cannot be treated here because of limitation of space. The authors of a recent symposium volume which it was my privilege to edit include further considerations of population as a factor in world politics. Especially pertinent are the articles by Kingsley Davis, Frank Lorimer, Irene Taeuber, and Quincy Wright, from which I have drawn material for this discussion.

[30] W. S. Thompson, *Population and Progress in the Far East* (Chicago: University of Chicago Press, 1959), chap. xviii.

natural increase. This is true for the world as a whole in the ultimate sense, with differences in timing for different parts of the world. For suggested solutions to the problems of present and prospective rates of population growth in the various subdivisions of the world through migration, foreign trade, redistribution of wealth, and similar means hold forth little promise, if any, even in the short run.[30]

There are only three ways to decrease natural increase: (1) by increasing the death rate; (2) by decreasing the birth rate; and (3) by some combination of the two.

Although it is true that decreased death rates were largely responsible for the population explosion in the past and are foreseen to be a large factor in the future, the adoption of a policy to increase mortality, or to diminish efforts to increase longevity, is unthinkable. Unless one is prepared to debate this, two of the three ways of decreasing natural increase are ruled out. For two of them involve an increase in death rates.

If longevity gains are to be retained, then, the only way to reduce explosive population growth is to decrease the birth rate. That is, the "death control" mankind has achieved can be retained only if it is accompanied by birth control. This proposition, even though it flows directly from the demographic facts of life, in view of prevalent value systems provokes heated debate of the type manifest in the press. Birth control has recently, indeed, made the front pages of the world press.

What is important about the value controversy under way is that it definitely affects global and international policy and action on matters of population and, therefore, on the crucial political problems involved. The most significant thing about all the available methods of birth control—a fact mainly obscured in the present public controversy—is that they are by no means adequate to the task of slowing down explosive world population increase, especially that in the underdeveloped areas. The great mass of mankind in the economically less advanced nations which are faced with accelerating rates of growth fail to limit their birth rates not because of the factors at issue in the controversy we are witnessing but because they do not have the desire, the know-how, or the means to do so. The desire to control fertility, arising from recognition of the problem, is, however, increasing. Japan is already well down the road to controlling its birth rate, although by methods which are not enthusiastically endorsed either by the Japanese themselves or by other peoples. China, India, Pakistan, and Egypt[31] have population limitation programs under way or under serious consideration, and other underdeveloped areas are showing increasing interest in this problem.[32] The changes in value systems which will create mass motivation to adopt methods of family limitation are not easily brought about,[33] but they are at least under way.

[31] "Japan's Population Miracle," *Population Bulletin*, XV, No. 7 (1959); "The Race between People and Resources—in the ECAFE Region," Part I, *Population Bulletin*, XV, No. 5 (1959), p. 89.

[32] *Asia and the Far East, Seminar on Population* (United Nations, New York, 1957).

[33] F. W. Notestein, "Knowledge, Action, People," *University—A Princeton magazine*, No. 2 (1959); P. Streit and P. Streit, "New Light on India's Worry," *New York Times Magazine*, March 13, 1960.

Birth control methods in use in the economically more advanced nations are not, in the main, well adapted for use in the underdeveloped areas. But the results of increased research and experimentation with oral contraceptives are encouraging,[34] and there may soon be a breakthrough on obtaining adequate means for the task of limiting population growth in the underdeveloped areas.

[34] See, for example, G. Pincus *et al., Science,* CXXX (1959), 81;——, "Field Trials with Norethnyodrel as an Oral Contraceptive" (Worcester Foundation for Experimental Biology, Shrewsbury, Mass., in preparation).

[35] Data are based on the following: J. J. Spengler, *Proceedings of the American Philosophical Society,* XCV (1951), 53; original data (for 1937) from "Energy Resources of the World," *U.S. Department of State Publication* (Government Printing Office, Washington, D.C., 1949), p. 102 ff.

CONCLUSION

The demographer and the increasing number of his allies, in directing attention to the implications of world population growth, are in fact pointing to major global and international political problems—problems that cannot be ignored. Needless to say, the solution to the problems is not to be found in appeals to the traditions of the past, sacred or secular. The solution is to be found in the policies and actions which man himself, as a rational animal, must work out and implement. The mind of man, which has conceived remarkable methods for increasing life expectancy, is probably ingenious enough to devise methods by which the population explosion can be controlled within the framework of man's diverse value systems.

Forms of Government and Socioeconomic Characteristics of Suburbs[*]

Leo F. Schnore and Robert R. Alford

The topic of metropolitan government has been widely discussed for a number of years, but there is a surprising dearth of information about forms of government employed by municipalities in metropolitan areas.

We are aware, of course, of the great

[*] Leo F. Schnore and Robert R. Alford, "Forms of Government and Socioeconomic Characteristics of Suburbs," *Administrative Science Quarterly,* 8 (June, 1963), 1–17.

number of separate municipalities to be found in these areas and of the fact that they have increased rapidly over the years.[1] Indeed, it is the proliferation of incorporated places and other units of government that is thought to give rise to "the metropolitan problem." In spite of much concern with this problem among urban planners and administrators, a recent critique by Sayre and Polsby concluded:

> Knowledge about suburban politics is at best highly generalized, for the most part unabashedly impressionistic. There are quite obviously many different kinds of suburbs—old, new, homogeneous, heterogeneous, Republican, Democratic, residential, industrial, populous, sparsely settled, upper class, middle class, restricted, unrestricted, and others. Most current generalizations ignore or blur these variations.[2]

Why do we find so little documentation of contemporary suburban political forms? One hypothesis is that the sheer variety of suburbs makes the task overwhelmingly difficult. Wood has offered the following tentative explanation:

> By and large, no muckrakers have appeared on the scene to describe in chapter and verse the inner workings of suburban politics in the way that big city bosses and urban political-business alliances were detailed fifty years

ago. This is not surprising; the number and variety of possible suburban political patterns make the documentation needed for sound generalizations an exceedingly formidable job. It is little wonder that we know most about our national, less about state, and least about local politics. The task of research expands geometrically as we go down the scale.[3]

Certainly the full diversity of suburban political patterns would be difficult to chart and analyze in any full and comprehensive fashion, but it is literally impossible to analyze any social or political phenomenon in its totality. It is probably the case study approach of many social scientists, which emphasizes the unique historical features of each city or political system, that has hindered the full development of comparative urban studies. It might be better to regard the great numbers of suburbs as an opportunity to gain general knowledge of the factors related to different political forms, since modern analytical techniques readily permit the handling of masses of data.

It is easy to classify cities according to form of government. Once this is done, other characteristics can be examined. The materials in Table 1, for example, are frequently cited. It is clear that the mayor-council form is most frequently found in the very largest and smallest cities. In contrast, the council-manager and commission plans are more often encountered in cities of intermediate size.[4]

---

[1] Amos H. Hawley, "The Incorporation Trend in Metropolitan Areas, 1900–1950," *Journal of the American Institute of Planners*, XXV (February, 1959), 41–45.

[2] Wallace S. Sayre and Nelson W. Polsby, "American Political Science and the Study of Urbanization," a paper prepared for the Committee on Urbanization, Social Science Research Council, July, 1961. See also Robert T. Daland, "Political Science and the Study of Urbanism," *American Political Science Review*, LI (1957), 491–509.

[3] Robert C. Wood, *Suburbia: Its People and Their Politics* (Boston, 1959), p. 177.

[4] Generalizations concerning city size and form of government may be found in Charles R. Adrian, *Governing Urban America* (New York, 1955), chap. viii; Stuart A. Queen and David B. Carpenter, *The American City* (New York, 1953), pp. 310–13; and Alvin Boskoff,

TABLE 1. Forms of City Government (U. S.), by Size

Population[a]	Per cent Commission	Per cent Mayor-council	Per cent Council-manager	Number
500,000 or more	0.0	94.1	5.9	17
250,000–500,000	21.8	39.1	39.1	23
100,000–250,000	20.6	42.6	36.8	68
50,000–100,000	19.7	34.1	46.2	132
25,000–50,000	15.5	37.1	47.4	283
10,000–25,000	14.6	45.6	39.8	800
5,000–10,000	10,0	60.6	29.4	1,146
All cities	13.0	51.2	35.8	2,469

[a] Population classified according to size in 1950.
Source : Adapted from Orin F. Nolting and David S. Arnold, eds., *The Municipal Year Book, 1958* (Chicago, 1958), p. 62.

If one should ask about systematic variations in social and economic characteristics of suburbs with different forms of government, however, the literature yields little more than a scattering of speculative assertions that are entirely undocumented. Adrian, for example, has held that "the upper-middle-class suburbs which are the homes of metropolitan businessmen are characteristically administered by a manager."[5] Even more typical is the kind of loose linkage between style of government and socioeconomic status postulated by Banfield and Grodzins:

The Sociology of Urban Regions (New York, 1962), pp. 230–33. The most sophisticated treatment of this subject came to our attention after this study was completed; see John H. Kessel, "Governmental Structure and Political Environment: A Statistical Note about American Cities," *American Political Science Review*, LXVI (1962), 615–20. Kessel deals with city size, rate of population growth, ethnic composition, location, and economic base. Each of these variables enters into our analysis, but here we confine our attention to *suburbs* rather than all cities for which data are available.

[5] *Op. cit.*, p. 206.

The independent suburban corporations, clustered around the central cities, exhibit a variety of social characteristics. There are fashionable communities inhabited by wealthy business and professional people who want and can easily pay for a high level of governmental services. Suburbs of this kind are generally very proud of their schools and of the business-like and impartial way in which their affairs are managed.... There are middle-class suburbs in which, characteristically, the residents are anxious to have a high level of local governmental service but, somewhat inconsistently, are also anxious to keep taxes down, at least until their mortgages have been reduced.[6]

The vast and sprawling literature on metropolitan government includes only one study that offers an empirical examination of the association between political characteristics and socioeconomic attributes of suburbs. A case study of the Chicago metropolitan area by Liebman posed the following question: "Do cities or suburbs,

---

[6] Edward C. Banfield and Morton Grodzins, *Government and Housing in Metropolitan Areas* (New York, 1958), pp. 18–19.

distinguished on the basis of their economic functions ... vary with respect to their political characteristics?"[7] It is the purpose of this paper to turn Liebman's question around, i.e., *to determine whether suburbs possessing different forms of government display measurable differences in social and economic characteristics.*

FORMS OF GOVERNMENT

The types of government recognized here are the three major forms employed by cities in the United States—*commission, mayor-council,* and *council-manager.* The problem of classifying these political forms along meaningful dimensions is a difficult one, and the following suggestions are necessarily tentative. The oldest form, of course, is the weak *mayor-council* system, under which the mayor possesses neither veto power over council legislation nor administrative power over city departments. The need for leadership in larger cities has strengthened the mayor's position in many cases, giving rise to the strong mayor-council forms. The various mayor-council forms remained the most popular mode of governmental organization in 1958, being found in over half of all U. S. cities having more than 5,000 inhabitants.

The *commission* form was created in 1900, and it spread rapidly to some 500 cities by 1918, but it has declined since that time. Under this form, three to seven persons serve as individual heads of separate administrative departments and act together as the policy-making body for the city. The use of the commission form de-

clined to 320 cities by 1958. The *council-manager* form is the newest, originating in 1908 and spreading since then to 885 cities by 1958. Under this form, a hired professional manager is responsible to the council for administration of the city's affairs.

The commission and council-manager forms were both essentially reform governments, but the council-manager form has proved to be more successful than the commission form, and it has replaced the mayor-council arrangement in a great many cities. This is probably related to the degree of *administrative centralization* characteristic of the three different forms. The commission form appears to be the least centralized of the three, since responsibility is divided among individual heads of departments, who apparently find it rather difficult to function collectively as a policy-making body. The weak mayor-council form is somewhat more centralized, since there is a council charged with appointing department heads, and responsibility can be fixed upon the council. The strong mayor-council form is still more centralized, and the council-manager form—under which the council functions much like a board of directors—is apparently the most centralized of all. The historical trend toward more centralized forms is probably due to the increased size and complexity of urban government. This may explain, at least partially, the decline of the weak mayor-council form, the failure of the decentralized reform government (the commission plan), and the success of the two strong forms: the council-manager system and the strong-mayor form, either with or without a chief administrative officer.[8]

---

[7] Charles S. Liebman, "Functional Differentiation and Political Characteristics of Suburbs," *American Journal of Sociology,* LXVI (1961), 486.

[8] The same view of the relative degree of administrative centralization produced by the different governmental

Both the commission and council-manager forms may be conceived as "businesslike" replacements for the mayor-council form, which was attacked at the end of the nineteenth century for its corruption. But the commission form was like an early nineteenth-century business: both were attempts to reflect the image of a few men working together for common ends—the "one big happy family" myth. Company unions emerged from the same ideology. (Although this myth has been perpetuated by twentieth-century corporations trying to promote employee loyalty, *structural* changes that embody the myth have seldom been contemplated.) Ideally, the commission was to operate like a small corporation with each member of the "family" running his own department and getting together once a week to talk over common problems. Urban conflicts and the exigencies of administrative requirements proved this conception of the nature of city problems to be unrealistic, at least in

its structural embodiment as the commission form. In contrast, the council-manager form is like a large twentieth-century corporation: the board of directors hires a plant manager, and there is no illusion of democracy, except through the distant intervention of the "stockholders" (the urban electorate), who get a chance to select members of the board at the annual meeting. This version of democracy, of course, is a far cry from the Jeffersonian ideal of direct democracy with continual checks upon representatives.

Here we are emphasizing the structural changes taking place as responses to new problems, rather than as conscious shifts in ideology. The commission form and the council-manager form were both seen as efficient and businesslike replacements of earlier forms when they emerged at the turn of the century, but cities have changed to other forms without any drastic revisions in ideological rationale. Businesslike efficiency was then and still is highly valued today, no matter what the form of local government. We do not know which structure is most likely to achieve this goal. And what of other goals? Democratic ideology, involving equitable representation to various socioeconomic groups and geographic areas, has continued to receive emphasis in American politics. Perhaps the conflict between these two ideologies—efficiency and representation—could be traced in cities which have experienced serious disputes over forms of government. More comparative research into urban history is needed on such topics.[9]

---

forms is presented in Amos H. Hawley, "Community Power and Urban Renewal Success," *American Journal of Sociology*, LXVIII (1963), 427–28. An early statement justifying the commission form held that "the essential elements of success, discarding, so far as city government is concerned, the theory of strict separation of powers, since the main functions of cities are similar to those of business corporations." Cf. E. S. Bradford, *Commission Government in American Cities* (New York, 1912), p. 193. This view implies that the commission form is more centralized than the mayor-council form, since there is no division of powers among commissioners. This may not be the case, however, if the functioning of commissioners as heads of divisions actually overrides their functioning as representatives of the city as a whole. Recent research on corporate, military, and governmental bureaucracies suggests that generalized responsibilities tend to be superseded in practice by highly specific responsibilities.

[9] Since World War II, school district reorganization has been a fertile field for the study of the conflict between the ideologies of representation and efficiency. See Robert R. Alford, "School District Reorganization and Community

Both the commission and manager forms imply that the city is essentially like a business, with few conflicts of interest, and therefore can function like an administrative machine. This view is sometimes challenged by organized labor, and for much the same reasons that legitimate unionism challenges the undisputed leadership of management in the corporation. The more the city government is seen by important and politically sensitive groups as the arena for the contesting of crucial and conflicting interests, the more a form of government (and election) which gives representation to more than one interest group is likely to be sought. Therefore, wherever labor union (other than old-line, apolitical AFL unions) are strong, we may expect the prevalence of the mayor-council form, with election by wards on a partisan basis, which will give representation to minority and working-class areas, largely Democratic in orientation. The nonpartisan election will be more prevalent in the "businesslike" forms (commission and council-manager) than in the mayor-council form. Size of city is also a factor, since (other things equal) we may expect that unionism will be stronger in the larger cities; the mayor-council form, with partisan elections, should therefore be more prevalent in such cities. Regional location should also affect the form of government, since the absence of traditional forms in the newer cities of the West should promote the form that is thought to be most appropriate to modern conditions, i.e., the council-manager form.

To summarize, the various forms of government can be ranked in terms of their *degree of centralization* and

related to the type of social and economic composition that we would expect to find in cities with those forms.[10] The commission form is likely to be found in older, less, modernized cities, where (1) the city does not face the kinds of problems requiring more centralized governmental forms, or (2) it does not have the aggressive community leadership which can produce political change. Commission cities should be at one end of a continuum of city characteristics indicating growth and modernization. The more centralized mayor-council form is likely to be found (1) in larger cities or (2) in cities where class cleavages have become politically relevant. The mayor-council form is somewhat difficult to delimit precisely because it is still found in all types of cities, but it should be found between the commission and council-manager forms when social and economic characteristics are compared.

---

[10] The relationship of political to social and economic characteristics of cities may be obscured if there are legal obstructions to a city changing its political form to one more appropriate to its social and economic character. In any large study of American cities, such factors as state regulations must be taken into account. For example, all forty-seven of Pennsylvania's third-class cities were required to use the commission form as of 1955. It is probable that the social and economic character of commission cities would be even more clearly different from the other types if these cities were not considered. Actually, the commission form is prominent in only three . states: Pennsylvania, New Jersey, and Illinois (see Adrian, *op. cit.*, p. 194). How suburbs differ from other cities is a problem that is beyond the scope of this paper. The authors, together with Harry M. Scoble, are extending the analysis to all cities with a population of more than 10,000 in 1960. In the present study, we were not able to distinguish between strong and weak mayor-council forms, but our current work incorporates this distinction.

Integration," *Harvard Educational Review*, XXX (1960), 350–71.

TABLE 2.   Forms of Suburban Government by Size and Regional Location

Size and location	Per cent commission	Per cent mayor-council	Per cent council-manager	Number
Size of suburb, 1960[a]				
100,000 or more	12.5	37.5	50.0	16
50,000–100,000	13.8	41.4	44.8	58
25,000–50,000	13.6	39.8	46.6	103
10,000–25,000	13.8	61.0	25.2	123
Regional location				
Northeast	21.2	63.6	15.2	132
North central	11.0	50.5	38.5	91
South	16.7	33.3	50.0	18
West	0.0	16.9	83.1	59
All suburbs	13.7	48.7	37.6	300

[a] Population classified according to size in 1960.

Source : Form of government was taken from Orin F. Nolting and David S. Arnold, eds., *The Municipal Year Book, 1959* (Chicago, 1959), Table VI.

The most centralized form of government—the council-manager system—should be found (1) in younger cities, (2) in cities facing problems requiring centralized leadership, or (3) in cities lacking a sustained challenge to twentieth-century business leadership.

Evidence for all these assertions is regrettably lacking, but at least some of them can be checked by means of census data and materials from the *Municipal Year Book.*

THE SUBURBS IN THE STUDY

For our purposes, we have assembled data on 300 suburbs lying within the twenty-five largest "Urbanized Areas,"[11] The aggregate sub-

[11] The "Urbanized Areas," with the number of suburbs they included given in parentheses, are: New York (74), Los Angeles (34), Chicago (30), Philadelphia (14), Detroit (22), San Francisco-Oakland (18), Boston (16), Washington (4), Pittsburgh (22), Cleveland (12), St. Louis (12), Minneapolis–St. Paul (4), Milwaukee (7), Houston (3),

urban population under study was 12,023,674 in 1960. Each unit in the study was an incorporated municipality having at least 10,000 inhabitants in 1940, and a series of some eighteen social and economic characteristics were assembled for each unit from various publications of the United States Bureau of the Census on population and housing in 1960. Table 2 provides some data on our sample in terms of the size and regional location of the 300 suburbs. The council-manager form tends to predominate in the very largest suburbs, while the mayor-council arrangement is most prevalent in the smaller suburbs, occurring in over six out of every ten in the smallest-size class. The commission form, which has lost popularity over the years since World War I, is found in a minority of suburbs in each size

Buffalo (5), Cincinnati (4), Dallas (4), Kansas City (1), Seattle (1), Miami (4), New Orleans (1), San Diego (3), Denver (2), and Atlanta (3). Baltimore, the twelfth largest area, contained no suburbs meeting the specifications of the study.

class. Regionally, the suburbs in the Northeast are notable for the frequency of the mayor-council form. Even more noteworthy is the large number of councils and managers in the West, where more than eight of every ten suburbs are administered by managers and where the commission form is lacking altogether. These western suburbs are of more recent origin.

Suburbs with each of the three forms of government show distinctive age profiles. If one measures "age" by observing the census year in which the suburb first included 10,000 inhabitants, commission suburbs are 47.5 years old, on the average. This compares with 37.5 years for mayor-council suburbs, and 28.3 for council-manager suburbs. With respect to the suburban economic base, over seven out of every ten commission suburbs (70.7 per cent) and 62.3 per cent of mayor-council suburbs are predominantly manufacturing subcenters. In sharp contrast, two out of every three council-manager suburbs (67.3 per cent) are predominantly trade and service centers, conforming to the popular image of the "bedroom town" or "dormitory city."[12]

---

12 The suburban economic base was taken from Victor Jones and Andrew Collver, "Economic Classification of Cities and Metropolitan Areas," in Orin

Before proceeding to a detailed enumeration of the social and economic characteristics of suburbs with different forms of government, it is desirable to indicate the association between form of government and form of elections. As Wood has remarked, "we know at least the extent to which nonpartisan elections prevail in the suburbs and the number of streamlined city-manager forms of government that have been established."[13] Actually, suburbs with both the council-manager form and the commission plan—products of the urban reform movement of the early part of the century—are likely to have nonpartisan elections. Table 3 shows that seven out of every ten commission suburbs and over eight out of every ten council-manager suburbs have nonpartisan elections. In contrast, well over half the mayor-council suburbs maintain partisan elections. The popularity of nonpartisanship in the suburbs, however, is evidenced by the fact that over six out of every ten suburbs in

---

F. Nolting and David S. Arnold, eds., *The Municipal Year Book, 1959* (Chicago, 1959), Table VI.

13 *Op. cit.*, p. 176. An association between form of government and form of election is noted by Adrian, *op. cit.*, pp. 190, 204. For a general discussion, see Charles R. Adrian, "Some General Characteristics of Nonpartisan Elections," *American Political Science Review*, XLVI (1952), 766–76.

TABLE 3. Forms of Suburban Government by Forms of Election

Form of government	Per cent partisan	Per cent nonpartisan	Number
Commission	26.8	73.2	41
Mayor-council	56.9	43.1	146
Council-manager	15.9	84.1	113
All suburbs	37.3	62.7	300

Source : As in TABLE 2.

TABLE 4. Social and Economic Characteristics of Suburbs by Form of Government

Characteristics	Commission	Mayor-council	Council-manager
Age and ethnic composition (%)			
Foreign-born	9.5	9.3	8.0
Nonwhite	8.7	5.1	4.3
Aged 65 years and over	10.3	9.2	8.9
Fertility and dependency			
Nonworker-worker ratio	1.42	1.43	1.43
Families with children under 6 years (%)	26.8	28.6	28.9
Cumulative fertility rate	1,477	1,542	1,556
Employment and socioeconomic status			
Married women in labor force (%)	28.6	29.2	30.3
Working 50–52 weeks in 1959 (%)	58.5	59.5	59.8
In white-collar occupations (%)	47.4	48.2	55.6
Completing high school (%)	42.1	45.6	56.0
Median family income, 1959	$6,816	$7,379	$7,977
Population growth and mobility (%)			
Median rate of change, 1950–60	−0.7	17.4	28.5
Suburbs losing population, 1950–60	53.7	20.5	15.8
Migrant, 1955–60	12.1	13.4	20.6
Moved since 1958	19.6	19.7	25.5
Housing (%)			
Housing units built since 1950	17.9	25.8	35.3
Dwelling units occupied by owner	56.9	64.7	65.7
Families living in one-family units	60.5	67.1	73.7

Sources : See footnote 15.

the total sample have adopted this mode of electing officials.

SOCIAL AND ECONOMIC CHARACTERISTICS

Table 4 shows the characteristics of the three types of suburbs. Unless otherwise noted, the values shown are unweighted means. Taken together, they provide convenient summary profiles.

AGE AND ETHNIC COMPOSITION. The three types of suburbs appear to differ systematically with respect to certain compositional features. Commission-plan suburbs contain not only higher proportions of foreign-born inhabitants, but also larger percentages of nonwhites.[14] The representation of

[14] The proportions of nonwhite and aged 65 and over were taken from U.S. Bureau of the Census, *U.S. Census of Population: 1960, General Population Characteristics* (Washington, D.C., 1961), Table 13 for each state. Unless otherwise indicated, the remaining characteristics were taken from U.S. Bureau of the Census, *U.S. Census of Population: 1960, General Social and Economic Characteristics* (Washington, D.C., 1961), Table 32 and 33 for each state. The growth rates for 1950–1960 were computed on the basis of data taken from *U.S. Census of Population: 1960*, Vol. I, *Characteristics of the Population* (Washington, D.C., 1961), Part A, "Number of Inhabitants," Table 8 for state; the rates of growth were adjusted for annexations of territory and population between 1950 and 1960 by ref-

minority populations is lowest in the suburbs with the council-manager form of government. With respect to age composition, commission suburbs also tend to have larger proportions of older persons. Both in age and ethnic composition, the values for suburbs with the mayor-council form are found to be intermediate between those of the commission and council-manager suburbs.

FERTILITY AND DEPENDENCY. Table 4 also shows the nonworker-worker ratio for the three types of suburb; this is the ratio of the number of persons *not* in the labor force (including children under 14 years of age) to the number within the labor force. It is clear that the three types are not distinguished from each other in terms of dependency, for their ratios are virtually identical. With respect to fertility, however, the suburbs reveal systematic differences according to type. Two measures are shown: (1) the proportion of families with children of preschool age, and (2) the cumulative fertility rate, i.e., the number of children ever born per 1,000 women 15 to 44 years old of all marital classes. Both measures reveal the highest values in the manager cities, intermediate values in the mayor-council suburbs, and the lowest values in the suburbs governed by commissions.

EMPLOYMENT AND SOCIOECONOMIC STATUS. Equally clear differences appear when the three types of suburbs are compared with respect to various indicators of employment and socioeconomic status. Employment stability (the proportion working from 50 to 52 weeks in the year preceding the census) is found to be highest in council-manager suburbs, where higher proportions of married women are found in the labor force. Again, mayor-council suburbs occupy intermediate positions on both measures, with commission-governed suburbs ranking lowest on the average.

Even sharper differences are encountered when various indicators of socioeconomic status are examined. Manager suburbs reveal the highest proportion in white-collar occupations (professional, managerial, clerical, and sales positions). Similarly, the highest proportions completing high school among those aged 25 or older are found in these suburbs. Finally, median family income is highest in manager-administered communities. In clear contrast, commission-governed suburbs rank lowest on each of these three measures, while suburbs with the mayor-council form of government occupy an intermediate position.

POPULATION GROWTH AND MOBILITY. The three forms of suburban government are associated with distinctive growth patterns over the past decade. Table 4 shows that over half the commission suburbs lost population between 1950 and 1960; their median rate of change, as a consequence, was negative. Mayor-council and council-manager communities, in contrast, grew quite rapidly, with the largest increments occurring in suburbs with the council-manager form of government.[15] In addition to the

---

erence to Table 9. For the importance of this adjustment, see Leo F. Schnore, "Municipal Annexations and the Growth of Metropolitan Suburbs, 1950–1960," *American Journal of Sociology*, LXVII (1962), 406–417. All the housing data were taken from U.S. Bureau of the Census, *U.S. Census of Housing: 1960*, Vol. I, *States and Small Areas* (Washington, D.C., 1962), Table 1 for each state.

[15] As noted, population change over the decade was measured within 1950

fertility differences previously noted, the three types of suburbs vary in the extent to which they have attracted migrants from other areas. The proportions "migrant"—defined as those persons aged five years or over who have lived in different counties in 1955 and 1960—are highest in the council-manager suburbs, lower in mayor-council suburbs, and lowest in commission suburbs. Moreover, exactly the same pattern is revealed in the statistics on residential mobility, where the question relates to the proportions who have moved into their current residences since 1958. As in the preceding comparisons, the striking feature of the data shown in Table 4 is the consistency of the results.

HOUSING CHARACTERISTICS. The final array of characteristics examined here refers to selected aspects of the housing stocks found in the three types of suburb. Table 4 reveals higher proportions of new housing in the council-manager suburbs, where over one-third of all the dwelling units were built between 1950 and 1960. Roughly one out of every four units is new in the mayor-council suburbs, and the comparable fraction is less than one out of every five in the commission suburbs. This finding, of course, is in accord with the expectations suggested by the differentials in population growth. Another set of differences has to do with housing tenure. Table 4 shows that although in all suburbs the dwelling units are more likely to be occupied by owners than by renters, the proportion is highest in council-manager suburbs and lowest in commission suburbs. Finally, the three

types of suburbs differ systematically with respect to type of residential structure. Although only three out of every five dwellings in commission suburbs are of the one-family style, almost three out of every four are designed for single-family occupancy in council-manager suburbs. Again, as in almost every comparison in Table 4, suburbs with the mayor-council form of government occupy a position that is between those of the manager and commission suburbs.

CONCLUSIONS

"Politically, the suburbanite is becoming increasingly important. His numbers alone make him a political factor to be counted."[16] It would seem that because of sheer numbers the suburbs themselves also warrant attention and analysis. This paper has been predicated on the assumption that we might begin the long-neglected study of suburban politics by giving some attention to the variety of political forms manifested in suburban municipalities and to their social and economic characteristics.

We found a whole series of systematic differences between suburbs having the three principal forms of government—commission, mayor-council, and council-manager. Although these differences were not great in every case, they were remarkably consistent. In general, we found the popular image of the council-manager suburb verified; it does tend to be the natural habitat of the upper middle class. In addition, however, we found this type to be in-

---

boundaries in order to control for differences in the extent to which the three types of suburb were able to annex surrounding territory.

[16] Robert H. Connery and Richard H. Leach, *The Federal Government and Metropolitan Areas* (Cambridge, Mass., 1960), p. 183.

habited by a younger, more mobile, white population that is growing rapidly. The type that is least similar to the mayor-council suburb in terms of political structure—the commission suburb—we found to be least similar to it in social and economic characteristics. Commission suburbs tend to include persons of lowest socioeconomic status and to be occupied by a slightly older population and by more members of minority groups. We also found that over half the commission cities were losing population during the 1950–1960 decade. In one characteristic after another, we found mayor-council suburbs occupying a position intermediate between those with council-manager and commission forms of government.[17]

We must introduce a note of caution concerning the problem of characterizing suburbs in terms of *differences* rather than predominant characteristics. Clearly none of the suburbs under study is heavily nonwhite nor populated by an absolute majority of persons over 65 years of age. Therefore, we cannot explain the differences in political structure in terms of these compositional characteristics per se. The causal connections are not as clear as they might be if we had found, for example, that nine out of every ten commission cities had over 70 per cent in working-class occupations, while only one out of every ten council-manager suburbs had such a high proportion of workers. It would then be far easier to argue that there was a

causal relationship present and to proceed to theorize about the connection between suburban occupational composition and political structure.

The kind of systematic tendencies actually found in the data argue for a different kind of connection between the social and economic composition of the suburb and its political structure. It is possible that there is a threshold effect in operation; thus if the white-collar population (with its typical characteristics, such as better education, higher income, single-family residence, and the like) constitutes a majority, then the political attitudes of this socioeconomic stratum will come to influence the political structure of the suburb, e.g., by favoring the nonpartisan and managerial forms. How these compositional features actually become effective through organizations and political parties must inevitably be examined by means of detailed case studies of the political histories of specific suburbs varying in these several dimensions.

Some of the implications of these patterned differences are obvious. The council-manager suburb, for example, tends to be in a more favorable position with respect to its tax base; not only does it have a white-collar population with higher average income, but it also tends to have a somewhat higher proportion of homeowners. Offsetting these advantages, of course, is the necessity for providing educational facilities for its younger, more fertile population. Other implications, however, are somewhat less obvious. To take an example from the political arena, we might consider the question of territorial annexation. Suburbs with different forms of government have had quite different kinds of experience in this area over the past intercensus decade. Only 28.1 per cent

---

17 It may be noted that most of these relationships between form of government and socioeconomic characteristics remain when partisan or nonpartisan suburbs are examined separately. Indeed, the ideal type of upper-middle-class suburb appears even more sharply delineated when only nonpartisan council-manager places are examined.

of mayor-council suburbs annexed territory between 1950 and 1960, and only a slightly higher proportion (31.7 per cent) of commission suburbs were able to add to their legal areas. In contrast, well over half the council-manager suburbs (54.0 per cent) were successful in extending their territorial limits.[18] Political *forms*, then, in conjunction with social and economic characteristics that accompany them, would seem to make a difference in certain phases of the political *process;* we find different outcomes consistent with the more centralized, modern character of the council-manager form.

Almost all of the foregoing discussion has been geared to a cross-sectional view of suburban government. We have examined various characteristic of three formal types of suburban government at a particular time. The pressing need would now seem to be for longitudinal analyses showing developments over time. Changes in form of government may be studied with relative ease.[19] In any case, the investigations should be broadly comparative in approach.

---

[18] Annexation data were taken from *U.S. Census of Population: 1960*, Vol. I, *Characteristics of the Population*, Table 9 for each state.

[19] See, for example, Edwin K. Stene and George K. Floro, *Abandonments of the Manager Plan: A Study of Four Small Cities* (Lawrence, Kansas, 1953); and Arthur W. Bromage, *Manager Plan Abandonments* (rev. ed.; Chicago, 1949).

The common denominator of health, welfare, and educational institutions is the function of maintaining or improving the quality of the population of societies in which they operate. The concept of *quality* implies the existence of norms or standards that serve as bases for evaluating the status of a society and its individual members. Such norms vary not only from one to another society but also within any given society over time. In large measure this variation is related to

8

HEALTH, WELFARE, AND EDUCATIONAL INSTITUTIONS

the organization and technology of the society, which are nearly always in a state of flux. Education adequate for an agrarian society is obviously not adequate for an industrial-commercial society, for example, nor are the institutional arrangements suited to the provisions of one type of education usually suited to the provision of another. Further, the norms of a given society are usually linked to the perceived potential for improvement. The so-called "revolution of rising expectations" reflects the shifting of norms in transitional societies.

Mass communication together with industrialization have probably lessened the variation in acceptable standards of living between societies. This tendency toward universal norms is perhaps best seen in the evaluation of health status. Good health is valued in all societies, and modern techniques to reduce illness and prolong life are diffused with relative rapidity even in preindustrial societies. The diffusion of health and medical technology has been a major factor in the sharp drop in mortality levels and a consequent rapid acceleration of population growth in many transitional societies. This, in turn, has created new problems for other institutional systems, including those of welfare and education.

Health institutions have served to accelerate population growth in ways other than simply reducing the death rate. They have also increased fertility rates, partly by permitting more people to survive to the reproductive ages and partly by reducing diseases and physical disabilities that cause sterility. Only in recent years has control of fertility been accepted as a major function of health institutions. Whether health institutions will be as effective in reducing fertility as in reducing mortality is problematical, since the norms supporting fertility control are neither so universal nor so strong as those supporting disease control.

Relatively few studies have been concerned with the influence of health institutions on migration. Indirectly, of course, a great deal of migration has been stimulated by rising population pressure on limited land resources stemming from reduced mortality. It is also probable that the urban concentration of health personnel and facilities has been a factor stimulating rural-to-urban migration, particularly for persons requiring specialized services.

Health institutions not only affect demographic changes but are also affected by such changes. The growth and distribution of population are important variables to be considered in the provision of health personnel and facilities. So, too, are the age and sex composition for the pattern of illness and injury varies widely for different age and sex categories. A thorough understanding of demographic structure and processes is basic to any rational planning of health services, while mortality and mortality rates serve as basic indicators of the effectiveness of such services.

Welfare institutions have traditionally cared for those whose conditions of life are below accepted standards, especially for reasons beyond their personal control. Like many other institutional functions, the responsibility for the provision of welfare has shifted in modern society from relatives and neighbors to specialized public and private organizations. Undoubtedly population growth and increased mobility have figured in this shift. Declining fertility has also entered into the pattern by increasing the ratio of aged dependent to those in the economically productive ages.

The demographic processes of mortality, fertility, and aging have always figured prominently in the creation of welfare needs. The loss of a family head is a major cause of economic deprivation. For example, 40 per cent of the families headed by a female in the United States were in poverty in 1963, compared with only 12 per cent of the husband-wife families.[1] Mortality was not responsible for all the broken families, but the figures do indicate the effects of the loss of a family head even in modern society. Economic deprivation is associated with relatively high mortality at all ages, especially among the very young, and thus may be viewed as a determinant as well as a consequence of mortality. There is also a positive association between high fertility and poverty in the United States. The linkage between these two factors is complex, with education probably serving as an important intervening variable. It is relatively easy to explain poverty as a consequence of high fertility, but less simple to explain why those already in poverty should have higher rates of reproduction, which also appears to be the case.

The aged constitute a disproportionate share of the welfare population in the United States and most other modern societies. Here it may appear that declining mortality is the principal cause, but, as Davis points out in an accompanying reading, the decrease in fertility has been the major factor in creating high proportions of aged in industrial society. Furthermore, continued fertility decreases needed to achieve population control will have the effect of further increasing the proportion of dependent aged in the future.

The relationships between migration and welfare institutions have not been extensively studied. On an international basis most of the early restrictive immigration legislation was aimed at barring those who seemed likely to become public charges, such as paupers, debtors, and the mentally deficient and diseased. It is a plausible assumption that differentials between states in welfare provisions influence internal migration in the United States, but the extent of the influence is yet to be determined. What is certain is that the extensive migration of low-income families and individuals from rural to urban locales and from the South to other regions has placed heavy burdens on the welfare institutions of the receiving areas.

Both health and welfare are intimately related to education in that those with substandard education are less likely to be healthy and more likely to be welfare recipients. Like all other institutional systems, education systems must constantly adapt to population changes produced by natural increase and migration. Migration usually provides the more difficult problems for educational systems because it is more variable and its effects are more immediate. Rural to urban migration has placed heavy strains on the urban school facilities in the United States as well as in many other nations. Rural areas that have sustained heavy population losses are usually forced to consolidate school districts or face

[1] Mollie Orshansky, "Counting the Poor: Another Look at the Poverty Profile," *Social Security Bulletin*, XXVIII, No. 3 (January 1965), 3–29.

excessively high operating costs. Population size also plays a part in the quality of education in that large numbers of students permit specialized programs which are not feasible where the number is small.

Although fertility and mortality are generally inversely related to educational level, it is difficult to measure the influence of education alone on these demographic variables because of the joint effects of other socioeconomic factors closely related to educational level. Robert O. Carleton has posited in the form of hypotheses a number of ways in which education might indirectly affect fertility through influencing the ends and norms of social action and altering conditions that obstruct family realization of desired family size.[2]

The accompanying readings provide a sampling of recent considerations given to the relations between demographic variables and health, welfare, and educational institutions. In the first selection, Mortimer Spiegelman provides a panoramic view of the implications of demographic changes in the United States for its health institutions. He emphasizes in particular the effects of population growth and its redistribution.

In the second paper, Kingsley Davis examines some of the welfare implications of population changes in industrial societies. Among the significant points he makes is that lowering fertility has created a high proportion of dependent aged, yet it must be lowered further if undesirable population growth is to be checked. Industrial nations therefore face the dilemma of population congestion or an increasingly high proportion of aged persons, both of which pose difficult welfare problems.

Frederick Jaffe, in the third selection, deals with the question of why low-income families have more children than they want, as indicated by numerous studies. The difference is explained in large part, he suggests, by their lack of access to guidance in effective birth control methods.

Another issue relating fertility to social welfare concerns the effects of income-maintenance programs that provide family allowances for each child. Earlier in this century a number of European nations used such allowances as a means of encouraging large families. Now they are more commonly incorporated in general welfare programs. (In a sense, tax deductions for minor children in the United States constitute a form of family allowance.) Critics of family allowance measures have argued that they tend to encourage population growth and may be self-defeating if intended to help the poor if poor families are thereby encouraged to have more children. Alvin Schorr examines the various arguments concerning the influence of family allowances and reviews the actual experiences of programs in Canada and France. The available evidence is

[2] Robert O. Carleton, "The Effect of Educational Improvement on Fertility Trends in Latin America," in *Proceedings of the World Population Conference, 1965*, IV (New York: United Nations, 1967), 141–45.

inadequate to permit refined measures of the fertility effects of family allowances, but Schorr considers them to be insignificant relative to the effects of other influencing factors.

The fifth paper, by J. Mayone Stycos, examines the effects of the rapid rise in the educational level of the Puerto Rican population on fertility. His data show a strong relationship between educational level, birth rates, and the practice of birth control methods. Stycos points out, however, that the drop in the birth rate lagged far behind the rise in educational levels in Puerto Rico despite a "most propitious milieu for fertility decline." The implications for other Latin American societies with less advantageous social and economic conditions are not favorable, Stycos concludes.

In the sixth selection, Harry Schwarzweller deals with another population living in unfavorable social and economic circumstances, one in the Southern Appalachian region of the United States. His concern is with the effects of education and migration on the living conditions of young men ten years after they had enrolled in the eighth grade of public schools in eleven mountain counties of eastern Kentucky. A majority of the former students had migrated from the region during the ten-year period. Comparing the migrants who could be located with those who remained in the region, Schwarzweller found surprisingly little evidence of educational selectivity. Migrants, however, scored significantly higher than nonmigrants on a level-of-living index. The amount of schooling completed was positively associated with level of living for the non-migrant population but did not appear to be an important influence on the level of living of migrants to other areas. Schwarzweller offers several possible explanations for this anomalous finding.

In the final selection, B. Alfred Liu examines the relationship between the educational development of nations and their population growth. Although he is able to demonstrate an inverse relationship between educational development and birth rate, his evidence does not warrant the conclusion that raising the educational level is an effective means of fertility control. However, he does suggest that the reduction of birth rates is a necessary step for educationally disadvantaged nations that wish to accelerate their educational development.

The Changing Demographic Spectrum and Its Implications for Health*

Mortimer Spiegelman

Both private enterprise and governmental agencies at all levels—Federal, State, and local—have come to recognize the need for an understanding of population characteristics and trends in their planning and administration. Depending upon the issues at hand, questions arise not only with regard to population size, composition, and distribution, but also on social and economic characteristics. The present paper explores the major implications that the structure and trends of the population have for health problems.

POPULATION CHANGE FROM 1940 TO 1970

POPULATION GROWTH. During the century ending in 1940, population growth in the United States was largely a product of a more rapid decline in the death rate than in the birth rate. Immigration was secondary to natural increase in this growth, but still an appreciable factor.[1] Since 1940, the situation has changed materially. Immigration is no longer an important element in our population growth, and a sustained high birth rate, rather than further mortality reduction, has since given us a large population increase. The 1960 census of population yielded a count of more than 180,000,000, including Americans abroad (Table 1). This marked an increase of almost one-fifth since 1950. According to projections by the Bureau of the Census, the population is expected to increase by about one-sixth in the 1960s, or to a total of around 210,000,000 by 1970. Viewed in longer perspective, a population increase of more than 50 per cent is in sight for the span from 1940 to 1970, which approximates the length of a generation.

Scientific advances and recent rapid population growth have contributed to present shortages in public health and medical care facilities and personnel. Because of the increase in numbers alone, there is urgent need for an expansion in both facilities and personnel during the present decade. For example, in 1959 the country had a ratio of 141 physicians per 100,000 population.[2] Simply to maintain this ratio, the number of graduates in medicine and osteopathy would have to be raised from 7,400 in 1959 to 9,600 in 1970. Merely to keep the ratio of dentists to the

---

* Mortimer Spiegelman, "The Changing Demographic Spectrum and Its Implications for Health," *Eugenics Quarterly*, 10 (December, 1963), 161–74.
[1] C. Taeuber, and I. B. Taeuber, *The Changing Population of the United States* (New York: John Wiley & Sons, Inc., 1958), pp. 292–97.

[2] This ratio includes both doctors of medicine and osteopathy. Public Health Service, 1959. *Physicians for a Growing America*, Report of the Surgeon General's Consultant Group on Medical Education, Washington, D.C. (Oct.), pp. 2, 3, and 67; Public Health Service, 1959. *Health Manpower Source Book*, Section 9, "Physicians, Dentists, Nurses." Division of Public Health Methods, Washington, D.C.

TABLE 1. United States Population from 1940 to 1960 and Projection to 1970 According to Age, Sex and Race[a]

			Age			
Year	All ages	Under 18	18–24	25–44	45–64	65 and over
			Population (thousands)			
July 1970 projected	208,931	74,148	24,317	48,166	42,265	20,035
April 1960	180,698	64,588	16,009	47,381	36,140	16,579
April 1950	151,807	47,026	16,128	45,610	30,748	12,296
April 1940	132,284	40,471	16,758	39,867	26,152	9,037
			Per cent increase in population during decade			
1960 to 1970	15.6	14.8	51.9	1.7	16.9	20.8
1950 to 1960	19.0	37.3	— 0.7	3.9	17.5	34.8
1940 to 1950	14.8	16.2	— 3.8	14.4	17.6	36.1
			Per cent distribution according to age			
July 1970 projected	100.0	35.5	11.6	23.1	20.2	9.6
April 1960	100.0	35.7	8.9	26.2	20.0	9.2
April 1950	100.0	31.0	10.6	30.0	20.3	8.1
April 1940	100.0	30.6	12.7	30.1	19.8	6.8
			Females per 100 males in population			
July 1970 projected	103	96	98	102	108	132
April 1960	102	97	100	104	104	121
April 1950	101	97	102	103	100	112
April 1940	99	97	102	101	95	105
			Per cent nonwhite in population			
April 1960	11.4	13.6	12.3	11.1	9.4	7.6
April 1950	10.7	12.7	11.7	10.6	8.6	7.4
April 1940	10.4	12.4	11.1	10.6	7.9	7.2

[a] Includes armed forces overseas and Americans living abroad; the age distribution for these in 1940 was estimated. Data include Alaska and Hawaii in all years.

Sources: Various reports by the Bureau of the Census and Current Population Reports, P-25, No. 98 (Aug. 13, 1954) and No. 241, Series III (January 17, 1962).

population near its present level of 57 per 100,000, the number of dental graduates would have to be doubled by 1975. In the case of nurses, both population growth and an increasing demand for services in the hospital, the doctor's office, and the home, and also in industry and public health have given rise to an estimate that about one-third more will be needed during the present decade.[3] Closely associated with these increased needs are the corresponding requirements for more paramedical personnel at all levels of training, from the professional to the semi-skilled.[4] Beyond these needs for health personnel engaged in providing services are the additional opportunities being created

[3] *Health Objectives for the Nation,* Public Health Service, 1961.

[4] G. St. J. Perrot and M. Y. Pennell, *Health Manpower Chart Book,* Division of Public Health Methods, Public Health Service, Washington, D.C., 1957, p. 1.

for research scientists in the medical and allied fields.[5]

Changed population attitudes and growth in voluntary health insurance, as well as advances in medical care practice, have led to a rise in the hospital admission rate from about 6 per 100 in 1931 to about 14 per 100 in 1960.[6] Although hospitals, nursing homes, and other medical care facilities must be accommodated to the size, characteristics, and trends of the population to be served, shifts in the patterns of disease and of patient care require important consideration in planning for economical administration. The importance of planning in order to meet population needs is clear in the implementation of the Hill-Burton program enacted in 1946 for the construction of hospitals and amended in 1954 to encourage construction of nursing homes, diagnostic or treatment centers, and rehabilitation facilities. An insight into population characteristics and trends will also be required to implement the Community Health Services and Facilities Act of 1961, with its provisions for the support of such out-of-hospital services as nursing care of the sick at home, homemaker services, and screening clinics for periodic health appraisal.[7] The demographic

structure and trends in localities and larger areas enter into the consideration of problems of environmental health, where the concern is essentially with preventive measures and safeguards against pollution of the air, water, food, and land.[8]

AGE. Since the pattern of illness and injury varies strikingly with age and sex, the structure of a population with regard to these two characteristics will bear upon its medical care and public health programs. At the two extremes of life—the ages under 18 years and ages 65 and over—the population in the country increased by more than one third from 1950 to 1960. Although smaller rates of increase are expected from 1960 to 1970, the gains in numbers will be very appreciable—almost 10,000,000 at ages under 18 years and about 3,500,000 at ages 65 and over. The number of young people—those at ages 18–24— actually declined from 1940 to 1960, but an increase of more than 50 per cent is expected in the decade ending in 1970. However, only a small increase is in sight by 1970 for the number at ages 25–44. For ages 45–64, a steady growth of somewhat over one-sixth is in evidence for each decade from 1940 to 1970 in Table 1.

As a result of these shifts, the proportion of the total population at ages 18–24 years and at ages 65 and over will rise from 1960 to 1970. On the other hand, a decrease is expected for the proportion at ages 25–44, while the proportions at ages under 18 and at ages 45–64 will be practically unchanged. With almost 30 per

[5] *Department of Health, Education, and Welfare, Part IV, Report on Manpower for Medical Research*, 1962. (Hearings before a Subcommittee of the Committee on Appropriations, U.S. House of Representatives, 87th Congress, 2nd Session).

[6] R. E. Brown, "Forces Affecting the Community's Hospital Bill," *Hospitals, J.A.H.A.*, XXXII (Sept. 16, 1958), p. 28, and (Oct. 1, 1958), p. 51.

[7] "Increasingly, communities are turning to surveys of their health needs as a means of determining benchmarks for planning, coordination, and the allocation of funds and services." D. W. Clark, P. H. Rossi, and R. Morris, "Community Health Studies," in *Public*

Health Reports, LXXVII (February, 1962), 114.

[8] Public Health Service, *Report of the Committee on Environmental Health Problems to the Surgeon General*. Washington, D.C., 1962.

cent of the total population at ages 45 and over during the current decade, chronic disease and mental health will continue as outstanding health problems.

SEX. The more rapid reduction in the mortality of females than of males is giving the country an increasing excess of women. However, this is not the case under age 18, which is influenced in favor of males by the sex ratio at birth. For the broad range from 18–44 years, during which most marriages occur, males and females will be practically equal in number by 1970, following a 30-year period with an excess of females. Most noteworthy is the trend in the sex ratio at ages 65 and over, from 105 females per 100 males in 1940 to an estimated 132 females per 100 males in 1970.

RACE. A relatively high birth rate and a rapid reduction in mortality have brought the proportion of nonwhites in the population to 11.4 per cent of the total in 1960, compared with 10.4 per cent in 1940. Each age group shared in this rise. With a social-economic stratification different from that for the white population, the nonwhites have a relatively greater concentration of the health problems usually associated with a lower level of living. However, the health situation of the nonwhites should improve the more rapidly with their economic advancement and also with an expansion of public health and medical care programs.

INFANCY AND THE SCHOOL AGES

However favorable the rates of morbidity and mortality in infancy and childhood may appear for the country as a whole, the many cases

of illness and death point up important health problems. Thus, in a total population of almost 65,000,000 children under age 18 in 1960, there were about 150,000 deaths during the year, of which nearly three-fourths were in the first year of life. In fact, about 70,000 deaths were recorded within the first week of life. Adding to this figure the like number of fetal deaths yields an annual toll of about 140,000 perinatal deaths, with prematurity as a major factor. It has been pointed out that the rate of decrease in infant mortality has slackened since about 1950, and the question has been raised as to whether further substantial reductions can be realized until significant gains are made with such problems as prematurity, congenital malformations, and other conditions associated with early infancy.[9]

For children under 15 years of age, the National Health Survey recorded recently 2,158,000 impairments, or at a rate of 41.0 per 1,000 persons in that age group.[10] Over one-third of these were orthopedic impairments, over one-fourth involved speech, nearly one-sixth related to hearing, and one-twelfth were visual. The same source also shows that more than one-sixth of the children under 15 years had some chronic condition; for 8 per cent of those affected, the condition involved some limitation of activity.

Data from the Crippled Children's Program of the Children's Bureau are also indicative of the magnitude of the problem of chronic conditions and

[9] I. M. Moriyama, "Recent Change in Infant Mortality Trend," *Public Health Reports*, LXXV (May, 1960), 391.
[10] U.S. National Health Survey, *Children and Youth, Selected Health Characteristics, United States, July 1957–June 1958.* Series C-1, October, 1959.

physical impairments in early life.[11] This program reported that 339,000 children under age 21 years, or 4.9 per 1,000, were under care in 1959. Here also congenital malformations play an important role, accounting for more than one-fourth of the cases. Nearly one-fifth of the cases were attributed to diseases of the bones and organs of movement; other conditions of appreciable frequency were cerebral palsy, crippling due to poliomeylitis, disorders of the eye and hearing, and impairments from accidents. Many of these crippled and handicapped children own their survival to improved pediatric care. For such handicapped children, their schooling may also lead to emotional problems if they are treated differently from the others. Also important among children are problems of dental health, nutrition, safety in a wide variety of circumstances, physical fitness, and the growing incidence of venereal disease.[12]

Such, in brief, are the major health issues in a child population increasing by an average of about 1,000,000 each year during the current decade. With the child as the focus, the issues involve the family, the physician, and both voluntary and public community agencies, particularly the school. Each has a vital part in an integrated program for child health and welfare.

EDUCATION

An educated public is highly health-conscious. Through articles on health in newspapers, magazines, and other mass-media, the public soon becomes aware of new medical and public health problems and of the scientific findings that may benefit health status. Such a public is receptive to improved public health and medical care services, especially those made known through community health education, and is also concerned with any undue lag in the application of new knowledge.[13]

An index to the rise in the educational status of our adult population is provided by the median school years completed by those aged 25 years and over. This median rose from 8.6 years in 1940 to 10.6 years in 1960, and the outlook is for a further rise to 12.0 years by 1970.[14] Contributing to this rise are increasing proportions enrolled in school, particularly at the early adult ages. Largely because of compulsory requirements, practically all children at ages 6–15 years are in school. At ages 16–17 years, the proportion increased from 68 per cent in 1947 to 83 per cent in 1959. Even at ages 25–29 years, there was a rise from 3 per cent to 5 per cent for the same period. Also noteworthy is the rise of 5-year-old children in kindergarten from 53 to 63 per cent.[15]

These increasing numbers and proportions of young people in school emphasize the role of school health programs in the national well-being. Although some generalities may be set out for such programs, they must

---

[11] *Crippled Children's Program Statistics, 1959*. Children's Bureau Statistical Series No. 63, Washington, D.C., 1961.
[12] Public Health Service. *VD Fact Sheet, 1960*. Venereal Disease Branch, Communicable Disease Center, Atlanta, Ga.

[13] H. Neal, ed., *Better Communications for Better Health*. The National Health Council, New York, 1962.
[14] Public Health Service, *The Costly Time Lag*. Washington, D.C., 1961.
[15] U.S. Bureau of the Census, *Current Population Reports*, Series P-20, No. 91 (Jan. 12, 1959) and No. 99 (Feb. 4, 1960).

necessarily be adapted to local circumstances and characteristics of the population served. The school offers unique opportunities for observing and securing care for health problems and remedial defects, for the formation of health habits, and for inculcating lifetime health attitudes.

Currently there is frequent reference to shortages of personnel with professional and subprofessional training. The principal ages at which such skills are acquired fall in the 18–24 year range, where an increase of over 8,000,000 is expected from 1960 to 1970. If the proportions remaining in school continue to rise, these shortages may be alleviated in some degree; the health professions and allied occupations will naturally look for their fair share.[17]

MARRIAGE AND THE FAMILY

Both morbidity and mortality data indicate a better health status for the married than for the unmarried.[18] This is usually attributed to selective factors; many in a seriously impaired state of health elect to stay out of marriage and others in poor physical condition, but willing to marry, are passed by. Marriage is also presumed beneficial to emotional health and offers the advantage of family care to a spouse in case of illness.

The advantages of family life have been accruing to increasing proportions of the population since 1940, as evident in Table 2. For example, the

proportion of young women at ages 18–24 years who are married rose from 42.5 per cent in 1940 to 55.5 per cent in 1961. Over the same period, the proportion of married men at ages 25–44 years increased from 75.6 per cent to 83.7 per cent. However, it may be asked whether the selective factors related to health have weakened with the rapid rise in proportions married, particularly in view of the marked reduction in average age at marriage.[19] Not only have the proportions married increased, but also the proportions with dependent children. In the short period from 1952 to 1960, the proportion of husbands at ages 25–44 years with dependent children under 18 years rose from 79.1 per cent to 86.3 per cent.

Improved chances of survival have increased the average length of married life and, by the same token, have decreased sharply the proportion of families broken prematurely by the death of a spouse. This, in turn, has greatly reduced the social and economic burden of orphanhood, with its attendant health problems.[20] However, the more rapid improvement in the chances of survival for women than for men has increased the probability that a wife will outlive her husband; in other words, the chances of eventual widowhood have increased. Moreover, the average length of widowhood

[16] U.S. Bureau of the Census, *Current Population Reports*, Series P-20, No. 101 (May 22, 1960). For a longer-term trend, see E. H. Bernert, *America's Children*, chap. v (New York: John Wiley & Sons, Inc., 1958).

[17] *New Careers in the Health Sciences*, National Health Council, New York, 1961.

[18] D. Shurtleff, "Mortality and Marital Status," in *Public Health Reports*, LXX (March, 1955), p. 248. Several reports in Series B of the reports of the U.S. National Health Survey present data separately for women working and women usually keeping house.

[19] U.S. Bureau of the Census, *Current Population Reports*, Series P-20, No. 114 (January 31, 1962).

[20] M. Spiegelman, *Significant Mortality and Morbidity Trends in the United States Since 1900* (Philadelphia: American College of Life Underwriters, 1962), p. 11.

TABLE 2. United States Population According to Marital Status, Living Arrangements, Child Dependency, and Family Income and Education of Husband, for Broad Age Groups, at Various Times From 1940 to 1961

Year ; characteristic	All ages	Under 18	18–24	25–44	45–64	65 and over
			Per cent married			
	Ages 14 and over	*Ages 14–17*				
Males						
March 1961	68.8	0.4	32.4	83.7	86.6	72.3
March 1950	68.0	0.3	33.5	82.7	82.7	65.8
April 1940	59.7	0.3	20.1	75.6	81.0	63.8
Females						
March 1961	65.3	3.9	55.5	87.3	73.8	37.4
March 1960	66.1	5.9	56.7	84.6	72.0	36.0
April 1940	59.5	3.5	42.5	78.9	70.7	34.3
	Living arrangements of civilian population, March 1961					
	All ages	*Under 18*				
Males						
In families	94.1	99.2	93.3	92.6	91.1	83.5
Unrelated individuals	4.8	0.4	5.3	6.2	7.5	14.1
In institutions	1.1	0.4	1.4	1.3	1.4	2.4
Females						
In families	92.0	99.3	92.5	95.4	86.2	67.6
Unrelated individuals	7.4	0.4	7.1	4.0	13.0	30.0
In institutions	0.7	0.3	0.4	0.6	0.8	2.4
	Per cent of husbands with own children under 18[b]					
March 1960						
No own children	40.7	35.4		13.7	57.3	96.2
One or more	59.3	64.6		86.3	42.7	3.8
All under age 6	15.0	62.1		24.3	1.2	0.0
Some under 6, some 6–17	17.9	1.9		33.4	6.3	0.4
All 6–17	26.4	0.6		28.6	35.2	3.3
April 1952						
No own children	44.8	42.4		20.9	62.6	96.2
One or more	55.2	57.6		79.1	37.4	3.8
	Family income and education of husbands, March 1957[b]					
Family income	100.0%	100.0%		100.0%	100.0%	100.0%
Under $2,000	12.8	11.4		6.4	12.8	41.4
$2,000–$3,999	21.9	38.1		20.0	20.0	28.4
4,000–5,999	29.8	33.1		35.7	25.9	14.8
6,000 and over	35.5	17.5		37.9	41.4	15.4
Median school years completed	10.8	12.2		12.1	9.0	8.2

[a] All data relate to the civilian population except for April 1940, which relate to the total population. The data for 1960 and 1961 include Alaska and Hawaii.

[b] Data relate only to families with both husband and wife present.

Source : Bureau of the Census, *Current Population Reports,* Series P-20, Nos. 44, 83, 106 and 114.

has also increased with improvement in longevity.

At the older ages—65 and over—in 1961, only 37.4 per cent of the women were married, compared with 72.3 per cent for men, as Table 2 shows. This differential is produced not only by the greater likelihood of widowhood for women (since they have the lower mortality and are usually younger than their husbands), but also by the higher remarriage rates for widowers than for widows.[21] The advantage of family life for older men is also evident in their living arrangements. Thus, 83.5 per cent of the men were living in families in 1961, but for women the proportion was only 67.6 per cent. Of these older persons living in families, those who had lost their spouse still had the advantage of care by another relative.[22]

ECONOMIC ACTIVITY

Issues of health in relation to economic activity arise at most stages of life, even before entry into the labor force. An unhealthy or physically handicapped youngster would hardly prepare for a strenuous occupation. In fact, it is not at all unusual for industry to set some minimum physical requirements to applicants for employment. For the working years of life, health programs of industry, government, and voluntary agencies are geared to problems of accident prevention, the control of occupa-

tional disease, and general health maintenance. Finally, discussions of health problems during the later years have a role in preretirement programs offered by some companies.[23] The magnitude of these issues depends on the numbers and characteristics of the population involved and also upon the changes in the patterns of industry.

Most men up to 65 years are in the labor force. For ages 65 and over, the proportion has been declining steadily due to the shift from agricultural to nonagricultural occupations, the movement from rural to urban areas, and the development of our Social Security program and of private pension plans. For women, labor force participation rates have been moving upward at all but the young ages, where they are starting family life. For both sexes, the outlook is that these trends will continue.[24]

Although most males at the prime ages are in the labor force, the participation rates are greater for the married than for the single—most likely a reflection of their better health status and a sense of family responsibility. For example, in 1960 the labor force participation rates for males at ages 25–44 years were 98.7 per cent for those married with their spouse present, and 90.5 per cent for the single, while the others had a midway rate of 94.7 per cent (Table 3).

[21] P. H. Jacobson, *American Marriage and Divorce* (New York: Holt, Rinehart & Winston, 1959), p. 82.

[22] Two pertinent references are P. C. Glick, *American Families*, 1957, and H. D. Sheldon, *The Older Population of the United States*, 1958 (New York: John Wiley & Sons, Inc.).

[23] M. T. Wermel, and G. M. Beideman, *Retirement Preparation Programs: A Study of Company Responsibilities* (Pasadena, California: California Institute of Technology, April, 1961); W. H. Franke, *Preparing Workers for Retirement*, Institute of Labor and Industrial Relations, University of Illinois, Bull. 27 (January, 1962).

[24] U.S. Bureau of Labor Statistics, *Populations and Labor Force Projections for the United States, 1960 to 1975*. Bull. 1242, Washington, D.C., 1959.

TABLE 3. Characteristics of Workers According to Age and Sex, United States, 1960

Characteristic	All ages	Under 18	18–24	25–44	45–64	65 and over
		Civilian labor force as a per cent of the civilian noninstitutional population[a]				
Males	80.4	34.0	82.2	97.6	91.9	33.1
Married, spouse present	89.2		97.1	98.7	93.7	36.6
Single	60.2	33.9	74.8	90.5	80.1	31.2
Other	63.1		82.7	94.7	83.2	22.7
Females	36.7	20.9	47.6	39.8	44.3	10.7
Married, spouse present	31.9	16.8	31.6	33.1	36.0	6.7
Single	48.0	20.9	67.6	83.2	79.8	24.3
Other	41.6		56.0	67.1	60.0	11.4
		Employed persons as a per cent of the civilian labor force				
Males	94.6	86.7	89.5	95.7	95.7	95.8
In agriculture	9.9	25.0	9.7	6.8	10.4	24.2
In nonagricultural industries	84.7	61.7	79.8	88.9	85.3	71.6
Females	94.1	87.1	90.1	94.6	96.1	97.2
In agriculture	4.4	10.1	2.4	4.0	4.8	7.5
In nonagricultural industries	89.7	77.0	87.7	90.6	91.3	89.7
		Persons in occupational group as a per cent of employed persons				
		Ages 14–19	Ages 20–24			
Males	100.0	100.0	100.0	100.0	100.0	100.0
White-collar occupations	37.3	22.4	30.5	40.2	37.8	38.4
Blue-collar occupations	46.2	44.9	55.1	48.2	44.7	25.9
Service occupations	6.6	10.8	5.9	5.1	7.2	11.0
Farm occupations	9.9	21.9	8.5	6.5	10.3	24.7
Females	100.0	100.0	100.0	100.0	100.0	100.0
White-collar occupations	54.6	50.7	69.1	55.4	51.8	43.1
Blue-collar occupations	16.4	7.2	12.2	19.4	17.2	11.1
Service occupations	24.5	35.9	16.5	21.2	26.2	38.4
Farm occupations	4.5	7.2	2.2	4.0	4.8	7.4

[a] Per cent not shown where base is less than 50,000.

Source : Bureau of the Census, Current Population Reports, Series P-20, No. 105, Table 1 (Nov. 2, 1960); Bureau of Labor Statistics, Special Labor Force Report, No. 14, Tables B2, B4, C1, C2, C3, C8 (April 1961).

As expected, the pattern of labor force participation is quite different for women, family responsibility keeping the rate low for the married and the need for self-support making it high for the unmarried. Most men under 65 work full-time, but about one-fourth of the women workers of that age period are on a part-time basis.[25]

[25] U.S. Bureau of Labor Statistics, Special Labor Force Report, No. 10 (November, 1960).

The upward trend in labor force participation by women was shared by the married and also by those who had been married and had dependent children with them, as evident in Table 4, where 1951 and 1960 are compared. The only category of women not sharing in this rise are those who had been married but were separated, divorced, or widowed at the time of the survey and had no dependent children present.

In 1960, 18.6 per cent of the married women with dependent children under 6 years of age were in the labor force; the proportion was 39.0 per cent where the dependent children were all over 6 years of age. Substantially higher are the proportions for women with dependent children but without their husbands—39.8 per cent where the children were under 6 years of age and 66.2 per cent where all were over 6 years. For these sizable proportions of mothers at work there are important problems in the health care of their children during their absence; they may also experience strains on their own physical resources in tending to both their jobs and their homes.

The postwar era has witnessed the

TABLE 4. Women in the Labor Force as a Per Cent of Population According to Their Marital Status and Age, and Presence of Children, United States, March 1960 and April 1951

Presence and age of children; marital status; year	All ages	Age				45 and over
		14–19	20–24	25–34	35–44	
No children under 18 years						
Married women, husband present						
March 1960	34.7	57.4		66.2	55.1	26.7
April 1951	31.0	51.5		56.0	45.4	20.3
Other ever-married women						
March 1960	35.7	59.1		71.1	73.2	31.9
April 1951	35.8	58.9		81.1	75.5	29.7
Children 6–17 years only						
Married women, husband present						
March 1960	39.0		41.4		39.9	36.4
April 1951	30.3		35.0		32.3	23.8
Other ever-married women						
March 1960	66.2		71.1		73.3	56.3
April 1951	61.8		69.6		70.4	46.7
Children under 6 years						
Married women, husband present						
March 1960	18.6	9.7	18.3	18.6	19.4	27.3
April 1951	14.0	8.7	13.0	14.5	14.7	13.3
Other ever-married women[a]						
March 1960	39.8		48.2	38.3	38.5	
April 1951	37.2		30.5	35.2	46.9	

[a] Per cent not shown where base is less than 100,000.
Source: U. S. Bureau of Labor Statistics, *Special Labor Force Report*, No. 13, Table H, Washington, D. C. (April, 1961).

introduction of new and complex industrial and agricultural processes, new types of industries, and a growth of services in health, education, and recreation. With these developments has come a shift in the occupational structure of the working population. Between 1947 and 1960, the proportion of employed persons engaged in white collar occupations rose from 35 to 43 per cent and those in service occupations from 10 to 13 per cent.[26] Meanwhile, the proportions in blue collar occupations fell from 41 to 36 per cent and those in farm occupations from 14 to 8 per cent. There are marked variations according to age and sex in the proportions engaged in these broad occupational categories, as evident in Table 3. Thus, white collar occupations involved 54.6 per cent of the employed women, but only 37.3 per cent of the employed men. Similarly, larger proportions of women than of men are in the service occupations. On the other hand, blue collar occupations accounted for 46.2 per cent of the men, but for only 16.4 per cent of the women; a corresponding situation is found in the farm occupations. With advance in age after 20–24 years, the proportion of employed women in white-collar occupations falls off steadily, while the proportions in service occupations and farm occupations rise. For men, advance in age after 20–24 years brings declining proportions in blue-collar occupations, but for white-collar occupations a level of about 40 per cent is maintained from age 25. Both the service and farm occupations take added importance among men after age 25.

These differentials in patterns of economic activity obviously enter into consideration in program planning for occupational health.[27] A case in point is provided by the rapid automation of industry, with its increased demand for special skills and its virtual eradication of opportunities for the unskilled. A study group of the World Health Organization "observed that automation must be considered both as a source of possible improvements in mental health and as a source of new types of strain which will require full consideration and fully planned preventive action."[28] As an example of the favorable impact of automation on physical health, it has been remarked that ". . . closed equipment and control at a distance will reduce tremendously medical problems where they are related to chemicals."[29]

Studies in England and Wales have shown that the higher mortality of the less favored social economic classes is a product of their environment rather than of occupational hazards.[30] It seems likely that, with recent health trends, social-economic

---

[26] U.S. Bureau of Labor Statistics, *Economic Forces in the U.S.A. in Facts and Figures* (6th ed. May 1960), p. 41; and *Special Labor Force Report*, No. 14 (April, 1961), Tables C-8.

[27] H. N. Doyle, "Summary of Seminar on Administrative Practices in Occupational Health," *Journal of Occupational Medicine*, IV (February, 1962), p. 76; Maisel, A. Q. (ed.) *The Health of People Who Work*. The National Health Council, New York, 1960.

[28] World Health Organization, *Mental Health Problems of Automation*, Tech. Rept. Series No. 183, Geneva, 1959, p. 9.

[29] J. H. Foulger, "The Anticipated Effect of Automation on Industrial Medicine." *Industrial Medicine and Surgery*, XXIX (February, 1960), p. 86.

[30] The Registrar General's Decennial Supplement, England and Wales, 1951, *Occupational Mortality*, Part II, Vol. 1, "Commentary," H. M. Stationery Office, London, 1958, p. 20; and W. P. D. Logan, "Occupational Mortality," *Proceedings of the Royal Society of Medicine*, LII (June, 1959), p. 463.

class variations may have been reduced materially.[31]

TABLE 5. Net Migration of Population for Regions of the United States, and Population Change within Standard Metropolitan Statistical Areas, 1950 to 1960, by Color.

Area, year	Total	White	Nonwhite
	Net migration from 1950 to 1960, thousands[a]		
United States	+2,660	+2,685	− 25
Northeastern States	+ 336	− 206	+ 541
North Central States	− 121	− 679	+ 558
The South	−1,404	+ 52	−1,457
The West	+3,850	+3,518	+ 332
	Population in standard metropolitan statistical areas (SMSA's), thousands		
Total SMSA's			
1960	112,885	99,688	13,198
1950	89,317	80,343	8,973
Per cent change	26.4	24.1	47.1
Central cities of SMSA's			
1960	58,004	47,655	10,350
1950	52,371	45,499	6,872
Per cent change	10.8	4.7	50.6
Outside central cities of SMSA's			
1960	54,881	52,033	2,848
1950	36,946	34,844	2,102
Per cent change	48.5	49.3	35.5

[a] This includes net immigration from abroad.

Source : C. Taeuber, H. G. Brunsman, and H. S. Shryock, Jr. "Trends as Revealed by the 1960 Population Census of the United States," presented before the American Statistical Association, New York, December 28, 1961.

---

31 E. G. Stockwell, "Socioeconomic Status and Mortality in United States," *Public Health Reports*, LXXVII (December, 1961), p. 1081.

POPULATION REDISTRIBUTION AND MIGRATION

The decade from 1950 to 1960, which witnessed a marked growth of population, also saw a great redistribution of population within the country consequent to a movement to the West, a shift from rural areas to urban places and from cities to suburbs, and the migration of nonwhites from the South to the cities of the North.[32] During the decade, the West gained a net of 3,850,000 persons by migration, while the South lost 1,404,000 (Table 5). The Northeastern States had a gain of only 336,000, but the North Central States lost 121,000; each of these regions of the North had a gain of over one-half million nonwhites and a loss of whites. The outstanding feature with regard to age is that both Arizona and Florida more than doubled their population of persons 65 and over between 1950 and 1960. Although social and economic considerations are undoubtedly the leading influences in this great internal migration, health is also an element of some importance.[33]

As a result of the movement from rural areas, the urban population rose from 64.0 per cent of the total in 1950 to 69.9 per cent in 1960. In the latter year, Standard Metropolitan Statistical Areas (SMSA's) contained over three-fifths of the total population of the country; these areas are

---

32 C. Taeuber, H. G. Brunsman, and H. S. Shryock, Jr., "Trends as Revealed by the 1960 Population Census of the United States," Presented before the American Statistical Association, New York City, December 28, 1961.

33 For an interesting study with regard to health, see B. Malzberg, and E. S. Lee, *Migration and Mental Disease*, Social Science Research Council, New York, 1956.

essentially made up of adjacent counties economically and socially oriented to one or more central cities of 50,000 and over.[34] These SMSA's increased in population by 26.4 per cent between 1950 and 1960, but the central cities within them grew by only 10.8 per cent, and most of this was by annexation of adjoining territory. On the other hand, the area within SMSA's but outside the central cities, in which the suburbs are contained, had an increase of 48.5 per cent.

The migration of nonwhites to the central cities of SMSA's becomes evident in an increase of 50.6 per cent in their number from 1950 to 1960, compared with only 4.7 per cent for the whites. In 1960, almost 95 per cent of the SMSA population outside the central cities was white. The shift from city to suburb has been largely by the more affluent families, while the migrants to the cities are in poorer circumstances for the most part.

The sprawl of population outside the cities and the changed character of the population within them has given rise to new health problems in both areas.[35] Rapidly growing communities find they must develop or expand facilities while the older central cities face the task of modernization. These problems relate to hospitals and their associated services, the private practice of medicine, and the functioning of voluntary health associations and like community organizations.[36] Also affected impor-

tantly are the programs of local health departments and community plans for health services, including environmental and industrial health. Rapid shifts of population have made these problems acute because the issues must be faced by complex structures of local government, and frequently in the presence of competing needs.[37]

In addition to these problems arising from the movement of population seeking new permanent residence, there is the health problem of migratory workers, who are largely young persons of limited education, and include a relatively high proportion of nonwhites.[38] These health problems are important to the migrants themselves, to their employers, and to the communities through which they travel and in which they live temporarily. The problems arise not only in the provision of health services, but in gaining acceptance by the migrant workers and their families. It has been generalized that, "In many areas, the usual living and working conditions of seasonal farmworker families contribute to disease and disability."[39] Furthermore, "There can be no assurance that a service started in one location will be

---

34 U.S. Bureau of the Census: *U.S. Census of Population: 1960. Number of Inhabitants, U.S. Summary.* Final Report PC (1)–1A, p. xxiv.

35 *Urban Sprawl and Health,* 1958. Report of the 1958 National Health Forum conducted by the National Health Council, March 17, 18, 19, in Philadelphia, Pa.

36 J. D. Thewlis, "Metropolitan Hospital Planning—Conference Report."

Public Health Reports, LXXV (February, 1960), p. 141.

37 F. B. Taylor, "Governmental Aspects of Sanitation in the Urban Fringe," *Public Health Reports,* LXXV (February, 1960).

38 U.S. Department of Labor, *Farm Labor Fact Book,* Washington, D.C., 1959, pp. 71 and 112.

39 J. K. Shafer, D. Harting, and H. L. Johnston, "Health Needs of Seasonal Farmworkers and Their Families," *Public Health Reports,* LXXVI (June, 1961), p. 469; see also, Social Security Administration, "Health Services for Migrant Workers and Their Families," Research and Statistics Note No. 24 (October 8, 1962), Division of Program Research.

completed in another, even when a migrant follows instructions." Meeting these health problems is the responsibility of local, State, and Federal government, the employers of migratory workers, and also the workers themselves.

THE OLDER AGES

The population at the older ages— 65 years and over—has already been described as one with rapid growth in numbers and with an increasing predominance of women, about two-thirds of them unmarried and a sizable proportion not living with relatives. These characteristics become more pronounced with advance in age toward the terminal years. Thus, between 1950 and 1960, the population at ages 85 and over increased by 61 per cent, compared with a 25 per cent rise at ages 65–69 years. In 1960, the sex ratio was as high as 115 females per 100 males at ages 65–74 years, and 133 females per 100 males at ages 75 and over. The proportion unmarried among older women, according to data for 1961, rose from 53.4 per cent at ages 65–74 years to 78.5 per cent at ages 75 and over; a corresponding situation is found for males at the older ages, although the proportions unmarried are much smaller.

With advance in years at the older ages, the proportions remaining in the labor force fall off rapidly; among those still in employment, the proportions decline for wage or salary workers, but rise for the self-employed and private household workers. Although much is heard of the movement of older persons to milder climates after retirement, on the whole the migration rates of those 65 and over are smaller than those for younger persons. Increasingly poor health with advance in age is a factor in the declines in labor force participation and also the lesser rates of migration.

Aging, in all of its aspects from the biological to the social, has become a matter of national concern in the postwar period. The biological area—considered in a broad sense— encompasses studies in the physiology, biochemistry, and structural changes of aging.[40] A separate topic is the psychology of aging. The social aspects of the aged under study include their demography, their housing, their income maintenance (with due consideration to employment and retirement), and their health maintenance. On each of these topics, the literature continues to accumulate rapidly and is already vast.[41] Underlying this literature, either explicitly or implicitly, is the common theme of health.

Many demographic features related to the health problems of the aged require elucidation. Thus, it may be asked to what extent medical care needs are complicated by social needs. For example, it has been noted that the hospital admission rates and stays of the unmarried exceed those of the married.[42] Inquiry in this area may

[40] National Institutes of Health, *Research Highlights in Aging*, 1960 (Bethesda, Maryland, 1961), p. 4.

[41] Some convenient references are *The Background Papers*, White House Conference on Aging, Washington, D.C., January 9–12 1961; M. Spiegelman, *Ensuring Medical Care for the Aged* (Homewood, Ill.: Richard D. Irwin, Inc., 1960); Blue Cross Association and American Hospital Association, *Financing Health Care of the Aged*, Chicago, Ill. 1962; N. W. Shock, *Trends in Gerontology* (2d ed., Stanford: Stanford University Press, 1957).

[42] M. Spiegelman, *op. cit.*, pp. 110–15.

be extended to take into account the family status and living arrangements of the aged. This brings up another area in the demography of the aged about which very little is known, namely, the extended family.[43] This concept relates to those relatives of the aged living nearby, some even next door, but in another household, who may be available in time of need. So far, census data show nothing on this matter, although the monthly population survey by the Bureau of the Census furnishes a convenient vehicle for its collection.

Further study is needed on health as an influence toward retirement, and also on the effect retirement may have upon health.[44] In commenting on the relatively high mortality rates observed in some pension plans soon after retirement, Myers inferred that the effect was produced by a tendency for those in an unhealthy state to retire as soon as permitted. Thompson and Streib stated that "people in poor health tend to retire, and not that retirement affects health. It should be noted, of course, that our data does *not* necessarily refute the notion that a radical withdrawal from sustaining activities results in a decline of health." A point may be made as to what, if any, stresses are raised by retirement and how they manifest themselves.

Another pertinent question is whether or not the population is accumulating an increasing proportion of physically or mentally impaired lives at the older ages. On the one hand, the control of infections may be reducing the proportion of lives that would otherwise reach the older ages with organic impairments as sequelae. On the other hand, medical advances have prolonged the lifetime of many with physical impairments and thus brought them into the older ages; diabetics are a prime example. In fact, scientific advances and the consequent increased opportunities for "medicated" survival have added to the complexities of medical care at the extreme ages.[45]

An insight is needed into the changing social, economic, health, and medical care patterns in a sample of persons in their late productive years traced to their terminal ages. Inferences from such a life history may differ in many respects from those currently based upon comparisons of contemporaries at different ages. For example, the relatively poor economic status of those now aged 75 and over reflects a productive lifetime of low earnings by present standards, the experience of the depression of the 1930s, little opportunity to save, erosion of savings by inflation, small proportions in receipt of Old-Age and Survivors Insurance benefits, and rather low benefits. On the other hand, when those now in late productive life reach these advanced ages, they will have the advantage of savings by home ownership, life insurance and otherwise, many will have an income from private pensions, and all but a small fraction will be in receipt of OASI benefits of sizable amounts.

CONCLUSION

The boundaries of demography are hard to define.[46] Because of space

---

[43] M. Spiegelman, *op. cit.*, pp. 8–9.
[44] ———, *op. cit.*, pp. 14–19; note references to Thompson and Streib, Sheldon, Myers, and Hinkle and Wolff.

[45] In this connection, see J. Fletcher, "The Patient's Right to Die," in *The Crisis in American Medicine*, ed. M. K. Sanders (New York: Harper & Row, Publishers, Inc., 1961), chap. x.
[46] G. A. Lundberg, "Quantitative Methods in Sociology: 1920–1960," *So-*

limitations, the present discussion does not refer to such topics as wealth and religious affiliation, nor has it said anything on health attitudes in relation to demographic structure.[47] For many segments of the population, there are important gaps in the information on such matters as health

expectations, self-appraisal of health status, attitudes toward health maintenance, and attitudes toward financing and utilization of health services. Whatever the health attribute under consideration may be, it should be recognized at all times that the demographic structure of the country is dynamic, and that plans and programs are more properly guided by trends than by the current situation.

---

cial Forces, XXXIX (October, 1960), p. 19.

[47] For examples, see M. Spiegelman, *op. cit.*, pp. 63–80, 150–161; see also reports of the Series in Rural Health, Agricultural Experiment Station, University of Missouri, Columbia, Missouri; various reports on health problems and attitudes from the Agricultural Experi-

ment Stations of the Universities of Kentucky and North Carolina; and reports and papers based on a study of the health needs of older people by the National Opinion Research Center, University of Chicago.

Population and Welfare in Industrial Societies[*]

Kingsley Davis

In choosing a topic for the Dorothy B. Nyswander Lecture of 1960, I sought one that would explore the basic relationships between demography and public health, and the best way to do this seemed to be to discuss the population problems of the most advanced industrial societies. It is in such societies that medical science has brought the greatest improvements in death control, and where con-

sequently the ultimate demographic implications are more clearly foreshadowed. Further, by turning our attention to the demographic problems peculiar to the industrial nations, we can avoid the unconscious assumption that it is only in the poorer and less developed countries that welfare is affected by population trends. The truth is that each type of society has its characteristic populations structure—hence its own kind of problems and its own policy issues.

The industrial societies, as yet embracing less than a third of the world,

[*] Kingsley Davis, "Population and Welfare in Industrial Societies," *Population Review*, 6 (January, 1962), 17–29.

are still so new, particularly the recent arrivals like Japan and the Soviet
Union, that their demographic potentials have not fully evolved. It is clear,
however, that among their most
distinctive population traits are: (1)
their high proportion of aged persons,
(2) their high degree of urbanization,
and (3) their moderately low birth
rates. Two other traits that once distinguished them—their long life-expectancy and their rapid population
growth—are no longer theirs alone.
The underdeveloped countries are
rapidly coming abreast of the industrial nations in life-expectancy and
have for some time surpassed them
in population growth.

Whatever they are, the demographic features of industrial societies are
mutually interconnected and dependent in their causation and in their
consequences upon the defining trait
of industrialism itself—high per
capita output. This does not mean
that the relationships are obvious at
first glance, for indeed they are not.
It means, rather, that none of the
demographic traits is alterable without affecting other such traits or the
bases of industrialism itself. By definition, the problem of an industrial
society is not poverty. There is no
question of populations lacking the
means of subsistence. The problem,
rather, is how to distribute rights
and obligations in such a way as to
guarantee the continued progress of
industrial civilization. It is in terms
of this problem that I wish to discuss
the distinctive population trends of
advanced countries.

THE STRUCTURE AND CAUSES
OF AGING POPULATIONS

The problem of an aged population
is usually phrased as how to achieve

the welfare of older persons despite
their rising population. Another way
of phrasing it is how to deal with
older persons in such a way as to
maximize the welfare of all members
of society. With this in mind let us
first look at the changing dimensions
of the aged population.

Perhaps the best single index of
the entire age distribution is the
median age. In the United States the
median age rose consistently with
each census, from 1800 to 1950, but
the most marked rise was from 1900
to 1950.

	White population	
	Median age[a]	Years added in prior period
1800	16.0	—
1850	19.1	3.1
1900	23.4	4.3
1950	30.8	7.4
1959	30.2	−0.6

[a] For 1800 through 1950, from Henry D. Shel-
don, *The Older Population of the United States*
(New York: John Wiley & Sons, Inc., 1958), p.
138; for 1959, from U.S. Census Bureau, Current
Population Reports—Population Estimates (Series
P-25, No. 212, Jan. 26, 1960), "Estimates of the
Population of the United States, by Age, Color,
and Sex, July 1, 1957 to 1959," p. 5.

The slight reduction in 1959 is insignificant compared to the enormous
rise that preceded it.

The median age of course tells us
nothing about the relation between
specific age groups. Interesting from
an economic point of view is the relation of those in the dependency-prone
ages to those in the productive ages.
If we take the dependency-prone to
consist of those under 20 and those
60 or over, we find (as seen in the
last column of Table 1) that there
were, in the United States in 1900,

TABLE 1. Dependency-Prone Age-Groups in United States Population, 1900, 1950, 1959

	Ages 20–59 (000's)	Ages under 20 Number (000's)	Ages under 20 Per 100 Age 20–59	Ages 60 and over Number (000's)	Ages 60 and over Per 100 Age 20–59	Under 20 and 60+ Number (000's)	Under 20 and 60+ Per 100 Age 20–59
1900	37,340	33,771	90.4	4,884	13.1	38,655	103.5
1950	81,269	51,099	62,9	18,329	22.6	69,428	85.4
1959	86,708	67,883	78.3	22,512	26.0	90,395	104.2

TABLE 2. Age Distribution of Persons Aged 60 or Over, United States, 1900, 1950, 1959

	Total 60+	Aged 60–64	Aged 65–70	Aged 70–74	Aged 75–79	Aged 80+
1900	100.0	36.8	26.7	18.1	10.7	7.7
1950	100.0	33.1	27.3	18.6	11.7	9.3
1959	100.0	31.7	25.5	19.0	13.2	10.6

about 104 of them for each hundred persons aged 20 through 59. By 1950, interestingly enough, the ratio had sunk to 85. This was an exceptionally favorable ratio, but note that the dependency-prone group was now much more heavily composed of older people. In 1900 the latter made up less than an eighth of the dependency-prone class, whereas in 1950 they constituted more than one-fourth of it. In fact, from 1900 to 1950 the child-adult ratio declined by a third, while the elderly ratio rose by three-fourths. Between 1950 and 1959, however, *both* dependency-prone groups rose in ratio to persons in productive ages. As a consequence, the total ratio of the dependency-prone to those in the productive ages returned to where it was in 1900, substantially higher than it had been 9 years before. Further, among those in the 60-plus category, the proportion in the upper ages, where dependency is more likely, showed a steady rise (Table 2). The age groups 60–65, in which most peo-

ple are still vigorous, declined from 37 to 32 per cent, whereas those 75 and over rose from 18 to 24 per cent.

The position of the industrial countries in relation to the nonindustrial ones can be seen from Table 3. The industrial countries have fewer proportions of children and youth but greater proportions in the older ages. The contrast is particularly marked for the older industrial nations of northwestern Europe.

As the researches of Valoaras proved some years ago,[1] the over-

---

[1] Vasilios G. Valoaras, "Patterns of Aging of Human Populations" in Eastern States Health Education Conference Proceedings, *The Social and Biological Challenge of Our Aging Population* (New York: Columbia University Press, 1950) pp. 67–85: "Young and Aged Populations," *Annals of the American Academy of Political and Social Science*, CCCXVI (March 1958), 69–83. See also U.N. *Population Bulletin*, No. 1 (December, 1951), pp. 42–57, and U.N. *The Aging of Populations and Its Economic and Social Implications* (New York: United Nations, 1956), chap. ii.

TABLE 3.   Dependency Indices of the Age Structure in Selected Countries

	Child-dependency ratio (children under 15 per 100 adults 20–59)	Youth adult ratio (youths 15–19 per 100 adults 20–59)	Old age dependency ratio (oldsters 60-plus per 100 adults 20–59)	Total dependency ratio (under 20 and 60 and over adults 20–59)
Underdeveloped countries				
Libya, 1954	87	20	22	129
Algeria (Moslems), 1954	101	24	12	137
Ceylon, 1956	90	19	12	121
Costa Rica, 1957	105	25	11	141
India, 1931	85	19	9	113
India, 1951	80	21	12	113
Industrial countries				
Old World				
Belgium, 1956	41	11	31	83
Denmark, 1956	51	14	28	93
France, 1957	47	12	33	92
New World				
U. S. A., 1958	62	15	26	103
N. Zealand, 1956	65	15	26	106
Life-table populations				
U.S.A. White Female, 1957, with life-expectancy of 73.5	39	13	43	95
Hypothetical future U.S.A. with life-expectancy of 83	38	13	60	111
Projected population				
Great Britain 2017[a]	30	11	57	98

[a] Mortality decline between 1947 and 1977 at same rate as in prior 50 years, then stable. Fertility declines 20 per cent between 1947 and 1967 and then remains fixed.

whelming factor in the aging of populations in the industrial countries is the long secular decline in the birth rate. This is shown clearly by the United States data. In 1960 the proportion of children and youth was reduced because of the long decline in the birth rate during the first 50 years of this century. Those under 20 were the survivors from the relatively few births of the 1930s and 1940s, whereas those aged 20 to 59 were survivors from the more prolific decades of 1890 to 1930. The rebound of the birth rate in the 1940s and particularly in the 1950s swelled the number of persons under 20, whereas by then the depression trough had moved up to the 20–59 group. In 1950 the elderly were numerous because they were the survivors of births in the prolific years of 1860–1890, and by 1959 they had grown proportionately more numerous because the 20–59 group had been drastically affected by past lower fertility.

Popularly, the cause of the aging population is still often thought to be declining mortality. It has been shown experimentally, however, by letting mortality decline while fertility is held constant and vice versa, that the rising proportion of elderly persons in the population of industrial countries is due almost entirely to the secular decline in fertility.[2] Since the reduction of mortality has been greater for younger than for older ages, it has tended to make the population more youthful in most cases. The postwar boom in births, a phenomenon common to all the industrial nations, lowered the median age of the population. It will eventually reduce the proportion of the aged, but not until birth cohorts of 1920 to 1940 have reached the elderly status, which will be after 1980.

OLD-AGE POLICIES IN AGING SOCIETIES

Changes in the sheer age-structure of the population, impressive as they may be, do not automatically bring any particular consequence.

The progressive aging just described constitutes a major factor in the further evolution of industrial societies, but its actual consequences depend upon medical and economic development as well as welfare policies. If, for example, the aging is accompanied by an extension of the average period of health and vigor, so that organic decline is postponed on the chronological scale, then an aging population will represent less cost to society than it seems to imply. Again, if the economic and social role of the elderly is redefined and reorganized in such a way as to increase their productive performance, this will make an aging population less costly than it would otherwise be. Indeed to see the flexible possibilities, one has simply to remember that an individual's chronological age affords no sure judgment as to either his organic condition or his social and economic capacity. A healthy man of 65 is likely to have more capacity for work than a sick man of 40. An outstanding man of science, though he may not be at *his* best at 70, may still be better than the run of the mill younger men in his field. To adopt a position of hopeless demographic determinism in this matter of aging populations would therefore be scientifically erroneous.[3] But it would be

---

[2] Valoaras, "Patterns of Aging," *loc. cit.*, showed that if the U.S. population of 1900 had been constantly subject to the same fertility as in 1900–1914 but experienced the declining mortality that it actually did experience, the result would be to make the population more youthful by 1940. If the 1900 population had been constantly subject to the same mortality as in 1900–1914, but experienced the declines in fertility that it actually did experience after 1900, the result would be to enhance the proportion of older persons. Using stable populations, the U.N. study, *Aging of Population and Its Economic and Social Implications,* found "that reductions in mortality such as have occurred in the past led to an increase in the proportion of young people from 0–14 years, a decrease in the proportion of adults from fifteen to fifty-nine years and a very slight increase in the number of persons of sixty years and over" (p. 28).

[3] For an exhaustive account of the changes in intellectual and artistic achievement with age, see Harvey C. Lehman, *Age and Achievement* (Princeton, N. J.: Princeton University Press, 1953). For a brief summary of evidence that organic aging proceeds at some compound rate, see Hardin B. Jones, "Some Notes on Aging" in *Symposium on Information Theory in Biology* (New York: Pergamon Press, 1958), pp. 314–46; and his "Relation of Human Health to Age, Place, and Time" in *Aging and the Individual,* ed., James E. Birren (Chicago: University of Chicago Press, 1960), chap. xi. A thoughtful analysis

equally erroneous to ignore the new demographic situation, for it requires great effort and ingenuity if its potentially unhappy consequences are to be evaded or mitigated.

Since an aged population is brought about by demographic factors—specifically up to now, by a low birth rate—one obvious solution is to eliminate the demographic cause. As a matter of fact, this is sometimes proposed in an oblique way, by condemning birth control because it creates the evil of an aging population. We shall later deal with the paradoxes of a demographic solution, but first let us analyze the social *mechanisms* either used or proposed for dealing with the swollen ranks of the elderly in industrial societies.

THE QUESTION OF LABOR-FORCE PARTICIPATION. As with any other major social problem, so in the case of the aged there are several problems rolled into one. A given policy may be addressed to one of the subproblems as if this were the sole consideration, or there may be ambiguity as to just what is being attempted. A conflict exists in modern industrial societies between providing a comfortable and dignified old age for increased numbers of people and keeping the rising load of taxes within bounds. Since there is no question but that the needs of the elderly must be met, even if more meagerly than some would desire, the further problem arises of how the financial responsibility is to be allocated.

The ideal solution—and one that

of an aging population from a mental health point of view is contained in Torsten Sjögren and Tage Larsson, "The Changing Age-Structure in Sweden and Its Impact on Mental Illness," *Bulletin of the World Health Organization*, XXI (1959), 569–82.

gets immediately to the crux of the problem—is to reduce the main source of both economic drain and social hazard in an aging population: namely, the higher risk of disemployment as age advances. In the United States, according to 1959 data, the proportion of males aged 65 and over who are either unemployed or not in the labor force is 65 per cent. The figure rises rapidly with age:

	Percentage of males not employed, not in school, not in the labor force, 1959[a]
20–59	6.4
60–64	20.4
65–69	52.2
70+	72.8

[a] Based on estimated populations in Census Bureau, Current Population Reports, Series P-25, No. 212, p. 9, and on labor force data in Ibid., Series P-57, No, 204, p. 12.

The number of disemployed at ages 60 and over is greater than the entire number either employed or in school in the age group 25–29. Obviously, if the disemployment ratio could be reduced, say, to 10 per cent for those 60–64, 15 per cent for those 65–69, and 25 per cent for those 70 or over, and if the increased employment in these ages was efficient, the net gain to national production would be substantial—probably substantial enough to meet the cost of keeping unemployed elderly population in decent circumstances. When we add that to continue in active work would save the morale of many an older person, the argument in favor of a policy of increased employment in the upper age brackets seems irrefutable.

Yet, if this is the most favored

policy, it shows a singular lack of success. As is well known, the trend is the other way. As industrialization proceeds, fewer and fewer of the aged are working. A tabulation of male activity rates in three classes of countries about 1950 shows the following:

Type of country	Percent males age 65 or over who are active[a]
Underdeveloped	78.5
Semideveloped	62.5
Developed	40.6

[a] United Nations, *Aging of Population and Its Economic and Social Implications*, p. 52.

Today in the United States, the proportion of aged persons in the labor force—34 per cent for males, 8 per cent for females—is the lowest on record, as Table 4 shows. A survey covering 1958 finds that 43 per cent of the men aged 65 or more and 14 per cent of the women had work experience *during some or all of the year;* but, even among those who did work, less than two-thirds of the men and less than half of the women had full-time jobs. Furthermore, among those who worked either full- or part-time, 26 per cent of the men and 29 per cent of the women worked only half the year or less.[4] It is also of interest that despite the great rise in the labor-force participation of women during the last half century, the proportion of participation among those aged 60 and over has not risen at all.

Unless the causes of this long downward trend in employment are

[4] U.S. Census Bureau, *Current Population Reports—Labor Force,* Series P. 50, No. 91 (June 30, 1959), p. 12.

TABLE 4. Proportion of Persons Aged 65 or More Who Were in the Labor Force, United States, 1890–1958

	Per cent in labor force	
	Males	Females
1890	68.2	7.6
1900	63.2	8.3
1910	n.a.	n.a.
1920	55.6	7.3
1930	54.0	7.3
1940	42.2	6.0
1950	44.4	7.0
1959	34.0	8.0

Source : For 1890 to 1940, from John D. Durand, *The Labor Force in the United States* (New York : Social Science Research Council, 1948), p. 208. For 1950, from Henry D. Sheldon, *The Older Population of the United States,* p. 166. For 1959, derived from U.S. Census Bureau, Current Population Reports—Population Estimates, Series P-25, No. 212 (Jan. 26, 1960), p. 9, and Current Population Reports—Labor Force, Series P-57, No. 204 (June 30, 1959), p. 12.

understood, there can be no intelligent policy with respect to the aged. For instance, one common interpretation is that the employers are to *blame,* since they often refuse to employ people in the upper age brackets. Although surveys indicate that preference is in fact given to younger workers,[5] this cannot automatically be laid to "prejudice," nor can it be easily demonstrated that "prejudice" has been on the increase.

[5] In seven labor market areas in 1956 the Federal Bureau of Employment Security found that 20 per cent of the job orders filed with public employment offices specified workers under 35 years of age; 41 per cent called for workers under 45 years; and 52 per cent for recruits under 55. U.S. Bureau of Employment Security, BES No. E152 (1956), p. 28. Cited by Margaret S. Gordon, "The Older Worker and Hiring Practices," *Monthly Labor Review,* LXXXII (November, 1959), 1199.

If careful investigation should prove that preference for younger workers is mainly a matter of irrational prejudice, then state laws barring discrimination against elderly workers on the basis of their age would be the answer. Such measures, however, assume falsely that there are no economically important differences associated with age. Yet we know that if an employer pays no attention whatever to age, but hires people solely on the basis of their proficiency in the work he wants them to do, he will wind up by taking some older persons, to be sure, but not an equal share of them. To force him by law to take an equal share particularly at ages above 65, would be to lower the efficiency of his business.

Fortunately, the factors tending to lower the efficiency of elderly workers are not irremediable. Even the slowing down and worsening health that generally come with advanced years may in the future be postponed far beyond the usual age when they appear now. The obsolescence of skills that comes with age is known to be remediable, because reeducation is possible in many cases. The employer, however, cannot base his hiring policies on the wonders of science in the future or on the maintenance of a costly reeducation system. He can hardly be expected to bear the entire burden of reversing the downward trend of labor force participation among the elderly, especially at a time when the proportion of the elderly in the population has reached an all-time high. Before trying to force the employer to take the entire responsibility, one would be wise to explore other possible causes of disemployment than prejudice and other possible remedies than legal restraint.

To see what improved health could accomplish, we have to realize that a sizable fraction of the elderly are now disabled. Approximately 35 per cent of American men aged 65 or more are either in institutions or ill or disabled. Among those not in institutions and not working during 1958, 30 per cent gave "illness or disability" as their reason, and fewer than 2 per cent cited "inability to find work." The proportion with obsolete skills is harder to estimate, but expert opinion suggests that it is substantial and that reeducation therefore has an important place in gerontological policy.

> During the last decade, and particularly in the last 3 or 4 years, the most rapid expansion of employment has been occurring in professional and technical occupations especially inaccessible to an individual who does not have the appropriate education and training and in which the proportion of persons aged 45 and over is relatively low. Meanwhile, the supply of younger workers is increasing, as the teenagers born in the high birth rate period of the early 1940s reach the labor market age.[6]

Important as organic disability and obsolescence may be, they do not explain, any more than prejudice does, the long association between a declining rate of labor-force participation by the elderly and an advancing trend of economic development. A more likely explanation can be glimpsed by recalling that work is not the whole of life, or production the whole of society. Although from many points of view it is desirable to keep the elderly engaged in productive activity, there are weighty reasons for excusing them from work too. Some people view the release from the necessity of working as a boon rather

---

6 Gordon, *op. cit.*, p. 1198.

than a catastrophe: a just reward for a life of useful activity, something to look forward to and prepare for. Business firms and other employers do not view retirement schemes as just a means of protecting themselves from aged employees, but also as a part of the incentive, or "fringe benefit," system. It is not so much that the elderly wish to shirk, but rather that they want the option of working or not working according to their own individual circumstances.[7] Those who are not in the labor force today are in numerous instances better off than those of the same age in previous decades who *were* occupied. A high proportion of the latter worked in spite of serious handicaps because they *had* to. Today the productivity of industrial societies is such that they can afford to relieve the aged of the necessity of working, just as they can relieve children and adolescents.

It therefore seems hard to escape the conclusion that the shrinkage in the labor-force participation of the elderly is due fundamentally to economic development itself.[8] Earlier retirement, plus some increase in life-expectancy even at advanced ages,

has given a long holiday to huge numbers of older people. Although there can be no doubt that for many this has been involuntary and disorganizing, there can equally be no doubt that for many it has been welcome.

THE ALLOCATION OF COSTS FOR OLD-AGE SUPPORT. If one of the potential gains of modern society is more opportunity for older persons to retire or work as they desire, then the question remains as to how the costs of those who elect to retire or who cannot work are to be met. In the oldest system, which still prevails more or less intact in much of the world, the aged continue to work if able and, if not able, receive support by kinsmen, usually their own children. This system has a certain symmetry; parents support their dependent offspring but put them to work as early as possible; and, in turn, the offspring (when mature) support their aged parents but keep them at work as long as possible. The immemorial tenacity of the system is explained by several factors. First, the prospect of being supported in old age encourages young adults to get married and reproduce. Second, the close and constant personal contact between those giving and those receiving support tends to minimize rigidity, neglect, fraud, etc. Third, in static primitive or agrarian societies, the old are more useful than in industrial societies, for they are valuable storehouses of culture and their skills, if retained, are not obsolescent.[9]

---

[7] How many do not wish to work is hard to say, because everyone is supposed to want to work and therefore gives some other reason for an inactive status than disinterest. In the University of California supplement to the Current Population Survey of April 1952, only 12.4 per cent of the 65 + men claimed they were able to work and yet not in the labor force. Of these, two-thirds were either not interested in working or wanted to work just occasionally. (Cited by Sheldon, *op. cit.*, p. 167).

[8] Sheldon, *op. cit.*, pp. 53–60, examines several explanations of the downward trend in labor force participation: changing occupational structure, declining self-employment, altered age structure among the aged. Rejecting these on empirical grounds, he leans to

the view that the rising level of living with retirement schemes etc., has been responsible.

[9] See Kingsley Davis and Jerry W. Combs, Jr., "The Sociology of an Aging Population" in *Social and Biological Challenge of Our Aging Population*, pp. 147–59.

Fourth, in such societies the birth rate is high and consequently the aged form a small portion of the population. In 1931, for example, India had 11.5 persons aged 20–59 for each one aged 60 or more, whereas the United States in 1958 had less than 4 to one and France in 1957 had only 3 to one.

It is only in industrial societies that the family-support system becomes superseded, and then only haltingly, partially, and with misgivings. Curiously, the system tends to persist so far as the support of children is concerned. Although public schools, family allowances, tax reductions, and other measures universally help in the support of children in developed countries, the main burden still rests on the parents. On the other hand, the aged are increasingly being supported in some other way than through reliance on their mature offspring. The reason for this difference is doubtless partly due to the fact that children are as a whole more attractive and enjoyable than old people; consequently, the industrial society can penalize parents by placing upon them most of the burden of child support and yet escape major difficulties of enforcement, whereas the reverse cannot be accomplished with respect to the aged. But there is a demographic factor as well. In an industrial society, due to the low birth rate, parents are more numerous in relation to young children than in an agrarian society. For identically the same reason, as we have seen, the aged are more numerous in relation to the younger adults. The effect of the demographic changes accompanying industrialization is therefore to reduce the burden per parent of supporting young children and to maximize the burden per young adult of

supporting aged parents. This is demonstrated in three model populations, each representing a different combination of fertility and mortality. The ratio of elderly parents to adult children, as exhibited in Table 5, is twice as high in industrial societies (column 3) as in transitional ones, and more than twice as high as in societies that have not started on the demographic transition (column 1). Although all of the models are made on the basis of certain formal assumptions, they illustrate clearly the *purely demographic* source of resistance to supporting the aged by having their children bear the burden.

TABLE 5.   Ratios of Aged Parents to Children in Three Model Populations

	Population I: high fertility high mortality	Population II: high fertility low mortality	Population III: low fertility low mortality
Parents surviving to age 60 for each surviving child	.289	.301	.601
Average number of years a parent lives beyond age 60 for each year lived by child between ages 30 and 60	.14	.18	.36

Source: United Nations, *Aging of Population and Its Economic and Social Implications* (1956), p. 75.

The demographic elements do not, however, solely determine the support situation. For instance, the burden on the parents of young children is enormously increased in industrial

societies by the ever-longer postponement of the child's entry into the
labor force. However necessary this
may be for education adequate to run
a complex economy, there can be no
question about its direct and indirect
costs to parents. It follows, then, that
parents do not receive the full benefit
provided by the low birth rate of
industrial countries. This means in
turn, that they are not in a good position to support *their* aged parents,
especially since this burden has increased both from the aging population and from some factors leading
to involuntary disemployment of the
aged. As a consequence, the support
of the aged, if left entirely in the
hands of sons and daughters, would
be not only onerous but unequal and
inadequate; it would force the elderly
into the labor market in maximum
numbers and on bad terms. Instead,
individuals have sought to make provisions for their old age in their own
right, independently of their children.
Since however, only a minority can
accomplish this, the society at large
has come to their rescue, and to the
rescue of their adult children, by collective systems of old age security.
In this way the erstwhile symmetry
has been destroyed. Although many
people still contribute to the support
of aged parents, the trend is the other
way. The parent-child bond, at least
economically, is broken when the
child becomes independent; the economic sacrifice of the parent for the
young child is not rewarded by a
return sacrifice by the adult child.
The family structure is such that
emphasis is placed on the married
pair and their dependent offspring,
with few ties remaining between
them and their four elderly parents.
Geographical and social mobility add
to this break between the generations,
a break between persons who were
once close.

Collective systems of support for
the aged tend to diffuse the cost to all
of the producers. They are equitable
—from each according to his capacity and to each according to his need;
but they are also impersonal. There
is "no personal link between the aged
persons who receive retirement pensions and the workers who pay the
contributions."[10] Consequently, the
rule of *caveat emptor* applies to a
greater extent. The aging generation
tends to be bilked of its expectations
by heartless inflation and in return it
sometimes turns to political pressure
to wring from the active population
all that it can. It has been stated that
persons over 60 receive 20 per cent
of the national income and compose
23 per cent of the electorate in
France.[11] In the United States, although the average income of the
elderly is below that of younger
groups, the senior citizen lobbies have
had considerable success in liberaliz-
ing state and federal legislation in
their behalf.[12] There are more voters
age 65 or over in the United States
than there are Negro voters, farm
voters or foreign-born voters. It
would be a major tragedy if their
situation became such that they would
vote as a solid bloc.

---

[10] United Nations, *Aging of Population and Its Economic and Social Implications* (1956), p. 78.

[11] Alfred Sauvy, "Social and Economic Consequences of the Aging of
Western European Populations," *Population Studies*, II (June 1948), 117.

[12] See John J. Corson and John
W. McConnell, *Economic Needs of Older
People* (New York: Twentieth Century
Fund, 1956), chap. v; and Frank A.
Pinner, Paul Jacobs, and Philip Selznick,
Old Age and Political Behavior (Berke-
ley: University of California Press,
1960).

THE FUTURE AGE
DISTRIBUTION

Although the aging of industrial populations in the past has been due to declining and low fertility, an added influence may arise in the future. As was mentioned earlier, the past declines in mortality were greater at the younger than at the older ages. So great have been the reductions at ages under 35 that little room for improvement is left. If *nobody* died before reaching age 35, it would increase the number who do reach that age by only 6.4 per cent. At higher ages, however, there is great room for improvement.[13] It follows that if continued improvement in mortality is to be made, it will have to be in the advanced ages, and this will contribute to a further aging of the population. In Table 3 it can be seen that the projected population for Great Britain, made on the assumption that mortality would decline for 30 years as it did in the previous 50 and that fertility would be at a low level, yields an extremely high proportion of persons over 60.[14] Actually, the projected decline of mortality was conservative, for the highest expectation of life at birth that would be reached would be 69.0 for males and 76.2 for females. If a more drastic drop in mortality is assumed, a greater rise in the proportion of the

aged takes place regardless of the level of fertility assumed.[15]

There is no reason to believe that the pace of death control will not continue. The resources of scientific talent now being poured into medical research may soon bring a major breakthrough in precisely those diseases which, being degenerative, are associated with age—such as cancer and cardiovascular-renal disorders. Having saved people from infectious disease, we now let them die from the chronic maladies; but we shall be increasingly postponing these too. One can visualize a time when most people will die of accident, homicide, suicide, and warfare. Civilizations are mirrored in their causes of death. One of the most vital questions facing industrial civilization is whether the prolonging of life to ever more advanced ages will be an extension of senility or an extension of vigor.

FERTILITY, PROSPERITY, AND
POPULATION GROWTH

I stated at the beginning that contemporary industrial societies exhibit moderate birth rates. Although these rates are approximately only half as high as those in nonindustrial countries, they nevertheless are sufficient, with low mortality, to yield substantial population growth (Table 6).

Between 1950 and 1960 the industrial regions as a whole added 14 per cent to their population—a rate sufficient, if continued, to double the

---

[13] The life table for the United States shows that, under the mortality conditions of 1957, 94 per cent of those born reach age 35. If nobody died, this would amount to only 6.4 per cent more survivors. Since, however, only 78 per cent of those born survive to age 60 under 1957 conditions, an increase in the survivors say up to 92 per cent would represent an 18 per cent rise.

[14] Royal Commission on Population, *Papers*, II (London: His Majesty's Stationery Office, 1950), 281.

[15] United Nations, *Aging of Populations* ..., pp. 28–30. The breaking point seems to be the life-expectation of 70 years, the point now approximated by most advanced countries. Beyond that point further declines in mortality tend to age the population at an accelerating rate.

TABLE 6. Population Growth, 1920 to 1960
Developed and Underdeveloped Regions

	Population (million)		Per cent
	1920	1960	gain
Underdeveloped	1,245	2,109	69
Developed	565	801	42
New[a]	338	521	54
Old[b]	227	280	23

[a] Australia-New Zealand, Canada, Japan, U.S.S.R., U.S.A.

[b] Northwest and Central Europe.

number every 60 years.

The problem of rapid population growth in industrial countries is not scarcity of basic necessities.[16] Just the opposite. It is the glut of goods as well as people. The explosive combination of multiplying possessions and multiplying people is causing an ever larger portion of our high level of living to be used to escape from the consequences of congestion.

This circumstance is exacerbated by another feature of industrial societies—their urbanization. More than half of the American population now lives in urbanized areas of more than 50,000 inhabitants, including some giants such as the New York area with about 15 million. As a consequence, more than half are living at an average density in the neighborhood of 6000 per square mile, which is nearly four times the average density of the settled parts of Egypt. Yet, while an ever greater proportion of people in industrial countries are concentrating in urban areas of such size and density as to give the average Indian or Indonesian a sense of

---

[16] Cf. Arnold C. Harberger, "Variations on a Theme by Malthus" in *The Population Ahead*, ed. Roy G. Francis (Minneapolis: University of Minnesota Press, 1958), pp. 108–24.

claustrophobia, their mode of life is making such density increasingly intolerable. In seven years, from 1950 to 1957, the number of motor vehicles in the United States rose by 37 per cent, while the population grew by less than 13 per cent. In the latter year, the average number of cars per square mile of land was 23. However, if half of them were stabled in urbanized areas of 50,000 or more inhabitants, the average density of this half was more than 2,500 cars per square mile.

As is well known, our urban masses are spreading from the more central to the peripheral portions of the urban areas in a frantic search for room in which to store and use their ever-growing number of material possessions—automobiles, boats, trailers, television sets, freezers, king-size beds, saw-tables, archery equipment, golfing carts, and fishing tackle. Even their move to the suburbs requires extra equipment, such as a power mower, an extra car, longer utility lines, more super-highways. Not only residences, but stores, offices, factories are moving out in an effort to satisfy rising space demands. But this attempt to escape the city is hopeless, because the conditions that make the city intolerable—the multiplication of goods and people—are carried to the suburbs (in fact stimulated by the suburbs), so that the erstwhile fringe becomes a part of the spreading city. Furthermore, the costs and wastes increase as the urban area, the population, and the goods expand. An ever greater fraction of our energy promises to be dissipated in meeting the costs of commutation, air pollution, water pollution, traffic congestion, noise abatement.

One finds it difficult, therefore, to justify continued population growth in industrial countries. Indeed, those among these countries which seem to enjoy the best life, and which are consequently magnets of immigration, are precisely the ones that have the fewest people in relation to resources. Why, then, does the birth rate remain so high?

It remains high in part because of the opposition of some religious groups to efficient birth control. This has the effect of not only increasing the proportion of unplanned births among adherents of such faiths, but, since municipal, county, state and federal administrative and welfare agencies are often influenced by the religious opposition, the availability of efficient birth control to the ordinary citizen, regardless of his faith, is reduced. A recent field study of a national sample of urban white women found that 16 per cent of the most recent pregnancies were not wanted by the wife, husband, or both. The percentage rose sharply according to how many pregnancies had preceded the last one. If the last pregnancy was the first, only 6 per cent reported it as unwanted by one or both married partners; if it was the ninth, the figure rose to 62 per cent.[17] The study also found that the percentage of Catholic couples using contraception is less than the percentage of Protestant couples doing so, but that the difference diminishes with wife's age. The people who need help from welfare agencies and who, on the average, are poorer and less educated than the ordinary citizen are particularly likely to be deprived of access to help in birth control. In this connection it

| | Percentage practicing contraception[a] | |
	Wife aged 18–24	Wife aged 30–34
Protestant	74	76
Catholic	51	63

[a] Ronald Freedman, Pascal K. Whelpton, Arthur A. Campbell, *Family Planning, Sterility and Population Growth* (New York: McGraw-Hill Book Company, 1959), p. 108.

is of interest to note that the illegitimate birth rate has risen substantially in the United States. In 1940 the estimated illegitimacy rate was 7.1 per 1000 unmarried women aged 15–44 years; in 1957 it was three times as high (20.9).[18] It is also of interest to note that the nonwhite birth rate, always higher than the white, has tended to increase its advantage:

| | Birth rate[a] | | Per cent by which nonwhite exceeds white |
	White	Nonwhite	
1925–29	22.4	30.9	38
1953–57	24.0	34.9	45

[a] National Office of Vital Statistics, *Vital Statistics—Special Reports*, National Summaries, L, No. 19 (November 27, 1959), 72. The rates are based on births corrected for underregistration.

But in addition to the inadequate use of birth control, another factor plays a part, and probably a larger part, in the continuance of a moderately high birth rate. Children are liked in industrial societies, and families of a congenial size are desired. Even if all pregnancies were planned,

17 Ronald Freedman, Pascal K. Whelpton, Arthur A. Campbell, *Family Planning, Sterility and Population Growth* (New York: McGraw-Hill Book Company, 1959), p. 75.

18 National Office of *Vital Statistics —Special Reports*, National Summaries, L, No. 19 (November 27, 1959), 69.

it seems likely that the birth rate would be high enough to yield substantial population growth. Indeed, as family planning has come to characterize a greater portion of all couples, the percentage of childless and one-child families has declined noticeably, just as has the percentage of families of six or more children. A greater portion of couples are now clustered in the two-, three-, and four-child range. With a low mortality in industrial societies, the average couple would need to have less than 2.2 children. In other words, some population growth would occur even if eight out of every ten couples had two children and the other two couples had only three. As the mortality is improved still further, the required number of births for replacement will approach ever closer to two per couple. This, along with the extension of life, means that a shorter and shorter portion of each person's existence would be spent with a young child in the household. It is questionable whether the tiny replacement-size family will ever be congenial to people.

Furthermore, a rate of reproduction low enough just to replace the population at the present low mortality would produce an extremely aged population. For example, in Table 3 are shown two life-table populations. Since a life-table population is one that has exactly the same fertility as mortality, it can be seen that in a population which has just enough births to replace itself and a mortality equaling that of United States white females in 1957, there would be more people aged 60 or above than children under 15. If mortality were improved only a bit further, to where a life-expectation of 83 was attained, the number aged 60 or over would be

greater than the number under age 20. This prospect of a further aging of the population has become a key argument in the anti-birth-control movement in France,[19] and may become so in this country. However, the implication that we should maintain a high birth rate as the means of solving the problem of an aging population overlooks the possibility that there are other, less heroic, means of doing so. It also overlooks the fact that family planning has other goals than simply the control of population, and that to ban it solely out of consideration for the age structure would be both short-sighted and ineffective.

THE DEMOGRAPHIC DILEMMA OF INDUSTRIAL SOCIETIES

Looking back over the history of the advanced countries, we can see that their demographic changes during the process of industrialization—the decline of mortality, the reduction of fertility, the rising proportion of adults in the active ages, the growth of cities, the rise of internal and overseas migration—all contributed greatly to the efficiency and hence to the industrialization of these nations. But the later stages of the demographic transition have turned up certain unanticipated problems that require, for solution, the utmost care and strategy on the scientific side as well as in governmental and welfare

[19] C. Watson, "Birth Control and Abortion in France since 1939," *Population Studies*, V (March, 1952), 263; A. Sauvy, *De Malthus à Mao Tse-Toung* (Paris: Denoel, 1958), pp. 275–77; Population Reference Bureau, " 'Children in Spite of Ourselves': France Struggles with a Dilemma," *Population Bulletin*, XII (November, 1956), 109–26.

policy. These problems are in large part the ultimate consequences of the decline in mortality that set off the demographic transition in the first place. This decline, which did so much to free the industrial peoples from the spectre of early death, caused the traditional level of the birth rate to yield families that were too large and populations too expanding. As a consequence, the birth rate during the latter part of the nineteenth and the first third of the present century was reduced with unprecedented speed—faster, in fact, than the death rate during the same period, with the result that the problem of extremely rapid population growth was diminished. But the lower fertility in turn brought an age structure which, though at first quite favorable from an economic point of view, eventually turned unfavorable as the bulge began moving from the young to the older adult ages. Yet the birth rate was still not low enough to cause population growth to cease, even though the latter has been complicated by urbanization. In the meantime, the recent and quick transfer of the latest scientific death control measures from industrial to the nonindustrial countries has caused their populations to grow at a rate never even approached in past human history, to a point fast enough to double their numbers every 40 years, bringing a tremendous inflation in the growth of world population. The immigration pressure on the industrial countries has accordingly been, and will be, greatly heightened. The population of most of the industrial countries, including the United States, is growing from immigration as well as from natural increase.

The industrial nations thus face today a peculiar demographic dilemma. On the one hand, they can conceivably reduce their birth rate to the point where their populations are just replacing themselves. This would solve the problem of rapid population growth at home, and would serve as an example of self-control to those abroad who are in poorer circumstances. But it would involve such small families, would give most people such a minimum exposure to young children during a long life, that they seem unwilling to take this course. Furthermore, it would increase still more the proportion of elderly persons in the population and would expose the borders to almost irresistible immigration pressure. On the other hand, the advanced countries can keep their moderately high birth rates and their moderately high rates of population growth. This would exert some influence in keeping the age structure younger than it would otherwise be, and give some basis for restraining immigration. However, the probability is very high that such a policy, if continued indefinitely, would be followed by almost incredible congestion. Also, the truth is that further declines in the death rate in the advanced countries will cause the proportion of the aged to rise regardless of the birth rate. Indeed, whatever the path taken, short of increased mortality, the industrial societies appear to be destined to have an aging population. This does not present them with an insuperable handicap, but it does place a profound burden upon them to find the means to mitigate the hardships and the inefficiencies that might otherwise result. To be successful, the means will have to be sought at all levels—biological, economic, governmental, familial—and will have to be compatible with the competitive viability of the industrial nation.

Family Planning and Poverty[*]

Frederick S. Jaffe

The main finding of United States fertility studies during the last decade has been that many of the historic differentials are rapidly disappearing. Almost all Americans are coming to share a quite similar set of fertility values and practices. Some of the ancient differentials, such as those between urban and rural families, are narrowing considerably, and even the traditional inverse relationships between income (and related measures of socioeconomic status) and family size have been reduced, and, for the most prosperous groups, even reversed.[1]

Yet within this over-all and clear trend toward uniformity, there remain many paradoxes which demonstrate that control over fertility has not yet been realized universally in America. Despite the progress of the last 20 years, many low-income families, and a disproportionate number of nonwhite families, still remain very significantly outside the area of effective fertility control.

Among the factors which are responsible for this situation are the institutional and social mechanisms which are amenable to modification and correction by the serving professions. First, some data are presented which will help to establish the parameters of the problem.

FAMILY SIZE PREFERENCES

A number of recent studies have shown, with remarkable consistency, that working-class Americans want as few children as, or fewer than, those of higher socioeconomic status.

This is fully demonstrated in the 1960 Growth of American Families study,[2] which is a replication of the 1955 GAF study of a representative national sample of white wives in their childbearing years. Nonwhite as well as white wives were sampled in 1960, thus providing the first overview of recent nonwhite fertility attitudes and practices.

The GAF investigators found that nine out of ten American wives, white and nonwhite, thought two to four children is the "ideal" size family, with the average minimum number 3.4 and the average maximum 3.5. In this study, "ideal" is a slightly different concept than "wanted." The number wanted at the time of the interview was smaller than the ideal. The average minimum number for all wives was 3.1, the average maximum

---

[*] Frederick S. Jaffe, "Family Planning and Poverty," *Journal of Marriage and the Family*, 26 (November, 1964), 467–70.

[1] Cf. especially the 1955 Growth of American Families study (Ronald Freedman, P. K. Whelpton, and Arthur Campbell, *Family Planning, Sterility, and Population Growth*, New York: McGraw-Hill Book Company, 1959), and the Princeton Study (Charles F. Westoff *et al.*, *Family Growth in Metropolitan America*, Princeton N.J.: Princeton University Press, 1961).

[2] The author is indebted to Dr. Arthur Campbell of the Scripps Foundation for Research in Population Problems for permission to cite data from completed sections of the 1960 GAF study, the report of which will be published by Princeton University Press.

3.4. Lower-income couples wanted somewhat smaller families than higher-income couples. While the average maximum number of children wanted by husbands with family incomes of $10,000 or more was 3.3, the average maximum among those with incomes under $3,000 was 3.1.

It is especially noteworthy that nonwhites wanted a significantly smaller average number of children than whites. White wives wanted a minimum of 3.1 and a maximum of 3.5, while nonwhites wanted 2.7 and 3.0 Forty-six per cent of nonwhites wanted no more than two children, compared to 29 per cent of whites.

In a similar manner, the recent Princeton study showed that white collar wives wanted 3.3 children, compared to 3.2 for blue collar wives.[3] And in a study by Bogue among Chicago families, the same preference of nonwhites for smaller families was shown. He found, the example, that 38 per cent of nonwhites regarded one or two children as ideal, compared to 21 per cent of whites.[4]

There is some evidence that these findings apply also to the most impoverished Americans—those who are on relief and those who depend on public health facilities. The Greenleigh study of ADC families in Chicago reported that 90 per cent of mothers of out-of-wedlock children did not want to have the child.[5] A 1963 paper from the Florida State Health Department showed that 70 per cent of more than 2,600 women attending maternity clinics wanted to have no more children. Two-thirds of this group were nonwhite, and they expressed a consistent desire to have fewer children than did white respondents.[6]

Whether or not these findings can be regarded as definitive, they do tend to challenge some widely prevalent notions about lower-class fertility attitudes. Stycos has noted the remarkable similarity in many diverse societies of upper-class explanations for the high fertility of lower-class groups. The key proposition, he pointed out, is that "...the lower classes want many children...or do not care how many they have."[7] The same explanation is commonly offered in this country—and it appears to bear approximately the same relationship to reality as most other middle-class explanations of lower-class behavior.

FERTILITY LEVELS

If lower-class attitudes favor small families, however, it is quite clear from census data and recent research that the wish is not quite the deed. In 1962, 34 per cent of the families with five children, and 44 per cent of those with six, had incomes below $4,000, compared to 20 per cent of the families with two children, and 22 per cent of those with three.[8]

The 1960 GAF data show that one

---

[3] Westoff *et al., op. cit.,* p. 187.
[4] D. Bogue, "Experiments in Use of Mass Communication and Motivation To Speed Adoption of Birth Control in High Fertility Populations," presented at Sociological Research Association, 1962.
[5] Greenleigh Associates, *Facts, Fallacies, and Future,* 1960, p. 19.

[6] R. Browning and L. L. Parks, "Child Bearing Aspirations of Public Health Maternity Patients," presented at American Public Health Association, 1963.
[7] J. M. Stycos, "Obstacles to Programs of Population Control—Facts and Fancies," *Marriage and Family Living,* 25: 1, February 1963.
[8] U.S. Census Bureau, *Current Population Reports—Consumer Income,* P-60, No. 41, Table 5, October 21, 1963.

out of five couples with children have excess fertility, defined as those whose last child was unwanted by either husband or wife. Not surprisingly, the study found that "...the problem of unwanted pregnancies is most severe in the lower income and education groups." Among couples with excess fertility, it was found that those with lowest incomes expect more births than those with highest incomes (4.2 vs. 3.9) although those with lowest incomes want fewer (2.5 vs. 3.1). If the husband had an income of less than $3,000 and the last pregnancy was unwanted, the excess of births expected was 70 per cent. Only 11 per cent of the college-educated group fall into the excess fertility category, compared to 32 per cent of the grade school group. The authors conclude: "A relatively high incidence of severe Excess Fertility in lower education and status groups explains most of the differences in expected family size between higher and lower status couples. In other words, lower status couples don't have more children...simply because they want more. They have more children because some of them do not use contraception regularly and effectively. If the wife has a grade school education and if the husband has an income of less than $3,000 a year, then 39 per cent have excess fertility...the judgment that their fertility is too high is their own opinion."

CONTRACEPTIVE PRACTICES

Thus the fertility problems of impoverished Americans must be considered against the background of current family planning practices in the United States. Here the 1960 GAF findings are in the main familiar in that they reinforce and extend the results of the 1955 investigation.

In 1960, fertility control of some sort was favored by 96 per cent of Protestants, 98 per cent of Jews, and 85 per cent of Catholics. Among whites, 81 per cent had used *some* form of fertility control by 1960, 6 per cent expected to begin practicing it some time in the future, and 10 per cent were subfertile. Thus almost everyone was practicing family planning after a fashion, although there still were some socioeconomic differentials—e.g., 93 per cent of college-educated wives had practiced fertility control or planned to, compared to 72 per cent of grade school wives.

Data on nonwhite practices and the breakdown of methods employed by different classes are not yet available. In the 1955 study, however, lower-status (e.g., grade school) wives more often utilized such relatively unreliable methods as douching (32 per cent vs. 23 per cent) and less often used such reliable methods as diaphragms (16 per cent vs. 52 per cent) than higher-status (college) wives.

THE GAP BETWEEN ASPIRATION AND PERFORMANCE

The gap between lower-class fertility aspirations and performance is usually explained by the fact that lower-class couples do not use contraception as regularly as higher-class couples, nor do they employ methods which are as effective. This, in turn, has led to studies, most notably by Rainwater,[9] of what is generally

9 Lee Rainwater, *And the Poor Get Children* (Chicago: Quadrangle Books, 1960).

termed the "motivation" problem. These studies have been valuable in pointing up the partly different cultural settings of lower-class families, not to speak of the quite different living conditions. In so doing, they should reinforce the need for more extensive and intensive services to make fertility control a reality for low-income Americans.

Yet, by a curious inversion, these useful explorations have been distorted by some public health and welfare officials into a justification for failure to offer any contraceptive services to indigent families on the ground that "they won't use it anyway." More generally, the motivational analysis has been employed by some to obscure what would seem to be the first order of business—the study of the concrete conditions under which impoverished Americans receive their medical care, and the bearing that these conditions and other institutional factors may have on the availability of contraception to these families.

For example, 82 per cent of married nonwhites in New York City between 1955 and 1959 delivered their babies in municipal hospitals or on ward services of voluntary hospitals, compared to 14.5 per cent of whites;[10] in 1955, only 11.1 per cent of nonwhite mothers had a private physician in attendance during delivery.[11] In a Washington, D.C. study published in 1961, 75 per cent of nonwhite births

were staff cases.[12] The 1961 report of the Obstetrical Statistical Cooperative, based on 66,000 discharges at approximately 20 hospitals in New York, New Haven, Hartford, Philadelphia, Denver, San Francisco, Baltimore, and Salt Lake City, showed that nearly 94 per cent of nonwhite deliveries were on ward service, compared to 35 per cent of whites.[13]

These figures make clear that the vast majority of nonwhite mothers do not have ready access to a private physician during the childbearing period. Most tax-supported hospitals still do not make contraceptive services routinely and easily available to their patients, and only the exceptional voluntary hospital operates a birth control clinic which ward patients can attend. Since the most effective methods of birth control are usually prescribed by private physicians for their private patients during the postpartum period, do not these related facts suggest a significant set of factors limiting the actual availability of effective fertility control measures for nonwhite families—and influencing their subsequent fertility performance? To what extent do similar considerations apply to impoverished whites?

Even before the advent of the oral birth control pills in 1960, contraception was acceptable to many low-income families. The 1960 GAF study, based still on conventional birth control methods, showed that the increase in contraceptive use over 1955 was greatest among couples in the lowest socio-economic group. The

---

[10] J. Pakter *et al.*, "Out-of-Wedlock Births in New York City, No. 1—Sociologic Aspects," *American Journal of Public Health*, 51:5 (May, 1961).

[11] S. Shapiro *et al.*, "Further Observations on Prematurity and Perinatal Mortality in a General Population and in the Population of a Prepaid Group Practice Medical Care Plan," *American Journal of Public Health*, 50:9 (September, 1960).

[12] E. Oppenheimer, "Population Changes and Perinatal Mortality," *American Journal of Public Health*, 51:2 (February, 1961).

[13] *Obstetrical Statistical Cooperative —1961 Combined Report*, Table IV.

proportion of users of all forms of birth control among grade school graduates increased from 49 per cent in 1955 to 66 per cent in 1960.

It will be most interesting to see a study of the period after 1960, because there is considerable evidence that oral contraception has radically changed the picture. In Mecklenburg County, North Carolina, for example, the Health and Welfare Departments have been cooperating since 1960 in a joint project offering oral contraceptives free to a group consisting primarily of relief recipients. Of the 673 patients who enrolled in the clinic, 75 per cent are still taking the pills regularly and effectively, and there have been no pregnancies in this group, although these patients previously had been quite prolific. Similar evidence of the acceptability of the oral pills among poor families comes from Bellevue Hospital in New York, where an active clinic serving a relief and impoverished population was established in 1959, and where more than 90 per cent of the patients choose the orals.[14] In Planned Parenthood clinics throughout the country, 70 per cent of the patients have incomes of under $4,000, and the pills have sparked a doubling of the patient load in the last five years. Between 1962 and 1963 alone, there was a 25 per cent increase in contraceptive patients and a 60 per cent increase in those on the pills.[15]

This recent experience should prompt the development of a more precise concept of the elements that go into motivation for family planning—and particularly of the relationship between ease of access to competent instruction and the level of motivation required for successful practice. Do all Americans today have equal access to fertility control? Would it not be fruitful to study the access problem of impoverished Americans realistically, to examine critically the obstacles society places in the way of effective fertility control guidance and instruction for poor families —and then to remove these obstacles? For it is certainly still true that most public hospitals, health departments, and welfare agencies either do not provide contraceptive service at all— or compel a couple to run an obstacle course in order to secure what everyone else in the society regards virtually as part of the Bill of Rights. In this connection, the significance of the fact should be pondered that in many public hospitals, it is considerably easier for an impoverished mother to be sterilized than for her to receive instruction and supplies for contraception.

Among these obstacles are those who manage to transform what has become an everyday practice for most American families into a traumatic experience, such as the caseworker who told a Planned Parenthood field worker not long ago, quite seriously, that she "wouldn't dream of suggesting birth control to a client unless the client had been in deep therapy for at least two years."[16] And, of course, there are the very physical arrangements of many public institutions, not to speak of the attitudinal problems of the serving professionals. How

---

14 Personal communication from Dr. Hans Lehfeldt.

15 A. F. Guttmacher, *1963 Annual Report*, Planned Parenthood Federation of America.

16 For a contrasting—and much more positive—view in the context of social work thinking, cf. *The Right to Birth Control Information in Family Planning*, Community Service Society of New York, 1964.

many middle-class couples would be practicing birth control effectively if it required first that the wife spend a half day in a dingy clinic waiting room, only to find that she has to defend her integrity against the indifference and hostility of a doctor who tells her that she ought to stop her sex life if she doesn't want children?

If that sounds extreme, it is useful to recall the story of Sadie Sachs which started Margaret Sanger on her work for birth control. As a public health nurse on New York's Lower East Side in 1912, Mrs. Sanger had carefully nursed back to life Mrs. Sachs, who was hemorrhaging after self-induced abortion. When Mrs. Sachs finally recovered, she asked the doctor to tell her how to keep from becoming pregnant. The doctor's immortal reply was: "Tell Jake to sleep on the roof."[17]

A half century later, in 1962, CBS did a telecast on the birth control situation in Chicago. The program contained the following equally immortal words from a white Tennessee mother of six who had delivered her last baby at Cook County Hospital. Like Sadie Sachs, she had asked the doctor for birth control information. "Well," she told CBS, "I asked him what I could do and he said that was up to me to decide. He said one thing that—the best thing for me to do would not be close to my husband, and if I didn't want to get that way, it was up to me to stay away from getting pregnant until I had the operation coming up in April. Well, I didn't like it, 'cause I figure my husband's a human being just like he is, and I don't think he'd like to be told that—to stay away from his wife, if he's married."[18]

---

[17] L. Lader, *The Margaret Sanger Story* (New York: Doubleday, 1955).

[18] *CBS Reports on Birth Control and the Law*, May 10, 1962.

Income Maintenance and the Birth Rate[*]

Alvin Schorr

Population growth is a recurring issue in the United States. In the 1930s there was widespread anxiety that the population was not replacing itself. In the 1960s there is anxiety because the population, not content with replacing itself, increases rapidly—with consequent crowding, dislocation, and pressure on services. In and out of public discussion weaves a strain concerned specifically with the birth rates of poor people. With a generally declining birth rate, it seemed that the poor might have most of the children; population quality—whether regarded as genetic or not—might decline. With a general rise in birth rate, the concern is that families already poor are handicapped by too many children and so are kept poor.

If there is to be public consideration of a major income-maintenance program for children, questions will naturally be asked about the birth rate. Will total births rise? Especially, will those who are poor be encouraged to have more children? Neither consequence is much to be desired. Viewing these questions in terms of probable effect on large population groups, the available evidence is here approached in two ways: through the experience of other countries with rising income and with family allowances; then, by examining what factors affect fertility patterns in general.

NATIONAL EXPERIENCES

Viewed most broadly, concern with the impact of income-support programs on birth rate is a variant of a historic argument about economic growth and birth rate. The view of classical economists was put by Adam Smith in these terms:

> If this demand [for labor] is continually increasing, the reward for labor must necessarily encourage in such a manner the marriage and multiplication of laborers, as may enable them to supply that continually increasing demand by a continually increasing population.[1]

As David McClelland points out, the argument that economic growth would lead to population growth was put forward at a time when population was indeed increasing. The number representing birth rate minus death rate in England was 0.7 or 0.8 in the period from 1750 to 1800 and rose to 1.2 in the period 1800 to 1950.[2] Population increase and economic growth were moving forward side by side. As so often happens, observers saw a law in the correlation.

Security Bulletin, XXVIII:12 (December, 1965), 22–30.

[1] Adam Smith, *An Inquiry into the Nature and Causes of the Wealth of Nations* (New York: Random House, Inc., 1937), p. 80

[2] David C. McClelland, *The Achieving Society* (Princeton, N.J.: D. Van Nostrand Company, Inc., 1961), p. 27.

---

[*] Alvin Schorr, "Income Maintenance and the Birth Rate," *Social*

If one abandons the perspective of the early 19th century, however, and looks backward from 1940, quite the opposite trend is apparent. "The large declines in fertility in economically developed countries in the 19th and 20th centuries are probably unprecedented."[3]

Now a plausible correlation seemed to reflect a reverse law of human behavior: rising wealth is associated with *declining* birth rates. Many explanations were advanced for this law. Their core was more sociological in tone: family functions, structure, and expectations change in an advancing industrial society. The new law gains an appearance of breadth by spreading its umbrella over two observations that are of rather a different quality. Inside the developed countries, those people with higher income have lower birth rates. And the underdeveloped nations, where wealth is slight, have higher birth rates.

There matters rested until after World War II, when rates of fertility in some of the developed countries suddenly moved upward again. It was impossible for the sophisticated to return to the simple view represented in the Adam Smith quotation above. Speculation about the reversal has ranged all the way from an unconscious reaction against a threat to human survival (atomic testing) to the notion that, after a certain level of adequacy has been reached, people in effect buy another child with additional income. It is not necessary to explore the merits of various theories but only to note that broad national trends support no sweeping generalization. Economic growth in a highly industrialized country may be coupled with a rising or a declining birth rate. There is no indication here of the likely effect of an income-maintenance program on birth rates.

Economic growth is so broad a concept that it may mask relationships that do exist. A look at national experience with income maintenance may perhaps reveal a clearer relationship. As a number of countries established family allowances *in order to* increase the population, it seems reasonable to use this program for exploration.

In neighboring Canada, with a delicate mixture of Protestant and French Catholic citizens, the population issue received due attention before a program of family allowances was enacted. For more than a decade, Canadian officials made recurrent attempts to evaluate the influence of the allowances on the birth rate. In 1957, the Director of Research of the Department of National Health and Welfare reported:

> There is little or no evidence to support the contention that the Canadian legislation has resulted in a birth rate higher than otherwise would have been the case. If there is any demographic influence it may be through a favorable effect on the survival rate rather than through any impact the program may have on the birth rate, but this would also be difficult to substantiate through statistical evidence.[4]

Although official attention to the issue apparently waned with the evaporation of Canadian criticism of family allowances, data concerning

---

[3] Ronald Freedman, "The Sociology of Human Fertility: A Trend Report and Bibliography," *Current Sociology*, V. X–XI, No. 2, 1961–62, Oxford, England, p. 53.

[4] Joseph W. Willard, "Family Allowances in Canada," *International Labor Review* (March, 1957), p. 22.

the last decade are also consistent with Joseph Willard's judgment.

The Canadian birth rate had started slowly up when allowance payments began (1945) and then rose sharply. This was, of course, the immediate postwar period. Since 1959, the birth rate has started down again. Close analysis of these figures would make it clear that any effect of allowances in the first decade cannot be disentangled from the effects of demobilization and postwar prosperity. Perhaps the most telling illustration of this point is the close correspondence between birth rates in Canada and in the United States (Fig. 1). U. S. and Canadian fertility patterns are not identical (Canadians marry later, for example); probably some differences between the two countries cancel out. Nevertheless, it would be difficult to argue that the Canadian birth rate is responding to family allowances while the United States birth rate accompanies it up and down.

If one explores fertility trends within Canada, the vital statistics suggest responses that may seem divergent and even perverse. If allowances are to produce larger families, it might be argued that this would be seen most markedly in Catholic Quebec. The money is made available where large families are presumably most desired or most accepted. Yet the increase in births through 1956 had been smaller in Quebec than in any other province. The fertility of married women at each specific age—a more complex but more accurate measure than total births—actually declined for every age group in Quebec except the youngest.[5]

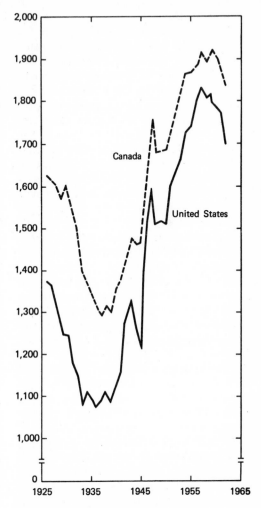

FIG. 1. Gross Reproduction Rates, United States and Canada, 1926–62

It is important now to note that Quebec was undergoing rapid urbanization in this period, as compared with the other provinces. Any population response to family allowances through increased childbearing that might conceivably have appeared was

[5] Bernice Madison, "Canadian Family Allowances and Their Major Social Implications," *Journal of Marriage and the Family* (May, 1964).

overwhelmed by the response to urbanization.

The Canadian program was not intended to increase the birth rate; moreover its cash payments are modest. That it produces no demonstrable effects on birth rates may tell nothing about more ambitious programs of family allowances. It is useful, therefore, to turn to France, the country that pays the most substantial benefits and deliberately sought a demographic result. As in other developed countries, the birth rate moved steadily downward from 1800 to World War II. In 1945, the French social security system was reorganized and family allowances made virtually universal. In the five years before World War II, France had averaged 630,000 births a year. In the five years after the war (and the new family allowance program), the Nation averaged 856,000 births a year. Total births declined slightly from this peak to a low point in 1953 and have shown a modest rise since.[6] As total population has also been rising, the birth rate per thousand population has varied little since 1954.[7]

One may understand from the marked reversal in 1945 why French officials sometimes take the position that family allowances have increased fertility. Moreover, they are impressed by the more marked recovery of fertility in France than among its neighbors. (Still other European countries, such as Portugal and Poland, have higher fertility rates than France.)[8] French demographers seek a more cautious position. They say, for example, that family allowances contributed to a general natalist spirit which is now a force in itself. They account in this way for stable fertility rates during the past decade, despite a relative decline in the significance of family allowances. (Family benefits have been permitted to fall behind while wages were rising rapidly.)[9] Yet Canada, with a modest family allowance program, and the United States, with none, experienced concurrent dramatic increases in birth rate. It is therefore necessary to be sceptical about even the more cautious formulation.

As with Canada, the components of the general increase in the French birth rate are difficult to reconcile with a view that family allowances are the causal element. One would expect family allowances to influence chiefly rural and other very poor French families. There is, for example, a wry country saying: "Let's make a baby to buy a motor bike."[10] But the data indicate that it is the urban families and those with comfortable incomes—not the others—who are showing the substantial increases in children. Because of the way French family allowances are calculated, the major advantage is felt by families with three children or more. If births were a consequence of family allowances, the number of large families should be increasing. Actually, in the sharp rise of the

---

[6] Roland Pressat, "La population Française au recensement de 1962," *Population*, No. 4, 1962, Paris.

[7] *Informations Sociales*, "La population Française, recensement 1962," August–September 1964, Paris.

[8] United Nations, *Demographic Yearbook* (New York, 1961).

[9] Paul Paillat, "Influence de nombre d'enfants sur le niveau de vie de la famille-évolution de 1950 à 1961," *Population*, No. 3, 1962, Paris.

[10] A more sophisticated statement of the same sort is the opening sentence of a satirical autobiography: "I was born of Allowances and a Holiday, of which the morning stretched out happily to the sound of 'I love You You love me' played on a sweet trumpet." Christiane Rochefort, *Les Petits enfants du siècle* (Paris: Bernard Grasset, 1961).

decade after the war, more families were having one, two, or three children and the proportion of large families diminished.[11]

The major difficulty in determining what lesson Canada and France teach is, as seen in retrospect, that they initiated their programs when fertility rate would naturally have risen anyway. The range may be extended by noting countries where the birthrate barely rose or even declined. Italy experienced a decline through the 1940s, despite all its efforts. Sweden suffered a continuing decline in birth rate through the 1950s, when the rate in most western countries was high.[12] As for Nazi Germany, its "whole vast apparatus...was used with a concentrated ferocity to raise the birth rate."[13] Not only were allowances paid; bachelors were taxed and men with large families were given preference in employment. Births rose from 14.7 per thousand population in 1933 to 19.7 in 1938 but never approached the figures achieved earlier in the century (29.5 in 1910–1913). Even the modest increase has been attributed to improved economic conditions and the suppression of abortion in combination with cash allowances.[14] It cannot be said of these countries that allowances failed to influence births any more than of France and Canada that they succeeded. It seems clear that in Italy and Sweden, at least, the birth rates were declining in continuation of long-term trends. Whether allowances prevented a sharper decline will never be known.

At the 1964 meetings of the International Social Security Association, the Permanent Committee on Family Allowances entertained a suggestion to study the effects of allowances on birth rates. The Committee declined to undertake such a study at that time, reasoning that sufficient data would not be available to support responsible conclusions. The extent of the difficulty is clear. If some conclusion must be derived from national experiences, it must be guarded: Neither proved nor disproved; the question remains open.

Having proffered the obligatory judgment, perhaps it is possible to press one step further to a plausible judgment: On one hand, it seems likely that some undetermined number of families, particularly with scant or moderate incomes, would have an additional child *because* it would invoke a government payment. These families may want a motor bike or they may simply enjoy children. On the other hand, national experiences suggest that the effect of these families on the national birth rate or its major elements (family size, low-income births compared with middle income, etc.) would probably be undetectable. Compared with other factors that seem to govern population trends (general level of living, infant survival, etc.) an income-maintenance program, however large, is small.

FACTORS INFLUENCING FERTILITY

Apart from the experience that other countries have had with income

---

[11] *Les Institutions sociales de la France*, Documentation Française, Paris, 1963, p. 31. Pressat, *op. cit.*, p. 527. *Informations Sociales*, *op. cit.*

[12] Murray Gendell, *Swedish Working Wives, A Study of Determinants and Consequences* (Ph.D. Thesis, Totowa, N.J.: The Bedminster Press, 1963).

[13] Richard and Kathleen Titmuss, *Parents Revolt* (London: Secker and Warburg, 1942), p. 105.

[14] Dudley Kirk, *Europe's Population in the Inter-War Years*, League of Nations, 1946.

maintenance, there is another question. What factors of any sort appear to influence fertility in the United States one way or another? Phrasing the question in this fashion makes it possible to deal directly with such special tendencies of low-income families as may be discerned.

The birth rate in the United States has moved steadily downward over the long term, consistent with the experience in western Europe. It is said that the long-term decline is compounded of (1) a shift in population from rural to urban areas, where many children are not economically useful to a family; (2) the spread in an urban society of efficient contraceptive devices and knowledge; (3) the shift from large geographically stable families to small, movable families; and (4) new views of the relationship of the individual to society and God which tended to depreciate the value of children.[15] The decline reached bottom, so far as can now be seen, with women born between 1906 and 1910. They averaged 2.3 children each.[16]

Despite the long-term trend, in the short run the birth rate moves up and down in a manner distinctly related to economic prosperity or depression. Hope Eldridge has made this observation in the following terms:

> Within this [long term] process, fluctuations in the birth rate show a positive correlation with fluctuations in the economic situation. People, like crops, are more prolific in "good years" than in "bad years." In population where fertility is largely subject to voluntary control [as in the developed countries] the timing of

births adjusts itself to changes in the economic outlook. If, as recent studies suggest, levels in completed fertility are influenced by the duration and intensity of these adjustments, then it follows that economic policy... is in effect population policy.[17]

The point seems plausible: When times are bad, families restrict the number of their children in order to avoid expense. When times are good, they may catch up and even have more children. (The long-term trend is nevertheless maintained.)

For some time now, researchers have been interested in the possibility that it is not prosperity in any absolute sense that influences families.[18] Rather, families are influenced by the feeling that they have more or less income than others like themselves; or the feeling that their own prospects are looking up or deteriorating. Deborah Freedman has calculated the income that men may expect to have, based on their occupation, education, and age. Studied in relation to these predictions, men whose income exceeds what is normal have more children than average. Men with low incomes in relation to others like themselves have fewer children. Number of children is directly related to *relative* income.[19] More pointedly, it has been argued that the link between prosperity and a high birth rate is the young adult entering the job market. If he has

---

[15] Ronald Freedman, *op. cit.*

[16] Charles F. Westoff, "The Fertility of the American Population," *Population: The Vital Revolution*, ed. Ronald Freedman (Chicago: Aldine Publishing Co., 1965).

[17] Hope T. Eldridge, *Population Policies: A Survey of Recent Developments* (Washington, D.C.: The International Union for the Scientific Study of Population, 1954), p. 121.

[18] R. Heberle, "Social Factors in Birth Control," *American Sociological Review* (December, 1941).

[19] Deborah Freedman, "The Relation of Economic Status to Fertility," *The American Economic Review* (June, 1963).

had little income but his prospects are good, he will have rather a large family. If he is accustomed to substantial income but jobs are hard to find, he will have fewer children. Thus, young adults who grew up in the Depression and married and worked after World War II had a high birth rate.[20] Those who grew up in better circumstances since 1940 and face the (for youth) highly competitive job market of the mid-1960s, may be expected to have fewer children.[21] Indeed, they seem to be doing so.

This material offers several hints about the effect of an income-maintenance program on birth rates. Any substantial increment in family income will improve a family's situation relative to self if not to others. There may, therefore, be an immediate reflection in a higher birth rate. On the other hand, birth rates may be influenced by the circumstances of other similar people—which would not change—and by independent economic factors such as the job market. Speaking of economic factors alone, the tendency of the birth rate to respond to financial improvement would be muffled. Whatever the immediate response of the birth rate, after several years the contribution of an income-maintenance program would be incorporated into families' standard of living and lose its influence on their birth rate.

These hints, such as they are, much oversimplify the matter, for birth rate is affected by many quali-

ties other than family income. These factors appear when researchers compare one population group with another. The Growth of American Families Study conducted in 1955 selected religion and level of education as the major factors influencing family size. The effect of income on family size appeared to be weaker than either education or religion.[22] A similar study, repeated in 1960, confirmed these findings. The effect of religion has been summarized as follows:

> Religion is a major factor in sculpturing completed family size. Religious fertility differentials—Catholics, high; Jews, low; with Protestants in between—appeared to be diminishing a decade ago, but recent studies indicate that since 1955 the traditional gap between Catholics and Protestants has widened again. It is unlikely that this trend will change even where economic and social differences between the groups are eliminated, because the greatest fertility differences often are found at the highest educational and income levels.[23]

So, too, education is an important "regulator" of fertility. The more highly educated groups of the population have increased their average family size in each of the last several decades, moving towards the averages of the poorly educated. Nevertheless, 1,000 married women born in the late 1920s will, if they had less than an eighth-grade education, probably have between 3,600 and 3,900 children. Those who have completed college will probably have between 2,500 and

[20] R. A. Easterlin, "The Baby Boom in Perspective," *The American Economic Review* (December, 1961).

[21] R. A. Easterlin, "On the Relation of Economic Factors to the Recent Fertility Decline," Meeting of the Population Association of America, Chicago, April 23, 1965.

[22] Ronald Freedman, Pascal K. Whelpton and Arthur A. Campbell, *Family Planning, Sterility and Population Growth* (New York: McGraw-Hill Book Company, 1959).

[23] "New Patterns in U.S. Fertility," *Population Bulletin* (September, 1964), pp. 114–15.

2,900 children.[24] To some extent, education seems to govern fertility.

If women work after marriage, the chances are that they will have fewer children. The evidence on this point is "systematic" and independent of family income.[25] It can only in part be attributed to the fact that women who cannot have children may choose to work. Presumably families postpone having children and, in some cases, avoid having additional children *in order to* make it possible for the women to work. In this sense, family patterns that encourage women to work—increasingly characteristic of the United States—are restraints on fertility.

Other factors affecting fertility should be mentioned. Rural families and city families with rural background tend to have more children than average;[26] with the continued movement to cities, the significance of this factor should diminish. It may be expected that housing policies affect family size.[27] In the last analysis, the decision to have a child is made or evaded by people; styles about family size and other psychological factors must play a role. Paul H. Douglas wrote of one kind of psychological factor when responding, on one occasion, to the claim that family allowances would cause an increase in population. He said as follows:

> There are other than economic barriers to large families. Children tax the endurance and patience of their mothers, and even

were women assured that their children would be provided with sufficient food and clothing, few would wish to bring large families into the world.[28]

There speaks not a distinguished economist and professor but an attentive father.

Demographic developments that are, in a sense, accidental, influence the number of births in a given year or decade. A baby boom after World War II leads to a marriage boom in the late 1960s and a rise in total births shortly afterwards. No real trend may be reflected but only the annoying human predilection for moving in fits and starts rather than in ideal curves. It has been noted that people are marrying younger and having their children earlier. Such trends produce a temporary rise in annual birth rate; they may or may not affect the total number of children women have in a lifetime. There has been as well an increase in the proportion of people who marry, leading to an increase in birth rate per thousand population but not in births per family.

This catalogue of factors affecting birth rate in the United States, though far from exhaustive, leads to a simple conclusion. A roughly similar conclusion has already been drawn from the experience of other countries. With care, researchers can distinguish a role that income may play in increasing the short-term birth rate. Total personal income in the United States approximates $500 billion a year. A fair-sized new income-maintenance program might constitute 1 per cent of this amount. And total personal income is only one—not

---

[24] Arthur A. Campbell, "Recent Fertility Trends in the United States and Canada," paper presented to the United Nations World Population Conference, Belgrade, Yugoslavia, August–September 1965.

[25] Ronald Freedman, *op. cit.*

[26] Westoff, *op. cit.*

[27] Eldridge, *op. cit.*

[28] Paul H. Douglas, *Wages and the Family*, 2nd edition (Chicago: University of Chicago Press, 1927), p. 253.

the most powerful—item in the catalogue. The birth rate is compounded of income and one's conception of income, of education and ignorance, of conviction and faith, of geography and technology, of love and covetousness, of accident, and design. It does not seem that the over-all birth rate would be markedly affected for the short run or affected at all for the long run.

The special question of low-income families must be considered separately. Society cannot be content if they are led to handicap themselves with large families, even if the development does not loom very large in national statistics.

Concern about the relationship of poverty and family size arises from more or less overlapping bodies of information. First is the prevalence of poverty among large families. It is sometimes assumed that the association of poverty and family size is a consequence of disorganized families. It may be found also with intact families. Young married women, through their early twenties, have fewer children if their husbands have less income. College students, whose income is low and who postpone having children, must account somewhat for this tendency.[29] In any event, the older families that are poor surpass other families in number of children. For example, white mothers in their early forties averaged 3.6 children each if their husbands earned under $2,000 in 1959. Similar mothers, if their husbands earned over $5,000, averaged 2.7 children each.

A second source of concern is a large number of studies that "document an inverse relationship between status measures and fertility..."[30] Many of the explanations proffered for this relationship center about the consequences of upward mobility for families—better education, later marriage, access to the best means of contraception, and so forth—all may lead to having fewer children. On the other hand, it is possible to view the relationship as a consequence of determination to achieve improved status: ambitious families arrange to control births in order to achieve their ends. Probably, each view is partially correct.

A third source of concern is undoubtedly the body of observations about Negro family patterns. The low-income white mother mentioned above has 3.6 children but a nonwhite mother at the same age and income has 5 children. Negro families more commonly than white families show symptoms of disorganization—separation, illegitimacy. Breathes there a man educated beyond monosyllables who has not heard of the Negro matriarchal family? Much of the contrast between Negro and white family patterns—contrast of *average* behavior—reflects the far larger proportion of Negroes who are poor. (The fertility of Negroes with higher education and higher occupational status is actually less than that of their white counterparts.) How much difference, if any, may be allocated to other factors than poverty (discrimination? ethnic patterns?) must, in the absence

---

29 If one considers family rather than husband's income, fewer children are associated with *more* income, except in the youngest group of white wives, aged 15 to 19. Presumably, the woman who works because her husband earns little tends to have fewer children in the first years of marriage. See Bureau of the Census, *U.S. Census of Population 1960–Women by Number of Children Ever Born*, Final Report, PC(2)–3A, 1964, tables 37 and 38.

30 Ronald Freedman, *op. cit.*, p. 59.

of relevant research, rest on judgment or bias.

Each stream of material in its own way establishes a connection between fertility and low income. Poverty and large families may both result from the same unfortunate circumstances—premature family and occupational choices, limited education and competence in general, limited resources. Poverty, family breakdown, and family size interact; year by year, they contribute to one another.[31] One can find in the relationship between low income and family size reason to believe that more income would lead to more children. One can also find reason to believe the opposite.

These arguments may be examined separately. Poor education and relative incompetence will not immediately be altered by a cash payment to families. Children may improve in these qualities; some parents may gain in education but many will not. It may be difficult to believe that families generally will seize on the prospect of an additional $25 or $50 a month deliberately to have an additional child. Such a belief requires the conviction that poor families are now limiting the number of their children because they are miserable, as Ronald Freedman has observed. Nevertheless, it is plausible that some uneducated families—apathetic, impulsive, grateful for the prospect of any cash income at all—may set out to have additional children. Whether the number might be large may be assessed in the light of the contrary argument.

The tendency of poor families to have somewhat more children might be altered in comparatively immediate, simple ways. The provision of a more nearly adequate income might lead to the knowledge and materials that are needed for limiting family size. Especially may this be true with the development of oral contraceptives and the intra-uterine device, both apparently more acceptable than devices previously used, along with the availability of services in public health and private medical sectors. Studies indicate that, when approached directly with birth-control information, "large numbers" of low-income families take advantage of such measures.[32]

Beyond the simple response, the family-income cycle of poor families can be interrupted. Providing income with which to do the things that lead to self-improvement is one method of altering family-income development. From this point of view, a cash payment adequate to its purpose would lead out of poverty and act to limit family size as well. Joseph Willard has put one reason that higher income will lead to smaller families as follows:

> It can be argued ... that as the income of the family unit is raised the birth rate will decline. Numerous studies have recorded differences in family size associated with differences in income and nearly all have led to similar conclusions, that the size of family becomes smaller as income rises and prosperity increases. It might be reasoned therefore, that the addition of disposable income for the family ... may sufficiently raise their standard of living so that they behave, after a time lag for adjustments, in accordance

---

[31] This point will be examined in detail in an article, "The Family Cycle and Income Development," by Alvin L. Schorr, in *Social Security Bulletin.*

[32] Elizabeth C. Corkey, "A Family Planning Program for the Low-Income Family," *Journal of Marriage and The Family* (November, 1964), p. 480.

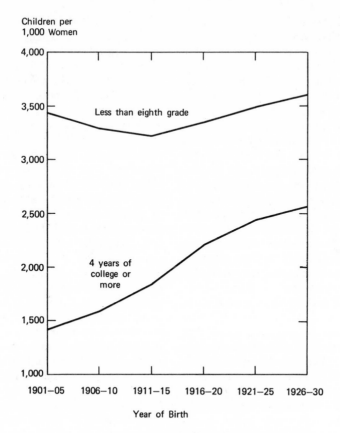

Children per
1,000 Women

FIG. 2. Education and Fertility: Estimated Number of Children per 1,000 White Women, by Women's Educational Attainment and Date of Birth

with social standards of typical persons at the new level rather than the old.[33]

The crux of this argument is not knowable. If lower-income people are provided with more money, will they become similar in fertility patterns to people with more money? Those who will hesitate to answer "yes" are conscious that the question is complex. Is it partly because they have limited the number of their children

that many people have decent income? If a disorganized family is simply provided with income, will family patterns be affected? Is money by itself so powerful? Perhaps accumulating data on the desires of low-income families hold a hint of what might happen. As Fig. 2 shows, in 25 years, the difference in fertility between the least- and best-educated women (more or less comparable to the lowest- and highest-income families) has narrowed from 2 children per woman to 1 child per woman. What women say they want is even more alike. It is difficult to discover

[33] Joseph W. Willard, "Some Aspects of Family Allowances and Income Redistribution in Canada," *Public Policy*, V. V, 1954, p. 231.

much difference in the number of children that low-income and high-income families say they want;[34] two to four children is the universal ideal. Then would not poor families, if they were given the means, attempt to have the number of children they say they want—and no more?

As with the material on over-all population trends, the discussion has once again come full circle to the conclusion based on the experience of other countries. An income-maintenance program might prompt some number of low-income families to have an additional child; people respond inscrutably to their personal perception of events. On the other hand, an income-maintenance program might well prompt some poor families to have fewer children. On the whole, the tendency to increase family size, if it occurred, would be a short-range tendency. The tendency to limit family size, arising from changes in attitude, education, and family patterns, would be a long-range tendency. In retrospect, it would prove impossible to find any alteration in the relationship between low-income and other birth rates that could be atributed to a new income-maintenance program.[35]

Having looked into the birth rates of poor people, it is only fair to note the argument that an income-maintenance program would increase births among those families who have more income. As has been seen, French births increased among those with comfortable incomes concurrent with the development of family allowances. One French demographer argues, therefore, that family allowances increase the birth rate by permitting those who are interested in the future of their children—those with the fewest children and the highest status —to have additional children.[36] Such a point of view is lent support by an American study of family behavior with respect to fertility. The study concludes that there is "one central norm" about family size: "One should not have more children than one can support, but one should have as many children as one can afford."[37] Those who have deliberately limited births in keeping with their view of what they can afford—presumably middle-class families or those moving up— might, with a government payment, decide to have an additional child.

[34] Lee Rainwater, *Family Design* (Chicago: Aldine Publishing Company, 1965); Ronald Freedman and L. Coombs, "Working Paper on Family Income and Family Growth," Appendix B to Social Security Administration Grant Progress Report, June 1963, mimeographed.

[35] Figure 2 provides the opportunity to test this point with regard to a large income-maintenance program for children. The aid to families with dependent children program was introduced in 1935; its effects would have been felt by 1936 or 1937. Well-educated women who were in their early twenties in 1935 (and were presumably to be having children through the 1950s) were to average more children than comparable women 5 years earlier. Five years later,

comparable women increased their family size even more sharply. In contrast, poorly educated women in their early twenties in 1935 show a decline in average number of children from a comparable group 5 years earlier. Five years later, a comparable group records a small increase in average family size.

The point of this exercise is negative. The trends charted probably responded to general economic improvement, to the onset of war, and other major forces. But one who seeks a relation between fertility and income maintenance finds, in the United States as in Canada, that the data are not merely uninformative but seem to move in the wrong direction.

[36] M. Febay, "Niveau et évolution de la fécondité par categorie socio-professionelle en France," *Population*, October–December 1959.

[37] Lee Rainwater, *op. cit.*, pp. 281–82.

Here again, the possibility must be acknowledged that a program would lead to some number of additional children. In the same sense, however, increased national income may lead to more births. It is difficult to regard an income-maintenance program as a substantial factor.

A rigorous scientific demonstration has not been provided that income maintenance will lead to a higher birth rate or that it will not. A new income-maintenance program would in all probability lead some people, in-cluding some people who are poor, to have additional children. But this effect would probably be trivial in re-lation to concurrent developments and not discernible in subsequent popula-tion figures. Balancing any small effect, a substantial income-mainte-nance program should significantly improve the circumstances of many families. In their children's genera-tion, at least, it may provide the com-petence and climate to achieve the family size that that generation genu-inely wants.

Education and Fertility in Puerto Rico[*]

J. Mayone Stycos

One of the most important ques-tions for nations where population growth is impeding economic develop-ment refers to the relation between education and fertility. Interest is motivated by the belief that western fertility declines have been caused, at least in part, by advances in educa-tion for the general population. As a consequence of this belief, modern-izing countries sometimes argue that direct programs to induce fertility

[*] J. Mayone Stycos, "Education and Fertility in Puerto Rico," in *Proceedings of the World Population Conference, 1965* (New York: United Nations, 1967), IV, pp. 177–80.

control are unnecessary, since educa-tional advances will take care of the problem. Others justify heavy outlays in population education, especially at the primary levels, partly in terms of the presumed effect on fertility.

At a very general level, some rela-tion between crude measures of fer-tility and education is found for most Latin American countries. Utilizing 1950 census data for eleven Latin American countries, child-woman ratios (persons aged 0–4 per 1,000 women aged 15–49) and literacy rates (percentage of adult population who can read and write) were computed for the smallest administrative units in each country reported in the censuses.[1] Although considerable variation in size of the relation between these two measures was apparent, in all cases the relation was negative, ranging from lows of −0.10 to −0.26 for Honduras, Panama, Mexico, and Venezuela, through moderate correlations of −0.36 and −0.46 for Guatemala and Colombia, to correlations of −0.60 and over for El Salvador, Costa Rica, Nicaragua, Chile, and Argentina.

While of considerable interest, the interpretation of such findings is made difficult by the crudeness of the measures themselves, the difficulty of holding constant such related variables such as urbanization,[2] and by the general limitations on causal inference based on ecological correlations. Furthermore, for any nation engaged in systematic planning, the question is not so much whether education produces a reduction in human fertility, as how much education produces how much of a change in fertility among which categories of the population. To answer such a question, while avoiding the limitations of ecological data, direct cross tabulations of educational achievement and fertility are needed, holding constant other relevant variables.

One of the few attempts of this kind for Latin American populations occurs in A. Jaffe's study of Puerto Rico. Utilizing 1955 sample survey data from the Puerto Rican Bureau of Labour Statistics, Jaffe concluded that "...at least six and possibly nine years of schooling for women is required before any significant decline in the birth rate occurs..."; and "the combined influence of increasing education and increasing participation of women in modern economic enterprises is likely to be more effective than either factor by itself."[3] The present paper continues this discussion by utilizing 1960 census data for Puerto Rico.

Jaffe's important thesis that at least 6 years of schooling was needed in order to have a real influence on fertility was somewhat limited by the broad educational categories reported in his analysis: zero to 4 years, 5 to 9, and 10 or more years of schooling. As Jaffe pointed out, "The data do not show at what point the education of women begins to take effect, i.e., whether 6, 7, 8, or 9 years of schooling are needed...." Table 1, utilizing 1960 special tabulations, increases the number of categories. In order to simplify the analysis, the data have been confined to legally married women of completed fertility whose spouses were present.

The total range in fertility is very great. Woman with no education have had 3.3 times as many births as those with one or more years of college. If the progression were distributed evenly over the approximately 14 years of education, it would mean that each additional year of schooling produced 0.4 fewer live births—or

---

[1] The countries were Argentina, Chile, Colombia, Costa Rica, El Salvador, Guatemala, Honduras, Mexico, Nicaragua, Panama, and Venezuela. The number of units ranged from fourteen in El Salvador to sixty-five in Costa Rica.

[2] While the mean correlation between the fertility ratio and the percentage of literate persons for the eleven countries is −0.46, it is −0.58 between the fertility ratios and the percentage of urban population. Unpublished data of the International Population Program. For a more extended analysis of a single country, using similar data, see J. M. Stycos, "Culture and differential fertility in Peru," *Population Studies*, XVI, No. 3 (March, 1963).

[3] A. J. Jaffe, *People, Jobs and Economic Development* (New York, N.Y.: The Free Press of Glencoe, Inc., 1959), pp. 196–97.

TABLE 1. Total Live Births per 1,000 Married Women Aged 45 and Over,[a] by Education, Puerto Rico, 1960

Years of school completed	Births per 1,000 women	Change from preceding category (percentage)	Women in category (percentage)
0	7,421	—	35.2
Primary :			
1–4	6,896	−7.0	32.8
5–6	5,836	−15.4	11.7
7–8	4,288	−26.5	8.5
Secondary :			
1–3	3,367	−21.5	4.0
4	2,453	−27.1	3.4
College :			
1+	1,920	−21.7	4.4
Total	6,224	—	100.0

Source : Special tabulations of the 1960 census of Puerto Rico.
[a] Legally married women with spouses present.

well over one birth for every three years of schooling. However, the progression is not even. There is only a difference of 7 per cent in the number of live births between those with no education and those with 1 to 4 years of education. Between the latter category and those with 5 or 6 there is a 15 per cent reduction in fertility. Thus, women with about 6 years of schooling, a major educational goal for many modernizing countries, have only 1.6 fewer live births by completion of the childbearing period than do women who have had no education. Each year of education over this range means only 0.28 fewer births and much less than this at the lower end of the educational continuum.

The data indicate an accelerating effect of education on fertility, starting very slowly in the lower primary school,[4] and reaching a high level

toward the end of junior high school, which is maintained thereafter. Differences are especially marked at the points of completing primary school and high school, which is maintained thereafter. Differences are especially marked at the points of completing primary school and high school,[5] but from the seventh grade on there are marked differences in fertility with each increment of education.[6]

[4] The accelerating effect of education

on fertility may even occur within the first category, zero to 4 years. Published data for ever-married women aged 35–44 (including consensually married, divorced, separated or widowed) show a 2.7 drop in live births between those with no education and those with one or two years, and a drop of 3.5 per cent between the latter category and those with three or four.

[5] See *United States Census of Population, 1960: Puerto Rico*, Series PC (1), No. 53D (Washington, Government Printing Office), Table 95.

[6] It is of interest that even women with 7 or 8 years of education are having more than twice as many live births as the average Puerto Rican woman con-

TABLE 2.   Total Live Births per 1,000 Married Women Aged 45 and Over,[a] by Education and Residence, Puerto Rico, 1960

Years of school completed	San Juan SMSA	Urban	Rural
0	6,936	6,454	7,830
Primary :			
1–4	5,962	5,865	7,626
5–6	5,078	4,942	6,886
7–8	3,924	4,106	5,271
Secondary :			
1–3	3,032	3,295	4,454
4	2,386	2,525	2,648
College :			
1+	1,909	1,938	1,931
Total	4,878	5,200	7,422

[a] Legally married women with spouses present.
Source : Special tabulations of the 1960 census of Puerto Rico.

As noted earlier, in evaluating or explaining the influence of education on fertility, one must control other variables, probably the most important of which is residence. In Puerto Rico, there is a marked relation between residence and education. For example, of legally married women aged 45 and over in 1960, 49 per cent in San Juan, 59 per cent in other urban areas, and 83 per cent in rural areas have had less than 5 years of schooling.

In Table 2, a three-category residential classification—the San Juan Standard Metropolitan Statistical Areas, other urban areas and rural areas—has been introduced.

Although there is little difference between San Juan and other urban areas when education is controlled, both education and residence (rural and nonrural) show independent relationships with fertility. Over the total educational range, i.e., from those with no education to those with one or more years of college, the rural areas show the greatest absolute and relative declines in fertility. Rural women of no education have had four times as many births as rural college women.

Urban fertility starts at a higher level than rural, but declines somewhat less over the entire educational range. The net effect is that toward the upper end of the educational range, differences in fertility by residence have virtually disappeared.[7] High educational inputs serve to equalize fertility at low levels among

siders the ideal number of children to have (two or less)—and only a fifth of the women get this far in school. See P. K. Hatt, *Backgrounds of Human Fertility in Puerto Rico* (Princeton: Princeton University Press, 1952), p. 53, Table 37.

[7] Jaffe found that urban and rural differences disappeared after 10 years of education. Since part of the San Juan metropolitan area was classified as rural, he speculated that "a higher proportion of the better educated 'rural' women were residing in the metropolitan area and conforming to urban rather than rural ways of life", *op. cit.*, p. 181.

women of varying residence. The leveling out, however, does not occur until completion of high school.

An important question for the strategy of modernization relates to the timing and amounts of rural *versus* urban investments in education. In terms of effects on fertility, will the dollar invested in rural schools go as far as the dollar invested in urban schools?

Looking at the degree of change in fertility associated with successive increments of education within each residential area (Table 3), one finds

TABLE 3. Percentage Change in Fertility (Live Births per 1,000 Legally Married Women 45+) between Successive Educational Categories, by Residence, Puerto Rico, 1960

Between educational categories	San Juan SMSA and Urban	Rural
0 and 1–4	−11.5	− 2.6
1–4 and 5–6	−15.2	− 9.7
5–6 and 7–8	−20.1	−23.4
7–8 and 1–3 high school	−21.9	−15.5
1–3 and 4 high school	−22.4	−40.5
4 high school and college	−20.9	−27.1

that rural and urban areas have somewhat different patterns. The modest declines in fertility which are characteristic for the Commonwealth as a whole at the primary school level are especially characteristic of rural areas. Despite the fact that education eventually levels out fertility differences between urban and rural areas, the same increases in education do not have the same effect on fertility in rural and urban areas at the same time. Thus, urban fertility drops by 25 per cent between women with no education and women with five or six

years, but only by 12 per cent for rural women. It would appear that modest inputs of education have a negligible impact in rural areas, but a more important effect in urban areas. To summarize, a little education goes a longer way in the urban areas, but a lot of education goes farthest in rural areas.

If fertility is closely related to education, even when other variables are controlled, what accounts for this relation? While physiological and nutritional factors should not be ignored, there is good reason to believe that the major explanation lies in deliberate attempts by couples to limit their fertility. As obvious as this point may seem, it is sometimes seemingly denied by nondemographers who imply that education could be a substitute for birth control.

Table 4 shows data from a sample survey conducted in Puerto Rico in 1953, relating the practice of birth control to residence and education.

TABLE 4. Percentage Who Have Used a Birth Control Method, by Residence and Education, Puerto Rico, 1953[a]

Years of education	Urban	Rural
0	40	26
1–4	40	35
5–8	57	37
9+	71	64

[a] While the sample was representative of the population of Puerto Rican households, the reported data for 767 couples refer to the married or consensually married population. See R. Hill, J. M. Stycos, and K. W. Back, *The Family and Population Control* (Chapel Hill: University of North Carolina Press, 1959), p. 164, Table 78.

Consistent with the foregoing findings on fertility, one sees that:

(1) Urban residence and years of education are independently and positively related to the practice of birth control;

(2) At the high school level, differences in contraceptive practice virtually disappear between urban and rural families;

(3) The largest impact of education on contraceptive practice occurs after elementary school in both urban and rural areas. However, the data do not support the hypothesis that a little education has more impact in the urban areas.

CONCLUSIONS

Over the past half-century, Puerto Rico has shown remarkable gains in education. According to census data, 55 per cent of its population over age 10 was illiterate in 1920, 41 per cent in 1930, 32 per cent in 1940, 25 per cent in 1950, and 19 per cent in 1960. The birth rate, however, showed no signs of change until the turn of the half-century, when it began dropping from about forty to its current rate of about thirty-one. However, other evidence indicates that much of this decline was caused by the out-migration of Puerto Ricans in the reproductive ages. It would appear that major improvements in education do not produce automatic fertility declines within the time span discussed.

On the other hand, the analysis presented here shows marked differential fertility by education. The fact that the differentials accelerate with education, with major declines occurring only after elementary school is achieved, accounts for the apparent discrepancy, for much of Puerto Rico's educational gains have been at lower levels.

The implications of the foregoing for Latin American countries with currently high birth rates are not favourable. Educational gains in Puerto Rico have been accomplished in a most propitious milieu for fertility decline, i.e., they have been accompanied by marked gains in per capita income, urbanization and industrialization. (In 1950 its per capita commercial energy consumption was exceeded only by Argentina, Chile and Venezuela; its per capita income only by Venezuela.) Thus, educational gains have not occurred in a "socioeconomic vacuum," as may occur with some Latin American countries.

In any event, most Latin American countries are well behind Puerto Rico in education. In 1950 at least eleven Latin American countries showed higher illiteracy rates than did Puerto Rico in 1930, and the average level of schooling in most Latin American countries is well below the point where crucial drops in fertility were seen to take place in Puerto Rico. In 1950, in at least nine Latin countries, more than three quarters of the males aged 25 and over had completed less than 4 years of primary school; in only two countries and Puerto Rico was this figure under 50 per cent.[8] For the sixteen Latin American countries where data were available, only about 7 per cent of the total population aged 15 years and over had more than 6 years of education. The average years completed in these countries were 2.2, as opposed to 4.5 in Puerto Rico.[9]

[8] *United Nations Compendium of Social Statistics: 1963* (United Nations publication, Sales No.: 63, XVII.3), Table 60.

[9] See O. Vera, "The educational situation and requirements in Latin America," in *Social Aspects of Economic*

Most striking of all are data from the mid-1950s which indicate that only about one in every four or five who begin school in Latin America

ever completed the elementary level, and only one in twenty complete the secondary level.[10] Latin American countries which wait for "education" to reduce birth rates may wait a long time.

Development in Latin America, eds. E. De Vries and J. Medina Echevarria, I (Paris, United Nations Educational, Scientific and Cultural Organization, 1963), p. 286, Table 3.

---

[10] *Ibid.*, pp. 291, 303.

Education, Migration, and Economic Life Chances of Male Entrants to the Labor Force from A Low-Income Rural Area[*]

Harry K. Schwarzweller

It is a well-founded generalization of economic behavior that labor tends to flow in the direction of higher wages.[1] Eastern Kentucky, a part of

the Southern Appalachian Mountain Region, is an area of chronic underemployment, and its people, particularly those young adults newly recruited into the labor force, tend to migrate in very large numbers to industrial centers in the Ohio Valley

---

* Harry K. Schwarzweller, "Education, Migration, and Economic Life Chances of Male Entrants to the Labor Force from a Low-Income Rural Area," *Rural Sociology*, 29 (June, 1964), 152–167.

[1] The generalization may not be a universal principle that holds true in all cultures at all times; however, this phenomenon has been observed consistently in the case of migration patterns within the more urbanized, industrializing nations of the Western world during modern times. In the United States, for example, see: Carter L. Goodrich *et al.*, *Migration and Economic Opportunity* (Philadelphia: University of Pennsylvania Press, 1936); Donald

J. Bogue, Henry S. Shryock, Jr., and Siegfried A. Hoermann, *Subregional Migration in the U.S., 1935–40*, Vol. I, *Streams of Migration Between Subregions* (Oxford, Ohio: Miami University, Scripps Foundation in Population Distribution No. 5, 1957); K. M. George, *Association of Selected Economic Factors with Net Migration Rates in the Southern Appalachian Region, 1935–1957*, Unpublished M. A. thesis (Lexington: University of Kentucky, June, 1961).

where more job opportunities are available.[2]

In numerous studies dealing with the low-income area labor force in this and other regions, research designs usually focus either on (1) the area of origin, in which case the problem is generally couched in terms of labor potential, labor commitment, propensity to migrate, potential adaptability to the industrial work situation, etc.; or (2) on the areas of destination, in which case the problem is very often conceptualized as a comparison between rural-recruited workers and their urban counterparts. In the latter case, rural-recruited workers often rank lower on indices of adjustment, status mobility, job-holding stability, and work efficiency.[3]

Little research attention has been given to assessing the structural characteristics of the low-income area labor force from the point of view of the area of origin as well as the areas of destination receiving migrants. A great deal of evidence suggests that these two areas tend to function as a single migration system. One can conceive of both the migrant and nonmigrant segments as being linked together as a sociocultural system through which the demands of the labor market, external to that system but disturbing its boundaries, influence the movement of men and families between the subsystems.[4] Recently, theoretical inter-

ests have been renewed in this more holistic approach to the problem of rural-urban migration.[5]

The purpose of this paper is twofold: (1) to compare the occupational placement of two segments of a low-income area labor force, one segment of which is in the area of origin and the other segment of which is in the area of destination; and (2) to explore the influence of education and migration on the occupational placement and economic life chances of youth entering the labor force from a low-income, rural situation.

THE RESEARCH DESIGN[6]

The population selected for study were males enrolled in the eighth grade during the school year of 1949–

[2] See Robert E. Galloway, *Rural Manpower in Eastern Kentucky*, Lexington: Kentucky Agr. Exp. Sta. Bull. 627 (June, 1955), p. 8.

[3] For contrary evidence, see Richard A. Lester, "Southern Wage Differentials: Developments, Analysis and Implications," *Southern Economic Journal*, XIII (April, 1947), 386–394.

[4] The term "migration system" is used and discussed in reference to demog-

raphic data by James S. Brown and George A. Hillery, Jr., "The Great Migration, 1940–1950," in *The Southern Appalachian Region: A Survey*, ed. Thomas R. Ford (Lexington: University of Kentucky Press, 1962).

[5] Early classic works in sociology that utilized a holistic approach to the problem of rural–urban migration, are, of course, Pierre Guillaume Frédéric Le Play, *Les ouvriers européens*, 2nd ed., 6 volumes, Paris: Imprimerie Impèriale, 1877–1879; W. I. Thomas and Florian Znaniecki, *The Polish Peasant in Europe and America* (Boston: R. G. Badger, 1918–1920); Conrad M. Arensberg and Solon T. Kimball, *Family and Community in Ireland* (Cambridge, Massachusetts: Harvard University Press, 1940).

[6] For a more detailed description of the research project from initiation to analysis, see Harry K. Schwarzweller, *Research Design, Field Work Procedures, and Data Collection Problems in a Follow-Up Study of Young Men from Eastern Kentucky*, Lexington: University of Kentucky, Department of Rural Sociology, RS 21, May, 1963.

For additional information on the sociocultural background of these young men, see Harry K. Schwarzweller, *Sociocultural Origins and Migration Patterns of Young Men From Eastern Kentucky*, Lexington: Kentucky Agr. Exp. Sta., Bull. 686, December, 1963.

50 in eleven low-income counties of eastern Kentucky.[7] These counties do not have urban centers; they have few if any industrial opportunities for youths; they have an economic base of small-scale commercial and subsistence-type agriculture along with some marginal mining operations; they have a large net out-migration (particularly of the age category studied); and they are relatively isolated geographically, culturally, and economically from the mainstream of American society. It was anticipated that at least half of these men would have migrated from the eastern Kentucky area and would have taken up residence in the Ohio Valley.

Eighth grade enrollment lists were obtained from school records with the cooperation and assistance of county school superintendents. The original base population list totaled 757 individuals. After 10 years, as anticipated, a tremendous technical difficulty was encountered in the attempt to trace the whereabouts of these men; this is a highly mobile age-group in a population characterized by high rates of out-migration.

Field work was limited to Ohio and Kentucky and excluded individuals in mental, penal, military, and other institutions. Last known addresses were obtained from school records, informants in the home counties, letters to parents, and by various other techniques described in detail elsewhere.[8] A total of 307 interviews were completed; they provided the data upon which the paper is based.[9]

The follow-up nature of the research design yielded a rather low per cent, by traditional standards, of the base population (41 per cent). However, comparison with data obtained through mailed questionnaires from over 100 individuals not contacted by interviewers indicates a reasonable degree of representativeness.[10]

The larger project, of which this study is a part, is based on the general proposition that "schooling is a good thing." Thus, it is expected that the more schooling an individual completes (1) the greater the contribution he can make to the public welfare; (2) the greater will be his rewards from the society in which he lives; and (3) the greater will be his adaptation to the sociocultural circumstances in which he works and makes his home. However, statements of relationships such as these presuppose certain specified environmental conditions. In this study, major interest focuses on the situational conditions under which the working hypotheses, derived from the above

---

[7] The age factor, therefore, was held constant by design. The mean age for the total study population was found to be 24.9 years, with 80 per cent falling between 24 and 26 years of age at last birthdays. It was expected that these youths, by and large, would have normally completed formal education and military service and would be more or less established in their work careers.

[8] Schwarzweller, *Research Design, op. cit.*

[9] The interview schedule was prepared in consultation with various professional personnel in the U.S. Department of Agriculture, the Cooperative Extension Service, the Sociology Department at the University of Kentucky, the State Department of Education, and local county school systems. It was pretested on a similar age-group under similar circumstances in rural and urban situations of western Kentucky. A team of interviewers, including a field supervisor and editor, were trained, and the field work undertaken during the early summer months of 1960.

[10] Schwarzweller, *Research Design, op. cit.*

statements, are put to an empirical test.

The young man who decides not to drop out of school before graduation generally is considered to have made a wise and rational decision that will enhance his future life chances. Likewise, it is recognized that a youth's decision to remain in the home county or to migrate after leaving school has a decided bearing on his future career alternatives, particularly if the home county is in an area of chronic underemployment and limited economic opportunity. But what effect does the latter decision have upon his career alternatives, and what effect does the combined influence of migration and education have upon the youth's life chances? This study is designed to explore such questions. In one sense, an assessment is made of the relative importance of education in the occupational placement and economic life chances of youths entering the labor force from low-income rural area backgrounds *when the effects of regional variations in the structure of occupational opportunity are controlled.*

SELECTIVITY OF MIGRATION

The selectivity of migration may account for some of the observed differences between the two segments of the original base population under consideration. Certainly one would be hard pressed indeed to defend the thesis that migrants and nonmigrants are drawn from a single population homogeneous in personality traits and sociocultural origins.[11] For the purposes of this study these antecedent differences, if any, need to be stated, particularly where they bear upon the variables under consideration.

Comparisons between the two segments of this study population in terms of (1) number of siblings in family-of-origins; (2) occupational status of fathers; (3) education of mothers; (4) education of fathers; (5) rural farm or rural nonfarm backgrounds; and (6) the most crucial variable for the present study, the level of schooling completed by respondents (see Table 1), reveal no statistically significant differences. Chi-square tests were employed throughout, with the criterion for rejecting the null hypotheses set at the 0.05 level of probability. Thus, for the purposes of analyses undertaken in the remainder of this paper, one can argue with some measure of assurance that the two segments of this study population are drawn from more or less similar sociocultural circumstances.[12]

A word of caution should be interjected at this point. One of the distinctive characteristics of the eastern Kentucky sociocultural complex is its emphasis upon strong intergenerational and family group ties.[13] Migrants probably differ in some ways from nonmigrants by the simple fact

---

[11] However, Brown and Buck, in their follow-up study of Pennsylvania rural youths, demonstrate that this is the case in terms of I.Q., father's oc-cupation, and educational levels of youths. See C. Harold Brown and Roy C. Buck, *Factors Associated with the Migrant Status of Young Adult Males from Rural Pennsylvania*, University Park: Pennsylvania Agr. Exp. Sta., Bulletin 676, January, 1961.

[12] These data are reported by Schwarzweller, *Sociocultural Origins and Migration Patterns, op. cit.*

[13] This familistic orientation is vividly portrayed by James S. Brown, *The Family Group in a Kentucky Mountain Farming Community*, Lexington: Kentucky Agr. Exp. Sta., Bull. 588, June, 1952.

TABLE 1. Level of Schooling Completed by Male Entrants to the Labor Force from Eastern Kentucky by Region of Residence, 1960

| Level of schooling completed | Region of residence, 1960 | | | |
| | Within E. Kentucky (nonmigrants) | | Outside E. Kentucky (migrants) | |
	Number	Per cent	Number	Per cent
No high school	47	29.9	49	32.7
Some high school	36	23.0	36	24.0
High school graduate	47	29.9	50	33.3
Some college	27	17.2	15	10.0
Total	157	100.0	150	100.0

$$\chi^2 = 3.809 \; ; \; df = 3 \; ; \; P > 0.05$$

that they did move away from parents, kinsfolk, and friends in the home county. Pursuing the motivational and situational factors which cause individuals to migrate is beyond the scope of the present paper. However, the fact that there are no significant differences between the two segments in the sociocultural background data cited above suggests that "what has happened" to these individuals during the decade 1950–60 can be attributed to regional variations in the structure of opportunity and the intervening cultural experiences of the individuals during that decade.

REGIONAL VARIATIONS IN OCCUPATIONAL OPPORTUNITY

There are great variations among economic regions and subregions in the United States, not only in the regional structure of the labor force but also in the availability of jobs for new entrants to the labor force. Concerning the latter point, for example, replacement ratios in the eleven counties, from which the study

population is drawn, range from 154 to 226.[14]

Furthermore, concerning the first point, the kinds of jobs available to these new entrants to the low-income area labor force are, categorically speaking, quite different in the respective regions. The occupational structure of eastern Kentucky is founded on a base of extractive industries, whereas migrants from the area move into situations where the predominating industry is manufacturing. The data in this study reflect this difference.

The jobs in which the men in this study were employed at the time of interviewing were classified according to the occupational situs categories developed by Morris and Murphy, the major criterion of which is the nature of the work task.[15] Those who were unemployed at that time, or who were students, and those for

---

[14] James S. Brown and Ralph J. Ramsey, *The Changing Kentucky Population*, Lexington: Kentucky Agr. Exp. Sta., Progress Report 67, September, 1958, Table 26.

[15] Richard T. Morris and Raymond J. Murphy, "The Situs Dimension in Occupational Structure," *American Sociological Review*, XXIV (April, 1959), 231–39.

whom information about the specific work task was too ambiguous for classification purposes were eliminated from this analysis (see Table 2).

No significant differences are observed in comparing the proportion of the migrant segment to the non-migrant segment with respect to: the arts and entertainment category (combined total—2 per cent); the education, research, and health and welfare categories (combined total—6 per cent); the transportation and commerce categories (combined total—15 per cent); and the building and maintenance category (combined total—26 per cent). In the case of legal authority, finance, and records categories, no respondents held such occupations in the nonmigrant segment, and only five were so classified among the migrants (all, incidentally, had completed high school).

As expected, the distinctive feature in the structure of occupations between these two segments is the large proportion of the migrants holding jobs in manufacturing (49 per cent) as compared with their non-migrant counterparts (5 per cent); and, similarly, the large proportion of nonmigrants holding jobs in extractive industries (43 per cent) as compared with the migrants (1 per cent). The kinds of occupations available are quite different in the two regions. This fact must be considered in evaluating the influence of education on the occupational placement and economic life chances of these youths.

REGIONAL VARIATIONS IN ECONOMIC LIFE CHANGES

The concept "life chances" is usually linked with social stratifica-

tion theory. It has been defined as "the probability of attaining culturally defined goals and avoiding culturally defined misfortunes."[16] In this sense, it differentiates between social strata in terms of the statistical prediction of certain ends or achievements which are deemed desirable by the culture. The present study attempted to tap one important dimension of life chances, namely, the economic or material, by employing a "static" measure and assuming prediction by degree of association in a comparative analysis.

The nine-item Cornell level of living scale was employed as a measuring instrument.[17] Level of living is often utilized as one component in composite measures of socioeconomic status. One can readily produce evidence demonstrating the high degree of correlation between this component and other components of SES such as educational level and occupational status. The reason is clear: given a cultural value consensus which defines the pursuit and acquisition of material amenities as "good," then those people with greater ability, better jobs, more money, in more powerful social positions, and so on, will possess greater means for acquiring these things.

The argument in this study is that material level of living is a meaningful measure of occupational success in the group studied. A major moti-

---

16 Harold F. Kaufman, Otis Dudley Duncan, Neal Gross, and William H. Sewell, "Problems of Theory and Method in the Study of Social Stratification in Rural Society," *Rural Sociology*, XVIII (March, 1953), 12–24.
17 Robert A. Danley and Charles E. Ramsey, *Standardization and Application of a Level of Living Scale for Farm and Nonfarm Families*, Ithaca, N.Y.: Cornell Agr. Exp. Sta., Memoir 362, (July, 1959).

TABLE 2. Occupational Situs of Jobs Held[a] by Male Entrants to the Labor Force from Eastern Kentucky, by Region of Residence, 1960

Occupational situs of jobs held	Region of residence, 1960			
	Within E. Kentucky (nonmigrants)		Outside E. Kentucky (migrants)	
	Number	Per cent	Number	Per cent
Manufacturing	7	5.1	70	48.6
Agriculture	41	30.0	2	1.4
Other extractive industries	18	13.1	0	0.0
Transportation and commerce	21	15.3	20	13.9
Building and maintenance	37	27.0	37	25.7
All other situs categories	13	9.5	15	10.4
Total	137	100.0	144	100.0

$$\chi^2 = 104.60; \; df = 5; \; P < 0.01$$

a. Those individuals who were unemployed, students, or for whom specific work task information was lacking were excluded from the analysis.

vation for migration is the quest for employment opportunities. Furthermore, data from this study reported elsewhere indicate a high level of aspiration for the acquisition of material amenities and a strong, realistic awareness of regional variations in opportunity among both segments of this population.[18] Since occupation is a major means by which a desirable level of living can be attained, and since the two regional situations which were studied differ in their structure of occupational opportunities, it is expected that the data will reflect these differences in occupational placements and consequently, in economic life chances.[19] It is hypothesized, therefore, that migration from this low-income area will be positively associated with level of living.

An operational assumption is made that the tendency to migrate is a more or less normally distributed characteristic. Correlation analysis, using a point biserial r correlation coefficient corrected for coarse groupings, produces an r of $+0.478$ (significant above the 0.01 level).[20] See Table 3. This moderately high correlation is interpreted as being indicative of regional variations in economic life chances that confront young men entering the labor force from low-income rural areas of eastern Kentucky. Any exploration of the influence of education on the occupational placement and economic life chances of these youth will have to take these regional variations of opportunity into account.

18 Harry K. Schwarzweller, *Career Placement and Economic Life Chances of Young Men from Eastern Kentucky*, Lexington: Kentucky Agr. Exp. Sta., Bull. 686, March, 1964.

19 Strictly speaking, these data show only occupations held, not occupations available. Other data, for example, from the U.S. Census, could be used to document this point. However, to do that would go far beyond the scope of the present paper or project.

20 See James B. Wert, Charles O. Neidt, and Stanley Ahmann, *Statistical Methods* (New York: Appleton-Century-Crofts, Inc., 1954), pp. 256–63.

TABLE 3. Level of Living Scores[a] of Male Entrants to the Labor Force from Eastern Kentucky by Region of Residence, 1960

Level of living[a] (grouped categories)	Region of residence, 1960			
	Within E. Kentucky (nonmigrants)		Outside E. Kentucky (migrants)	
	Number	Per cent	Number	Per cent
Low (0–3 pts.)	94	60.2	39	26.0
Middle (4–6)	50	32.1	89	59.3
High (7–9)	12	7.7	22	14.7
Total	156	100.0	150	100.0

$\sigma = 1.98$; $\bar{X} = 3.94$
$rp = +0.393$; $P < 0.01$
r (corrected) $= +0.478$

[a] Level of living measured by the nine-item Cornell Scale developed by Danley and Ramsey.

EDUCATION AND OCCUPATIONAL PLACEMENT: SITUS DIMENSION

It was established earlier that a major difference in the occupational placement between the two regional segments is that about half of the nonmigrants are engaged in the extractive industries, whereas almost half of the migrants are employed in manufacturing-type occupations. It was further established that the two segments do not differ significantly with respect to level of schooling completed. Thus, if high school tends to sort out individuals for particular occupational roles, as Sorokin and others assert, this phenomenon should be reflected by the data.[21]

In the case of the nonmigrant segment, analysis reveals that a larger proportion of the school "dropouts" hold jobs in the extractive industries ($\chi^2 = 5.209$; df=1; $P < 0.05$). The only other significant relationship observed from these data is that of

the eleven individuals in the education, research, and health and welfare categories, all had completed high school. One concludes that the extractive industries (agriculture and marginal mining) in this area tend to attract that portion of the labor force with less ability, at least as measured by the possession of a high school diploma.

In the case of the migrant segment, when focusing on the proportion of individuals engaged in manufacturing occupations compared with those in all other occupational pursuits, no significant difference in terms of high school completion is observed ($\chi^2 = 0.033$; df=1; $P > 0.05$). The only other significant relationship noted is that the building and maintenance occupations tend to attract a larger proportion of school dropouts (73 per cent of individuals in this situs category did not complete high school). Thus, one concludes that level of schooling is not significantly related to the occupational placement of youths in the migrant segment. In other words, the educational system in the low-income rural area does not appear to func-

21 Pitirim A. Sorokin, *Social and Cultural Mobility* (New York, N.Y.: The Free Press of Glencoe, Inc., 1959), pp. 187–93.

tion as a social mechanism for sorting out individuals on the basis of ability to qualify for and perform work roles in the occupational structure of the areas to which considerable numbers of them migrate.

EDUCATION AND OCCUPATIONAL PLACEMENT: STATUS DIMENSION

The status or prestige ranking of an occupation in relation to other occupations is an important dimension in occupational placement. It suggests, to some extent, the nature of the job performed. However, classification of occupations according to a status ranking scheme is more meaningfully interpreted as a measure of career achievement, since it more directly implies a hierarchical ordering of the occupational structure. In this sense, it is a component of the complex phenomena of socioeconomic status and is therefore, on the basis of arguments previously stated, a theoretical correlate of material level of living. A positive association is hypothesized between occupational status and high school completion.

For analysis, occupations are classified in two ways: (1) according to "status," using the Edwards Scale,[22] and (2) according to "prestige," using the North-Hatt Scale.[23] Cross-regional comparison of oc-

cupation rankings is difficult to defend in terms of validity, particularly where one situation is dominated by manufacturing industry and the other small-scale agriculture. In this study, occupations are grouped into two gross categories according to the Edwards criteria, and into three categories according to the North-Hatt criteria.[24] To compensate for the obvious fact that farm operators in eastern Kentucky are at a considerably lower level of status prestige than farm operators in, for example, Iowa or New York, a farm operator is classed in the lower category on status, and in the middle category on prestige (lowered 10 points on the North-Hatt Scale). This places farmers in a position more or less equivalent to semiskilled craftsmen in industry; thus, meaningful comparisons are possible.

In the case of the nonmigrant segment for both sets of data (Tables 4 and 5), a positive relationship is observed between level of schooling and the dependent variable. As hypothesized, a greater proportion of the nonmigrants who completed high school are found in the upper occupational strata when compared with their dropout counterparts.

In the case of the migrant segment, however, no significant difference is revealed in either set of data (Tables 4 and 5). High school education does

[22] A. M. Edwards, _Population: Comparative Occupation Statistics for the United States, 1870 to 1940_, U.S. Bureau of the Census, Washington: U.S. Government Printing Office, 1943.

[23] National Opinion Research Center, "Jobs and Occupations: A Popular Evaluation," in _Class, Status, and Power_, eds. Reinhard Bendix and Seymour M. Lipset (New York, N.Y.: The Free Press of Glencoe, Inc., 1953), pp. 411–26.

[24] In coding according to the Edwards Scale, it was possible to refer to the U.S. Census _Dictionary of Occupational Titles_. However, to code specific jobs according to the North-Hatt Occupational Prestige Scale, such a complete reference is not available. To assure a reasonable degree of judgment reliability, particularly where interpolation was necessary, the occupations were coded by two different coders, and discrepancies were arbitrated by the research directors.

TABLE 4. Occupational Status[a] of Jobs Held by Male Entrants to the Labor Force from Eastern Kentucky, by Level of School Completed, with Region of Residence Controlled

	Region of residence, 1960						
	Within E. Kentucky (nonmigrants)				Outside E. Kentucky (migrants)		
Occupational status of job held[a]	Did not complete high school		Completed high school		Did not complete high school		Completed high school	
	Number	Per cent	Number	Per cent	Number	Per cent	Number	Per cent
White collar and skilled[b]	13	16.5	27	39.7	25	30.5	22	36.1
Farm, semiskilled, and unskilled[c]	66	83.5	41	60.3	57	69.5	39	63.9
Total	79	100.0	68	100.0	82	100.0	61	100.0

$\chi^2 = 9.982$; $df = 1$; $P < 0.01$ $\chi^2 = 0.518$; $df = 1$; $P > 0.05$

[a] Jobs classified according to the Edwards Scale, utilizing the *Dictionary of Occupational Titles*, U. S. Census Bureau.

[b] Includes professionals, semiprofessionals, managerial, clerical, etc.

[c] Includes farm laborers, domestics, etc.

not appear to function as a sorting out mechanism in the occupational status placement of the migrant segment of this low-income area labor force as it does with the nonmigrant segment.

Before attempting to interpret these findings in the light of previous discussion, let us briefly turn to the relation between education and economic life chances.

TABLE 5. Occupational Prestige Status[a] of Jobs Held by Male Entrants to the Labor Force from Eastern Kentucky, by Level of Schooling Completed, with Region of Residence Controlled

	Region of residence, 1960						
	Within E. Kentucky (nonmigrants)				Outside E. Kentucky (migrants)		
Occupational prestige of job held[a]	Did not complete high school		Completed high school		Did not complete high school		Completed high school	
	Number	Per cent	Number	Per cent	Number	Per cent	Number	Per cent
High	7	10.3	18	31.6	17	21.0	21	35.6
Intermediate[b]	37	54.5	25	43.8	53	65.4	27	45.8
Low	24	35.3	14	24.6	11	13.6	11	18.6
Total	68	100.1	57	100.0	81	100.0	59	100.0

$\chi^2 = 8.887$; $df = 2$; $P < 0.05$ $\chi^2 = 5.539$; $df = 2$; $P > 0.05$

[a] Jobs classified according to the North-Hatt Scale by interpolation. Scores for farm operators were adjusted so as to be comparable to semiskilled jobs in industry.

[b] Includes farm operators.

TABLE 6. Level of Living Scores[a] of Male Entrants to the Labor Force from Eastern Kentucky, by Level of Schooling Completed, with Region of Residence Controlled

	Region of residence, 1960						
	Within E. Kentucky (nonmigrants)				Outside E. Kentucky (migrants)		
Level of living (grouped categories)	Did not complete high school		Completed high school		Did not complete high school		Completed high school	
	Number	Per cent	Number	Per cent	Number	Per cent	Number	Per cent
Low (0–3)	64	78.0	30	40.5	18	21.2	21	32.2
Middle (4–6)	16	19.5	34	46.0	58	68.2	31	47.7
High (7–9)	2	2.5	10	13.5	9	10.6	13	20.0
Total	82	100.0	74	100.0	85	100.0	65	99.9

$$\sigma = 1.92; \quad X = 3.17$$
$$rp = +0.355; \quad P < 0.01$$
$$r \text{ (corrected)} = +0.433$$

$$\sigma = 1.71; \quad X = 4.73$$
$$rp = +0.018; \quad P > 0.05$$
$$r \text{ (corrected)} = +0.023$$

[a] Level of living measured by the nine-item Cornell Scale developed by Danley and Ramsey.

EDUCATION AND ECONOMIC LIFE CHANCES

If the school system helps to prepare young people for roles in the work world, and if the school system functions as a sorting out mechanism for ability, then it should follow that young people who complete high school thereby are enhancing their life chances. A positive association between level of living and completion of high school is hypothesized.

As noted earlier, the correlation (point biserial r corrected) is +0.478 between migration and level of living. In the analysis presented in this section, migration (*i.e.*, regional structure of occupational opportunity) is controlled. Incidentally, for the total study population the correlation (point biserial r corrected) is +0.209 between education and level of living.

In the case of the nonmigrant segment (see Table 6) the correlation (point biserial r corrected) between schooling and level of living was +0.434, significant above the 0.01 level. As expected, there is a moderately high association between these variables.

In the case of the migrant segment (Table 6), the relationship is not significant; there is no association between schooling and level of living as measured by the Cornell Scale.

One concludes that the young man who remains in eastern Kentucky enhances his economic life chances by completing high school; if he migrates, however, a high school education appears to have little consequence on his level of living.

SUMMARY AND ELABORATION

This study focuses on a population of young men who were reared in a low-income rural situation. Ten years after enrollment in the eighth grade, a large number had migrated and established residence elsewhere. Since the migrant and nonmigrant segments do not differ significantly in antecedent sociocultural characteristics (prior to 1950), it is argued that differences in occupational placement and material level of living which do exist between the segments at the time of interviewing (in 1960) are largely due to regional variations in the structure of opportunity and cultural experiences which intervened during the decade.

A moderately high correlation is shown between migration and material level of living. This may be explained, in part, by the fact that almost half the migrants are employed in manufacturing industries mainly at a semiskilled level but drawing high wages, whereas nearly half the nonmigrants are engaged in the marginal farming and mining operations characteristic of this low-income area, which return relatively low wages for the labor input of workers.

As expected, high school completion is related to type of job (situs) and status of occupational placement, as well as to the economic life chances of youths who remain within the low-income area. School experience appears instrumental in determining the level of achievement and kind of work performed by these men in their home environs of eastern Kentucky. On the other hand, in the case of migrants, these data do not demonstrate the expected relationship between school completion and occupational situs, status, or material level of living. The question "Why not?" must be asked.

It is clear that the sociocultural origins from which this population stems can be described as a "depressed" situation. For example, in most cases the educational level of parents is less than eight grades.[25] Because the socioeconomic status of these families is at a low position relative to the American stratification system (which is what is generally meant by a "low-income" area), these families possess very little functional power to assist in the vertical circulation of their members in the competition for higher status positions outside the home country environs. Thus, in Sorokin's terms, the task of testing individuals for placement in life careers falls largely to the school systems in these low-income areas; as Sorokin puts it, "... The school is the next agency which retests the 'decisions' of a family and very often and very decisively changes them."[26]

From the findings on hand in this study, one is tempted to formulate a hasty conclusion that school systems in the low-income rural countries of eastern Kentucky do not function very effectively as testing and selective agencies which control the social distribution and economic life chances of youths who migrate to areas of greater opportunity. However, there are a number of reasons why that conclusion cannot be drawn from these observations and, indeed, why such a conclusion may be quite fallacious.

First, the interrelationships between level of schooling, region of residence, and level of living need to be reexamined. The purpose here is to attempt an explanation of the de-

---

[25] In only 16 per cent of the cases did the father have more than eight grades of schooling; in only 23 per cent of these cases did the mother complete more than eight grades.

[26] Sorokin, *op. cit.*, pp. 187–93.

pendent variable, level of living, in terms of the other two variables. Four comparative subgroupings are possible: (1) nonmigrant dropouts, (2) nonmigrant high school graduates, (3) migrant dropouts, and (4) migrant high school graduates.

Very little difference is revealed in levels of living between high school graduates in either regional situation ($\chi^2 = 1.48$;   df$=2$; $P > 0.05$). Migration does not appear to affect the high school graduate's economic life chances.

However, a comparison of levels of living between nonmigrant dropouts and migrant dropouts reveals marked differences in favor of the latter ($\chi^2 = 53.89$;   df$=2$; $P < 0.001$). Furthermore, migrant dropouts exhibit a higher level of living than nonmigrant high school graduates ($\chi^2 = 8.65$; df$=2$; $P < 0.05$) and, as noted earlier, the level of living of migrant dropouts is no different from that of migrant high school graduates.

In the light of reexamination, these data point to migration (i.e., regional structure of opportunity) as an important contingent condition explaining the economic life chances of high school dropouts. Couched in more practical terms, the economic life chances of high school dropouts appear to be influenced a great deal by their decision to migrate, and for that reason, youth advisory programs in low-income rural areas ought to encourage school dropouts to seek opportunities via migration to industrial areas elsewhere. Nevertheless, one can argue that completion of high school is strategic for the enhancement of a youth's life chances because in the course of a normal career, it is antecedent to the individual's decision to migrate.

DISCUSSION

Three important questions emerge from this study: (1) Why do migrant dropouts do better than nonmigrant dropouts?; (2) Why do not migrant high school graduates do better than nonmigrant high school graduates?; and (3) Why do not migrant high school graduates do better than migrant dropouts? These questions are interrelated, of course.

Comparing the labor market situation of the respective regions—the area of origin and the area of destination—may yield some plausible explanations. For example, a reasonable argument can be formulated that differences in economic life chances between migrant dropouts and nonmigrant dropouts are a consequence, in large part, of the more favorable economic circumstances and structure of opportunity in the industrial Ohio Valley as compared with the small-scale commercial and subsistence agricultural areas of eastern Kentucky. It may be that the kinds of opportunity available to rural migrants in the recipient areas are, regardless of their level of schooling, at the lower end of the occupational hierarchy.[27] Thus, migrant high school graduates do not do better than migrant dropouts; rural migrants, in that sense, form a single, more or less homogeneous labor pool. One can support that argument by referring to the much publicized belief that high school education is only a minimum level of training required for a posi-

_____

[27] From his Oakland Bay Area study, Lipset concluded that migrants tend to fill manual occupations while residents move up to nonmanual occupations. See Seymour Martin Lipset, "Social Mobility and Urbanization," *Rural Sociology*, XX (September–December, 1955), 220–28.

tion in the contemporary industrial order and that, in this case, dropouts make as good assembly-line workers as do those migrants who have completed high school.

The fact that all of these men are recent entrants to the labor force also must be considered. In the process of migration with its concomitant "uprooting" from familiar environs, the influence of education has not yet had time to become a manifest advantage for the migrants. High school education may not function as a selective mechanism for job placement, but it may serve as a necessary credential for future advancement within the industrial context.[28] Furthermore, it may well be that the dropout migrants had been working longer in the areas of destination than the migrants who had graduated from high school and, therefore, have, at that point in their careers, a considerable advantage over the migrant graduates.

It is also likely that the familistic orientation characteristic of this Southern Appalachian subculture tends to regulate the level of aspiration and performance of individuals who migrate.[29] In the setting of career goals, and in the evaluation of career attainments, the low-income area migrant may have as his reference those primary groups with which he was associated back in his old home neighborhood, and from this perspective, he is "doing well" if, by simply drawing high wages from a semiskilled job, he can acquire those material amenities that are so scarce "back home" in the low-income area. In that sense, the high school graduate migrant would not judge his performance vis-à-vis other migrants, but rather vis-à-vis nonmigrants.

Alternative explanations such as these which bear on the problems posed by the findings reported here indicate areas of much needed research. As this and other studies reveal, the potentials of human ability and talent that one assumes to be more or less normally distributed in a low-income area population seem to be systematically smothered and held in check by social influences characteristic of these situations.[30] With increasing concern for the development of talent resources in society, the labor force from low-income rural areas offers a research challenge.

---

[28] With increasing automation in industry, rudimentary literacy skills are becoming ever more important requisites for advancement, which, in turn, is beginning to influence recruitment policies. This observation is drawn from informal interviews with professional persons (personnel managers, welfare officers, and the like) working with eastern Kentucky migrants in the industrial areas of Ohio.

[29] Concerning this point, see, for example, the excellent discussion by Robert E. L. Faris, "Reflection On the Ability Dimension in Human Society," *American Sociological Review*, XXVI (December, 1961), 835–43.

[30] *Ibid.*, p. 842.

Population Growth and Educational Development*

B. Alfred Liu

The educational development of a country is conditioned by many historical, cultural, and socioeconomic factors. A factor of major importance is the rate of population growth, particularly the level and trend of the birth rate. In this paper we shall examine the rates of population growth, and specifically the recent levels and trends of the birth rate, for some seventy countries of the world, each with a population of five million or more, and discover what relationship, if any, exists between these rates and the present stage of educational development of each country.

As a measure of educational development we shall use, in combination: (1) an *adult literacy rate*, defined as the percentage of the population 15 years old an over who can both read and write; and (2) a *school enrollment ratio*, defined as a ratio based on the number of pupils enrolled in primary and secondary schools compared to one hundred persons in the population aged 5 to 19 years inclusive, adjusted for the normal duration of schooling in the particular country.[1]

As a measure of population growth we shall use, in combination: (1) an annual percentage rate of increase 1958–1963, published by the United Nations in the *Demographic Yearbook 1964;* and (2) an annual rate of natural increase, for 1964 or the latest year available, from the same source or from the United Nations *Compendium of Social Statistics: 1963.* Also from these sources we have taken the crude birth rates (number of live births per one thousand population), averaged for three periods: 1945–1949, 1955–1959, and 1960–1964 or the latest years avail-able.

EDUCATIONALLY MOST ADVANCED COUNTRIES

On the basis of our educational indices we have selected the following seventeen countries, each with a

Australia	Japan
Austria	Netherlands
Belgium	Poland
Canada	Sweden
Czechoslovakia	Switzerland
France	U.S.S.R.
Germany, East	United Kingdom
Germany, West	United States
Hungary	

---

* B. Alfred Liu, "Population Growth and Educational Development," *Annals of the American Academy of Political and Social Science*, 371 (January, 1967), 109–120.

[1] For explanations of these indices and their application to all countries of the world, see: United Nations Educational, Scientific and Cultural Organization (UNESCO), *World Illiteracy at Mid-Century* (Paris: UNESCO, 1957);

and *Statistical Yearbook, 1964* (Paris: UNESCO, 1966).

population of five million or more, as relatively *most advanced* in educational development.[2]

All these countries have adult literacy rates of 95 per cent or higher and, with one or two exceptions, school enrollment ratios of 75 or higher. They are all situated in the northern, eastern and western parts of Europe, except Australia, Canada, Japan and the United States. Pertinent data on the educational and demographic situation in these countries are presented in Table 1.

EDUCATIONALLY LESS ADVANCED COUNTRIES

Another group of twenty-seven countries are classified as educationally *less advanced,* in comparison to the first group, but they meet our two minimum criteria for educational development: an adult literacy rate of 50 per cent or more, and/or a school enrollment ratio not lower than fifty.

Argentina	Malaysia
Brazil	Mexico
Bulgaria	Peru
Burma	Philippines
Ceylon	Portugal
Chile	Rumania
China, Mainland	South Africa
China, Taiwan	Spain
Colombia	Thailand
Cuba	Venezuela
Greece	Vietnam, North
Italy	Vietnam, South
Korea, North	Yugoslavia
Korea, South	

[2] Other countries which may be classified as educationally most advanced, such as Denmark, Finland, Ireland, Israel, New Zealand, and Norway, are not included in this list because they have less than five million population.

One-fourth of these countries are situated in Asia; nearly one-third are in Latin America; the rest are found in southern and eastern Europe and one in Africa. Educational and demographic data relating to these countries are set out in Table 2.

EDUCATIONALLY LEAST ADVANCED COUNTRIES

Finally, twenty-four countries are classified as educationally *least advanced* because they have less than half of their adult population able to read and write and, with one marginal exception, less than half of their school-age population enrolled in school. They are found situated geographically, almost in equal numbers, in Africa and in Asia, with a large concentration in the Mediterranean or Middle East region.

Countries in this group are listed in Table 3, together with such data as are available concerning their educational and demographic development.

Afghanistan	Morocco
Algeria	Mozambique
Cambodia	Nepal
Congo (Leopoldville)	Nigeria
Ethiopia	Pakistan
Ghana	Saudi Arabia
India	Sudan
Indonesia	Tanzania
Iran	Turkey
Iraq	Uganda
Kenya	United Arab Republic
Madagascar	Yemen

We shall now examine some of the demographic factors associated with the different levels of educational de-

TABLE 1. Some Educational and Demographic Indices for Seventeen Selected Countries (Educationally Most Advanced)

Country	Adult literacy rate: 1960 or latest	School enrollment ratio: 1960	Total population in millions: 1960	Annual % rate of increase: 1958-1963	Natural rate of increase per 1,000: 1964 or latest	Birth rate per 1,000 population:			Trend in birth rate: 1945-1964	5-14 Age group as % of total population: 1960	Educational expenditure as % of national income: 1960 or latest
						Average 1945-49	Average 1955-59	Average 1960-64			
	(1)	(2)	(3)	(4)	(5)	(6)	(7)	(8)	(9)	(10)	(11)
Australia	98–99a	93	10.3	2.1	13	23	23	22	Remaining at moderate level	20	3.9
Austria	98–99a	68	7.1	0.2	6	17	17	19	Low level and rising	15	4.0
Belgium	97	101	9.2	0.5	5	17	17	17	Remaining at low level	15	6.2
Canada	97–98a	81	17.8	2.0	16	27	28	25	Remaining at moderate level	22	7.6
Czechoslovakia	97–98a	85	13.7	0.7	7	23	19	16	Falling to low level	19	6.5
France	96	88	45.5	1.3	7	20	18	18	Falling to low level	17	3.6
Germany, East	98–99a	78	16.2	−0.2	4	13	16	18	Low level and rising	17	6.0
Germany, West	98–99a	83	53.4	1.3	7	17	17	18	Remaining at low level	14	3.7
Hungary	97	79	10.0	0.4	3	20	18	14	Falling to low level	17	4.7
Japan	98	91	93.2	0.9	11	30	18	17	Falling to low level	22	7.2
Netherlands	98–99a	93	11.5	1.4	13	26	21	21	Moderate level and falling	20	6.3
Poland	95	93	29.7	1.3	11	28	27	20	Moderate level and falling	23	5.1
Sweden	98–99a	80	7.5	0.5	6	19	15	15	Low level and falling	15	5.7
Switzerland	98–99a	73	5.4	2.1	10	19	18	18	Remaining at low level	15	3.4
U.S.S.R.	98	78	214.4	1.7	14	b	b	23	Moderate; trend unknown	b	6.1
United Kingdom	98–99a	82	52.5	0.7	7	18	16	18	Remaining at low level	15	5.8
United States	98	102	180.7	1.6	12	23	25	22	Remaining at moderate level	20	6.8
Group median	98	83	17.2	1.3	7	20	18	18		17	5.8

a Estimated.   b Not available.

Source: Educational data from UNESCO, Statistical Yearbook, 1964 (Paris, 1966) and World Illiteracy at Mid-Century (Paris, 1957). Demographic data from United Nations, Demographic Yearbook, 1961, 1964 (New York: United Nations, 1962, 1965) and Compendium of Social Statistics: 1963 (New York: United Nations, 1963).

TABLE 2. Some Educational and Demographic Indices for Twenty-Seven Selected Countries (Educationally Less Advanced)

| Country | Adult literacy rate: 1960 or latest | School enrollment ratio: 1960 | Total population in millions 1960 | Annual % rate of increase: 1958-1963 | Natural rate of increase per 1,000: 1964 or latest | Birth rate per 1,000 population: | | | Trend in birth rate: 1945-1964 | 5-14 Age group as % of total population: 1960 | Educational expenditure as % of national income: 1960 or latest |
| | | | | | | Average 1945-49 | Average 1955-59 | Average 1960-64 | | | |
	(1)	(2)	(3)	(4)	(5)	(6)	(7)	(8)	(9)	(10)	(11)
Argentina	91	72	20.0	1.6	14	25	24	22	Moderate level and falling	20	3.5
Brazil	49	51	70.8	3.1	27-36a	43a	b	b	High level ; trend unknown	26	2.2
Bulgaria	85	81	7.9	0.9	8	25	19	17	Falling to low level	18	4.7
Burma	55-60a	43	20.7	1.0	15a	b	50a	b	High level ; trend unknown	21	2.5
Ceylon	68	74	9.9	2.5	27	38	37	35	Remaining at high level	25	5.9
Chile	84	74	7.3	2.3	22	36	36	35	Remaining at high level	24	3.2
China, Mainland	45-50a	58	646.5	2.3	23a	b	34a	b	High level : trend unknown	b	b
China, Taiwan	54	74	10.6	3.5	29	40	43	37	Remaining at high level	27	4.1
Colombia	62	50	14.1	2.2	26-32a	34	42	44	High level and rising	26	3.4
Cuba	78	72	6.8	1.8	17-25a	30	b	32	Remaining at high level	24	b
Greece	80	70	8.3	0.7	12	19	19	18	Remaining at low level	17	1.4
Italy	86	59	49.4	0.6	10	21	18	19	Falling to low level	16	6.3
Korea, North	b	b	8.3	2.2	23	41	39	b	Remaining at high level	b	b
Korea, South	71	64	24.7	2.8	28a	18	37	41a	Rising to high level	27	6.8
Malaysia	47	63	7.7	3.2	31	41	44	41	Remaining at high level	26	b
Mexico	65	53	35.0	3.2	35	44	46	46	Remaining at high level	28	3.0
Peru	61	55	10.9	2.7	24-35a	29	38	35	Rising to high level	27	4.9
Philippines	72	70	27.8	3.2	22	25	30	22	Moderate level and falling	28	3.6
Portugal	62	62	8.9	0.7	14	26	24	24	Remaining at moderate level	19	2.0
Rumania	89	60	18.4	0.8	7	25	23	17	Falling to low level	17	b
South Africa	40-45a	69	15.8	2.4	b	b	b	b	b	b	4.0
Spain	87	70	30.1	0.8	14	22	21	22	Remaining at moderate level	18	1.4
Thailand	68	58	26.3	3.0	22a	25	37	34	Rising to high level	29	2.9
Venezuela	66	79	7.5	3.4	30-40a	39	47	45	High level and rising	25	4.8
Vietnam, North	64	b	15.9	3.4	b	b	b	b	b	b	b
Vietnam, South	b	47	14.1	3.4	17a	b	36	26	Falling to moderate level	b	1.8
Yugoslavia	76	75	18.5	1.1	11	28	25	22	Moderate level and falling	21	5.1
Group median	68	64	15.8	2.3	22	28	36	32		24	3.5

TABLE 3. Some Educational and Demographic Indices for Twenty-Four Selected Countries (Educationally Least Advanced)

| Country | Adult literacy rate: 1960 or latest (1) | School enrollment ratio: 1960 (2) | Total population in millions: 1960 (3) | Annual % rate of increase: 1958-1963 (4) | Natural rate of increase per 1,000: 1964 or latest (5) | Birth rate per 1,000 population: | | | Trend in birth rate: 1945-1964 (9) | 5-14 Age group as % of total population: 1960 (10) | Educational expenditure as % of national income: 1960 or latest (11) |
						Average 1945-49 (6)	Average 1955-59 (7)	Average 1960-64 (8)			
Afghanistan	1-5a	5	13.8	2.8	b	b	b	b	b	b	b
Algeria	8	26	11.0	2.2	23	41	37	39	Remaining at high level	25	3.0
Cambodia	31	41	5.0	b	22a	b	45a	41a	Remaining at high level	b	b
Congo (Leopoldville)	15	39	14.2	2.2	23a	b	38	43	High level and rising	23	4.4
Ethiopia	1-5a	4	20.0	1.7	b	b	b	b	b	b	b
Ghana	20-25a	31	6.7	4.1	30	33	50	56	High level and rising	25	4.3
India	28	31	432.6	2.3	19	40a	b	40a	Remaining at high level	24	2.6
Indonesia	43	40	92.6	2.3	22a	b	b	43	High level; trend unknown	b	b
Iran	13	30	20.2	2.4	25-28	29	b	45-48a	Rising to high level	25	3.1
Iraq	15	50	7.1	1.6	10	6	12	21	Rising to moderate level	26	6.6
Kenya	20-25a	41	7.1	2.9	b	b	b	b	b	b	5.1
Madagascar	33	30	5.4	3.0	22	24	35	38	Rising to high level	b	b
Morocco	14	27	11.6	2.9	27	b	b	47a	High level; trend unknown	b	4.7
Mozambique	1-2a	26	6.5	1.7	b	47a	b	b	High level; trend unknown	b	b
Nepal	5	10	9.4	1.6	15a	b	b	45a	High level; trend unknown	23	b
Nigeria	11	30	35.1	5.7	b	b	49a	b	High level; trend unknown	b	2.1
Pakistan	19	26	92.7	2.1	26-30a	21	b	43-46a	Rising to high level	27	1.8
Saudi Arabia	1-5a	6	6.0	1.9	b	b	b	b	b	b	b
Sudan	12	12	11.8	2.8	33a	b	52a	b	High level; trend unknown	b	5.6
Tanzania	5-10a	15	9.5	1.9	21-22a	44a	b	b	High level; trend unknown	b	4.5
Turkey	38	47	27.6	2.9	b	b	b	b	b	23	2.9
Uganda	25	31	6.7	2.5	22a	42a	b	b	High level; trend unknown	24	4.0
United Arab Republic	20	43	25.9	2.5	22	42	40	43	Remaining at high level	24	3.8
Yemen	1-5a	8	5.0	2.6	b	b	b	b	b	b	b
Group median	14.5	30	11.3	2.4	22	b	b	b	b	24	4.0

a Estimated.　b Not available.
Source: See Table 1.

velopment in these three groups of countries.

SIZE OF POPULATION

First, we might ask: Does the size of population, by itself, bear any relationship to the level of a country's educational development? The answer is definitely: No. Three of the most populous countries of the world, each with more than ninety million people, are found in the first group (Japan, Soviet Union, and United States). One such country (China, Mainland) is found in the second group; three others (India, Indonesia, Pakistan) are in the third group. Among thirty-seven countries, each with a population between ten and ninety million, ten are in the first group, seventeen in the second group, and ten in the third group. Among twenty-four countries in the five to ten million population size group, four are educationally most advanced; nine are relatively less advanced; and eleven are in the least advanced category. Hence our first general observation:

(1) *The size of a country's population does not, by itself, show any direct relationship to its level of educational development.*

RATE OF POPULATION GROWTH

Next we address ourselves to the question: Is there any significant difference in the rates of population growth among countries at different levels of educational development? The answer to this question is a qualified yes. The rates of total population increase between 1958 and 1963, shown for our first group of

countries, are all, with three exceptions, less than 2 per cent per year. Excluding the effects of external migration, the current rates of natural increase (excess of births over deaths within the country) for all but one of these countries, are less than fifteen per thousand population or an annual growth rate of about 1.5 per cent. The countries of this group show annual growth rates, based on natural increase, ranging from 1.6 per cent (Canada) down to 0.3 per cent (Hungary). The median growth rate for the group is 0.7 per cent based on natural increase in or close to 1964; or 1.3 per cent based on total population increase between 1958 and 1963 (see Table 1, columns 4 and 5).

For our second group of countries, the median rate of increase between 1958 and 1963 is 2.3 per cent. The median rate of natural increase currently is 2.2 per cent. The rates of natural increase range from 3.5 per cent (Mexico) down to about 0.7 per cent (Rumania). (See Table 2, columns 4 and 5.) Thus, it may be seen that half of the countries in our first group are growing in population at a rate equal to or less than the lowest rate shown for any country in the second group. Conversely, more than half of the countries in our second group are growing in population faster than the fastest-growing country in the first group. It may therefore be concluded that the countries educationally most advanced tend to have lower rates of population growth than countries in the educationally less advanced group.

Regarding our third group of countries, we are handicapped by the lack of adequate statistics for the calculation of population growth rates for many of the countries. From such data as are available, we find a median growth rate for this group almost identical to that for the second group: about 2.2 per cent. The range of rates shown, whether registered or estimated, goes from 3.3 per cent (Sudan) down to 1.0 per cent (Iraq). (See Table 3, columns 4 and 5). Compared to the first group of countries, all but two of the rates shown for this group are higher than the highest rate reported for any country in the first group, while the lowest rate reported for any country in the third group is still higher than the rates for half of the countries in the first group. Unquestionably, the educationally most advanced countries do tend to have lower rates of population growth than countries in the least advanced group. However, no significant difference can be attributed to the population growth rates between the *less* advanced and the *least* advanced groups of countries. We may thus state our next two general observations:

(2) *Countries which are most advanced educationally tend to have lower rates of population growth than those which are relatively less advanced or least advanced in educational development.*

(3) *There is no evidence of any significant difference in the population growth rates between countries in the educationally less advanced and those in the least advanced groups.*

LEVELS OF BIRTH RATE

Natural increase of the population results from a combination of two demographic factors, the birth rate and the death rate, the first being normally in excess of the second. With the over-all death rate generally on the decline throughout the modern world, quite substantially in some instances, it is the level of the birth rate and its changes which will become the principal determinants of future population growth. We shall, therefore, attempt to answer another question: Are the birth rates of various countries a significant factor in the differentiation of countries according to their levels of educational development? Here we shall confine our attention to average birth rates published by the United Nations for three time periods: 1945–1949; 1955–1959; and 1960–1964 or for the latest years available (see columns 6 to 8 in Tables 1, 2, and 3). To simplify comparisons, we shall consider a crude birth rate of thirty or more per thousand as relatively high; between twenty and thirty as moderate; and any rate less than twenty as low. These are arbitrary limits chosen for convenience in this study, and do not imply any criteria of optimum birth rates for national development planning and other purposes. On this basis, our answer to the question stated above is a substantial yes.

Taking our first group of countries, those classified as most advanced in educational development, we find only one country (Japan) which may be considered at any time since 1945 as having a relatively high birth rate. About half of the other countries have had moderate birth rates, at least during part of the period in question. The other countries in the group have had consistently low birth rates throughout the postwar years. The average rates reported for the 1945–1949 period range from about thirty per thousand (Japan) to about thirteen (East Germany). The median rate for this group of countries, excluding the Soviet Union, for which data for those years are not available, stands at about twenty, just above our arbitrary borderline between moderate and low rates. For the period between 1955 and 1959, the highest average rate, about twenty-eight, is reported for Canada; the lowest, about fifteen, is reported for Sweden. The median rate for the group dropped to eighteen, definitely on the low side. For 1960 and later years, the median rate stands at eighteen (see Table 1, columns 6 to 8).

Among our second group of countries, relatively less developed educationally, we find no less than sixteen countries—a clear majority—which can be classified as having high birth rates. Half of the countries starting with moderate rates for the 1945–1949 period have either moved up to the high category (Peru, Thailand), or moved down to the low category (Bulgaria, Italy, Rumania). Five countries have remained at the moderate level. Only one country in this group, Greece, has consistently reported low birth rates since the 1945–1949 period. The highest rate shown for any country in this group is an estimated rate of fifty for Burma, referring to the 1955–1959 period. The lowest rate shown is about seventeen for Bulgaria and Rumania, referring to the period 1960–1964. The median rate for this group was about twenty-eight for the 1945–1949 period, rising to about thirty-six for the 1955–1959 period, and dipping to about thirty-two for the latest years available (see Table 2, columns 6 to 8).

Finally, for the third group of countries (educationally least advanced), we are again handicapped by inadequate data on birth rates. From the spotty data available, it seems that practically all the countries, with the possible exception of one, have to be classified as high-birth-rate countries, according to our criteria. Pakistan reported only moderate birth rates for the period 1945–1949; Iran and Madagascar seem to have moved up from moderate to high rates. Only one country, Iraq, has reported low-to-moderate rates of birth. Because of the grossly incomplete, and possibly misleading, data, we have not attempted to compute median rates for this group of countries (see Table 3, columns 6 to 8).

A comparison, even based on incomplete data, clearly shows a pattern which may be tentatively described as follows. Countries which are most advanced in education are characterized by low to moderate birth rates; those less advanced tend to have moderate to high birth rates; those least advanced have practically all high birth rates, reported or estimated at levels ranging from thirty up to fifty or more. We shall therefore state the following additional observations:

(4) *Countries which are educationally most advanced may be expected to have relatively low or moderate birth rates as compared to countries less advanced or least advanced in educational development.*

(5) *Countries which are educationally less advanced may be expected to have birth rates ranging from moderate to high levels when compared to countries which are relatively most advanced.*

(6) *Countries which are least advanced in educational development may be expected to have the highest birth rates when compared to other countries which are educationally more advanced.*

TRENDS IN CHANGING BIRTH RATES

Birth rates, however, are not static phenomena. For almost any country they may change, sometimes dramatically, from year to year and from one period to another. We shall therefore raise one more pertinent question: Is there any noticeable difference in the *trends* of changing birth rates, when countries are compared on the basis of their level of educational development? Our answer to this last question, based on the same data which we have examined above, is almost emphatically: Yes. In Tables 1, 2 and 3, we have summarized the trends, where discernible, of changes in the birth rates of individual countries, over a period extending approximately twenty years since the end of the Second World War. The following pattern emerges.

Of all countries which we have classified as educationally most advanced, leaving out the Soviet Union for which we do not have the pertinent data, almost half have registered declines in their birth rates since 1945. One country (Japan), starting with an average birth rate of about thirty in the early postwar period, has drastically reduced that rate to about seventeen. Five countries (Czechoslovakia, France, Hungary, Netherlands, Poland) registering moderate rates of twenty or more in the same earlier period have since reduced their rates below that level. One other country (Sweden) which had relatively low rates at the beginning of the postwar period has further declined to still lower levels. Of the other half, three countries (Australia, Canada, United States) have remained at moderate levels; three countries

(Belgium, West Germany, United Kingdom) have stabilized around their relatively low levels. Only two countries (Australia, East Germany) have shown a rising trend from their postwar low levels, but their current rates are still low in comparison with most other countries (see Table 1, column 9).

Among those countries classified as less advanced in education, seven countries have shown a falling trend in birth rates, three of them (Bulgaria, Italy, Rumania) shifting from moderate to low levels. Ten countries have maintained their relative positions in their respective levels; while five have apparently shown a rising trend (see Table 2, column 9).

In the group of countries which we have classified as educationally least advanced, *not one* has shown a trend of falling birth rates. Four countries (Algeria, Cambodia, India, United Arab Republic) have maintained their positions among the high-birth-rate countries. Six other countries have shown rising trends, one of which (Ghana) reporting in 1960 a rate of about 56, which possibly qualifies it as the country with the highest known birth rate among all the 68 countries included in our study (see Table 3, column 9).

We shall now state two more general observations from our study of the relationship between population growth and educational development:

(7) *Countries at more advanced levels of educational development are apt to be found with falling trends in their birth rates, even where these rates are already at a moderate or low level.*

(8) *Countries at the least advanced levels of educational development are more apt to be found with rising trends in their birth rates,*

even where these rates are already at a relatively high level.

SOME PRACTICAL CONSEQUENCES

Let us see what are some of the practical consequences of population growth, particularly of high birth rates, on the level of educational development of a country. First, it is obvious that a country with a high birth rate and a rapidly growing population must have a higher proportion of its people in the younger ages, especially in the school-going ages. For our first group of countries, around the year 1960, the proportion of the total population in the age group 5 to 14 years inclusive ranges from 23 per cent in Poland to 14 per cent in East Germany. The median percentage for the group is about 17. For our second group of countries, these percentages range from 29 for Thailand to 16 for Italy. The median for this group is about 24 per cent. For those countries in the third group for which we have comparable data, the percentages run from 27 for Pakistan down to 23 for Congo (Leopoldville), with a median for 11 countries at about 24 per cent (see column 10 in Tables 1, 2 and 3). Comparing the three groups, we find that more than half of the countries in the second, and practically all countries in the third group for which we have available data have a higher proportion of their population in school-going ages than *all* the countries in the first group. It follows that the country with a higher proportion of its population in the school-going ages imposes a heavier educational burden on the rest of its people. It is reasonable to surmise that most of such countries find their educational

development impeded largely as a result of their demographic situation.

One measure of a country's effort toward meeting its educational needs is furnished by its total public expenditure on education in relation to its national income. Data on this index, as available for each country around 1960, are shown in column 11 of Tables 1 to 3. For the first group of countries, these percentages range from nearly 8 for Canada to about 3 for Switzerland, with a median for the group at about 6 per cent. For the second group of countries the range is from about 7 per cent for South Korea down to less than 1.5 per cent for Greece and Spain. The median for this group is 3.5 per cent. Available data for the third group of countries show a range from about 7 per cent for Iraq down to less than 2 per cent for Pakistan. The median for these countries, however, is 4 per cent, which is somewhat higher than the median percentage for the second group. We may therefore say that the countries educationally less advanced could possibly increase their efforts further toward meeting their educational needs, although we recognize that such needs constitute a relatively heavier burden on their national economy than in the case of the more favored countries.

A question might be posed here as to whether by raising the educational level of its people, a country can thereby reduce its birth rate and slow down its population growth. Unfortunately, there is not enough consistent and conclusive evidence to support such an expectation. At best it may be surmised that in countries with currently high fertility levels, raising the educational level of the population, particularly of women, and more especially up to completion of secondary school, could bring about a lowering of the birth rate, perhaps directly through extending the knowledge and practice of family planning, or perhaps indirectly through increasing the age of marriage, improving the socioeconomic status of the family, and in other ways.[3]

ONE CONCRETE EXAMPLE

We shall conclude our study with one concrete example of a country with a large and growing population, faced with a heavy burden of educational needs which demands the utmost use of the country's resources.

India is the second largest country of the world, with a total population estimated at about 450 million. It is growing at an annual rate of almost 2 per cent, adding some 9 million persons to the population each year. Approximately 187 million persons 15 years old and over are unable to read and write, constituting more than 72 per cent of India's population at that age level. Although the rate of illiteracy had been reduced from about 81 per cent in 1951, there were thirteen million *more* illiterate persons in 1961 than there were in 1951, due to the

rapid population growth. Almost one-fourth of India's population are in the 5 to 14 years age group. Between 1950 and 1960, the total number of pupils in primary schools increased by more than 80 per cent (from 18.7 million to 34.2 million), while secondary school enrollment more than doubled (from 4.9 million to 10.4 million). During the same decade, the percentage of national income which went into public expenditure on education increased more than threefold (from 0.8 to 2.6 per cent). Yet there was only a 50 per cent improvement in the school enrollment ratio, rising from 21 in 1950 to 31 in 1960. As of the latter date, nearly seven out of ten school-age children were still without the advantages of any formal schooling.

SOME GUIDELINES AND TARGETS

The example of India is by no means unique. Similar situations may be found among many other educationally disadvantaged countries. What, then, can these countries do to speed up their own educational development? There is, of course, no answer which can serve for all countries; much depends on the particular circumstances, traditions, and value systems of each nation. However, our present study, based on a limited analysis of available official statistics relating to population growth and educational development, may be useful in suggesting a few guidelines and targets, such as the following:

(1) A country can speed up its educational development by providing enough schools, classrooms and teachers to accommodate at least 50 per cent of its school-age children. The optimum tar-

---

[3] For recent summary discussions on this subject, see United Nations, *Population Bulletin* No. 7 (1963), chap. viii; also various papers presented to the World Population Conference (Belgrade, 1965), in particular: Philip J. Idenburg, "Educational Consequences and Determinants of Population Trends" (Background paper A.6/25/E/495); George W. Roberts, "Fertility" (Background paper A.1, B.1, B.2/18/E/483); Robert O. Carleton, "The Effect of Educational Improvement on Fertility Trends in Latin America" (A.6/I/E/152); Robert M. Dinkel, "Education and Fertility in the United States" (A.6/V/E/414); J. Mayone Stycos, "Education and Fertility in Puerto Rico" (A.6/I/E/236).

get should be a school enrollment ratio of not less than 75 per cent.

(2) A country can carry out an intensive literacy program to bring up the educational level of its adult population, so that at least 50 per cent of those persons 15 years old and over will have the basic skills of written communication. The ultimate aim should be an adult literacy rate of 95 per cent or higher.

(3) A country can devote still more of its material and financial resources to the task of education, increasing its public expenditure to no less than 5 or 6 per cent of its total national income. Eventually, total educational expenditure should be raised to a level equaling no less than 7 or 8 per cent of the national income.

(4) In order to achieve these targets, it would be imperative for most of the disadvantaged countries to reduce their annual birth rates to no more than twenty births per one thousand population, and their rates of population increase to no more than 1 per cent per year.

These are not utopian dreams. They are specific objectives already achieved or surpassed by many of the world's larger countries. They should be within reach by all.

part

4

Social
Aggregate
Systems
and Demographic
Structure
and Processes

In the introductory chapter a distinction was drawn between two different types of social systems whose linkages with demographic systems establish the interest field of social demography. One type—social action systems—distinguished by the social interaction of component members has been dealt with in Chaps. 3–8. The other type we have termed social aggregate systems and does not involve social interaction. Rather, the systems are defined by the possession of one or more common traits. Several different types of aggregate systems are treated in the chapters of this section.

We have also distinguished between aggregate systems defined by traits for which members of a society have developed certain norms, i.e. behavioral expectations, and systems defined by traits primarily of interest to·the researcher. The former we have called socially defined aggregates. Some of the more important socially defined aggregates in American society are those based on traits of race, ethnic origin, and social class. Social demographic studies dealing with these aggregates are provided in Chaps. 9 and 10.

The establishment of analytical aggregates is a relatively primitive stage of theoretical formulation, which probably explains why so many social demographic studies deal with this type of social system. A concrete illustration may help to demonstrate both the utility and limitations of the analytical aggregate approach. In studying fertility differences of social class groupings in Detroit, David Goldberg recognized that a high proportion of the lower-class population had rural backgrounds. It occurred to him that this characteristic might be more closely related to fertility differences than the usual social status variables. His subsequent analysis proved this to be the case, at least for his particular population.[1]

In one respect the finding of Goldberg might be considered analogous to Ansley Coale's finding for demographic systems that fertility rates account for changes in the age composition to a greater extent than do mortality rates.[2] But there is an important difference in that Coale's finding can be explained by analytical theory that tells us why particular relationships exist among variables within the system. This is not so in the case of Goldberg's finding. The explanation for the differences does not lie within the system itself. To further scientific understanding, we must go beyond the recognition that differences or relationships exist. We must develop and test systematically related propositions that explain their existence. In the case of social demographic behavior this almost always means knowing a great deal more about the members of a social system than that they possess certain common traits.

The inclusion of a chapter on attitudes, values, and beliefs in this section on aggregate systems rather than in a separate section on social psychological systems reflects the general failure of social demography to develop a more comprehensive social psychology of demographic behavior. Rarely do we know much more about the individuals whose attitudes, values, or beliefs are related to their demographic attributes

---

[1] David Goldberg, "The Fertility of Two-Generation Urbanites," *Population Studies* 12 (March, 1959), 214–22.

[2] Ansley J. Coale, "The Effects of Changes in Mortality and Fertility on Age Composition," *Milbank Memorial Fund Quarterly* 34 (January, 1956), 80–114.

than that they possess the traits used to define the aggregates. In Chap. 11, an effort was made to choose reading selections in which the theoretical assumptions were relatively clear. The social psychology of demographic behavior is a field of tremendous potential in which research findings promise to be of great practical value as well as of theoretical importance.

9

Racial and ethnic identification along with social class status are highly significant aggregate traits for understanding and predicting sociological phenomena. Some of the more reliable generalizations in the social sciences are based on these aggregate system characteristics. Certainly the major, and perhaps the best, source of racial and ethnic group data is the census. It is not surprising, then, that social demographic research constitutes an important part of the intergroup

RACIAL

AND ETHNIC

GROUPS

relations literature.

Several theoretical strands can be identified in contemporary race and ethnic group relations research. A wide range of research concerns the general problem of "adjustment," which is usually discussed in the context of such basic interactive processes as assimilation, amalgamation, segregation, acculturation, and accommodation. Studies indicate that various racial and ethnic groups are at different points along the "adjustment" continuum, and that intergroup tensions remain. Factors in intergroup tensions, notably the factors of prejudice and discrimination, constitute other areas of intergroup research. Theories of prejudice explore not only the normative cross-cultural perspectives but also the psychological, psychoanalytic, and economic bases of this intergroup phenomenon.[1] A correlate of prejudice is

[1] Frank R. Westie, "Race and Ethnic Relations," in

the practice of discrimination. Here intergroup studies have investigated the various methods of practicing discrimination and their social and psychological consequences for individuals and groups. A further area of interest is action research which seeks to develop and evaluate interaction patterns that reduce racial and ethnic group prejudice and discrimination.

Social demographers have contributed most notably to the first of these areas of research—factors in racial and ethnic group "adjustment" processes. The migration of racial and ethnic groups has been a major social factor throughout world history. The United States provides an excellent example, since all Americans are of immigrant stock, including the "indigenous" Indian population. They were the first immigrant group, coming from the Mongolian area several centuries before the early Colonists from Europe laid claim to American soil. The Colonists —Spanish, English, Dutch and French—were quite well established by the time the first Negroes were brought to America in 1619. However, the big crush of immigrants came during nineteenth and early twentieth centuries with first northern and then southern and eastern European nationality groupings constituting the major proportion of new arrivals. Included among these immigrants were many European Jews. At the same time as the great Atlantic migration was taking place, new Americans were coming from the Orient, especially China and Japan. This era in American demographic and intergroup history was delimited by the restrictive legislation that nearly closed the great doors of immigration, first to the Orientals and then, in the 1920s, to most other groups. Latin Americans, and particularly Puerto Ricans, constitute the newest American minority group members. The majority of these have entered the United States in the past two decades. The various immigrant groups came to the United States for a wide range of reasons, but most sought a new and better way of life. It is in the interactive processes of attaining these goals that the relationship between demographic and general sociocultural factors is most clearly demonstrated.[2] The relationship between migration and residential segregation is a salient example.[3]

Fertility and mortality trends frequently differ for various majority and minority groups.[4] The reasons for the differences are tied to a variety of sociological factors such as education, communication pat-

---

Handbook of Modern Sociology, ed. Robert E. L. Faris (Chicago: Rand McNally & Co., 1964), pp. 576–618.

[2] For example, see Oscar Handlin, *The Newcomers* (Garden City, New York: Doubleday & Company, Inc., 1959).

[3] Karl E. Taeuber and Alma F. Taeuber, *Negroes in Cities* (Chicago: Aldine Publishing Co., 1965).

[4] William Petersen, *Population* (New York: The Macmillan Company, 1961), pp. 222–28; Earl E. Huyck, "White-Nonwhite Differentials: Overview and Implications," *Demography,* III (1966), 548–65.

terns, and status differences.[5] The combined results of fertility, mortality, and migration trends produce demographic balances between majority and minority groups which can be important conditions in understanding prejudice and discrimination.[6]

The readings included in this section afford a sample of the wide range of social demographic research in problems involving racial and ethnic populations. The first selection by Mayer and Marx considers the fertility behavior of Polish immigrants as they are assimilated into a new community in the United States. Four concomitants of high fertility were present—foreign birth, rural origin, low socioeconomic status and Roman Catholicism. However, these attributes did not prevent very rapid acceptance of the control of births. The authors feel the explanation for the decline in fertility lies in the complex of attitudinal and behavioral expectations which accompany the process of assimilation into a new culture. It is interesting to speculate about alternative explanations.

Racial, ethnic, and income factors in the epidemiology of neonatal mortality is the topic of the second reading. This study was designed to investigate differentials in neonatal mortality of Negro, native White, Italian, and Polish populations in census tracts with similar socioeconomic status levels. While Negro and native White mortality levels were quite similar, family income was an important differentiating factor. Professors Willie and Rothney discuss several possible reasons why women in lower-income families do not seek prenatal care, even when it may be available without charge.

Racial and ethnic group discrimination is influenced by many factors, some of which concern the size of the minority group. In the selection "Per Cent Nonwhite and Discrimination in the South," Blalock investigates some of the relationships between various indices of discrimination, the rate of nonwhite increase and the proportion of the population nonwhite in a sample of Southern United States counties. The results indicate that population increase was only moderately correlated with discrimination but that size of the nonwhite population was quite strongly correlated with indices of discrimination. The author suggests

---

[5] Pascal K. Whelpton, Arthur A. Campbell, and John E. Patterson, *Fertility and Family Planning in the United States* (Princeton, N.J.: Princeton University Press, 1966), pp. 334–70; and selected chapters in Donald J. Bogue (ed.), *Sociological Contributions to Family Planning Research* (Chicago: Community and Family Study Center of the University of Chicago, 1967).

[6] Philip M. Hauser, "Demographic Factors in the Integration of the Negro," *Daedalus*, XCIV (Fall, 1965), 847–77; Robert C. Weaver, "Washington, D.C., Nonwhite Population Movements and Urban Ghettos," *Phylon*, XX (Fall, 1959), 235–41; Hubert M. Blalock, Jr., "Per Cent Nonwhite and Discrimination in the South," *American Sociological Review*, XXII (December, 1957), 677–82; and David M. Heer, "The Sentiment of White Supremacy—An Ecological Study," *American Journal of Sociology*, LXIV (May, 1959), 592–98.

there may be a size threshold below which discrimination is not a significant phenomenon.

In the last reading in this selection, "The Negro in New Orleans: A Functional Analysis of Demographic Data," Hillery poses a sociological hypothesis to explain white–Negro population differentials. Specifically, the hypothesis is advanced that one function of the white man's definition of the racial situation is to create demographic differentials between his own and the Negro population. The basic theory used in explaining the differentials is the self-fulfilling prophecy: If men define situations as real, they are real in their consequences. In testing the proposition this article points out some interesting theoretical issues in social demography.

Social Change, Religion, and Birth Rates[*]

Albert J. Mayer and Sue Marx

The process by which a population makes the transition from very high to low fertility rates is still largely unknown. It has been found in the Western world for 150 years and is associated with industrialization and urbanization. It is supposed to take several generations before the large family is supplanted by the small.

A generally accepted proposition is that, if a people whose cultural background may be classed as traditional comes into contact with a fully urbanized and industrialized population, they will assimilate traits of the latter culture in an order inversely proportional to the strength and intensity of the attitudes and values which bear upon these traits. Superficial characteristics, such as clothing, manners, etc., change rapidly, but birth control, being highly associated with both the basic religious and family structures, will be very slowly accepted.

An example of acculturation is found in the Polish immigrant community of the United States, the sub-

[*] Albert J. Mayer and Sue Marx, "Social Change, Religion, and Birth Rates," *American Journal of Sociology*, 62 (January, 1957), 383–90.

ject of one of the most extensive studies ever made—*The Polish Peasant in Europe and America*. The authors of it, Thomas and Znaniecki[1] with others, have led us to believe that this immigrant group would retain its traditional family values, including high birth rates, for many years after its arrival in this country.

Four qualities characterized the Poles in America: rural origin, foreign birth, identification with a religion which does not sanction active forms of birth control, and a standard of living associated with laboring and semiskilled occupations. The Polish community of Hamtramck, Michigan, has provided a place to test the more general sociological proposition as well as the findings of Thomas and Znaniecki. A community totally inclosed within the city of Detroit, it stands as a landmark of the explosive industrial development of America. In the ten years following 1910, the automobile industry changed a suburban, largely farming community of 3,559 persons into a manufacturing center. Packed into the interstices between giant industrial plants were, and still are, the dwellings of newly arrived workers. By 1920, Hamtramck was a completely functioning city with a population of 48,615 predominately Catholic Polish immigrants.

---

[1] William I. Thomas and Florian Znaniecki, *The Polish Peasant in Europe and America* (New York: Alfred A. Knopf, 1927), pp. 1516–17; also Niles Carpenter, *Immigrants and Their Children* ("Census Monographs," Vol. VII [Washington: Bureau of the Census, 1920; Government Printing Office, 1927], p. 189); also Warren S. Thompson, *Ratio of Children to Women, 1920* ("Census Monographs," Vol. XI [Washington: Government Printing Office, 1921], p. 75).

RURAL ORIGIN AND FOREIGN BIRTH

In 1930, when the community was at its largest, 38 per cent of the white population was foreign-born, and, of these, at least three-quarters were originally Polish. Of the native-born, 27,901, or 88 per cent, had at least one foreign-born parent, and, of these, a minimum of 22,797, or 80 per cent, were of Polish origin. Thus over 80 per cent of the white population was either of Polish birth or immediate descent. How much of this culture has been retained? A walk down Joseph Campau, the main street of Hamtramck, makes it apparent that if one knew only the Polish language, he would have no difficulty, even today, in communicating. The names of the stores, the signs, and the conversations are almost as frequently in Polish as in English. Little imagination is needed to realize how much more prevalent were the Polish language and Polish customs 25 years ago. Indeed, many residents of Hamtramck refer to Detroit as the "outside" and speak of Hamtramck itself as "little Warsaw."

Regarding the rural origin of Hamtramck's population, the only quantitative statement is that of Arthur Wood. He states that 83 per per cent of the 1,247 applicants for citizenship by persons born in Poland gave their birthplace as a village or farm, while only 13 per cent claimed to be city-born.[2] Also a survey made in Hamtramck in 1915 reported:

> The population (some 20,000 in 1915) is approximately 80 per cent Polish, 15 per cent German and the remainder largely Negro. Most of the Poles have come within ten

---

[2] *Hamtramck Then and Now* (New York: Bookman Associates, 1955), p. 30.

years and are not yet citizens while a larger proportion neither speak, read, nor write English. They are hard working, hard drinking, thrifty people, originating in rural Poland. Characteristic of their origins are superstitions and low standards of living which are revealed in fatalism as to the care of the sick and abnormal, and in their personal relations.[3]

The last decade has seen a substantial decrease in the population of Hamtramck, particularly among white persons. Young people with small children have been moving to the new Detroit suburban areas of residence in the typical way. Their houses and flats are being taken over by Negros, although the rate of replacement was not particularly rapid until the last few years. However, many of these younger people still return for the important events of life; their marriages and funerals are held in Hamtramck as well as their church services.

RELIGION

Hamtramck is, by and large, a Roman Catholic community. Our data on fertility pertain to the whole white population, but the total number of white Protestant families is too small to justify calling the derived rates other than *Catholic* birth rates. There is much evidence to justify this.

That most of the population was, and still is, of Polish stock is a most important clue to religious affiliation. In 1955 Hamtramck had three Roman Catholic parishes, with a total membership of approximately 29,000 persons, or what would amount to 80

per cent of the local white population. However, not all persons of Roman Catholic background are included in the church registers, and Catholics living outside may, for many reasons, belong to one of the Hamtramck churches.

The Census of Religious Bodies in 1926 indicated that, of Hamtramck's total population, only 2,645 persons were reported as belonging to a church (the Roman Catholics did not report on Hamtramck in this census). Of these, 1,443 persons belonged to Negro churches and 734 persons to other Protestant churches, some of which could be Negro. On the other hand, in 1936, the Roman Catholic church did report on Hamtramck. Of the 18,787 reported, 16,126, or 95 per cent, were Roman Catholic.[4] This, of course, does not preclude the possibility that Protestants in Hamtramck might have joined Protestant churches in Detroit or might not belong to a church at all. However, the almost total absence of Protestant churches within Hamtramck certainly supports the conclusion that there are very few local Protestants.

Further evidence, though not definitive, was secured by the classification of each birth as Protestant or Roman Catholic on the basis of the information contained on the birth certificate. The names of the parents, their birthplace, hospital, etc., were used to identify indirectly the religious affiliation of the parents. While this technique is undoubtedly crude, results were impressively in accord with the other data. In 1920, 94 per

---

[3] Walter Kruesi, *Social Survey of Hamtramck* (publisher unknown, 1915).

[4] Only 423 of the remaining 2,661 persons belonged to the Polish National Catholic church, which is not a Romanist body, while 1,773 belonged to Negro churches and 505 persons belonged to other Protestant churches, some of which may have been Negro.

TABLE 1. Total Fertility Rates by Nativity, Hamtramck and Detroit, Michigan, 1920–50[a]

Year	Total white	Hamtramck native white	Foreign-born white	Total white	Detroit native white	Foreign-born white
1920	5,767.5	4,293.0	6,331.0	3,019.0	2,468.5	4,151.5
1930	2,492.0	2,486.5	2,773.5	2,131.0	2,023.0	2,793.5
1940	1,759.5	1,872.0	2,062.5	1,829.5	—	—
1950	2,262.5	—	—	2,604.5	—	—

a Data on births were gathered from primary sources—birth certificates on file with the Hamtramck Health Department. Births were tabulated on the basis of residence, with the out-of-city births to residents located in the files of the Michigan Department of Health in Lansing. There was some initial underregistration in 1920, but during World War II a birth certificate was mandatory to obtain factory employment in Hamtramck and Detroit. Because of this, most of the nonregistered were later post-registered. Birth totals for all years were checked against federal and local school census and national Office of Vital Statistics records. A high degree of correspondence and internal consistency was found. Population data came from the appropriate U. S. censuses.

cent; in 1930, 94 per cent; in 1940, 96 per cent; and in 1950, 91 per cent of the births were classified as Roman Catholic.

In summary, it appears that, while no single bit of evidence is conclusive, taken together the data clearly indicate that, at the very least, 90 per cent of the population is of the Roman Catholic faith.

OCCUPATION AND ECONOMIC STATUS

Dwelling units in Hamtramck are almost all frame one- and two-family houses, constructed with little regard for anything but the bare essentials of living and maximum utilization of land. They were frankly planned for sale or rent to workers with low incomes. The town was virtually without an upper or middle class. The special situation of Hamtramck, that is, its total inclosure within Detroit, does not allow for expansion. Therefore, the high degree of homogeneity as a working-class district has been maintained.

The occupational distribution in 1920 and 1930 as seen in the United States census shows this economic segregation clearly. Of course, the nature of the classification "gainful worker" obscures the level of skill within the manufacturing category, but very small numbers appear in the classifications "professional service" and "clerical." Included in the professional category in 1920 were six clergymen, two dentists, seven lawyers, twelve doctors, and one engineer. As this was a community of almost 50,000 persons, it is obvious that professional needs were largely met outside the city or not at all. Data concerning employed persons in the labor force in 1940 and 1950 are a more valid indication of the occupational structure. Even in 1950 Hamtramck remains a predominantly working-class community, although some changes in the upward direction can be seen when the situation is compared with that of 1940. Part of this, of course, is a reflection of postwar prosperity and the general upgrading of job classification.

THE FINDINGS

Given the four traits, each usually associated with high fertility, one would expect local fertility to be initially high and to remain high for a considerable time, since the congeries of attitudes and values associated with each trait is thought to be deep-seated. However, fertility rates in the Hamtramck population declined greatly in a short time. If Hamtramck is a specific example of a general phenomenon of change in birth rates, as we assume it to be, there may, after all, be no correlation between the depth of a value and the length of time needed for change. This decline in fertility must therefore be analyzed and related to the four conditions by which high fertility is supported. The essential findings of this study are shown in Table 1.

There was an enormous decline in the total fertility rate in Hamtramck between 1920 and 1930, and it was greater among the foreign-born than among the native. Beginning in 1940, the total fertility rate in Hamtramck

was similar to Detroit's.[5] It evidently took less than 20 years for Hamtramck to conform to the norm of the larger community, despite the prevalence of so many attributes associated with high fertility. Why did fertility begin to decline almost as soon as the community was formed?

NATIVITY

In Hamtramck the total fertility rate of foreign-born women in 1920 was 47 per cent greater than the corresponding rate for native white women. Only a decade later all but 12 per cent of this differential had disappeared: by 1940 it was only 10 per cent. In 1950 there were so few foreign-born women in the childbearing years that fertility rates could not be computed. It can be concluded that foreign-born mothers accepted fertility controls almost as readily as the native-born.

[5] Detroit's population includes large numbers of Catholics (35–40 per cent), Poles, and production workers.

TABLE 2.   Age-Specific Fertility Rates by Nativity as a Per Cent of 1920[a] Hamtramck, Michigan, 1930 and 1940 (Percentages)

Age	Total white		Foreign-born white		Native white	
	1930	1940	1930	1940	1930	1940
15–19	40	17	48	44	63	27
20–24	59	35	66	43	60	37
25–29	43	41	40	44	74	61
30–34	32	32	30	18	47	50
35–39	31	21	32	19	54	36
40–44	35	15	36	9	30	38
45–49	b	6	b	5	b	b

a Each per cent in the table is a proportion of the 1920 fertility rate of the same age group.
b Only a few births occurred to women in this age group.

TABLE 3. Average Birth Order by Age of Mother for Occupation of Husband, White Women, Hamtramck, Michigan, 1920–50

Age of Mother	Un-skilled	Semi-skilled	Skilled	White collar	Un-skilled	Semi-skilled	Skilled	White collar
			1920				1930	
15–19	1.28	1.31	1.28	1.00	1.25	1.03	1.00	1.08
20–24	2.39	2.12	1.83	1.66	1.75	1.70	1.17	1.39
25–29	3.51	3.53	2.83	3.42	2.96	2.97	1.69	3.06
30–34	5.19	4.80	5.89	5.18	4.81	4.29	3.33	4.07
35–39	6.12	6.70	7.25	6.38	6.57	6.34	3.50	4.50
40–44	9.63	9.60	11.41	—	10.05	7.44	4.76	11.00
No. of births	1,399	288	279	85	493	277	120	82
			1940				1950	
15–19	1.37	2.00	1.11	1.00	1.25	1.19	1.43	1.33
20–24	1.54	1.44	1.52	1.52	1.50	1.42	1.47	1.25
25–29	2.02	2.00	1.81	1.73	1.92	2.13	1.96	1.70
30–34	3.29	3.00	4.14	2.43	2.37	2.46	2.06	2.41
35–39	5.45	4.85	5.25	4.16	3.05	4.07	4.18	3.22
40–44	7.57	7.00	6.66	7.00	4.00	4.00	—	3.50
No. of births	434	134	141	80	185	270	203	159

Comparison with the foreign-born population of Detroit provides further evidence. While in 1920 foreign-born women in Hamtramck had a total fertility rate 35 per cent higher than the corresponding group in Detroit, only ten years later the two rates were the same. After 1930 fertility rates by nativity were not available for Detroit, but it is apparent that before their numbers in the childbearing years became small the nativity of mothers no longer was an important element in the differences. Since the foreign-born women were also of rural birth it can be concluded that this, too, did not prevent the decline in fertility.

Table 2 shows that changes in the marriage pattern are pretty well eliminated as a direct cause of declining fertility. The greatest reduction in fertility rates from 1920 to 1940 occurred in those age groups where the percentage of married women is high and relatively unchanging. This may not be true of the native women aged 15 to 24, where decline in birth rates might be due to a change in age at marriage. There seems to be only one possible cause for the decline—conscious, deliberate planning.

ECONOMIC LEVEL

Fertility and economic level are generally highly associated. In the absence of data on the economic level of all families by mother's age, the father's job, as given on the birth certificate, was substituted,[6] the average birth order was used as a measure of fertility. Admittedly, neither

---

[6] Each birth certificate was classified, according to the father's occupation, in one of four broad occupational groups: laborer, semiskilled, skilled, and "white collar." The latter was a catch-all of the few persons in the white-collar, professional, and managerial occupations. In addition, a few jobs (less than 3 per cent for any period) were either not reported or could not be classified.

of these measures is precise, but, nevertheless, broad differences are apparent (Table 3).

If we compare the change in birth order from 1920 to 1950 by occupational categories, we note distinct patterns. From 1920 to 1930 the decrease in average birth order was not nearly so marked for the two lower occupational groups (laborer and semiskilled) as for the two higher occupational groups; i.e., there is a time lag in reduction of births between the upper and lower occupational groups. However, by 1940 the decrease in both the skilled and the white-collar categories was not nearly so great as it was in the lower occupational groups or as it had been in the former in 1930. In fact, in the skilled group the average birth order increased for all age groups. Since the latter group had already reached greatly reduced family size, little further decrease could normally be expected. By 1950 the decreases in average birth order in all four occupational groups were very slight except for the highest age groups.

In summary, the average birth order in the higher occupational categories decreased sooner than did that of the lower occupational categories. However, by 1940 the rate of decrease in the laborer and semiskilled groups was greater than that of the other two occupational groups, possibly stimulated by the behavior of the skilled and white-collar groups.

RELIGION

The birth rates of Catholics and Protestants cannot be compared directly. We can only relate the Catholics of Hamtramck to the mixed population of Catholics and Protestants in Detroit. However, if we compare the total white population of the two communities over the entire period, we see that in 1920 the total fertility rate in Hamtramck was 92 per cent above Detroit; in 1930 it was 18 per cent higher; by 1940 it was actually 3 per cent *lower* than Detroit; and in 1950 it was 13 per cent lower.

It is quite evident that today the birth rate in Hamtramck is lower than the birth rate of the general white population in Detroit. Since no clear Catholic-Protestant comparison is possible, several interpretations can be suggested. The birth rate of Catholics in Detroit may be assumed to be about the same as that of Catholics in Hamtramck. If so, it follows that Protestants in Detroit have substantially higher birth rates than Catholics, which is difficult to believe, although not outside the range of possibility. Another assumption is that birth rates among Catholics in Detroit are higher than birth rates among Catholics in Hamtramck—a more plausible idea. The fertility ratio for the white population for Hamtramck for 1950[7] was slightly lower than that of Detroit women (323 and 348 per 1,000 women, respectively)—facts consistent with the data obtained from the more precise age-specific fertility rates. Next, a group of census tracts comprising the nucleus of the west-side Detroit Polish community and the five census tracts in Detroit comprising another identifiable foreign-born group—the

---

[7] The fertility ratio as used throughout this study is defined as the number of children under five years of age divided by the number of women 15 to 44 years of age. All fertility ratios used in this study have been adjusted by the method of indirect standardization for age of women. The standard population utilized was the 1940 Detroit white population.

Italian Catholics—were found to have only a slightly smaller degree of ethnic concentration than did the Polish community of Hamtramck, thus making them fairly comparable with the latter.[8] Fertility ratios among Italian Catholics and Polish Catholics in Detroit in 1950 were found to be slightly higher than those of Hamtramck (364 and 333 per 1,000 women, respectively), especially in the case of the Italian Catholics. The same results were found for 1940.[9]

In summary, the available data, admittedly limited, indicate little relationship between religion and fertility rates. That is, although the two Catholic communities in Detroit had higher fertility ratios than those found in Hamtramck, they were not high enough to account for the fertility differential between the latter and the total Detroit population. Rather, other factors must be investigated in order to determine what groups are contributing the most to the birth rates in Detroit. For example, recent studies indicate that when religion is held constant, there is a *direct* relationship between economic level, by both income and occupation, and birth rates.[10] Although not directly related to this paper, this is further evidence of the increasing lack of relationship between religion and fertility.

GENERALITY OF THE FINDINGS

There are no equally detailed data for Polish groups elsewhere; still there is a strong indication of a general decline in fertility among Polish immigrants (Table 4).

TABLE 4. Fertility Ratios in Polish Areas of Selected Cities, 1940 and 1950[a]

City	1940	1950
Hamtramck	238	323
Detroit	248	348
Chicago	212	330
Cleveland	218	340
Pittsburgh	271	393
Buffalo	257	328

[a] These cities were selected as being the principal centers of Polish immigration in this country. The age-adjusted fertility ratios were calculated for only those census tracts in them which contain at least the same degree of concentration of Polish-born as found in Hamtramck.

In 1940 and 1950 the fertility ratio in Hamtramck was neither outstandingly high nor outstandingly low. There is a considerable range to the fertility ratios, particularly in 1940, but Hamtramck was close to the center. Of course, the fertility ratio is a relatively crude index, and small differences are not necessarily real. The pattern seems clear, though; in 1940 the fertility ratios in each city were at one level, and in 1950 each had increased. The amount and proportion of increase was also within a reasonable range. We can conclude, although

---

[8] The concentration of Italians in these tracts was not quite so great as among the Poles in Hamtramck. Of the total white population, 25 per cent was foreign-born, and, of the foreign-born, 59 per cent were of Italian birth.

[9] Fertility ratios in 1940 were as follows: Detroit, 248; Hamtramck, 238; Polish tracts (Detroit), 258.

[10] Albert J. Mayer and Carol Klapprodt, "Fertility Differentials in Detroit, 1920–1950," *Population Studies*, IX, No. 2 (November, 1955), 148–57. Much information was obtained from a study conducted by the Detroit Survey Research Center of the University of Michigan. We are deeply indebted to Mr. David Goldberg for allowing us to examine the data in advance of publication.

our evidence is not precise, that the fertility trends in Hamtramck were not the product of unique circumstance but, on the whole, were experienced in other Polish immigrant communities throughout the United States.

On the other hand, we do not know whether this is true of such groups as the Italian and Irish Catholics. Analyzing them would be a method of holding religion constant, in order to determine the relationship between the national culture and fertility rates.

THE CAUSES OF DECLINING FERTILITY

As our statistical data do not tell us anything about basic causes or how the transition to small families was accomplished, we questioned representatives of each social agency operating in Hamtramck since 1925, as well as women who had raised families there during the 1920s. We learned that the main inducement for the reduction of families was the difficulty of raising a large family on the then current wages of a factory worker. However, this situation was customary in Poland. Moreover, there were other groups in this country at the same income level who did not exhibit such a drastic reduction in births in such a short time. Rather, if we remember that, on the one hand, these people were attempting to become assimilated, while, on the other, they were constantly aware of the differences between themselves and the Americans "on the outside" (native-born Detroiters), it becomes apparent that the relative standard of living may have been a strong stimulant. That the wages of a work-

er might have been greater in Hamtramck than in Poland was not to the point. The proximity of a reference group with a higher standard of living, particularly for the children, was possibly a far more powerful incentive to family limitation. Furthermore, the statements of those interviewed make it appear as a comparatively conscious and rational process.

The ease with which social change takes place is generally held to be dependent on the intensity of the attitudes and values associated with the cultural trait in question. However, this may also be related to the intensity of the attitudes and values associated with the conflicting and substituting traits. The avoidance of group ridicule, the desire to enjoy the higher standard of living of the reference group, the difficulty in supporting a large family at even subsistence level, and the strong prejudice of Poles against accepting welfare funds were sufficiently powerful to make them prefer small families and resort to birth control.

This still does not explain how these changes took place. While interviewers from the social agencies agreed that there must have been deliberate birth control, none would admit that their agency had abetted the process. Thus no formal procedure for the dissemination of birth-control information existed. This does not, however, preclude the possibility that an individual social worker might have given information to Hamtramck women. Nevertheless, the desire for such information must have been strong if no easily accessible group was volunteering it. It would seem that the important pressure was exerted informally in the factory both by Poles living in Hamtramck who were to some degree identified with

TABLE 5. Fertility Rates of White Women by Age and City, Hamtramck and Detroit, Michigan, 1920–50

Age and city	1920 Total white	Native white	Foreign-born white	1930 Total white	Native white	Foreign-born white	1940 Total white	Native white	Foreign-born white	1950 Total white
Ham-tramck total	5,767.5	4,293.0	6,331.0	2,492.0	2,486.5	2,773.5	1,759.5	1,872.0	2,062.5	2,262.5
15–19	96.1	53.8	167.8	38.0	33.5	80.7	15.9	14.3	73.1	31.9
20–24	298.1	281.4	303.9	175.4	166.9	199.8	103.1	102.1	129.1	146.0
25–29	266.9	180.1	279.2	119.1	127.2	110.0	109.8	108.6	121.9	136.0
30–34	246.1	178.3	257.8	78.2	83.9	76.3	76.6	88.8	46.7	93.5
35–39	177.9	106.0	187.0	57.1	57.3	57.0	36.7	38.1	35.6	38.9
40–44	64.9	59.0	66.5	23.1	17.7	23.8	9.5	22.4	6.0	6.0
45–49	3.5	—	4.0	7.5	10.8	7.1	0.2	—	0.2	0.2
Detroit total	3,019.0	2,468.5	4,151.5	2,131.0	2,023.0	2,793.5	1,829.5	—	—	2,604.5
15–19	60.0	52.5	92.3	49.7	47.2	64.3	27.1	—	—	46.4
20–24	169.7	149.1	227.7	131.7	123.0	168.6	113.5	—	—	165.1
25–29	154.1	127.6	207.6	118.1	107.2	141.8	112.4	—	—	157.7
30–34	115.0	94.9	148.8	58.5	71.5	98.8	68.8	—	—	96.3
35–39	72.8	49.6	105.9	49.4	41.7	60.3	34.4	—	—	44.6
40–44	29.2	18.1	44.0	17.3	12.9	23.0	8.9	—	—	10.2
45–49	3.0	1.9	4.0	1.5	1.1	1.9	0.8	—	—	0.6

native Detroiters and by the native Detroiters themselves. Thus the pressure to practice birth control came from within the community as well as from the reference group rather than from an organized source.

Furthermore, these pressures were abetted by the cohesiveness and solidarity of the community. On occasion, these qualities may present a formidable barrier to the transmission of new cultural traits. Nevertheless, once the new trait meets favor, they become highly effective in its rapid diffusion. In Hamtramck, once the values related to lower birth rates began to be accepted, the knowledge of birth-control methods could spread rapidly through the community. Although the formal sanction of a social agency might have stimulated this process even more, the informal in-group was, no doubt, an excellent substitute.

These facts demonstrate that predictions of the speed of assimilation or social change must reckon with the intensity of conflicting and substituting attitudes and values and the proximity of a reference group. Furthermore, the hypothesis is suggested that the change in values concomitant with this pattern of decreasing fertility rates to some extent requires a concentrated cultural community. It is very likely that Polish families living in native-white areas may exhibit a different pattern of birth rates due to a local difference in their self-image.

Racial, Ethnic, and Income Factors in the Epidemiology of Neonatal Mortality*

Charles V. Willie and William B. Rothney

Evidence on the difference in infant mortality rates between white and nonwhite populations is inconclusive. For example, a report of the National Office of Vital Statistics (from 1949 to 1951 which include the first two years of this study) indicates that the infant mortality rate of 45.5 per 1,000 live births in the nonwhite population is 65 per cent greater than the infant mortality rate of 27.7 in the white population of the United States.[1] However, Alfred Yankauer in a 1947 study of the New York City population found that in neighborhoods where more than 75 per cent of nonwhite parents reside the neonatal mortality rate of 52.7 per 1,000 live births among nonwhite persons is less than two points greater than the rate of 51.0 among white persons who reside in the same neighborhoods.[2] Clearly, discrepancy exists in the findings of these reports. This discrepancy has not been resolved because studies of variation in infant mortality rates between racial and ethnic populations seldom control adequately for socioeconomic status.

The purpose of this study is to determine whether infant mortality rates, particularly neonatal mortality rates, vary by racial and by ethnic neighborhoods when socioeconomic status is held constant.

Also, the distribution of neonatal mortality is studied in relationship to the distribution of families of varying income levels within racial and ethnic neighborhoods and within the total city. In a previous report, it was pointed out (1) that the distribution of median family income, by census tracts, had only a modest association, intercorrelating at 0.53, with the distribution of socioeconomic status (consisting of occupation, education, and housing items), and (2) that family income correlated significantly with the distribution of neonatal mortality rates, by census tracts, while the socioeconomic status index did not.[3] Thus, it would seem that socioeconomic status as subsequently defined in this study and family income are not interchangeable variables. This study is designed to hold socioeconomic status constant. However, it cannot be assumed that family

* Charles V. Willie and William B. Rothney, "Racial, Ethnic, and Income Factors in the Epidemiology of Neonatal Mortality," *American Sociological Review*, 27 (August, 1962), 522–26.

[1] National Office of Vital Statistics, "Infant Mortality, United States, 1915–50," *Vital Statistics Special Reports*, 45 (July 27, 1956), p. 13.

[2] Alfred Yankauer, Jr., "The Relationship of Fetal and Infant Mortality to Residential Segregation," *American Sociological Review*, 15 (October, 1950), p. 645.

[3] Charles V. Willie, "A Research Note on the Changing Association Between Infant Mortality and Socio-Economic Status," *Social Forces*, 37 (March, 1959), pp. 222–25.

income is also held constant. A secondary consideration in this investigation, then, is the three-way association, if any, between neonatal mortality, racial or ethnic neighborhood, and family income.

DATA AND METHOD

The study area is Syracuse, New York, an industrial city of approximately 25 square miles, with a population of 220,583 persons in 1950. Because of the small numbers of infant deaths that occur during a single year, it is necessary to combine several years. The study utilized data for the years 1950 through 1956 and is limited to the neonatal period, since 80 per cent of all infant deaths (excluding still births) occur during the first month of life.

The study includes four racial and ethnic populations in Syracuse—Negro, Native White, Italian, and Polish—that have neighborhoods in the lowest socioeconomic area of the city. The study is limited to these groups that have significant populations in Area VI, lowest in the hierarchy of residential areas according to an ecological investigation,[4] so that socioeconomic status and age of parents are held relatively constant.

Median age of women in the childbearing years, 20 to 44, is, computed for each racial and ethnic neighborhood. Medians for Negro, Native White, Italian, and Polish populations are 30, 31, 30, and 31 years, respectively. Thus, age of mother appears to be constant for the four neighborhoods and cannot account for varia-

---

[4] Charles V. Willie, *Socio-Economic and Ethnic Areas in Syracuse, New York,* unpublished Ph.D. thesis, Syracuse University, 1957, pp. 167–222.

tions, if any, in neonatal mortality rates.

Census tracts are the basic units of analysis. A socioeconomic status score, derived for each census tract, is a composite of five factors representing occupation, education, and housing characteristics of the population. Specifically, the variables are (1) percentage of persons in the combined occupational categories of operatives, service workers and laborers; (2) median school year completed by the adult population over 25 years of age; (3) average monthly rental; (4) average market value of own homes; and (5) percent of single-family dwelling units. (The first factor is inverted so that it will vary directly with the other four.) All factors in the socioeconomic index, except one indicating house type, intercorrelate with each other at 0.80 and above. The Pearsonian correlation coefficients between per cent of single-family dwelling units and the other four factors range from 0.59 to 0.70. Thus, a significant and high association exists between all variables in the socioeconomic status index. Distributions of all variables are converted into standard scores with assigned means of 100 and assigned standard deviations of 10. Standard scores for the five factors are averaged into a composite socioeconomic score for each census tract, and tracts with similar standard scores are combined into a single socioeconomic area. Six areas incorporating several neighborhoods are delineated; they range from Area I, high in socioeconomic status, to Area VI, low in socioeconomic status. Composite index scores, for individual census tracts, range from 85 to 123. The average socioeconomic status score for the four racial and ethnic neighborhoods is 92, well below the city assigned mean of 100. A difference of five between the highest and lowest average score of the four neighborhoods, is, of course, not statistically significant at the 5 per cent level of confidence. Thus, socioeconomic status is held constant for all four neighborhoods.

Racial and ethnic neighborhoods are delineated by a method similar to one used by Shevky and Williams to measure ethnic segregation.[5] When the percentage of a racial or ethnic population in a census tract is three or more times greater than the percentage of that population in the total city, a census tract is designated as part of the racial or ethnic neighborhood. This is the method used to identify neighborhoods with high proportions of Italian and Polish foreign born. Data on foreign born only are available in census publications for determining the boundaries of the two ethnic neighborhoods. Because of the high degree of segregation of the Italian and Polish populations (40 to 50 per cent of their foreign born are concentrated in identifiable neighborhoods), it is assumed that many second and third generations of these families also lived near their foreign-born kinsmen.[6] The same method is used to delineate the Negro neighborhood. However, the total Negro population is included. The Native White neighborhood consists of those census tracts in socioeconomic Area VI, with few Negroes and few foreign born, in which the percentage of Native White is greater than that in the total city population; more than 90 per cent of the residents in these census tracts are native born and white.

A few census tracts are eliminated from the study because they are neighborhoods that include two or more racial or ethnic populations in significant numbers. The final study area consists of 15 census tracts, two in the Negro neighborhood, three in the Native White neighborhood, and five each in the Italian and Polish neighborhoods. There are 52,497 persons in these tracts, about one-fourth of all persons in the city. The final study population consists of 8,626 live births and 197 neonatal deaths.

Unless otherwise stated, associations resulting from the statistical analysis are considered significant if they would occur by chance less than 5 times out of 100.

FINDINGS

For the total city, principal causes of death during the neonatal period are congenital malformations, complications associated with prematurity, and injuries at birth.[7] There are 34,700 live births and 658 neonatal deaths in the total city for the seven-year study period, resulting in a neonatal mortality rate of 19 per 1,000 live births.

As seen in Table 1, socioeconomic status is fairly similar for all neighborhoods. The neonatal mortality rate for the four racial and ethnic neighborhoods combined is only slightly higher at 23 than the total city rate. By individual neighborhoods, however, there is great variation with the

5 Eshref Shevky and Marilyn Williams, *The Social Areas in Los Angeles* (Berkeley: University of California Press, 1949), pp. 47–57.

6 Charles V. Willie, *Socio-Economic and Ethnic Areas in Syracuse, New York, op. cit.,* pp. 223–69.

7 Syracuse Department of Health, *Annual Report of the Bureau of Vital Statistics,* 1956 (typewritten).

TABLE 1. Neonatal Mortality Rate per 1,000 Live Births and Socioeconomic Status by Racial and Ethnic Neighborhoods Syracuse, 1950–56

Neighborhood	Live births	Neonatal deaths	Mortality rate	Average socio-economic score[a]
Negro	1,442	46	32	96
Native White[b]	1,749	52	30	91
Italian	3,226	66	20	90
Polish	2,208	33	15	91
Total	8,626	197	23	92

[a] The average socioeconomic status score for the total city is 100. Socioeconomic status is derived from a composite standard score of five variables reflecting occupation, education, and housing characteristics of the population. The composite score ranges from 85 in the census tract of lowest status to 123 in the tract of highest status.

[b] That portion of the neighborhood in the lowest socioeconomic area.

Negro and Native White rates of 32 and 30 respectively, being significantly higher than the rates of 20 and 15, and in that order, in the Italian and Polish neighborhoods. It should be noted that Negro and Native White neighborhoods consisting of two different racial populations have similar, almost identical, rates. At the same time, the neonatal mortality rate in the Native White neighborhood contrasts with and differs significantly from the mortality rates found in neighborhoods populated by white persons of Italian and Polish ancestry.

The analysis, thus far, demonstrates that Negro and Native White populations, though different racially, have similar neonatal mortality rates when socioeconomic status is held constant. Also, it demonstrates that the neonatal mortality rate of white native-born persons in a lower socioeconomic neighborhood differs from rates of other Caucasian populations in neighborhoods of similar socioeconomic status. Because the Native White and Negro neighborhoods with different racial populations have similar rates, and because the neighborhoods of white native born and white foreign born have different rates, though racially similar, doubt is cast upon any hypothesis that racial factors directly contribute to variations in the distribution of neonatal mortality by residential neighborhoods.

Since socioeconomic status as defined in this study and family income are not interchangeable variables, the family finance factor is introduced into the analysis at this point to see if it helps to explain the wide variations in neonatal mortality rates among different neighborhoods. Family income data are reported by census tracts and include the total earnings of all family members in one household for a single year. As seen in Table 2, income is unequally distributed among the racial and ethnic populations included in this study.

TABLE 2. Annual Median Income of Family by Racial and Ethnic Neighborhood, Syracuse, 1950–56

Neighborhood	Median family income
Negro	$1,584
Native White[a]	2,101
Italian	2,676
Polish	3,121

[a] That portion of the neighborhood in the lowest socioeconomic area.

Median family income varies from a low of $1,584 in the Negro neighborhood to a high of $3,121 in the Polish neighborhood. The Italian and Native White populations are second and third, respectively, following the Polish in the hierarchy of annual family income by racial and ethnic neighborhoods.

Using all 15 census tracts in the racial and ethnic neighborhoods, a Spearman rank correlation coefficient was computed because of the small numbers of units in the analysis. For the variables, median family income and neonatal mortality rates, a correlation coefficient of -0.75 gave definite evidence of a significant negative association. As median family incomes decrease neonatal mortality rates increase. The Negro and Native White populations in the lowest socioeconomic area of the city have similar high neonatal mortality rates notwithstanding their racial difference. It would appear that the similarities in high neonatal mortality rates is explained by the low-income status of families that populate these two neighborhoods. More than half of the families in the combined census tracts of these two neighborhoods received less than $40 per week in 1950. As a contrast, the Polish neighborhood has a low infant mortality rate of 15 and a median family income of $3,121, indicating that half of its families received incomes of $60 per week or more in 1950.

The high association between family income and neonatal mortality found to exist in some neighborhoods of the lowest socioeconomic area is quite different from the association between these two variables throughout the entire city. When family income and neonatal mortality rates were intercorrelated for the remaining forty-two census tracts not included in the racial and ethnic neighborhood analysis, the Pearsonian correlation coefficient of -0.06 was small and obviously not statistically significant. This finding corresponds with a conclusion arrived at in an earlier investigation that the historical association between infant mortality and economic conditions of life is diminishing.[8]

Nevertheless, a highly significant association exists between neonatal mortality and family income in part of the city, indicating that a critical income level must exist at some point along the continuum of family finances above which there is little, if any, association and below which there is significant association between neonatal mortality and this economic variable. To determine that critical level, a histogram was constructed as seen in Fig. 1. By median family income, census tracts were grouped into 11 income intervals ranging from $1,500 to $4,500 and over. By inspection, it is seen that $2,700 is the critical level below which there is a regular increase in neonatal mortality rates as the median incomes of families decrease. Above $2,700, fluctuations in the distribution of family income and neonatal mortality rates by census tracts are irregular and insignificant. Illustrating the very definite association between low-income status and neonatal mortality, two census tracts in which half of the families earned less than $1,600 a year in 1950 have mortality rates of 40 or above; these are twice as great as the neonatal mortality rate for the total city.

---

[8] Charles V. Willie, *Social Forces, op. cit.*, pp. 225–27.

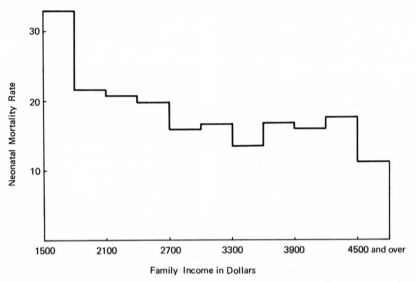

FIG. 1. Median Annual Family Income and Neonatal Mortality Rate per 1,000 Live Births, by Census Tracts, Syracuse, N. Y., 1950–56

CONCLUSIONS

Under the conditions of this analysis, it may be concluded: (1) that Negro and Native White populations have similar neonatal mortality rates when socioeconomic status is held constant; (2) that Native White populations in lower-income neighborhoods have neonatal mortality rates greater than the rates of white populations in higher income neighborhoods; (3) that neonatal mortality rates are intercorrelated with family income in neighborhoods where at least half of the households receive less than $2,700 per year; and (4) that no association exists between the distribution of neonatal mortality by neighborhoods and family financial status above the critical median income level of $2,700 per year.

The association between infant mortality and economic circumstances of life is diminishing. As with all generalizations, however, the condi-

tions under which a phenomenon will or will not occur should be specified. Our data refine this generalization by indicating that the probability of death during the neonatal period is heightened in neighborhoods where at least half of the families have incomes of less than $2,700 per year. The specific income level, below which the occurrence of neonatal mortality is significantly increased, may vary in time and by region. But the principle of a *critical income level* should persist as long as poverty exists.

While better care of premature children and more skillful handling of mother and child in the delivery room might further reduce the neonatal death rate, the importance of medically attended pregnancies cannot be overemphasized. Although our data do not indicate this, it is quite possible that part of the increased incidence of neonatal mortality among families below the critical income level of $2,700 is due to inadequate prenatal care experienced by pregnant women in these families. A nationwide family survey sponsored by the Health Information Foundation in 1953 discovered that "medical skills were utilized less fully in families with annual incomes of less than $3,000. . . . One out of seven mothers in this group did not see a physician during pregnancy, and approximately two thirds had fewer than seven prenatal physician visits."[9] In Rochester, New York in 1951, Alfred Yankauer and associates found that difference in the neonatal mortality rate between two populations of women in the lowest social class "was related to the amount of prenatal care sought."[10]

Why pregnant women in lower-income families do not seek prenatal care, even when it may be available without charge, is a sociological problem worthy of further research and

study. One possibility is that lower-income people are constricted in their ability to reach out to community health and welfare services for help. Were this hypothesis confirmed it would indicate the importance of professional workers in health and welfare seeking out the poor rather than waiting for community services to be sought. A second possibility is that many lower-income women do not know what services are available. A third possibility is that variations in the use of medical services during pregnancy may be a function of variation in cultural values of different populations of people. As stated by Odin Anderson, "the next steps in research in infant mortality which may yield useful information. . .should be directed toward relationships between infant mortality. . .and *mother-craft*, specific infant-care customs and practices. . . ." (Italics added.)[11] As the total rate decreases, the proportion of infant deaths attributable to different causes may increase. Thus, several hypotheses should be studied.

[9] Health Information Foundation, "Maternity Care and Its Costs in the United States," *Progress in Health Service*, VI (January, 1957), 4.

[10] Alfred Yankauer, Jr., Kenneth G. Goss and Salvator M. Romeo, "An Evaluation of Prenatal Care and Its Relationship to Social Class and Social Disorganization," *American Journal of Public Health*, XLIII (August, 1953), 1003.

[11] Odin W. Anderson, "Infant Mortality and Social and Cultural Factors," in *Patients, Physicians and Illness*, ed., E. Gartly Jaco (New York: The Free Press of Glencoe, Inc., 1958), p. 23.

Per Cent Nonwhite and Discrimination in the South[*]

H. M. Blalock, Jr.

The purpose of this paper is to investigate the relationships between various indices of discrimination and rate of nonwhite increase and per cent nonwhite in a random sample of 150 Southern counties. The present study is a follow-up to a previous study of non-Southern Standard Metropolitan Areas (S.M.A.'s) in which some of the same variables were interrelated but with different conclusions.[1] In the earlier study it was found that for non-Southern S.M.A.'s neither rate of nonwhite increase nor per cent Negro was highly related to the discrimination indices used. There was some evidence, however, that negative results such as these would not be obtained if the analysis were carried out on units having a larger percentage of nonwhites. Certain predictions concerning both the strength and the form of relationships were suggested by the first study. These predictions have been stated in terms of explicit hypotheses to be tested in the present study.

> *Hypothesis 1.* The correlations between rate of nonwhite increase and indices of discrimination will be either low positive or nonsignificant when relevant variables have been controlled. (Partial cor-

relations should range roughly between 0 and .40.)

For non-Southern S.M.A.'s relationships between rate of nonwhite increase and indices of income and job discrimination were slightly negative. It was anticipated that correlations for Southern counties might be slightly positive because of a tendency for rural nonwhites to migrate to urban areas that are characterized by relatively high white levels of living. Although no definite hypothesis was formulated concerning nonlinearity of relationships, it was suspected that areas having substantial nonwhite increases might have disproportionately high rates of discrimination.

> *Hypothesis 2.* The correlations between per cent nonwhite and indices of discrimination will be positive and moderately high (between .40 and .70) when relevant variables have been controlled.

Although a moderate positive correlation between per cent Negro and income differentials in non-Southern S.M.A.'s did not hold up under controls, evidence suggested that correlations would be considerably higher for Southern counties.

> *Hypothesis 3.* The correlations between per cent nonwhite and *white* levels of living will be negative when relevant variables have been controlled.

This hypothesis was not suggested by the earlier study but by the frequently stated argument that a large number of low status minority mem-

---

[*] Hubert M. Blalock, Jr., "Per Cent Nonwhite and Discrimination in the South," *American Sociological Review*, 22 (December, 1957), 677–82.

[1] H. M. Blalock, Jr., "Economic Discrimination and Negro Increase," *American Sociological Review*, XXI (October, 1956), 584–88.

bers will depress job and income standards in the entire area. According to this argument any advantages whites may obtain through exploitation of the disadvantaged group will be more than counterbalanced by job competition on the part of nonwhites willing to work for low wages.

> *Hypothesis 4.* The relationships between per cent nonwhite and indices of discrimination will tend to be nonlinear at the upper end of the per cent nonwhite continuum, with discrimination in counties having very large percentages of nonwhites tending to be less than would be expected on the basis of a linear model.[2]

Several lines of reasoning suggested Hypothesis 4. First, it seemed likely that a difference between 20 and 30 per cent nonwhite, for example, should be much more visible to members of a community than a difference between 60 and 70 per cent nonwhite. Second, it was assumed that the relationship between per cent nonwhite and discrimination is not a direct causal one but is mediated by the amount of competition between the two groups. It might be expected that the greater the degree of discrimination and therefore the greater the socioeconomic barriers between the two groups, the smaller the fraction of the nonwhite group directly in competition with most whites. Therefore, a given increase in the proportion of nonwhites should produce a relatively small increase in the total amount of competition between the two groups in situations where there is already a high degree

of discrimination, i.e., near the upper end of the per cent nonwhite continuum according to Hypothesis 2. On the other hand, the same increase in per cent nonwhite should produce a much larger increase in intergroup competition in instances where the two groups are more nearly equal in status. This hypothesis was also directly suggested by the first study in which it was found that slopes of regression equations were most steep in regions having the smallest minority percentages and least steep in the South.

> *Hypothesis 5.* The relationships between per cent nonwhite and indices of discrimination will also tend to be nonlinear at the lower end of the per cent nonwhite continuum, there being less discrimination in counties having very small percentages of nonwhites than would be expected on the basis of a linear model.

Evidence in the first study pointed to the existence of a threshold in the neighborhood of 10–15 per cent nonwhite, below which competition may not be defined primarily along group lines. It was therefore expected that counties having very small percentages of nonwhites would have considerably lower discrimination rates than other counties in spite of the fact that all counties studied are located within a region in which discrimination has a well-established historical heritage.

METHODS

The sample consisted of 150 counties selected at random from all Southern counties having at least 250 nonwhite households. Counties having fewer than 250 nonwhite households were excluded because certain data

---

[2] Hypotheses 4 and 5 predict an increasing function with a decreasing slope. Several alternative mathematical models were used in order to predict the exact form of this curve. Since Hypothesis 4 was not supported by the data, these models will not be discussed.

for nonwhites were not available. Virginia was not included since county data were not comparable with data for other states. States included consisted of the remaining ten states in Odum's Southeast.[3] For the purpose of investigating Hypotheses 4 and 5 concerning nonlinearity, 95 additional counties were selected so as to obtain counties with more extreme percentages of nonwhites.[4] The measure of rate of nonwhite increase was obtained by subtracting the percentage of nonwhites in the county in 1940 from the comparable figure for 1950.

Indices of discrimination were computed from 1950 census data using the following variables: (1) *Homeownership:* percentage of occupants who were homeowners; (2) *Overcrowding:* percentage of dwelling units with one or fewer persons per room; (3) *Rentals:* percentage of urban renter-occupied dwelling units with gross monthly rentals of $15 or more; (4) *Income:* percentage of families having annual incomes of $1500 or more; (5) *Education:* percentage of males 25 and over having completed more than six years of schooling; (6) *Occupation:* percentage of the urban male labor force in semiskilled, skilled, or white collar positions.

Figures were obtained for both whites and nonwhites, and since in each case a high percentage indicates a high level of living, an index of discrimination was obtained by subtracting the nonwhite percentage from that of the whites. A factor

analysis of the 6×6 matrix of discrimination indices was carried out on this sample of Southern counties in order to determine whether or not a single factor could account for most of the intercorrelations among indices. Since the second and subsequent factors accounted for a negligible fraction of the variance, it was decided to consider the first factor as a general socioeconomic discrimination factor and to compute a combined discrimination index by weighting each separate index in proportion to its loading with the first factor.

The control variables finally selected included white levels of living (as obtained above), states, percentage of residents classified as urban, per cent rural farm, percentage of females in the labor force, per cent in manufacturing, the average valuation of farm land and buildings, and percentage of total crop acreage planted in cotton. Since differentials between white and nonwhite figures were expected to be a function of the relative proportions of each group living in urban areas, an urbanization ratio measuring the degree to which nonwhites were underrepresented in urban areas was also used as a control variable. Since many of the control variables were highly interrelated, it was found that the use of three or more controls yielded partial correlations that are practically identical with those produced by the operation of two simultaneous controls. Only those controls that yielded the greatest departures from zero-order correlations have been reported in this paper.

[3] See H. W. Odum, *Southern Regions* (Chapel Hill: University of North Carolina Press, 1936), pp. 7 ff.

[4] This supplementary sample consisted of all remaining counties having fewer than 5 or more than 60 per cent nonwhites plus a random sample of counties having between 5 and 20 or 55 and 60 per cent nonwhites.

FINDINGS

The correlation between per cent nonwhite and rate of nonwhite increase was a nonsignificant −0.01.

Intercorrelations among indices of discrimination were moderately high with the exception of correlations with the occupational index. Intercorrelations among the first five indices varied from 0.33 to 0.68, and correlations between these indices and the combined index ranged between 0.68 and 0.86. Correlations with the occupational index were all positive, but two were not significant at the 0.05 level and the remainder were less than 0.30. Some reasons for these low correlations are discussed below in connection with Hypothesis 2.

TABLE 1. Correlations Between Indices of Discrimination and Nonwhite Increase and Per Cent Nonwhite

Type of discrimination	Nonwhite increase		Per cent nonwhite	
	Total correlations	Partial correlations	Total correlations	Partial correlations[c]
Homeownership	0.04	0.06	0.60[a]	0.52[a]
Overcrowding	−0.06	−0.04	0.69[a]	0.56[a]
Rentals	0.10	0.11[d]	0.53[a]	—[d]
Income	0.43[a]	0.46[a]	0.54[a]	0.46[a]
Education	0.33[a]	0.42[a]	0.72[a]	0.68[a]
Occupation	0.08	0.03[d]	−0.03	—[d]
Combined index	0.22[a]	0.37[a]	0.80[a]	0.73[a]

[a] Only these correlations are significant beyond .05 level.

[b] With simultaneous controls for per cent urban and per cent nonwhite.

[c] With simultaneous controls for per cent urban and urbanization ratio.

[d] Since measure involves urban data only, controls for per cent urban and urbanization ratio are unnecessary.

Hypothesis 1. Correlations between nonwhite increase and the various indices of discrimination summarized in Table 1 tended to support the first hypothesis to the effect that correla-

tions would be nonsignificant or low positive. Correlations with occupational differentials and the three housing indices were nonsignificant. Relationships with income and educational differentials were somewhat higher than anticipated, however. There is some evidence that a partial explanation for these correlations can be made in terms of selective migration of nonwhites into areas having high white levels of living. Correlations between rate of nonwhite increase and white income and educational levels were 0.39 and 0.29 respectively. Since measures of discrimination involved differentials between white and nonwhite figures, such selective migration would serve to inflate the correlations between discrimination indices and rate of nonwhite increase. Unfortunately, the data did not permit isolation of the effects of migration from those of actual discrimination.

Notice that correlations were generally increased slightly when controls were introduced for per cent urban and per cent nonwhite. Tests for nonlinearity produced nonsignificant results, although there was a slight tendency for income and educational differentials to be disproportionately high in counties having an increase of more than 4 per cent nonwhite during the decade. Thus there is a hint of the possibility that very large rates of increase may be associated with higher differentials. On the other hand, no positive correlations were found for non-Southern S.M.A.'s where rates of increase have been much more striking.

Hypothesis 2. Table 1 indicates that correlations between per cent nonwhite and all indices except occupational differentials were at least moderately high and that these correlations were only slightly reduced by controls for per cent urban and urbanization ratios. In the case of the combined index, about 64 per cent of the variation in discrimination was associated with per cent nonwhite without controls and 53 per cent when controls were introduced.

The low correlations generally found between the occupational index and other variables deserve further comment. It is possible, of course, that these results were due to inadequacies in the measure itself. Certain variables may also have operated in a direction opposite to the per cent nonwhite factor, producing very low correlations with other discrimination indices as well. We would expect to find a higher percentage of professionals, businessmen, and clerical workers among nonwhites whenever the minority percentages were sufficient to stimulate the development of a dual economy. This factor alone, however, cannot account for the low correlation, since the proportion of white-collar workers among nonwhites was found to be very low in all counties. Actually, the size of the measure for nonwhites was largely determined

by the ratio of the number of unskilled laborers to operatives. It seems plausible to argue that if there were a large number of nonwhites in urban occupations, some of these persons would occupy positions as operatives simply because the available number of unskilled jobs had already been filled by other members of their own group. In other words, a large percentage of nonwhites might tend to produce an overflow of the minority group into semiskilled positions. This does not mean that nonwhites in these positions would necessarily receive the same pay as whites or that they would be afforded comparable status. Consistent with this explanation is the fact that with a control for per cent urban the correlation between per cent nonwhite and white occupational levels was positive (0.38).

Hypothesis 3. It was anticipated that correlations between per cent nonwhite and white levels of living would be negative. As shown in Table 2, results tended to be opposite to those predicted when controls were introduced for per cent urban. The data therefore do not support the thesis that whites in areas with the largest percentages of nonwhites tend to have the lowest standards of living. For example, the writer was surprised to find that whites in counties with more than 60 per cent nonwhites had average or higher than average levels of living as compared with whites in other Southern counties. This does not mean that low white levels in the region as a whole cannot at least partially be attributed to the presence of a cheap source of labor.

Hypothesis 4. This hypothesis, which predicted nonlinearity at the upper end of the per cent nonwhite continuum, was not supported by the data. For each of the six discrimina-

TABLE 2. Correlations Between White Levels of Living and Per Cent Nonwhite

White levels	Total correlations	Control for per cent urban
Homeownership	−0.16	−0.21[a]
Overcrowding	0.15	0.22[a]
Rental	−0.17[a]	—[b]
Income	0.07	0.31[a]
Education	0.35[a]	0.38[a]
Occupation	0.23[a]	—[b]

[a] Only these correlations are significant beyond .05 level.
[b] Control unnecessary since measures involve urban data only.

TABLE 3. Comparion of Observed Discrimination Scores with Scores Expected under the Linear Model, for Counties with 65–69.9 and 70–84.9 Per Cent Nonwhite

Type of discrimination[a]	Counties with 65–69.9 per cent nonwhites (N=25)			Counties with 70–84.9 per cent nonwhites (N=24)		
	Obs. score	Exp. score[b]	Diff.[c]	Obs. score	Exp. score[b]	Diff.[c]
Homeownership	47.8	48.6	−0.8	53.4	50.5	2.9
Overcrowding	44.3	46.1	−1.8	49.3	47.9	1.4
Rental	47.5	50.7	−3.2	53.8	53.4	0.4
Income	42.5	42.9	−0.4	46.1	44.9	1.2
Education	67.8	66.0	1.8	69.7	69.2	0.5
Combined index	50.9	50.9	0.0	54.0	53.0	1.0

[a] Occupational differentials omitted since correlation with per cent nonwhite was not significant.

[b] Expected scores obtained by extending regression equations for remaining counties.

[c] The *t* test was used to test for significance of adjusted differences between observed and expected scores. Since computation of the regression equation involved possible sampling error, 95 per cent confidence bands for the true equations were computed and adjustments made so as to reduce the differences between observed and expected figures to values that would be obtained if the true regression equations were the most " unfavorable " ones possible within the confidence bands. Probability levels indicated are therefore likely to be on the conservative side. All differences are nonsignificant at the 0.05 level.

tion indices for which a significant relationship was established, the form of the relationship with per cent nonwhite turned out to be remarkably linear except at the very low end of the continuum.[5] There was no noticeable tendency for discrimination scores to level off in the case of the 49 counties having over 65 per cent nonwhites. Table 3 indicates the direction and magnitude of differences between mean scores to be expected if relationships were linear and mean scores actually obtained for counties having 65–69.9 and 70–84.9 per cent nonwhites. Observed scores were slightly below the expected figures for counties having between 65 and 69.9 per cent nonwhites, but just the

opposite tendency can be noted in the case of counties with 70–84.9 per cent nonwhites. All differences were extremely small, however, and none were significant at the 0.05 level. Clearly, either the reasoning that motivated Hypothesis 4 is basically wrong or there were forces counterbalancing a tendency for a decreasing slope. One such factor might be the threat of political or economic dominance posed by a very large nonwhite group unless it were completely subordinated. It is also possible that a very large number of nonwhites might produce a situation in which the market for unskilled labor could become supersaturated to such a degree that nonwhites depressed their own standard of living without markedly affecting that of the whites.

Hypothesis 5. The final hypothesis predicted that counties having very

---

[5] In tests for over-all nonlinearity using all 245 counties, results were nonsignificant at the 0.05 level except in the case of the combined index.

TABLE 4. Comparison of Observed Discrimination Scores with Scores Expected under the Linear Model, for Counties with 0–4.9 and 5–9.9 Per Cent Nonwhite

Type of discrimination[a]	Counties with 0–4.9 per cent nonwhite (N=17)				Counties with 5–9.9 per cent nonwhite (N=27)			
	Obs. score	Exp. score[b]	Diff.	Sig. level[c]	Obs. score	Exp. score[b]	Diff.	Sig. level[c]
Homeownership	26.1	30.7	−4.6	N.S.	26.5	32.1	−5.6	N.S.
Overcrowding	21.4	29.9	−8.5	<.01	29.0	31.1	−2.1	N.S.
Rentals	14.1	27.1	−13.0	<.02	30.0	29.0	1.0	N.S.
Income	15.9	23.7	−7.8	<.05	25.1	25.1	0	N.S.
Education	28.7	37.4	−8.7	<.01	34.4	39.6	−5.2	N.S.
Combined index	21.4	29.7	−8.3	<.01	28.8	31.2	−2.4	N.S.

[a] Occupational differentials omitted since correlation with per cent nonwhite was not significant.

[b] Expected scores obtained by extending regression equations for remaining counties.

[c] See Table 3, footnote c for explanation of significance test.

small minority percentages would have unusually low discrimination scores. Table 4 indicates the direction and magnitude of differences between observed and expected mean scores for counties having 0–4.9 and 5–9.9 per cent nonwhites. Counties with 0–4.9 per cent nonwhite had substantially lower discrimination scores than would be expected under the linear model. There was much less of a tendency for counties with 5–9.9 per cent nonwhite to deviate in the predicted direction, however. Although deviations for four of the indices were as predicted, none of the differences was significant at the 0.05 level. There therefore seems to be a threshold somewhere between 5 and 10 per cent nonwhite below which nonwhites tend to fare relatively well.

CONCLUSIONS

This study was designed to test certain hypotheses concerning the relationships between various indices of discrimination and rate of nonwhite increase and per cent nonwhite. Moderate positive correlations were obtained between rate of nonwhite increase and income and educational differentials, but correlations with other indices of discrimination were nonsignificant. On the basis of these findings and those of a previous study, the writer concludes that the relationship between discrimination and rate of minority increase is at most a relatively weak one.

Correlations between per cent nonwhite and all indices except occupational differentials were moderately high. These relationships were remarkably linear except for counties with less than 5 per cent nonwhites that had substantially lower discrimination scores than other counties. In view of the fact that comparable correlations for non-Southern S.M.A.'s were considerably lower than those obtained in the present study, the conclusion is that the relationship between these two variables is by no means a necessary one, but is depenlent upon other variables. An increase in the relative size of the minority may directly increase the total amount of competition with the majority, but this competition need not be defined along group lines and therefore may not result in increased discrimination. There may be a threshold below which discrimination and minority percentage are only slightly related. The exact level of the threshold may be determined by such factors as the amount of prejudice toward the minority, the degree to which the minority is easily visible, and the presence of group norms sanctioning discrimination. Further study is needed to determine whether or not such thresholds do in fact exist and to investigate the exact nature of the relationships among the variables involved.

The Negro in New Orleans:
A Functional Analysis of
Demographic Data*

George A. Hillery, Jr.

Population study and sociology have shown a tendency toward convergence. From separate origins the fields have moved towards an increasing interdependence.[1] All too seldom, however, has the relevance of sociological theory for demographic analysis been verified.[2] Probably one of the

---

* George A. Hillery, Jr., "The Negro in New Orleans: A Functional Analysis of Demographic Data," *American Sociological Review*, XXII, 2 (April, 1957), 183–88.

[1] Whether one begins the history of demography with Sir Walter Raleigh, John Graunt, or Thomas Malthus, a considerable period of time elapsed before Herbert Spencer (probably the first clearly recognizable sociologist to write in this field) put forth his theories of population. Cf. James Bonar, *Theories of Population from Raleigh to Arthur Young* (New York: Greenberg, 1931); Warren S. Thompson, *Population Problems* (4th ed., New York: McGraw-Hill Book Company, 1953); and Harry Elmer Barnes (ed.), *An Introduction to the History of Sociology* (Chicago: The University of Chicago Press, 1948).

[2] The writer is not speaking here of logical analyses of the relations between the two areas. *Cf.* Kingsley Davis, *Human Society* (New York: The Macmillan Company, 1949), chap. xx; and Amos H. Hawley, *Human Ecology* (New York: Ronald Press, 1950), pp. 70, 77–79, *et passim* for excellent attempts in this direction. Rather the claim is made that there is a deficiency of empirical tests of the relation of sociological theory of data which describe the changing sizes of populations, i.e., demography.

	Nonwhite[a]	White	Difference (white-nonwhite)	Ratio[b] $\left(\dfrac{nonwhite}{white}\right)$
Number	182,631	387,184	205,183	.47
Per cent	32.0%	68.0%	36.0%	.47
Median age (years)	28.2	32.3	4.1	.87
Dependency ratio[c]	54.2	43.6	−10.6	1.24
Sex ratio	87.0	92.0	5.0	.95
Index of family instability[d]	55.0	27.4	−27.6	2.01
Persons living as married couples	50.5%	59.9%	9.4%	.84
Median years of schooling completed (population 25 years of age and over)	6.5	9.6	3.1	.68
Males in service production work[e]	30.6%	60.1%	29.5%	.51
Males in physical production work[e]	68.4%	39.0%	−29.4%	1.75
Males in white collar work[e]	11.4%	52.8%	41.4%	.22
Males in blue collar work[e]	87.6%	46.3%	−41.3%	1.89
Median income of families and unrelated individuals (1949)	$1,381	$2,900	$1,519	.48
Median contract monthly rent	$16.49	$31.57	$15.08	.52
Voters per 100 eligible voters (males, 1952)	29.9	81.8	51.9	.37
Crude birth rate	33.3	21.9	−11.4	1.52
Fertility ratio[f]	480	396	−84	1.21
Gross reproduction rate	187	128	−59	1.46
Three-year mean death rate (males, 1949–1951)	13.2	11.6	−1.6	1.14
Three-year mean death rate (females, 1949–1951)	10.7	8.8	−1.9	1.22
Infant mortality rate	34.5	27.0	−7.5	1.28
Persons residing in different county in 1950 than in 1949 (preliminary count)	2%	4%	2%	.50
Net migrants per 1,000 population	22.0	50.7	28.7	.43

a Nonwhites in the city of New Orleans were 99.5 percent Negro in 1950.

b The ratio is computed by dividing the statistic for nonwhites by the comparable statistic for whites. A ratio above 1.00 thus measures the proportion by which nonwhites exceed whites for a given measure, whereas a ratio below 1.00 shows the reverse.

c Persons under 15 years and 65 and over per 100 persons 15 to 64 years of age.

d Number of broken families per 100 persons living as married couples. Letting M equal persons married, Mc equal married couples, D equal persons divorced, W equal persons widowed, the index is computed as follows: $\dfrac{D+W+M-2Mc}{2Mc} \times 100$, where M−2Mc equals persons separated for whatever reasons.

e These categories are the functional and status groupings of occupations employed by Ronald Freedman in his Recent Migration to Chicago (Chicago: The University of Chicago Press, 1950), pp. 26–27.

f Children under 5 per 1,000 women 15 to 44 years of age.

Sources: George A. Hillery, Jr., "The Negro in New Orleans: A Demographic Analysis," unpublished doctoral dissertation, Louisiana State University, 1954; United States Bureau of the Census, U. S. Census of Population: 1950 (Washington: Government Printing Office, 1952), Vol. II, Part XVIII; U. S. Census of Housing: 1950 (Washington: G. P. O., 1952), Vol. I, chap. xviii; 1950 Census of Population: Preliminary Report, Series PC-5, (Washington: G. P. O., June 10, 1951), No. 32; National Office of Vital Statistics, Vital Statistics of the United States, 1949 (Washington: G. P. O., 1951), Part II; Vital Statistics of the United States, 1950 (Washington: G. P. O., 1953), Vol. III; Louisiana State Department of Health, Statistical Report of the Division of Public Health Statistics, 1951 (New Orleans: n.d.); State of Louisiana, Report of Secretary of State to his Excellency Robert F. Kennon, Governor, From January 1, 1951 to December 31, 1952 (Baton Rouge: Thos. J. Moran's Sons, 1953).

more crucial questions in this connection is the relation between population characteristics and processes[3] on the one hand and social values on the other. It is the task of this paper to indicate such a relationship and to reach this goal through an explanation of some observed demographic differentials by means of a particular sociological theory. Specifically, the hypothesis is advanced that *one function of the white man's definition of the racial situation is to create demographic differentials between his own and the Negro population.* One would logically expect that such a hypothesis could be verified. This paper attempts to show by empirical and theoretical demonstration that the hypothesis is tenable for at least one city.

Racial differentials constitute an important focus of this paper, but explaining an entire pattern of race relations represents a broader and more complex approach than that employed here. A new theory is not resented; the one to be used is well established.[4] Instead, selected data of one area are used with a theory of another. The problem is this: Why are there a host of demograhic differences between two races in a southern city? (See Table 1.) Em-

phasis is given (1) a relatively comprehensive set (though only one type) of *demographic* data and (2) differentials rather than absolute levels. To the writer's knowledge, no single theory has yet been offered which integrates such information.[5] This paper represents an effort in that direction.

THE DATA

The data for the study are taken from an extensive demographic investigation of the Negroes of New Orleans.[6] To better emphasize demographic differentials, the condition of the Negro was described in relation to that of whites. This method found definite and important demographic differences between the two races and these are summarized for 1950 in Table 1. Numerically speaking, Negroes were a minority people. Compared with whites, they were disproportionately concentrated in the younger ages. Females were also relatively more numerous. Measured by the prevalence of broken families, family life was more unstable. Negroes received less education and had occupations with less status and smaller income. Disproportionately

---

For the purpose of this paper, it matters not whether demography is considered as a sister discipline or a subfield of sociology. What is more relevant is the importance of delineating the relationship, whatever it may be, through actual research.

[3] Population characteristics are here defined to include age, sex, and familial composition, marital status, educational status, economic status, and political status, whereas population processes refer to birth, death, and migration. Religious status was excluded because of lack of data.

[4] Cf. Robert K. Merton, "The Self-Fulfilling Prophecy," *The Antioch Review*, VIII (June, 1948), 193–210.

[5] More concretely no theory will explain demographic differentials within a single biracial population and will extend over all major aspects of population composition and processes. The present theory is applicable only where a socially more powerful group defines a subordinate group as inferior. See also the section "Theoretical Integration of the Data," below.

[6] Hillery, *op. cit.* The focus of investigation was the Standard Metropolitan Area of New Orleans and its constituent parts. For the sake of abridgment, only data for the city of New Orleans, proper, are presented in this paper.

fewer of them achieved the right to vote. Their fertility was higher, their mortality greater, and they were less often found as migrants.

These differentials are not confined to the New Orleans area, but are generally recognized in demographic literature. An understanding of the factors underlying dissimilarities in New Orleans may thus have wider application.

THE THEORY

The basic theory to be used in explaining the differentials is derived from one originally set forth by Thomas: "If men define situations as real, they are real in their consequences."[7] Although numerous earlier investigators had anticipated this statement, it remained for Thomas to state it in what could be termed codified form. Yet perhaps the very succinctness and simplicity of the principle were disarming, for few bothered to inquire more fully into what Thomas had said.[8] Merton, however, has provided an interpretation whereby the abstraction may be employed to lend form to empirical data. According to Merton, the first part of the theorem indicates that men respond not only to objective features

of a situation; they respond to the meaning this situation has for them. And once that meaning has been assigned, it determines not only men's behavior, but also some of the consequences of that behavior.[9] Thus, the act of making the definition is also an act of making a prophecy, and the very fact that the definition comes into existence creates conditions whereby the prophecy will be realized. The definition is accordingly a "self-fulfilling prophecy," as Merton has termed it. The degree of objective truth in the assertion has no effect on its eventual social fulfillment. The essential quality is initial belief. In fact, as Merton has so aptly stated:

> The self-fulfilling prophecy is, in the beginning, a *false* definition of the situation evoking a new behavior which makes the originally false conception come *true*. The specious validity of the self-fulfilling prophecy perpetuates a reign of error. For the prophet will cite the actual course of events as proof that he was right from the beginning.[10]

Possibly the most difficult point to grasp in this connection is that there is no conspiracy to "make" the definition come true. Rather, in my opinion the "fulfillment" occurs unintentionally—or, more precisely, comes about through unforeseen and unintended consequences. The problem, however, is not simple. There are several aspects that must be investigated, two of which have divergent consequences. For example, the "white man's" definition that the Negro is inferior is intended to accomplish nothing, for its believers feel that the definition is gospel—it is taken as a given. In this sense, the definition has no in-

---

[7] W. I. Thomas and Dorothy S. Thomas, *The Child in America* (New York: Alfred A. Knopf, 1928), p. 572.

[8] This statement does not, of course, imply that the principle has not been accepted as valid by social scientists nor that it has not been subjected to verification. One of the more notable attempts at demonstrations is represented by Gunnar Myrdal, with the assistance of Richard Sterner and Arnold Rose, *An American Dilemma* (New York: Harper & Row, Publishers, Inc., 1944). Even this treatment is deficient in not explicitly showing the connection between the Thomas theorem and the data presented.

---

[9] Merton, *op. cit.*, p. 194.
[10] *Ibid.*, p. 195.

tended consequences, no manifest functions. One cannot deny, however, that there are certain crucial consequences of this definition: the "inferiors" are awarded a lesser share in the privileges and opportunities of society. The reasoning may run somewhat as follows: "These people are inferior. Thus, they can receive only inferior benefits from *any* material provided them. It follows that one is wasting time and effort if he provides them with anything more than inferior material." The "definers" do not give the "inferior material" to prove their point. They do so because their point (to them) is proven. That is, the definers intend only to act in accordance with their initial definition that the Negro is inferior. There is thus a two-edged sword: the whites have no intention of proving the definition, but they do intend to live up to its stipulations. This intention and the acts accompanying it (awarding lesser shares in the society, etc.) can properly be labeled manifest functions, or intended consequences of the definition.

These manifest functions, further, provide additional and now unintended consequences (or latent functions) in creating other deficiencies. These deficiencies, together with the original lesser share of privileges and opportunities, have in turn the unintended consequences or latent functions of providing "unquestionable" evidence that the definition is really what it purports to be—a truth.

These functions can be outlined as follows:

> *Initial definition:* The out-group is inferior (or, at least, "not as equal" as the in-group).
> *First intended consequence:* The in-group assumes the definition is true and treats the out-group as inferior, giving the mem-

bers certain "inferior materials" or privileges.

> *Resulting unintended consequence:* The out-group is placed in situations where its members receive additional unequal privileges, and inequalities relative to the in-group spread to most if not all segments of their life.
> *Unintended consequences of the above two consequences:* (1) The out-group does become inferior (at least in a social sense); and (2) the definition is accordingly accepted by the in-group as proven.

The important point in the foregoing is that most of the functions of the initial definition are latent, not manifest, unintended, not intended.[11] Without this realization, it is a simple matter to overlook the importance of values for guiding social action and to impute to white southerners the unsubstantiated traits of stupidity and dishonesty.

THEORETICAL INTEGRATION OF THE DATA

The testing of the relation between the theory and the data is done primarily by indicating the logical nature of the connection. Beginning with the self-fulfilling prophecy and utilizing functional analysis, the writer hopes to show that the ethnic differences as found demographically (see Table 1) are what would be anticipated if the self-fulfilling prophecy is a valid concept.[12] For example, it

---

[11] This observation is in general agreement with the finding that prejudiced persons do not tend to realize that they are prejudiced. See Gordon Allport and B. M. Kramer, "Some Roots of Prejudice," *Journal of Psychology*, XXII (July, 1946), 34–36.

[12] Thus, in addition to describing the relation between sociology and demography, another effort will be directed towards validating the theory of the self-fulfilling prophecy, itself. Merton's ex-

can be noted that, according to the theory, when A exists, B can be expected to follow. If the data show such a condition, the theory is validated *to that extent*. The more theoretical expectations that are verified, the greater validity of the theory. To claim, however, that this paper can *prove* the theory would disregard canons of scientific research. The relationship is indicated here for only one city (New Orleans), one brief segment of time (mainly 1950 and the preceding decade), and two groups (white and Negro). There *could* be wider applicability, as has been noted. Nothing more is claimed.

That the New Orleans white population defines the Negro as inferior can be readily demonstrated, particularly in such matters as restrictions on Negro voting, poorer educational facilities allocated, and enforced segregation. More important, data from an earlier study indicate that the Negroes themselves believe that white persons define them as inferior.[13] Such a definition (or prophecy) is the initial stimulus in activating a series of consequences. Hence, the Negroes are given poorer educational facilities, both in cost and in space. They emerge with a lower educational level, and this condition in turn (and that of discrimination in general) has the unintended consequence of handicapping their search for jobs, a handicap reflected in the disproportionate concentration in jobs requiring more

cellent analysis relies more on illustration rather than demonstration, though admittedly the distinction between the two techniques is vague. In this connection, see also footnote 8.

[13] George A. Hillery, Jr., "The Presence of Community Among Urban Negroes: A Case Study of a Selected Area in New Orleans," unpublished master's thesis, Louisiana State University, 1951, pp. 203–8.

physical effort and vested with less authority. As an additional latent function, the level of living would be expected to be lower than the whites', and the evidence attests to that expectation.

The lower educational level also has the functional consequence of lowering the degree to which the mores of the larger society are inculcated in the Negroes. In addition, a lower economic level signifies a closer proximity to marginal subsistence. These two factors could be expected (at least as one consequence) to influence the Negro family to deviate in form from that of the larger society. Such deviation is also a matter of record, especially in the more unstable family pattern as measured by the greater number of broken families. The relationship that relative ignorance, poverty, and familial instability bear to mortality would lead one to expect the latent function of higher mortality to be realized. In fact mortality rates for Negroes are higher than those in the white population.

In a sense, the chain of consequences approaches completion when mortality is recognized as an index of the incidence of disease. A higher disease level would tend to lower the educational and economic levels, and high mortality rates can have as one of their immediate consequences broken families (though again unintended). Even the sex ratio of Negroes does not go untouched: the larger study showed evidence of a connection between high stillbirth rates and low sex ratios at birth—the former influencing the latter.[14] High stillbirth rates can be regarded,

[14] Hillery, "The Negro in New Orleans," *op. cit.*, pp. 198–99.

of course, as a consequence of the educational, economic, and mortality levels.

The self-fulfilling prophecy, however, has varied ramifications, and accordingly there is no simple chain of consequences. Education may be singled out for emphasis, for this factor clearly reveals the absence of any unilinear causality. The lower educational level makes for a lower level of knowledge of birth control. Accompanying this observation is the higher fertility of the New Orleans Negroes. This higher fertility is reflected also in the higher dependency ratios, which further affect the level of living. Just which of these two variables is without consequences for the other is difficult to say. There is possibly an additional function: low economic levels and a felt discrimination would be expected to depress in-migration rates, and such lowered rates were found among the people studied.[15]

Meager educational attainments are also intimately related to political activity, since education is to a large degree in the hands of the local government. A smaller political voice means a smaller degree of political control. Practically nonexistent until quite recently, the Negro's political voice is still numerically weak. When accompanied by a definition of Negro inferiority, such a situation would be expected to have the consequences of

inadequate educational facilities and lower educational status for Negroes. Again the data uphold the expectations.

An interesting feature of this complex of relationships is the relative dearth of any dysfunctional elements. Thus, most of the consequences of the definition of the Negro's situation tend to sustain that definition, i.e., they are functional for the definition. The few dysfunctional elements arising from the definition, i.e., elements that tend to destroy it, are either unimportant or are accompanied by functional elements. For example, a functional consequence of the definition of Negro inferiority has been segregation—functional because it emphasized that there were Negro-white differentials distasteful to the whites, or, practically speaking, represented inferior qualities. This consequence of segregation, however, has favored the creation of a Negro professional and business class (especially doctors, teachers, and undertakers), which has the consequence of standing as disproof of the definition and is thus dysfunctional for it. However, it must be remembered that this situation is accompanied by segregation, which itself has the functional consequence of isolating this upper stratum of Negroes from the whites, a condition which serves as a cushioning effect for any dysfunctional consequences arising from that condition.

The ultimate effect of this relative lack of dysfunctional consequences is that the entire system has a high degree of functional autonomy. There is little that tends to destroy the system. We can then expect it to exhibit a high degree of resistance to change. This point, of course, does not have to be labored. The lineage of the sys-

---

15 More specifically, discrimination and low economic levels would be expected to raise out-migration rates and lower those for in-migration, *provided* that the migrating population believed migration would alleviate their situation. Otherwise, the only remaining effect would be to lower the general incidence of migration. The writer had data only for in-migration and net migration. Both sets of data showed lower rates for Negroes than whites.

tem extends over several centuries, and the tenacity with which white New Orleanians are presently resisting the effects of the Supreme Court's 1954 public school desegregation decision are only too well known.

CONCLUSION

The analysis is obviously incomplete. It has been handicapped by a lack of data on values and attitudes. These have not as yet become the proper—or perhaps even the available—tools of demographic investigation, but, as the discussion has possibly indicated, they are nevertheless fundamental in interpreting demographic phenomena.

It would be a truism to add that the situation as depicted greatly simplifies, perhaps oversimplifies, a complex matter. Numerous specific questions remain unanswered: What purely biological processes (if any) accentuate (or lessen) the fertility and mortality differentials? What has been the influence of historical factors, such as the formation of the self-fulfilling prophecy, the source of varying types of migrants, etc.? Urbanism has probably had an influence in modifying the self-fulfilling prophecy—how much of an influence? The reader can easily complicate the situation further.

The fundamental goal of this paper is more modest: to delineate empirically and theoretically at least one aspect of the relation between two areas of investigation. One type of demographic phenomenon, racial differentials, was related to one sociological theory, and the evidence has been consistent with that theory. Briefly, the members of the dominant group have defined the Negro as inferior. This definition, or prophecy, has set in motion forces that tended to fulfill it, and the forces have served to create differences in the manner in which the two groups have changed their numbers. In other words, the self-fulfilling prophecy has helped to bring about differences in the population processes of these two races, and these differences have created further differences in their population characteristics, the characteristics in turn influence the processes and are influenced by the self-fulfilling prophecy. Finally, these influences of the prophecy stand as evidence, regardless of how circular, of the fulfillment of the prophecy and accordingly tend to perpetuate it.

A universal characteristic of societies is the differentiation of their members into various groupings on the basis of selected distinguishing traits. Usually such groupings are social aggregates made up of persons who possess certain traits in common, such as sex, age, occupation, or wealth either singly or in combination. Less often they may be true social groups exhibiting an organized pattern of interaction, such as the members of a religious sect in a community.

10

SOCIAL DIFFERENTIATION, STRATIFICATION, AND MOBILITY

The categorization of individuals into differentiated groupings is generally accompanied by a ranking of the groupings on the basis of power or prestige into a hierarchy of social strata. The prestige strata of a society or community are often referred to as social classes, although some sociologists would reserve this designation for those strata that possess shared perceptions and interests, or "class consciousness."[1]

Social mobility refers to the movement from one differentiated grouping or stratum to another. When the movement entails a change in social rank, it is termed *vertical mobility*. Not only

[1] Leonard Broom, "Social Differentiation and Stratification," in *Sociology Today*, eds. Robert K. Merton, Leonard Broom, and Leonard S. Cottrell, Jr. (New York: Basic Books, Inc., 1959), p. 434.

individuals but entire groupings (such as an occupation or religious denomination) may engage in vertical mobility either upward or downward.

Unlike many areas of sociology, the study of social differentiation and mobility has long been marked by an explicit consideration of the influence of demographic variables. Indeed, such influence was a specific concern of Durkheim in his classic study *The Division of Labor in Society* in which he posed the proposition that "the division of labor varies in direct ratio with the volume and density of societies, and, if it progresses in a continuous manner in the course of social development, it is because societies become regularly denser and generally more voluminous."[2]

Various students of social differentiation and stratification since Durkheim have stated propositions relating population size and growth to organizational complexity and the existence of social ranks. It has also been widely recognized that the generally lower fertility of upper strata is conducive to upward social mobility.[3] The observed inverse relationship between social status and fertility in industrial societies has led to a significant body of research testing the proposition that fertility control is an aid to social mobility, if not a requirement for it.[4] The results of these studies, however, have been inconclusive.

The pattern of lowering mortality rates with rising social status has been even more consistent than the lowering of fertility rates, although recent evidence suggests that the differentials are lessening. It might be noted that the influence of differential mortality on mobility is contrary to the influence of differential fertility. The hypothesis that social mobility is accompanied by physical and emotional stresses that increase mortality has not been consistently supported. However, a number of studies have reported higher frequencies of cardiovascular disease among persons who are upwardly mobile.[5]

Studies of migration have conclusively established that different social groups have different rates of migration, but the rates for the different groups vary according to whether the migration is internal or international as well as according to the circumstances under which the migration takes place. As Bogue has summed up, "migrants must be expected to reflect, in their characteristics, the social and economic changes

[2] Emile Durkheim, *The Division of Labor in Society*, trans. George Simpson (New York: The Macmillan Company, 1933), p. 262.

[3] Seymour Martin Lipset and Reinhard Bendix, *Social Mobility in Industrial Society* (Berkeley and Los Angeles: University of California Press, 1959), p. 86.

[4] For a bibliography of studies relating fertility to stratification and mobility, see Ronald Freedman, "The Sociology of Human Fertility, A Trend Report and Bibliography," *Current Sociology*, Vol. X/XI, No. 2 (1961–62), pp. 95–98.

[5] S. Leonard Syme and Leo G. Reeder, eds., "Social Stress and Cardiovascular Disease," *The Milbank Memorial Fund Quarterly*, XLV, No. 2, Part II (April 1967).

that are taking place. Because these changes vary from place to place and from time to time it is to be expected that the characteristics of migrants cannot remain fixed."[6] Even so, it may be possible to associate regularities in characteristics of migrants with specific circumstances under which migration occurs. Everett S. Lee has hypothesized, for example, that migrants who are motivated by perceived opportunities tend to be drawn from the higher educational and occupational ranks, while those who are forced to migrate by conditions at the place of origin tend to be negatively selected.[7]

Considering that social mobility aspirations are believed to be one of the major causes of migration, surprisingly few studies have investigated the direct relationship between social mobility and migration. Such studies as have been made suggest that the intergenerational effects of migration are greater than the intragenerational effects. A difficult methodological problem presented by intragenerational mobility is the comparison of status in the areas of origin and destination. Lower-class migrants from rural areas to cities typically move into lower-status positions whereas native urbanites of similar social class backgrounds move upward,[8] but whether the migrants have advanced relative to those of similar class who remained in their rural communities is difficult to ascertain. One of the most comprehensive studies of social mobility, carried out in Denmark by Kaare Svalastoga, revealed that rural males who migrated to the city had a better chance of social ascent than those who remained at home, but also a higher percentage moved downward in social status.[9] It was also found that interurban migrants were more upwardly mobile than nonmigrant urban residents.

In the first reading of this section, Bertram Hutchinson reports on the relationships between fertility, social mobility, and urban migration in Brazil. His findings support the existence of an inverse relationship between social status, as indicated by occupation, and also a slight lowering of fertility with upward mobility. Contrary to the hypothesis advanced by David Goldberg based on fertility studies in Indianapolis and Detroit, Hutchinson found that the differentials by socioeconomic status were not accounted for by the presence of large rural-born elements in the lower status categories.

The second reading presents the results of correlations between occupational status and standardized mortality rates for men 20–64 years of age in the United States in 1950. An inverse relationship was

---

[6] Donald J. Bogue, "Internal Migration," in *The Study of Population*, eds. Philip M. Hauser and Otis Dudley Duncan (Chicago: The University of Chicago Press, 1959), p. 505.

[7] Everett S. Lee, "A Theory of Migration," *Demography* 3, No. 1 (1966), p. 56.

[8] Lipset and Bendix, *Social Mobility in Industrial Society*, p. 216.

[9] Kaare Svalastoga, *Prestige, Class and Mobility* (Copenhagen: Glydendal, 1959), p. 395.

found for fifteen of eighteen specific causes of death, thus supporting a number of earlier studies.

The third reading compares the intergenerational occupational mobility of migrant and nonmigrant sons from families in a small urban community in Kentucky. Sons of manual workers were found to migrate in greater proportions than sons of white-collar workers, and chances of upward mobility were appreciably greater for the migrants.

The fourth study deals with immigrants to Canada and examines both intergenerational and intragenerational mobility. Immigrants from the United Kingdom in general experienced upward mobility, but this was not found to be the case for those from non-English-speaking nations.

Fertility, Social Mobility and Urban Migration in Brazil*

Bertram Hutchinson

The publication in 1952 of Berent's study of fertility and social mobility in England and Wales[1] seemed to offer a satisfactory basis for future and more detailed studies of the relationship between these two variables. It will be remembered that Berent's data showed not only the theoretically expected inverse association between family size, social class and social mobility, but also that the socially promoted, while less fertile than their class of origin, were more fertile than the class into which they moved. Some years later, however, the results of two other studies, although both less broadly based than that of Berent, provided evidence of populations in which Berent's conclusions did not appear to hold good. The first of these, a study by W. Scott, of fertility and social mobility among teachers in England and Wales, found none of the expected tendencies for fertility to vary with degree and direction of social mobility.[2] The second, a study

* Bertram Hutchinson, "Fertility, Social Mobility, and Urban Migration in Brazil," *Population Studies*, 14 (March, 1961), 182–89.

[1] J. Berent, "Fertility and Social Mobility," *Population Studies*, V, No. 3, 1952.

[2] W. Scott, "Fertility and Social

of an urban sample of the population of Detroit[3] by D. Goldberg, examined separately data from urban dwellers of two generations' standing, and from rural migrants. Among the established urban population Goldberg found socioeconomic differences in fertility to be small and generally insignificant statistically, and he attributed the inverse fertility pattern found in the total Detroit population to the effect of migration to the city of the rural-born. Berent's useful and apparently reasonable conclusions, insofar as they might be thought of general application to the problem of class differences in fertility, have therefore been called in question; and the moment seems opportune to offer new evidence relevant to the social mobility hypothesis obtained in a social and economic milieu differing radically from that of England and the United States.

I

For the purposes of a general study of the process and social consequences of urban growth in southern Brazil,[4] interviews were taken during 1959 and early 1960 from a sample of 5,250 men and women selected from the population of eight cities in this region. The cities were Rio de Janeiro, São Paulo, Belo Horizonte, Curitiba, Londrina, Americana, Volta Redonda, and Juiz de Fora. Information was obtained from the sample respecting

marital status,[5] number of marriages, year of marriage, age of both spouses at marriage, number of liveborn children and the year (but not the month) of their birth and decease, occupations of father and father-in-law at the time of the informant's marriage, and (for the male sample) the informant's, and his father's, current or last main occupation. The occupational data were later marshalled in six categories of social status, an adaptation of the Hall-Jones scale,[6] although for certain purposes and where the numbers involved were too small, to allow the more elaborate analysis in six groups (as in the problem discussed in the present paper) occupations were divided into two categories only; manual and nonmanual. All informants who at the time of interview had been married for ten years or more (that is, marriages of 1949 or earlier) were separated from the main sample, giving a total of 2,224 men and women for whom there was complete information as to fertility in relation to social class of origin, and 1,347 men for whom there was information as to fertility related to intergenerational mobility.

A preliminary assessment of the larger group's mean family size after ten or more years of marriage was related to the status at the time of

---

Mobility among Teachers," *Population Studies*, XI, No. 3, 1958.

[3] D. Goldberg, "The Fertility of Two-Generation Urbanites," *Population Studies*, XII, No. 3, 1959.

[4] The study referred to forms part of the current work of the Brazilian Centre of Educational Research, Rio de Janeiro, to which the author is attached under the auspices of the UNESCO Technical Assistance Programme.

[5] "Marriage" was so defined as to include not only registered civil and religious marriages, but also couples who were *amasiados*, or common-law consensual unions. These were not recorded separately.

[6] The six status categories were: (1) professional and high administrative; (2) managerial and executive; (3) higher grade inspectional, supervisory and other nonmanual; (4) lower grades of inspectional, supervisory and routine grades of nonmanual; (5) skilled manual; (6) semiskilled and unskilled manual.

TABLE 1. Mean Family Size after Ten or More Years of Marriage, Related to the Status of the Husband's Father and Father-In-Law

Status	Father	Father-in-law
Nonmanual	3.33	3.43
	(753)	(719)
Manual	4.67	4.59
	(1471)	(1505)
Total	4.21	4.21
	(2224)	(2224)

the husband's marriage of his father and father-in-law. The results (Table 1) followed the expected inverse relationship. That is, in our sample, a man marrying at a time when his father or his father-in-law, or both, were of nonmanual status subsequently had a significantly lower fertility than would have been the case had either or both of these relatives been of manual status. The small horizontal differences visible in Table 1 are not statistically significant, from which we may conclude that the choice of father's or of father-in-law's status is immaterial to an examination of differences in fertility.

The question is taken a stage further when we consider mean family size in its relation to the four possible combinations of parental origin. Thus we find (Table 2) that a man marrying a woman of social origin higher than his own had a smaller average family than he would have had from an endogamous marriage; while a man marrying "beneath" him had an average family slightly larger than he could have expected from marriage with a woman of his own origin.[7] The same pattern prevails when the matter is viewed conversely, wives marrying upwards having a smaller, and those marrying downwards a larger average family than their class of origin. Moreover, it is noteworthy that the mean family size of exogamous marriages lies between the means of unmixed marriages (the differences are statistically significant

---

[7] This difference, while consistent with the general pattern observed here, is not statistically significant.

TABLE 2. Mean Family Size after Ten or More Years of Marriage Related to Husband's and Wife's Class of Origin

	Status of wife's father		
Status of husband's father	Nonmanual	Manual	Total
Nonmanual	3.24	3.44	3.33
	(501)	(252)	(753)
Manual	3.82	4.82	4.67
	(218)	(1253)	(1471)
Total	3.43	4.59	4.21
	(719)	(1505)	(2224)

TABLE 3. Mean Family Size after Ten or More Years of Marriage: Husband's Status Related to That of His Father

| | Husband's status | | |
Father's status	Nonmanual	Manual	Total
Nonmanual	3.09[a]	4.08	3.33
	(387)	(126)	(513)
Manual	3.57	5.02	4.64
	(217)	(617)	(834)
Total	3.26	4.86	4.14
	(604)	(743)	(1347)

[a] All differences between pairs of means, both horizontal and vertical, are statistically significant.

with the exception already noted). A party to a mixed marriage, that is to say, failed to adopt completely the fertility of the spouse's class—a conclusion similar to that reached by Berent for intergenerational mobility in England and Wales. In other words, the ultimate fertility of a class-exogamous marriage appears to be the result of a compromise between the respective family-building traditions of the spouses.

Our data for intergenerational mobility offer evidence of a similar compromise. In our male sample, the average family of a husband who was born and had remained in the manual category was approximately 60 per cent greater than that of a man born and remaining in the nonmanual class (Table 3). Class differences in fertility, visible throughout our material, are at their greatest between the groups retaining their father's social status. Social mobility modified the position in certain respects. A husband who had lapsed from the non-manual status of his father had an average family significantly greater than his fellows who had retained their status of origin. Yet the increase in mean size was of the order of only

TABLE 4. Mean Family Size after Ten or More Years of Marriage: Rural-Born Husband's Status Related to That of His Father

| | Husband's status | | |
Father's status	Nonmanual	Manual	Total
Nonmanual	3.77[a]	4.97	4.11
	(170)	(67)	(237)
Manual	4.07	5.71	5.34
	(103)	(349)	(452)
Total	3.88	5.59	4.91
	(273)	(416)	(689)

[a] Differences between horizontal pairs of means are statistically significant. Vertical differences, with the exception of the totals in column 3, are not significant.

TABLE 5. Mean Family Size after Ten or More Years of Marrige: Urban-Born Husband's Status Related to That of His Father

	Husband's status		
Father's status	Nonmanual	Manual	Total
Nonmanual	2.76[a]	3.63	2.96
	(177)	(51)	(228)
Manual	2.81	4.05	3.65
	(77)	(166)	(243)
Total	2.78	3.95	3.32
	(254)	(217)	(471)

[a] Differences between horizontal pairs of means are statistically significant. Vertical differences, with the exception of the totals in column 3, are not significant.

30 per cent, so that loss of status, while encouraging fertility, failed to promote it sufficiently to produce an average family as large as that of the adoptive class. Similarly, men moving upwards into the nonmanual category had a mean family only 29 per cent smaller than their class of origin, although that of their adopted class was 38 per cent smaller. In short, the data from our sample show an inverse relationship between fertility and social class of origin and of adoption; and that for a given established class the lower the class of origin the higher the fertility. These conclusions corroborate those of Berent for England and Wales.

We now turn to Goldberg's finding that among two-generation urbanites in Detroit "mobility has little effect on completed family size." We divided our sample of married men into two groups: those born in the city in which they were interviewed or in one similar in size, and those born in rural areas and small rural townships. Our urban group was therefore composed of men who had a record of one or more generations of urban

TABLE 6. Mean Family Size after Ten or More Years of Marriage: Foreign-Born Husband's Status Related to That of His Father

	Husband's status		
Father's status	Nonmanual	Manual	Total
Nonmanual	2.54[a]	2.28	2.45
	(35)	(18)	(53)
Manual	3.68	4.49	4.28
	(34)	(95)	(129)
Total	3.10	4.14	3.75
	(69)	(130)	(182)

[a] Differences between vertical pairs of means are statistically significant. Horizontal differences with the exception of the totals in row 3, are not significant.

TABLE 7. Mean Family Size after Ten or More Years of Marriage: Two-Generation Urban Husband's Status Related to That of His Father

	Husband's status		
Father's status	Nonmanual	Manual	Total
Nonmanual	2.41[a]	3.11	2.55
	(69)	(18)	(87)
Manual	2.96	3.91	3.60
	(26)	(53)	(79)
Total	2.56	3.70	3.05
	(95)	(71)	(166)

[a] Differences between vertical and horizontal pairs of means are not statistically significant, with the exception of the totals, where the differences are significant.

life, so that the effect Goldberg observed, although it would presumably be visible, would be likely to be less pronounced in our analysis.

The data for rural-born males are presented in Table 4. It will be seen that, comparing rural migrants with the sample as a whole, mean family size is considerably greater in every status category among the migrants, the over-all mean being 4.91 compared with 4.14 in the entire sample. The inverse relationship between status and fertility is evident; and, as in the sample as a whole, men falling to manual status had a mean family approximately 30 per cent greater than their class of origin, while men rising to nonmanual status had an average family some 30 per cent smaller. There is some indication of a failure to assume fully the fertility of the adopted class, but here the differences between means are not statistically significant. These were the results expected on Goldberg's view that the apparent inverse relationship between social class and fertility is brought about by the presence in urban populations of the rural-born.

But on the same view we would also expect no, or at any rate less, evidence (since our sample was of less-established urban dwellers than that of Detroit) of such a relationship between social mobility and fertility among the urban-born. This is manifestly not the case (Table 5). It is true that this group in every category has a smaller average family than the rural-born (the over-all mean is 3.32, compared with 4.91), but fertility as before remains inversely related to class status. Men falling in status show a tendency to increase the size of their family, and those rising to increase it, by approximately 30 per cent. Hence we find that the same relationships persist, and persist to the same degree, among the urban-born as among the rural migrants.

There were also in our sample 182 men whose birthplace was outside Brazil. Of these roughly 60 per cent were Portuguese, Spanish, and Italian. The remainder included Poles, Lithuanians, Germans, Austrians, Rumanians, Russians, Yugoslavs, Levantines, Japanese, and a small number of west Europeans. While the numbers involved were small, the heterogeneous national origin of this group made a closer examination of it seem of possible interest, and we therefore calculated mean family size in the same manner as before (Table 6). The inverse relationship between fertility and social status was again evident, and there was an indication that for a given established status the lower the class of origin the higher the fertility.

Finally, we separated from the main sample those men who, urban-born themselves, were the sons of urban-born parents—that is, whose father and mother were both born in the city in which the interview took place or in another of similar size. There were only 166 of these in the sample, and the wisdom of a separate analysis would have been doubtful had these individuals not been the equivalent of Goldberg's two-generation urbanites, and hence capable of showing a pattern of fertility different from any of our other categories. While differences in mean family size were, of course, not always significant statistically, the relationships emerging from our analysis (Table 7) were those familiar to us from preceding analyses. The lack of statistical significance in the central cells of Table 7 may probably be more justly attributed to the small numbers involved than to any real divergence of our two-generation urbanites from the general pattern.

II

Our data therefore seem to confirm Berent's general findings, and to this extent we may be nearer the establishment of the inverse relationship between fertility, social class and social mobility as a fairly widespread feature of western populations. On the other hand, we found nothing to support Goldberg's suggestion that this relationship may be merely a reflection of rural-urban migration. But the explanation of this negative result has already been implicitly offered by Goldberg himself when he writes, "where the family size decision is shared equally by husband and wife, socioeconomic differences are not likely to produce different levels of fertility."[8] He then describes the decay of the traditional family in the American urban community, the transformation of the male into "the servant-class husband," and the emergence of the "egalitarian" family.

While this may be happening in urban America (with its possible consequences for chosen family size), in urban Brazil the process is, at most, incipient. The "traditional" roles of the sexes have been as yet little affected by social and economic change, and even in the largest cities and at the highest social levels the wife remains responsible for domestic matters and for child-rearing. Yet, though the revolution in woman's status which has occurred elsewhere has barely begun in Brazil, she is by and large the arbiter of family size. As such she is the object of a number of forces tending to high fertility. The Brazilian male may perhaps welcome numerous children as (among other reasons) outward evidence of a virility which, particularly among the poorer classes, he is under considerable social pressure to establish by continual sexual activity. Religious teaching (more than 90 per cent of the Brazilian population is Roman Catholic) encourages high fertility, and the Church's influence, while less dominating than elsewhere in Latin America, is considerable, especially

---

[8] D. Goldberg, *op. cit.*, p. 221.

among women. Large families, often welcome in a rural subsistence economy, may remain of material assistance to domestic income even in the larger cities, where legal restrictions on juvenile employment are easily evaded. Underlying these and similar encouragements to fertility is the central importance of the family as a unit of social structure and social relations, with its concomitant emphasis upon family loyalty, the ramification of family connections and influence, and the special provision for the continuance of a family connection for the orphan through the institution of *compadresco.* If to these we add other circumstances compatible with high fertility such as widespread poverty, a high rate of illiteracy, limited knowledge of contraceptive measures, the difficulty and expense of obtaining appliances and the preference for the control of conception by the safe period method (appropriate only for the literate), we find the Brazilian women enmeshed in a complex of pressures which tend toward a large average family.

But, at least in the urban communities, the higher the class status the less powerfully do these pressures impinge upon her, and the less willingly does she subordinate her outside interests to repeated childbearing. Among the comfortably-off the phrase "a good Catholic" is used ironically and disparagingly to describe a woman whose family is thought excessively large (it is significant that the husband is rarely mentioned). Women's personal freedom has been somewhat extended in recent decades as urban and cultural interests in Brazil have multiplied, and the proportion of women in employment has increased. At the same time, decisions respecting family size remain largely

hers; and only among the small intellectual middle class do we find any tendency toward a greater participation of the husband in domestic matters. It follows that social class and social mobility are inversely related to fertility in Brazil because women are still comparatively free to modify the number of children they have in accordance with the claims that their other interests make upon them; and this is still true of the urban as of the rural born. In Detroit, as Goldberg indicated, this freedom is opposed by the countervailing wishes of the husband respecting the size of his family. In short, we did not confirm Goldberg's findings because the conditions he stipulates are not yet present to a significant degree among either the rural or the urban population of Brazil.

It is difficult to estimate the ultimate effect of social mobility on population growth, for clearly this will depend not only upon the amount of social mobility taking place, but also upon its net direction and the differences in fertility of the upward and the downward mobile. In Brazil, where there appears to be considerably more upward than downward mobility, the problem is made more complex by the effect on fertility of rapid urbanization accompanying economic growth. Between 1940 and 1950 while the annual rate of population increase was 1.9 per cent, in cities of 20,000 or more inhabitants the rate was slightly over 4 per cent. The urbanization of the population which these figures indicate seems likely to continue (Brazil, with equal or greater economic resources, is less urbanized than some other Latin American countries such as Argentina, Chile and Venezuela) and to bring with it a decreasing fertility rate. The fertility of urban married women in 1950 was only 67 per cent of the fertility of the Brazilian population as a whole.[9] But we have at present no means of isolating the effect of urban migration itself upon the fertility of the rural-born migrant, and we do not know how far his fertility differs from others who have remained in the country. On the other hand, we have seen that if urban migration is followed or accompanied by a rise in socioeconomic status, fertility tends to fall. We can therefore reach a tentative estimate of the net consequence to the fertility of our sample which social mobility, considered apart from migration, has had.

It will be seen (Table 3) that, owing to the movement of nearly a quarter of the nonmanual-born section of the sample to positions of lower status, mean family size among men of this origin was raised from 3.09 to 3.33—an increase of about 8 per cent. There was also a reduction in average family size of about the same magnitude due to the upward mobility of men of manual origin. Considering the current status of the sample, we find that mean family size

_____

9 United Nations Social and Economic Council, *Demographic Aspects of Urbanisation in Latin America*, E/CN. 12/URB/18, New York, 1958, Table 9, p. 21.

among nonmanuals is about 5 per cent greater and that of manuals about three per cent smaller, owing to the movement into these classes of persons of different origin. Social mobility thus brought about an increase in the fertility of the upper status group and did not, contrary to earlier theoretical speculation, reduce it. But the effect on average family size in the sample as a whole is smaller. The total number of children reported by the sample after ten or more years of marriage was 5,582. Had none moved from the social status of his father, and assuming the mean family sizes indicated by the two nonmobile groups, they would have had 5,772 children, or 3.3 per cent more. It seems, therefore, that the net consequence to the sample of social mobility was to reduce total births by about 3 per cent. Of this apparent loss, two-thirds was caused by the upward mobility of men of manual origin for whom there was no compensating downward mobility from the nonmanual class—that is, social mobility brought about by changes in the economic structure, and not by the lowering of class barriers in a static society. Hence, had the economy been in equilibrium, thus permitting only the exchange of status positions, the loss in total births caused by social mobility would have been of the order of 1 per cent.

Occupational Level and Mortality*

Jacob Tuckman, William F. Youngman, and Garry B. Kreizman

Spiegelman,[1] using data prepared by Whitney[2] on age-specific rates for gainfully occupied males in ten selected states, based on the 1930 Census of Population, demonstrated an inverse relationship between social-economic status and mortality. In general, age-specific rates tended to rise as social-economic status decreased from professional workers to unskilled laborers. In a recent, more comprehensive study based on deaths for all males in the United States in 1950, Moriyama and Guralnick indicated a similar relationship.[3]

The findings of these two studies referred to mortality from all causes. One question raised by Moriyama and Guralnick was whether there are particular causes of death which account for the relationship. For example, it would be expected that deaths from cardiovascular disorders, constituting almost 50 per cent of all deaths, would contribute more to the relationship than suicide, constituting approximately three percent of all deaths. The purpose of the present study is to estimate the relationship between occupational level and various specific causes of death.

PROCEDURE

Data for this study were obtained from a national report of mortality by occupation and cause of death among men 20–64 years of age in the United States in 1950.[4]

The report presents standardized mortality ratios (S.M.R.'s) for seventy-two causes of death, some highly specific and others broadly classified, for twenty-six occupational groups. The S.M.R. compares the tabulated number of deaths in an occupational group with the number to be expected if the death rate for the total male population with work experience had prevailed in that occupational class. Since there are race differences with respect to mortality[5] and occupational distribution,[6] and the data were fragmentary for nonwhites, the study was limited to white males. In seven occupational cate-

* Jacob Tuckman, William F. Youngman, and Garry B. Kreizman, "Occupational Level and Mortality," *Social Forces*, 43 (May, 1965), 575–77.

[1] Mortimer Spiegelman, *Introduction to Demography* (Chicago: The Society of Actuaries, 1955).

[2] J. S. Whitney, *Death Rates by Occupation Based on Data of the United States Census Bureau, 1930* (National Tuberculosis Association, New York, 1934).

[3] I. M. Moriyama and L. Guralnick, "Occupational and Social Class Differences in Mortality," in *Trends and Differentials in Mortality* (New York: Milbank Memorial Fund, 1956).

[4] U.S. Public Health Service, *Mortality by Occupation Level and Cause of Death among Men 20 to 64 Years of Age. United States, 1950*, Vital Statistics—Special Reports, Vol. LIII, No. 5 (Washington, D.C.: U.S. Government Printing Office, 1963).

[5] U.S. Public Health Service, *Vital Statistics of the United States, 1960: Life Tables*, Vol. II, Sec. II (Washington, D.C.: U.S. Government Printing Office, 1960).

[6] U.S. Department of Commerce, *Statistical Abstract of the United States, 1962* (Washington, D.C.: U.S. Government Printing Office, 1962).

gories, data were not shown separately for whites and nonwhites because the number of nonwhites was very small; therefore it was necessary to use data for all males. For practical purposes the data in the seven categories can be considered to represent the S.M.R.'s for whites since the effect of race was negligible.[7]

Although there were seventy-two causes of death, gaps in the data made it necessary to use broad classifications whenever possible. Only one, major cardiovascular-renal disease, accounting for almost one-half of all deaths, was divided into two categories. Even using broad classifications, six causes of death were excluded from computation but examined graphically to determine trends because S.M.R.'s were missing for more than two occupational groups. These were: benign neoplasms and neoplasms of unspecified nature, diseases of blood and blood-forming organs, appendicitis, cholelithiasis and cholecystitis, hyperplasia of prostate, and congenital malformation. After selecting broad classifications and eliminating those from computation for the reason given above, there were eighteen causes of death, including all causes. The S.M.R.'s for the eighteen causes of death were correlated with occupational level in the following manner. The twenty-six occupational categories were ordered into a hierarchy of eight from professional workers to laborers, based on social status or social class: professional, semiprofessional and technical; managerial and proprietary; clerical; sales; craftsmen; operatives;

service workers; and laborers. Professional, semiprofessional, and technical occupations were given a weight of eight, managerial and proprietory occupations a weight of seven, and so on until laborers were given a weight of one. Then, these weights were assigned to the twenty-six occupational groups and the correlations between causes of death and occupation were computed.

RESULTS AND DISCUSSION

The correlations between occupational level and S.M.R.'s for the eighteen selected causes of death shown in Table 1, ranged from −0.20 for diabetes mellitus to 0.69 for alcoholism. Fifteen of the eighteen correlations were significantly different from zero. The three exceptions were diabetes mellitus, diseases of cardiovascular system, and chronic and unspecified nephritis and other renal sclerosis. For the six causes of death excluded from computation, the graphic representation showed the same trend as that evident in the correlational data.

It is clear that the inverse relationship between occupational level and mortality, reported by Moriyama and Guralnick for death from all causes, also applies to specific causes. Obviously, job hazards have a bearing on mortality but their contribution will vary with the particular cause of death. For example, it would be expected that deaths from respiratory diseases or from accidents would have greater relevance to job hazards than deaths from syphilis or from homicide. Undoubtedly, both hazards on the job and those related to lower social class membership contribute to mortality rates. However, the consist-

---

[7] Personal communication with Lillian Guralnick, Chief, Mortality Statistics Branch, U.S. Department of Health, Education, and Welfare, Public Health Service, National Vital Statistics Division.

TABLE 1. Standard Mortality Ratios for Selected Causes of Death, by Twenty-Six Occupational Categories, for White Males, 20–64 Years of Age, in the United States, 1950; and Correlation Coefficients Between Occupational Level and Standard Mortality Ratios

Cause of death and international classification code

Occupational category	All causes	Tuberculosis, all forms 001-019	Syphilis & its sequelae 020-029	Malignant neoplasms 140-205	Asthma 241	Diabetes mellitus 260	Alcoholism 322	Diseases of cardiovascular system 330-334, 400-468	Chronic & unspecified nephritis & other renal sclerosis 592-594	Diseases of the respiratory system 470-527	Ulcer of stomach 540	Ulcer of duodenum 541	Hernia & intestinal obstruction 560, 561, 570	Cirrhosis of liver 581	Symptoms, ill-defined & unknown causes 780-793, 795	Accidents E800-E962	Suicide E963, E970-E979	Homicide E964, E980-E985
Professional workers	83	36	41	89	71	98	68	98	73	62	54	70	68	90	49	50	90	18
All other professional, technical and kindred workers	89	60	60	94	89	122	57	100	92	59	86	96	81	91	72	69	89	23
Officials & inspectors and specified managers	82	32	49	90	73	91	50	93	64	48	66	80	66	87	44	68	85	33
Managers, officials, and proprietors (n.e.c.), wholesale and retail trade	98	40	55	101	92	166	69	112	92	58	81	107	86	146	50	66	111	54
Clerical and kindred workers	85	76	59	93	95	112	49	97	88	81	95	120	84	102	54	45	73	19
Salesmen & sales clerks (n.e.c.), retail trade	102	74	92	109	100	139	118	115	105	83	102	140	86	127	70	70	106	24
All other sales workers	92	53	69	97	70	111	63	107	83	66	92	124	54	93	52	64	100	19
Mechanics & repairmen, except radio	83	65	63	94	120	74	a	83	69	70	99	81	69	85	60	93	97	39
Foremen (n.e.c.)	73	34	35	88	a	77	77	80	68	50	48	84	71	52	36	71	54	35
Metal craftsmen	116	91	88	132	124	105	107	121	102	112	135	133	93	118	65	106	118	35
Cabinetmakers & carpenters	84	75	74	97	124	57	98	81	76	68	63	100	81	50	78	102	50	52
Painters & plasterers	114	141	109	126	123	90	204	107	83	121	165	130	96	122	98	123	115	71
All other craftsmen	108	101	89	126	119	107	108	110	96	94	109	135	97	131	65	94	148	36
Engine & construction machinery operators	104	67	79	110	105	122	87	109	78	79	103	96	96	88	55	129	106	38
Transportation & public utility workers	114	97	116	122	147	104	95	112	122	98	100	96	120	120	104	153	93	53
Metal operatives	72	56	50	85	71	61	61	74	59	78	64	90	54	76	40	69	91	24
Drivers & deliverymen	99	91	87	98	91	97	76	95	88	89	131	106	84	108	55	135	84	54
Operatives in selected manufacturing industries	82	70	54	96	76	84	80	85	82	76	74	105	87	79	64	73	83	29

TABLE 1. Standard Mortality Ratios for Selected Causes of Death, by Twenty-Six Occupational Categories, for White Males, 20-64 Years of Age, in the United States, 1950; and Correlation Coefficients Between Occupational Level and Standard Mortality Ratios (Cont.)

Occupational category	Cause of death and international classification code																	
	All causes	Tuberculosis, all forms 001-019	Syphilis & its sequelae 020-029	Malignant neoplasms 140-205	Asthma 241	Diabetes mellitus 260	Alcoholism 322	Diseases of cardiovascular system 330-334, 400-468	Chronic & unspecified nephritis & other renal sclerosis 592-594	Diseases of the respiratory system 470-527	Ulcer of stomach 540	Ulcer of duodenum 541	Hernia & intestinal obstruction 560, 561, 570	Cirrhosis of liver 581	Symptoms, ill-defined & unknown causes 780-793, 795	Accidents E800-E962	Suicide E963, E970-E979	Homicide E963, E980-E985
Mine operatives & laborers (n.e.c.)	185	263	120	169	275	88	155	149	137	438	232	123	144	120	200	301	179	149
All other operatives	79	71	71	90	72	64	68	78	71	81	108	84	111	122	66	78	83	21
Guards & protective-service workers	117	82	78	117	138	133	a	129	101	105	94	181	111	134	77	85	128	120
Service workers	117	175	98	115	149	140	229	112	84	138	145	128	135	277	93	93	130	90
Laborers in metal manufacturing (n.e.c.)	145	207	165	160	264	127	191	127	121	208	231	171	167	185	97	151	163	97
Laborers in other manufacturing (n.e.c.)	143	163	161	150	179	111	327	124	129	156	210	156	106	a	129	190	177	97
Construction & outdoor laborers	122	160	84	106	84	78	209	99	96	136	115	126	106	167	124	223	156	93
Laborers in other nonmanufacturing industries	106	144	101	104	127	83	234	94	93	146	117	139	120	148	98	131	127	73
Correlation between occupational level & SMR[b]	.49	.63	.63	.47	.47	-.20 N.S.	.69	.19 N.S.	.37	.43	.53	.53	.61	.45	.49	.58	.53	.58

a No data available

b All correlations significant at <.05 level except where indicated.

Source: U.S. Public Health Service, Mortality by Occupational Level and Cause of Death among Men 20 to 64 Years of Age: United States, 1950, Vital Statistics—Special Reports, Vol. 53, No. 5 (Washington, D. C.: U.S. Government Printing Office, 1963).

ency of the findings of the inverse relationship between the S.M.R.'s for specific causes and occupational level, as well as the fact that a similar relationship was found for causes of death which appeared to have little relevance to job hazards, suggests the relatively greater contribution of social class to mortality than job hazards. This suggestion is supported by data from a British population study which showed that married women, when classified according to the occupation of their husbands, had the same pattern in mortality variation as men.[8]

---

[8] The Registrar – General's *Decennial Supplement, England and Wales, 1951,* Part I, "Occupational Mortality" (H. M. Stationery Office, London, 1954).

Social Mobility of Immigrants in Canada[*]

Anthony H. Richmond

The object of this paper is to examine some of the operational problems that arose in studying the social mobility of postwar immigrants in Canada and to present the findings of a survey concerning the pattern and degree of mobility exhibited by the immigrants. The research was part of an extensive survey of the economic and social absorption of postwar immigrants carried out in association with the Dominion Bureau of Statistics and the Research Division of the Canadian Department of Citizenship and Immigration.[1]

The sample was based upon a monthly labor force survey carried out by the Dominion Bureau of Statistics. The latter is a 1 per cent sample of the total Canadian population, but the immigrant households studied were drawn from a subsample

---

[*] Anthony H. Richmond, "Social Mobility of Immigrants in Canada," *Population Studies,* 18 (July, 1964), 53–69.

[1] The study was initiated when the author was appointed Canada Council and Koerner Visiting Fellow and Lecturer at the University of British Columbia, 1960–61. I am indebted to the Milbank Memorial Fund of New York and to the Government of Canada for grants towards research expenses. I should like to express my thanks to the Director and staff of the Research Division, Department of Citizenship and Immigration, Ottawa, for their practical assistance at every stage of the research.

of 1 in 6 households in the general sample, giving a sampling ratio of 1 in 600. The initial sample consisted of 692 heads of households or economically independent persons, including eighty-six women, who were postwar immigrants. Information was collected by means of a questionnaire completed by the immigrants themselves and mailed to the Research Division in Ottawa in February, 1961. A response rate of 69 per cent was obtained, after the enumerators who had originally distributed the questionnaire had called a second time upon those who had not responded within one month. This gave a total of 478 completed questionnaires for the national sample.[2] Information about nonrespondents provided by the Dominion Bureau of Statistics showed that the sample of respondents was fully representative with regard to age, sex, and occupation. There was, however, a slight underrepresentation of single people and of immigrants from Mediterranean countries.

Various measures were designed to assess the changes which have taken place between the socioeconomic position of the immigrants in their former countries and that which had been achieved in Canada. An objective measure of standard of living was devised based upon the difference between the number of household amenities possessed in the former country and the number possessed in Canada.[3] On this basis it was found

that 9 per cent of the immigrants had the same or fewer amenities as in the former country; 63 per cent had up to six more amenities and 27 per cent had between seven and ten more amenities. A subjective measure of the change in the immigrants' standard of living was used in which 36 per cent of the respondents said that they were very much better off in Canada, 40 per cent that they were a little better off, 17 per cent that they were the same, 4 per cent that they were a little worse off, and 3 per cent that they were very much worse off. A subjective measure of social status mobility was also used in which the respondent was asked to indicate whether he thought his position in the community had risen, remained the same, or fallen, compared with his former country. Thirty-three per cent of the respondents thought their position had risen, 53 per cent that it was the same, and 14 per cent that it had fallen.

However, the main source of information used in the study of social mobility was the information provided by the informants concerning their own and their fathers' occupations. The immigrants were asked to indicate the father's occupation when he was the same age as the informant; their own occupation in their former country; their first occupation in Canada and the occupation at the time of the survey. This enabled an assessment to be made of intergenerational mobility before migration, and intergenerational mobility achieved since migration, together with the pattern of intragenerational mobility consequent upon the migration itself.

The question immediately arose as to how the occupations were to be classified. The immigrants came from a large number of different countries

---

[2] Information was also obtained from a special sample of immigrants in Vancouver for comparison with the national sample, but the results are not discussed in this paper.

[3] Amenities included central heating; exclusive use of hot and cold running water, inside toilet and bath or shower, refrigerator, washing machine, vacuum cleaner, telephone, television, and automobile.

whose economic structure differed. While the majority of immigrants came from urban backgrounds about 17 per cent had been in agriculture or other primary industries in their former country. It was necessary to adopt a single classification of occupations that could be used for all countries and for all stages in the intergenerational and intragenerational comparisons. This procedure overcame some of the difficulties which have been faced by sociologists attempting international comparisons of rates of social mobility where different occupational scales have been adopted in the various countries.[4] At the same time it did not remove the objection that the occupational structure varied from country to country and that the criteria for evaluating social status were probably also different. However, the comparative studies by Inkeles suggested that the difference in occupational prestige between urban industrial societies is not substantial and that some consensus probably exists between them.[5]

The four occupations reported by the respondent, that of his father, his own occupation in his former country, his first job in Canada, and his job at the time of the survey were, first of all, coded on the classification used by the Dominion Bureau of Statistics in the 1961 census of Canada.[6] This classification was a modified version of the International Standard Classification of Occupations recommended by the I.L.O. but it had certain basic disadvantages as a means of measuring occupational status mobility. Its main categories were descriptive of the type of employment but grouped together people of very different levels of education and income. Thus, for example:

Division 1: Managerial occupations on the Dominion Bureau of Statistics classification include owners of one-man businesses and persons in lower levels of administration.
Division 2: Professional and technical occupations include laboratory technicians as well as the higher professional occupations.
Division 7: Consists of farm owners and farm workers.

In other divisions manual occupations are grouped according to the kind of work without regard to the level of skill required.

In order to overcome this difficulty use was made of the scale of occupational status devised by Professor Bernard Blishen of the University of British Columbia.[7] The Blishen occupational class scale was based upon the 1951 census of Canada. The 343 main occupational groupings in the census classification of occupations were first ranked according to the mean income and mean years of schooling. From these data standard scores were computed for education and income, and each occupation

---

[4] For a discussion of the problems involved in making international comparisons of social mobility see S. M. Lipset and Reinhard Bendix, *Social Mobility in Industrial Society* (Berkeley, 1959), and S. M. Miller, "Comparative Social Mobility," *Current Sociology*, IX, No. 1, 1960.

[5] A. Inkeles and P. Rossi, "National Comparisons of Occupational Prestige," *American Journal of Sociology*, LI, No. 4 (1956), 329–39.

[6] *Occupational Classification Manual*, Census of Canada, 1961, Dominion Bureau of Statistics, Ottawa (April, 1961).

[7] Bernard R. Blishen, "The Construction and Use of an Occupational Class Scale," *Canadian Journal of Economics and Political Science*, XXIV (1958), 519–31.

rated according to this combined score.[8] The scores ranged from 32.0 for hunters and trappers at one end of the scale, to 90.0 for judges at the other end. Bus drivers scored 47.6; compositors 50.4 and university professors 72.0. Blishen assumed that the combination of income and education as criteria would reflect the prestige ranking of occupations in Canada and in other countries. The only other Canadian study with which he was able to make comparisons was that of Tuckman.[9] The latter included only eighteen occupations in its list which were ranked by informants in order of prestige. Blishen showed that the rank correlation between his classification and Tuckman's was 0.91. He found, also, that his scale correlated closely with the one devised by the National Opinion Research Center in the United States (with a correlation of 0.94) and with prestige scales used in Germany, Great Britain, New Zealand, and Japan.

In addition to scoring occupations on the basis of average income and education at the time of the 1951 census Blishen divided his occupations into seven classes, though the

boundaries between classes were somewhat arbitrary. They were based upon his own awareness of the relative prestige ranking of occupations. In view of the close correlation of Blishen scores and other classifications of occupational status used in studies of social mobility in various countries, it was felt that Blishen scores would be a useful means of measuring the occupational status mobility of immigrants in Canada. However, the Blishen scale of classes had the disadvantage of cutting across the broad occupational distinctions between professional, managerial, clerical, skilled, semiskilled and unskilled workers that are a familiar feature of such scales as those by the Registrar General in Britain or the Hall–Jones classification of occupational prestige.[10] In the Blishen classes there is no clear-cut distinction between manual and nonmanual workers which has been shown to be in important boundary in the study of social mobility.

Therefore, a third occupational classification was devised for analyzing the data on the social mobility of immigrants in Canada.[11] This was a combination of the Dominion Bureau of Statistics census classification and the Blishen score, or the known years of education. The occupations of immigrants were coded on the Dominion Bureau of Statistics scale and the Blishen score. When the information was punched on to cards a further sort was undertaken which eliminated

[8] Insofar as these scores reflected *average* education and income in each occupational category, they did not take into account the considerable range of income often exhibited within the category. This presented difficulties when Blishen scores were used to compute the social mobility of immigrants. For example, if an immigrant's first job in Canada was reported as "Civil Engineer" his score would be 75.0. If he subsequently became manager of a firm, his Blishen score, strictly speaking, fell to 63.8. However, when the internal evidence from the questionnaire showed that the change of occupation had resulted in an increase or no loss of income his original Blishen score was retained.

[9] Jacob Tuckman, "The Social Status of Occupations in Canada," *Canadian Journal of Psychology*, I (1947), 71–94.

[10] John Hall and D. Caradog Jones, "The Social Grading of Occupations," *British Journal of Sociology*, I (March 1, 1950).

[11] I am indebted to Dr. R. Sylt of the Research Division, Department of Citizenship and Immigration, Ottawa, who undertook the technical preparation of this scale.

from the Dominion Bureau of Statistics category of professionals all those with less than 13 years of education. These were grouped into a special intermediate category of lower professional, other managerial and technical workers. Manual occupations were divided into two according to Blishen score, providing a group of highly skilled manual workers with scores above 44.0 points and a further group of other skilled, semiskilled, and unskilled workers. The new scale of socioeconomic status consisted, finally, of six classes and residual groups of persons not in the labor force or about whom sufficient information was not available. The classes were as follows:

1. *Managers, executives and senior civil servants*: consisting of D.B.S. Division 1 (excluding small owners and junior managers) together with such occupations as real estate agents and stockbrokers from Division 4.
2. *Higher Professional*: consisting of D.B.S. Division 2 (excluding the lower professional and technical occupations) together with commissioned officers from Division 5.
3. *Intermediate*: consisting of lower professional, junior managerial and technical occupations.
4. *Clerical and Sales*: consisting of the whole of D.B.S. Division 3 together with the remainder of Division 4.
5. *Highly skilled*: consisting of all manual workers with Blishen scores above 44.0, ranging from locomotive engineers to construction machine operators.
6. *Other skilled, semiskilled and unskilled*: consisting of manual workers with Blishen scores of 44.0 and below, ranging from blacksmiths, carpenters, and cooks to general laborers.

An attempt was made to validate the new scale by calculating the mean incomes and average years of education of immigrants in each class as reported in the survey. The results showed that the managers in Class 1 had the highest incomes, but the professionals in Class 2 the longest period of education. Managers in Class 1 had more education than the immigrants in the intermediate Class 3. The latter had more education and higher incomes than the clerical workers in Class 4, among whom there was a high proportion of women. Skilled workers had less education but earned more than clerical workers, and the immigrants in Class 6 had the lowest levels of education and income. The scale, therefore, appears to be consistent with expected distributions of income and education and to be a valid measure of socioeconomic status.

Table 1 shows the distribution of occupations on this scale, comparing immigrants from the United Kingdom with those from other countries in terms of father's occupation, own occupation in former country, first job in Canada (held for two months or more),[12] and occupation at the time of the survey. Immigrants from the United Kingdom constituted about a quarter of the total immigrant population in 1961. Those from other countries consisted of 3 per cent from other English-speaking countries, 2 per cent from Asian countries and the remainder, constituting 70 per cent of the total, from various countries of Europe. When United Kingdom immigrants are compared with the others at the time of the survey

---

[12] Immigrants are encouraged to take any job they can get as a temporary measure on first arriving in Canada. By asking for "first job held for two months or more" purely stopgap employment of this kind was excluded from consideration.

TABLE 1. Socioeconomic Status of Immigrants and Their Fathers

| | United Kingdom | | | | | | | |
| | Father's occupation | | Former occupation | | First job in Canada | | Job : February 1961 | |
Code :ᵃ	No.	Per cent	No.	Per cent	No.	Per cent	No.	Per cent
1	11	8.9	10	8.1	7	5.7	15	12.1
2	14	11.3	7	5.7	6	4.8	7	5.7
3	5	4.0	18	14.5	16	12.9	19	15.3
4	14	11.3	26	21.0	24	19.4	21	16.9
5	51	41.1	37	29.8	32	25.8	33	26.6
6	13	10.5	15	12.1	31	25.0	18	14.5
7	1	0.8	8	6.5	4	3.2	11	8.9
—	15	12.1	3	2.4	4	3.2	—	—
Total	124	100	124	100	124	100	124	100
	Non-United Kingdom							
1	29	8.2	10	2.8	5	1.4	11	3.1
2	28	7.9	21	5.9	14	4.0	19	5.4
3	15	4.2	16	4.5	6	1.7	12	3.4
4	20	5.6	37	10.5	10	2.8	30	8.5
5	105	29.7	94	26.6	70	19.8	116	32.8
6	110	31.1	119	33.6	218	61.6	151	42.7
7	2	0.6	33	9.3	10	2.8	15	4.2
—	45	12.7	24	6.8	21	5.9	—	—
Total	354	100	354	100	354	100	354	100

ᵃ Code : 1–Higher managerial.   5–Highly skilled.
2–Higher professional.   6–Other skilled, semiskilled and unskilled.
3–Intermediate.   7–Not in labor force and nonemployed, including students.
4–Clerical and sales.   —No reply.

it is found that 43 per cent of the latter fell into the bottom social class compared with only 14.5 per cent of the immigrants from the United Kingdom. At the other end of the scale approximately 18 per cent of the United Kingdom immigrants were in the top two social classes compared with only 8.5 per cent of the others. In this respect the postwar immigrant population reinforced the status differences which were already evident in the Canadian population between those of British descent and those who were of some other ethnic origin. Blishen showed that, at the time of the 1951 census, Canadians of British descent were underrepresented in the lowest social classes and over-represented in the top class compared with French-Canadians and those of other ethnic origins.[13]

INTERGENERATIONAL MOBILITY

It is evident, therefore, that in studying the social status and social mobility of postwar immigrants in Canada it is essential to distinguish between the experience of the United Kingdom immigrants and those from other countries. We may begin by

[13] *Loc. cit.*, p. 524.

TABLE 2. Intergenerational Mobility of Postwar Immigrants in Canada (Outflow Analysis)

	1-4		5		6		7		Total	
Father's occupation[a]	Former Per cent	Can. 1961 Per cent	Former Per cent	Can. 1961 Per cent	Former Per cent	Can. 1961 Per cent	Former Per cent	Can. 1961 Per cent	Per cent	No.
Non-United Kingdom Origin Migrants' Occupations										
1-4	51	40	25	30	10	28	14	1	100	92
5	18	14	35	43	31	33	15	10	100	105
6	7	12	23	21	58	66	12	1	100	110
7	21	15	19	43	28	36	32	6	100	47
United Kingdom Origin Migrants' Occupations										
1-4	66	77	16	7	9	9	9	7	100	44
5	37	37	37	43	16	14	10	6	100	51
6	31	31	54	38	15	31	—	—.	100	13
7	56	31	25	19	6	19	13	31	100	16

[a] Code: 1-4 Nonmanual.
    5 Highly skilled.
    6 Other skilled, semiskilled and unskilled.
    7 Not in labor force and not known: includes students and other nonemployed together with those about whom information was not available.

examining the pattern of intergenerational mobility. When the occupations of fathers are considered there are no significant[14] differences between United Kingdom immigrants and others in the proportion having fathers in Classes 1, 2, and 3. However, the United Kingdom immigrants have a higher proportion of fathers in Classes 4 and 5 consisting of

14 In this paper no differences are described as "significant" that could occur more than once in 40 times in a random sample of the same size. When allowance is made for "clustering" and other effects this is equivalent to $P<0.05$. See Appendix for results of tests of significance.

routine clerical workers and skilled manual workers. They have a significantly lower proportion in the category of other unskilled and semi-skilled workers. It is possible to compare the father's occupation with that of the migrant in his former country and that pursued by the migrant at the time of the survey. Table 2 shows that among the United Kingdom immigrants whose fathers were nonmanual workers, 66 per cent were in nonmanual employment in the former country and 77 per cent in nonmanual employment in Canada. This contrasts with the experience of immigrants from other countries. In their case, of those with fathers in nonmanual occupations 51 per cent were themselves in nonmanual employment in their former country and only 40 per cent in Canada. In other words, the process of emigration had enabled the children of white-collar workers in the United Kingdom to retain or improve their position, whereas those from other countries fell in status. Clearly, this process was related to the question of language and of professional qualifications, both of which presented greater obstacles to the immigrant from Europe than from the United Kingdom. In the case of highly skilled workers there was almost exactly the same proportion of those from the United Kingdom and those from other countries who had the same status as their fathers in their former country. Furthermore, in the case of both United Kingdom immigrants and the others, the same proportion of those whose fathers were in highly skilled occupations achieved this status in Canada. However, of those who moved out of highly skilled occupations the majority of the United Kingdom immigrants moved up into white-collar employment, whereas the majority of other immigrants moved down into semiskilled or unskilled types of employment. Only a very small proportion of the immigrants from the United Kingdom had fathers in semiskilled or unskilled employment and of these only 15 per cent in the former country and 31 per cent in Canada remained in this status. In contrast, immigrants from other countries had the highest proportion with fathers in the lowest category and 58 per cent were in this group in the former country compared with 66 per cent in Canada.

It is evident, therefore, that the intergenerational mobility of United Kingdom immigrants compared with the others is of a rather different character. Whether one considers the occupations of the immigrants in their former country or those of their fathers it appears that the emigration from Britain is, principally, of people with middle-class or upper working-class backgrounds. Only 12 per cent of the British immigrants, compared with one-third of those from other countries, were from semiskilled or unskilled occupations. In the case of the fifteen United Kingdom immigrants in the sample who were in semiskilled or unskilled employment in their former country, twelve had fathers who were in higher status occupations. This suggests that British people with lower working-class backgrounds do not often emigrate to Canada. In contrast, the movement of European immigrants is much more proletarian. There are a number of reasons for this difference. In the first instance, it is well known that unskilled manual workers in Britain appear to have a strong attachment to the locality of their birth and upbringing and are often reluctant to move, even to another part of Britain, let alone to emigrate.[15] If they are tempted to do so, they might be more attracted by the prospects in Australia as an almost free passage is provided. Furthermore, Canadian Government immigration officers in Britain would probably discourage a prospective emigrant who had no special skills to offer. In contrast, Canadian immigration policy in Europe has tended to

---

[15] For a discussion of the relation between occupational status and internal migration see, R. Illsley, A. Finlayson and B. Thompson, "The Motivation and Characteristics of Internal Migrants," *Milbank Memorial Fund Quarterly*, XLI (April and July, 1963), No. 2 and 3.

encourage the migration of unskilled workers. In the period immediately after the Second World War there was a demand for farm labor, and the movement from refugee camps in Europe tended to be of people with relatively low educational levels. Subsequently, the Canadian Government adopted stricter occupational requirements for its open-placement immigrants, but unskilled workers with low educational attainment continued to enter Canada sponsored by their close relatives. Under the Canadian Immigration Act and Regulations certain Canadian residents could sponsor a first-degree relative so long as they guaranteed that the new immigrant would not become a public charge. Over a period of years this movement of sponsored relatives tended to snowball and was particularly marked from Italy. The Canadian Government attempted, in 1959, to impose an occupational skill requirement upon sponsored immigrants but was prevented from so doing by political pressures.

Before leaving the question of intergenerational mobility, it is interesting to compare the experience of postwar immigrants from Britain to Canada with that of the population studied by Professor D. V. Glass and his associates.[16] Obviously the small size of the migrant sample makes it necessary to be very cautious in interpreting the evidence. Furthermore, there is an age and sex difference between the sample studied by Glass and the sample of postwar immigrants in Canada. The latter contains a proportion of women who were excluded from Glass's study and, on the whole, the migrants are a younger

generation. Excluding students and others not in the labor force, 54 per cent of the migrants were in nonmanual employment in Britain compared with 37 per cent in Glass's sample. The proportion of skilled workers was almost exactly the same, 33 per cent, but the proportion of semiskilled and unskilled workers was only 13 per cent compared with 29 per cent in the national sample studied by Glass. This confirms the underrepresentation of unskilled workers and the overrepresentation of white-collar workers among emigrants to Canada. Glass used an index of association to measure the extent to which children tended to have the same social status as their fathers. An index of unity implied perfect mobility. Glass found that, in his sample of adult males, the nonmanual workers had an index of association of 1.6 compared with an index of 1.2 for skilled manual workers and 1.8 for semiskilled and unskilled workers. It is only possible to make a very crude comparison with the migrants in view of the very small size of the sample. However, an examination of the proportion of those whose fathers were in nonmanual occupations and who were themselves in nonmanual employment in the United Kingdom, compared with the proportion that one would expect from the total proportion of nonmanual workers in Glass's sample, would appear to give an index of association of 1.8. The experience of migration for the children of white-collar workers was, as has been shown, to increase further the association between parental occupation and that of the migrant. Glass found an index of association for skilled manual workers of 1.15 and the index for the migrant sample was almost exactly the same when the

---

[16] D. V. Glass, ed., *Social Mobility in Britain* (London, 1954).

TABLE 3. Blishen Score Difference Between Father's Occupation and Son's Last Occupation in Canada

Score difference Blishen Points[a]		Non-U.K. No.	Per cent	U.K. No.	Per cent	Total No.	Per cent
Up	11 and higher	20	6.8	12	11.9	32	8.1
	6–10	24	8.1	9	8.9	33	8.4
	3–5	44	14.9 {39.0	15	14.8 {43.5	59	14.9 {41.2
	1–2	27	9.2	12	11.9	39	9.8
No change		46	15.6	14	13.9	60	15.2
Down	1–2	26	8.8	13	12.9	39	9.8
	3–5	38	12.9	11	10.9	49	12.4
	6–10	33	11.2 {45.4	6	5.9 {38.6	39	9.8 {43.6
	11 and higher	37	12.5	9	8.9	46	11.6
		295	100	101	100	396	100
Movement not known		59	16.7	23	18.5	82	17.2
		354		124		478	

[a] Ignoring third digit (decimal point) in Blishen score.

occupation in the United Kingdom was considered. However, there was a slight increase in the association between parental occupation and the occupation of migrants with fathers in this class when employment in Canada was considered. In the case of semiskilled and unskilled workers, Glass found an index of association of 1.8 while the index for the migrant sample was a negative one, suggesting that those whose fathers were in semiskilled and unskilled employment had more than the expected proportion who had risen to skilled manual or nonmanual status. However, the move to Canada slightly increased the association between the status of the parent and of the migrant for this group, bringing it close to unity, but the numbers are too small for the change to be regarded as significant. Only the most tentative and hypothetical conclusions can be drawn from this analysis. Provisionally, it would appear that emigrants to Canada from Britain whose fathers were in nonmanual employment have a larger than expected chance of themselves being in nonmanual employment in Britain, and that this expectation is further increased by their experience in Canada. Those with fathers in skilled manual employment have about the expected proportion who are themselves in skilled manual employment in Britain and a slightly higher proportion in Canada. In the case of those whose fathers were semiskilled and unskilled workers, the proportion of the emigrants in this type of employment in Britain is below expectation but may be increased by the experience in Canada. *Thus, it seems that for some sons and daughters of white-collar and skilled workers, emigration to Canada provided a means of avoiding downward mobility, relative to the occupation of the father.* The migrant children of semiskilled and unskilled workers tended already to be upwardly mobile, but emigration to Canada did not improve their status further.

When United Kingdom immigrants and others are compared in terms of the over-all degree of intergenerational mobility as measured by the Blishen score, the differences are comparatively small.[17] (See Table 3.) This is despite the variation in class composition initially. At the time of the survey 15 per cent of those about whom information was available had the same score as their father, or less than one Blishen point difference, and there was no variation between British immigrants and others. Of the United Kingdom immigrants 44 per cent had risen and 39 per cent had fallen, while 39 per cent of the others had risen and 45 per cent had fallen. These differences were not statistically significant. However, the purely quantitative measure ignores the qualitative differences in types of movement between classes to which attention has been drawn. It also ignores the range of downward movement which was greater in the case of non-United Kingdom immigrants.

INTERGENERATIONAL MOBILITY

At this point it is appropriate to examine more closely the actual pattern of social status mobility exhibited by postwar immigrants in Canada, comparing their jobs in their former country with their first job in Canada, and the job at the time of the survey. The period of residence in Canada is clearly relevant to any examination of occupational status mobility. The maximum number of years that a postwar immigrant could have been resident at the time of the survey was 15 years and the minimum

---

[17] Blishen scores movements exclude the "not known" categories and ignore the third digit (decimal points) in Blishen scores.

1 year. The average for the sample as a whole was 7½ years. Thirty-eight per cent of the immigrants had been in Canada for 5 years or less, 42 per cent 5 to 10 years, and 20 per cent 11 to 15 years.

The Blishen score provides a useful measure of the change in status between the job in the former country, the first job held for two months or more in Canada, and the job at the time of the survey. In order to appreciate the implications of the distribution of score differentials, it is useful to consider the number of points which certain typical movements up or down the scale involve. A worker in the construction industry, for example, who moved between unskilled laboring and a skilled job would gain or lose between three and four points. A skilled worker who became a foreman or vice versa would gain or lose three points. The difference between the score of a foreman and a manager in the construction industry was approximately sixteen points. In the professional field, the movement from a school teacher to a university professor or vice versa would mean a gain or loss of four points and the difference between a practical nurse and a graduate nurse was thirteen points. The difference between a dental mechanic and a qualified dentist was thirty-two points.

Forty-one per cent of all respondents about whom information was available had no change or a change of less than one point in their Blishen score between their job in their former country and the first job in Canada (Table 4). About 15 per cent had a higher score and 44 per cent a lower score than formerly. There were significant differences between immigrants from the United Kingdom

TABLE 4.   Blishen Score Difference Between Occupation Abroad and First Occupation in Canada

Score difference Blishen points[a]		Non-U. K. No.	Per cent	U. K. No.	Per cent	Total No.	Per cent
Up	11 and higher	—	— ⎫	3	2.7 ⎫	3	0.8 ⎫
	6–10	11	3.9 ⎬ 14.8	3	2.7 ⎬ 14.5	14	3.5 ⎬ 14.7
	3–5	24	8.4	2	1.8	26	6.6
	1–2	7	2.5 ⎭	8	7.3 ⎭	15	3.8 ⎭
No change		104	36.5	58	52.7	162	41.0
Down	1–2	20	7.0 ⎫	11	10.0 ⎫	31	7.8 ⎫
	3–5	42	14.7 ⎬ 48.7	9	8.2 ⎬ 32.8	51	12.9 ⎬ 44.3
	6–10	43	15.1	7	6.4	50	12.7
	11– and higher	34	11.9 ⎭	9	8.2 ⎭	43	10.9 ⎭
		285	100	110	100	395	100
Movement not known		69	19.5	14	11.3	83	17.4
		354		124		478	

[a] Ignoring third digit (decimal point) in Blishen score.

and from other countries in this respect. Thirty-seven per cent of those from other countries compared with 53 per cent of those from the United Kingdom had no change or a change of less than one point in their score. Approximately the same proportion, just under 15 per cent of both groups, moved up, but a higher proportion of the non-British fell; 49 per cent compared with 33 per cent of those from the United Kingdom. There was also a substantial difference in the degree of downward movement. In the case of immigrants from the United Kingdom the median downward movement was four Blishen points, whereas that of the immigrants from other countries was seven. The highest upward movement experienced by a British immigrant in his first job in Canada was fourteen points compared with a highest score of ten points in the case of an immigrant from another country. The largest downward movement was twenty-five points in the case of one British, and thirty points in the case of one non-British migrant. The

most dramatic examples of scores falling twenty or more points were the consequence of migrants with higher educational and professional qualifications finding it impossible to obtain employment in their own fields and, consequently, being compelled to accept employment at the level of semiskilled or unskilled workers in Canada.

When the first job in Canada is compared with the job at the time of the survey, it is found that a little under half of the immigrants experienced no change, or a change of less than one Blishen point in their score (Table 5). About 7 per cent had a lower score at the time of the survey and 46 per cent a higher score. The proportion of immigrants from the United Kingdom and from other countries who retained the same Blishen score or who rose, was approximately the same, but the proportion of British immigrants who fell was slightly higher, although the difference was not statistically significant. About 5 per cent of the sample had been in

TABLE 5. Blishen Score Difference Between First Occupation and Occupation in Canada, February 1961

Score difference Blishen points[a]		Non-U. K. No.	Per cent	U. K. No.	Per cent	Total No.	Per cent
Up	11 and higher	21	6.6	12	10.9	33	7.7
	6–10	61	19.2	15	13.6	76	17.8
	3–5	47	14.8 } 46.6	10	9.1 } 42.7	57	13.3 } 45.6
	1–2	19	6.0	10	9.1	29	6.8
No change		152	47.8	51	46.4	203	47.4
Down	1–2	7	2.2	5	4.5	12	2.8
	3–5	7	2.2 } 5.6	5	4.5 } 10.8	12	2.8 } 7.0
	6–10	4	1.2	1	0.9	5	1.2
	11 and higher	—	—	1	0.9	1	0.2
		318	100	110	100	428	100
Movement not known		36	10.2	14	11.3	50	10.5
		354		124		478	

[a] Ignoring third digit (decimal point) in Blishen score.

Canada for only about a year and might reasonably be expected to experience further mobility in due course. The over-all mobility due to migration can be estimated by comparing the Blishen score of the migrant in his former country with that at the time of the survey. Table 6 shows that, at the time of the survey 43 per cent of all migrants, about whom information was available, had the same Blishen score as in their former country and the proportion was the same for United Kingdom immigrants and others. Thirty-one per cent had risen and 27 per cent fallen. A higher proportion of British had experienced upward and a smaller

TABLE 6. Blishen Score Difference Between Occupation Abroad and Occupation in Canada, February 1961

Score difference Blishen points[a]		Non-U. K. No.	Per cent	U. K. No.	Per cent	Total No.	Per cent
Up	11 and higher	6	2.1	4	3.8	10	2.6
	6–10	17	5.9	11	10.5	28	7.1
	3–5	40	13.9 } 28.5	12	11.4 } 37.1	52	13.3 } 30.9
	1–2	19	6.6	12	11.4	31	7.9
No change		121	42.2	46	43.8	167	42.6
Down	1–2	13	4.5	8	7.6	21	5.3
	3–5	40	13.9 } 29.2	6	5.7 } 19.1	46	11.7 } 26.5
	6–10	18	6.3	3	2.9	21	5.4
	11 and higher	13	4.5	3	2.9	16	4.1
		287	100	105	100	392	100
Movement not known		67	18.9	19	15.3	86	18.0
		354		124		478	

[a] Ignoring third digit (decimal point) in Blishen score.

TABLE 7. Special Matched Groups of Migrants. Blishen Score Difference Between Occupation in Former Country and in Canada, February 1961

	Higher	Same	Lower	Not known	Total
U. K.	13	15	7	2	37
Non-U. K.	4	16	12	5	37

proportion downward mobility, but the differences were not statistically significant.

COMPARISONS OF SPECIAL MATCHED GROUPS. Due to the heterogeneity of the samples it is doubtful whether the tests of significance applied to the Blishen score movements are a strictly valid indication of the differences between United Kingdom and non-United Kingdom immigrants. The χ^2 test in such cases assumes that the groups being compared have equal statistical chances of rising or falling. This was manifestly not the case, since the United Kingdom group had a larger proportion in the higher social classes in their former country and, therefore, a greater theoretical chance of falling. By the same token non-United Kingdom migrants tended to start nearer the bottom and consequently their purely statistical chances of rising were superior to the United Kingdom group.

In order to overcome this difficulty and to allow for other differences between the samples, two special matched groups of United Kingdom and non-United Kingdom migrants were compared. The comparison was confined to males between the ages of 24 and 55 years who had been in Canada five years or more and who had expressed an original intention to remain in Canada rather than re-migrate. Immigrants from all non-European countries were eliminated from the non-United Kingdom group

as were refugees from East European countries. The groups so matched also had a similar distribution of marital status and of Blishen social class in their former country. If language and nationality had ceased to be important determinants of social class after migrants with similar education and class backgrounds in their former country had been in Canada for more than five years, then the distribution of Blishen score movements at the time of the survey should have exhibited no significant difference. Table 7 shows that, in fact, a larger proportion of United Kingdom migrants rose and a smaller proportion fell in status. When the "not known" cases are eliminated, the differences are of an order that would occur less than 1 in 20 but more than 1 in 40 times in a simple random sample of the same size. It is reasonable to conclude, therefore, that United Kingdom immigrants in Canada did have some advantage over non-United Kingdom immigrants, when other things were equal, but that this advantage was a comparatively small one.

MOVEMENTS BETWEEN SOCIOECONOMIC CLASSES. Although the Blishen score gives a useful quantitative estimate of social mobility, an analysis by socioeconomic classes throws more light on some qualitative aspects of the movement. In particular it draws attention to important differences in the experience of manual and non-

TABLE 8. Intragenerational Mobility of Postwar Immigrants in Canada (Outflow Analysis)

	Non-United Kingdom Origin Job in Canada									
	1–4		5		6		7		Total	
Job in country of origin[a]	First per cent	1961 per cent	First per cent	1961 per cent	First per cent	1961 per cent	First per cent	1961 per cent	Per cent	No.
1–4	32	54	21	25	43	17	4	4	100	84
5	—	5	42	68	56	24	2	3	100	94
6	—	3	9	14	86	80	6	3	100	119
7	14	32	7	25	46	35	33	8	100	57
	United Kingdom Origin Job in Canada									
1–4	77	74	8	12	13	7	2	8	100	61
5	8	30	70	57	22	13	—	—	100	37
6	7	7	—	33	80	47	13	13	100	15
7	18	46	9	—	27	18	46	36	100	11

[a] Code: 1–4 Nonmanual.
      5 Highly skilled.
      6 Other skilled, semiskilled and unskilled.
      7 Nor in labor force and not known: includes students and other nonemployed together with those about whom information was not available.

manual workers, especially those who were not from English-speaking countries.

Table 8 shows intragenerational movements in terms of the socioeconomic classes, and confirms the differences between United Kingdom immigrants and others in their first job in Canada. Whereas 77 per cent of the British immigrants who were formerly in white-collar occupations retained this status in their first job in Canada, only 32 per cent of the immigrants from other countries did so. Those who fell into manual employment were twice as likely to enter the lowest category rather than Class 5, for which they would rarely have suitable qualifications. For example,

seven out of ten non-United Kingdom immigrants who had been in higher managerial posts in their former country fell in status, all of them into manual employment, and only one out of the seven entered Class 5. United Kingdom immigrants who fell from Classes 1 or 2 were more likely to remain in nonmanual employment, but clerical workers from the United Kingdom and from other countries who failed to retain their status were more likely to drop to Class 6.

There were considerable differences between the experience of immigrants from the United Kingdom and from other countries, who were formerly in Class 5. Whereas 70 per cent of the skilled workers from the United Kingdom retained this status in their first job in Canada, only 42 per cent of those from other countries did so. The remainder of the non-United Kingdom group fell into the lowest class, whereas some of the skilled workers from Britain entered clerical employment. There was less difference in the experience of semiskilled and unskilled workers in Class 6, only 7 per cent of whom improved their status in their first job in Canada, irrespective of origin.

When the situation at the time of the survey is examined, it appears that some of the non-United Kingdom migrants who were in white-collar employment in their former country, but who fell initially into the manual category, had at least partially recovered their position. The proportion in nonmanual employment had risen from 32 to 54 per cent, but only 40 per cent had actually returned to their original class. Skilled workers did rather better. By the time of the survey 68 per cent were in their former class and 5 per cent had moved into nonmanual employment. There was only a slight decline in the proportion in the lowest class, compared with the first job in Canada, although 17 per cent had moved up mainly into more highly skilled manual employment.

In the case of immigrants from the United Kingdom there was very little difference between the position of former nonmanual workers at the time of the survey compared with their first job in Canada. About the same proportion were still in manual employment, although the more detailed figures show that some who had dropped from the managerial, professional or intermediate classes subsequently recovered their position. Recovery or improvement upon their former position was most marked in the case of highly skilled workers. Only 13 per cent of this class were still downwardly mobile and 30 per cent had moved to nonmanual employment, mainly in Class 4. A substantial number of those formerly in Class 6 moved up into Class 5 by the time of the survey.

CONCLUSION

The over-all picture suggests that immigrants from the United Kingdom began with a very strong advantage insofar as they had fewer language problems to overcome and their occupational qualifications were more immediately acceptable to Canadian employers. This initial advantage diminished over a time as immigrants from other countries became more acculturated. Although British immigrants continued to be markedly underrepresented in the lowest social class and overrepresented in nonmanual employment, compared with other immigrants and the Canadian population as a whole, the over-all degree of upward mobility achieved by migration was hardly any higher than that of the non-British. Semiskilled and unskilled manual workers stood the greatest chance of improving their status by entering employment requiring greater skill, although hardly any, even from the United Kingdom, entered the white-collar category. Nonmanual workers, particularly those who were not from English-speaking countries, suffered the largest initial decline in status and had the greatest difficulty in recovering.

In interpreting the evidence concerning both intergenerational and intragenerational mobility, it must be remembered that the subjective significance of movement for the individual concerned may differ from the objective implications for a system of stratification. There may have been some sons who did not wish to follow their father's footsteps in a white-collar job and some migrants who positively preferred an outdoor job to one in an office, particularly if the decline in status did not necessarily mean a fall in the migrant's standard of living. Since the standard of living in Canada generally is high, so long as a migrant was fortunate enough to avoid prolonged unemployment or ill-health he could improve his material conditions despite a fall in status. In fact, 8 per cent of the immigrants said that their standard of living had risen in Canada although their position in the community had fallen; only 3 per cent said that their position in the community and their standard of living had both fallen.

APPENDIX

TESTS OF SIGNIFICANCE

TABLE 1.: *Socioeconomic status of immigrants and their fathers*

DIFFERENCES BETWEEN U.K. AND OTHERS

Father's

Class 1–3	No significant difference.
4	$P < 0.05$
5	$P < 0.025$
6	$P < 0.001$

Former

Class 1	$P < 0.025$
2	No significant difference
3	$P < 0.001$
4	$P < 0.01$
5	No significant difference.
6	$P < 0.001$

First in Canada

Class 1	$P < 0.01$
2	No significant difference.
3	$P < 0.001$
4	$P < 0.001$
5	No significant difference.
6	$P < 0.001$

Canada 1961

Class 1	$P < 0.001$
2	No significant difference.
3	$P < 0.001$
4	$P < 0.001$
5	No significant difference.
6	$P < 0.001$

TABLE 2:

NON-U.K.

Fathers' occupations compared with migrants' in former country:

No significant movement in either direction

Fathers' occupation compared with migrants' in Canada 1961:

Movement from nonmanual to manual: McNemar test of change (one-tailed): $P < 0.05$

Movement from nonmanual to manual between former country and Canada 1961 of children of nonmanual fathers: McNemar test of change (one-tailed): $P < 0.005$

U.K.

Fathers' occupation compared with migrants' in former country:

No significant movement in either direction

Fathers' occupation compared with

migrants' in Canada 1961:

Movement from manual to non-manual: McNemar test of change (one-tailed): $P < 0.05$

Movement from manual to non-manual of children of nonmanual fathers: McNemar test of change (one-tailed): $P < 0.05$

TABLE 3:

Blishen score movement between father's occupation and that of migrant in Canada, 1961.

No significant difference between United Kingdom and others.

TABLE 4:

Blishen score movements between occupation abroad and first occupation in Canada.

Significantly less downward mobility of United Kingdom $P < 0.025$

TABLE 5:

Blishen score movement between first occupation in Canada and occupation in February 1961.

No significant difference between United Kingdom and others.

TABLE 6:

Blishen score movement between occupation abroad and occupation in Canada, February 1961.

No significant difference between United Kingdom and others.

TABLE 7:

Special matched groups. Difference between United Kingdom and Non-United Kingdom $P < 0.05$.

TABLE 8:

Non-U.K.

First occupation in Canada compared with former country:

Movement from nonmanual to manual: McNemar test of change (one-tailed): $P < 0.001$

Movement from skilled to semi- and unskilled:

McNemar test of change $P < 0.001$

Occupation in Canada 1961 compared with former country:

Movement from nonmanual to manual:

McNemar test of change (one-tailed): $P < 0.001$

Movement from skilled to other: McNemar test of change—no significant change in either direction.

U.K.

First occupation in Canada compared with former country:

Movement from nonmanual to manual:

McNemar test of change (one-tailed): $P < 0.025$

Movement from skilled to semi- and unskilled:

McNemar test of change (one-tailed): $P < 0.025$

Occupation in Canada 1961 compared with former country:

McNemar test of change—no significant changes in any direction.

Migration and Vertical Occupational Mobility[*]

Richard Scudder and C. Arnold Anderson

Studies of social stratification in the United States have shown a striking contradiction in findings. The few studies of vertical mobility[1] report that a large minority or even majority of men are engaged in occupations with socioeconomic status different from their fathers. The community-focused investigations of social classes, on the other hand, either neglect to report any observed vertical mobility or imply strongly that mobility is rare and class lines are firm.[2] An exception is a recent community study by Deasy,[3] who took the novel step of inquiring directly about new and former members of the elite group and about families who had failed in their attempts to enter the elite. It is significant that she found a considerable influx into the upper-upper class.

Some of the sociologists engaged in the study of stratification have found it possible to reconcile these divergent findings. First of all, it is apparent that certain of the more active students of American stratification are not diligently looking into evidence on mobility. A second interpretation, which has been discussed at some length by Florence Kluckhohn,[4] is based on observation of the failure in the community studies of stratification to record the origins and careers of individuals migrating into or away from the community. It is to be expected that individuals who leave their home communities become detached from stable status relationships and manifest unusual mobility. The present study attempts to test this hypothesis.

The Kentucky community studied, containing about 1500 white households, is within an hour's drive of two moderate-sized cities and within a hundred miles of two metropolitan centers. The "fathers" reported on are the white male household heads residing in the community and having one or more sons aged 15 or older who have completed their schooling. The sons are divided into two groups: those who have remained in the community, and those who have migrated. For each of these two groups, occupations of fathers and sons are scaled

[*] Richard Scudder and C. Arnold Anderson, "Migration and Vertical Occupational Mobility," *American Sociological Review*, 19 (June, 1954), 329–34.

[1] Richard Centers, "Occupational Mobility of Urban Occupational Strata," *American Sociological Review*, XIII (1948), 197–203; H. D. Anderson and P. E. Davidson, *Occupational Mobility in an American Community* (Palo Alto: Stanford University Press, 1937); C. C. North and P. K. Hatt, "Jobs and Occupations: A Popular Evaluation," in *Sociological Analysis*, eds. L. Wilson and W. L. Kolb (New York: Harcourt, Brace and World, Inc., 1949), p. 473.

[2] The widely known studies published by W. L. Warner and his associates are particularly in point here.

[3] Leila Calhoun Deasy, *Social Mobility in Northtown* (Cornell University Dissertation), 1953.

[4] Florence R. Kluckhohn, "Dominant and Substitute Profiles of Cultural Orientation," *Social Forces*, XXVIII (1950), p. 388.

TABLE 1. Distribution of Father and Sons by Occupational Category and by Residence of Sons

Occupational category of fathers	Number	Percentage distribution of sons by occupational category						
		1 Pro-fessional	2 Pro-prietors[a]	3 Minor busi-ness-men[b]	4 Clerical	5 Skilled manual	6 Semi-skilled manual	7 Unskilled manual
					Resident sons			
1 Professional	32	50	47			3		
2 Proprietors	80	8	49	12	16	9	5	1
3 Minor businessmen	88	1	14	27	27	23	7	1
4 Clerical	68		3	12	34	26	15	10
5 Skilled manual	128		2	5	9	56	17	11
6 Semiskilled manual	51		2	13	8	24	41	12
7 Unskilled manual	43			2	12	30	16	40
Total	490	5	14	12	17	29	14	9
					Migrant sons			
1 Professional	23	52	31	9	4	4		
2 Proprietors	42	21	24	17	14	17	5	2
3 Minor businessmen	92	13	12	41	19	12	3	
4 Clerical	56	5	29	11	23	27	5	
5 Skilled manual	113	3	11	13	11	45	11	6
6 Semiskilled manual	22			10	27	27	18	18
7 Unskilled manual	16	6	6	26	19	19	12	12
Total	364	11	16	20	16	26	7	4

[a] Group 2 is composed of all proprietors and major executives.

[b] Group 3 includes business executives above the clerical level. See W. Lloyd Warner, Marchia Meeker, and Kenneth Eells, *Social Class in America* (Chicago: Science Research Associates, Inc., 1949), pp. 132–41.

and compared with each other. In addition, intergeneration occupational mobility is related to general social status scores of the fathers based on four combined indices: occupation, type of house, dwelling area, and prestige ratings by local judges.[5]

The combinations of occupations for each set of sons and fathers are

shown in Table 1; the complete table is included because of the paucity of similar mobility data in the literature. The patterns of occupational inheritance and mobility here displayed resemble those found in the studies cited in footnote 1 above.[6]

[5] The scales used, except for prestige, were those presented in W. L. Warner, M. Meeker, and K. Eells, *Social Class in America: A Manual of Procedure for the Measurement of Social Status* (Chicago: Science Research Associates, 1949). Perforce, parental reports of migrant sons' occupations were used.

[6] The report deals with sons only; the results for the sons-in-law are similar. A father may appear in both sections of Table 1 if he has one son in the home community and one elsewhere. Although these data cannot settle the question posed in this paper, they may open the discussion on the basis of facts hitherto lacking. More extensive data would permit classifying the sons by age, distance of migration, and other factors.

TABLE 2. Occupational Status of Migrant and Resident Sons in Relation to Combined Status Score and Occupational Stratum of Fathers

Father's combined status score[a]	Father's occupational stratum[b]	Numbers of sons		Percentage of sons in white-collar stratum[c]		Percentage distribution of sons' occupations compared to fathers' occupations[d]					
						Resident			Migrant		
		Resident	Migrant	Resident	Migrant	Higher	Same	Lower	Higher	Same	Lower
		(1)	(2)	(3)	(4)	(5)	(6)	(7)	(8)	(9)	(10)
All	White collar	268	213	72	80	11	38	51	27	34	39
	Manual	222	151	18	40	32	49	19	47	38	15
	Total	490	364	47	63	20	43	37	35	36	29
4–14	White collar	107	107	92	89	8	57	35	28	40	32
	Manual	0	0	—	—	—	—	—	—	—	—
	Total	107	107	92	89	8	57	35	28	40	32
15–18	White collar	115	92	69	73	11	32	57	31	24	45
	Manual	44	51	32	43	43	48	9	45	45	10
	Total	159	143	59	62	20	37	43	36	32	32
19–27	White collar	39	16	28	38	5	18	77	6	31	63
	Manual	173	110	16	40	34	43	23	52	33	15
	Total	212	126	18	40	29	39	32	46	33	21

[a] On each status index scores range 1–7; since four indices are combined, the possible scores for the combined or general social status index range from 4–28.

[b] The manual stratum includes categories 4–7 of the occupational scale and white-collar includes categories 1–3.

[c] In each cell the difference between the percentage given and 100 is the portion of sons in manual occupations.

[d] Here both the fathers' and sons' occupations are in seven groups, as shown in Table 1.

This table does not, however, sufficiently display the effects of migration upon mobility.

Table 2 groups the white-collar and the manual occupations of the fathers into separate strata and further subclassifies the parents by general or combined status scores. These composite scores take account of elements of status that are more varied and complex than occupational ratings alone, Columns (1) and (2) give the numbers of resident and migrant sons respectively for fathers in each of the designated occupational and general status categories. In columns (3) and (4) are shown the proportions of those sons who were pursuing white-collar occupations. In the last six columns of the table the mobility of the resident and of the migrant sons is portrayed in terms of the percentages who were at the same, a higher, or a lower occupational level than fathers on the seven-point occupational scale.

Though in total fewer than half of the sons left the community, the likelihood that a son would migrate was increased when the father's general social status was high. At a given level of general status sons of manual workers were more likely to migrate than were the sons of white-collar fathers. There were, however, no manual worker fathers in the highest general status bracket.

Achievement of a white-collar

TABLE 3. Ratio of Actual to Expected Numbers[a] of Sons in Occupations Higher, Similar to, or Lower than the Parental Occupation by Residence of Son and Combined Social Status Score of Father

Son's position relative to father's	Occupation of father				Combined status score of father		
	All	White-collar	Manual		4–14	15–18	19–27
				Resident sons			
Higher	0.56	0.93	0.51		0.33	0.67	0.85
Same	2.55	3.41	2.21		1.78	1.75	1.49
Lower	0.79	0.66	1.08		0.81	0.87	0.81
				Migrant sons			
High_r	0.79	1.09	0.72		0.77	0.85	0.92
Same	1.91	2.15	1.74		1.61	1.41	1.20
Lower	0.80	0.65	1.21		0.83	0.92	0.95

[a] The expected numbers were computed from the separate sections of Table 1 in the usual manner for contingency analysis. That is, the actual numbers of fathers in each of the seven occupational categories were multiplied by the percentages of sons in each category (for the resident and migrant groups separately) to get the "expected" figure in each father-son cell. The same values would of course result from multiplying the numbers of sons by the percentages of fathers.

position was of course more frequent among the sons of white-collar fathers than among the sons of manual workers. This differential advantage was much less marked, however, among the migrant than among the resident sons—percentages for the migrants were 80 against 40, for the resident sons they were 72 against 18. General social status of the parent was influential along with parental vocation in determining the white-collar or manual status of sons. The lower the parental general status, the less likely were sons to become white-collar workers. This relationship was clear-cut for all the resident sons and for the migrant sons of white-collar workers, but it was virtually obliterated for the migrant sons of manual workers. In each instance, irrespective of the vocational or general status of the father, migrant sons entered white-collar positions more frequently than their nonmigrant contemporaries. The migrants, it would seem, were not just restless incompetents.

A more adequate conception of occupational mobility can be developed by using seven occupational categories rather than the crude dichotomy of manual versus white-collar vocations. Mobility along this seven-point scale is summarized in the right section of Table 2.

Among resident sons there is an excess of moves into ranks below the father's position, among migrant sons the upward shifts exceed the downward. A fifth of the sons who remained in the home community rose to a position higher than that of the father and 37 per cent came to occupy a lower position. Of the sons who moved to another community 35 per cent moved up the occupational scale while only 29 per cent moved down. If the sons remaining on the same level as the father are excluded, the relation of migration to direction of occupational mobility is even more striking. Of all the sons who did not leave the home community but did move into a vocational level different from that of the father, two-thirds dropped in status. Among sons who went elsewhere but did not pursue the same sort of job as the father, over half rose vocationally. The chances of going up rather than down, if mobile at all, were definitely greater for the migrants, and fewer of the migrants entered occupations rating at the same level as those of their fathers.

The least mobile group was the resident sons of white-collar fathers with the highest composite social status. Sons of white-collar fathers whose parents were of rather low repute in terms of the combined index of status had a particularly unpromising outlook; a large majority of such sons dropped below their fathers' positions and few rose vocationally.

Among sons of manual workers quite a different mobility pattern is evidenced; the effects of low general status of parents are mixed. The resident sons of manual worker fathers are less likely to advance occupationally and more likely to drop down the scale when the general status of the parents is low. But the one group of sons showing a majority rising above their fathers' positions are the migrant sons of the manual workers with the lowest general status.

The proportions that would rise or fall vocationally as compared with their parents, on the hypothesis that sons' occupations were unaffected by those of their fathers, vary with the relative positions of the fathers along the occupational scale. It is of interest, therefore, to ask how the mobility patterns actually displayed among sons of each of the two main groups, the resident and migrant, compare with the "expectancy" patterns derived from the null hypothesis, of no correlation between father and son vocations.[7] Table 3 provides some evidence on this point. As the first column of Table 3 shows, occupational inheritance was two-and-a-half times "expectancy" for the resident and twice "expectancy" for the migrant sons. In both groups downward shifts occurred to the extent of 80 per cent of "expectancy," as did upward shifts also among the migrants. However, resident sons moved upward only about half as often as would be expected on the null hypothesis. While (as noted above) the absolute percentages of upward mobility were considerably greater for the sons of manual than of white-collar fathers, this absolute excess of upward mobility of sons of manual workers was less than the excess to be hypothetically expected. Among both migrant and resident sons upward mobility within the white-collar ranks, and downward mobility within the manual ranks were about equal to expectancy, but downward mobility of sons of white-collar and upward mobility of sons of manual workers were considerably below the hypothetical rate. It seems probable that these figures reflect a discontinuity in the occupational scale between the top manual and the low white-collar categories regardless of the group of sons involved. Migrant sons of both white-collar and manual workers fathers moved up the scale more fre-

---

[7] An intensive exploration of alternative measures of mobility is to be found in the following study: C. Arnold Anderson, James C. Brown, and Mary Jean Bowman, "Intelligence and Occupational Mobility," *Journal of Political Economy*, LX (1952), 218–39.

quently in relation to expectancies than did sons who remained in the community.

Once more it is instructive to take account of the father's combined or general status score as distinct from his occupational rank alone. As is shown in Table 3, inheritance of paternal occupation exceeded the hypothetical figures to a somewhat greater extent when fathers had high status than when they scored low. Cases in which the son dropped below the father's position occurred in about the same ratio to expectancy irrespective of the father's general status. The proportion of sons rising above their father's occupations more nearly approximates expectancy when fathers are of low general status than when they score high.[8] This effect is much greater among resident sons. Thus the number of resident sons of fathers with combined status scores of 4 to 14 surpassing their fathers in occupation was only a third of expectancy; for those whose fathers' combined status score was 15 to 18, the ratio was two-thirds; but for the fathers with general status scores of 19 to 28, the proportion of expectancy was 85 per cent. For the corresponding three groups among migrant sons the proportions of the hypothetical rates were 77, 85, and 92 per cent respectively.

In general, the occupations of migrant sons of low status fathers come remarkably close to a zero correlation with parental vocations. Among these sons occupational inheritance is only 1.2 times expectancy

---

[8] This is the more noteworthy in that upward mobility was greater, relative to expectancy, when fathers were white-collar, and there is a positive association between white-collar vocation and high general status.

on the null hypothesis and both upward and downward mobility exceed 90 per cent of the expected value. In view of the strong tendency toward inheritance of vocation among the migrant as well as resident sons generally, approach to the hypothetical distribution in this particular set of sons is noteworthy. Also migrant sons of middle status fathers and resident sons of low status fathers show a departure from inheritance of vocational status that testifies to the impulsions toward mobility revealed in this population.

Up to this point consideration has been given only to the proportions of sons moving up or down the occupational ladder, but not how far they move. In this as in other studies concerned with vertical mobility, it is evident that the majority of sons find themselves in strata which are the same as or adjacent to those of their fathers. This concentration of sons in the vicinity of the parental position is shown in Table 1; the vocational "distances" between fathers and sons are summarized in Table 4. The column headed "expected distribution" in Table 4 shows the percentage distribution of father-son differences in occupational position that would be expected if the over-all percentage of sons in the several occupational categories matched that for fathers but with no correlation between father and son in vocational status. It differs from the expectancies underlying Table 3 in that the latter were derived from the actual distributions of occupations of the two groups of sons as well as fathers. Thus in Table 4 the parameters used in quantifying the hypothesis of zero father-son occupational inheritance are so defined as to admit the possibility of 100 per cent inheri-

Table 4. Percentage Distribution of Father-Son Differences in Occupational
Status Level

Number of ranks difference in status		Expected distribution[a]	Resident sons		Migrant sons	
			Total	Mobile only	Total	Mobile only
Son higher	6	0.6	0	0	0.3	0.4
	5	2.1	0	0	0.3	0.4
	4	5.0	0.4	0.7	1.9	3.0
	3	8.3	2.9	5.0	5.8	9.0
	2	11.9	5.5	9.7	14.3	22.2
	1	13.7	11.6	20.4	12.6	19.7
No difference	0	16.9	43.1	—	35.7	—
Father higher	1	13.7	19.4	34.1	17.0	26.5
	2	11.9	11.6	20.4	8.0	12.4
	3	8.3	4.1	7.2	3.0	4.7
	4	5.0	1.2	2.2	0.8	1.3
	5	2.1	0.2	0.4	0.3	0.4
	6	0.6	0	0	0	0
Number			490	279	364	234

[a] The "expected distribution" is the percentage distribution of numbers of steps from father's status shown in an expectancy table derived on the hypothesis of zero inheritance of occupation, taking the initial over-all distribution of fathers as the parameter for both generations and for both resident and migrant sons.

tance; they abstract from the shift between the generations in the over-all occupational distribution.

From Table 4 as from Table 3 it is immediately evident that occupational inheritance exceeds the hypothetical rates and is greater for the resident than the migrant sons. The downward drift of the mobility distribution among the resident sons is marked, while there is a moderate upward drift among the migrants. The migrant sons were the more likely to depart markedly from the positions of their fathers. In the expected mobility figures of Table 4, 56 per cent of the sons would have departed from their fathers' vocational status by two or more steps along the occupational scale; in actuality among the migrant sons 35 per cent and among the resident sons only 26 per cent moved that far.

While this study can constitute only a footnote to empirical information concerning occupational mobility, its findings are sufficiently clear-cut to support at least two basic hypotheses. First, vocational status of sons is affected by general social status of parents as well as by their vocational rankings, especially within the group of white-collar fathers. Second, sons who migrate out of small or moderate-size communities are more likely to rise above their parents' occupational status than sons who remain in the home town. Students of social stratification in American communities would do well to turn more of their attention toward the dynamic aspects of the situation before drawing conclusions concerning the fixity of status over time or even the nature of the over-all status structure at a given point in time.

11

Perhaps nothing typifies the area of social demography as much as research into demographic-related attitudes, values, and beliefs. Foremost in quantity are studies of fertility attitudes.[1] These have usually focused on the relationship between fertility and attitudes about family size and family planning.[2] Interest in the process of migration has precipitated increased concern for the value and attitude base of geographic mobility. Attitudes and values on such issues as famil-

ATTITUDES, VALUES, AND BELIEFS

ism, type of neighborhood, quality of housing, social mobility, and life style have been investigated in an effort to increase understanding and prediction of migration.[3] Relatively few demogra-

[1] For an extensive review see Ronald Freedman, "The Sociology of Human Fertility," *Current Sociology*, Vols. X–XI, No. 2 (1961–62).

[2] For examples, see Pascal K. Whelpton and Clyde V. Kiser, *Social and Psychological Factors Affecting Fertility* (New York: Milbank Memorial Fund, 1943–58), 5 vols; Ronald Freedman, Pascal K. Whelpton, and Arthur A. Campbell, *Family Planning, Sterility, and Population Growth* (New York: McGraw-Hill Book Company, 1959); Pascal K. Whelpton, Arthur A. Campbell, and John E. Patterson, *Fertility and Family Planning in the United States* (Princeton, N.J.: Princeton University Press, 1966); Charles F. Westoff, Robert G. Potter, Jr., Philip C. Sagi, and Elliot G. Mishler, *Family Growth in Metropolitan America* (Princeton, N.J.: Princeton University Press, 1961); and Charles F. Westoff, Robert G. Potter, Jr., and Philip C. Sagi, *The Third Child* (Princeton, N.J.: Princeton University Press, 1963).

[3] Peter H. Rossi, *Why Families Move: A Study in the Social Psychology of Urban Residential Mobility* (New

phers have explored the ties between belief systems and mortality or population size.

Despite the volume of attitudinal research, the theoretical links between attitudinal factors and demographic behavior remain somewhat vague. There is the general recognition that attitudes are component elements which help govern human behavior. But behavior and attitudes may be similar or they may be different; they may be conforming or deviant.

Few need to be convinced that an individual's attitudes are largely a product of interaction, and that some kind of communication is basic to all forms of interaction.[4] Perhaps the majority of attitudes result from the interaction of an individual with other individuals or with groups. Since the characteristics of individuals and groups can vary significantly, individual and group properties become important analytical components of attitude research. Furthermore, aspects of the immediate situation can impose contextual limits that are reflected in the attitudes of individuals. A research emphasis on certain of these major components helps distinguish the psychological, social psychological, and sociological perspectives of attitudes. The sociological perspective focuses on the relations between attitudes and the determinants and consequences of the structure and functioning of groups and, to a lesser degree, the situational aspects of interaction in group settings. Largely within the bailiwick of psychologists and social psychologists are problems concerning the relevant properties of individual attitudes and the interpersonal perception processes in interaction.

The existence of a group is a key component of attitude research for both the sociologist and social demographer. Some groups are easy to recognize, such as the family, fraternal clubs, or community organizations, while others, such as abstract reference groups, are more difficult to identify or characterize. In any case, their importance for attitude research rests primarily on an identification of shared behavioral expectations among group members. Knowledge of such group-based attitudes about reciprocal ways of behaving is a requisite step to explaining attitude-behavior congruities and incongruities in sociological as well as social demographic research.

Most social demographic studies of attitudes, unfortunately, do not

---

York: The Free Press of Glencoe, Inc., 1955); Edgar W. Butler, George Sabagh, and Maurice D. Van Arsdol, Jr., "Demographic and Social Psychological Factors in Residential Mobility," *Sociology and Social Research*, XLVIII (January, 1964), 139–54; Gerald R. Leslie and Arthur H. Richardson, "Life-Cycle, Career Pattern, and the Decision to Move," *American Sociological Review*, XXVI (December, 1961), 874–902; and Wendell Bell, "Familism and Suburbanization: One Test of the Social Choice Hypothesis," *Rural Sociology*, XXI (Sept.–Dec., 1956), 276–83.

[4] Theodore M. Newcomb, Ralph H. Turner, and Philip E. Converse, *Social Psychology* (New York: Holt, Rinehart, and Winston, Inc., 1965).

define meaningful social groups. As was indicated in Chap. 1, the vast majority of studies report findings based on a sample survey of sociologically unrelated individuals. Although the surveyed attitudes are *assumed* to be influenced by group interaction, seldom are the groups or the interaction processes a subject of investigation. This type of social demographic investigation appears to be primarily aimed at identifying attitude uniformities. Categories established on the basis of such studies (for example, persons who approve of birth control measures and persons who do not) constitute what we have earlier termed "analytically defined aggregates." Even though the important sources and processes of attitude formation are not explained, attitudinal differences of social groupings often provide insight into differences in behavior and norms.

The readings included in this section are exemplary of social demographic attitude research. First is Judith Blake's study of ideal family size among white Americans during the past quarter of a century. Using sample survey data collected by several public opinion research organizations, Professor Blake discusses attitude stability and change for respondents with different social and demographic characteristics. Despite notable differences in the fertility rates of the 1930s, the late 1940s, and early 1950s, and the 1960s, the data on ideal family size for these periods show remarkable stability. The lack of congruence between these two trends is a mjor point of discussion.

The second reading by Lee Rainwater and Karol Weinstein follows a similar investigative logic but deals with qualitative rather than quantitative data. The authors describe various social and psychological factors related to contraceptive behavior of a sample of nearly one hundred white-working class respondents in Chicago and Cincinnati. The results of the "depth interviews" indicate the importance of personal values and attitudes as conditioning factors in the disparity between family planning goals and the ability to practice contraception effectively.

In Peter Field's study, the third reading, an aggregate index of the social-psychological concept of aggression is developed and correlated with death rates. The research stems from cross-cultural studies that have posited the general thesis that socialization and behavioral factors are important in explaining differential mortality. Using data from each state of the United States, significant differences were noted between causes of death correlated with the "anger-out" and the "anger-in" dimensions of aggression.

Why people decide to move is the problem which Leslie and Richardson consider in the next reading. The study tests the hypothesis that life cycle stage and social mobility, as exhibited in career plans, are the major decision-making influences. These variables are tested in relation to statements on mobility intentions and follow-up checks on actual mobility experience. From the results the authors develop a decision-to-migrate paradigm which, along with similar research, provides a basis for assessing the complex interaction of demographic, social psychological, and areal characteristics related to residential mobility.

The influence of attitudes pertaining to family population composition is discussed in the final selection by Deborah and Ronald Freedman and Pascal Whelpton. The research question is whether the number of children Americans expect to have is influenced by their desire to have at least one child of each sex. This norm of family composition is not necessarily shared by families in other societies where the sex of the child may have important family economic considerations. The findings, based on data from a national probability sample of white married women in the child-bearing years, suggest the importance of understanding the differential functions of boys and girls in family life as a guide to comprehending differences in family size in various societies.

Ideal Family Size Among White Americans: A Quarter of a Century's Evidence[*]

Judith Blake

Since most Americans exert some control over the size of their families, their reproductive desires are obviously a determinant of their reproductive performance. This fact received explicit recognition during the 1950s through the Growth of American Families Study and the two so-called Princeton Studies, but for periods prior to this no published analyses relating to the nation as a whole may be found.[1] For how long

[*] Judith Blake, "Ideal Family Size Among White Americans: A Quarter of a Century's Evidence," *Demography*, 3 (1966), 154–73.

[1] The report of the 1955 Growth of American Families Study may be found in Ronald Freedman, Pascal K. Whelpton, and Arthur A. Campbell, *Family Planning, Sterility, and Population Growth* (New York: McGraw-Hill Book Company, 1959). The first Princeton Study has appeared as *Family Growth in Metropolitan America*, by Charles F. Westoff, Robert G. Potter, Jr., Philip C. Sagi, and Elliot G. Mishler (Princeton, N.J.: Princeton University Press,

have Americans idealized an average of approximately three children? Did their ideals fluctuate greatly during periods of social change? Was the baby boom presaged by a marked upturn in family-size desires? Are men and women consistently different or similar in the number of children desired? Have religious, educational, occupational, and other differences in reproductive ideals changed significantly over time? Incredibly, the nation lived through the depression, the war, and the baby boom, without generating a national survey directed to answering such questions. The Growth of American Families Study in 1955 was, in fact, the first national survey concentrating on reproductive motivation and behavior.

However, although national studies of reproductive motivation for the period between the depression and the GAF study are unavailable, it is not true that national data on reproductive goals are nonexistent for these years. National surveys conducted by polling agencies like Gallup and Roper have periodically included questions on family-size ideals together with additional demographically relevant information. Such surveys are frequently used successfully by social scientists for nondemographic analyses (such as those relating to social stratification or political behavior), and there seems to be no valid reason why they cannot be used profitably for demographic analysis as well.

The present paper is the first in a series reporting on previously un-

analyzed survey data regarding family formation in the United States. Although derived principally from Gallup and Roper surveys conducted at intervals between 1936 and 1961, our analysis includes comparable materials as well from the 1955 and 1960 Growth of American Families Studies. This initial report will devote some attention to methodological aspects of the research and then present information on family-size ideals as represented by thirteen surveys. Other papers will deal with important social differences, such as education, religion, city size, economic status, and occupation in relation to family-size desires over time. Since the presentation here concerns white Americans only, separate consideration will be given subsequently to our data for nonwhites.

FINDING AND USING THE SURVEYS

Since our analysis rests on many studies originated by other researchers over a protracted period of time, it has obviously required much cooperation from both individuals and research agencies. This help enabled us to solve the two major initial problems of locating the appropriate studies and acquiring them for our detailed analyses. The subject index at the Roper Public Opinion Research Center showed which polls and surveys on file there contained a question on family-size ideals. These polls, together with the two GAF studies, appear to be the principal national surveys including such a question in this country. The Roper Center also rented us the actual data—interview schedules, IBM decks, codebooks, and so forth—from each of the studies.

1961), and the second Princeton Study is reported in *The Third Child*, by Charles F. Westoff, Robert G. Potter, Jr., and Philip C. Sagi (Princeton, N.J.: Princeton University Press, 1963).

Acquisition of these materials allowed us to compile comparative tables from all the surveys. In addition, Ronald Freedman, of the University of Michigan, and Arthur Campbell, of the National Center for Health Statistics (formerly of the Scripps Foundation), were extraordinarily generous in supplying us with IBM decks and other materials from the 1955 and 1960 GAF studies.[2]

NATURE OF THE SURVEYS

With the exception of two polls under the auspices of Roper Associates (those for 1943 and 1948) and the 1955 and 1960 Growth of American Families Studies, all the surveys reported on in this paper were conducted by the American Institute of Public Opinion (the Gallup Poll). Except as otherwise noted in the tables, the AIPO surveys conformed to the usual sampling procedures of that organization. The Gallup Poll samples the civilian, noninstitutional, adult population. Typically, the sampling units are of 1,500 persons, but since we have deleted nonwhites in the present analysis, our male/female totals do not amount to the full number sampled by AIPO. When compared with Census data, the Gallup Polls have generally been found to be representative not only of major regions of the country but also of age, sex, and white–nonwhite groupings.

[2] Although we did not have an opportunity to use any of the studies on file at the Survey Research Center of our own university (they contained no questions of interest to use), the staff of the International Data Library was of continuing assistance to us. They suggested sources of data and allowed us to canvass their files of interview schedules and questionnaires for additional studies of relevance.

More detailed discussion of relevant characteristics of these particular polls will be found below.

The 1955 GAF study is already widely known, but we shall remind the reader of the fact that it consisted of a probability sample of white, American, married women between the ages of 18 and 39 who were living with their husbands. It differs from typical AIPO surveys, therefore, in constituting a more restricted age and sex group of presently married individuals. The 1960 GAF sample was selected so as to be similar to and comparable with the 1955 study.

The two Roper surveys were also national studies, but they dealt with special age or sex groups in the population. The 1943 study sampled women aged 20–34 only, whereas the 1948 survey sampled a youthful group (aged 18–25) and a middle-aged

Percentage Who Are Farm Residents

Year	U. S. population[a]	Polls and surveys
1936	24.8	16.3
1941	22.7	21.5
1943	19.6	16.9
1945	18.1	18.8
1947	18.9	16.1
1948	17.7	12.7
1952	15.5	15.7
1953	14.3	14.5
1955	13.6	10.5
1957	12.7	13.6
1959	12.0	12.1
1960	11.4	9.4

[a] *Statistical Abstract of the United States, 1962,* p. 608. The entire series, including the figure for 1960, conforms to the definition of farm residence in use prior to the 1960 Census. The census data refer to the total population, whereas the poll results relate only to the white population.

TABLE 1.   Age Distribution of Male and Female Respondents in the Sample Surveys, 1936–61, and in the United States Census—Whites (Percentage by Age)

Date	Age range	Under 30	30–44	45+	N. A.	Total Per cent	Total Number
			Females				
1930[a]	20+	27	35	38	—	*100*	33,138[d]
1936	21+	15[b]	52[c]	30	3	100	704
1940	20+	26	33	41	—	*100*	39,112
1941	21+	22	35	41	2	100	974
1943	20–34	65	31	—	4	100	2,787
1945	21+	17	35	47	1	100	1,449
1947	21+	23	34	42	e	100	1,396
1948	(18–25) (40–55)	49	—	51	—	100	1,756
1950	20+	23	33	44	—	*100*	45,852
1952	21+	20	38	40	2	100	987
1953	21+	22	39	39	e	100	677
1955	18–39	47	53	—	—	100	2,713
1957	21+	20	41	39	e	100	679
1959	21+	18	37	44	e	100	716
1960	20+	19	32	49	—	*100*	51,118
1960	18–39	46	54	—	—	100	2,414
1961	14–23	100	—	—	—	100	1,148
			Males				
1930	20+	26	35	39	—	*100*	34,108
1936	21+	15[b]	48[c]	35	2	100	1,975
1940	20+	25	33	42	—	*100*	39,228
1941	21+	19	37	42	2	100	2,037
1945	21+	12	31	56	e	100	1,279
1947	21+	12	31	56	e	100	1,388
1948	(18–25) (40–55)	52	—	48	—	100	1,900
1950	20+	23	33	44	—	*100*	44,432
1952	21+	15	35	49	e	100	963
1953	21+	16	31	53	—	100	728
1957	21+	14	35	51	e	100	629
1959	21+	14	30	55	e	100	673
1960	20+	19	33	48	—	*100*	48,023
1961	14–23	100	—	—	—	100	1,002

a Italicized figures are from the census.
b 24 and under.
c 25–44.
d For the census totals, the numbers are given in thousands.
e Less than 1 per cent.

group (aged 40–55) of both sexes. Table 1 shows the age distributions of the populations sampled by sex in all the surveys and gives com-

TABLE 2. Religious Affiliation of Male and Female Respondents in the Sample Surveys, 1943–61—Whites (Percentages)

Date[a]	Age range	Protestant	Catholic	Jewish	Other	N. A.	Total Per cent	Total Number
				Females				
1943	20–34	74	20	3	2	1	100	2,787
1948	(18–25)	60	22	4	14	—	100	854
	(40–55)	64	17	3	16	—	100	902
1952	21+	71	22	4	2	b	100	987
1955	18–39	66	28	2	4	—	100	2,713
1957	21+	70	28	2	—	b	100	679
1959	21+	66	26	4	4	—	100	716
1960	18–39	66	28	4	2	—	100	2,414
1961	14–23	59	23	4	4	10	100	1,148
				Males				
1948	(18–25)	52	23	4	21	—	100	979
	(40–55)	52	16	3	29	—	100	921
1952	21+	70	23	5	2	b	100	963
1957	21+	69	25	2	2	2	100	629
1959	21+	64	26	5	5	—	100	673
1961	14–23	55	24	7	4	10	100	1,002

[a] The question on religious affiliation was not asked in the AIPO studies of 1936, 1941, 1945, 1947, and 1953. No males were questioned in 1943, 1955, and 1960.

[b] Less than 1 per cent.

parable figures for the census populations as enumerated in 1930, 1940, 1950, and 1960. In the surveys sampling the adult population in general (rather than a special age group), females tend to be concentrated somewhat more in the age group 30–44 than they are in the adult population of women in the country as a whole. Among males, there is a decided deficiency of those under 30 and an excess of those aged 45 and over. Because of the age differences among some of the samples (i.e., those where a special group, such as respondents aged 18–39, was chosen), all of our summary historical materials are presented with information as to the age range of respondents in each poll.

Some interest naturally attaches to the composition of these samples with respect to major socioeconomic characteristics and to the comparability of the respondents with white adults in the nation as a whole. We shall, therefore, consider briefly the distributions of the surveys with respect to religion, farm residence, years of school completed, and region.

RELIGION. The percentage distributions of the samples by sex and religious affiliation are presented in Table 2. The proportion of Catholics sampled has risen in recent years, presumably because Catholics now make up a larger proportion of our white population. In any event, the distributions by religion for the middle and late 1950s correspond very closely with the distributions found by the sample survey conducted in March,

1957, by the Census Bureau. For example, the Bureau found that among white women aged 14 and over in 1957, 65.1 per cent were Protestant, 27.9 per cent Catholic, 3.6 per cent Jewish,. and 3.4 per cent "other."[3]

[3] United States Department of Commerce, Bureau of the Census, "Religion

It should be noted, however, that the 1961 AIPO Youth Study of high school and college students contained

Reported by the Civilian Population of the United States: March, 1957," *Current Population Reports—Population Characteristics*, Series, P-20, No. 79 (Washington, D.C.: Government Printing Office, February 2, 1958), 8 pp.

TABLE 3.   Years of School Completed in Surveys and Censuses—White Population (Percentages by Years of Education)

Date	None	1-8	High school 1-3	4	College 1-3		4+	N. A.	Total Per cent	Number
					Females					
1940[a]	3	52	16	17	7		4	1	100	33,886[b]
1943	—	13		53		22		12	100	2,787
1945	1	29	19	30	12		9	—	100	1,449
1947	1	28	20	31	12		8	—	100	1,396
1948[c]	—	10		60		30		—	100	854
1948[d]	1	25		49		25		—	100	902
1950	2	41	18	24	8		5	2	100	40,704
1952	1	26	23	33	8		9	—	100	987
1953	1	31	22	35	6		5	—	100	677
1955	—	14	25	46		15		—	100	2,713
1957	1	24	23	35	9		8	—	100	679
1959	2	22	23	39	8		6	—	100	716
1960	2	34	20	29	9		6	—	100	46,322
1960	—	10	24	48	11		7	—	100	2,414
1961[e]	—	5	22	27	13		25	8	100	1,418
					Males					
1940	3	57	15	13	5		6	1	100	34,114
1945	1	37	18	23	8		13	—	100	1,279
1947	2	30	20	24	11		13	—	100	1,388
1948[c]	—	8		59		32		g	100	979
1948[d]	—	32		39		27		2	100	921
1950	2	44	17	19	3		8	3	100	38,753
1952	1	29	20	26	9		15	—	100	963
1953	1	37	22	24	9		7	—	100	728
1957	2	32	20	29	8		9	—	100	629
1959	5[f]	28	19	27	9		12	—	100	673
1960	2	37	19	22	9		6	5	100	43,259
1961	—	6	26	26	13		21	8	100	1,002

[a] Census data are for the white population by sex aged 25 and over.
[b] For the census totals, the numbers are given in thousands.
[c] Ages 18–25.
[d] Ages 40–55.
[e] Education of the respondent's father, or head of household.
[f] None and 1–4.
[g] Less than 1 per cent.

almost 10 per cent nonresponse on the religious question. As can be seen, the nonresponse rate is negligible or nonexistent for the other studies. The "other" category in the 1948 Roper Fortune poll is made up primarily of those who do not attend church. Aside from these anomalies, the distributions by religious affiliation appear to be reasonable and consistent.

FARM RESIDENCE. As with religious affiliation, reproductive desires are known to vary according to whether respondents have a farm background. Although we do not have data on the respondents' previous residence, we do have information concerning their present locations. The tabulation on a previous page shows that the proportion of farm residents in our polls generally corresponds closely to the proportions in the same years for the population as a whole.

EDUCATIONAL LEVEL. There are, as Table 3 shows, conspicuously lower proportions of the sampled populations who have only a grade-school education than of the white population in general. Since grade-school respondents in the surveys have somewhat higher family-size ideals than those with more education, this bias in the sampling means that in general the respondents' ideals are slightly lower than would be the case for the national population of whites at the relevant dates. The selection against respondents having only a grade-school education is particularly great among the younger members of

TABLE 4. Regional Distribution of Respondents in the Sample Surveys, 1936–61, and of the Population of the United States in 1930, 1940, 1950, and 1960—Whites (Region of the Country)

| | | North | | | | Total | |
Dates	Northeast	Central	South	West	Per cent	Number
1930	31	34	25	10	100	108,864[a]
1936	35	32	18	15	100	2,679
1940	29	33	27	11	100	118,215
1941	34	38	14	14	100	3,011
1943	27	30	32	11	100	2,787
1945	33	39	13	15	100	2,726[b]
1947	32	37	13	18	100	2,784
1948	28	31	27	14	100	3,655[b]
1950	28	31	27	14	100	134,942
1952	34	36	17	13	100	1,878[b]
1953	33	32	21	14	100	1,405
1957	37	29	21	13	100	1,308
1959	29	33	22	16	100	1,389
1960	26	30	28	16	100	158,837
1960	24	30	31	15	100	2,414
1961	33	30	22	15	100	2,002[b]

[a] For the census totals, the numbers are given in the thousands.

[b] Cards unpunched for region of the country are not included here. The 1955 Growth of American Families Study is also not included because its regional breakdown is not comparable with the other surveys.

the 1948 sample (aged 18–25), the 1955 and 1960 GAF studies, and the 1961 sample of high-school and college students whose parents' educational levels are used in this breakdown. In part, the higher educational level of the two GAF studies is a function of the limitation of these samples to the reproductive ages.

REGION OF THE COUNTRY. Table 4 demonstrates a fairly good correspondence between the surveys and the decennial censuses in many cases. There is, however, a tendency for the Northeast (and occasionally the North Central) regions to be overrepresented and for the South to be underrepresented. This bias is particularly great for the 1941, 1945, 1947, and 1952 studies.

INTERVIEWING

As far as we can ascertain, all the studies were the results of personal interviews with respondents except the AIPO study conducted in 1961 among high-school and college students by means of a self-administered questionnaire. This questionnaire was different from the ordinary Gallup schedule in being unusually long and focused entirely on questions (some very personal) of relevance to young people. AIPO considered that its results would be more valid if these youngsters were allowed to fill out the questionnaires themselves rather than being interviewed by adults.

Obviously, we are unable to offer assurances concerning many refinements in the data-gathering process, such as comparability of interviewing. It may perhaps be significant, however, that the AIPO organization rarely varied the family-size question. Since, as will be seen, the stability

and patterning of answers to this question are remarkable, we have little reason to search for gross differences in data gathering. The accompanying tabulation gives the percentage of nonresponse to the question on ideal family size for each of the studies by sex. Although the

Percentage

	Females	Males
1936	10.1	11.4
1941	5.5	8.0
1943	a	b
1945	1.9	2.8
1947	5.2	6.6
1948	—	—
1952	3.1	3.0
1953	1.2	1.8
1955	0.5	b
1957	7.5	8.6
1959	9.4	8.0
1960	0.3	b
1961	1.5	4.0

a Dashes indicate that all respondents replied.
b No males sampled.

AIPO nonresponse percentages are higher than the nonresponse rate in studies like GAF which were devoted exclusively to the topic of fertility, in only one case did as many as 10 per cent of the respondents fail to reply.

NATURE AND COMPARABILITY OF THE QUESTION ON FAMILY-SIZE IDEALS

Two principal types of questions have been asked in surveys concerning attitudes on family size. One pertains to the respondent's opinion of the "ideal" number of children in a family ("What do you think is the ideal size of family— a husband, a wife, and how many children?"), and it is this type of question with which we shall be dealing. The other concerns the size family the respondent "expects" to have ultimately, and this has come to be a preferred question in recent American fertility research. In order to suggest some of the problems involved in the use of the question on "ideal" family size, let us discuss its possible drawbacks and ambiguities briefly, including its relation to the question on "expected" number of children.

Clearly any question regarding "ideal" family size which specifies no conditions or points of reference for the respondent to take into account leaves him free to answer in whatever terms seem relevant to him. But are these terms similar for all respondents? Or, rather, is one respondent thinking of an "ideal" number of children who will appear under "ideal" conditions, whereas another is thinking of the best number under the stress of realistic limitations? Equally, are some respondents answering in personal terms and others in terms of some hypothetical "average man"? There are no satisfying and elegant answers to such queries for the studies under consideration, since typically only one very general question was asked. Fortunately, however, some experimentation with the phrasing of the question on ideal family size has been done, and this gives a sense of how much hidden variability may exist. A study by Freedman and his colleagues in West Germany contained a question on "ideal" family size for the "average" family in Germany, and another question on the number the respondent

would himself desire if "conditions of life were very good." The difference in mean family size between the "ideal" for average Germans (2.6 children) and the number desired for one's self under good conditions (2.7 children) was obviously slight. Since more than one facet of the question was allowed to vary here, we do not know exactly the reason for the similarity of response. We can only say that, given a considerable variability in frame of reference, the similarity was great. It is also possible to compare these data with a question in the same study on "expected" family size. Here the "expected" size of family was only 2.2 children.[4]

In addition to the German study, two surveys in the Detroit area (one conducted in 1952 and the other in 1954) varied the "ideal" family-size question somewhat. In 1952 the question was asked with reference to the "average American family," whereas in 1954 it referred to "a young couple ...if their standard of living is about like yours." The first study produced a mean "ideal" of 3.15 children, whereas the 1954 figure was 2.94. Because the "ideal" expressed by the higher socioeconomic strata remained relatively constant between the two studies, whereas the lower economic groups showed a definite decline, the authors believe that the more specific reference to level of living brought down the average for the lower economic groups.[5]

---

[4] Ronald Freedman, Gerhard Baumert, and Martin Bolte, "Expected Family Size and Family Size Values in West Germany," *Population Studies*, XIII (November, 1959), 136–50.

[5] Ronald Freedman, David Goldberg, and Harry Sharp, " 'Ideals' about Family Size in the Detroit Metropolitan Area, 1954," *Milbank Memorial Fund Quarterly*, XXXIII (April, 1955), 187–97.

Percentages

Ideal family size	For high-income family	For average American family	For low-income family
0	—	} 0.1	5.0
1	—		8.8
2	4.0	17.6	61.8
3	9.0	29.4	12.0
4	36.6	43.4	9.7
5	15.8	4.2	} 2.2
6	24.2	4.3	
7	2.8		
8	5.5	} 1.0	} 0.5
9+	2.1		
Total	100.0	100.0	100.0
	(2291)	(2377)	(2320)
5+	50.4	9.5	2.7

Finally, the 1960 Growth of American Families Study demonstrates that the "ideals" will change considerably if *extremes* of economic status are explicitly brought before respondents. The table [above] shows the "ideal" family-size distributions resulting from three variants of the question: "ideal" for the "average American family," for a "high-income family," and for a "low-income family."[6]

Clearly, a general question on "ideal" family size leaves much to be desired methodologically, since we cannot be sure that respondents are answering in terms of similar frames of reference. It may, however, be heartening that Americans tend to think of themselves as "middle class" or "average," hence their answers to a general question on family ideals may refer to their notion of the "average" (including themselves). They

[6] The previously unpublished materials in this table were derived from the IBM decks of the Growth of American Families, 1960.

may answer with reference to socioeconomic extremes only if the latter are explicitly pressed upon them by the questionnaire. We shall see that answers to the general question from studies other than the 1960 GAF study (for proximate years) are closer to the 1960 GAF "average American family" answers than to either the high- or low-income family distributions. However, the more data we accumulate and analyze on this topic, the more we are led to realize that greater precision is required in formulating the question itself if its usefulness is to be maximized.

IDEAL VERSUS EXPECTED FAMILY SIZE. One effort at improving the family-size question has been made in the Growth of American Families Studies of 1955 and 1960. The studies inquired about the number of children respondents "expected" to have, in addition to asking about "ideals." Although this question has the advantage of specifying a personal reference (the respondent himself), the responses are in other respects very difficult to standardize. The problem of predicting fertility is shifted to the respondent—he is being asked for a calculus of the number of children he would *like* to have as a family (presumably thinking in terms of the family as an isolated goal), combined with the number that he thinks he will have, taking into account a wide variety of conditions (known factors over which he has no control). In some cases, the latter will be some fecundity problem of which he already has knowledge, but the younger he is the less likely he is to know of this difficulty. He will also probably take into account some notion of his long-term financial situation and whether he is in any way inhibited from effectively using contraception. But, in

TABLE 5. Percentage Distribution of Total Number of Children Considered Ideal by White Females in the United States, for Selected Years, 1936-61

Ideal family size[a]	1936 (21+)	1941 (21+)	1943 (20-34)	1945 (21+)	1947 (21+)	1948 (18-25)	1948 (40-55)	1952 (21+)	1953 (21+)	1955 (18-39) Min.	1955 (18-39) Max.	1957 (21+)	1959 (21+)	1960 (18-39) Min.	1960 (18-39) Max.	1961 (14-23)
0	—	3	5	—	1	1	—	1	—	—	—	1	—	—	—	1
1	2	2	5	1	2	1	1	1	1	—	—	1	1	—	—	1
2	33	28	40	21	26	31	20	26	27	21	17	17	16	22	18	19
3	33	25	25	27	28	35	32	28	29	34	30	36	27	32	30	27
4	24	30	19	37	33	26	36	33	30	39	44	37	44	39	43	32
5	5	5	3	7	6	4	5	5	7	3	5	4	7	3	4	10
6+	3	7	3	7	4	2	6	6	6	3	4	4	5	4	5	10
Total	100%	100%	100%	100%	100%	100%	100%	100%	100%	100%	100%	100%	100%	100%	100%	100%
(N)[b]	(633)	(920)	(2690)	(1421)	(1324)	(825)	(859)	(937)	(648)	(2684)	(2684)	(622)	(637)	(2378)	(2377)	(1115)
$\bar{X}$	3.1	3.2	2.7	3.5	3.2	3.1	3.4	3.3	3.4	3.3	3.5	3.4	3.6	3.4	3.5	3.6
2-4	90%	83%	84%	85%	87%	92%	87%	87%	86%	94%	91%	90%	87%	93%	91%	78%

[a] All of the Gallup Polls (those dated 1936, 1941, 1945, 1947, 1952, 1953, 1957, and 1959) except the Gallup Youth Study of 1961 asked the following question: "What do you consider is the ideal size of a family—a husband, wife, and how many children?" The Gallup Youth questionnaire (1961) asked, "How many children would you like to have?" The Roper Poll of 1943 asked, "How many children would you like to have, if you had your choice?" and that of 1948, "How many children do you think makes the nicest size family?" The Growth of American Families Studies of 1955 and 1960 inquired concerning "the ideal number of children for the average American family." The minimum distribution arises from coding range answers (e.g., "two or three") to the lowest figure, and the maximum distribution results from coding them to the highest figure.
[b] Total number of respondents giving codable answers to question on ideal family size.

any event, the question scrambles together the issue of "ideals" or "desires" and the facts of life as the respondent is able to know them and assess them. Variability in the answers thus reflects to an unknown degree variability in many factors—family-size "ideals" (presumably under some conditions), knowledge and judgment, moral restraints. We have no way of knowing what weights each respondent should be assigned on the different elements in the mixture because all we are presented with by him is the result itself—"expected" family size.[7]

We therefore believe that future sophistication in research on family-size goals will emerge from separating rather than agglomerating the elements in the respondent's motivation. One separate element will always be some "ideal" or desired family size that the respondent holds for himself under certain conditions, as against other factors influencing "expected" family size. Consequently, although the data on ideal family size presented in this paper and others to come are the result of a relatively crude question, we believe that such a series of materials will form a backdrop for cumulatively valuable methodological improvements in the future.

Although we cannot be sure that respondents were thinking of the same issues during the quarter of a century under consideration, we are most fortunate that at least they were *asked* approximately the same question in most of the studies. As may be seen from the footnotes to Table 5, eight polls inquired, "What do you think is the ideal size of family—a husband, a wife, and how many children?" Another survey asked essentially the same question ("How many children makes the nicest size family?"), and the two GAF studies asked for "ideal" family size in terms of the "average American family." Two additional studies inquired as to the number of children the respondent would like to have.

---

7 "Expectations" of family size have been found to be relatively good predictors of actual family size in the *aggregate*, apparently because involuntary factors (particularly infecundity and excess fertility) cancel each other out. For example, Campbell, Whelpton, and Tomasson have shown that expectations expressed by respondents in 1955 were remarkably accurate in predicting the number of children actually born between 1955 and 1960, as reported in the 1960 GAF study. However, the 1960 distribution of actual births is compared in the aggregate with the 1955 expectations. See A. A. Campbell, P. K. Whelpton, and R. F. Tomasson, "The Reliability of Birth Expectations of U.S. Wives," *International Population Conference* (London: UNESCO, 1963), pp. 49–56. The congruence between responses and behavior is less impressive where the two factors for the same individual are matched. The unexplained variance due to involuntary factors has been examined in detail in Philip C. Sagi and Charles F. Westoff, "An Exercise in Partitioning Some of the Components of the Variance in Family Size," *Emerging Techniques in Population Research* (Milbank Memorial Fund, 1963), pp. 130–40.

TRENDS IN IDEAL FAMILY SIZE

Recent research on American fertility has established that parental desires currently fall within a range of two to four children. Whether this range is evaluated as "wide" or "narrow" depends, of course, on one's criteria of relevance. If one is concerned with the determinants of differential family-size desires, then one might claim (as Freedman and others have done) that the two-to-four-child range represents a remarkable con-

TABLE 6. Percentage Distribution of Total Number of Children Considered Ideal by White Males in the United States, for Selected Years, 1936-61

Ideal family size[a]	1936 (21+)	1941 (21+)	1945 (21+)	1947 (21+)	1948 (18-25)	1948 (40-55)	1952 (21+)	1953 (21+)	1955 (18-39) Min.	Max.	1957 (21+)	1959 (21+)	1960 (18-39) Max.	1961 (14-23)
0	—	2	1	1	1	1	1	—	1	1	—	—	2	3
1	2	1	1	1	2	1	—	2	5	5	1	1	6	1
2	33	31	23	29	36	31	30	29	34	32	21	22	30	27
3	32	28	27	32	33	32	31	31	26	25	40	34	23	36
4	21	23	28	26	22	24	25	27	23	24	27	27	25	23
5	7	8	11	5	4	4	6	6	4	5	8	8	6	5
6+	5	7	9	6	2	7	7	5	7	8	3	8	8	5
Total	100%	100%	100%	100%	100%	100%	100%	100%	100%	100%	100%	100%	100%	100%
(N)[b]	(1750)	(1874)	(1241)	(1297)	(905)	(854)	(916)	(694)	(1893)	(1893)	(564)	(593)	(2191)	(943)
$\bar{x}$	3.2	3.2	3.5	3.3	2.9	3.2	3.3	3.2	3.1	3.2	3.3	3.5	3.2	3.1
2-4	86%	82%	78%	87%	91%	88%	85%	87%	83%	81%	88%	84%	78%	86%

a See footnote a, Table 5, for discussion of the family size question asked on the various schedules. The 1955 data from the Growth of American Families Study are responses by wives about the number their husbands wanted, and the ages given are the ages of the wives who were interviewed.
b Total number of respondents giving codable answers to question on ideal family size.

sensus among Americans on a family of limited proportions.[8] Even here, however, it could be argued that there is a profound sociological difference between having two and having four children and that the determinants of such different ideals within the range require investigation along with the determinants of the limitations on the range itself. Such attention to the width rather than the narrowness of the range becomes particularly relevant if one is concerned with the implications for population growth of having twice two instead of two children. A family pattern of four as against two children not only has yearly manifestations in birth rates

---

[8] Ronald Freedman, "The Sociology of Human Fertility: A Trend Report and Bibliography," *Current Sociology*, X/XI, No. 2 (1961–62), 35–68; and "American Studies of Family Planning and Fertility: A Review of Major Trends and Issues," in *Research in Family Planning* (Princeton, N.J.: Princeton University Press, 1962), pp. 211–27.

but builds into the population a much faster rate of demographic escalation. Therefore, we shall place as much emphasis in our trend analysis on shifts in preference for two, three, and four children as on any changes in the upper and lower limits of the range itself.

Mean ideal family size during the last quarter of a century has varied for both sexes by about one child at the most (Tables 5 and 6). For women, the mean never rises above 3.6 children or falls below 2.7, and for men the picture is similar. Moreover, the sex difference in the mean seems to exhibit a definite pattern. Men typically either want the same size family as do women on the average or they want fewer children. In only two cases, are men found to want a slightly larger family than women. There would therefore seem to be an important consensus between the sexes concerning the number of children desired, and, if anything, a tendency for men to wish for smaller families

Mean Family Size Considered Ideal

Year	Men	Women	Difference[a]
1936	3.2	3.1	0.1*
1941	3.2	3.2	0
1945	3.5	3.5	0
1947	3.3	3.2	0.1*
1948	2.9	3.1	0.2
1948	3.2	3.4	0.2
1952	3.3	3.3	0
1953	3.2	3.4	0.2
1955	Min. 3.1	3.3	0.2
1955	Max. 3.2	3.5	0.3
1957	3.3	3.4	0.1
1959	3.5	3.6	0.1
1960	Max. 3.2	3.5	0.3
1961	3.1	3.6	0.5

[a] Cases where men want more children are marked with an asterisk.

than women. The following table clarifies this point [see page 580]: Although the variability in means has been relatively small—especially for men—there is some tendency among women for mean ideal family size to rise in recent years. This will show more clearly when the samples are broken down by age. As it is, the later samples (with the exception of 1957 and 1959) are younger than most of the earlier ones and, since younger respondents want smaller families than older ones regardless of time period, this age difference in the samples somewhat obscures the rise in means.

Turning to the percentage distributions themselves, one finds that the preference for a family of between two and four offspring has been with us at least since the thirties. The percentage of women choosing this number varies only between seventy-eight and ninety-four for the entire period and for men between seventy-eight and ninety-one. These data for the last quarter of a century thus confirm the view that family-size ideals do not respond very greatly to upheavals such as war, depression, and economic boom—the moderate-to small-size family prevails as the ideal.

On the other hand, if we look at variability within the two-to-four-child range, the picture is different—particularly for women. Among them, families of two children have declined markedly in popularity and the four-child family has become the modal "ideal." From the 1955 GAF study onward, approximately 40 per cent of the women consider a family of four children ideal, whereas in 1936, 1941, and 1943, this many offspring were favored by 24, 30, and 19 per cent of the females, respectively. Among men,

there appears in the late 1950s to be some increase in those idealizing three children at the expense of those preferring two. Apparently, the baby-boom experience in the United States has been at least in part a result of a long-term shift in preferences among women from families of two and three children to families of three and four.

**TREND IN IDEAL FAMILY SIZE
AMONG COMPARABLE AGE
GROUPS**

A division of our surveys into comparable age groups removes the effect of differences in age classification and, in addition, enables us to study family-size ideals by age itself. Let us start with the ideals of youthful respondents—those under 30—over time. Looking at the means for women in Table 7, one observes a rise in ideal family size among those in the prime reproductive period. The three earliest polls show an average of three or fewer children; none of the studies prior to 1953 exceed 3.3 children as a mean, and most fall below this figure. After the early 1950s, a mean of 3.3 children becomes the low rather than the high figure, and a number of polls exceed this average. Comparison of the three early polls with those of the fifties indicates, for these young women, approximately a doubling of the percentages desiring four children. Conversely, the two-child family has moved from being the choice of a third or more of young women to being selected by a poor fifth of them. Among young men, the means have changed less than among women. The former idealize a mean as high as 3.3 children in only one instance. There has been some decline

TABLE 7. Number of Children Considered Ideal by Male and Female Respondents, Aged under 30, 1936–61—Whites (Ideal Family Size—Percentages and Means)

									Total		
Year	0	1	2	3	4	5	6+	Per cent	Number[c]	$\bar{X}$
					Females						
1936[a]	—	2	36	43	16	2	1	100	94	2.8
1941	1	2	39	30	22	1	5	100	213	3.0
1943	4	6	40	26	19	2	3	100	1771	2.7
1945	—	1	24	34	33	5	3	100	342	3.3
1947	1	1	29	32	30	4	3	100	310	3.1
1948[b]	1	1	31	35	26	4	2	100	825	3.1
1952	1	1	31	32	30	2	3	100	195	3.1
1953	—	1	32	29	26	5	7	100	146	3.3
1955 Min.	—	1	23	34	37	3	2	100	1259	3.3
Max.	—	—	17	32	43	5	3	100	1259	3.4
1957	—	1	16	44	34	3	2	100	128	3.3
1959	—	1	18	26	48	5	2	100	121	3.5
1960 Min.	—	—	23	34	37	3	3	100	1099	3.3
Max.	—	—	18	32	42	4	4	100	1099	3.4
1961	1	1	19	27	32	10	10	100	1115	3.6
					Males						
1936[a]	—	3	38	34	17	4	4	100	261	2.9
1941	1	2	43	30	15	6	3	100	369	2.9
1945	—	—	32	36	22	7	3	100	148	3.1
1947	2	—	36	33	21	4	4	100	249	3.0
1948[b]	1	2	36	33	22	4	2	100	905	2.9
1952	—	1	38	35	20	4	2	100	138	3.0
1953	—	1	43	29	21	3	3	100	117	2.9
1957	—	—	32	37	26	5	—	100	81	3.0
1959	—	2	26	32	26	8	6	100	86	3.3
1961	3	1	27	36	23	5	5	100	943	3.1

[a] Ages 24 and under.

[b] Ages 18–25.

[c] Total number of respondents giving codable answers to questions on age and ideal family size.

in the percentage choosing two children and some increase in those selecting four, but in neither case has the shift been as great as for women. Young women in recent years quite consistently prefer a larger family than do young men.

The age group 30–44 shows the same trends over time (Table 8). For the women in this category, the mean ideal family size becomes consistently stabilized at around 3.5 children, whereas in earlier years it is closer to three. As early as 1945, the four-child preference is established as the modal category, with two-child families declining as a choice. Men in this age group exhibit little trend in the average number of children desired, but evince a continuous increase in the percentage preferring three children at the expense primarily of those

TABLE 8. Number of Children Considered Ideal by Male and Female Respondents Aged 30–44, 1936–60—Whites (Ideal Family Size—Percentages and Means)

Year		0	1	2	3	4	5	6+	Total Per cent	Total Number[b]	$\overline{X}$
					Females						
1936		—	1	35	32	25	5	2	100	339	3.1
1941		2	2	34	24	27	6	5	100	321	3.1
1943[a]		6	5	37	26	19	3	4	100	807	2.7
1945		—	1	25	31	33	7	3	100	503	3.3
1947		1	2	29	28	31	5	4	100	461	3.2
1952		—	3	27	26	34	5	5	100	358	3.3
1953		—	1	25	29	33	8	4	100	252	3.3
1955	Min.[c]	—	—	20	34	39	3	4	100	1425	3.4
	Max.	—	—	16	30	45	4	5	100	1425	3.5
1957		—	1	19	36	37	3	4	100	258	3.4
1959		—	1	13	33	40	7	6	100	243	3.6
1960	Min.[c]	—	—	20	31	40	4	5	100	1279	3.4
	Max.	—	—	17	28	44	4	7	100	1278	3.6
					Males						
1936		—	2	34	35	19	6	4	100	854	3.1
1941		2	2	34	31	21	5	5	100	683	3.1
1945		—	1	26	29	29	8	7	100	393	3.4
1947		1	1	34	35	22	3	4	100	425	3.0
1952		1	1	35	34	20	4	5	100	322	3.1
1953		—	1	27	37	24	7	4	100	217	3.3
1957		1	1	22	46	22	6	2	100	203	3.1
1959		—	1	21	41	27	4	6	100	177	3.3

[a] Ages 30–34.
[b] Total number of respondents giving codable answers to questions on age and ideal family size.
[c] Ages 30–39.

choosing two. Small, erratic changes in other family-size categories for men compensate for this shift and leave the averages relatively unaffected over time.

Older women, those aged 45 and over (Table 9), exhibit little consistent pattern of change in the averages. Beginning with 1941, their preferences run consistently in favor of about 3.5 children, and, except for 1936, the modal category is four children. The two latest polls for women of this age—1957 and 1959—show a pronounced drop in two-child preferences and an increase in four children as the ideal compared with the ten years preceding. With the exception of 1936, the means in this age group among men tend to be high—around 3.5 children—with little trend beyond the depression year. There does, however, seem to be some rise in the proportion selecting three- and four-child families.

This analysis by comparable age groups over time shows that the shift to a three-and-four-child preference characterizes younger women and women in their thirties, whereas old-

TABLE 9. Number of Children Considered Ideal by Male and Female Respondents, Aged 45 and Over, 1936–59—Whites (Ideal Family Size—Percentages and Means)

Year	0	1	2	3	4	5	6+	Total Per cent	Total Number[b]	$\bar{X}$
				Females						
1936	—	3	28	30	28	6	5	100	185	3.3
1941	5	2	18	22	36	7	10	100	368	3.5
1945	1	1	15	21	42	8	12	100	559	3.8
1947	1	1	21	26	38	7	6	100	544	3.5
1948[a]	—	1	20	32	36	5	6	100	859	3.4
1952	—	—	22	28	34	7	9	100	364	3.5
1953	—	—	26	28	29	9	8	100	249	3.5
1957	2	1	15	32	39	6	5	100	232	3.5
1959	—	1	16	23	45	9	6	100	268	3.6
				Males						
1936	—	2	28	28	25	9	8	100	605	3.4
1941	3	1	24	24	27	10	11	100	792	3.5
1945	2	1	18	26	29	13	11	100	691	3.7
1947	1	2	23	29	30	7	8	100	611	3.5
1948[a]	1	1	31	32	24	4	7	100	854	3.2
1952	1	—	25	28	30	7	9	100	449	3.5
1953	—	2	26	30	31	6	5	100	359	3.3
1957	—	2	17	37	30	10	4	100	277	3.4
1959	—	1	20	31	28	10	10	100	325	3.6

[a] Ages 40–55.
[b] Total number of respondents giving codable answers to questions on age and ideal family size.

er women have remained more stable in the proportions desiring families this large. That older women do not push up their ideals markedly beyond four children seems to indicate that the "distance" between four and more-than-four is substantial and not readily bridged even by an age group consistently at the top of the two-to-four-child range. Of course, it remains for us to examine in later papers how the composition of these age groupings has changed over time with regard to important social and economic characteristics. Among men, the analysis by age groups leads us to suspect that larger family ideals may "grow" on men after the fact and that, if we had more masculine data

for later years and older age groupings, we would find more of an overall masculine increase in the number of children considered ideal. It does seem important that our series of data gives little indication of a masculine desire for large families. In so far as women want them, their reactions cannot be ascribed to male pressure.

CONTRASTS IN FAMILY-SIZE IDEALS AMONG AGE GROUPS

A comparison of age groups themselves, rather than a trend for each age group separately, shows that, regardless of the period, older people

TABLE 10. Number of Children Considered Ideal by Females by Age, 1936–60—Whites (Percentage Distributions and Means)

Dates	Under 30						30–44						45+					
				Total						Total						Total		
	0-1	2-4	5+	Per cent	N	X̄	0-1	2-4	5+	Per cent	N	X̄	0-1	2-4	5+	Per cent	N	X̄
1936 (21+)	2	95	3	100	94	2.8	1	92	7	100	339	3.1	3	86	11	100	185	3.3
1941 (21+)	3	91	6	100	213	3.0	4	85	11	100	321	3.1	7	76	17	100	368	3.5
1943 (20–34)	10	85	5	100	1771	2.7	11	82	7	100	807	2.7	—	—	—	—	—	—
1945 (21+)	1	91	8	100	342	3.3	1	89	10	100	503	3.3	2	78	20	100	559	3.8
1947 (21+)	2	92	6	100	310	3.1	3	88	9	100	461	3.2	2	85	13	100	544	3.5
1948 (18–25) (40–55)	2	92	6	100	825	3.1	—	—	—	—	—	—	1	88	11	100	859	3.4
1952 (21+)	2	93	5	100	195	3.1	3	87	10	100	358	3.3	—	84	16	100	364	3.5
1955 (18–39) Min.	1	94	5	100	1259	3.3	—	93	7	100	1425	3.4	—	—	—	—	—	—
Max.	—	92	8	100	1259	3.4	—	91	9	100	1425	3.5	—	—	—	—	—	—
1957 (21+)	1	94	5	100	128	3.3	1	92	7	100	258	3.4	3	86	11	100	232	3.5
1959 (21+)	1	92	7	100	121	3.5	1	86	13	100	243	3.6	2	84	14	100	268	3.6
1960 (18–39) Min.	—	94	6	100	1099	3.3	—	91	9	100	1279	3.4	—	—	—	—	—	—
Max.	—	92	8	100	1099	3.4	—	89	11	100	1278	3.6	—	—	—	—	—	—

TABLE 11. Number of Children Considered Ideal by Males by Age, 1936–59—Whites (Percentage Distributions and Means)

Dates	Under 30 Total						30-44 Total						45+ Total					
	0-1	2-4	5+	Per cent	N	X̄	0-1	2-4	5+	Per cent	N	X̄	0-1	2-4	5+	Per cent	N	X̄
1936 (21+)	3	89	8	100	261	2.9	2	88	10	100	854	3.1	2	81	17	100	605	3.4
1941 (21+)	3	88	9	100	369	2.9	4	86	10	100	683	3.1	4	75	21	100	792	3.5
1945 (21+)	—	90	10	100	148	3.1	1	84	15	100	393	3.4	3	73	24	100	691	3.7
1947 (21+)	2	90	8	100	249	3.0	2	91	7	100	425	3.0	3	82	15	100	611	3.5
1948 (18–25) (40–55)	3	91	6	100	905	2.9	—	—	—	—	—	—	2	87	11	100	854	3.2
1952 (21+)	1	93	6	100	138	3.0	2	89	9	100	322	3.1	1	83	16	100	449	3.5
1953 (21+)	1	93	6	100	117	2.9	1	88	11	100	217	3.3	2	87	11	100	350	3.3
1957 (21+)	—	95	5	100	81	3.0	2	90	8	100	203	3.1	2	84	14	100	277	3.4
1959 (21+)	2	84	14	100	86	3.3	1	89	10	100	177	3.3	1	79	20	100	325	3.6

tend to have larger family ideals. Within each study, we typically find a linear relationship with age. Among the nine means for the age group 45 and over, eight are as high as 3.4 children or more; among the seventeen means among those under 30 and the 15 averages among those 30–44, only five are this high. The percentage distributions show the same picture (Tables 10 and 11).

Is this relationship with age a function of some characteristic—such as education—which is independently associated with family-size ideals? Subsequent analyses will be addressed to this point. An alternative, or additional, hypothesis is that the individual's position in the family cycle is influential. Those who have completed their families and reared their children may either rationalize the three, four, or five children they have had or, if their families have been smaller, they may feel that they could have taken on more, that they were too cautious, or that the family is more important than they believed when they were young and distracted by diverse aims and ambitions. A sense of regret for not having had more children may be a highly patterned characteristic of older people in societies where great pressure is experienced among the young to limit their families severely. Whatever interpretation turns out ultimately to be correct, it seems clear that the relatively substantial family ideals of the older generation during this period in American history must have had some influence on young people. During the past 25 years, the latter have grown up in a society where their elders believed a family of three or, more typically, four children ideal. Just what influence this apparently familistic orientation of the elders

has had may perhaps be evidenced in the increasing family ideals among those under 30 once the depression years were over. It certainly seems to be true that new generations were not discouraged by their elders from investment in the three-to-four-child family.

SUMMARY

Our data on ideal family size from thirteen surveys and polls over the past quarter of a century show a variability among white women of about one child from the lowest to the highest mean, with a rise in family-size ideals in recent years. Among men, the picture is similar but the variability is less. It is apparent, therefore, that a time period which included the depression, the war, and the years of postwar prosperity did not give rise to a drastic realignment of reproductive desires among white Americans. Whether one looks at averages or percentage distributions, the two-to-four-child range has encompassed the ideals of approximately 80 to 90 per cent of our men and women since the middle of the 1930s.

However, although respondents did not go to extremes of change during the period under consideration, they did vary their reproductive goals within the two-to-four-child range in a demographically significant manner. Our analysis, which allows us to look at shifts in the number of respondents desiring two, three, and four children, respectively, shows a definite movement away from the two-and-three-child to the three-and-four-child family among women. Among men in the late 1950s, there seems to be some increase in the proportion desiring three children at the expense of two. It would appear, therefore, that the baby-boom experience in the United States has been in part a result of shifting preferences, especially among women, from the lower and middle parts of the family-size continuum to the middle and upper reaches. Hence, although fertility ideals are still compressed within the two-to-four-child range, the four-child family has become the modal category for the mid-century woman, and the two-child family is chosen by less than a fifth of female respondents in recent surveys. Such a result implies that the image of a "planned family" of two or, at the most, three children is archaic. For approximately 40 per cent of female respondents, "excess" fertility (fertility over and above the ideal) begins only with the fifth child.

The shift to the three-and-four-child preference is particularly sharp among women in the reproductive ages—those under 30 and 30–44—since older women, those aged 45 and over, choose a family size close to the top of the range throughout the time period. The net result of rises in family-size ideals among younger women and relatively static desires among older ones is to make women of all ages more similar in reproductive goals than was previously the case. Among men in the various age groups, there is some proportionate shift away from an ideal of two children to an ideal of three or four, but the changes are not as marked as for women. In particular, young women in recent years prefer larger families than do young men.

Despite the fact that differences between old and young women are diminishing, family-size ideals exhibit a consistent pattern of increase with age in the various studies. Such a finding may perhaps be explained, on the one hand, by distinctive socioeconomic characteristics of older as against younger people at every date and, on the other hand, by a change in attitudes toward family size as individuals move through the life cycle. Regardless of the antecedents, however, we are led to ask whether such pronatalist ideals among the grandparent generation have not constituted a moral backdrop for the reproductive renaissance among the young. In the future, therefore, it may be valuable to study the familial preferences of both the older and the reproducing generation in more detail, because the former—through their moral, as well as their tangible support—may influence the reproductive performance of young people.

A Qualitative Exploration of Family Planning and Contraception in the Working Class[*]

Lee Rainwater and Karol Kane Weinstein

Our study involves a qualitative examination of various social and psychological factors related to contraceptive behavior among that large group in our society called the working class—the families of medium- and low-skilled manual and service workers who live in neighborhoods and housing of below average reputation and quality, and who these days are earning from $3,000 to $6,000 a year but from whom, nevertheless, most of the problem cases which most social agencies deal with are recruited. One basic dimension of the social problem which this group represents is the tendency to have more children than they really want and can care for—a condition which arises from the fact that so many of the couples in this group are not able to practice contraception effectively.

Several excellent studies have defined the extent to which lack of effective family planning characterizes the working class, most particularly the lower status portion of that group. The Indianapolis Fertility Study by Whelpton and Kiser in the 1930s and the 1955 study by Freedman, Whelpton, and Campbell have indicated the statistical dimensions of the problem.[1]

Such studies show that most middle-class families do not have more children than they want. This is not so with the working class, where the hardships imposed by too many children are a common problem—again, most particularly in the lowest part of the class. Previous research, then, has defined the extent of the problem, and some of its socioeconomic correlates. However, relatively little has been known of the deeper psychological and psychodynamic conditions which lead to lack of effective contraception in this group.

The role of attitudes, motives, needs, and symbolic meanings in the area of contraception and the sexual behavior of which it is a part has been little explored. Our study represents a pilot exploration of these factors in relation to concrete contraceptive practices and to such broader background factors as sexual relations, attitudes toward spouse and children, and ideas about conception and pregnancy.

SAMPLE AND METHOD

The study involved a quota sample

[*] Lee Rainwater and Karol Kane Weinstein, "A Qualitative Exploration of Family Planning and Contraception in the Working Class," *Marriage and Family Living*, 22 (August, 1960), 238–42.

[1] See P. K. Whelpton and Clyde V. Kiser, *Social and Psychological Factors Affecting Fertility* (Milbank Memorial Fund, 5 volumes, 1946, 1950, 1952, 1954 and 1958). Also, Ronald Freedman, P. K. Whelpton, and Arthur A. Campbell, *Family Planning, Sterility, and Population Growth* (New York: McGraw-Hill Book Company, 1959).

of white working-class respondents in Chicago and Cincinnati; forty-six were men and fifty were women. The limited budget available for the study prevented any systematic examination of ethnic factors or inclusion of Negroes in the sample. However, the sample did include a range of European ethnic backgrounds and a good representation in Cincinnati of respondents from rural Southern homes. About one-third of the respondents were Catholic, almost all the rest were Protestant. Slightly over half of the respondents were from the lower portion of the working class, the lower-lower class; the rest were placed socially in the upper-lower class.[2] From our data it appeared that about 75 per cent of those in the upper-lower class were now reasonably consistently practicing an effective contraceptive method while only about one-third of those in the lower-lower class were doing so.

Each respondent was interviewed at length following a pattern of conversational, relatively free discussion (the so-called depth interview). A wide range of topics in the areas of the family, family planning, conception, contraception and contraceptive methods, and sexual relations was taken up with each respondent. In addition, respondents were given a shortened and specially designed version of the thematic apperception technique to tap information on personality and on feelings about family planning and contraception.

The interview covered a number

---

[2] For a discussion of the characteristics of upper- and lower-lower class persons see W. Lloyd Warner, M. Meeker, and K. Eels, *Social Class in America* (Chicago: Science Research Associates, 1949).

of quite intimate topics, and thus posed a problem in design of the interviewing guide. Preliminary interviews indicated that if respondents were told at the beginning of the interview that contraception and sexual relations would be discussed we could expect a high refusal rate. The introduction to respondents was then revised so that interviewers told respondents only that we were generally interested in family life and child rearing. The first questions of the guide dealt with these topics, then with the number of children desired and only then with family limitation and contraceptive practices. Sexual relations were covered in the last part of the interview. This procedure yielded a low refusal rate, and less than 5 per cent of the respondents failed to cooperate in the latter, more intimate half of the interview.

PLANNING AND PROBLEM OF CHOICE

Central to effective family planning is a particular world view on the part of the planner. To plan means to look ahead, to orient oneself toward the future, and to make commitments both to oneself and to others. To plan is to choose consciously between alternative courses of action and to pursue the course chosen in an energetic and consistent manner. Planning requires an active mastery of one's impulses, energies and capacities, and to a considerable extent of one's environment. In order to plan, one must have some trust in the future and believe that one's world is more or less stable and predictable so that one may intelligently project action into the future. A view of life in which planning is a real possibility because f trust in a predictable future and confidence in one's ability to maintain a chosen course of action embodies a rational as opposed to a nonrational or mystical orientation to living. In our society, the value on planning and belief in its efficacy is most solidly developed in the middle class.

Many researches into working-class psychology suggest that such a view is difficult for the lower-class person to maintain. His upbringing and his contemporary world encourage neither trust in a secure, predictable future nor belief in one's ability actively to master oneself and the world around. These people tend instead to see the world as on the chaotic and unpredictable side, a world controlled more by fate and chance than by intellectually apprehensible regularities and causal effects. Similarly, lower-class people find it difficult to believe that they can actively master themselves and their futures in such a world; one can simply do one's best and then hope uncertainly for the best.[3]

PLANNING A FAMILY

Such an orientation on the part of the working class is of considerable importance for understanding family planning, since what is planned is not really *parenthood* but *nonparenthood*, which seems to these people an artificial status sought by artificial means and maintained, if at all, against the pressure of natural and spontaneous forces. To insist on nonparenthood until parenthood is desired requires a

[3] For an extended discussion of the personality world view of the working class housewife see Lee Rainwater, Richard P. Coleman, and Gerald Handel, *Workingman's Wife* (New York: Oceana Publications, Inc., 1959).

most consistent exercise of the world view, self-mastery, and trust of the planner and chooser.

Working-class people are in general concerned about the number of children they have, and have reasonably definite ideas about how many they want. Recent studies suggest that they do not want more children than middle-class couples.[4] Their conscious concerns in thinking about family planning involve health and finances most centrally. Having children is the dictate of nature, but poor health or insufficient income are legitimate arguments against nature's intention, a view argued as emphatically by Catholics as by Protestants.

The desire and hope to have three or four children, and to space them about two years apart, are very common in this group. Doing something which may result in that hope being realized, however, is another question. The tendency for many lower-class people to *fantasy* rather than to *act out* a plan is strong and for many of these respondents birth control is almost literally a fantasy, as is nicely illustrated in the comment of a 21 year old lower-lower class woman with two children who says:

> "We thought about maybe three or four children would be nice. That's ideal I would say. (What do you do?) We don't use anything, we just trust to luck."

The trusting to luck so common in this group ranges from the extreme of doing nothing through the use of a system such as douching in which one really has very little faith to the sporadic use of an effective method such as the condom. The latter pattern is quite common, illustrated by

[4] Freedman, *et al., op. cit.*

one woman who told us that when her husband ran out of condoms he did not get a new supply until sometime later when he got around to it. At least two-thirds of our noneffectives are so because of careless or sporadic use rather than nonuse. It is as if these people believe that impregnation is additive, that one can be "a little bit pregnant," or that backsliding in contraception may be forgiven by the fates if one does better next time. It seems likely that while the effective contraceptive user regards what he does as a rational way of achieving some predictable result (even though he allows for the possibility of method failure on a very rare occasion), many lower-class noneffective contraceptive practitioners see contraceptive action as merely part of a larger situation in which fate, luck, and chance play a large part—the contraceptive often seems to serve them more as a magical talisman than as a method—a function attested to by many of the jokes about contraceptives.

The results of fantasied birth control without planful action are, of course, greatly disappointing to many lower-class men and women, particularly women. As time goes on they are often forced into a more rational attitude by the pressures which four, five, or six children represent. Their contraceptive histories often show a progressive shift from just trusting to luck to sporadic use of less effective methods to a desperate insistence on regularity with the condom or the diaphragm. Such movements toward active rather than fantasied birth control often take place against the resistance, both overt and covert, of husbands who fail to understand why their wives are so demanding about "protection."

SENSE OF FAMILY PARTICIPATION AND CONTRACEPTION

Several characteristic attitudes toward one's family participation differentiate those who do and do not practice contraception effectively. By and large, the courtship periods of noneffective couples show much less planfulness about the couples' prospective life together. These people seem to just drift together; they give little indication of having planned a future together. Generally, there is little or no discussion of family planning and none of contraception, either during courtship or in the early period of the marriage. Almost none of the noneffectives in our sample had concerned themselves with the issue this early in the marital relationship, while over two-thirds of the effectives seem to have done so.

In the established family, there is a tendency (apparent in about two-thirds of our cases) among the noneffectives for the father to go his own way. His relation to the family is less close and less involved than that of the effective contraceptive practitioner. Often, the father prides himself on the number of children he has rather than the quality of his fatherliness; this latter is more important to the effective group of fathers.

The mothers often feel isolated from their husbands and tend to concentrate their attention on their children. Though they might prefer to have had fewer, the children become their main source of emotional gratification. Because they find it difficult to communicate with their husbands about common family goals, and about the necessity for limiting children in order to accomplish these goals, they often reconcile themselves to recurrent pregnancies. Because of their rather primitive relations to their children there is real consolation value in having another baby to mother intimately as a way of forgetting their larger family troubles.[5] Such a mother's attitude is often simply this: "Men don't understand, they can't be trusted, they won't discipline themselves in contraceptive use so I might as well enjoy myself with the children I must inevitably have."

SEXUAL RELATIONS AND CONTRACEPTIVE PRACTICE

Several attitudes toward the sexual relation in marriage strongly interfere with effective contraception. Such attitudes inhibit doing anything about contraception or, when the couple becomes desperate about the number of children they are having, operate as a strong force against which the couple must struggle in their effort to be rational about family limitation.

Among men, the most common interference is an attitude of impatience and demandingness (65 per cent of the noneffective women criticize their husbands on this score). Such men feel that having sexual relations is their central right in marriage, and that their wives are duty-bound to make themselves available on demand. They tend to think of sex as an eliminative function by which they get rid of tension and of their wives as a necessary vehicle for doing so. They tend to be rather hostile in their sexual attitudes, regarding what they do as a legitimate hostile act toward the woman, an act she must put up with. Given such attitudes, they tend to be highly impatient with the interferences which contraception represents, whether it be pausing to put on a condom or for the wife to insert the diaphragm. They are also inclined to reject condoms as interfering with pleasure—they tell us that "you don't go swimming with your boots on"—and their demandingness is such that they prefer to forget the consequence of no contraception.

Among women, two attitudes commonly limit contraceptive effectiveness. When, as is not uncommon, the woman believes that sex is strictly for the man, and rejects sexual experiences for herself, she may also feel that she has no responsibility for contraception—"he's the one that always wants it, let him worry about the protection." Such women (slightly over a third of our noneffectives) are unable to separate their emotional rejection of the sexual act from contraceptive action even though the latter represents an issue of their own well-being. Such women are unlikely to be receptive to any other method than the condom both because the man is responsible for its use and because their rejections of sexuality include a desire not to come into contact with semen.

A second interfering attitude (present in about one-fifth of our noneffectives) also involves an inability to separate sex and contraception, but in a context of greater acceptance of sexuality. These women value their sexual relations in a kind of desperate way—they are fond of saying that during intercourse they "go crazy." Intercourse is valued as an act which overwhelms the ego and allows the woman to forget herself. How, then,

---

[5] Rainwater, *et al.*, *op. cit.*

can she pause to see that something is done about contraception? For her, sex is not integrated into the rest of the marriage relation but is instead a kind of illicit activity within it— often the woman prefers to isolate sex from any family considerations, including family planning ones.

THE MYSTERY OF CONCEPTION

We find that among noneffective couples knowledge about how conception takes place is minimal and often quite incorrect at the most elementary level. The result is that many men and women cannot understand the effectiveness of any contraceptive other than the condom.

We find that while half of the effective women have a fairly clear idea of the separate contributions of sperm and ovum to conception, less than a quarter of the noneffectives have such understanding. At the opposite extreme, one-third of the noneffective women have practically no clear idea, correct or incorrect, of how conception takes place, compared to only 16 per cent of effective women. Men, on the other hand seem generally disinterested in the mechanisms of conception; half of both the effective and noneffective groups have no clear idea of what might be involved, and less than 10 per cent of each group speak of the sperm and ovum as separate entities. It seems apparent, however, that even those who have no clear idea do know that the man's ejaculation has something to do with impregnation, since these "know-nothing" respondents are usually strong supporters of the condom as the only effective contraceptive. On the other hand, three-fourths of the women who demonstrate sperm-ovum understanding either now use, or wish to use a feminine method such as the diaphragm.

One common incorrect belief (held by about a quarter of the men and women in our sample) ascribes the most important functions to the man —he lays the egg in the woman, she then nurtures and hatches it. Or, there may be a belief that the male and female both have "eggs" which must get together in order to start the "hatching" process. Here, too, mechanical ideas seem to dictate a mechanical barrier—there is not sufficient understanding of the complexity of the process to make chemical contraception seem reasonable.

CONTRACEPTIVE METHODS AND THEIR MEANINGS

We can only sketch here the main ideas which working-class people have about existing or proposed contraceptive methods of particular interest.

The condom, by far the most widely known and used method, appeals to those people for several reasons. Nearly half of our effective couples use condoms, and almost as many of the noneffectives have had experience with the method. As we have suggested, it makes the most sense in terms of the oversimplified ideas these people have about contraception. Further, it protects both parties from contact with the other's genitals, something which tends to be regarded as unpleasant and dangerous. The condom also goes well with the feeling that sex, even in marriage, is illicit—it is the method of the single man who wants to keep out of trouble in his philandering. The main drawback of the method is its interference with the man's pleasure—for men who fit the impatient, demanding pattern described above there is strong resistance to consistent use of the condom.

The diaphragm is very seldom used in this group; often women acquire diaphragms in clinics or from physicians but quickly give up using them. Slightly over 10 per cent of our sample use the diaphragm; an equal number have tried the method and given it up. Most of these women have strong resistances to handling their genitals as the diaphragm requires (we also know they less often use tampons than middle class women). The masturbatory taboo for these women easily extends to any such applicance as the diaphragm. Further, many of them feel that a woman shouldn't have to put something inside herself because it is dangerous, and they often fear that the diaphragm will be lost since they have a very poor understanding of their genitalia. The diaphragm and jelly method is seen as more complicated than the condom and therefore a greater interference with spontaneity. In general, the diaphragm requires greater rationality on the part of the user than most working-class women (or their husbands) are able to bring to bear.

Vaginal jellies and tablets are similarly not widely used in this group (there were only two users in the sample). First reactions to the idea tend to be negative—women tell us they "don't want all that mess inside me" or that they don't believe a nonmechanical method will work. On the other hand, the appeal of simplicity compared to the diaphragm is strong. In many ways, these methods seem most promising for those lower-class couples who cannot be expected to use the condom consistently.

The oral pill which has received a great deal of publicity recently is both appealing and frightening to this group. On the one hand, a method which does not require contact with the genitals or use at the time of intercourse is very attractive; on the other, a pill which must obviously affect the body chemistry worries these people a great deal—they resist taking potent drugs in general and usually only do so when very sick. They tend to fear being poisoned or "de-sexed" by oral contraceptives. Finally, the lack of rationality in the contraceptive area which most lower-class women show makes it quite unlikely that they would consistently take the pill every day as they must if it is to be effective.

CONCLUSION

Intensive qualitative study of the attitudes, values, and personality characteristics of working-class husbands and wives indicates that lack of ability to practice contraception effectively in line with family planning goals is conditioned by a variety of psychosocial factors which are part of the world views and personalities of working-class people. Conceptions of oneself as capable of successful planning in any area of life, as a participant in family life as spouse or parent, as a sexual partner with certain needs and preferences, all have a role in determining how effectively the individual is able to operate with contraceptives. Also, knowledge and feelings about conception seem to influence the individual's ability to understand particular contraceptive devices, and to predispose many working-class individuals to such simple mechanical devices as the condom.

Those who advise working-class couples on family planning and contraception must take such attitudes and orientations into account if they are to be successful in counseling or persuasive activities on an individual basis, in clinics or through the mass media.

Mortality Rates and Aggression Management Indices*

Peter B. Field

The cross-cultural method was originally developed to test behavioral hypotheses across a sample of primitive tribes. For example, Whiting and Child[1] tested the psychoanalytic hypothesis of projection of aggression by rating ethnographic reports on (1) the degree of anxiety the typical child in a tribe experiences during aggression training, and (2) the belief that illnesses are caused by the machinations of sorcerers. Whiting and Child included a wide variety of tribes from all over the world in their sample, counting each tribe as a single case and scoring each tribe on the pair of variables to be related.

They found a significant positive correlation between their two measures, and concluded that this finding supported the theory of projection of aggression.

While working in Professor Whiting's research group, the present author considered the possibility of testing psychoanalytic theories of psychosomatic diseases by applying the cross-cultural method. If primitive tribes could be reliably rated on deaths from various diseases, it should be possible to correlate mortality rates with Whiting's psychoanalytic indices. A preliminary survey, however, showed that information on causes of death in primitive tribes was not usually well enough reported to permit the construction of meaningful scales. Since the data on primitive tribes proved insufficient, a better-reported sample was adopted: states of the United States. While information on

* Peter B. Field, "Mortality Rates and Aggression Management Indices," *Journal of Health and Human Behavior*, 4 (Summer, 1963), 99–104.
[1] J. W. M. Whiting and I. L. Child, *Child Training and Personality* (New Haven, Conn.: Yale University Press, 1953), p. 276.

mortality rates in the United States is by no means perfect, it is much better than the information available on primitive tribes; at the same time, this kind of sample of course violates Whiting's assumption of cultural independence of each case.

The next research step was to score each state on a meaningful psychological variable, just as is done in the cross-cultural method. Many psychosomatic hypotheses center around unconscious aggressive impulses; since homicide and suicide rates are available for each state, perhaps a simple index of aggression management could be derived from these rates through cross-cultural statistical techniques. The ambitious goal of testing theories with such an index was soon modified in favor of the more realistic goal of determining what sorts of empirical correlations exist between mortality rates and aggression-management indices.

METHODS AND PROCEDURES

A technique for handling homicide-suicide rates to make them theoretically more relevant was suggested by an unpublished statistical research paper by David G. Beswick. Beswick observed that Whiting and Child present separate, independent ratings on the degree to which primitive tribes attribute responsibility for illness to the activities of sorcerers, and also on the degree to which illness is blamed on something the patient himself has done. Beswick reasoned that societies that both attribute the causation of illness to sorcerers and also deny any responsibility to the patient were showing the psychological mechanism of projection: they consistently blame others for illness. Similarly, tribes that deny that sorcerers cause illness

and believe that the patient himself caused his illness would be very low on projection and high on introjection. Beswick therefore suggested the statistical creation of a new psychological dimension of "projection-introjection" by subtracting the Whiting-Child ratings of patient-responsibility for illness from sorcerer-responsibility for illness. (Another possible combination—high on both patient-responsibility and sorcerer-responsibility—would produce a different dimension that might be called "human responsibility.") Beswick noted that this procedure was similar to factor rotation through an angle of 45 degrees. He produced two new orthogonal factors by transforming the two Whiting-Child ratings to standard scores (with a mean of zero and a standard deviation of one), and then subtracting the two groups of normalized ratings to produce the "projection-introjection" factor, and adding the two groups of normalized ratings to produce the "human responsibility" factor. He found that his derived "projection-introjection" factor was superior to the unmodified ratings in explaining certain cross-cultural variables.

In the present report, Beswick's technique was applied to the homicide and suicide rates in each state. Subtracting these rates produces a new dimension that might be called "aggression directed outward" versus "aggression directed inward." That is, a state with a high homicide rate and a low suicide rate (such as Mississippi) would be an "aggression-out" or "anger-out" state. A state with a high suicide rate and a low homicide rate (such as Wyoming) would be an "aggression-in" or "anger-in" state. This factor might be theoretically relevant to Funkenstein's psychophysiological anger-in versus anger-out dimension.[2]

If we assume, with Henry and Short,[3] that suicide and homicide are comparable acts of aggression, differing mainly in whether the aggression is turned in or out, then we might be justified in adding together homicide and suicide rates to get a new measure that might be loosely labeled "general aggressiveness." States with a high homicide rate and a high suicide rate (such as Nevada) would be high in general aggression, while states with little homicide or suicide (such as Rhode Island) would have little of this general surface aggression. This second derived factor might be theoretically relevant to the psychoanalytic theory of the expression of aggressive impulses.

In computing these new factors, raw homicide and suicide rates were not used. Instead, age-adjusted homicide and suicide rates for both sexes in the years 1949–1951 were used,[4] and these rates were normalized by conversion to standard scores before they were added or subtracted.

The resulting factors were then correlated with the leading causes of death in the United States. These were age-adjusted mortality rates, by state of residence of the deceased person, for both sexes, including whites and nonwhites, for the years 1949–1951.[5] A few causes of death were excluded, since in some disease there were not enough deaths to provide a stable base for calculating age-adjusted rates, or since some reports provided only slightly different data (e.g. total death rate for tuberculosis and death rates for different forms of tuberculosis).

Table 1 shows tetrachoric correlation coefficients between the two aggression-management factors and fifty leading causes of death for the forty-eight continental states and the District of Columbia. The fourfold tables underlying each correlation coefficient were evaluated for statistical significance by Chi-square corrected for continuity with one degree of freedom.

The first column of Table 1 represents correlations of mortality rate with the homicide-minus-suicide ("anger-out") dimension; homicide of course correlates highly with this factor (0.90), and suicide of course correlates negatively (−0.72). Causes of death are listed in order of the magnitude of their correlation with this column. The second column represents correlations of mortality rate with the homicide-plus-suicide ("general aggression") factor. Both homicide and suicide correlate positively with this factor (0.67 and 0.35 respectively), but not as highly as they correlate with the first factor; the shrinkage of these correlations probably reflects the empirical negative correlation (tetrachoric $r = -0.31$ between homicide and suicide rates in these data. The two derived factors ("anger-out" and "general aggression") were designed statistically to be independent, and empirically the Pearson product-moment correlation between the two is 0.01; but when dichotomized, as they were in computing all the correlations in Table 1

---

[2] D. H. Funkenstein, S. H. King, and M. E. Drolette, *Mastery of Stress* (Cambridge, Mass.: Harvard University Press, 1957).

[3] A. F. Henry and J. F. Short, Jr., *Suicide and Homicide* (New York: The Free Press of Glencoe, Inc., 1954).

[4] *Vital Statistics: Special Reports*, "Death Rates for Selected Causes by Age, Color, and Sex: United States and Each State, 1949–51." Vol. 49, Nos. 1–62, 1958–59, National Office of Vital Statistics, Dept. H.E.W., P.H.S.

[5] *Ibid.*

TABLE 1. Tetrachoric Correlation Coefficients Between Age-Adjusted Mortality Rates (1949–1951, Both Sexes), and (a) Difference and (b) Sum of Normalized Age-Adjusted Homicide and Suicide Rates

	Columns:			Columns:	
	(a)	(b)		(a)	(b)
	Homicide minus suicide	Homicide plus suicide		Homicide minus suicide	Homicide plus suicide
1. Homicide	0.90	0.67	25. Bronchitis	0.35	0.22
2. Hypertension with heart disease	0.87	0.22	26. Diseases of heart	0.22	−0.16
3. Tuberculosis, all forms	0.84	0.57	27. Accidents, except motor vehicle accidents	0.16	0.62
4. Chronic and unspecified nephritis and other renal sclerosis	0.84	0.22	28. Malignant neoplasm of respiratory system	0.16	0.03
5. All causes	0.81	0.57	29. Benign neoplasms and neoplasms of unspecified nature	0.10	0.10
6. Meningitis, except meningococcal and tuberculosis	0.80	0.62	30. Motor vehicle accidents	0.09	0.67
7. Syphilis and its sequelae	0.80	0.67	31. Cirrhosis of liver	0.09	−0.04
8. Influenza and pneumonia (except pneumonia of newborn)	0.76	0.67	32. Appendicitis	0.04	0.29
9. Gastritis, enteritis, duodenitis, colitis (except diarrhea of newborn)	0.76	0.76	33. Rheumatic fever	0.04	0.41
10. Hypertension without mention of heart	0.76	0.22	34. Scarlet fever and streptococcal sore throat	−0.04	0.22
11. Malignant neoplasms of genital organs	0.76	0.22	35. Diabetes mellitus	−0.09	−0.72
12. Dysentery, all forms	0.63	0.63	36. Anemias	−0.09	−0.57
13. Other diseases of heart (residual category)	0.63	0.40	37. Malignant neoplasms of urinary organs	−0.10	−0.35
14. Malignant neoplasms of buccal cavity and pharynx	0.63	−0.22	38. Malignant neoplasms, including neoplasms of lymphatic and hematopoietic tissues	−0.16	−0.46
15. Acute nephritis and nephritis with edema, including nephrosis	0.63	0.52	39. Malignant neoplasm of digestive organs and peritoneum, not specified as secondary	−0.22	−0.57
16. Malignant neoplasms of other and unspecified sites (residual category)	0.62	0.40	40. Arteriosclerotic heart disease, including coronary disease	−0.22	−0.22
17. Hernia and intestinal obstruction	0.52	0.28	41. Other diseases of circulatory system (residual category)	−0.22	0.35
18. Nonrheumatic chronic endocarditis and other myocardial degeneration	0.46	0.22	42. General arteriosclerosis	−0.28	−0.16
19. Major cardiovascular-renal disease	0.46	0.03	43. Chronic rheumatic heart disease	−0.28	−0.16
20. Meningococcal infections	0.41	0.63	44. Malignant neoplasm of breast (female)	−0.35	−0.57
21. Vascular lesions affecting central nervous system	0.35	0.03	45. Ulcer of stomach and duodenum	−0.46	−0.10
22. Symptoms, senility, and ill-defined conditions	0.35	0.47	46. Lymphosarcoma and other neoplasms of lymphatic and hematopoietic tissues	−0.52	−0.28
23. Diseases of the cardiovascular system	0.35	−0.09	47. Acute poliomyelitis	−0.57	−0.62
			48. Congenital malformations	−0.57	−0.35
24. Hyperplasia of prostate (males)	0.35	0.10	49. Suicide	−0.72	0.35
			50. Leukemia and aleukemia	−0.88	−0.52

= ±0.62, p < 0.01.
= ±0.52 and ±0.57, p < 0.05.
= ±0.47, p=not significant at 0.05 level.
Note: All correlations are listed in order of their degree of relationship with column (a), and are each based on an N of 49 (48 continental states plus District of Columbia).

their correlation is 0.28 (not significant at the 0.05 level).

Both factors in Table 1 correlate highly and significantly with death rates from all causes (Item 5); consequently the positive correlations between the aggression factors and specific diseases may be spuriously inflated because of this correlation, while the negative correlations may be spuriously low for the same reason.

Items 2 and 10 (hypertension with and without mention of heart) correlate highly with the "anger-out" factor, but not significantly with the "general aggression" factor. This is consistent with Funkenstein's theory of the relationship between the outward expression of anger and a rise in blood pressure mediated through the release of norepinephrine,[6] and with some reports concerning hostility in patients with hypertension.[7] Also positively correlated with this factor are a number of infectious diseases such as tuberculosis, syphilis, and influenza; this may reflect a correlated third factor, such as low income, poor housing, and poor sanitation.

Negatively correlated with the "anger-out" factor are Items 46 and 50, leukemia, aleukemia, lymphosarcoma, and other neoplasms of lymphatic and hematopoietic tissues. If we assume with Funkenstein *et al.* that anger-in is the pattern found in depression, then this result is consistent with a series of papers by Greene[8, 9] reporting that patients with leukemias and lymphomas have experienced loss, separation, or the threat of separation, and feelings of "sadness and hopelessness" prior to disease onset. Le Shan[10] suggests that a similar psychological pattern is implicated in other types of cancer as well. He reports that time-series correlations between the cancer mortality rate and the suicide mortality rate in the United States tends to be positive, although in younger age groups some negative correlations are found. The present results, however, indicate a good deal of variability from one type of cancer to another; while leukemias and lymphatic cancers and possibly breast cancer fall at the "anger-in" pole, cancers of the genital organs, buccal cavity, and pharynx fall at the "anger-out" pole, and other types fall between these extremes.

Gastric and duodenal ulcers show a nearly signifiant correlation with the "anger-in" pole. Funkenstein *et al.*[11] have found that physiological reactions to stress are similar in individuals who show "anger-in" and those who show a "severe-anxiety" pattern. This correlation therefore may be consistent with the evidence relating fear or anxiety to peptic

---

[6] D. H. Funkenstein *et al.*, *op. cit.*

[7] S. M. Kaplan, L. A. Gottschalk, E. B. Magliocco, D. D. Rohovit, and W. D. Ross, "Hostility in Verbal Productions and Hypnotic Dreams of Hypertensive Patients: Studies of Groups and Individuals," *Psychosomatic Medicine*, XXIII (1961), 311–22.

[8] W. A. Greene, Jr., "Role of a Vicarious Object in the Adaptation to Object Loss: I. Use of a Vicarious Object as a Means of Adjustment to Separation from a Significant Person," *Psychosomatic Medicine*, XX (1958), 344–50.

[9] W. A. Greene, Jr., L. E. Young, and S. N. Swisher, "Psychological Factors and Reticuloendothelial Disease. II. Observations on a Group of Women with Lymphomas and Leukemias," *Psychosomatic Medicine*, XVIII (1956), 284–303.

[10] L. Le Shan, "Cancer Mortality Rate: Some Statistical Evidence of the Effect of Psychological Factors," *AMA Archives of General Psychiatry*, V (1962), 333–35.

[11] Funkenstein *et al.*, *op. cit.*

ulcers. Brady[12] has shown that monkeys on a shock-avoidance schedule develop gastric ulcers, and Sawrey and Weisz[13] have found similar results in hungry rats who are prevented from reaching food by a shock grid. Conger *et al.*[14] have reported that isolation during stress and during rearing increases susceptibility to gastric ulcers in rats, and isolation seems to be correlated with anger-in (suicide) in humans.[15]

Deaths from congenital malformations also correlate highly with the "anger-in" pole, but this relationship is difficult to understand. A similar correlation appears for deaths from acute poliomyelitis. This may be an indirect relationship, reflecting a correlation between homicide rates, poor sanitation, and poor housing. In states with high homicide rates there may have been many subclinical immunizing cases of poliomyelitis; and therefore individuals in states with little homicide may show higher poliomyelitis mortality because they have not had these mild immunizing infections.

The second column shows correlations of mortality rates with the homicide-plus-suicide or "general aggression" factor. One possible interpretation of this factor would be in terms of superego strength: superego controls on expression of aggression

might be weak where there is a good deal of surface aggression, and strong where there is little surface aggression. An alternative interpretation, however, must also be considered: that the degree of general aggression reflects in part the strength of aggressive drives, not the strength of control of the drives. This alternative interpretation would be more consistent with Henry and Short's[16] analysis of homicide and suicide rates as aggressive responses to varying degrees of frustration. The first (or "superego") interpretation, moreover, is not entirely consistent with the results of Wright,[17] who found that acts of aggression in folktales tended to be *more* intense in tribes that were anxious about aggression than in tribes with little anxiety about aggression; since homicide and suicide are both examples of Wright's intense forms of aggression they might indicate repression and displacement of aggression rather than free expression and a weak superego.

Items 27 and 30 show that both motor vehicle accidents and other kinds of accidents correlate significantly with the "general aggression" factor, but neither correlates significantly with the "anger-out" factor. This result supports a previous finding by Porterfield,[18] who showed that states with high rates of motor vehicle accident deaths also have high death rates from homicide and suicide. The present result extends this finding to accidents other than motor

---

12 J. V. Brady, "Ulcers in 'Executive' Monkeys," *Scientific American*, CIC (3) (1958), 95–104.

13 W. L. Sawrey and J. D. Weisz, "An Experimental Method of Producing Gastric Ulcers," *Journal of Comparative and Physiological Psychology*, XLIX (1956), 269–70.

14 J. J. Conger, W. L. Sawrey, and E. S. Turrell, "The Role of Social Experience in the Production of Gastric Ulcers in Hooded Rats Placed in a Conflict Situation," *Journal of Abnormal and Social Psychology*, LVII (1958), 214–20.

15 Henry and Short, *op. cit.*

16 Henry and Short, *op. cit.*

17 G. O. Wright, "Projection and Displacement: A Cross-cultural Study of Folk-tale Aggression," *Journal of Abnormal and Social Psychology*, XLIX (1954), 523–28.

18 A. L. Porterfield, "Traffic Fatalities, Suicide, and Homicide," *American Sociological Review*, XXV (1960), 897–901.

602   Attitudes, Values, and Beliefs

vehicle accidents, and is consistent with the possibility that fatal accidents may in part be expressions of aggressive impulses. This finding also tends to support the construct validity of this factor as a "general aggression" factor.

The pattern of correlation with this "general aggression" factor shows a number of similarities to the correlations with the "anger-out" factor. For example, a number of infectious and inflammatory diseases correlate positively with this factor, while acute poliomyelitis, leukemia and aleukemia, and breast cancer correlate negatively with it. Diabetes mellitus and anemias, however, are significantly related to absence of general surface aggression, while they are uncorrelated with the "anger-in versus anger-out" factor.

A number of diseases fail to show any important correlation with either factor. These include vascular lesions of the central nervous system, respiratory neoplasms, heart diseases, scarlet fever and streptococcal sore throat, cirrhosis of the liver, and others. An estimate of the prevalence of alcoholism in each state,[19] based on cirrhosis of the liver mortality, also failed to correlate significantly with either factor (tetrachoric $r = 0.10$ and -0.10 for the first and second factors respectively).

There are a number of cautions that must be observed in interpreting these data. Certainly causation cannot safely be inferred from a simple correlation without other evidence. Some of the correlations presented, in fact, have been interpreted as the effects of mutual correlations with other causes,

such as poor sanitation. It is entirely possible that most or all of the correlations in Table 1 are in fact merely reflections of quite different variables. The consistencies noted between these correlations and certain psychosomatic hypotheses are only consistencies and not claims of direct supporting evidence. These correlations, moreover, are not relationships across individuals but only relationships across political units. It might be true that these correlations have some meaning at the individual level, but the present data do not establish this.

It would be desirable to determine whether these findings could be replicated with other samples (such as other nations, or other years in the United States), or in subgroups within the present sample (such as within different races, ages, sexes, and socioeconomic strata). A time-series correlation approach might easily produce different results, since year-to-year shifts in psychological variables probably have different implications for disease than chronic maintenance of a variable at a certain level.

One final important qualification on these relationships is the possible nonindependence of cases, which may cast some doubt on their level of statistical significance. The lack of cultural independence of these cases has been previously mentioned, but there is also a lack of geographical independence. Each state is geographically correlated with other states and with broader regions of the country. Perhaps it is not really justified to count each southern state (for example) as an independent "anger-out" unit; perhaps they simply represent a single geographical region in which because of common historical factors all tend to express anger outwardly rather than inward-

19 M. Keller and V. Efron, "The Prevalence of Alcoholism," *Quarterly Journal of Studies on Alcohol*, XVI (1955), 619–44.

ly. While computing these correlations it became apparent that there were in fact very important regional variations in both the aggression indices and the mortality rates. This often appeared to inflate many of the correlations, but may have lowered some. Because of this lack of geographical independence, the rank-order of a correlation with each factor may be more meaningful than its absolute magnitude or statistical significance.

SUMMARY

Mortality rates for the fifty leading causes of death in the United States were correlated with two indices of aggression management derived statistically from homicide and suicide rates. The results indicated (in part) that the "anger-out" dimension appeared to correlate with hypertension and several infectious diseases, while "anger-in" appeared to be related to leukemia and aleukemia, lymphatic neoplasms, acute poliomyelitis, and possibly gastric and duodenal ulcers. The "general aggression" dimension correlated positively with mortality from motor vehicle accidents and also with other accidents, with certain infectious diseases, and negatively with diabetes mellitus, anemias, breast neoplasm, acute poliomyelitis, and other diseases. It was emphasized that correlation does not necessarily imply causation, and other qualifications on interpretation of these correlations were noted.

Life-Cycle, Career Pattern, and the Decision to Move*

Gerald R. Leslie and Arthur H. Richardson

The analysis of urban residential mobility is not new.[1] As a phenome-

---

* Gerald R. Leslie and Arthur H. Richardson, "Life-Cycle, Career Pattern, and the Decision to Move," *American Sociological Review*, 26 (December, 1961), 894–902.
[1] Among the earlier studies are William Albig, "The Mobility of Urban Population," *Social Forces*, XI (March, 1933), 351–67; Donald O. Cowgill, "Residential Mobility of an Urban Population," Master's Thesis, Washington University, St. Louis, 1936; Charles E. Lively, "Spatial and Occupational Changes of Particular Significance to the Student of Population Mobility," *Social Forces*, XV (March, 1937), 351–55; Andrew W. Lind, *A Study of Mo-*

non involving peculiar convergence of social structure with demographic and social psychological influence, however, it is of broad theoretical significance and of considerable research interest.[2] As "urban residential mobility," we shall treat here, not upward social mobility nor urban migration rates, but the process whereby families and individuals change their places of residence. Explanation will be sought in two contrasting approaches—life-cycle and career pattern—for the decision to move.

LIFE-CYCLE ANALYSIS

It is reasonably well established that residential mobility is high among young families and declines with increased age of the household head.[3] In 1950, the mobility rate was twice as high in families where the head was under 35 years of age as in those where he was from 35–44 years old and five times higher than where he had reached age 65.[4] The high

---

bility of Population in Seattle (Seattle: The University of Washington Publications in Social Sciences, 3, October, 1925); and Bessie A. McClenahan, *The Changing Urban Neighborhood* (Los Angeles: The University of Southern California, 1929).

[2] Sidney Goldstein, *Patterns of Mobility, 1910–1950; The Norristown Study* (Philadelphia: University of Pennsylvania Press, 1958); Arthur H. Richardson, "The Prediction of Household Mobility from an Urban Subdivision," Ph.D. Dissertation, Purdue University, 1958; and Peter H. Rossi, *Why Families Move: A Study in the Social Psychology of Urban Residential Mobility* (New York: The Free Press of Glencoe, Inc. 1955).

[3] Paul C. Glick, *American Families* (New York: John Wiley and Sons, Inc., 1957), p. 89. Data from 1950 Census of Population, Vol. IV, Special Reports, Part II, chap. A, General Characteristics of Families, Table 15.

[4] Glick, *op. cit.*

mobility rates for young persons presumably reflect new marriages, families expanding with the birth of children, and moves associated with the husband's employment. Each of these factors operates with less force at older ages. Thus, viewed in terms of migration rates, residential mobility appears to be associated with the expansion stage of the family life-cycle.

A major attempt to explain individual household mobility in terms of life-cycle appeared in Rossi's, *Why Families Move.*[5] Rossi sampled four Philadelphia census tracts, selected to represent areas of high and low mobility rates and high and low socio-economic status, to: (1) illustrate the application of modern survey research to the study of residential mobility; and (2) draw generalizations concerning the social psychology of residential mobility.[6] Rossi affirmed that his study design could not serve both aims with equal efficiency and emphasized the application of survey research to the discovery of causal factors in residential mobility. However, he concluded that his "empirical generalizations are so strongly supported in the data that they are almost certain to hold up in subsequent researches."[7]

Rossi's analysis focused upon mobility patterns in each of the four residential areas, upon household mobility, and upon the factors entering into the individual decisions to move. Household mobility was defined in terms of desires and plans for moving: mobile households were considered to be those who were anxious to move and who planned to do so while stable households were defined as those who expressed no inclination

[5] *Op. cit.*
[6] *Ibid.*, p. 4.
[7] *Ibid.*

o move.[8] The major characteristics that were found to differentiate mobile from stable households were variables closely related to the family life-cycle. Thus, large families were more prone to move than were small ones, the younger the household head, the more likely the family was to move, and renters—particularly those who desired to own—were more likely to move than were owners.[9] Mobile households also differed from stable ones in the frequency of the complaints they expressed about the dwelling and the neighborhood.[10] Two arbitrary indexes, the Mobility Potential Index (composed of age, household size, and tenure preference) and the Complaints Index, were found to correlate well with mobility inclinations but not too highly with one another. The two indexes, combined, permitted approximately 75 per cent accuracy in the prediction of mobility inclinations.[11]

The decision to move was seen as a function of various "pushes" from the original dwelling and various "pulls" toward the new one.[12] About one-fourth of the moves were involuntary —the result of evictions and destructions, or accompaniments of other decisions such as to marry, to divorce, or to take a job in a distant location. Among the voluntary moves, dissatisfaction with the amount of space in the dwelling was the most important factor; then came dissatisfaction with the neighborhood and the costs associated with the present dwelling. The most important feature of the new dwelling sought was its size. When two dwellings of equal size were available, the cheaper one generally was chosen.

Rossi concluded that the major function of residential mobility is to enable families to "adjust their housing to the housing needs that are generated by the shifts in family composition that accompany life-cycle changes."[13]

CAREER PATTERN ANALYSIS

Several early studies showed a general association between migration and upward vertical mobility.[14] These early works failed to compare the amount of upward mobility experienced by migrants and nonmigrants and were succeeded, in a sense, by Hobbs' analysis of migration in an economically depressed region. He found that the relationship held even when a control group was used.[15] However, Hobbs' conclusion that

---

[8] The correspondence between moving inclinations and actual mobility experience was tested by returning to the 924 households eight months after the initial interviews to see whether the dwellings were still occupied by the original respondents. The respondents had been asked to predict their own behavior over a ten-month period. Of those who definitely planned to remain in their present homes, 96 per cent did so. Eighty per cent of those definitely planning to move did so, and of those who gave themselves an even chance to move or stay, 26 per cent moved. This evidence was regarded as justifying the use of mobility intentions to stand for actual mobility behavior. *Ibid.*, pp. 105–7.

[9] *Ibid.*, pp. 68–71.
[10] *Ibid.*, pp. 80–85.
[11] *Ibid.*, p. 94.
[12] *Ibid.*, pp. 8–9.

[13] *Ibid.*, p. 9.
[14] C. J. Galpin, *Analysis of Migration of Population of and from Farms* (U.S. Department of Agriculture, Bureau of Agricultural Economics, Washington, D.C., 1927); Carle C. Zimmerman, "The Migration to Towns and Cities, II," *American Journal of Sociology*, XXX (September, 1927), 237–41.
[15] Albert H. Hobbs, *Differentials in Internal Migration*, Ph.D. Dissertation, The University of Pennsylvania, 1942.

"migrants are superior to nonmigrants in those characteristics necessary for socioeconomic occupational success,"[16] has not been systematically tested in further research. Instead the emphasis shifted toward use of residential mobility as a dependent variable.

The influence of individual career patterns, involving upward vertical mobility, upon residential mobility received attention in William H. Whyte's analysis of Park Forest, Illinois. Whyte pictured Park Forest and, by implication, other residential suburbs as the dwelling areas of young lower-echelon management officials in commerce and industry. He stressed the homogeneity of backgrounds, present positions, and tastes of suburbanites, and the inevitability of their residential mobility with occupational advancement.[17] The idea of a distinctive suburban pattern also received support from Jaco and Belknap in their analysis of a new family form emerging in the urban fringe.[18]

Analysis of one Lafayette, Indiana, residential subdivision showed that it did not conform completely to Whyte's description. Partridge did find, in North Park, a young management group who had definite expectations of both social and geographical mobility, but she also found residential mobility not associated with occupational advancement. Some 80 per cent of North Park residents were not Whyte's upwardly mobile management group.[19] She concluded that the superficial homogeneity found among North Park residents in age, income, and life-style concealed fundamental differences in the career patterns that male residents of the area follow.

Since the data to be reported in the next section of this paper were gathered, several studies have appeared that bear upon the influence of career pattern upon residential mobility, and that offer some prospect of reconciling Whyte's and Partridge's divergent findings. Mowrer, studying Chicago suburbs, found evidence of a suburban cycle in which multiple life styles and family forms follow upon the migration of young family units of husband, wife, and one or more children to the suburbs.[20] He concluded that suburban patterns are not homogeneous but that "the cycle of suburban life is in microcosm the cycle from the rural to the urban both with respect to the family relationship and community organization."[21]

Other studies have suggested selective migration to the suburbs as a function of factors that might or might not be directly linked to oc-

---

16 *Ibid.*, p. 87.

17 The substance of this argument was later included in William H. Whyte, Jr., *The Organization Man* (Garden City: Doubleday Anchor Books, 1957).

18 E. Gartly Jaco and Ivan Belknap, "Is a New Family Form Emerging in the Urban Fringe?" *American Sociological Review*, XVIII (October, 1953), 551–57.

19 Janice Partridge, "A Descriptive Analysis of the Social Characteristics of Residents of a Prefabricated Housing Subdivision," Master's Thesis, Purdue University, August, 1956. North Park residents ran the gamut of occupations found in small mid-Western cities. They included young executives, small-businessmen, civil servants, white-collar workers, and skilled and semiskilled workers. This does not mean, of course, that Park Forest was not the homogeneous community that Whyte found it to be. It does mean that Whyte's model cannot be uncritically generalized to all residential suburbs.

20 Ernest R. Mowrer, "The Family in Suburbia," in *The Suburban Community*, ed. William A. Dobriner (New York: G. P. Putnam's Sons, 1958), pp. 147–64.

21 *Ibid.*, p. 163.

cupational advancement and upward social mobility. Fava, in a study of urban and suburban residents in the New York City area, found evidence for a selective migration to the suburbs "on the basis of nonrational elements of habit, belief, feelings, and experience," and concluded that the suburbs may attract those who are willing to be neighborly.[22]

The idea of an association between life-style and suburban migration was carried further by Bell.[23] He postulated three general preference patterns for life-styles in modern society: (1) a high valuation on family living (familism); (2) upward vertical mobility (career); and (3) striving for a high standard of living in the present (consumership). He hypothesized that persons moving to the suburbs are principally those who have chosen familism over either career or consumership and presented supporting data from two interview studies in the Chicago area. Thirty-one per cent of his moves involved pure familism with no other reason being given, and familism entered into the decision to move in 83 per cent of the cases. Ten per cent of the cases were cited as pure examples of the consumership pattern, and 43 per cent gave consumership along with other reasons. Only 10 per cent had upward mobility aspirations involved in their moves, while 20 per cent said that the husband's job was in some way a factor in the move. Bell recognized that his findings might not hold for different types of suburbs and recommended study of more neighborhoods of many different types.[24]

Bell's emphasis upon the importance of familism in residential mobility and his conclusion concerning the small influence of the occupational pattern are at variance with our thesis here.[25] Unfortunately, Bell's data were not available to us at the time the Vinton Homes survey was designed, and we cannot present a test of the relative influence upon household mobility of life cycle, career pattern, familism and consumership. Instead, we seek adequate explanation for residential mobility in a combination of life cycle and career pattern variables and propose a model for use in further research.

THE VINTON HOMES SURVEY

The Vinton Homes survey applied Rossi's methodology to analysis of residential mobility in a relatively new urban subdivision. Vinton Homes is an area of 402 two- and three-bedroom single houses in Lafayette, Indiana. In March, 1957, the area was approximately six years old. The houses currently range in value from just over ten to twenty thousand dollars. Lafayette is a diversified industrial city of approximately 40,000 population. The Purdue University community of West Lafayette is

---

[22] Sylvia F. Fava, "Contrasts in Neighboring: New York City and a Suburban County," in William A. Dobriner, editor, *ibid.*, pp. 122–31.

[23] Wendell Bell, "Social Choice, Life Styles, and Suburban Residence," in William A. Dobriner, editor, *ibid.*, pp. 225–47.

[24] *Ibid.*, p. 238.

[25] A very recent article points out that explanations of occupational residence patterns have stressed either occupational differences in resources or in style of life. Its authors conclude that residential association is a function of similarity in rank and reflects education more directly than income. See Arnold S. Feldman and Charles Tilly, "The Interaction of Social and Physical Space," *American Sociological Review*, XXV (December, 1960), 877–84.

located across the Wabash River and is a separate municipality.

A 50 per cent probability sample of the households was interviewed. The three life-cycle items comprising Rossi's Mobility Potential Index and five items reflecting the influence of the career pattern were included in the interview schedule. These eight items available for predicting residential mobility were: (1) age of the household head; (2) household size; (3) tenure status;[26] (4) years of formal education completed by the household head; (5) the respondent's estimate of his social class position compared with that of his neighbors;[27] (6) the respondent's estimate of his prospects for upward social mobility;[28] (7) the respondent's attitude toward his present dwelling; and (8) the respondent's attitude toward his present neighborhood.[29]

To select items for inclusion in a predictive equation, the eight variables were intercorrelated and were also correlated with stated mobility intentions.[30] The resulting point correlations are shown in Table 1. A multiple correlation regression design was then formulated for processing through a datatron computer. The correlation of all eight variables to mobility intentions was found to be 0.76.

Table 2 represents the square of the correlations of stated mobility intentions to succeeding independent variables along a path of greatest increments. The path started with X_8, social mobility expectations; then X_7, perceived class differences; then X_4, house attitude; and finally X_6, education. The selection of variables by the computer stopped there, for the addition of others would have done nothing to increase the correlation with stated mobility intentions.[31]

A predictive equation based upon these correlations was then developed.[32] For each household appropriate variable data were inserted into the equation. The values assigned to stated mobility intentions were 0.00 if there was no intention to move during the year and 1.00 if there was intention to move during the period. The predicted values for individual households ranged from 0.22 to 2.12. The 0.05 level of sig-

---

[26] Whereas Rossi had asked whether respondents preferred to own or rent, tenure status in the Vinton Homes study referred to whether the respondents actually owned or rented.

[27] Each respondent was asked to place himself and then to place most of his neighbors into one of four classes: upper, middle, working, or lower. The ratings "above," "same as," and "below" neighbors then were used.

[28] Respondents were asked to indicate the reasons why they might move from their present dwellings. These reasons were then probed to see whether they involved any significant increases in income or other occupational advancement.

[29] Both "dwelling" and "neighborhood" attitudes were assessed by means of Likert-Type items providing five alternatives ranging from "excellent" to "unsatisfactory."

[30] Like Rossi, we used stated mobility intentions (for one year) to rep-resent household mobility. We reinter-viewed our respondents ten months after the initial contact to check the correspondence between mobility intentions and actual mobility experience. Of forty-seven households predicting mobility within a year, forty actually moved within ten months. Of 154 households not planning to move, only four did so (Phi coefficient, 0.84).

[31] The Summerfield-Lubin method was used to test each succeeding increment. See A. Summerfield, and A. Lubin, "A Square Root Method of Selecting A Minimum Set of Variables in Multiple Regression," *Psychometrika* XVI (September, 1951), 271–84.

[32] $Y^1 = 0.10X_4 + 0.06X_6 + 0.46X_7 + 0.42X_8$.

TABLE 1. Intercorrelations of Eight Mobility Variables and Their Correlation with Stated Mobility Intentions, 201 Households, Lafayette, Indiana

	Age	Household size	Ownership	House attitude	Subdivision attitude	Education	Perceived class differences	Social mobility expectations	Stated mobility intentions
Age	—	0.10	0.02	0.07	0.05	0.10	0.20	0.18	0.17
Household size		—	0.06	0.11	0.08	0.10	0.13	0.06	0.02
Ownership			—	0.02	0.05	0.01	0.10	0.06	0.01
House-attitude				—	0.54	0.32	0.34	0.36	0.45
Subdivision attitude					—	0.30	0.16	0.16	0.25
Education						—	0.47	0.48	0.52
Perceived class differences							—	0.54	0.62
Social mobility expectations								—	0.64
Stated mobility intentions									—

nificance was used to test the differences between the predicted and actual values. For 182 of the 201 households the differences between predicted and actual values were not significant. With a sample of this size, ten households would be expected to fall outside these limits purely by chance.

For 19 of the 201 households, the equation failed to predict the respondent's mobility intentions. In 17 of the 19, however, the equation did predict the actual mobility experience. Apparently, in this instance, the discrepancy between stated mobility intentions and actual mobility experience is considerably greater than the error in predicting mobility from the equation.

TABLE 2. Multiple Correlations of Eight Variables to Stated Mobility Intentions along the Path of Greatest Increments, 201 Households, Lafayette, Indiana

i	X_1	X_2	X_3	X_4	X_5	X_6	X_7	X_8
r^2_{yi}	0.0303	0.0006	0.0001	0.2043	0.0613	0.2728	0.3861	0.4040
$R^2_{y\ 0.8i}$	0.4075	0.4042	0.4047	0.4609	0.4261	0.4646	0.5144	—
$R^2_{y\ 0.78i}$	0.5148	0.5172	0.5174	0.5466	0.5282	0.5392	—	—
$R^2_{y\ 0.478i}$	0.5472	0.5502	0.5492	—	0.5474	0.5648	—	—
$R^2_{y\ 0.4678i}$	—not obtained—			—	0.5648	—	—	—

y = stated mobility intentions
X_1 = age of head of household
X_2 = household size
X_3 = owning or renting status
X_4 = house attitude
X_5 = subdivision attitude
X_6 = number of years of education
X_7 = perceived class differences
X_8 = social mobility expectations

Two things stood out at this point. First, a high degree of predictive accuracy had been achieved; and, second, the variables that had proved useful in making the predictions were not life-cycle variables. The correlations of age, household size, and tenure status with mobility intentions were all quite low (see Table 1), while the correlations of social mobility expectations, perceived class differences, education, and house attitude with mobility intentions were substantial. Consequently, further exploration of the link between career pattern and residential mobility was suggested.

We looked to comprehensive job history data and to data on the respondents' present occupations for clues. In some instances the data showed obvious career mobility through promotions, salary increases, and transfers extending over periods of ten or more years. Such respondents generally replied affirmatively to the question whether further upward mobility was anticipated. Other respondents had held the same position for many years and did not anticipate upward mobility. With these cases as guides all respondents were classified into potentially mobile and nonmobile groups. Though this classification occasionally resulted in persons who followed superficially similar occupations being placed in different categories, an independent ranking of the respondents verified the reliability of the procedure. Forty-seven of the 201 household heads were classified as having significant upward mobility potential. They came entirely from professional, business, and upper white-collar ranks. The 154 household heads who were classified as nonsocially mobile came from the lower white-collar, skilled, and semiskilled ranks.[33]

When the residential mobility intentions of the 201 households were related to their upward social mobility potential, a striking pattern emerged. The pattern is shown in Table 3. Forty-four of the forty-seven upwardly mobile households planned to move within the year. Only 20 of the 154 non-upwardly mobile households planned to do so.[34] Of forty-four households who moved during the year, forty-two were judged to

TABLE 3. Upward Mobility Potential and Residential Mobility Intentions over a One-Year Period, 201 Households, Lafayette, Indiana

	Upward mobility potential	No upward mobility potential
Residential mobility intentions	44	20
No residential mobility intentions	3	144

have done so as part of the process of upward social mobility and only two moves occurred independently of upward mobility.

---

[33] As may be apparent from the text, persons presently in the lower ranks were never classified as potentially mobile, while some upper white-collar and business people were classified as nonmobile.

[34] When actual mobility experience over the next ten months was added to the picture, still another relationship was discovered. When households fail to predict their mobility behavior correctly, the direction of the error is a function of the household's upward mobility potential. Among upwardly mobile households the tendency is to underestimate the chances for residential mobility, whereas non-upwardly mobile respondents overestimate the opportunities for residential mobility.

These data are not completely consistent with those presented by Bell for two Chicago suburbs where he found the influence of upward mobility upon the suburban move to be almost negligible.[35] Unfortunately, Bell's data were not available to us at the time and we made no effort to assess the relative influence of familism and career pattern in our sample. The association between upward mobility and residential mobility was so striking, however, that we are inclined to believe that the samples are from different populations. We have consistently described Vinton Homes as a residential subdivision rather than as a suburb because it is located within the corporate limits of a small city and may not involve the same selective migration that occurs in the commuter suburbs of larger metropolitan centers.

It seemed apparent that in Vinton Homes upward social mobility far outweighed all other considerations in producing residential mobility. While at first glance these findings might be interpreted as refutation of Rossi's conclusions concerning the importance of life-cycle variables in residential mobility, there is no necessary inconsistency between the findings of the two studies. Rossi's respondents were drawn from diverse economic circumstances and from a wide variety of living conditions.[36] Moreover, the predictive accuracy demanded for his study was not so high as in the Vinton Homes study. The Vinton Homes sample was a more homogeneous one. The operation of age as a factor in residential mobility was limited by the fact that only seven heads of household in Vinton Homes were more than 50 years old.[37] Nor was it possible for household size to operate with equal effect in Vinton since there were no one-person households in the area.[38] Vinton also is an area of home owners, with only 18 of 201 households renting their dwellings.

If the conclusions from these two studies are not necessarily inconsistent, however, one or both of their theoretical bases must be inadequate.[39] An adequate explanation of residential mobility would need to encompass the significant factors operating in a wide variety of residential circumstances. An approximation of a model for the explanation of *voluntary* residential mobility can be found in the following paradigm based upon both family life-cycle and upward social mobility.

Stage of family life-cycle	Upward mobility potential		No upward mobility potential	
	Move	Stay	Move	Stay
Expansion Stage	1	2	5	6
Non-Expansion Stage	3	4	7	8

The paradigm assumes that both the need for more living space as the

---

[35] *Op. cit.*

[36] The fact that 25 per cent of the moves from his areas were involuntary suggests a significant number of demolitions, fires, evictions, and so on, all of which failed to appear in Vinton Homes.

[37] None of these seven households moved or otherwise displayed significant mobility potential.

[38] Rossi distinguished one-person households, two-person households, and households with three or more persons.

[39] Either of the two studies may be based upon such atypical samples as to cast doubt upon the generalizability of their findings. Rossi has confidence that his data, based upon four census tracts,

family increases in size and the need to adjust housing to changes in social status are potent forces inducing families to move. The push toward residential mobility would be greatest when the two forces act in concert and least when neither is operative. The expected distribution of cases, for heterogeneous universes, in the eight cells might be summarized as follows:

Cell No. 1. There should be many more cases in cell No. 1 than in cell No. 2.

Cell No. 2. Families socially tied to an ancestral home or experiencing similar restriction upon moving would be found here. The arbitrary time period covered in the prediction would force some potential movers into this cell.

Cell No. 3. Upward social mobility alone would produce a significant number of moves. Luxury features in the new dwelling would take priority over additional space.

Cell No. 4. There should be fewer cases here than in cell No. 3. The absence of pressure for additional space would permit some households to shunt their resources into values other than housing. Conscious rejection of the ideology of status striving through material possessions should be common.

Cell No. 5. Increased household size alone would produce a significant number of moves. Additional space would take priority over luxury features.

Cell No. 6. Lack of resources would prevent a large number of households from moving even when there is a pressing need for additional space.

Cell No. 7. Cases would appear in this cell only in response to factors not included in the theoretical framework: demolitions, evictions, fires, straight job transfers, etc. These moves would be involuntary.

Cell No. 8. No significant pushes toward residential mobility. At any one time, this cell likely would contain the largest number of cases.

It would be highly desirable to test this model in a variety of urban circumstances: with probability samples drawn from small and large cities, and from metropolitan areas; and with more homogeneous samples from deteriorated areas, middle-class suburbs, and so forth. Any gross deviations from the expected distributions of cases in the various cells would require revision of the model and the introduction of additional causal factors.[40]

---

are not seriously so-limited. Since the Vinton sample was much more homogeneous, a follow-up study using a probability sample of Lafayette households is now being completed. Preliminary screening of the data indicates that career pattern and upward social mobility will remain as highly significant determinants of residential mobility.

[40] The point has been made that age of household head, household size, and tenure preference do not provide an adequate index of family life-cycle. With this, the authors agree. Use of the above items provides comparability with Rossi's study, but future studies might get at family life-cycle more directly through tracing changes in family composition. Such data, coupled with data on values placed upon family living versus career striving would permit a definitive test of the theoretical positions assumed by Rossi, Bell, and the present authors.

THE DECISION TO MOVE

Thus far we have surveyed the empirical evidence and incorporated family life-cycle and career-pattern variables into a framework for the description and explanation of residential mobility. One task remaining is to consider the process whereby life-cycle and career-pattern variables become translated into individual decisions to move.

Complaints about the present dwelling can be put into fuller perspective if they are treated as intervening variables in the development of the decision to move. Viewed thus, in terms of the Philadelphia and Lafayette studies, the independent variables become "stage of the family life-cycle" and "career pattern," and the dependent variable is "residential mobility."

It seems plausible that complaints

Independent variables	Intervening variable	Dependent variable
Stage of family life-cycle $\searrow$	Complaints about $\rightarrow$	Residential mobility
Career pattern $\nearrow$	present dwelling	

Rossi sought to illuminate the development of the decision to move through the method of reason analysis.[41] The decision to move was seen as the making of a conscious choice among explicit alternatives, with the emphasis upon the household's attitudes toward the present dwelling and upon the attractions of the new dwelling.[42] His assumption was that "a household starts out with some kind of complaint, decides to move, has definite ideas about the kind of dwelling it wants, and finally, makes a choice among several dwellings according to their relative merits."[43] The method of reason analysis, however, necessarily limits the time span over which complaints as causes operate, and draws attention away from life-cycle variables as major determinants of residential mobility.

about a dwelling are not simply a function of such objective characteristics as improper construction, inadequate storage facilities, deteriorating neighborhood, and so on, but also reflect the opportunities that a household sees to escape these conditions by moving to another dwelling. Families without significant residential mobility potential may well rationalize the same features which potentially mobile families list as objectionable. And even the same families who find a dwelling satisfactory at one point may become dissatisfied with it as the pressure of additional household members makes it inadequate and/or as the financial means are acquired to make a move possible. That verbalized complaints about the dwelling reflect more basic underlying factors is also suggested by Rossi's finding that complaints about one feature tend to be accom-

[41] Paul F. Lazarsfeld, "The Statistical Analysis of Reasons as a Research Operation," *Sociometry*, V (February, 1942), 29–47.

[42] Rossi, *op. cit.*, pp. 123–32.

[43] *Ibid.*, p. 128. It should be pointed out that Rossi's selection of complaints as the starting point in the development of the decision to move did not imply that he assigned particular theoretical significance to this factor. Since he was interested in helping modify policy in the construction of housing units, he appropriately focused on recent conscious factors affecting the decision to move. He did note that one can be interested in why complaints arise and then search for changes in the household or dwelling unit that made the current housing unsatisfactory (p. 212).

panied by complaints about other features of the dwelling.[44] The verbalization of specific complaints about the present dwelling and the anticipation of more satisfactory features in the new dwelling may be the vehicle for the translation of mobility potential into mobility intentions.

It should not be implied, of course, that the general model to account for residential mobility developed in this article has adequate empirical foundation. The relevant studies to date have differed sufficiently in general

purposes, in populations studied, and in methodological detail to make it possible that the differences in their findings are artifacts thereof. Yet a theoretical scheme including both life-cycle and career-pattern variables is in accord with the general complexity of social relationships and threatens the integrity of neither Rossi's analysis nor the present study. Further, consideration of complaints as immediate precondition for mobility places independent, intervening, and dependent variables in the potentially most fruitful relation to one another.

---

[44] *Ibid.*, p. 83.

Size of Family and Preference for Children of Each Sex*

Deborah S. Freedman, Ronald Freedman, and Pascal K. Whelpton

This paper deals with the question whether the number of children Americans expect and have is influenced by their desire to have at least one child of each sex. The maintenance of every society depends on a reasonable balance of the sexes. Preference for one or the other sex and

* Deborah S. Freedman, Ronald Freedman, and Pascal K. Whelpton, "Size of Family and Preference for Children of Each Sex," *American Journal of Sociology*, 66 (September, 1960), 141–46.

the desired ratio between the sexes probably will vary with the nature of the society, particularly with reference to the difference between male and female roles at various stages of the life cycle and how the sex of a member affects ability to discharge certain responsibilities in the family.

In Western society, preferences for male or female children are not, to any important extent, dependent on economic considerations. The economic significance of children of either sex has declined with the disappearance of child labor, the separation of economic activity from the family, and the relative economic independence of new families of their parents. Nevertheless, it is a common observation that a majority of couples want children of each sex. Presumably, this is because boys and girls play different roles in the family apart from any economic considerations.

From one point of view, children can be regarded as consumer goods—yielding direct satisfactions which will vary according to whether they are boys or girls; hence, some value is involved in having at least one of each. For example, boys bring about relations of their parents to outside groups which differ from those effected by girls; they involve their parents in different kinds of leisure pursuits (e.g., hunting and certain sports for a boy and his father as contrasted with dolls and an interest in clothes for mother and daughter), and children of either sex permit the parents to relive vicariously their childhood experiences, or experiences they wish they had had. (The parent may derive satisfaction from vicarious participation in the childhood role of the opposite sex: the mother who really wanted to be a boy may get special satisfaction from a son's activities.) If such differential satisfactions are enjoyed by couples with any given number of children, those with children all of the same sex will be more likely than will others to have an additional child. Whether it is, in fact, the case that couples whose children are all boys or all girls are more likely to go on to have more children is reported in this paper, on the basis of data for a national sample.

PREVIOUS STUDIES

There have been some previous studies of the problem, with more limited samples. Clare and Kiser analyzed ex post facto statements by married couples in the Indianapolis Study[1] as to how important the desire for a child of each sex was in their decision to have their last child. They found that it was important to a small group at each parity. However, as the authors indicate, this kind of ex post facto statement of reasons for actions is suspect as rationalization. In the Princeton American Family Study of two-child couples in large metropolitan areas, Westoff[2] used factor analysis to isolate the variables which are related to the desire for another child. He found sex preference to be important to Protestants but not to Catholics or Jews.

Results similar to Westoff's are reported by De Wolff and Meerdink[3] in a study of births in Amsterdam between 1948 and 1955. They found that the first two children of couples having a third child in those years were more likely to be of the same sex among Protestants and those professing no religion than among Catholics. In families with a third birth, the first two children were of

---

[1] Jeanne E. Clare and Clyde V. Kiser, "Preference for Children of Given Sex in Relation to Fertility," *Milbank Memorial Fund Quarterly*, XXIX, No. 4 (October, 1951), 440–92.

[2] Charles F. Westoff, "The Social-Psychological Structure of Fertility," in *International Population Conference* (Vienna: International Union for the Scientific Study of Population, 1959), pp. 355–66.

[3] P. de Wolff and S. Meerdink, "La fécondité des marriages à Amsterdam selon l'appartenance sociale et religieuse," *Population*, XII, No. 2 (1957), 289–318.

one sex in 50 per cent of the Catholic and 52 per cent of the non-Catholic. (A considerable proportion of both Protestants and Catholics stopped at the second child.) These differences are not large, but they are statistically significant.

All these studies show that the desire to have a child of each sex is a relevant but not decisive factor determining the size of a family. Given the current norm of two, three, or four children in American families,[4] it is inevitable that this will affect only a small percentage of the families. By virtue of the nearly equal sex ratio at birth, most families will have children of both sexes in the course of having the moderate size of family they desire. On a chance basis, about 50 per cent of the two-child families, 75 per cent of the three-child families, and 87 per cent of the four-child families will have at least one child of each sex.

The data for this paper come from the Growth of American Families Study.[5] That study included 2,713 wives, chosen to constitute a national probability sample of all white wives who, in 1955, were 18 to 39 years old, married, and living with their husbands. The present investigation is limited to a subsample: those classified as fecund,[6] in their first mar-

riage, having borne two, three, or four children to date, all still living. This involves 889 couples—521 with two children, 266 with three, and 102 with four.

Only fecund couples were studied, which seemed reasonable in an analysis of expectations of additional children. The investigation is limited to women who had been married only once, to eliminate the influence a second marriage might have on expectations of additional children, and to those who have never had a child who died, since when a child dies the parents frequently desire to replace it and there are too few such cases for proper assessment.

In analyzing preferences in size of family, the variable we have used is the expected, instead of desired, number of children. The stated desires in size do not necessarily represent a couple's probable performance; nor are expectations of size of family to be equated with the desires, intentions, or plans of a family. Many parents do not plan the size of their families; others have attempted to plan, but have been unsuccessful. Such families may not want more children and may not intend to have more, but a realistic appraisal leads them to expect a certain number of additional children. The expectations of a couple with regard to size of family reflect not just their hopes or intentions but also a more or less realistic appraisal of their future fertility. For most couples, expectations and desires will be identical, but the minority for whom there is a discrepancy is substantial.

---

[4] For evidence on the marked consensus on the two-, three-, or four-child family, see Ronald Freedman, "Social Values about Family Size in the United States," (*International Population Conference, op. cit.*, pp. 173–83).

[5] The methodology and major findings of this study are reported in R. Freedman, P. K. Whelpton, and A. Campbell, *Family Planning, Sterility, and Population Growth* (New York: McGraw-Hill Book Company, 1959).

[6] The "fecund" wives are those in couples for whom there is no reason to

suspect any physical limitation to the ability to have additional children (for a more complete operational definition, see Freedman *et al.*, *op. cit.*, chap. ii).

FINDINGS

For our subsample of 889 families, the hypothesis investigated is that, at a particular parity, couples with only boys or only girls are more likely than others (1) to expect to have additional children in the future and (2) actually to have gone on to have additional children in the past. We deal first with what people expect and then with actual behavior at each parity.

Two types of data were used to test the two parts of this hypothesis: (*a*) The sex composition of the family—whether or not the children were both (or all) of one sex—was related to the expressed expectation of additional children. This was done separately for two-child, three-child, and four-child families. The question is whether the proportion expecting additional children is larger among couples who, to date, had had just girls or just boys, or among those who already had at least one child of each sex. We are also interested in whether this relationship, if it exists, is more pronounced in larger than in smaller families. (*b*) The sex composition of the first two children of the three-child families was compared to that of completed two-child families—that is, those in which additional children were not expected. Here the question is whether couples with two children who actually went on to have three children might have been influenced by the fact that their first two children were of the same sex. This influence was measured by comparing the proportion of such couples whose first two children were of the same sex with the comparable proportion among completed two-child families. The same comparison

was made for the first three children of four-child families and of the completed three-child families.

The relationship of sex of the children already born to expectations of additional children is shown in Table 1 separately for two-, three-,

TABLE 1. Expectations of Additional Children of Two-child, Three-child, and Four-child Couples, by Sex Distribution of Children Already Born

| | Couples expecting an additional child | | | |
| | Families with children of just one sex | | Families with children of both sexes | |
No. of children already born	Per cent	N[a]	Per cent	N[a]
Two	63	259	59	261
Three	61	69	53	197
Four	76	17	49	85

[a] Total sample on which the percentage figure was based.

and four-child families. At each parity level the mothers with children of the same sex are more likely to expect additional children than are the other mothers. Among the two-child mothers, 63 per cent of those who had had only boys or only girls expected additional children, as against 59 per cent of those who had both boys and girls—a difference of four percentage points.

For mothers of three children, 61 per cent of those with children of just one sex expect additional children, compared to 53 per cent of those with children of both sexes —a difference of eight percentage points.

When mothers of four children are considered, the difference becomes much larger. Seventy-six per cent of the mothers with children of just one sex hope for additional children, as compared to 49 per cent of those families with children of both sexes—a difference of twenty-seven percentage points.

For both the two- and the three-child families the differences are small.[7] Though the difference is large for the four-child families, the number of cases is too small to yield a statistically significant difference. However, in all three cases the differences are in the expected direction and increase progressively with size of family.

A comparison was also made between the sex composition of completed two-child families and that of the first two children of those couples who had had a third child. The same comparison was made between the sex distribution of completed three-child families and that of the first three children of four-child families. In both comparisons a higher proportion of couples who actually had the additional child earlier had had children of only one sex. Among the 266 couples with three children, 55 per cent had only boys or only girls among their first two, compared with 47 per cent of the 203 couples stopping at two. Among the 102 couples with four children, 31 per cent had children of only one sex among the

first three, as compared with 23 per cent among the 119 couples stopping at three.

Thus, five comparisons have been made between couples with children of both sexes and couples with children of just one sex—three comparisons of expectations to have additional children and two of the sex composition of groups of differing performance. In all five comparisons, whether the couples have children of only one sex is consistently related to expecting or having an additional child. The relationship is admittedly small, but it is consistent throughout and becomes larger as the family increases. It is reasonable to infer that this relationship demonstrates a preference for children of both sexes.

Given this small but consistent relationship between sex preferences and fertility expectations and behavior, a next step is to determine whether the relationship persists if controls are used for certain variables which are related to size of family. As control variables, four characteristics were used which, in the Growth of American Families Study, were found to have a significant relationship to size of family: number of years wife worked, education of wife, religion of wife, and duration of marriage. Since the number of cases was limited, each control variable was simply dichotomized, and the relationship between sex distribution and fertility expectations or achievements was investigated within the two categories of each control variable. The two types of comparisons made for each pair of subgroups were identical with those discussed previously, namely, (1) between those couples at each parity (two, three, or four) who do and

---

[7] Tests for significance, allowing for the clustered character of the sample, show the relationships to be significant at about the 0.10 level. The numbers in our sample are so small that a relatively large percentage difference is necessary for statistical significance at the 0.05 level. However, the consistency of the results at all three parities makes it unlikely that the results are due to chance fluctuations in sampling.

those who do not expect to have additional children, and (2) between those couples who had completed families of two (or three) children and those who had at least one additional child. Thus, for each control variable ten comparisons were made of fertility as related to sex distribution.

The results are as follows:

1. *Years wife worked.*—This control does not change the relationship previously found between sex distribution and fertility. The differences in eight out of ten cases are in the expected direction. There is no apparent relationship between the size of the differences and the length of work experience.
2. *Education of the wife.*—This does not change the relationship. In eight out of ten comparisons the differences are in the expected direction. The amount of education has no consistent relationship with the size of the differences.
3. *Duration of marriage.*—In all ten comparisons, the differences are in the expected direction. Duration of marriage does not affect the size of differences consistently.
4. *Religion of the wife.*—This variable affects the size of the relationship but not its direction. The validity of the general findings is not altered in that the differences are in the expected direction in five out of five comparisons for Protestants and in four out of five comparisons for Catholics. But the size of the differences is greater for Protestants than for Catholics in all five comparisons. It seems that a desired sex distribution is more important to Protestants than it is to Catholics. This is consistent with the findings of Westoff and of de Wolff and Meerdink.

The relationship between sex preference and fertility was investigated with another control—success in family planning—but in a different manner. For this analysis the sample was restricted to couples who said they had wanted all their children and who had never had an "accidental conception" (a conception occurring when the couple was practicing contraception to avoid a pregnancy). In four of the five comparisons made for this group, the differences are still in the expected direction and are about the same size as those for the total sample. For these couples who have planned size of family successfully, expectations and desires are most likely to be identical, so this particular test indicates that the discrepancy between expectations and desires does not affect the relationship under study.

Thus, a total of forty-four comparisons were made within control categories of various kinds. In thirty-nine of the forty-four, the difference is in the direction consistent with the hypothesis. While the overlapping samples and the interdependence of control characteristics make it improper to use a sign test to evaluate exactly the statistical significance of the pattern of differences, the cumulative evidence certainly supports the statement that the preference for children of both sexes persists in a wide variety of important subgroups in the population.

None of the evidence considered up to this point depends on statements by respondents about their reasons for having any given number of children. We have simply considered whether the failure to have a child of each sex is associated in fact with expecting or having additional children. This seems to us to be the best kind of evidence in view of the large element of rationalization and the unconscious motivations affecting a respondent's statement of reasons why she has or expects to have a family of a certain size. Nevertheless, we have examined statements by respondents as to why they wanted to have at least a certain number of children.

In the complete sample of the Growth of American Families Study, among all the respondents giving reasons for having at least a certain number of children, 10 per cent mentioned sex preference among other reasons. This is consistent with our earlier findings that sex preference is relevant for a small but significant minority. Clearly, it is not perceived as important by any large number.

For the special subsample analyzed in this paper, a further check was made by considering the reasons given by couples with three or four children who had children of only one sex and did expect to go on to a fourth or fifth child. Did such couples explicitly recognize a desire for a child of the sex they did not have? Among 42 such couples who had three children, 15 gave this reason among others for expecting to go on to a fourth child. A significant minority of the wives told us that they expected more children but did not want them. If we eliminate from the comparison these 9 couples who did not want the additional children expected, 15 out of 33—almost 50 per cent—gave this reason. Among the corresponding 13 four-child families of boys only or girls only expecting to have a fifth child, 7 gave sex preference as a reason. If we eliminate the 3 couples who did not want the additional child expected, the proportion rises to seven out of ten. Though these wives mentioned other reasons for wanting additional children, it was clear from the interviews that, for the majority, sex preference was the most important reason.

We have considered here the rea-

sons given by only a small number of couples of the third and fourth parities because most couples reaching these parities have children of each sex and some of the others can not or will not have additional children for a variety of other reasons.

Preference for a child of each sex appears to be a significant, if minor, influence in determining the size of a family in the United States. Such a preference exists in a variety of subgroups in the population. With the limited data available only one characteristic was found which affected the magnitude of this influence—religion. The preference apparently exists among both Catholics and Protestants, but it is less pronounced among Catholics. We may ask whether the special religious values attached to size of family and family planning for Catholics reduce the relevance of such matters.

The influence of sex preference was found to increase with size of family within the two- to four-child range considered. Although this needs confirmation with a larger sample, if it persists in replication it has interesting implications. One possible explanation is that, with increasing family size, those with children of only one sex are more and more "deviant" if they take as a reference group persons with families of similar size. Three-fourths of the couples will satisfy the preference if they have three children. Another possibility is that, within the range of two to four children desired and expected by most Americans, most of the gains derived from children can be realized with the smaller number. Those who go on to or beyond the upper end of the range may be increasingly those with special reasons, such as the desire for children of each sex.

There appears to be enough support for the idea that Americans do value having children of each sex to justify research on the differential functions of boys and girls in American family life.

Demographic Transition and the Socioeconomic Development of Societies

No population questions in recent years have received greater attention than those concerned with the relationships between population growth and the social and economic development of national societies. One reason for this interest lies in the efforts of most nations whose economies are largely preindustrial to achieve "modernization" through a variety of social and economic measures. One of the basic indexes of modernization is rising per capita income deriving from per

623

capita economic production. Unless aggregate production within a nation increases more rapidly than the population grows, per capita production will not rise. Effective social and economic development requires consideration of demographic factors in combination with those specifically relating to the social and economic structure.

If not the earliest, certainly the most famous exposition of the relationship between population growth and economic development was the principle enunciated in 1798 by Thomas R. Malthus that population has a constant tendency to increase beyond the means of subsistence unless curbed by certain preventive and positive checks.[1] Preventive checks include voluntary efforts to curb fertility, of which Malthus approved only the "moral restraint" of postponed marriage. Positive checks refer to those causes "which contributed to shorten the natural duration of human life" and included a variety of factors ranging from unwholesome occupations to diseases, wars, plague, and famine. Although in his earlier essays Malthus appeared pessimistic about the chances of achieving population control or the ability of mankind to rise above the level of bare subsistence, his position revealed in later essays was somewhat more sanguine. In the final edition of his essay published in 1826, he wrote:

> From a review of the state of society in former periods, compared with the present, I should certainly say that the evils resulting from the principle of population have rather diminished than increased, even under the disadvantage of an almost total ignorance of the real cause. . . . On the whole, . . . though our future prospects respecting the evils arising from the principle of population may not be so bright as we could wish, yet they are far from being entirely disheartening, and by no means preclude that gradual and progressive improvement in human society, which, before the late wild speculations on this subject was the object of rational expectation.[2]

There have been numerous criticisms of Malthusian theory on a variety of grounds, but, to quote Alan T. Peacock's summary evaluation, ". . . the Malthusian theory of population does at least give prominence to the relevant factors which influence economic development in the broad sense, even in the present century."[3]

[1] Thomas R. Malthus, *An Essay on the Principle of Population, as It Affects the Future Improvement of Society, with Remarks on the Speculations of Mr. Godwin, M. Condorcet, and Other Writers* (London: 1798).

[2] Thomas R. Malthus, *On Population*, edited and introduced by Gertrude Himmelfarb (New York: The Modern Library, 1960), pp. 592–93. The quotation reprinted in the Modern Library version is from the 7th edition of the Essay published in 1872, which was substantially a reprint of the 6th edition published in 1826. Malthus died in 1834.

[3] Alan T. Peacock, "Malthus in the Twentieth Century," in *Introduction to Malthus*, ed. D. V. Glass (London: Watts & Co., 1953), p. 73.

Among the severest critics of the Malthusian principle have been the Marxists, who have argued that overpopulation is an accompaniment of the capitalist economic system that will disappear with the adoption of a collectivist system without the necessity of population control measures. Significantly, however, in recent years the People's Republic of China in seeking to modernize through implementation of a collectivist system has also actively promoted fertility-control measures.

The analytical framework utilized most by social demographers when they study population change in countries becoming modernized is what has come to be called "transition theory." In general, transition theory relates type of population growth to the level of technological development of a society. The growth rate of a population whose technology is basically of a subsistence variety is largely governed by "natural" conditions. Characteristically, both birth and death rates are high, and population growth varies according to which is higher. At a higher level of technology, but yet preindustrial, a society may achieve greater control over mortality as improved methods of agriculture and animal husbandry provide a more stable food supply. Population tends to increase somewhat more rapidly, but is still subject to fluctuations resulting from forces such as epidemics that have not been brought under human control. In agrarian societies, as in primitive societies, both birth and death rates are relatively high.

The process of modernization, according to transition theory, introduces new techniques for reducing mortality, such as disease-control measures, which tend to be rapidly accepted. Fertility control measures are less likely to be either introduced or accepted, with the result that death rates decline as birth rates remain high, leading to a very rapid natural increase. Later, as fertility-control techniques are accepted, fertility rates decline and population grows more slowly or may even decline.

Donald O. Cowgill provides one of the most complete expositions of transition theory in the reading selection entitled "Transition Theory as General Population Theory." Cowgill presents some of the major principles of transition theory and shows how, as a special theory, it fits into a more general theory of population change. It should be noted that some of the principles set forth in this theoretical system involve only demographic variables while others include social variables as well.

Many demographers have raised questions about the validity and utility of transition theory. In the second selection, Leighton van Nort poses some of these questions. Among the issues he raises is whether the theory is an empirical one from which specific predictions can be made or whether it is simply a frame of reference that describes what happens to one set of variables when another set changes without claiming to predict how or when the latter will change in any specific situation. Despite current limitations of the theory, van Nort believes it to be a useful guide for observation and analysis.

The other selections in this section present demographic studies of societies representing different states of technological development. The first paper, by R. D. Harding, provides some limited vital statistics of a primitive African tribe. The fertility rate in this particular pre-industrial society was not as high as might have been expected of a group not controlling fertility, but the low rate is partly explained by the high prevalence of gonorrhea. The death rate in the period recorded by Harding was actually higher than the birth rate, although the author does not believe this was a general condition since other evidence suggested that the population was slowly growing. More than a third of the recorded deaths occurred among infants less than one year old. The infant mortality rate of approximately 42 per 100 births is not unusually high for a society at this level of technological development.

G. William Skinner in his study of the population of a minor civil division in China provides a microcosmic view of another preindustrial society at an agrarian level clearly more advanced than that of the African tribal group. Although no vital statistics data are reported, the author does provide information on family size, revealing in this parti-cular community a direct relationship with amount of landholdings. This direct correlation, although plausibly explained in terms of the economic system, contrasts sharply with the inverse relationship between size of family and socioeconomic status usually observed in Western industrial societies.

The final reading selection, "Demographic Cycles and Economic Development: Some Observations Based Upon Australian Experience," by W. D. Borrie, provides a case study of population change in a modernized Western society. The growth trend of Australia like that of other Western nations reveals some of the basic problems and limitations of transition theory. As late as the 1940s it was generally assumed that Australia's population, whose growth rate from natural increase was less than 1 per cent, had reached a plateau of the type predicted by transition theory. After World War II, however, the fertility rate increased rapidly and, as in the United States, continued at a high level for a much longer period than could logically be explained by a "catching-up" of marriages and births postponed because of the War. Borrie indicates that the clue to the fertility boom in developed countries may lie in the relationships between population and economic factors that have so far been little studied by demographers. In any case, it becomes evident that the transition model as currently developed offers little in the way of explaining the radical shifts observed in the reproduc-tive rates of modernized Western nations since 1945.

Transition Theory as General Population Theory*

Donald O. Cowgill

In his presidential address to the Population Association of America ten years ago, Rupert Vance lamented the dearth of theoretical work in the field of demography and challenged his colleagues to develop theories and hypotheses of somewhat greater generality.[1]

However, in the decade which has elapsed since Vance issued this challenge, little further theoretical work has been done. Instead we are still amassing facts and playing our theoretical cards close to our chests. No one has dared to propose a "loose" system of the order that Vance suggested.

I take it that Vance was not necessarily calling for "grand" theory of the level of abstraction of Malthus or Oswald Spengler or Talcott Parsons. It seemed that he might be content with theories of "the middle range" which Merton holds are of more value, given our present state of knowledge.[2]

At the same time, Gutman has contended that we are not as poverty-stricken in respect to theory as is often maintained and that our feeling of "relative deprivation" derives from too rigid or unrealistic notions of what constitutes theory.[3] I am inclined to agree with Gutman; it appears to me that we may have the elements of such a theory of limited range contained within the theory of the demographic transition and a variety of relatively "tight" generalizations about current population trends which have not yet been integrated into the more general theory. Therefore, I make bold to attempt to put these pieces together taking comfort in Vance's assurance that "...he who develops a theory capable of being proved invalid makes a contribution."[4] I also hope that this paper may in a measure provide the more extensive and explicit statement of the transition theory which was recently called for by Gutman.[5] Needless to say, there are no new facts nor even any new generalizations in this paper; the only novelty is in the way in which the various generalizations are integrated in what purports to be a theory.

First let me acknowledge that I do not think we are completely devoid of valid general or "grand" theory. The basic assumption underlying Malthusian theory was and is

* Donald O. Cowgill, "Transition Theory as General Population Theory," *Social Forces*, 41 (March, 1963), 270–74.

[1] Rupert B. Vance, "Is Theory for Demographers?" *Social Forces*, XXXI (October, 1952), 9–13. Reprinted in Joseph J. Spengler and Otis Dudley Duncan, *Population Theory and Policy* (New York: The Free Press of Glencoe, Inc., 1956), pp. 88–94.

[2] Robert K. Merton, *Social Theory and Social Structure* (Revised and enlarged; New York: The Free Press of Glencoe, Inc., 1957), pp. 5–10.

[3] Robert Gutman, "In Defense of Population Theory," *American Sociological Review*, XXV, No. 3 (June, 1960), 325–33.

[4] Rupert B. Vance, *op. cit.*

[5] Robert Gutman, *op. cit.*, p. 332.

sound, it is only in specific details and in misapprehension of limiting and qualifying conditions that Malthus erred. The basic proposition was that the human species, like every other species, had the capacity to reproduce itself at a geometric rate and that unless there were inhibiting factors, the rate of reproduction tended to approach the maximum capacity. Malthus recognized some of the grosser conditions which tended to dampen this tendency, but even his crude formulations were close approximations to reality for most of past human history and even for a considerable portion of today's population.

In spite of the insistent tendency toward population increase, the most common historical condition is not growth, but nongrowth, or seen at close range, short-term cycles of growth and decline which average out to stability, as noted by Ta Chen in China from the time of Christ to 1800.[6] Long-term growth in a geometric pattern within a limited space is impossible. With such a growth potential, every species tends very quickly to expand to the carrying capacity of its environment and at this point to achieve a relatively stable equilibrium with the other elements of its environment.[7] It was this generally sound aspect of Malthusian theory which furnished the basis for Darwin's theory of evolution.

Let me attempt to reformulate these basic postulates in a form which does no violence to our more sophisticated knowledge:

1. Any population has the capacity to increase at a geometric rate.
2. Unless inhibited by environmental factors, any population will tend to increase at a geometric rate approaching maximum capacity.
3. At a geometric rate of increase, any population will quickly fill up any finite environment, taxing its space and resources.
4. As a population begins to press upon the limits of its environment, inhibiting factors will come into play to slow down the growth.
5. If the limits of the environment cannot be expanded or the resources used more efficiently, population will cease to grow.
6. At any given time, most species have long since passed their maximum rate of growth and have achieved a condition of equilibrium characterized by a relatively stationary population.
7. Like other species, the most common, if not the normal, condition of man is stability of population.
8. However, the human species has a unique capacity for expanding the limits of his environment and of improving the efficiency of utilization of the resources of his environment.
9. Thus, man has from time to time achieved technological breakthroughs which have made it possible for him to utilize the resources of an enlarged environment and to make more efficient use of the resources of any specific area.
10. Any such technological advance increases the potential carrying capacity of the environment and, given the persistent tendency of population to increase, tends to increase the size of the population.
11. When such an advance occurs, it tends to be followed by a cycle of population growth.[8]

---

6 Ta Chen, "Population in Modern China," *The American Journal of Sociology*, LII, No. 1, Pt. II (July, 1946), 1–126.

7 The slow growth of primitive populations, as well as the accelerated growth resulting from technological advances are well illustrated by Louis-Rene Nougier in his article, "Essai sur le peuplement prehistorique de la France," *Population*, IX, No. 2 (April–June, 1954), 241–74.

8 This is strikingly illustrated in

The modern demographic transition is just one such era of growth. It was undoubtedly preceded by an extensive period of relative stability of population.

If then, we may assume that such a stable equilibrium is usual and that growth is sporadic and unusual, a significant part of population theory should pertain to the description and explanation of the conditions of stability and those of change. Transition theory deals with two conditions of stability and one of change. It asserts that the modern growth cycle is essentially a transition from: Stage 1, under which both birth and death rates are under a minimum of human control, through Stage 2, the period of growth, to Stage 3, under which both birth and death rates are extensively controlled and are balanced at a low level.[9] Stage one is the primi-

tive condition of high birth rates and high death rates, and equilibrium having been previously achieved, these vital rates tend to balance each other and the population tends to remain relatively stable.[10] Such change as occurs is of a cyclical order, resulting from fluctuations in the death rate. The birth rate tends to be stable while the death rate is the unstable variable varying with drought and epidemic.[11] This stage is usually referred to as the stage of "high potential growth." This term is a tacit acknowledgement of the variability of the death rate and of its susceptibility to control, or reduction, under modern conditions.

The second stage is that of transition or change; it marks the transition from a condition of high birth rates and high death rates to that of low birth rates and low death rates. Thus far the expected pattern is one in which the death rates fall first and most rapidly for a time, resulting in rapid population growth or what in recent times has been dubbed "the population explosion." This stage is terminated when the birth rate sinks to meet the death rate, and a new condition of equilibrium is approached. It may be assumed that this secular decline in the birth rate is the chief novelty about the mod-

---

Nougier's data concerning the increase of the population of France with the invention of agriculture, *op. cit.* For a description of the mechanics of such growth cycles under primitive conditions, see Donald O. Cowgill, "The Theory of Population Growth Cycles," *The American Journal of Sociology*, LV (September, 1949), 163–70. Reprinted in Joseph J. Spengler and Otis Dudley Duncan, *Population Theory and Policy, op. cit.*, pp. 125–34.

[9] The transition theory was first stated by Warren S. Thompson in his article, "Population," *American Journal of Sociology*, XXXI (May, 1929), 959–75. It was later reformulated by Frank W. Notestein in "Population—The Long View," in T. W. Schultz, *Food for the World* (Chicago: The University of Chicago Press, 1945). It has found wide acceptance among such scholars as: Kingsley Davis, "The World Demographic Transition," *Annals of the American Academy of Political and Social Science*, CCXXXVII (January, 1945), 1–11; Dennis Wrong, Population (New York: Random House, 1956); Joyce Hertzler, *The Crisis in World Population* (Lincoln: University of Nebraska Press, 1956); Dudley Kirk, "Dynamics of Human Populations," *Eugenics Quar-*

terly, II, No. 1 (March, 1955), 18–25 and others.

[10] For an explicit statement of the principles applying to "preindustrial cultures" see Warren S. Thompson, *Population and Progress in the Far East* (Chicago: The University of Chicago Press, 1959), pp. 15–16. He notes four characteristics of such "preindustrial" populations: (1) high birth rates —above 40 per 1000, (2) high death rates, (3) fluctuating death rates and relatively stable birth rates, (4) slow and uneven growth, varying from year to year.

[11] For the mechanics of such growth cycles see Donald O. Cowgill, *op. cit.*

ern population growth cycle and that without this decline in the birth rate, the death rate would eventually be forced upward and the cycle then would not differ in its fundamental features from a growth cycle under primitive conditions.[12]

Stage 3, as yet largely hypothetical, is that condition of low birth rates and low death rates which presumably follows the transition stage. In this stage the death rate becomes the stable variable, while the birth rate is most subject to variation. The conditions necessary to this stage are knowledge of and willingness to apply the technology of both birth control and death control.

At this point it appears desirable to state the transition theory in more abstract terms:

1. In the absence of effective technology of birth control and death control, population will increase to the maximum carrying capacity of the environment then achieve a stable equilibrium characterized by high birth rates and high death rates and limited longevity.
2. Under conditions of industrialization and urbanization, given the technology of birth control and death control, there is a marked tendency for the technology of death control to be applied earlier and more extensively resulting in rapid population growth and extensive structural changes in the population. Later, and less predictably, cultural values permitting, the technology of birth control may be employed to reduce the rate of growth and bring about a new condition of equilibrium.[13]

3. During the process of urbanization and industrialization, the nuclear form of the family tends to replace extended or consanguine forms, and
4. With a falling birth rate, the size of the nuclear family tends to decline.

While modern technology of death control and birth control makes possible rapid and dramatic changes, perhaps warranting the expression "population explosion," the transition never occurs all at once. Instead, the death rate starts falling in the upper

prediction of future events. William Petersen contends that modern population growth began with an increase in the birth rate and only later did the death rate start falling. See W. Petersen, "The Demographic Transition in the Netherlands," *American Sociological Review*, XXV, No. 3 (June, 1960), 334–47. Joseph S. Davis says that the United States, Canada, Australia, and New Zealand do not fit the model of the transition theory and with the continuation of their birth rates at medium levels a new category other than "incipient decline" is indicated. See J. S. Davis, "Population and Resources: Discussion of Papers by Frank W. Notestein and P. V. Cardon," *Journal of the American Statistical Association*, XIV (September, 1950), 348–49. Hatt, Farr, and Weinstein while finding evidence of the polar types, "high growth potential" and "incipient decline," found little evidence for a uniform pattern of correlation of levels of vital rates with the degree of modernization during the transition stage. See Paul K. Hatt, Nellie Louise Farr, and Eugene Weinstein, "Types of Population Balance," *American Sociological Review*, XX, No. 1 (February, 1955), 14–21. Others contend that the transition theory cannot be used for prediction. For example, see Irene Taeuber, "The Future of Transitional Areas," in *World Population and Future Resources*, ed. Paul K. Hatt (New York: The American Book Company, 1952), pp. 25–38. Even Thompson appears to doubt the predictability of the transition theory as applied to South and East Asia. See W. S. Thompson, *Population and Progress in the Far East*, op. cit., p. 27.

[12] The contrast between these two types of cycles is treated at length in the article by the author referred to under footnote 8.

[13] The transition theory has been criticized both for poorness of fit to historic data and lack of utility for

social and economic classes first, and only later similar developments occur in the lower classes. Thus a marked differential in the death rate is characteristic of the transition.

5. Given the technology of death control and a cultural disposition to make use of it, it will be applied first and most extensively in the upper social and economic classes and only somewhat later will it be applied with equal vigor within the lower classes. Hence, while the general death rate is falling, there will be marked differentials between the social classes.

There is no consensus of cultural values in favor of the application of the technology of birth control and frequently in the initial stages of the transition conservative cultural values are antithetical to it. Consequently it is those whose perspectives reach beyond their own culture who first break with these traditional values and begin to practice birth control. This results in a differential birth rate, the rate for the better educated, more culturally mobile elements declining first and more rapidly than that of the less well-informed. This leads to the formulation of the general principle that:

6. Given the technology of birth control, it will be applied first and most extensively in the upper socioeconomic classes. Thus, while the birth rate is manifesting a secular decline, there will be a marked differential between the rates of the upper and the lower socioeconomic classes.

Another uniform pattern during the transition has been for urban birth rates to be reduced first and thus characteristically there has been a decided differential between urban and rural birth rates. Hence, the further general principle:

7. During a secular decline in the birth rate, the rate will decline first in the cities; consequently, the urban birth rate is characteristically lower than the rural birth rate for the same region.

During the transition, the structural characteristics of the population undergo marked changes. A primitive population with uncontrolled birth rates and death rates will be predominantly a young population; the average life expectancy will be low. Partially because of the age structure, but also because of high maternal mortality, sex ratios, i.e., ratios of males to females, tend to be high. Occupational structures will lean heavily in the direction of primary production, hence, a high proportion of persons engaged in agriculture, fishing, herding, and the like. Residential patterns will be largely rural, the bulk of the population living either in the open country or in small villages.

8. A population in which birth rates and death rates are relatively uncontrolled will be a young population, dominantly male, concentrated in extractive industries, agrarian occupations, and predominantly rural in residence.

Marked changes occur in each of these structural variables during the demographic transition. As the death rate declines, the expectation of life increases and the population grows older.[14] If, later, the birth rate also

---

[14] Alfred Sauvy calls attention to the fact that the aging effect of the reduction of the death rate, in so far as this is measured by the increasing proportion of aged in the population, may be a delayed reaction. Since the

declines, the effect is to reduce the proportion of the population which is made up of children and hence to exaggerate the proportion which is older. As the population gets older, given a higher death rate among males, the sex ratio tends to decline; hence, highly urbanized populations usually have a surplus of females. The demographic transition is closely correlated with urbanization and industrialization; hence, it is almost self-evident that during the transition there will be a marked shift from agrarian occupations to industrial occupations and from rural residence to urban residence. The general principles may be stated as follows:

9. A population which is experiencing secular declines in both birth rates and death rates will also manifest a marked aging trend.
10. An aging population tends to be predominantly female.
11. During the demographic transition there is a marked shift from extractive industries and agrarian occupations to industrial and commercial occupations.
12. During the demographic transition, there is a marked tendency toward urbanization of the population.

While the shifts in age and sex composition are somewhat exaggerated during the transition, in comparison with primitive populations any population which achieves a new equilibrium characterized by low birth rates and low death rates after having passed through the transition will continue to be relatively old and highly female. But it is probably a bit early to speculate about the characteristics of such a post-transition population except to comment that while this stage is frequently referred to as the stage of "incipient decline," I have never seen a single cogent reason advanced for expecting decline at this point.[15] But if decline should occur, presumably because the birth rate would drop below the death rate, the structural changes already described would be further extended.

In retrospect, it appears that in the above formulations, I have shifted from the use of the economists's conventional variables—land, labor, and capital—to population, technology, and culture. The pertinent technological variables are not only those of economic production but also those of birth control and death control. Our technology of death control is highly advanced and extensively applied. Cultural values approach consensus in favor of the maximum application of this technology. Birth control technology is not as far advanced, but the prime inhibitor to its application is conflicting or antagonistic cultural values. Inherently there appears no reason for this order of cultural priorities, and logically it appears quite possible to have an earlier fall in the birth rate than in the death rate.[16] That the opposite

---

earliest reductions in the death rate relate chiefly to infant and child mortality, the immediate effect of reducing the death rate may be an increase in the proportion of children in the population; only decades later will the proportion of the aged begin to increase. See Alfred Sauvy, "Le viellessement des populations et l'allongement de la vie," *Population*, IX, No. 4 (October–December, 1954), 675–82.

[15] Hatt, Farr, and Weinstein also note that in the examination of those populations which most nearly approximated the pure type of "incipient decline" there were no facts which indicated actual decline. *Op. cit.*, p. 19.

[16] W. S. Thompson calls attention to the cultural determinants which are involved in the application of birth control technology in *Population and Progress in the Far East*, *op. cit.*, p. 24.

is the almost universal order of events wants explanation, and perhaps the anthropologist is in the best position to give us that explanation.

Certainly in the further development of population theory the prime needs are for more extensive knowledge of the factors inhibiting and promoting the application of birth control technology.

In the meantime, transition theory appears to offer a reasonably accurate model of the major population changes taking place in recent centuries. It describes the main processes resulting in the "population explosion" of modern times. As developed above, it describes the main structural changes which may be expected during such changes. It even anticipates and predicts with reasonable accuracy the demographic reaction to a considerable variety of factors inherent in modern technological and cultural changes.

As such it appears to fulfill the claims of a theory of the middle range. The modern transition is merely a special case in the dynamics of population change, but from it we may extract certain principles which have a considerable degree of generality.

Biology, Rationality, and Fertility: A Footnote to Transition Theory[*]

Leighton van Nort

Perhaps few disciplines are as modestly conscious of their limitations while as methodologically sophisticated as demography in its current phase of critical self-examination. Its most important theoretical statements are carefully hedged with restrictions and qualifications, and the tentativeness with which they are offered is matched by an urgency in the acquisition of new data and new knowledge. And yet modesty is self-defeating if it results in an avoidance of precision which makes theories difficult to confirm or disprove. A case in point is the body of generalizations which has become known as the "theory of demographic transition." This statement of the dynamic relations between declining mortality and fertility in the process of modernization is perhaps demography's

* Leighton van Nort, "Biology, Rationality, and Fertility: A Footnote to Transition Theory," *Eugenics Quarterly*, 3 (September, 1956), 157–60.

best claim to general theoretical development,[1] yet the controversy over the validity of these generalizations has provided evidence that there is little agreement either on the definition of the variables, the precise nature of their dynamic relationship, or the predictions implied.[2] This situation may be regarded as unfortunate, even if traceable to an acute sense of the theory's limitations on the part of its principal expositors.[3]

We may ask first of all what sort of theory we are dealing with—is it an empirical theory, or is it a frame of reference? If it is the former, it must account directly for the observed variance in mortality and fertility. If it is the latter, it must tell us what categories of variables are

important, and how we should relate them to one another. We can perhaps see the consequences of these alternatives most clearly in the case of fertility.

THE FERTILITY TRANSITION

Fertility has been a major focus of discussion. The problem of operationally defining it is discussed in a recent paper by Ryder.[4] Its status as a variable remains controversial. The prospective critic of the transition theory finds himself faced with the task of resolving this question before he can even attempt a rebuttal of the theory. For example, does the theory actually predict "incipient decline" produced by fertility below replacement levels in those countries which have already passed through the stage of "transitional growth"? What are the postulates which imply this prediction? Or is "incipient decline" simply a somewhat misleading but inessential label for the "mature" balance between low fertility and low mortality?

The transition in fertility described by the theory may be interpreted in either of two ways: (1) It may be treated as a simple statement of the empirical relationship between fertility and some other essentially unitary variable such as "modernization" which might, in principle, be represented by an index number.[5] Or (2) it may be regarded

---

[1] This is the conclusion of Rupert B. Vance in "Is Theory for Demographers?" *Social Forces*, XXXI (October, 1952), 9–13.

[2] See, for example, Joseph S. Davis, "Our Changed Population Outlook and Its Significance," *American Economic Review*, XLII (June, 1952), 304–25; "Population and Resources," *Journal of the American Statistical Association*, XLV (September, 1950), 346–49; "The Population Upsurge and the American Economy, 1945–80," *Journal of Political Economy*, LXI (October, 1953), 369–88; Paul K. Hatt, Nellie Louise Farr, and Eugene Weinstein, "Types of Population Balance," *American Sociological Review*, XX (February, 1955), 14–21; Leighton van Nort and Bertram P. Karon, "Demographic Transition Reexamined," *American Sociological Review*, XX (October, 1955), 523–27; and Weinstein's "Comment" on the latter and "Reply" by the authors, *American Sociological Review*, XXI (June, 1956), 369–73.

[3] Notestein, for example, in his most recent published statement of the theory, writes: "At present we cannot either list all the factors involved or attach precise weights to the factors we can list." Frank W. Notestein, "The Economics of Population and Food Supplies," *Proceedings of the Eighth International Conference of Agricultural Economists* (London: Oxford University Press, 1953), p. 18.

[4] Norman B. Ryder, "Problems of Trend Determination During a Transition in Fertility," *Milbank Memorial Fund Quarterly*, XXXIV (January, 1956), 5–21.

[5] A partial example of such an approach, apparently involving also an interpretation of the theory of demographic transition as a static typology,

as a description of the relations among *categories* of variables, that is, relations among more specific bodies of theory whose parameters can be obtained from direct observation. In this case it is a *frame of reference*, not a simple statement of an empirical relationship.

In the first interpretation, we are dealing with a theory from which we should be able to obtain a predicted level of fertility by specifying the observed values of the parameters. A test can be straightforward and direct. For example, can the theory predict the "baby boom," or tell us just how rapidly populations in "transitional" areas will grow? On the other hand, *frame of reference cannot be either confirmed or disproven from direct observation alone.* Only when the subordinate postulates are operationalized does the "transition" frame of reference become accessible to test. If we adopt the second interpretation, it follows that criticism of the theory for failing to supply specific predictions is wide of the mark. We wish to suggest a formulation involving the latter interpretation.

A POSSIBLE FORMULATION

Our proposed formulation can be put very simply and crudely as follows: the transition from "high" to "low" levels of fertility represents, in first approximation, a transition from a *biological* model of fertility to an *economic* model of fertility. By a *biological* model of fertility we mean the ideal-type situation in which levels of fertility are determined by the more or less direct operation of

is to be found in Hatt, Farr, and Weinstein, *op. cit.*

biological factors, conditioned by a set of social and psychological factors specific to a preindustrial society. By an *economic* model of fertility we mean the ideal-type situation in which levels of fertility are determined by decisions based on the rational allocation of resources among competing wants of the type normally denoted economic, conditioned by a set of social and psychological factors specific to a modern industrial society. The transition in fertility represents, in terms of this particular formulation, the gradual limiting of biological determinants of fertility by a process of rational decision-making.

This formulation is scarcely unconventional, for it leads to the sorts of questions which have characteristically been asked by "transition"-oriented demographers. These are questions such as the following:

COUNTRIES IN THE STAGE OF "HIGH GROWTH POTENTIAL."[6] Since fertility is seldom or never observed at the biological maxima, even in pre-industrial societies, (1) what are the levels of fertility which would be expected on the basis of purely biological factors, and (2) what are the social and psychological factors which serve to reduce observed levels of fertility below these maxima? What are the magnitudes of the reductions induced by specific factors within the framework of such societies?

COUNTRIES IN THE STAGE OF "TRANSITIONAL GROWTH." To what extent can the decline in fertility in

6 The descriptive labels for the three types of countries are those employed by Notestein. See Frank W. Notestein, "The Population of the World in the Year 2000," *Journal of the American Statistical Association*, XLV (September, 1950), 335.

"transitional" countries be attributed to the gradual substitution of rational decision-making of the type broadly denominated "economic" for the direct operation of biological factors within marriage? What is the relation of improvements in the technology of fertility control to the spread of such a rational orientation?

COUNTRIES IN THE STAGE OF "INCIPIENT DECLINE." To what extent can fertility in highly developed industrial countries be explained and predicted in terms of purely "rational" economic decisions about childbearing, together with deviations from such decisions resulting from inefficiencies in the available technology of fertility control and its application within the family? When the variance attributable to these factors is subtracted, what is the magnitude of the residual variance which must be explained in social and psychological terms?

SOME NEEDED RESEARCH

There is nothing very new or startling about this list of questions, except insofar as it suggests one critical gap in current work on fertility: the absence of any rigorous theorizing about the levels of fertility in the transitional and mature stages which would be implied by the operation of purely "economic" factors. To what extent does family investment in children follow the principles governing investment in other durable goods involving future costs which are relatively fixed and predictable? To what extent are children economically substitutable with such other commodities, and what sort of substitution effects result from variations in relative costs? What levels

of fertility would be predicted on the basis of variations in (1) expected costs of child-maintenance, and (2) expected income? Could some portion of the postwar rise in fertility be attributed to changes in income expectations, and in the prices of commodities competitive with children? These questions are of course supplementary to the currently more prominent question of the direct costs of childbearing, but they may be far more important than the latter.

There is ample evidence of interest in the refinement of the biological model of fertility, but notably little interest displayed in developing an adequate economic model. Almost all the other subordinate postulates incorporated in the "transition" frame of reference have been more thoroughly explored, and some further information on several will be provided by the "New Study of American Fertility."[7] Some information on the economic variables will probably also be forthcoming. Westoff, Mishler, Potter, and Kiser note in their recent article on the design of the new study that

> ... a fertility choice (whether implicit or explicit) involves a "cost" for the individual and the family, that is, certain desires and interests are either yielded or compromised in preference to others. (Decisions not to have children are as "costly," in a sense, as decisions to have them.)[8]

Mishler and Westoff, in a more technical paper, indicate interest in the process of family decision-making and in gathering some economic

---

[7] See Charles F. Westoff, Elliot G. Mishler, Robert G. Potter, Jr., and Clyde V. Kiser, "A New Study of American Fertility—Social and Psychological Factors," *Eugenics Quarterly*, II (December, 1955), 229–33.

[8] *Ibid.*, p. 232.

data.[9] Thus some information potentially useful for the construction of an adequate economic model probably will be collected. However, as Hauser pointed out in a discussion of the study design, relatively little attention will be given to the relation of the family decision-making process to the "general social-economic climate."[10] And perhaps equally as important is the exploration of the implications of what is already known about general economic behavior for the analysis of fertility under conditions of substantially complete voluntary control.

---

[9] Elliot G. Mishler and Charles F. Westoff, "A Proposal for Research on Social Psychological Factors Affecting Fertility: Concepts and Hypotheses," *Current Research in Human Fertility* (New York: Milbank Memorial Fund, 1955), pp. 145–49.
[10] Philip M. Hauser, "Some Observations on Method and Study Design," *ibid.*, p. 155.

If the foregoing comments have any validity, it follows that a great deal of theorizing about fertility remains to be done if the transition theory is to be stated in testable or operational form. If a "transition" frame of reference cannot at present be either confirmed or disproven, it *is* open to criticism if it fails to provide us with relative weights for the categories of variables it relates to one another. At present, the system of ideas known as the transition theory is perhaps most accurately described as a shrewd selection of materials from which to construct a theory. The particular fertility formulation discussed above is one of many possible ways of relating some of these factors to one another. We may expect a variety of others, for even in its present embryonic form the transition theory is a fruitful guide for observation and analysis.

A Note on Some Vital Statistics of a Primitive Peasant Community in Sierra Leone*

R. D. Harding

Though more or less reliable vital statistics are available for some of the larger and more sophisticated towns in British West Africa, as far as the writer knows none exist for peasant communities whose primitive living conditions have altered little in essentials since British occupation. The observations now offered, though referring only to a small community and therefore subject to a high sampling error, have the merit of being accurate as far as they go.

The data were collected by the writer and his wife as a by-product of an investigation into the seasonal variations in the manifestations of untreated yaws in a community over a period of a year, for which purpose all the members of the community were examined individually in alternate months, i.e. seven times in all. The first examination was preceded by an intensive census aimed at including all members of each family. At each reexamination pains were taken to obtain every person and there were but few absentees. Every pregnancy was noted as soon as definite signs appeared, so as to reduce the chance of any subsequent birth or miscarriage being missed, and the average period which elapsed between the registration of a preg-

nancy and its normal termination showed that the condition was nearly always recognized during the fourth or fifth month. Most careful inquiries about deaths were made from relatives, and corroborated from village chiefs and any other available sources. At the first examination the community comprised a population of 1406 persons, of whom 29.3 per cent were classed as men (over about 15 years), 36.2 per cent as women (over about 13), 18.6 per cent as boys, and 16.0 per cent as girls. This percentage composition is typical of the tribe in question, and indeed of other rural communities in Sierra Leone, and tends to confirm that the census was accurate.

By way of indicating the degree of accuracy of the observations it should be mentioned that none were based on returns rendered by African sanitary inspectors—a fertile source of error in such matters. Every individual was questioned on each of the seven occasions by the writer or his wife, who soon came to recognize most of them by face as well as name, while the detailed concomitant recording of the development of yaws lesions provided an additional check to identification. Since pregnancy could undoubtedly be recognized during the last four months or so there existed no loophole by which births could be concealed. As regards deaths, theoretically a person might have

---

* R. D. Harding, "A Note on Some Vital Statistics of a Primitive Peasant Community in Sierra Leone," *Population Studies*, 2 (December, 1948), 373–76.

been reported dead when he had really departed from the area, but, in fact, these primitive people are not capable of inventing, and maintaining systematically on repetition, the circumstantial detail which was asked for in connection with every death recorded. The converse possibility, of people who had died being reported as having gone away, was guarded against by a system of tracing absentees, and in fact nearly every absentee was sooner or later brought back for inspection. As an additional precaution an intelligent and reliable member of the tribe who had long been employed by the writer was sent from time to live in one of the villages and by means of casual conversation discover any useful details the writer might have missed.

The great majority of the population belonged to the *Kissi* tribe—one of the most primitive in Sierra Leone. The people live in dirty unventilated mud huts usually with an internal diameter of about 8 feet, each housing an average of four to five people. Children go mainly unclothed, while adults wear a variety of garments of native or imported cloth, very often ragged and nearly always dirty. Babies are suckled until two to three years of age, but breast milk is supplemented, starting usually within the first two months, by forcing "pap" of rice or mashed banana down the infant's throat. A hospital or dispensary is available within fifteen miles of all parts of the area for the treatment of all common diseases, but is attended chiefly for the treatment of yaws, sleeping sickness, and some chronic or minor ailments and singularly little for serious acute illness, so that the presence of these institutions has had very little influence on the death rate (apart from that formerly due to sleeping sickness). A high proportion of acute illness is attributed to witchraft, and recourse is had to native medicine men. Whatever the illness, native medicine is first tried, and it is usually only after an unsuccessful trial that a patient may, if still alive, be brought to hospital, often in an advanced condition.

Since venereal disease might have an influence on the birth and death rates it should be remarked that gonorrhoea was very prevalent in the area, though its complications, except perhaps stricture, do not seem to follow as frequently as might be expected. An independent inquiry of women who were over childbearing age, in a neighboring tribe of similar habits in whom gonorrhoea is equally prevalent, had shown that rather more than 10 per cent had borne no children. Syphilis is uncommon in the area, presumably as the result of the prevalence of yaws, and no recognizable case of congenital syphilis has ever been seen there by the writer.

BIRTH RATE

Birth and death rates have been calculated on the basis of the number of people in the community at the first examination, viz. 1406. In this community 48 live births occurred in a mean period of 12.46 months, giving a birth rate of 32.9 per thousand per annum with a probable error of ± 3.27. Since adults are unaware of their ages the fertility rate per thousand females aged 15–45 cannot be calculated, but the rate per thousand females who have passed puberty (at about 14 years) works out at 90.9.

MISCARRIAGES

Since pregnancy could be recognized at 4–5 months probably all pregnancies which terminated in a miscarriage or stillbirth after that time have been recorded. There were eleven such (a pair of twins born dead being counted as two stillbirths), giving a ratio of 22.9 miscarriages or stillbirths per 100 live births.

Five infants survived birth by only from one hour to four days, but these have been grouped under infant births and deaths.

DEATH RATE

Fifty-six deaths occurred in a mean period of 12.46 months, giving a death rate of 38.4 per thousand per annum with a probable error of ±3.52. There were no major epidemics, and the deaths were distributed fairly evenly over the year.

INFANT MORTALITY RATE

Twenty deaths occurred in infants of less than one year, giving an infant mortality rate of 417 per thousand per annum with a probable error of ±48.

CAUSES OF DEATH

The cause of death was inquired into in each case, but usually it was impossible to discover more than some cardinal symptom preceding death. Not uncommonly all that could be learnt was that the patient had had an acute illness lasting maybe a few hours, maybe two or three days, often attributed to witchcraft. Sometimes, as in children, the relatives stated that the patient just became suddenly ill and died without any one well-marked symptom; sometimes the chief symptom was given as headache, generalized body pains or fever. Such cases have been classified below as dying from acute febrile illness. Where cough or any other prominent symptom such as diarrhoea was mentioned in addition, the case has been classified under another appropriate heading. Since an epidemic of cerebrospinal fever might cause acute fatal illness without symptoms which the relatives would recognize, it should be mentioned that this disease was borne in mind but no cases were discovered in the area. In a few cases the cause of death was accurately known because the patient had been seen by the writer when already ill. The causes of death as reported are set out below.

INFANTS. Ten male, ten female deaths. Acute febrile illness, eight; neonatal (less than a week after birth), five; "cough," five; diarrhoea or vomiting, two; starvation, one. (The single death from starvation occurred in an infant whose mother died. Death of the mother is usually followed by the death of the infant owing to lack of alternative supplies of breast milk. It is rare to find another woman willing and able to feed such an infant.)

CHILDREN AGED ONE YEAR TO PUBERTY. Two male, six female deaths. Acute febrile illness, three; whooping cough, two; starvation in child aged 1¼ years owing to mother's death, one; acute dysentery, one; cancrum oris, one. Of these eight deaths six occurred between the ages of one and three years. There were no deaths in children between the ages of five and puberty.

ADULTS. Thirteen male, fifteen female deaths. Acute dysentery, six; acute febrile illness, five; old age, three; pulmonary tuberculosis, two; pneumonia, one; leprosy, one; sleeping sickness, one; intestinal strangulation, one; accident, one; snakebite, one; puerperal complication, one; cerebral haemorrhage, one; heart failure, one; Hodgkin's disease, one; chronic abdominal complaint, one; unknown, one.

The difference between the birth rate (32.9) and the death rate (38.4) is of course far from having any statistical significance in a population of this size, and furnishes no true indication that the population is declining. Independent evidence actually suggests it is slowly increasing. The rates quoted are subject to a high sampling error and are not to be regarded as providing more than very approximate figures. However, it is believed that the figures given for births and deaths are accurate and it is felt that information of value is more likely to accrue from a few accurate observations on small communities than from large-scale returns of doubtful accuracy. If other workers who had opportunities of studying a primitive West African tribe would obtain similar data for two or three communities of similar size it would then be possible by considering the results in conjunction to arrive at birth and death rates which are accurate within fairly narrow limits. The present writer feels that knowledge of these vital factors is a necessary prerequisite to any rational plan of social and hygienic betterment in the West African colonies, the population of which consists so largely of a more or less primitive peasant community. The only published comparable statistics from a

British African colony of which the writer has knowledge are contained in an article[1] concerning the Digo District of Kenya, though the facts that the data were acquired by African sanitary teachers, and that the ratio of stillbirths to livebirths found reached the almost incredibly low figure for the tropics, of 0.53 per cent, raises an element of doubt as to their accuracy. In the Digo District in 1932 the birth rate was found to be 49.36 per 1000 per annum, the death-rate 20.19, and the infant mortality rate 148.5 .

Three features concerning the recorded causes of death in the present inquiry deserve comment. Firstly, deaths in children aged 3 years or under, numbering 26, accounted for almost half the total deaths at all ages (56). Secondly, of these twenty-six deaths in young children 10, or 38.5 per cent, have been attributed to an acute febrile illness. There is no means of knowing what acute infections this term may have covered, but there is little doubt that in the majority of these cases the cause of death was malaria, which is hyperendemic in the area. Thirdly, an acute intestinal or gastrointestinal condition, probably most frequently bacillary dysentery, was the cause of death in nine cases at all ages, i.e. accounted for 16.1 per cent of all deaths. These findings may be compared with those obtained by the writer in a rural area (Kankara District) of Northern Nigeria.[2] There the relevant figures were as follows: (1) deaths in children under approximately 3 years of age accounted for 45 per cent of the

---

[1] J. H. S., *East African Medical Journal*, X (1933–4), p. 144.
[2] R. D. Harding, *Transactions of the Royal Society of Tropical Medicine and Hygiene*, XXXIII (1940), 483.

total deaths recorded for all ages; (2) 32 per cent of these deaths under 3 years were attributed to "fever" by the relatives; (3) dysentery and diarrhoea accounted for 29 per cent of total deaths at all ages.

A Study in Miniature of Chinese Population*

G. William Skinner

SETTING

Szechwan, the largest and most populous of the provinces in China proper, constitutes in its greater part a natural geographic region usually called the Red Basin. Except along the important rivers, its terrain varies from hilly to mountainous, though the region is nonetheless intensively cultivated by means of elaborate terracing and irrigation devices. In the west of this basin the waters of the Min river pour out from the mountains on to the Chengtu Plain, forming an alluvial fan some seventy miles from north to south. Due to a magnificent irrigation system devised over 2000 years ago, this fertile valley is the most productive and prosperous agricultural area in China. It is also among the most densely populated regions of its size in the world, averaging 2452 persons per square mile.[1] The provincial, capital Chengtu, is located at the eastern edge of the plain; a few miles outside the city's east gate the hills begin.

Sansheng *hsiang*, the subject of this paper, lies about six miles from Chengtu in the hills which rim the plain.[2] A *hsiang* is an administrative subdivision of the *hsien* (county), and resembles the American township. In Szechwan it always contains at least one, and usually only one, market town. Sansheng *hsiang* is one of thirty-five townships in Huayang *hsien*, a county embracing both hills and plains to the south and east of

* G. William Skinner, "A Study in Miniature of Chinese Population," *Population Studies*, 5 (November, 1951), 91–103.

[1] Calculated for eight *hsien* and one municipality which include all but a fraction of the Plain, from figures given in the 1946 *Szechwan Statistical Yearbook* (in Chinese). Chengtu, June 1947, pp. 14–18, 60–65.

[2] At an elevation of about 2000 ft., E. longitude 104° 5', about that of Singapore, and N. latitude 30° 40', about that of Jacksonville, Florida.

Chengtu. In 1947 the *hsien* had about 470,000 people[3] and the *hsiang* 15,-963.

Most of Szechwan is peculiar for its lack of villages, if by the term is meant a large number of dwellings grouped together separate from the land tilled. Szechwanese farmers, as distinct from those in other parts of China proper, live in scattered households and household clusters. Compact settlements are commercial rather than residential-agricultural centers; the larger ones with regular market days (nine each month) are market towns, and the smaller centers without periodic markets are called *yao-tien-tzu*, literally "small shops." Sansheng *ch'ang*, the market town which is the administrative seat of the *hsiang*, is nestled on a high rise of land away from the main lines of communication and urban influences. Through the northern tip of the *hsiang*, however, runs the Chengtu-Chungking highway, along which, in the *hsiang*, are located four *yao-tien-tzu*, two of considerable size. At the crossroads of the paths in the *hsiang* are perhaps ten more *yao-tien-tzu* consisting of only one or two shophomes. The limits of Sansheng *ch'ang's* natural marketing area differ from the *hsiang* boundaries; the marketing area is somewhat larger but includes about the same number of people as the *hsiang*.

Sansheng *hsiang* has had some fifteen years of experience with the *pao-chia* system.[4] It is now admin-

istratively divided into eleven *pao*, while each of these in turn is divided into about ten *chia* of twenty to thirty families. In this area *pao* are of functional importance in the social as well as the strictly political realm. Four of the *pao*, Nos. 8–11, touch on or are crossed by the highway; there the modernizing and commercial influences are strongest. The first *pao* corresponds to the market town itself, while *pao* 2–7 are strictly agricultural.

HISTORICAL BACKGROUND

The population of the Chengtu area was radically altered in size and composition by the catastrophic events of the period between the Ming and Ch'ing dynasties.[5] In the 1630s, the usual end-of-dynasty troubles had so weakened the Ming's control of Szechwan that bandits and petty rebels rose up throughout the land. Two of the rebel bandits active in Szechwan made permanent places for themselves in Chinese history: Li Tzu-ch'eng by capturing the Ming capital, Peking, and Chang Hsien-

---

holds form one *chia*, while from six to fifteen or more (ideally ten) adjacent *chia* constitute one *pao*. The *chia* and *pao* heads, theoretically elected but often appointed, are held responsible by their immediate superiors in the local governmental hierarchy for the behavior of the families in their respective constituencies. The Communists are now gradually abolishing the *pao-chia* system, replacing it in rural areas with village and *hsiang* "people's governments."

[5] The account of these events is based on articles in the *Huayang Hsien Gazetteer* (in Chinese), 17 vols., Chengtu, 1934; and on the *Record of Chang Hsien-chung's Szechwan Massacre* (in Chinese), 2 vols., Chengtu, 1950.

---

[3] *Statistical Yearbook, op. cit.*, p. 60.
[4] The *pao-chia* system, an old Chinese device for administrative and security purposes, was revived by the Kuomintang in the 1930s in part to strengthen centralized control at the local level and combat Communism. According to the modern system, from six to twenty or more (ideally ten) neighbouring house-

chung by precipitating the most thorough devastation known in the long history of Szechwan. Both men led armies into the province on several occasions in their bids for power, and it must be remembered that theirs were only the more spectacular of the hundreds of armed groups who pillaged, plundered and fought over the land during the half-century following 1630.

The stories told about Chang Hsien-chung are unbelievable; if even a small proportion of them has any basis in fact, he ranks among the more bloodthirsty tyrants of history. Chang was a native of Shensi province, but as a child he learned much about the rich and productive province to the southwest from his father, who took frequent trips there on government business. He also heard a biased account of the Szechwanese, for his father had some unfortunate experience with the natives and recounted his losses of face to the boy. It is also said that Chang, posing in his earlier forays into Szechwan as a liberator of the people from their Ming oppressors, was enraged on several occasions to find the common people rallying under Ming leadership against him. In any case, by 1645 when his army swept victorious into Chengtu, he had developed an exceptional brutality and conceived an undying hatred for the Szechwanese people.

Chang set himself up in Chengtu as "King of the West" and ruled by killing. He reputedly killed the city people for trying to flee from his capital and the country people for not bringing grain to the city. When the surrounding countryside had been stripped bare and agriculture had come to a standstill, it is said that he killed to feed his troops on human flesh. Finally in 1647, to meet the double threat of Li Tzu-ch'eng and Ch'ing troops, he razed the city to the ground and left for the north where he died in battle.

At the peak of his power, Chang controlled most of Szechwan, but the massacre was worse in and around Chengtu, where it is estimated a million people were slain during Chang's 15-month reign. After he left, epidemics, lack of food, bandits and tigers depleted the remaining population. When the Ch'ing governor moved to Chengtu in 1652, he is reported to have found wild animals roaming the streets. It was not until the beginning of K'ang Hsi (1662) that the city began to function normally, and only in 1681 did a Ch'ing general finally subdue all the bandits in the area.

With the Ch'ing governors and generals came troops from Kansu, Shensi, and north Szechwan, and they were the first to begin filling the population vacuum of the Chengtu plain. They were followed shortly by a trickle of immigrants from the neighboring provinces of Hupeh, Hunan, and Shensi. The trickle grew to a stream as the imperial government encouraged immigration and imposed compulsory migration on certain groups of Central Chinese. By the early eighteenth century, most of the rich rice lands of the plain had been repopulated; only the devastated areas in the hills east of the city remained largely unoccupied.

The news of the opportunities and prosperity in Szechwan was slow in getting as far afield as Kwangtung. When the northeast section of that province had some severe famine years at the end of K'ang Hsi (1662–1723), some of the more adventuresome Hakka families there set out for the west and eventually settled in the hills east of Chengtu, where they were reminded of their former homes in the Lingnan mountains.[6] The Hakkas in Kwangtung heard how well these pioneers fared, and during succeeding famine years all through Yung Cheng (1723–36) and up to the tenth year of Ch'ien Lung (1746) they migrated to Huayang *hsien,* and in smaller numbers to other parts of Szechwan.

The Hakka people are hardy and adaptable migrants. Their origin as a separate people dates back apparently to Liang Tsin (A.D. 265–419), when the depredations of such non-Chinese nomads as the Hsiung-nu caused a group of Honanese to leave their homes on the Yellow River plain and settle in the Yangtze valley. In succeeding dynasties the descendants of these first migrants moved farther south to Kiangsi and Fukien provinces, and it was probably not until Southern Sung (1127–1278) that later descendants moved in number to northeast Kwangtung. Intruding into these southern provinces of distinct language and culture, they were dubbed by the natives "guest families," whence the term Hakka. In the Ch'ing dynasty, the devastation of Szechwan and the increase in trade with Malaya and the East Indies opened up new avenues of migration for the Hakkas, and when hard-pressed by nature or the government they emigrated in swarms. Today, they form about 15 per cent of the large Chinese population in southeast

Asia.[7] In Szechwan, however, they form only cultural islands,[8] the largest being the 150,000 populating the east hills in Huayang *hsien,* in a sea of Szechwanese descended from natives of neighbouring provinces.

Little can be said of the population changes in the Chengtu area since the last major migrations. During the nationwide prosperity of Ch'ien Lung (1736–96), the population of the region increased probably more rapidly than elsewhere for its earlier devastation. In 1796, the official Manchu report for Huayang *hsien* listed 48,883 households with 113,446 males and 92,215 females,[9] which if true would give a household size of 4.2 and a sex ratio of 123.0. The Taiping rebellion little affected western Szechwan (though some of the Hakka soldiers from Kwangtung under the Taiping general, Shih Ta-k'ai, stayed on with their clansmen in Huayang *hsien*), and the population appears to have doubled during the next 150 years.

During the recent war with Japan,

---

[6] The data on Hakka migrations are taken from an unpublished thesis in Chinese written by Hsu Pao-t'ien for the Sociology Department of West China Union University in 1948, and from the clan books of the Lin, Pai, Fan, Chang, Hsieh, Liao, and Li clans of Huayang *hsien.*

[7] Recent estimates of the Hakka population in southeast Asia are to be found on p. 80 of the writer's *Report on the Chinese in Southeast Asia* (issued by the Southeast Asia Program, Cornell University, February 1951). The percentage of the total Chinese population which is Hakka is highest for three British territories (North Borneo 56 per cent, Sarawak and Brunei 31 per cent, Federation of Malaya 21 per cent) and Indonesia (21 per cent), sizeable for Thailand and Vietnam (12 and 10 per cent respectively) and smallest for Burma, Singapore, Cambodia, and the Philippines. A rough estimate for the total Hakka population of these ten political units is 1,450,000.

[8] The Szechwan Hakkas have preserved a few non-Szechwan social customs and are bilingual, speaking only their own language among themselves.

[9] *Huayang Hsien Gazetteer, op. cit.,* vol. IV, p. 1.

"down-river" Chinese migrated to Szechwan in great numbers, and Sansheng *hsiang* was not unaffected by their influx. In 1947, 7.8 per cent of the population of the four *pao* touching on the highway (Nos. 8–11) were natives of provinces other than Szechwan.[10] How little immigration there has been in recent generations into that part of the *hsiang* away from the main lines of communication is seen in the distribution according to place of birth of the population of *pao* 1–7: 97.0 per cent are natives of Huayang *hsien,* 2.9 per cent are from other *hsien* in Szechwan, with only 0.1 per cent from outside the province.

SOURCES OF DATA

In November 1949, the writer moved to Sansheng *hsiang* to make an anthropological community study. After 2½ months, however, he was requested by the newly arrived Communist Liberation Army to cease research; hence there are unfortunate gaps in the data collected. Most of the material presented below was tabulated from the raw statistics collected in 1947 by the *chia, pao* and *hsiang* officials in connection with a government "census."[11] Demographers

rightly deprecate the value of the published population statistics collected through the *pao-chia* system.[12] In this case, however, being familiar with the area from which the statistics were obtained, having access to the raw data themselves, and being in a position to discuss with the *pao-chia* leaders the methods of collecting materials and the definitions of terms used, the writer was able to glean meaningful and reasonably accurate data from the census statistics.

The eighth *pao* was selected for more detailed investigation because, more than any other *pao,* its population is similar to that of the whole *hsiang.*[13] As with the *hsiang,* the northern tip of the eighth *pao* touches the highway, while the remainder lies back in the less accessible hills. Just as two of the *hsiang*'s eleven *pao* are predominantly commercial, so are two of the eighth *pao*'s ten *chia.* A list of all the family heads in the eighth *pao* was obtained and, with the help of the *pao* head, brought up to date. Then from the heads of the various *chia* detailed information as to the landholdings, education, occupations, composition, etc., of each family was obtained. Thus the *chia* heads, in a position to know every detail about the twenty-five or so families for

---

10 Some of these outsiders were military personnel who have since left the *hsiang.* All figures in this paragraph are compiled from the 1947 Sansheng *hsiang* statistics; see the section below on Sources of Data.

11 In 1947, each *chia* head brought his records of each family in the *chia* up to date, interviewing family heads where necessary. Data as to age, sex, marital status, occupation, place of birth and educational attainment for each individual (by family) were submitted through the *pao* heads to the *hsiang* administrative office, where clerks copied off the raw data and compiled totals by

chia and *pao.* Of such statistics from each *hsiang* in the province were compiled the abstracts for the so-called 1947 "census."

12 See, for example, A. J. Jaffe, "A Review of the Censuses and Demographic Statistics of China," *Population Studies,* I, No. 3 (December, 1947), 320–22.

13 In representative characteristics the *pao* population compares respectively with that of the entire *hsiang* as follows: *fu* (household) size, 4.34 versus 4.36 persons; percentage married, 41 versus 43; percentage literate, 39 versus 38; percentage 0–14 in age, 31.2 versus 32.8; percentage over 12 years of age with business occupations, 9.7 versus 8.9.

which each had responsibility, were a second source of the data here presented.

Finally, a one-fifth sample of the families in the eighth *pao* was drawn up (52 out of 262) and the family heads interviewed.[14] The sample distribution conformed to that of the total population in all known particulars. In addition to checking the *hsiang* "census" figures and the information obtained from the *chia* heads, sampling made possible some tentative conclusions unwarranted by the other data alone.

---

[14] Ten one-fifth samples were selected at random by drawing numbered slips from a container. Each sample was tested for conformity to the total *pao* population in all known characteristics, and the sample which conformed most closely in most particulars was used.

AGE AND SEX DISTRIBUTION

The population statistics for Sansheng *hsiang* are tabulated according to age and sex in Table 1. It can be noted in column 5 that the percentage of the total population who are males in each age group under 50 is lowest for group 20–24 and increases in both directions to peaks at groups 10–14 and 35–39. From the writer's investigations it seems certain that these statistics are here in error due to faulty registration aimed at avoiding Kuomintang military conscription. That is, men and boys in their teens and early 20s tended to give younger than true ages, while men in their late 20s and 30s gave older than true ages.[15] Local officials connived

---

[15] It may also be that some young

TABLE 1. Distribution of the *Hsiang* Population According to Age and Sex

(1)	(2)	(3)	(4)	(5)	(6)	(7)	(8)
		Persons		Percentage of total population			Sex ratio (males per
Age group	Males	Females	Total	Males	Females	Total	100 females)
0–4	1025	1030	2055	6.42	6.45	12.87	99.51
5–9	861	682	1543	5.39	4.27	9.66	126.25
10–14	945	690	1635	5.92	4.32	10.24	136.96
15–19	716	562	1278	4.49	3.52	8.01	127.40
20–24	524	478	1002	3.28	3.00	6.28	109.62
25–29	589	487	1076	3.69	3.05	6.74	120.94
30–34	615	485	1100	3.85	3.04	6.89	126.80
35–39	663	596	1259	4.15	3.74	7.89	111.24
40–44	568	485	1053	3.56	3.04	6.60	117.11
45–49	630	454	1084	3.95	2.84	6.79	138.77
50–54	453	334	787	2.84	2.09	4.93	135.63
55–59	395	286	681	2.47	1.79	4.26	138.11
60–64	290	249	539	1.82	1.56	3.38	116.47
65–69	207	177	384	1.30	1.11	2.41	116.95
70 and over	214	273	487	1.34	1.71	3.05	78.39
Totals	8695	7268	15963	54.47	45.53	100.00	119.63

in these inaccuracies, because the conscription quotas laid down by the government were based on the number of males in military age groups, and these leaders were responsible for rounding up the conscripts. If compensation is made for this error, the percentages in each age group roughly decrease from younger to older, presenting a slightly bell-shaped population pyramid.

Of special interest are the distribution of the female population and the sex ratio, since these statistics clearly reflect certain Chinese culture values. If the data for southwest China are accepted as valid, it would appear that a larger proportion of girls are born than in the west.[16] Yet the proportion of females drops steadily with age for the childhood groups.[17] Even if compensation is not made for the faulty registration of young men, the sex ratio is well over 100 for every age group from 1 to 70. Clearly the data must be in error or the emigration and/or death rates for females must be considerably higher than for males. Disproportionate migration of females to the city is ruled out by the sex ratio for Chengtu, 152,[18] extremely unbalanced in favor of men. The only logical explanation of the surplus of females in the earliest ages and the deficits later is that there is either severe under-reporting of boy babies and young children or misreporting of boy babies as girl babies. Either practice may arise from the culturally sanctioned desire to conceal good fortune, of which male progeny is the symbol *par excellence,* and in particular to conceal the baby boy from begrudging evil spirits who might otherwise strike at the parents by bringing misfortune to their male infant.

The major explanation of the surplus of boys after the period of early infancy lies in the greater cultural value placed on boys, which operates mainly through denying to girls the same subsistence and health advantages given to boys. Probably little of this discrimination is deliberate policy on the part of parents, but rather their unthinking expression of attitudes and adherence to patterns common to the whole society. A mother may come to love sons more than daughters because birth of the former enhances her status in the eyes of her husband and the community; hence she may give preferential feeding and treatment to her sons. Boys are given the first opportunity to attend school, while girls still, for the most part, must stay at home and work hard for subsistence. In country homes sons are early allowed to move to the head table with their father and other adult males and guests, where the diet is appreciably better, while young daughters are commonly relegated to the table for hired laborers and babies.

In discussions of Chinese population problems it is invariably pointed out that the desire for male heirs to continue ancestor worship is an im-

---

men were intentionally not reported, though this practice was disclaimed by *pao-chia* officials who frankly told of other deliberate inaccuracies.

[16] The census of 1942 of three *hsien* in the Chengtu Plain gave a sex ratio at birth of 99.0. The 1939 census of Cheng Kung (Yunnan) and the 1942 census of the Kunning Lake Region gave respectively sex ratios at birth of 89.1 and 88.8. See Table 3 in Ta·Chen, "Population in modern China," *American Journal of Sociology,* LI, No. 1 (July, 1946), part 2, p. 81.

[17] Statistics for age group 0–4 are also available split into two groups, under 1 and aged 1–4, and these have sex ratios respectively of 96.5 and 100.1.

[18] *Statistical Yearbook, op. cit.,* p. 73.

portant factor contributing to the continuing overproduction of children. It is often forgotten, however, that the same complex of cultural values which emphasizes the desire for male progeny also operates to reduce drastically the number of women who reach childbearing age. The Chinese are a marrying people. In Sansheng *hsiang* 95.2 per cent of the women over 18 are married, and spinsters are virtually unknown. Once the culture patterns are so changed that the desire for male progeny is lessened, proportionally more females will live to childbearing age and marry. In Sansheng *hsiang* at the present time only 72.6 per cent of the men over 18 are married, for the scarcity of women leads to late marriage and bachelorhood.[19]

It may be noted (from column 8 of Table 1) that the sex ratio shows a downward trend from the 45–49 age group on to old age, and that, for the very old, women outnumber men. The end of the childbearing period may lessen the hazards for Chinese women, even giving them a greater probability of further life than men

at the same age. But an equally important factor is found in the cultural attitudes. The Chinese woman who has survived subtle discrimination in childhood and borne heirs for her husband's family has a position of respect. To her, as well as her husband, are due the patterns of filial piety which constitute an effective system of old-age insurance. In consequence, the usual demographic pattern whereby women outlive men is allowed, by the Chinese patterns of sex equality for the aged, to assert itself. It is not surprising to find that widows in Sansheng *hsiang* outnumber widowers by 994 to 509.

POPULATION ON THE LAND

The total area of Sansheng *hsiang* is in the neighborhood of 8.3 square miles, which gives a population density of about 1920 per square mile. In a hilly area such as this, however, at most two-thirds of the land is actually cultivated. Land ownership and tenancy figures for the whole *hsiang* are unavailable, while the statistics on occupations from the 1947 census are unreliable beyond salvage. Hence this section must depend solely on the eighth-*pao* data.

Cultivated land, according to local custom, is of two main kinds: *t'ien*, flat, terraced fields with comparatively abundant water supply, and *ti*, unterraced hillside and hilltop fields which must be irrigated, if at all, from the storage pools dotting the countryside. *T'ien* is planted in rice during the summer and either left fallow during the winter to collect water or put in wheat, beans, barley, or rape. For *ti* the main crops are corn and sweet potatoes in the summer, and wheat, barley, beans, and

---

[19] This argument is predicated on the assumption that the surpluses of males shown in this and other counts and compilations of the Chinese people are real. If so, then the major explanation must be the relatively higher mortality of the female, since major assumptions as to under-reporting of females are required for the assumption that the proportion of boys born is even as high as it is in the West. There are no vital statistics for Chinese living in the peasants situation in China that permit definitive analysis of this relationship of the sexes as a whole and by age. The relatively accurate statistics collected on Chinese populations by the Japanese in Taiwan and Manchoukuo are not relevant, for here the conditions of living and the pressures on subsistence were altered sharply from those in the local areas such as that studied here.

TABLE 2. Distribution of Eighth-*Pao* Families with Landholdings According to Landownership and Predominant Type of Land

	Number of families cultivating		
	Mostly *t'ien*	Mostly *ti*	Totals
Landowners	18	17	35
Part tenants	5	2	7
Tenants	32	80	112
Totals	55	99	154

peas in the winter. Since Sansheng *hsiang* is located near city markets, a considerable proportion of the *ti* is given over to vegetables and orchards. Rice is the most productive crop grown in the area, contributing, for instance, almost three times as much food per unit of land as wheat; consequently *t'ien* is far more valuable than *ti*. In Sansheng *hsiang* the proportion of *t'ien* to *ti* is almost two to one. The holdings of *t'ien*, however, are more concentrated than those of *ti*, and the fields larger, so that more farmers cultivate mostly *ti* than cultivate mostly *t'ien* (see Table 2).

The system of land utilization in Sansheng *hsiang* is too complex to be described in full here. Suffice it to say that most of the land is owned by absentee landlords living in Chengtu, by a few landlords living in the *hsiang*, and by several of the more prosperous clans. Tenants and subtenants actually manage most of farms, while the field labor itself is done as often by the landless workers as by the tenants or owners themselves. Without going into detail, Table 3 shows the number of families in the eighth *pao* with landholdings of different sizes. The local unit of land measure is the *mong* (*mou* or *mu* in other dialects), about 6½ of which equal 1 acre.

TABLE 3. Distribution of Landed, Eighth-*Pao* Families According to Size of Holdings[a]

Mong									
Owned and/or rented	0 to 1.4	1.5 to 2.9	3.0 to 4.4	4.5 to 5.9	6.0 to 7.4	7.5 to 8.9	9.0 to 10.4	10.5 to 11.9	12.0 to 14.9
No. of families	22	19	35	11	7	13	12	6	3

Mong									
Owned and/or rented	15.0 to 17.9	18.0 to 20.9	21.0 to 23.9	24.0 to 29.9	30.0 to 35.9	36.0 to 41.9	42.0 to 47.9	48.0 to 53.9	80
No. of families	6	4	4	2	3	2	0	4	1

[a] The class boundaries were so chosen because the farmers tend to round off the amount of their landholdings to the nearest lower integer. Note that the class intervals double at 12 *mong* and again at 24 *mong*; the vertical lines divide the data into uniform intervals of 6 *mong*.

It can readily be calculated from the table 81.2 per cent of all the families with land have less than 2 acres, while 56.5 per cent have less than 1. In view of the fact that non-agricultural production in the *pao* is negligible, the following percentage distribution of eighth-*pao* families is especially startling:

	%
Landed families with from 2 to 13 acres	11.1
Landed families with less than 2 acres	47.7
Landless families	39.7
Unknown	1.5
	100.0

This is the kind of situation that must be expected when more than 15,000 people live *off* an area of land which, if located in an upper middle-class residential suburb of a western city, a similar number of people would merely *live in*. Redistribution of the farmland in this area, scheduled by the Communist regime for the fall of 1951, while tending to equalize wealth and living standards, will increase income from the land for the whole rural populace only by the fraction which now goes in rent to absentee landlords.[20]

In the eighth *pao* there are 104 landless families. The chief bread-winners in forty-seven of these are petty merchants and professionals, while in fifty-seven they are workers: agricultural laborers, artisans, and those engaged in (manpower) transportation. Life is hardest in Sansheng *hsiang* for the landless.

---

[20] And by the same amount, generally speaking, private capital in the city available for the development of industry will be reduced.

FAMILY SIZE AND COMPOSITION

The value of many Chinese population statistics has been reduced by confusion between *de facto* and *de jure* populations and between family and household. As far as can be determined, the 1947 census in Sansheng *hsiang* enumerated the *de facto* population.[21] The average size of the *fu* (*hu* in other dialects, usually translated household) was calculated from the 1947 census data. By *fu* was meant relatives living together in the same house plus *ch'ang-nien*, year-round agricultural workers who room and board with their employers. Thus if in a single house were found one family of five members, one tenant family of three members, a *ch'ang-nien* working for the larger family, and a bachelor merchant unrelated to the others but boarding with the tenant family, the census would list three *fu* of sizes 6, 3, and 1. With *fu* thus defined, its average size for the whole *hsiang* was found to be 4.36.

For purposes of his own investigations, the writer defined a household as "those persons living in the same house who have a common board" and a family as "those *related* persons living in the same house who have a common board," with the added proviso that a single individual sharing room and board with a

---

[21] In Chinese and other oriental cultures in which family ties are particularly strong, the household is often considered to include persons not living therein but bound by kinship or semi-feudal obligations to the head of the household. A *de jure* report in many cases gives this "legal" household and results in the double enumeration of certain individuals living away from "home," A *de facto* report, however, never includes more than the co-living unit under one roof.

family to which he is unrelated should be counted neither in the family nor as a family, but only as a member of the household. If the writer came across the hypothetical house mentioned above, he would list two families of sizes 5 and 3, and two households of sizes 6 and 4. For the eighth *pao* the average family size was found to be 4.60 and the average household size 4.71.

The following outline divides families into types which will facilitate the presentation of data on family composition:

I. Families whose head is or was married.

   A. Those of which the family head's spouse is still a living member.

     (1) Those with no intact married couple other than the family head and wife.

      (*a*) Those with no widowed parents of the family head or of his wife.

      (*b*) Those with at least one widowed parent of the head or of his wife.

     (2) Those with at least one intact conjugal couple

other than the family head and his wife.

   B. Those in which the spouse of the family head is dead.

     (1) Those headed by widows.

     (2) Those headed by widowers.

II. Families whose head is single.

The percentage distribution, based on the results of the eighth-*pao* sampling, of these structural types is given in Table 4.

When the eleven *pao* are arranged in order of *fu* size, as in Table 5, factors relevant to family size can be pointed out. First of all it might be noted that the four *pao* on the highway, containing all the sizeable *yao-tien-tzu*, and the market town itself (first *pao*) have the lowest *fu* sizes. These *pao* have a greater proportion of landless workers and merchants, are more subject to urban influences, and have better educational facilities (each of these five *pao* has a public school, while only two of the other six do). The figures in the third column may be taken as an index of the relative importance of agriculture as an occupation, and they have a positive correlation of 0.936 with average *fu* size.

TABLE 4.   Average Family Size and Percentage Distribution of Families and Persons According to Family Type

Family type	Per cent of families	Per cent of persons	Average family size
IA1a: "conjugal"	55.8	48.1	4.0
IA1b: "stem"	15.4	21.3	6.4
IA2: "composite"	9.6	19.7	9.4
IB1: "widows"	11.6	7.9	3.2
IB2: "widowers"	3.8	1.7	2.0
II: "single"	3.8	1.3	1.5
Totals	100.0	100.0	4.6

TABLE 5. *Fu* Size and Percentage Employed in Agriculture by *Pao*[a]

Pao	Average fu size	Per cent of population employed in agriculture[b]
4	5.20	48.5
7	4.82	39.6
3	4.79	30.2
5	4.76	34.1
2	4.75	35.1
6	4.60	34.6
8	4.34	20.7
9	4.17	20.3
1	4.14	10.6
11	4.02	22.5
10	3.87	7.9

[a] Figures from the 1947 census data; *fu* as defined above.

[b] These figures from the 1947 data are meaningless as absolute percentages, since the definition of "agricultural occupation," insofar as any was adhered to, was unreasonably exclusive. But they are useful as an index of "agriculturalness."

The eighth-*pao* sample data show a positive correlation of 0.526 between the amount of land owned and/or rented and family size, and when the families are grouped according to landholdings, as in Table 6, the average family size is seen to increase steadily with the size of the holdings. The data further suggest four ways in which large landholdings operate to give large family size. (1) Men with little or no land find it hard to find a wife in view of the shortage of women; hence a disproportionate number of them fail to marry. The single men in the eighth-*pao* sample had either no land or a fraction of a *mong*. (2) Since most wealth in Sansheng *hsiang* comes from the land, families with little or no holdings suffer from inadequate diet, housing, sanitation, etc. Women and children in these families, therefore, tend to be in poorer health, which

TABLE 6. Average Size of Families Grouped According to Landholdings

Amount (in mong) of land owned and/or rented	Average family size	Percentage of families	
		Sample	Population
0	3.56	34.5	39.8
0–2.2	3.71	13.5	13.7
2.3–4.2	4.29	13.5	14.4
4.3–7.2	5.17	11.5	6.9
7.3–11.2	6.00	13.5	12.2
11.3 and over	6.57	13.5	11.5
Unknown	—	—	1.5
	4.60	100.0	100.0

results on the one hand, in more deaths of women in childbirth and fewer live births and, on the other, in more deaths of children, especially infants.[22] (3) The wealthier families tend to adhere more closely to upper-class standards, including especially the composite family, with its ideal of several generations under one roof. Of the five composite families in the sample, two are in the wealthiest group of families and one each is in the next most wealthy groups. (4) The wealthier families keep and attract a disproportionate number of relatives to live with them. The number of "extra" relatives (those not included in the conjugal unit or units forming the core of the family) per family increases from 0.17 for the landless families, to 0.40 for those

with holdings of 7.2 *mong* or less, to 0.57 for those with holdings of 7.3 *mong* or more.

One cannot escape the conclusions from these data that family size in this rural area is held down in large degree by poverty, that without concomitant cultural changes an appreciable rise in living standards would result in larger families, and that this larger family size would be due largely to an absolute population increase.

EDUCATION

Most of the population of the *hsiang* is still illiterate, and few have any public schooling. From Table 7 it is apparent, first of all, that the seven *pao* away from the main lines of communication and of modern influences, as compared with the whole *hsiang*, have a lower literacy rate and a far smaller proportion of persons with any public schooling (altogether only 8.34 per cent). Secondly, many fewer

---

[22] This statement of relationships between land, health and mortality is a hypothetical explanation for the population studied here, for no historical vital records were available for analysis. However, in the rural areas of Japan the relationship between land and mortality predicated here actually exists.

TABLE 7. Percentage Distribution of the Population over 6 Years, According to Highest Educational Attainment, for *Pao* 1–7 and the Entire *Hsiang*

Population	Sex	Illiterate	Old private schools	Primary school[a]		Middle school[a]		Higher education[a]	
				Some	Graduated	Some	Graduated	Some	Graduated
Pao 1–7	M.	48.82	41.86	6.53	0.92	1.22	0.47	0.08	0.10
	F.	86.00	6.91	5.49	0.72	0.54	0.25	0.03	0.06
	All	65.23	26.43	6.07	0.83	0.92	0.38	0.06	0.08
Entire *hsiang*	M.	46.16	37.12	10.26	1.07	3.29	1.12	0.25	0.73
	F.	81.73	6.09	8.38	0.71	2.21	0.56	0.11	0.21
	All	62.16	23.17	9.41	0.91	2.81	0.87	0.18	0.49

[a] "Primary School: Some" includes those who have had some or all lower primary schooling (first four grades) and those who have had some upper primary schooling (grades 5–6) but not graduated. Similarly, "Middle School: Some" includes those who have had some or all junior middle school training (grades 7–9) and those who have had some senior middle school training (grades 10–12) but not graduated. "Higher Education" includes those with training at military academies and advanced technical schools as well as in colleges and universities.

TABLE 8. Educational Attainments of Eighth-*Pao* Family Heads According to Economic-Occupational Status

Economic-occupational group	Highest educational attainment									
	Years of private schooling						Public schooling		Totals	
	None		2 or less		3 or more					
	No.	%	No.	%	No.	%	No.	%	No.	%
Landless workers	38	66.7	11	19.3	6	10.5	2	3.5	57	100.0
Landholders with 0–4.2 *mong*	44	59.4	17	23.0	12	16.2	1	1.4	74	100.0
Landholders with 4.3–11.2 *mong*	28	56.0	10	20.0	11	22.0	1	2.0	50	100.0
Landholders with 11.3 *mong* and over	11	36.7	10	33.3	7	23.3	2	6.7	30	100.0
Landless merchants and professionals	15	31.9	11	23.4	11	23.4	10	21.3	47	100.0
Unknown	4								4	
Totals	140	53.4	59	22.5	47	18.0	16	6.1	262	100.0

women than men are literate. Thirdly, most of the literate were educated in old-style private schools. And fourthly, the ratio between women and men with public schooling, being much less disproportionate than the sex ratio of those with old-style private schooling, indicates that girls now have far greater access to formal education than they did before public schools were introduced.

In the entire *hsiang* at present, fewer than 450 children (less than one-seventh of those aged 5–14) are enrolled in public schools. Six *pao* schools, all located in makeshift quarters, give instruction up to the fourth grade, while the one central school, in the town, goes up to the sixth. No education above the primary level is available in the *hsiang*. There are still more than ten old-style private schools giving instruction in the Chinese classics, but all of these together have less than 175 students.

Data on education were collected for the individual family heads in the eighth *pao*, making it possible to bring out the relation between highest educational attainment and economic and occupational status, as in Table 8. The proportion of literate family heads is lowest for landless workers, increases steadily for landholders with increase in size of holdings, and is largest for merchants and professionals. In an immobile society such as that of rural China, educational attainment is certainly more a result of economic status than vice versa. Education still tends to be a luxury which the poorer families cannot afford.[23]

A single study of this kind of a limited area can, of course, be no more than suggestive. No conclusions as to the population of China or the demography of the Chinese are justi-

[23] Tuition is charged for at public as well as private schools. However, the loss of students' labor is probably a consideration of equal importance in deterring parents from sending their children to school.

fied by these findings. This is, indeed, only a "study in miniature." However, if a sufficient number of detailed studies were made in China of the relationships of the people, economy and cultural values, some definitive hypotheses as to the demography of that fifth of the world's people who are Chinese might begin to emerge.

Demographic Cycles and Economic Development: Some Observations Based upon Australian Experience*

W. D. Borrie

Australia is a land of paradoxes. Covering about three million square miles, it is about as big geographically as the United States; yet in terms of population it is as small as Greater London or New York. Living substantially by export of a few primary products, and notably wool, it is yet more industrialized than the U.S.A., with almost 40 per cent of the Australian work force engaged in manufacturing and associated industries and only 15 per cent in occupations of a rural character. The most thinly populated nation-state on earth, with only three persons per square mile, Australia has at the same time one of the world's most highly urbanized societies, with 54 per cent of its people living in the capital cities of the six states and almost 79 per cent living in all urban areas.[1]

Yet, despite all these apparent paradoxes, economically Australia can be "typed" as a young, new-world country whose growth has been, and still is being, stimulated by high levels of public and private investment, which lead to and sustain high material standards of life. Demographically speaking Australia can also be "typed" as a Western society that has run through the typical cycle of high fertility—high mortality patterns to one in which fertility displays a high degree of rational control and in which mortality is amongst the lowest in the world.

* W. D. Borrie, "Demographic Cycles and Economic Development: Some Observations Based Upon Australian Experience," *Population Index*, 26 (January, 1960), 3–15.

[1] Defined as all incorporated cities and towns, and other towns with a population of 1,000 or more persons (750 in Tasmania).

THE COLONIAL PERIOD, 1788-1900

In terms of its nonindigenous population Australia is a very young country.[2] The first European settlement was in 1788; but so long as the eastern colonies were administered as convict settlements growth was slow. Until 1850 only 332,000 Europeans had settled in Australia. Of these 146,000 were convicts and 187,000 were free settlers. The young colonies still had little natural attraction for Britain's emigrants, and a high proportion of the free settlers were assisted by revenues raised from the sales of colonial lands along the general lines advocated by Wakefield and the "systematic colonizers." In New South Wales, by far the most populous colony, all but 28,000 of the 117,300 free settlers who arrived between 1829 and 1850 received assistance, most of it in the form of subsidized fares. A substantial part of such assistance was given to encourage female and family immigration. Even so, the young colonies carried heavy excesses of males. In 1851 in New South Wales and South Australia the male to female sex ratio at ages 21–44 was approximately 160:100. But on the other hand a high proportion of adult immigrants were in the childbearing age groups, and they both brought substantial numbers of children with them and bore

many more after their arrival in an environment in which mortality was comparatively low.

Yet, when the opening up of the rich gold fields in Victoria and New South Wales in 1850 gave the Australian colonies their first real "pulling" power as attractions for immigrants, they harbored only 405,400 persons. Then the pace quickened: the gold decade 1851–60 brought 601,000 immigrants, most of whom remained to make their homes in Australia. Again the assisted element (229,500) was very important in this growth.

In terms of both people and capital, the gold rushes of the 'fifties set the Australian colonies off on a long period of rapid growth which may be summarized as follows (figures in thousands):

Period	Growth from natural increase	Growth from immigration	Total growth
1861–1870	335	168	503
1871–1880	392	191	583
1881–1890	537	383	920
1891–1900	589	25	614
1861–1900	1,853	767	2,620

Growth from 405,400 in 1850 to 3,765,400 when the century closed may not be quantitatively spectacular; but in spite of the smallness of the base figure in 1850, a ninefold increase was very substantial.

The maturity of the population is also apparent in the fact that after 1860 the greater part of growth (69 per cent) came from Australian-born children. The demands created by expanding families provided one important factor stimulating the economic growth, which in turn acquired an expanding work force derived from immigration. Immigration, however, continued to be a significant comple-

[2] This article is restricted to the nonaboriginal population. The story of the aboriginal population since European settlement is as unhappy in Australia as in most other European-settled new-world areas. What their population was at the first white settlement in 1788 is still a matter of conjecture: they may have numbered 300,000. Today full-blood and half-caste aboriginals number only about 75,000, but there are signs that they are again increasing.

ment to natural increase until it was cut off by the economic collapse following 1891. For the 30 years preceding this point, the total rate of growth of the Australian population was one of the highest in the world. In four of those 30 years it exceeded 4 per cent; in 23 it exceeded 3 per cent; and in 21 years the growth from natural increase alone exceeded 2 per cent.

The financial crisis of 1891 applied the closure to this great era of economic development, and likewise to some aspects of population growth. Immigration was cut off; the colonies had no natural "attractive" power with the onset of economic recession, and policies of sponsoring immigration (which had been progressively pruned or abandoned with mounting economic difficulties of the 'eighties) were set aside in all colonies in the 'nineties. In addition, the years immediately around 1891 witnessed a sharp fall in birth rates and a check upon the decline in death rates. Consequently growth, now almost wholly dependent upon natural increase, fell sharply from an annual rate of 2.84 per cent in 1891 to 1.76 in 1896. Not until 1908 did the rate again exceed 2 per cent.

The birth rates of the Australian colonies had been falling steadily throughout these years of economic development (1861–1890). The average rate for all colonies remained above 40 per 1000 of population until 1868 and thereafter fell away to 35.5 in 1888. By the end of the century it was down to 27.3. Yet the decline in birth rates before the 'eighties was more the result of changes in the age structure of the populations than of decline in the fertility of married women. Legitimate birth rates per 1000 married women under the age of

45 years changed little between 1861 and 1881, but fell sharply in New South Wales over the next decade and in all colonies between 1891 and 1901.[3]

The differential timing of trends in the separate colonies offers scope for several interesting hypotheses: for example, the possible causal relation in Victoria between relatively low birth rates and a high degree of urbanization, or in Queensland between high birth rates and rapid rural development. Even more intriguing is the sharp decline in fertility in New South Wales between 1881 and 1891, well before the economic crisis of the latter year that marks the initial sharp downturn in the fertility rates of all other colonies.

These patterns suggest that while the impact of the economic crisis is clear, other factors than the purely economic were operating, at least in New South Wales. The latter hypothesis is further supported by the events after the revival of economic prosperity, which brought no return to high fertility patterns. The move towards the small-family system appears to have started in the 'eighties, to have been given an impetus by the events of the 'nineties, and to have taken firm and widespread root by the end of the century. Indeed from the 'eighties right through to the present there has been a very close corres-

---

[3] T. A. Goghlan, *The Decline in the Birth Rate of New South Wales* (Sydney, 1903), p. 3, gives the following legitimate birth rates per 1,000 married women under the age of 45 years:

Year	New South Wales	Victoria	Queensland
1861	340.8	302.2	—
1871	331.5	298.2	—
1881	336.3	298.4	316.2
1891	288.7	297.7	327.7
1901	235.3	228.6	254.0

pondence between trends in fertility in Australia and in a number of new world countries peopled by Europeans and enjoying high and improving material standards of living. The similarity has been particularly marked between the United States of America and Australia.

GROWTH AND
DISILLUSIONMENT, 1900–1940

The twentieth century opened with birth rates of approximately 26.5 per 1000 of population, the lowest ever recorded. Death rates were also well down to just over 12 per 1000 and were falling steadily, but the resultant natural increase of some 1.5 per cent a year was still below the levels of prefederation colonial days[4] and was widely felt to be insufficient for a young developing country.[5] The trend toward the small family was at least viewed with sufficient concern in New South Wales to lead in 1903 to the appointment of a Royal Commission to examine its cause and consequence and to recommend steps to reverse it.[6] The Commissioners con-

cluded that selfishness was the one motive common to all the reasons given by witnesses for the limitation of the size of the family, that "the effort of the race towards its increase in numbers is in inverse ratio to the effort of the individual toward his personal development," and that unless the nation could do better it would fall far behind the performance of Russia and Japan who were seen as "prospective rivals of Australia" in the Pacific.

This gloom was not entirely justified, for rates of growth were still high. The birth rate was now holding steady, and with improving mortality natural increase was showing a slight upward trend, from 14.21 per 1000 of population in 1900 to 17.44 in 1914. In addition, as more prosperous conditions returned, the traditional policy of priming the immigrant flow by offering passage assistance was revived. Modest net gains from immigration of 21,800 in 1909 and 29,912 in 1910 leapt to 74,400; 91,900; and 63,200 in 1911, 1912, and 1913 respectively, again raising annual growth well above 3 per cent a year.

The new prospect of rapid growth was cut short by the war of 1914–18, but Australia emerged from the war determined to press the pace of population growth. In 1920 the Federal government took over from the states the main responsibility for recruiting and assisting immigrants, and, in cooperation with the United Kingdom through the machinery of the Empire Settlement Act of 1922, set about peopling Australia. The net result fell far short of the oft-stated objective of "redistributing" the

---

[4] By 1861, six self-governing colonies had been developed in Australia; in 1901 these were brought together in a federal commonwealth with the central government having defined powers. There had, however, been close consultation on statistical matters long before federation, and censuses were taken on the same day and year and on approximately the same bases from 1881.

[5] In comparison with many young countries, knowledge about population trends was probably quite widely diffused in Australia through the comparative excellence of colonial censuses and registration systems and through the writings of people like H. W. Archer in Victoria and T. A. Coghlan in New South Wales, and later, in the Commonwealth period, of Sir George Knibbs.

[6] New South Wales, Parliamentary

Papers for 1904, Royal Commission on the Decline of the Birth Rate and on the Mortality of Infants in New South Wales, *Report.*

population of the British Empire, but between 1921 and 1930 the net gain from immigration was 313,000, and the extent of official promotion in this movement is apparent in the fact that over the same period 214,000 persons received passage assistance.

As in 1891, however, worsening economic conditions put an end to assisted immigration and again deprived Australia of any natural attractive power. Between 1931 and 1935 there was a small net loss of 10,800 through emigration; and even with improving economic conditions after 1935 there was no substantial support for the revival of large-scale sponsorship of immigration. A considerable part of the gain of 43,000 people between 1936 and 1940 represented refugees from Nazi persecution; there were few signs of the revival of the traditional flow from the British Isles (Table 1).

These prewar years appeared to confirm the findings of official United Kingdom Committees—particularly of the Overseas Settlement Board's final report in 1938—that the continued departure of large numbers of able-bodied workers was not in the best interests of the United Kingdom and that the Dominions might have to turn increasingly to continental Europe for new settlers.[7] Official concern in the United Kingdom about *emigration* was largely the result of published research which concluded from a study of reproduction rates that population decline was imminent. But even if the United Kingdom had emigrants to spare, Australia, with unemployment running at 8 to 10 per cent of the work force, was in no mood to receive them. In Australia pessimism about the future was deep-

ened by the revelation that the net reproduction rate had fallen below unity in 1931, and by projections based upon this fact which forecast impending population decline.[8] The picture was brightened a little by the further pessimism of the students of Australia's resources, who were busy whittling away the grand vision, current after the First World War, of an Australia carrying a hundred million people. The failure of the land settlement schemes of the 'twenties, the collapse of markets for Australia's primary exports, and a reemphasis of the theories that Australia was no more than a fertile rim with a dead and useless interior, all encouraged the view that the population-carrying capacity of Australia at reasonable living standards was more likely to be at the limit of 15 or 20 millions than 100 million.[9] Thus, if the era of growth from natural causes was drawing to a close, and if emigrants who could be spared from the British Isles were in short supply, there was at least comfort in the knowledge that Australian resources were severely limited anyway.

The concept of only limited population growth was prevalent until well into the years of the Second World War. As late as 1944 a report of the National Health and Medical Research Council[10] forecast a population that, in the absence of immigration, would never exceed 8.2 millions and would be declining by 1980. In the light of

---

[7] Cmd. 5766 for 1938.

[8] See W. S. Wolstenholme, "The Future of the Australian Population," *The Economic Record*, XII, No. 22 (June, 1936), 195–213.

[9] For an analysis of opinion of the time see W. D. Forsyth, *The Myth of Open Spaces* (Melbourne, 1942).

[10] *Report* of the 18th session, November 1944. Appendix I: Interim report . . . on the decline in the birth rate.

TABLE 1. Elements in Australian Population Growth, 1921–58; Annual Averages

Period	Population at end of period	Natural increase	Net immigration	Total increase[a]	Birth rate	Death rate[b]	Rates of increase per 1,000 of population		
							Natural increase	Net immigration	Total increase[a]
1921–25	6,003,027	81,693	36,653	118,346	23.9	9.5	14.3	6.4	20.7
1926–30	6,500,751	73,603	25,941	99,544	21.0	9.3	11.7	4.1	15.8
1931–35	6,755,662	52,650	−2,177	50,473	16.9	9.0	7.9	−0.3	7.6
1936–40	7,077,586	54,452	8,626	63,078	17.5	9.6	7.9	1.2	9.1
1941–45	7,430,197	67,536	1,562	69,098	20.3	11.0	9.3	0.2	9.5
1946	7,517,981	101,128	−15,148	85,980	23.6	10.1	13.5	−2.0	11.5
1947	7,637,963	108,777	10,611	119,388	24.1	9.7	14.4	1.4	15.8
1948	7,792,465	101,137	55,115	156,252	23.1	10.0	13.1	7.1	20.2
1949	8,045,570	106,001	150,001	256,002	22.9	9.5	13.4	19.0	32.4
1950	8,307,481	112,404	152,505	264,909	23.3	9.6	13.8	18.7	32.5
1951	8,527,907	111,510	111,433	222,943	23.0	9.7	13.2	13.2	26.4
1952	8,739,569	120,053	94,032	214,085	23.4	9.5	13.9	10.9	24.8
1953	8,902,686	122,047	42,897	164,944	22.9	9.1	13.8	4.9	18.7
1954	9,090,395	120,451	68,207	188,658	22.5	9.1	13.4	7.6	21.0
1955	9,313,291	125,641	97,255	222,896	22.6	8.9	13.7	10.6	24.3
1956	9,533,334	126,045	93,998	220,043	22.5	9.1	13.4	10.0	23.4
1957	9,747,471	135,405	78,732	214,137	22.9	8.8	14.0	8.2	22.2
1958	9,951,618	138,781	65,366	204,147	22.6	8.5	14.1	6.6	20.7

[a] These columns exclude official adjustments for the years 1933–54 calculated to bring the increase based on annual data into line with census results. The adjustments involved are, however, of minor importance from the aspect of trends, and in no year exceed 3,000. For years 1946–54 the adjustments bring rates of increase down slightly, but in no case by more than 0.2 per 1,000.

[b] Rates include deaths of defence personnel, which averaged 7,215 for each year, 1941–45.

the facts as they were then known the projections were reasonable. They were made at the latter end of a decade during which natural increase was consistently between 7 and 9 per 1000 of population. The rise in birth rates per 1000 of population from 17.4 in 1939 to almost 21.0 in 1944 was assumed to be but a reflection of peak wartime marriage rates, which averaged over 11 per 1000 of population between 1940 and 1943. In 1944 there was nothing in the history of marriage and fertility in Australia, or in the demographic lessons to be learned from the war of 1914–18, to justify an assumption of a long-term trend toward more or younger marriage or of any substantial increase in family size. In short, those making the projections in Australia were, like their contemporaries in the U.S.A., proved wrong for the right reasons, or because they would not speculate at the expense of assumptions that were reasonable in the light of all circumstances known at the time.

FROM SLUMP TO BOOM:
IMMIGRATION

The war of 1939–45 drastically altered Australian opinion about population growth. By 1945 there was virtually no opposition to the view that a much larger population was urgently necessary. In addition, the war effort on the industrial and technical fronts, as well as in the field and in the air, had engendered a new confidence in the future which contrasted sharply with the pessimism of the 'thirties. Further, in view of the widespread assertions that the small-family system was likely to remain the dominant feature of Western societies, it seemed obvious that the

rate of growth would again have to be primed through planned immigration. The first postwar government[11] planned to sustain growth at the rate of 2 per cent a year, and assumed that half of this would be supplied by natural increase, leaving the other half to be made up of immigrants. This implied an initial "target" of 70,000 new settlers a year.

State socialism and economic development were old bedfellows in the patterns of growth of the antipodean colonies of Australia and New Zealand. So there was nothing new in federal and state governments forcing the pace of growth through massive hydroelectric and irrigation schemes, through capital investment in public transport, soil conservation, pasture improvement, and housing. Nor was there anything new in the principle of planned immigration financed from public revenue. The only really new principle here was the extension of financial assistance on a broad scale to non-British as well as British settlers—a recognition of the prewar warnings that the British Isles were no longer an inexhaustible reservoir of surplus manpower.

The main demographic and social features of this immigration have been described elsewhere.[12] Particular aspects that need emphasizing here are:

1. In the eleven years ending 1958 net immigration added approximately one million to the population.
2. Of these slightly more than 700,000

---

[11] A Labor government led by Mr. J. B. Chifley.

[12] See W. D. Borrie, "The Growth of the Australian Population with Particular Reference to the Period Since 1947. Part I: The Role of Immigrants," *Population Studies*, XIII, No. 1 (July, 1959), 4–18.

were assisted immigrants. What the scope would have been had no assistance been offered is a question that cannot be answered; but undoubtedly it would have been much lower. The ratio of 7 assisted to every gain of 10 through net immigration may be compared with ratios of approximately 7:10 for the period 1901–40 and 6:10 for 1861–1900.

3. The new feature of postwar immigration was the extensive assistance given to non-British. Amongst those arriving between October 1945 and June 1958 with the intention of residing in Australia for a year or more (that is the statistical classification of "permanent arrivals"), the following was the pattern:

	British	Non-British	Total
Assisted	331,231	365,599	696,830
Full fare	301,588	333,639	635,227
Total	632,819	699,238	1,332,057

The most numerous group of non-British assisted were the displaced persons who came in 1949 and 1950 (171,000). Among the Dutch also, the assisted were predominant—56,900 assisted as against 43,300 full-fare immigrants. But the largest non-British national group, 179,000 Italians, were mostly unassisted (146,100 unassisted and 32,900 assisted). Thus while British comprised by far the largest single category of assisted immigrants, *all* non-British assisted exceeded them. Precisely what the position was amongst the unassisted is difficult to determine because here "British nationality" includes Australian residents returning after a year or more abroad. Excluding these from the "full-fare" category shown in the above figures, the dominance of non-British would be even greater and the proportions of British amongst all categories would be about 35 per cent instead of 47 per cent.[13]

The general conclusion from these patterns appears to be that while Australia has had considerable powers of attraction for the unassisted immigrant, and while some of those assisted probably would have immigrated in any case, the offer of passage assistance may well have doubled the immigrant flow. Without it Australia would certainly not have had 171,000 displaced persons and probably only about half the immigrants in all other categories.

4. Economically this postwar immigration provided the greater part of the annual increment to the population of working age. Between 1947 and 1957 the population aged 15–64 increased by 908,400 persons, amongst whom 678,700 were immigrants. Yet even with immigration of this magnitude, with its heavy concentration in the young adult age groups, those of working age were still increasing at a slower rate than total population, and in the 20–24 age group there was an actual decline. At these ages immigration did little more than build out the groups that were in deficit as a result of the very low birth rates of the 'thirties.

The great gaps in Australia's population structure arising from those prewar years have undoubtedly been one of the major factors facilitating the economic absorption of immigrants in these years.

5. While immigration thus provided labor which was in short supply, it nevertheless created its own demands, which in turn increased the immigrant absorptive capacity of the nation. For the period 1947–57 there was a surplus of 138,000 males in the net gain from immigration. Such a surplus is inevitable in any large-scale immigration program, and a more significant feature than this male surplus,

[13] For an analysis of problems of interpretation of this kind see C. A. Price, "The Effect of Post War Immigration on the Growth of Population, Ethnic Composition and Religious Structure of Australia," *Australian Quarterly*, XXIX, No. 4 (December, 1957), 28–40.

which will be considerably reduced over time,[14] has in fact been the high proportion of family units. Over one-quarter of all immigrants have been children under the age of 15, and over three-quarters of immigrant women aged 15 and over have been married when they arrived in Australia—with a good part of the remainder already affianced. Immigrants were in fact responsible for 44 per cent of the increase in married women in the intercensal period 1947–54 and for 33 per cent of the increase between July 1954 and December 1957.

The demand stimulated by this demographic pattern among the immigrants in terms of schools, housing, and consumer durables is self-evident. When statistics are produced to show that in June 1954, the date of the last census, 20 per cent of the nation's wage- and salary-earners were born outside Australia, it has to be remembered that between the censuses of 1947 and 1954 half the population increase and 44 per cent of the net addition in new families came from immigration.

6. While both the lack of increase in the non-immigrant work force, as a result of the low fertility of the 'thirties, and the demands created by postwar immigrants themselves have been important factors facilitating the economic absorption of new settlers in the past 12 years, other demographic factors of this period are beginning to create pressures of a new kind that may well render much more difficult the maintenance of the

annual immigration "target" of 1 per cent of the population, that is currently a net gain of 100,000 persons.

SLUMP TO BOOM: NATURAL INCREASE

As the purpose of this article is a general outline of the nature of population growth and structure, detailed analyses of Australia's postwar "baby boom" will not be attempted in this article.[15] Its essential characteristics for purposes required here can be stated quite briefly.

Since 1945 natural increase in Australia has remained between 13.1 and 14.4 per 1000 of population, a level much above that of the "depressed" years of the 'thirties and analogous to that of the 'twenties. The net reproduction rates have also been consistently high, with a tendency to rise still further in very recent years. The high reproduction rate of recent years has been accompanied by very high proportions of young persons marrying. The present proportions married at ages 20–24 and 25–29 certainly create an Australian record. The trend in net reproduction rates and in proportions married may be summarized as follows:

Year	Net reproduction rate	Proportion per cent of women aged 20–24 "ever married"
1921	1.313	33.6
1933	0.976	31.2
1947	1.493	49.0
1954	1.558	59.0
1957	1.597	59.8

There is as yet no adequate explanation for the change in marriage

---

[14] Among southern Europeans in particular there is a marked tendency for young men to emigrate first, and when they are economically established, to bring out their brides or to return to their native country to get them. The imbalance of sexes was more serious in the case of displaced persons who have been unable to have fiancées or families join them. Amongst northern European immigrants the sexes are fairly balanced. A fundamental aspect of "assisted" policy is to encourage family immigration.

[15] A paper treating this subject in detail is being prepared for publication.

proportions and marriage age, but almost certainly one factor in Australia as in the U.S.A. and New Zealand) has been the economic prosperity of the last decade. The marriage boom has in turn kept the birth and reproduction rates at high levels, but it also appears that young couples married in recent years are having more children within the first 5 and 10 years of marriage than did those who married in the 'thirties. Up to 10 years of marriage the pattern approaches that of the early 'twenties. The following figures summarize the confinements per 1000 marriages occurring between 1921–22 and 1952–53:[16]

Marriage cohort	At five years' duration	At ten years' duration
1952–3	1,477	
1947–8	1,426	2,207
1931–2	1,274	1,788
1925–6	1,307	1,872
1921–2	1,419	2,301

Whether the young mothers of today will go on to have larger *completed* families than their parents did is still a matter of some conjecture. But the high marriage rates, which have compensated for the lack of rapid increase in the age groups in which most marriages have been occurring, and the high fertility of the early years of marriage, together with an inflow of immigrants of whom over a quarter have consistently been under the age of 15 years, have all combined with consistently low death rates[17] to keep natural increase at a high level. The consequence of this, compared with the situation of no

16 These figures have not been corrected for the factor of immigration. More detailed analyses and interpretation of cohort trends are at present being prepared.
17 The most striking improvement in

immigration and low birth rates of the 'thirties, is readily illustrated by expressing the children in today's population as a ratio of those aged 20–24 years.

Age group	Population	Percentage change
20–24	624,900	100.0
15–19	688,100	110.1
10–14	908,500	145.4
5–9	992,300	158.8
0–4	1,042,000	166.7

These figures illustrate the extent to which changes in marriage and fertility patterns can alter the basic structure of a population. By contrast, immigration has greatly increased the numbers in each age group at least up to age 50; but it has not greatly altered the ratio of one age group to another, or the age profile of the population. . . . In this regard the postwar marriage and baby booms have been far more important than immigration. Appreciation of this fact helps to explain both why the economic absorption of a million immigrants since 1947 has been so simple and why new pressures will occur over the next decade or so.

CHANGING COMPOSITION AND GROWTH: SOME REFLECTIONS

The interrelations between economic and demographic factors at any point of time is complex and difficult to determine precisely. It can hardly be assumed that the economic crisis of the Australian colonies in 1891 was due to demographic factors, for there were economic pressures

death rates has been in infant mortality, which dropped from 29.38 per 1,000 births in 1945 to 21.41 in 1957.

building up in the late 1880s which made the crisis of 1891 almost inevitable. Yet rapid population growth between 1861 and 1890 as a result of high rates of both natural increase and immigration was probably one factor encouraging excessive borrowing abroad to stimulate investment. Is the converse true that after the recession immigration was discouraged to damp down investment? Probably not; more likely is the explanation that assisted immigration was *not* revived on a large scale until approximately 1910 because there was a rapidly increasing work force arising out of the population structure of 1861–1890. In 1871 the proportion of population aged 0–14 years was as high as 42 per cent, while in 1891 it was still 37 per cent. These were the young cohorts from which an ample supply of recruitment was available for the work force until well into the twentieth century.

The composition of the population in recent years has been the converse of this. After World War II the absorption of immigrants was simplified because of the near-stationary situation of the work force at a time when there was a keen demand for labor arising from the leeway that had to be made up in the nation's stock of capital and consumer goods. But while immigrants built out the deficit age groups, they also brought their own share of dependents. For the intercensal period 1947–54, the consequence was that while immigration lifted the annual increment to the work force from about 17,000 to 72,000, it also raised the total population increase from an annual average of some 95,000 to 201,000. Had Australia relied for its growth between June 1947 and June 1954 wholly upon natural increase, the

work force would have increased only by 3.7 per cent and the total population by 8.8 per cent. Immigration raised these figures to 15.8 and 18.6 per cent respectively. In a situation in which the demand for labor remained high as a result of heavy investments in both the public and the private sectors of the economy and in which the demand for goods was sustained by a high rate of family formation (substantially as a result of changing marriage patterns rather than of any growth in the age groups in which most marriages occurred) and by the immigration program itself, the proportion of the population of working age (15–64) was still declining. In 1947 that proportion was almost 67 per cent, compared with only 63.2 per cent in 1954.

However, in the last three years the increment to the work force has begun to increase again as a result of the increase in births occurring after 1942, and also as the result of the immigration of children since 1947. The annual increment to the work force without any further immigration will rise in the immediate future to some 46,000; and when the full force of the postwar baby boom hits the work force in 1963, the average annual increment without any immigration will jump to some 72,000, or approximately the same as the actual figure that has applied with immigration over the last ten years or so. With immigration continuing at the "target level" of 100,000 new settlers a year the increment to the work force will be as high as 123,000 by 1963.[18]

---

[18] See W. D. Borrie and Ruth M. Rodgers, *The Next Fifteen Years, a Study of Australia's Changing Population Structure*, Australian National University (Canberra, 1959).

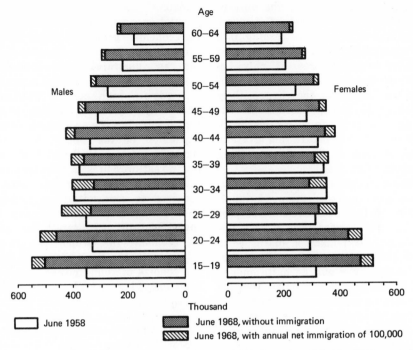

FIG. 1 The Australian Population of Working Age (15–64), 1958 and Projected to 1968

Assuming the new immigrants will have the same age and sex composition as in recent experience, they will include a high proportion of dependents whose requirements for capital and consumer goods will greatly augment the demand for labor. But, if marriage proportions in the population stabilize at recent levels, the rate of increase in families will remain below that of either the total population or of the work force despite very substantial increases amongst those reaching marriageable age.[19]

Thus the future would be the converse of the past, with work force increasing at a faster rate, and new family formation probably increasing at a slower rate, than total population. But the changes implied in these ratios should not be considered as changes from a "normal" to an "abnormal" situation; for it is the past rather than the future composition that has been abnormal, and the abnormality has been primarily the product of the birth deficits of the 'thirties. Nevertheless, demographic analysis sug-

[19] The ratios would be as follows:

	Base year 1958	Without immigration		With immigration of 100,000 each year	
		1965	1975	1965	1975
Total population	100	109	124	117	146
Work force	100	110	125	119	149
Families	100	108	123	115	143

gests very strongly that the absorption of the great waves of new recruits who will soon be passing into the work force will not be achieved without some stresses, if only because of the suddenness of their impact. The extent of the change likely to occur in the population in the younger working age groups, both without and with future immigration, is illustrated in the accompanying diagram (Fig. 1).

The ease with which full employment, and the absorption of immigrants, has been achieved in the past has been associated with a very low rate of natural increase in the work force. This situation is ending, and the change-over will be quite sudden and dramatic. Easy optimism that expanding numbers in the young age groups will generate their own demands overlooks the important change that may also occur in other facets of the nation's demographic structure, particularly in regard to marriage. The past has revealed clearly that there need be only a very low correlation between changes in total age distribution and the number of marriages or new family formation.

The general proposition from the foregoing analysis is that demographic variables have been and are still likely to be very important in a "developed" (or high per capita income), as well as in an "underdeveloped" (or low per capita income), country. In the latter, mortality tends to be the dynamic factor, and in the former, marriage and voluntary decisions regarding the size of the family and the spacing of children. The trends and changes observed and analyzed in the case of Australia apply substantially to other countries also, particularly to the U.S.A. and New Zealand, and to a lesser extent to

Canada.[20] On the assumption that population growth is itself a stimulus to economic growth,[21] there is no cause for pessimism in the long term for, as illustrated from the Australian experience, natural increase will remain high even if marriage and fertility patterns stabilize at recent levels; but the suddenness of the expansion of the work force, particularly between 1962 and 1965, will bring real pressures in the short run. Some stimulus to employment may be required to cope with this problem, and this may require stepping up investment in social capital in types of economies in which the major stimulus in the past has come from the cohorts of young people who have been marrying in such fantastic proportions and raising children in numbers beyond the dreams of demographers who wrote in the depressed era of the 1930s.

While the strongest incentive encouraging the study of the interrelation of economic and demographic factors may continue to come from the high-fertility, high-mortality, and economically "underdeveloped" areas, some new interrelations that pose difficult questions in terms of social and economic policy have also arisen out of slump and boom in many of the controlled-fertility, low-mortality and "developed" countries. These questions are all the more fascinating—

---

[20] The potential changes in rates of growth in different segments of the population of the U.S.A. can be read from the cover design of *Population Index*, Vol. 25, No. 4 (October, 1959), which illustrates estimated percentage increases of specific age groups in the U.S.A. between 1950 and 1959.

[21] For a challenge to what is fairly clearly the majority view on this subject see J. J. Spengler, "Population Threatens Prosperity," *Harvard Business Review* (January–February, 1956), pp. 85–94.

and all the more difficult—in highly industrialized countries with high material standards of life in which the pace of growth is being forced through planned immigration. A demographer, noting that in almost every one of these "developed" countries a decade and more of economic boom has occurred at a time when increments to the work force have been at abnormally low levels, wonders whether adequate attention has yet been given by economists to the study of current population structure which is now dominated by the advance of the cohorts of the postwar "baby boom" toward the labor market.

12

SYSTEMS

ANALYSIS

IN SOCIAL

DEMOGRAPHIC

RESEARCH

Social demography is concerned with relationships between social and demographic phenomena. In the introductory chapter to this volume we suggested that the most promising approach in the study of these relationships is through the conceptualization of intersecting demographic and social systems. We further suggested two different types of social systems that can be employed in social demographic analysis: social action systems and social aggregate systems. In the former,

interaction among members of the system is an important system process; in the latter, it is not. Social aggregate systems, it was noted, may be socially or analytically defined for research purposes. An example of the socially defined aggregate is a social class system, while an analytically defined type would be exemplified by a classification system based on "alienation."

The different types of social systems related to demographic systems provided the basic organizational principle for the volume. Part 3 dealt with various forms of social action systems, while Part 4 was concerned with aggregate systems.

These classifications, it is to be noted, were those of the editors, not of the authors of the readings. Relatively few of the readings provided clear conceptualizations of the analytical systems they were employing. The failure to make more explicit the systems involved in analysis poses a serious limitation to social demographic research.

The nature of this limitation becomes more clear if we look at a common problem of social demography—the explanation of a sudden decline in the birth rate in a given population. The social demographer would probably first consider explanations that could be handled entirely within the demographic framework. The birth rate may have dropped, for example, because there are fewer women in the productive age groups, perhaps as a result of out-migration. If analysis reveals that age-specific birth rates have remained unchanged, there is no reason to look outside the system for further explanation, unless he wishes to explain the migration pattern (or other possible reasons why the age structure may have altered). But that is really a different problem from the one he initially sought to explain.

Let us suppose, though, that the investigator finds that age-specific birth rates have in fact declined, and further analysis convinces him that this decline does not represent simply a change in the spacing of births. At this stage he has exhausted the explanatory utility of demographic analysis and must look outside the demographic system to find an explanation. The problem now is how best to continue his search.

What is frequently done is to search for individual variables that might be correlated with some aspect of fertility, with the assumption that if some high correlations can be found, changes in the fertility variable can be explained by changes in the social variable. Usually these relationships of covariation are expressed in the form of hypotheses. In the early Indianapolis fertility study, for example, there were 23 hypotheses relating social and psychological variables to fertility behavior but rarely relating them to other variables in a systematic framework.[1] The hypotheses were of the form "the greater the feeling of economic insecurity, the higher the proportion of couples practicing contraception effectively and the smaller the planned families." The directors of the Indianapolis Study, Whelpton and Kiser, were themselves critical of what they referred to as "the atomistic approach—i.e., the separate analysis of the variable under each hypothesis." They further observed, "In a very real way this approach necessitates the assumption that all other factors are equal when groups are classified on the basis of only

[1] P. K. Whelpton and Clyde V. Kiser, eds., *Social and Psychological Factors Affecting Fertility*, 5 vols. (New York: Milbank Memorial Fund, 1946–58). In their evaluative summary of the study, Kiser and Whelpton observed (p. 1362): "As indicated in a previous publication, the twenty-three hypotheses which form the basis of the Study are not systematically interrelated and little attempt was made to link the hypotheses to any basic social or psychological theory."

one variable at a time. The atomistic approach neglects the sociological and psychological axiom that motivations are multiple and complex."[2]

A similar analytical procedure was followed in the studies of family growth in metropolitan America,[3] although the researchers in the latter case were fully aware of the criticisms directed at the Indianapolis study because of its failure to employ a systematic theoretical framework. Unable to find "a unified body of thought that could serve as the source of hypotheses," they continued to search for meaningful correlations between fertility and other variables both singly and collectively.

Granted the greater simplicity of this approach, it presents some serious limitations to the advancement of social demography. In the first place, without some theoretical guidance the selection of independent variables is largely arbitrary—a trial-and-error process—governed largely by previous empirical experience. Second, without a systematic framework, which gives meaning to a particular concept, we may not even know what a particular variable signifies. We noted this earlier in connection with the concept "ideal size of family" so frequently used as an independent variable in fertility studies.[4] Consider the example of the personality characteristic "manifest anxiety," used as an independent variable in *Family Growth in Metropolitan America*. Without some supporting conceptualization of a "personality system," the concept is relatively meaningless, except for whatever connotations it may carry in ordinary language. It becomes something measured by a personality test that may have predictive value but certainly little explanatory value.

Finding no significant relationships between personality characteristics and fertility planning, the authors of *Family Growth in Metropolitan America* candidly admitted: "Whether the failure thus far to uncover stable relationships of any predictive value is due more to the unreliability and the primitive level of measurement of personality or to simple invalidity of theory is a critical, though unfortunately moot, question."[5] It was impossible to test the theory, because there was no theory to be tested; there was only a relationship between variables to be measured.

It should be clear from the above example that our explanation of a demographic phenomenon would not have been advanced very much

[2] Whelpton and Kiser, *Social and Psychological Factors*, p. 1366.

[3] Charles F. Westoff, Robert G. Potter, Jr., Philip C. Sagi, and Elliot G. Mishler, *Family Growth in Metropolitan America* (Princeton, N. J.: Princeton University Press, 1961); Charles F. Westoff, Robert G. Potter, Jr., and Philip C. Sagi, *The Third Child, A Study in the Prediction of Fertility* (Princeton, N. J.: Princeton University Press, 1963).

[4] Chap. 1, p. 12.

[5] Westoff, *et al.*, *Family Growth in Metropolitan America*, p. 319.

even if a high correlation had been found. Without an explanatory model, it is difficult to interpret correlations even when they occur. Even though particular variables may have predictive value, if we are concerned simply with forecasting, we will often do better to predict, at least for a short-range period, on the basis of previous experience. Our best predictor of the birth rate next year, for example, is usually the birth rate this year. From a purely practical standpoint, even if personality variables had remarkably high predictive value, one might question the feasibility of the mass administration of personality tests to obtain the needed data. Without an explanatory system, we have no basis for positing a continuation of any empirical relationship between variables found in any given study. Indeed, measures of association between individual social variables and demographic variables have often proved highly unstable in time and space. The search for consistently high correlation coefficients as a basis for proposing theoretical relationships is probably a vain quest. As Blalock has point out, "correlation coefficients, which in effect measure the amount of unexplained variation, have little or no theoretical significance in themselves, though they may be used to test the adequacy of any given causal model."[6]

The tendency of social demographers to examine isolated social variables instead of social systems in order to explain demographic variables can easily lead to erroneous conclusions—and often does. Consider, for example, the problem of the influence of the employment of married women upon their fertility behavior. The unwary investigator, who finds that employed women have much lower fertility than unemployed women when other social and economic factors are statistically controlled, may easily be led to the unwarranted conclusion that employment leads to lowered fertility. Why unwarranted? Because of the very strong possibility that fertility behavior affects the composition of the labor force system. Married women of low fecundity may be more likely to secure employment; other women may leave the labor force in order to have children or because they are pregnant. Until the investigator knows how fertility behavior affects participation in the labor force, he can only describe the association between employment and fertility; he cannot "explain" it.

THE USE OF DEMOGRAPHIC SYSTEMS IN EXPLAINING SOCIAL BEHAVIOR

Social demography, it should be kept in mind, is not exclusively concerned with the explanation of demographic behavior through reference

---

[6] Hubert M. Blalock, Jr., *Causal Inferences in Nonexperimental Research* (Chapel Hill: The University of North Carolina Press, 1961), p. 46.

to social systems; it is also concerned with the effects of demographic systems on the operation of social systems. As Beshers has observed in discussing the impact of population processes on social systems, the analysis involves two basic tasks. One is the specification of the links between the two systems; the other is formulating the consequences within the social system of changes occurring within the demographic system.[7]

As is evident from the reading selections in this volume, most social demographers concerned with demographic influences on social phenomena have used an approach emphasizing relationships between variables rather than between systems. This is probably less of a problem in dealing with demographic variables than with social variables, because the relations of variables within the demographic system are well known. Nevertheless, the analysis of demographic system processes can often provide explanations that variable analysis can not. As an example, consider the problem of a researcher seeking to explain why a county that has a long tradition of supporting conservative political candidates has now begun to elect liberal candidates. He is aware that there has been an influx of young adults into the community, so he decides to correlate voting preference with both age of voter and migrant status. Analyzing survey data, he finds that in both the group of voters under 30 and among recent migrants some 55 per cent preferred liberal candidates and 45 per cent preferred conservative candidates; among older and nonmigrant voters, the reverse percentages obtain. Since it is apparent that neither age nor migrant status explains much of the variation in voting preference, the researcher concludes that he must continue to look for other variables that will explain a larger amount of the variation.

Had the researcher considered how the process of migration changed the age composition of the voting population, he might have discovered there was no need to look further for an answer to his problem. It is quite possible that the in-migration brought in enough young people so they eventually constituted a majority of the voters. Consequently, even though the proportion of liberals among the younger voters was only slightly higher than the proportion of conservatives, their numerical strength had increased enough to offset the conservative majority among the older voters. Under these circumstances systems analysis provides an explanation that could not have been reached through correlating individual voting preferences with other individual attributes.

Considering how long we have recognized the influence of population processes on social systems, it is surprising that in contemporary sociological analyses so little attention is paid to these relationships. Some

---

[7] James M. Beshers, *Population Processes in Social Systems* (New York: The Free Press of Glencoe, Inc., 1967), p. 164.

relationships are sufficiently well established to serve as the logical propositions of at least one theory of organization behavior.[8] One of the propositions, for example, states: "As the population of a social organization increases, the proportion of the population deviating from its norms also increases." If the proposition has validity, the student of deviant behavior should be guided to demographic analysis when seeking to explain increasing rates of deviance. Again, we should be careful to note that it is not necessary to establish population growth as the cause of deviant behavior for such analysis to be useful. It is only necessary to show that population growth is significantly related to the increase of deviant behavior within a defined organizational system. Such an approach has practical, as well as theoretical, implications. We can tell the director of a growing organization that he can expect an increasing amount of deviation from organizational rules unless he adopts some different procedures to maintain social control. Or, assuming it possesses the relevant features of a social organization, the growing community that relies primarily on police to enforce legal norms can be warned that, to maintain the same crime rate, the police force will have to be increased at a faster rate than that at which the population grows, barring the introduction of other law enforcement mechanisms.

Changes in population growth and density have been used to explain social changes to a far greater degree than have changes in the demographic structure, such as age or sex composition. Yet the possible influences of population composition and the demographic processes producing them have long been recognized. Durkheim, for example, saw the concentration of youth in the cities resulting from migration as a primary reason why innovations are rapidly introduced and accepted while traditions are easily discarded in urban centers.[9] Was the high birth rate following World War II an important contributing factor to the widespread rebellion of youth against established authority in the latter 1960s? Sex differentials in mortality resulting in the concentration of property ownership by old women have sometimes been cited as contributing to business stagnation, but few have tried to relate systematically the changing age structure of central cities to urban blight. Similarly the influences of sex composition on the structure and functioning of social systems have been rarely explored, even though, as Etzioni has observed, "most forms of social behavior are sex correlated and hence . . . changes in sex composition are very likely to affect most aspects of social life."[10]

[8] Paul E. Mott, *The Organization of Society* (Englewood Cliffs, N. J.: Prentice-Hall, Inc., 1965).

[9] Emile Durkheim *The Division of Labor in Society*, trans. George Simpson (New York: The Free Press of Glencoe, Inc., 1964), pp. 295–96.

[10] Amitai Etzioni, "Sex Control, Science, and Society," *Science*, CLXI, No. 3846 (September 13, 1968), p. 1109.

Why social demographic studies have not been more widely pursued in the recent past is a matter of speculation, but it certainly cannot be because the subject area has been exhausted. On the contrary, even in the most advanced areas our studies are still in exploratory stages, as evidenced by the readings in this volume, and many areas remain virtually untouched by systematic research.

THE FUTURE APPLICATION OF SYSTEMS ANALYSIS

To summarize briefly the aim and argument of this chapter, it is our belief that social demography is an important area of study that will contribute to our understanding of both social and demographic behavior and provide us with needed knowledge for dealing with a number of significant social problems. Recent approaches to the study of social demographic phenomena, at least in the United States, have relied heavily on the analysis of statistical relationships between individual demographic and social variables. This approach, in our view, has failed to advance our knowledge significantly, because it is of limited productivity. The variable considered apart from some conceptual system has unknown explanatory value, however highly correlated it may be with some other variable.

We have suggested as a more promising alternative approach that attention be focused on how demographic systems are related to social systems rather than on how demographic variables are related to social variables. As we earlier noted, system conceptualization and techniques of system analysis have been more highly developed in demography than in sociology. A prerequisite to the successful employment of systems analysis in social demography is the devising of more refined social systems models. Where such models have been utilized in social demographic studies, the results have been quite promising. An excellent example is provided by the study "Intra-Family Communication and Fertility Planning in Puerto Rico," by Hill, Back, and Stycos, which appears in Chap. 4 of this volume. In this study the authors drew upon family interaction theory to develop an explanatory model that could be tested by predicting which families would engage in fertility planning. The failure of certain hypotheses to be supported indicated certain inadequacies in the model, but they were then in a position to modify their explanation at specific points.

In recent years the rise of general systems theory has aroused new interest in the conceptualization and analysis of systems models. The application of general systems concepts and analytical techniques to sociological data would appear to hold great promise for broadening our understanding of human relations.[11] We are less concerned with general systems models, though, than with devising specific social conceptual systems that will permit us to explain (a) how such a system significantly influences the operation of a demographic system, or (b) how such a system is significantly influenced by the operation of a demographic system.

Social system models useful in research will of necessity be limited in scope. Consequently, rarely can we expect them to account completely for changes in a demographic system to which they are linked. Neither can we expect to explain all changes in the social system models through reference to demographic systems, since social systems are always subject to the influences of other systems and environmental factors. But in this respect we shall certainly be no worse off than we are using present techniques of variable analysis. In most instances we shall probably be better off because systems analysis often guides us to specific other systems as explanatory sources, which analysis of variables using such techniques as simple correlation and regression rarely does. Furthermore, we should not preclude the probable development of better means of assessing the cumulative influences of a variety of systems operating in concert to produce a given change.

Within the field of demography, systems analysis is as old as the discipline itself, but it has not been carried over successfully into the field of social demography. There is no intrinsic reason why it cannot be applied with equal success in this developing disciplinary area, if we are able to design appropriate social system models. Adjusted to the more modest goal of partial explanation, systems analysis poses the potential for extending knowledge that will prove of inestimable value to both its parent disciplines.

[11] See Walter Buckley, *Sociology and Modern Systems Theory* (Englewood Cliffs, N. J.: Prentice-Hall, Inc., 1967).

Index